READINGS IN
CHILD AND ADOLESCENT
PSYCHOLOGY

READINGS IN
CHILD AND ADOLESCENT
PSYCHOLOGY

Edited by

LESTER D. CROW, Ph.D.

Professor of Education
Brooklyn College

and

ALICE CROW, Ph.D.

Formerly Associate Professor of Education
Brooklyn College

DAVID McKAY COMPANY, INC.
New York

READINGS IN CHILD AND ADOLESCENT PSYCHOLOGY

Preface

IN A DEMOCRATICALLY organized society every individual, young or older, plays an important role. The kind of person a child or adolescent becomes cannot be left to chance. Hence psychologists, sociologists, and educators, recognizing the significance of the developmental years, are devoting much time and energy to the study of young peoples' patterns of growth: their innate abilities, their gradually acquired attitudes and interests, their emotional experiences, their social relationships, and their learning potentialities.

Readings in Child and Adolescent Psychology is concerned with the dynamics of human behavior from birth through adolescence. Included in the book are reports of child and adolescent studies, and excerpts from the writings of men and women who through years of working with young people have acquired a constructive understanding of the internal and external behavior motivations of the developing individual. The materials are so organized that the *Readings* can be used either as a basic text or as a supplement to standard textbooks in child and adolescent psychology.

In their search for material, the editors have selected articles and excerpts that highlight significant considerations in human behavior, and have arranged them in such a way that the reader can (1) gain insight into the developmental pattern during childhood and adolescence, (2) recognize the responsibility of adults for guiding young people during the formative years, and (3) discover ways in which children and adolescents are motivated to engage in personally satisfying and socially acceptable behavior in a democracy. The selections can be of help to the student in enriching his understanding of growing individuals.

Due to limitations of space, most of the "References" associated with these reading selections were not included. If the student wishes, however, he may readily find them by consulting the original source given for each.

The editors wish to thank the authors, and the publishers of textbooks and professional journals for their cooperation in granting permission to reprint the materials included in this *Readings in Child and Adolescent Psychology*.

LESTER D. CROW
ALICE CROW

Contents

CHAPTER   PAGE

I. CHILD AND ADOLESCENT STUDY APPROACHES
    1. Commonly Used Study Approaches
                           LESTER D. CROW AND ALICE CROW   1
    2. Current Methods of Studying [Children and]
       Adolescents   WENDELL W. CRUZE   4
    3. Projective Techniques
                           LESTER D. CROW AND ALICE CROW   8
    4. Sociometric Aids   MARY R. ROUTH   11
    5. The Formal Case Study
              ALFRED SCHWARTZ AND STUART C. TIEDEMAN   13
    6. A Longitudinal Study of Sibling Resemblances in
       Intelligence and Achievement
                              SARAH M. SCHOONOVER   19
    7. Experimental Analysis of Behavior
                                HARRY F. HARLOW   26

II. BIOLOGICAL AND CULTURAL FACTORS OF DEVELOPMENT
    8. Hereditary Transmission
                  PAUL H. MUSSEN AND JOHN J. CONGER   37
    9. Biological Inheritance, Environmental Influence, and
       Cultural Heritage
                           LESTER D. CROW AND ALICE CROW   41
   10. Culture and Personality
                  MAX L. HUTT AND ROBERT G. GIBBY   47
   11. A Cross-Cultural Study of the Reinforcement of Child
       Behavior   WAYNE DENNIS   52
   12. Adolescence during the Middle Ages and Early
       Modern Times   LESTER D. CROW AND ALICE CROW   60

CHAPTER   PAGE

III. CHILD GROWTH AND DEVELOPMENT
    13. Concepts of Development   WILLARD C. OLSON   64
    14. The Period of the Embryo
                    PAUL H. MUSSEN AND JOHN J. CONGER   67
    15. Approximate Timetable of Prenatal Development
                                    ROBERT I. WATSON   69
    16. Developmental Changes in Needs during Infancy
                                    ROBERT I. WATSON   72
    17. How to Encourage Language Development
                                           LEIGH PECK   78
    18. If a Child Stammers   C. S. BLUEMEL   82

IV. ADOLESCENT GROWTH AND DEVELOPMENT
    19. Characteristics of Preadolescence: Ages 11 to 14
                EDWARD C. BRITTON AND J. MERRITT WINANS   87
    20. Characteristic Needs of Adolescence
                                 RAYMOND G. KUHLEN   93
    21. Physical Growth   HAROLD E. JONES   99
    22. Somatic Variations   HAROLD W. BERNARD   105
    23. Objectives of the Adolescent Period   LUELLA COLE   108
    24. The School, the Peer Group, and Adolescent
         Development
              RICHARD L. SIMPSON AND IDA HARPER SIMPSON   112
    25. Adolescents' Views on One Aspect of Their
         Development   RUTH STRANG   117

V. PROGRESS IN MOTOR DEVELOPMENT
    26. Concepts of Motor Development
                           J. M. LEE AND D. M. LEE   126
    27. Motor Activities   KARL C. GARRISON   132
    28. How the Infant Gains Control over His Arms and
         Hands   FRIEDA K. MERRY AND RALPH V. MERRY   138
    29. Infant Development under Conditions of Restricted
         Practice and Minimum Social Stimulation
                                       WAYNE DENNIS   143
    30. Study of Prehension in Infants   H. M. HALVERSON   153
    31. The Learning of Motor Skills as Influenced by
         Knowledge of Mechanical Principles
                                 FRANCES M. COLVILLE   161

CHAPTER   PAGE
VI.   DEVELOPMENT OF SOCIAL RELATIONSHIPS
      32.   Dimensions of Ego and Infantile Identification
                                              WANDA C. BRONSON   167
      33.   The Status of Adolescents in American Society:
            A Problem in Social Identity
                                 ROBERT D. HESS AND IRENE GOLDBLATT   178
      34.   Why Antisocial Children?   J. RESNICK   189
      35.   The New Importance at Adolescence of Social
            Relationships   RAYMOND G. KUHLEN   192
      36.   Language as a Social Skill
                                 MAX L. HUTT AND ROBERT G. GIBBY   195
      37.   Some Social Issues in Education   E. GEORGE PAYNE   200

VII. INTELLIGENCE AND APTITUDE
      38.   On the Meaning of Intelligence   GEORGE D. STODDARD   210
      39.   Three Faces of Intellect   J. P. GUILFORD   219
      40.   What Is an Aptitude?   ALEXANDER G. WESMAN   237
      41.   The Intelligence Test in School Use: Some Persistent
            Issues   JAMES B. STROUD   240
      42.   Boys and Girls—Are There Significant Ability and
            Achievement Differences?   WILLIS W. CLARK   247
      43.   The Relationship of Intelligence and Achievement to
            Birth Order, Sex of Sibling, and Age Interval
                                        SARAH M. SCHOONOVER   250

VIII. EMOTIONS DURING CHILDHOOD AND ADOLESCENCE
      44.   The Bases of Emotional Experiences
                                 LESTER D. CROW AND ALICE CROW   256
      45.   Factors Affecting Emotionality
                                      ELIZABETH B. HURLOCK   259
      46.   Developmental Differences in the Stability of Object
            Preferences and Conflict Behavior
                                      BETTY RHEA STEWART   263
      47.   Experimental Modification of Emotions
                                      HAROLD W. BERNARD   264
      48.   The Role of Social Class Differences and Horizontal
            Mobility in the Etiology of Aggression
                                      GERHARD J. FALK   268

CHAPTER   PAGE

IX.   FORMATION OF INTERESTS AND ATTITUDES
     49. A Survey of the Attitudes, Opinions, and Objectives of
          High School Students in the Milwaukee Area
                                        WILLIAM H. BOYER   278
     50. Attitudes Affect Pupils' Learning   CYRIL R. MILL   283
     51. Teen-age Traits, Interests, and Worries
                                        LESTER D. CROW   288
     52. The Reduction of Prejudice through the Arousal of
          Self-Insight
              EZRA STOTLAND, DANIEL KATZ, AND MARTIN PATCHEN   294
     53. Student Attitudes toward Child Behavior Problems
                                        ROBERT M. PORTER   305
     54. Life Problems and Interests of Adolescents in 1935
          and 1957   DALE B. HARRIS   310

X.   DYNAMICS OF CHILD AND ADOLESCENT BEHAVIOR
     55. Self: Missing Link for Understanding Behavior
                                        RICHARD M. BRANDT   320
     56. The Motivating Effects of Exteroceptive Stimulation
                                        D. O. HEBB   332
     57. Patterns of Personal Problems of Adolescent Girls
                                        RICHARD E. SCHUTZ   339
     58. General Characteristics of a Model of Mature Behavior
                                        ALFRED L. BALDWIN   346
     59. Resolution of Frustration and Conflict
                                 LESTER D. CROW AND ALICE CROW   353

XI.   CHILD AND ADOLESCENT LEARNING
     60. Changing Perceptions in Infancy   MILLIE ALMY   359
     61. The Development of Thinking and Reasoning
                                 LESTER D. CROW AND ALICE CROW   363
     62. Individual Differences in Memory
                          JAMES B. STROUD AND LOWELL SCHOER   366
     63. Cognition in Infancy   ALFRED L. BALDWIN   370
     64. Problem-Solving   LESTER D. CROW AND ALICE CROW   376
     65. The Multidimensional Contexts of Learning
                                        NATHANIEL CANTOR   381
     66. Animistic Thinking among College and High School
          Students in the Near East   WAYNE DENNIS   388

CHAPTER PAGE

    67. Sex Differences and Judgment Processes
        MICHAEL A. WALLACH AND NATHAN KOGAN   394

XII. PERSONALITY DEVELOPMENT AND THE SELF
    68. How the Home Affects Personality Development
        FRIEDA K. MERRY AND RALPH V. MERRY   399
    69. The Self-Image: A Theory of the Dynamics of Behavior
        CAMILLA M. ANDERSON   406
    70. The Adolescent Personality
        LESTER D. CROW AND ALICE CROW   419
    71. Boys Who Run Away from Home
        WILLIAM W. WATTENBERG   425
    72. Toward a Concept of Personality Integration
        JULIUS SEEMAN   433

XIII. CHARACTER FORMATION AND PSYCHOSEXUAL BEHAVIOR
    73. Discipline: Its Psychological and Educational Aspects
        HIRSCH LAZAAR SILVERMAN   441
    74. Moral and Spiritual Values   HENRY NEUMANN   453
    75. The Nature of Religious Controls
        MORTIMER OSTROW   456
    76. A Code of Moral and Spiritual Values
        PAUL S. ANDERSON   461
    77. Psychosexual Development
        L. JOSEPH STONE AND JOSEPH CHURCH   468
    78. The Nature and Origins of Psychological Sexual Identity
        THOMAS COLLEY   474
    79. Treated Sex Offenders and What They Did
        LOUISE VIETS FRISBIE   490
    80. Mate Selection and Marriage
        LESTER D. CROW AND ALICE CROW   495
    81. The Unmarried Mother of School Age as Seen by a
    Psychiatrist   FLORENCE CLOTHIER   502

XIV. PARENT-CHILD ADJUSTMENT
    82. How Can the Home Help a Child Make a Good
    School Adjustment?   HAZEL F. GABBARD   516

CHAPTER   PAGE

83. Reactions of Parents to Problems of Mental
    Retardation in Children
                EDMUND W. GORDON AND MONTAGUE ULLMAN   521
84. Parent-Child Conflicts   JOHN E. HORROCKS   528
85. Parent Education Groups in a Child Guidance Clinic
                                        HAIM G. GINOTT   535
86. Parents and Teen-agers: Differing Perspectives
                                        ROBERT D. HESS   541
87. Separation of the Parents and the Emotional Life of the
    Child   GEORGE E. GARDNER   545
88. Parental Attitudes toward Boy-Girl Relations
                                        ALICE CROW   554
89. Parent-Youth Code
                COMMUNITY DELINQUENCY ACTION COMMITTEE   562

XV. ADJUSTMENT TOWARD MENTAL HEALTH
90. Adjustment for What?   GAIL M. INLOW   565
91. Helping Young People to Deal with Their Problems
                                        WILLARD JACOBSON   571
92. How to Deal with Your Tensions
                GEORGE S. STEVENSON AND HARRY MILT   579

INDEX   587

READINGS IN
CHILD AND ADOLESCENT
PSYCHOLOGY

1. Commonly Used Study Approaches *

LESTER D. CROW
AND ALICE CROW

THERE ARE various possible approaches to the study and evaluation of human characteristics. More or less consciously, everyone constantly is attempting to discover why another person acts or thinks in one or another way. For the most part, the layman's evaluation of his respective associates is conducted informally and reflects his own attitudes, standards of values, and biases or prejudices. To be valid, a study of the development and adjustment of a young person of any age must represent an objective approach and follow scientific procedures to as great an extent as is possible. Conclusions subjectively arrived at can be avoided or minimized only if the person or group engaging in the study or evaluating process makes careful preparation for the project, observes or measures accurately and objectively, classifies obtained data completely, summarizes the results of the study correctly and impartially, and verifies the final conclusions through continued research and application.

Limiting factors of study. Regardless of the study technique employed and the carefulness of its utilization, general applicability of the resulting conclusions may be questionable. For example, many of the existing studies of individual development and behavior have centered around research concerning young people who have been reared in middle-class urban communities. We have emphasized the effect upon the developmental pattern of youth of subcultural influence, as well as of differences in

---

* From Lester D. Crow and Alice Crow, *Adolescent Development and Adjustment*, pp. 43–47. Copyright 1956 by McGraw-Hill Book Co., Inc., New York, and reprinted with their permission.

biologically inherited potentialities. Hence, as we consider the various commonly utilized techniques of adolescent study and evaluation, we need to be alert to at least two significant facts: (1) generalizations resulting from research applicable only to members of the group studied, e.g., behavior or attitudes that may seem to be general for younger adolescents or for teen-agers who are born and reared in a large metropolitan community such as New York City may not be representative of older adolescents or youth in the small agricultural village of Dundee, Ohio; (2) within the group studied there are likely to be some adolescents who, for one or another reason, deviate from the generally accepted norm of development or adjustment, e.g., an adolescent's personal and group behavior may be affected by too great difference between himself and the majority of the group in physical structure and constitution, mental potential, emotional balance, or socioeconomic status. With these cautions concerning the acceptance of study results, we now shall consider some of the generally used approaches to the study of child and adolescent nature.

The horizontal study approach. Much of the data now available concerning children has been obtained through the utilization of horizontal or cross-sectional study approaches. By means of this technique, often referred to as a "normative" study, specific characteristics of a large group of supposedly same-status subjects are investigated to discover what the general trend or average for that particular group appears to be. When a norm has been reliably ascertained, any individual who falls into the group studied can be compared to his group's average to determine the extent of his deviation from it, i.e., the degree to which he is atypical.

The utilization of cross-sectional studies has provided us with considerable information concerning general growth and development trends. Height and weight charts represent the results of studies that have been conducted at various age levels, respectively. The same is true of mental growth and of other phases of child and adolescent development. Comparisons of these developmental "average ages" have led to the acceptance of certain expected norms as standards for the evaluation of individual growth and progress. The many carefully conducted cross-sectional studies that have been and continue to be made have value in that they represent a convenient basis for evaluating the status of a young person at any given stage of his development.

The study limitations referred to in the preceding section apply to the utilization of the horizontal approach. When or if we critically examine all the factors involved in this method, we can recognize the danger of accepting without question any norm, no matter how reliable it may seem to be. The results of a cross-sectional study usually are supposed to represent a sampling of the whole population at a given stage of growth or development. Since it is difficult to obtain an adequate sampling, the obtained norm may not be representative of all possible cases. Hence apparent deviation from that norm may not be a reliable measure of individual evaluation. It is only as many different studies are conducted in the same area of investigation, and yield comparable results, that valid conclusions can be drawn.

Another cause of error in cross-sectional studies of growth and development lies in the fact that rate of progress differs with individuals. One cannot assume, for example, that all persons who have the same chronological age, say, 8, 10, 12, or 14 years, respectively, have reached the same maturational stage. Yet all or most of them may be fully mature by age 20. The factor of growth and development rate is particularly significant during the adolescent years. Another weakness lies in the fact that an eight-year-old group may yield a greater range of differences than is found in older age groups, with consequent unreliable "averages."

This situation can be illustrated by supposing that in a school or school system a simultaneous group study is undertaken to discover the average increase in mental ability that can be expected to take place in pupils from the fourth through the sixth to the eighth grade. Undoubtedly the study project will show that children grow mentally during these years. The average difference, however, between age and grade levels cannot be explained entirely in terms of the growth and development factors alone. Unless the school or school system is organized in terms of social promotions, i.e., according to chronological age, with no regard for success in the learning progress, the pupils of the higher grades constitute a more selective group from the standpoint of mental alertness. Since the mentally slower members of the fourth grade group have not been able to keep pace with their brighter classmates, the norms of intelligence in the upper-grade groups represent not only increasing maturation but also greater homogeneity in mental ability.

The vertical study approach. No one can deny the fact that in spite of their weaknesses, cross-sectional group studies have great value as means of furthering our general understanding of the maturational and developmental processes. Parents, teachers, and other adults who are responsible for the welfare of young people usually are interested in general "psychological" principles only to the extent that they apply to specific boys and girls. Parents are concerned about the developmental progress of their child. The teacher at any school level needs to understand each of his pupils in terms of the young person's particular developmental history, his present status, and probable future progress. The child, and especially the adolescent, should gain some awareness of personal strengths and weaknesses. These data can be obtained only by means of a continuous study of the individual from the prenatal period through the maturing and developing years. Such longitudinal or vertical studies are time-consuming and costly projects. They necessitate the continued application of research techniques which may be difficult to manage. Moreover, reliable conclusions concerning the individual's pattern of developmental progress cannot be made until he has reached maturity.

2. Current Methods of Studying [Children and] Adolescents *

WENDELL W. CRUZE

Directed observation. Directed observation is just what the phrase implies. It is observation of individuals and their activities when the observations are made according to a planned schedule and with a definite goal in view. It is a refinement of the superficial, uncontrolled observations that we make of the behavior of others during most of our waking hours. Everyone observes the behavior of adolescents, but few observe it under conditions satisfactory to science.

The method of directed observation has been used to great advantage in the study of child behavior. Psychologists using one-way vision screens and motion-picture cameras have been able to obtain a wealth of information concerning child development.[1] It hasn't been so satisfactory with adolescents, for these older individuals are much more observant, and they soon discover that they are being observed. When this occurs, spontaneity

* From Wendell W. Cruze, *Adolescent Psychology and Development*, pp. 36–41. Copyright 1953 by The Ronald Press Co., New York, and reprinted with their permission.

[1] The work of Arnold Gesell and his associates at the Yale University Clinic of Child Development provides excellent examples of the use of these techniques. See Arnold Gesell, *Studies in Child Development* (New York: Harper and Bros., 1948).

of behavior is likely to disappear, and the reactions observed and recorded may not be representative of the natural reactions of the individual.

Systematic questionnaires. The questionnaire is one of the devices developed in an effort to improve the accuracy of the observation of human behavior. In the nineteenth century it was widely used by Sir Francis Galton in his studies of individual differences. It was popularized in this country in the early part of this century by G. Stanley Hall and his co-workers in their studies of childhood and adolescence. In general, a list of carefully formulated questions is sent to a selected group of individuals, or the questions may be asked directly in an interview. The answers are recorded, classified, and analyzed. Eventually certain generalizations may appear to be justified.

Despite the fact that the questionnaire technique was one of the first to be employed in studying adolescents, it has never been too satisfactory when used with young people of this age level. Whenever a printed questionnaire is administered to a large group of adolescents simultaneously, the investigator has no way of ascertaining how many of his subjects took the questionnaire seriously and gave truthful answers and how many decided that it would be "smart" to falsify their answers and deceive the investigator. The psychologist who is a realist is well aware of this tendency among adolescents, but to date no technique has been devised to enable him to identify the papers of these noncooperative respondents. If the questionnaire is utilized as a part of a personal interview with an adolescent, the chances for obtaining adolescent cooperation and valid information are greatly increased. This technique, however, is time-consuming and cannot be utilized whenever large numbers of adolescents are to be studied.[2]

Retrospective reports. Since the time of G. Stanley Hall there has been a tendency to use the retrospective reports of older individuals to provide us with information concerning the experiences and attitudes of adolescents. This tendency has increased during the past decade or so, and while this particular technique undoubtedly yields some very valuable information, nevertheless it must be used with caution. In the first place, we must realize that many attitudes, experiences, and feeling states are forgotten with the passage of time. Secondly, the experiences that have transpired between the period of adolescence and the time the retrospective report is made will undoubtedly color some of the adolescent experiences and lead to inaccurate reports. On the other hand, older individuals are

---

[2] The study of current grooming practices of adolescent girls reported in Chapter 6 provides an illustration of the use of the questionnaire with an adolescent group.

more cooperative than adolescents. They are willing to talk about their past experiences, while adolescents resist strenuously attempts to get them to discuss their present experiences. Most people seem more willing to discuss past than present aspirations, desires, and experiences. This greater willingness is probably due to the fact that an appraisal of present status is not involved. Retrospective reports, interpreted cautiously, seem to provide a promising fund of information concerning adolescent development.[3]

Adolescent diaries. G. Stanley Hall also suggested that a study of adolescent diaries should provide a valuable fund of information concerning adolescent aspirations and experiences. Present-day psychologists are inclined to agree with him, for diary recordings are likely to represent spontaneous expressions of interests, feelings, emotions, and other attitudes. The statements written in diaries are likely to be spontaneous and unrestrained, since the adolescent feels that no one else will ever read what he has written. And since the materials are entered in the diary daily or at regular intervals, the experiences recorded are not likely to be distorted by the shortcomings of the human memory.

There are certain difficulties involved in the use of materials from the diaries of adolescents. In the first place, there is a paucity of such materials. Too few adolescents keep diaries, and many of those who do will not surrender them for analysis even though many years have elapsed since they were written. In the second place, it has been discovered that those adolescents who keep diaries usually are of superior intelligence; the materials contained therein would hardly be representative of adolescents as a group. Finally, the bulk of the materials written in the diaries deal with highly emotional experiences. Most of the occurrences during the day are not considered to be sufficiently important to record. Accordingly, one who depends upon a perusal of adolescent diaries for his concept of adolescent development will inevitably receive the impression that practically all experiences of the adolescent are highly tinged with emotion.[4]

The method of measurement. Measurement in modern adolescent psychology involves the utilization of quantitative techniques in evaluating both physical and psychological development. Physical measurements have been used for many years to chart the course of development in height, weight, muscular strength, muscular coordination, and various other aspects

---

[3] The study by Kirkpatrick and Caplow, reported earlier in this chapter, was based upon retrospective reports.

[4] See H. Meltzer, "Students' Adjustments in Anger," *Journal of Social Psychology,* 4 (1933), 285–308.

of physical growth. Visual and auditory acuity, speed of reaction, discrimination of weights, and muscular precision have also been measured with a high degree of accuracy.

The development of tests of mental ability has been of great importance in the field of adolescent psychology. The utilization of both individual and group tests of intelligence has provided us with much information concerning intellectual development that would be difficult if not impossible to obtain in any other way. More recently, psychologists have also developed objective tests and inventories for the measurement of personality characteristics and social adjustment. These tests and rating devices have furnished us with data that enable us to compare adolescent boys and girls of different age levels. They also enable us to measure the development that occurs in any individual over a period of months or years. All in all, we must conclude that the development of objective tests of various types has contributed much to our understanding of adolescent personality and development. . . .

The experimental method. The experimental method is the most accurate, precise, and reliable to the methods used in psychology. At times it has been referred to as the "scientific method," as though it were the only method that could be considered scientific. This is not the case, however, for each method or technique described in this section is scientific if the rigid requirements of the scientific procedure are satisfied. Nevertheless, because of its greater precision and reliability, the experimental method is to be preferred over any other technique, provided, of course, the topic under investigation lends itself to an experimental attack. A psychological experiment is a special kind of directed observation. The subjects used are selected carefully in accordance with the criteria established when the experiment is planned. The conditions under which the observations are made have been prearranged and are carefully controlled. The factors to be controlled vary greatly in different types of experiments, but in most experiments involving human subjects the following factors are usually considered important: (*a*) the age and sex of the subjects, (*b*) the past experiences of the subjects—education and training, (*c*) the present condition of the subjects—tired, sleepy, hungry, or rested, and (*d*) the stimuli acting upon the subjects—light, heat, sound, and others. The control of all these factors is a difficult task, even for a trained psychologist, but it must be accomplished if the results are to be valid and reliable. As a result, the experimental method has been used rather infrequently in the field of adolescent development. This method has been used more extensively in animal psychology than in human psychology, and in studying the simpler problems of reaction than in the study of broad and extensive problems of development.

3. Projective Techniques *

LESTER D. CROW
AND ALICE CROW

T HE PERSONALITY TESTS and inventories that were discussed in the preceding pages can be regarded as containing "structured" material. The subject or the rater responds to definite items according to an assigned pattern of responses from which he has to select the one that seems best to meet his reactions to the task. His responses are limited thereby to the *what* and the *how* of the stimuli-situations that comprise the test. The techniques here described do not place these restrictions upon the responder. For the most part, these techniques are individually administered. A projective technique presents a supposedly *"unstructured"* situation or task to which the subject responds freely. The administrator offers only brief general suggestions or directions and/or asks relatively vague questions. The situation is informal; the subject is permitted to give free rein to his imagination. Instead of being restricted in his responses, he is encouraged to *project,* through his responses, his characteristic opinions, aggressions, hopes and aspirations, fears and worries, likes and dislikes, and other expressive attitudes. However, the subject will cooperate with the clinician only to the extent that the atmosphere is informal and relaxed.

Because of the relative vagueness and ambiguity of the stimuli and the "looseness" of the entire evaluating experience, interpretation of responses is difficult. Explanatory manuals that accompany the materials suggest possible interpretations of various combinations of responses. A projective technique should not be administered by anyone except a clinician who has received intensive training in its administration and interpretation.

* From Lester D. Crow and Alice Crow, *Human Development and Learning,* pp. 409–14. Copyright 1956 by American Book Co., New York, and reprinted with their permission.

Many projective techniques have been devised, and more are in the process of construction. This new approach to personality analysis still is in an exploratory stage and needs much study and application before valid conclusions can be reached concerning its value. There are several of these techniques that have gained some attention among psychologists and are used in clinical testing situations.

The Rorschach technique. Probably the most widely known and most generally discussed projective technique is the Rorschach Inkblot Technique. The material consists of ten cards, each of which has printed on it an inkblot or an apparently meaningless, bilaterally symmetrical figure or form. On five of the blots, the shades are gray and black; two of them contain touches of bright red, and the other three have assorted colors. . . .

The person who is being tested is given the first card and encouraged to describe everything that he sees on the card. He may turn the card to any position. On a blank prepared for this purpose, the clinician notes down everything that the subject says. After the ten cards have been examined and described, the subject goes through them again, pointing to the areas of the respective inkblots that represented to him what he had described. Meanwhile, on a duplicate set of inkblots, the examiner marks the areas indicated by the subject.

The interpretation of the responses includes: location (area) determinants, color, shading, forms, "movements," contents (kind of figures: human, scenery, food, etc.), and popularity (frequency of response among different subjects). Differences can be found among scoring systems, especially for content. As yet, there are no definitive norms. Hence the clinician needs to interpret data carefully. He must give special attention to behavior and attitude tendencies that show themselves with relative consistency in reactions to all the inkblots. Although this technique is concerned primarily with emotional reactions, degree of mental alertness and educational background are reflected in the kind of responses given.

Pictorial techniques. There are various techniques that utilize pictures as the materials of evaluation. The pictures may seem to be a little more structured than are inkblots, but pictured material varies in degree of situational ambiguity and figure portrayal.

The Thematic Apperception Test (*TAT*). This test is relatively unstructured. It consists of nineteen cards, each of which presents vague pictorial material in black and white, and one blank card. The subject is asked to tell a story about each of the nineteen pictures, including: what probably has happened, what is happening now, what is going to happen, and how the depicted characters feel about the whole "situation." While the subject looks at the one blank card, he is supposed to imagine a picture on it and tell a story about it.

There is no general agreement regarding a scoring system. As the clinician listens to the subject talk, observes his behavior and takes notes, he usually finds a relatively consistent pattern of emotional reaction running like a thread throughout the stories. For example, one adolescent boy to whom the TAT was administered was consistent in his interpretations of the fact that someone had been murdered, would be murdered, or was doing something for which he deserved to be killed. This boy was known to resent his parents and teachers, and was suffering from deep-seated feelings of frustration. Another subject interpreted every picture as a "happy" picture. Several of her stories were accounts of young lovers who had been separated but were together again. This adolescent girl was irresponsible, extremely romantic, and given to much daydreaming.

Children's Apperception Test (CAT). Other pictorial techniques have been devised for specific age ranges. The TAT can be given to children as young as seven, but better results are obtained with older children, adolescents, and adults. The Children's Apperception Test (CAT) substitutes animals for humans, but the animals are portrayed in human situations. Stories about these pictures may reveal a child's emotional reactions to parent-child and parent-parent relationships, sibling rivalry, and other problem situations that arise in the child's home or neighborhood environment.

Situational Tests

The purpose of a situational test is to observe the subject's behavior in a situation that has been set up to resemble what might be an everyday situational experience.

The Character Education Inquiry. One of the earliest of these testing approaches includes the situations set up by Hartshorne and May when they were conducting the Character Education Inquiry. As part of their study of children's behavior in relation to character development, they established situations in which children's behavior was observed, without the subject's being aware of it. Many of these situations dealt with dishonesty in the form of cheating: accepting more change than was coming to them when they purchased something in a store, changing answers as they marked their own test papers (duplicates of which had been made), using materials to help them during the taking of a test and similar situations.

As a result of their findings, Hartshorne and May concluded that extent of cheating is determined by the ease or difficulty of cheating, and that probably no one is completely honest. To this conclusion were added other conclusions based upon situations that involved the degree of displayed generous behavior or of other forms of behavior that are associated with ethical and social values. Much protest was elicited from parents and from educational and religious leaders as a result of the published findings of Hartshorne and May. The Inquiry has continued to be a subject of controversy.

Value of the situational technique. The situational technique employed in the Inquiry has been applied to situational stress tests, such as those that were employed during World War II to discover reactions of men under stress. This technique was one of the "screening" devices by which men were evaluated for assignment to strategic and perhaps dangerous forms of service.

Tests that involve participation in disguised or partially disguised "life-like" situations are difficult and costly to set up. Moreover, they may not give complete or adequate insight into "habitual" behavior as such, unless the individual can be exposed to many such structured situations.

✓ 4. *Sociometric Aids* *

MARY R. ROUTH

SOCIOMETRIC TECHNIQUES are social measurements. From an educational standpoint, they are subjective rather than objective measures. They do not constitute a single science, but borrow from and blend with many fields—sociology, psychology, literature, history, drama, group therapy.

Sociometric techniques are a means to an end, for measurement has no value unless it is the basis for some action or knowledge. Specifically, for the classroom teacher, they are techniques by which she can find concrete evidence of the social relationships, desires, and frustrations of the students sitting before her. What she can do with this knowledge depends upon her ability.

* From Mary R. Routh, "Sociometric Aids," *Education* (January, 1960), pp. 307–8. Reprinted by permission of the author and The Bobbs-Merrill Co., Inc., Indianapolis, Ind.

In most elementary schools, children are assigned to a first grade class, and, substantially, the membership of the class remains the same until it leaves the school. A similar situation exists in high school report or home-room classes. For the child who is well adjusted, such an arrangement provides a secure framework of friendships within which he pursues his school work. For the poorly adjusted child, it is a social manacle. Similarly, a whole class group may be well or poorly adjusted to the school. For the teacher, no matter how she provides for individual differences, the child is still one of a class group, one of an age group, one of a family group, and must not be isolated from these relationships for teaching purposes.

School children's relationships should be studied from both the individual and the groups aspects. They include: (1) the relationship of the child to his classmates; (2) the interrelationships among the members of the class; (3) the social attitudes of the child; (4) the social attitudes of a class group; (5) the relationship of the child to his past experience; (6) the relationship of the class to its past experience; (7) the relationship of the child to his current experience; (8) the relationship of the class to its current experience; and (9) the relationship of the child to his dreams and plans for the future.

Interclass Relationships

A specific technique, called a sociogram, has been developed for the demonstration of the relationships within a class group, and of the individual child to the group. This simple tool consists of having the child record answers to one or more questions concerning his preferences for association within the group. The questions which are asked should be formulated by the teacher to fit some activity which is planned for the classroom.

Children who are chosen by many others are referred to as "leaders," "stars," or "overchosen." Those who are not chosen by others are termed "isolates" or "underchosen." The tabulation of choice scores will probably show one of two patterns: (1) a class in which the choices are concentrated on a few children and isolates appear, or (2) a class in which the choices are more evenly distributed and neither strong leaders nor isolates appear.

To the writer's knowledge, no study has been made as to whether children's social adjustment is better in one of these patterns than in the other. However, it has been found that, when children move from one class to another, their sociometric status shows little change; they assume approximately the same social status in the new group as they had in the old group.

Sociometric questions have been used to identify the child who arouses group antagonism. The writer does not advocate this technique—children should not be asked to express formal rejection of each other unless very intensive, skillful individual and group therapy is to be administered.

√ 5. The Formal Case Study *

ALFRED SCHWARTZ
AND STUART C. TIEDEMAN

SERIOUS PROBLEMS will occasionally occur even with the best of educational programs. It is for the investigation of these more complex and deep-seated maladjustments that the formal case study is a valuable tool. Although the formal case study includes the same steps, in general, as the informal, continuous study described in the preceding paragraphs, the formal case study has certain important characteristics which differentiate it from the more informal study.

1. Ordinarily only one student, or a very few, can be studied at any one time by any given teacher.
2. A rather well-structured form or pattern (although the form need not be identical for every case) is usually followed.
3. All (or at least most) of the information or data assembled relative to the case, as well as the interpretation of the data, the diagnosis, the remediation recommended or suggested, and the follow-up are accurately recorded in written form.
4. Much more data of a special or technical nature are usually obtained than is true with the informal study.
5. The services of specialists (doctors, nurses, psychiatrists, child guidance clinics, social workers, and the like) are frequently employed.

* From Alfred Schwartz and Stuart C. Tiedeman, *Evaluating Student Progress in the Secondary School*, pp. 244–50. Copyright 1957 by Longmans, Green and Co., Inc., New York, and reprinted with their permission.

6. Effort is most often directed at the diagnosis and solution of a rather severe problem.
7. Very complete and comprehensive cumulative record data are a must if teachers are to use the method at all.

The formal case study begins when a problem is detected, usually through observation of the student, and corroborated by a careful perusal of cumulative records. Once a problem is recognized the case study proceeds to include these principal parts:

1. Collection of data about the student
2. Organization of these data into meaningful, practical, usable categories
3. Interpretation of the data
4. Analysis of the problems, needs, and plans of the student in the light of the data
5. Tentative diagnosis of the basic problem
6. Discussion and agreement concerning the appropriate therapy or treatment
7. Implementing of the agreed-upon remedial procedure(s)
8. Follow-up (evaluation) of the results of the therapy

Although, typically, these are the major parts of a case study, it is not intended that they be regarded as a time-sequence procedure. There is bound to be considerable overlapping and running together of the various parts as the study proceeds. This is to be expected and should be anticipated by the teacher about to begin a case study.

Step one. Inasmuch as it is necessary, in conducting a case study, to obtain the facts about the student, the cumulative record should be consulted as the initial phase of the investigation. Most of the important data relating to the case will already have been assembled and organized there. The question of which data are important and should, therefore, be recorded as part of the case study is dependent to some extent upon the nature of the case and the purpose of the study. However, in any case, even with a very limited and specific difficulty, the problem can best be diagnosed and remediation suggested when the problem is interpreted against the background of the "whole student." Therefore, all the available data included in the cumulative record should be carefully examined, since every item of information may be important. It is assumed that a complete record will include the student's personal health and social history, test scores (principally achievement, intelligence, and aptitude), academic achievement, interests, and personality information. If any of these data are not included, those that seem pertinent or significant should be obtained as part of the first, or data gathering, phase of the study.

Step two. Since it is somewhat unlikely that very recent information about any student will be contained in his cumulative record (most facts are recorded or entered at specified times or intervals during the year), it is usually necessary to interview all persons who have had recent contact with the student, including classroom teachers, class counselors, homeroom teacher, gym teacher or coach, school nurse, and librarian, as well as the parents, clergyman, and even other students. Written records should be made of each interview, or each interested person should be asked to write a brief statement concerning the student in answer to the case worker's specific questions regarding him.

Step three. Information is obtained from the student himself through interviewing him, administering additional tests to him, particularly diagnostic tests, personality or adjustment inventories, attitude scales, and questionnaires. In many instances, the results of the administration of such instruments will provide convenient leads or cues for the interview which should follow.

Step four. The information is assembled in a written form convenient for reviewing, interpreting, and analyzing the data. Thus far the case study is not significantly different from a case history. The unique aspects of the case study appear in steps five, six, and seven which follow:

Step five. The assembled information is studied intensively, analyzed, and interpreted in the light of the original problem or difficulty with a view to arriving at a tentative conclusion or diagnosis concerning the cause or causes of the problem. Having arrived at such a diagnosis, the conclusions are written up and become a part of the case study record.

Step six. Having arrived at a diagnosis of the problem, it next becomes necessary to formulate a plan of action designed to alleviate or "cure" the difficulty or solve the problem in whole or in part, and to record, in writing, a plan of treatment or therapy. It may be assumed that having arrived at a plan of treatment or therapy that action would be taken to activate the plan at the appropriate time.

Step seven. As the treatment proceeds, the results should be *evaluated* in terms of the progress made by the student in overcoming his difficulty or solving his problem. This phase of the case study may be continued in some cases as long as the case worker has any contact with the student in a way that would lend itself to appraisal of the student, or at least until such time as it appears that the treatment is leading to definite success or failure.

It is not uncommon for a case study to be undertaken with a view to solving what appears to be a very obvious problem, only to discover during the course of the study that the "obvious problem" is only a symptom and that the real problem is not so evident or obvious. It is important, therefore, that the teacher conducting the case study *clearly differentiate between the overt or surface manifestations of difficulty and the basic problem* (which is usually not discovered until all the data are recorded, analyzed, and interpreted). In order to be perfectly clear, the initial statement of the problem should actually be termed "reason for study" rather than "the problem."

One further word of caution may prove helpful especially to the teacher inexperienced in case-study work. It is extremely necessary to approach every case with an open mind, with no preconceived conclusions, and with an attitude of readiness to switch courses if it appears that the original line of investigation is achieving no results. In other words, the case study should not become a technique for the purpose of corroborating the teacher's personal, invalidated judgment concerning the causes of the student's problem. As is true with every instrument or tool, regardless of its expressed purpose or function, the case study is no better than the person using it.

There is no single form or outline which will fit every teacher's needs when it comes to assembling and organizing the data for a case study. Similarly, there is no magic formula which tells one what specifications or areas of information are to be included in the study. Insofar as the outline to be followed in making the study is concerned, any pattern which is meaningful to the teacher and which arranges data in a convenient form is satisfactory. It is usually convenient, however, in those instances where a fairly complete cumulative record is kept for every student, to have the outline of the case study agree with the cumulative record. This facilitates transcribing data from the cumulative record to the written case-study report. As far as the items of information to be gathered and assembled for the study are concerned, the nature of the case, the teacher's time and skill, and the facilities available for obtaining data will determine *what* and *how much* information will be collected. In spite of the fact that many authors and authorities have presented outlines to be followed in the conduct of a case study with little agreement as to *specific* items of information to be included, there is rather general agreement concerning certain main elements. The authors present an adaptation of Rivlin's outline of the case-study method, not as a composite but rather as an illustration of an outline which embodies the essential elements of a complete case study and a guide to the teacher to help him give direction to his efforts.

I. *History and descriptive information*

   A. *Identifying data (the student)*: Name, address, school, grade, sex, age (birth date), teacher (homeroom teacher), nationality (race), color, religion, significant and objective comments describing physical appearance of the student, condition of clothing, obvious physical or mental limitations, mannerisms.

   B. *Reason for the study (the complaint)*: Specific incident(s), setting and probable causes, plus name(s) of person(s) making complaint.

   C. *Personality traits*

     General emotional tone; for example, cheerful, moody, etc.
     Attitude toward his family (father, mother, siblings, others)
     Attitude toward his school (teachers, administrators, others)
     Attitude toward his friends
     Attitude toward himself, his abilities, and problems
     Play life
     Hobbies
     Educational and vocational ambitions
     Marked likes and dislikes
     Unusual fears
     Results of special tests (projective, etc.)
     Any special personal problem?

   D. *Educational status*

     Age at entrance to first grade
     Present school achievements
     History of retardation or acceleration
     Special deficiencies and proficiencies (results of diagnostic tests)
     Past record in work and conduct
     Schools attended—type—location

   E. *Results of medical examination*

     Physical defects
     Efficiency of sensory organs (vision—hearing)
     General condition of health
     Nutritional status
     Comparison with normal height and weight (height-weight ratio)
     Muscular coordinations
     Reduced or exaggerated reflexes
     Twitchings, tics, tremors
     Peculiarities of gait or speech
     Previous health history

   F. *Results of mental examination*

     Mental age ⎱
     Intelligence quotient ⎰ also subtest scores, if available
     Results of achievement test
     Special abilities

Special disabilities
Vocational aptitudes and interests
G. *The home environment*
The individuals living at home (number, age, relationship, sex)
Apparent economic level
Apparent social status
Parental methods of discipline
Parents' emotional disposition
Attitude toward this child
Possibilities of securing the home's cooperation
Unusual customs, traditions observed
Cultural resources (educational level of parents, etc.)
Relations within home (parent-child, child-child, etc.)
Record at other social service agencies
H. *The neighborhood environment*
Recreational facilities
Housing and living conditions
Desirability of his playmates
Any special obstacle to adjustment
I. *Social background and activities (outside school and home)*
Church affiliation and attendance (also Sunday school)
Boy Scout, Girl Scout, Hi-Y, 4-H, Future Farmers, local youth groups
Summer camp attendance
Civic organizations (including municipal band, orchestra, athletic teams, etc.)
Gang affiliations
Sexual irregularities
Court record

II. *Summary of case data*
A condensation of the sum total of all significant facts assembled in light of the problem being investigated.

III. *Diagnosis*
A practical workable hypothesis or guess as to the cause or causes of the explanation of the problem under consideration, based upon all the evidence obtained and recorded. It is worth repeating that an original diagnosis is seldom final; new hypotheses may be formulated and new diagnoses made as new additional evidence is obtained.

IV. *Treatment and follow-up*
The actual treatment grows out of the diagnosis and may be considered the culmination of the case study. If the recommended treatment or therapy proves effective, it verifies the soundness of the diagnosis; if it proves ineffective, it suggests that either the diagnosis was in error, the wrong treatment was used, or conditions surrounding the case (either the individual himself or his environment) have changed. Under such circumstances the

case may need to be restudied or a different form of treatment be tried. In any event, an effective follow-up or evaluation of the case from the standpoint of the success of the treatment in bringing about an improvement in the student's adjustment is imperative.[1]

⌐6. A Longitudinal Study of Sibling Resemblances in Intelligence and Achievement *[1]

SARAH M. SCHOONOVER

THE MAJOR PROBLEM of this study is to determine the amount of sibling resemblance in longitudinal growth records of mental ability and educational achievement. The following specific points have been investigated: (a) To what extent do children of the same family resemble each other in intelligence and in educational achievement? (b) To what extent are differences between siblings reduced as compared to those that exist between unrelated pairs within the same population? (c) To what degree do the sibling resemblances in intelligence and achievement correspond to each other?

Investigations concerning familial resemblances in mental ability have been numerous since the initial studies were made by Galton nearly ninety years ago. Studies of the resemblances of siblings in mental ability and in school achievement have been reviewed in the writer's doctoral dissertation. The present study has utilized the longitudinal approach to this problem in a manner that has not been employed with data analyzing sibling resemblances in intelligence or achievement.

[1] Harry N. Rivlin, *Education for Adjustment: The Classroom Application of Mental Hygiene* (New York: Appleton-Century-Crofts, Inc., 1936), pp. 108–10.

* From Sarah M. Schoonover, "A Longitudinal Study of Sibling Resemblances in Intelligence and Achievement," *The Journal of Educational Psychology* (November, 1956), pp. 436–42. Reprinted by permission of the author and the publisher.

[1] This report is a portion of the writer's doctoral dissertation, "Sibling Resemblances in Achievement" (Supplemented by the mental-age data). See: *Dissertation Abstracts*, Vol. 13, No. 5, Publication No. 5726 (Ann Arbor: University Microfilms, 1953). Acknowledgment is made to Dean Willard C. Olson, University of Michigan, who directed the original research.

Siblings Selected for Study

Source of the data. The data were secured from the records of the University Elementary School at the University of Michigan. Of the children in this school, 70 per cent come from professional homes, while 30 per cent come from business and white-collar homes.

There are approximately seven applications for each vacancy at the University Elementary School. The primary purpose for which the school was established, i.e., the promotion of research in child development, is the main guide in admission policies. Consideration is given to the suitability of children as subjects for growth studies and for the type of educational program provided. Applications are not accepted for the blind, the deaf, the seriously crippled, nor the severely mentally retarded. Preference is given to children likely to remain through sixth grade, to children seeking entrance at an early age, and to children having siblings already enrolled. An attempt is made to keep a balance between the number of boys and the number of girls at each age level.

The school endeavors to provide for the development of the child as a whole in his social setting. It takes into account physical hygiene, mental hygiene, pacing of growth, individual differences, and active participation in group life. Its curriculum is flexible and emergent, is based upon a concept of learning through experience, and is determined in the light of children's interests and present needs.

Description of the data. The psychology division of the University Elementary School maintains an intelligence-test schedule on a yearly basis. The Stanford-Binet Revised Scale is administered annually within two weeks of each child's birth date, or six months following the birth date of children born in the summer. An achievement-test schedule is maintained on a six-month basis. The Gates Reading Test is given semiannually in October and in April, until the child achieves a score of 102 months, at which time he is given the Stanford Achievement Test, Primary Battery. The Intermediate Battery is administered in grades four through six.

Records of intelligence- and achievement-test scores have been filed in the Psychometric Unit for all children who have attended and who have been tested at the University Elementary School. Since the school was opened in 1930, longitudinal material has been collected over a twenty-five-year period.

Selection of the data. All true sibling pairs, with chronological age overlap, and with four or more scores per sib on the Stanford-Binet Test and on the Stanford Achievement Test, from the fall of 1929 through the spring of 1951, were utilized in this study. With these qualifications, fifty-nine sibling pairs were found for intelligence; sixty-four pairs for arithmetic, education, reading, and spelling; forty-two pairs for literature and social studies; forty pairs for language; and thirty-eight pairs for science. There were fewer sibling combinations in language, literature, science, and social studies because these tests are not found in the Primary Battery; therefore, there is less chance for a child to have four scores on these tests than for him to have that number on the other tests in the battery.

Methods for the Comparison of Longitudinal Sibling Records

The longitudinal approach. The longitudinal records, which involved measurement of the same children year after year, provided the data for this study. They have the following advantages: (a) Some of the variables found in the test situation, such as the child's disposition on any particular date or the child's reaction to being tested for the first time, are minimized. (b) Comparison of children at the same chronological age, rather than at dissimilar ages, is permitted.

For each family included in this study a mental growth graph and eight achievement growth graphs were constructed. This meant that 344 growth graphs and 757 individual growth curves were plotted.

Chronological, mental, and achievement ages were expressed in months. Chronological ages were plotted on the abscissas of the graphs, while mental and/or achievement ages were plotted on the ordinates of the graphs.

Fitting the linear equation. The linear equation best fitting the data was found to eliminate the observed variation and to determine some constant rate of growth which may be used to characterize the observed results. The equation of a straight line, $y = ax + b$, which gives the slope and the intercept of the line used to describe the growth-age relationship, was found by the method of the least squares fit. The linear fit for each child for intelligence and for each of the eight achievement variables was plotted graphically.

The method of the mean of the average differences. For each pair of siblings the limits of the overlap of their chronological ages were found, and from these the midpoint of the overlap was computed. Using the linear best fit, the age scores of each pair of siblings were read at these midpoints. The difference between these two ages was found, yielding the average difference for each sibling pair. The sum of these average differences was divided by the number of pairs, to secure the mean of the sib average differences. In addition to the group of siblings as a whole, the above was calculated for brother-brother, sister-sister, and brother-sister combinations.

It may be noted that the difference found for each pair is the average difference for the whole overlap period for the pair, because of the nature of the straight line. Also, because the linear best fit was found by utilizing a number of test scores for each child, a longitudinal effect is reflected in the average differences.

The unrelated pairs. To secure comparable data for unrelated pairs, siblings of this study were paired randomly with a nonrelated partner, and the means of the average differences were calculated for the unrelated pairs. By utilizing the same children for the sibling and for the nonsibling pairs, all group variables (such as age, sex, IQ, EQ, physical factors, emotional factors, social maturity, home environment, and school environment) are neutralized, resulting in two groups, comparable to each other in all of these respects.

The ratios. Ratios were computed by using the means of the average differences of the sib-pairs as dividends and those of the corresponding unrelated pairs as divisors. The resulting ratios were subtracted from 1.00 and then were multiplied by one hundred, producing in percentages the extent to which the sibling differences were reduced beyond those of the nonrelated pairs. To determine the significance of the differences between the sib-pair means and the unrelated pair means a t test for significance was employed.

The method of correlation. In addition to the ratio of the means, correlation coefficients were computed for the sibling pairs. A Pearson product-moment formula was used, as was the method of intraclass correlation. To discover the significance of these correlations a t test of an observed correlation was employed.

Sibling Difference and Resemblance

The mean of the average differences. The results obtained by the method of the mean of the average differences for sibling pairs and for unrelated pairs are given in Table 1 for intelligence and achievement.

The percentages of the reduction of the means of the average differences between the sibling and the nonrelated pairs in this study are given in Table 2.

These siblings consistently were found to have smaller means of average differences than the unrelated children for the group as a whole, as well as

Table 1

MEANS OF AVERAGE DIFFERENCES IN MENTAL AND EDUCATIONAL AGE SCORES,
EXPRESSED IN MONTHS

Mental or Achievement Age Measure	Total Group	Boy-Boy	Girl-Girl	Boy-Girl
Mental				
Sibling	9.9	9.4	8.1	11.5
Unrelated	18.3	23.5	14.2	18.1
Arithmetic				
Sibling	10.7	12.2	9.2	10.6
Unrelated	15.1	17.7	10.1	13.8
Education				
Sibling	12.6	12.2	12.3	13.0
Unrelated	19.3	23.6	17.7	15.8
Language				
Sibling	20.7	16.1	23.3	22.2
Unrelated	30.1	31.8	36.5	28.5
Literature				
Sibling	14.3	10.0	16.7	15.6
Unrelated	20.7	18.2	22.7	17.4
Reading				
Sibling	16.4	13.0	17.8	18.3
Unrelated	25.9	32.6	22.4	26.1
Science				
Sibling	16.0	14.3	16.1	16.7
Unrelated	20.5	24.1	23.3	23.0
Social studies				
Sibling	13.6	12.3	9.7	17.6
Unrelated	19.7	25.2	13.8	21.8
Spelling				
Sibling	14.7	13.1	14.3	16.1
Unrelated	21.5	25.5	20.3	20.8

Table 2

PERCENTAGES OF REDUCTION OF MEANS OF AVERAGE DIFFERENCES BETWEEN
SIBLING AND NONSIBLING PAIRS

Mental or Achievement Age	Total Group	Boy-Boy	Girl-Girl	Boy-Girl
Mental	45.6	60.4	42.8	36.5
Arithmetic	29.2	31.1	8.9	23.2
Education	34.8	48.3	30.5	17.8
Language	31.2	49.4	36.2	22.1
Literature	31.0	45.1	26.5	10.4
Reading	36.7	60.1	20.6	30.0
Science	22.0	40.7	31.0	27.4
Social studies	31.0	51.2	29.8	19.3
Spelling	35.4	52.6	42.0	25.6

for boy-boy, girl-girl, and boy-girl combinations. The greatest amount of reduction in variation, in each measure, was found in the boy-boy pairs. The question arises: are brother-brother combinations more alike than the other groupings, or are the differences between unrelated boy-boy pairs merely greater? The means of the average differences indicated that the differences between unrelated boys were greater than those of the other groupings, and that the brother-brother pairs showed only slightly less variation than what was found for the total group.

The smallest amount of reduction in variation, 8.9 per cent, was for girl-girl combinations in arithmetic. Girls as a whole in this study were more similar to each other in arithmetic ability than they were in other achievement-age measures. The largest amount of reduction in variation, 60.4 per cent, was found for boy-boy combinations in mental age. Unrelated boys varied to a greater extent in mental ability than did the other groupings, and brothers were slightly less variable than was the total group.

In general, the content subjects showed less reduction in variation than did the skill subjects. Perhaps this was caused partly by the greater unreliability of tests in the content subjects. All the differences between the sibpair means and unrelated pair means for the total group were significant at the 5 per cent level or lower, except for science. The number of sibling and unrelated pairs in science was the smallest of all the achievement measures, which may explain in part why the differences of the science means, though in the expected direction, did not meet the same test for significance.

Table 3

CORRELATIONS FOR THE TOTAL GROUP OF SIBLING AND NONSIBLING PAIRS

Mental or Achievement Age	Siblings	Nonsiblings
Mental	0.71	0.27
Arithmetic	0.49	0.08
Education	0.59	0.02
Language	0.40	−0.09
Literature	0.41	−0.11
Reading	0.51	0.01
Science	0.39	−0.02
Social studies	0.64	0.14
Spelling	0.53	0.08

The correlation coefficients. The results secured by the method of correlation coefficients for the total group of sibling pairs and for the total group of unrelated pairs are given in Table 3. For intelligence the correlation coefficient found for the siblings was high, indicating a marked relationship. The correlation for the nonrelated pairs was low, indicating a small relationship. Theoretically, the correlation expected for the unrelated pairs is zero. The fact that approximately 95 per cent of the children in this study have mental growth curves above the so-called norm may, in part, be responsible for the correlation for the unrelated pairs yielding a small relationship, rather than no relationship.

For achievement the correlation coefficients for the siblings were moderate, indicating a substantial relationship. The correlations found for the nonrelated pairs average $+0.01$ for the eight achievement measures.

According to the obtained t values, all the sibling correlations were significantly different from zero. It may be pointed out that these correlations substantiate each other and give some indication of the value of the correlations in the population, since they are all positive and are in a relatively narrow range.

The children involved in this study were a select and homogeneous group, since the large majority of them came from homes of superior economic, social, and intellectual status. It is possible that the differences between the unrelated pairs were smaller than they would have been if the total group had been less homogeneous.

Conclusions

All three methods of analysis utilized on the longitudinal growth records in this study, i.e., means of the average differences, percentage reduction of difference by family membership, and correlation, produced consistent results in describing the existence of a substantial amount of sibling resemblance in intelligence and achievement. Resemblances in intelligence were somewhat greater than they were in achievement.

7. Experimental Analysis of Behavior * 1

HARRY F. HARLOW

IT IS A privilege to be invited to appear before you on the occasion of the Semicentennial Celebration of the Establishment of the Psychological Laboratory of Saint Elizabeth's Hospital. The farsightedness of the program initiated in 1907 is evident in the prestige and leadership the laboratory has enjoyed in the field of clinical and abnormal psychology. At the time of its inception, the Psychological Laboratory was assigned the dual roles of diagnosis and research, and arrangements were made with George Washington University to provide for the mutual advantages that a mental hospital and academic psychology department can enjoy through cooperative enterprises. Its facilities were such even at the start that they would surpass those of some large mental hospitals of today. For one who regards himself as primarily a research psychologist, to be able to speak to a group with such rich research traditions is a pleasure, indeed.

It is my position that the experimental analysis of behavior is essentially the same whether we are dealing with the behavior of the paramecium or the man, whether we are analyzing behavior that appears to be simple or that which appears to be complex. As we ascend the phyletic scale, behavior becomes, or appears to become, progressively more intricate. The ultimate in apparent complexity is found at the human level, where we may measure indirectly such abstruse behavior as consciousness by using language as a dependent variable. Regardless, however, of the complexity of the behavior investigated, the fundamental techniques of the research psychologist are the same.

It is of interest to note that one of the pioneers in physiological and comparative psychology, a man who clearly recognized that the methods used in the experimental analysis of behavior were not species specific, was the first scientist to hold an appointment as psychologist on the staff of Saint Elizabeth's Hospital, Shepherd Ivory Franz. In William A. White's original report on the hospital's Psychological Laboratory in 1907 there are listed two published researches by Franz: one measuring the behavorial effects of brain abnormality in man, the other the effects of cortical lesions on learned

* From Harry F. Harlow, "Experimental Analysis of Behavior," *The American Psychologist* (August, 1957), pp. 485–90. Reprinted by permission of the author and the American Psychological Association.

1 This paper was presented at the Semicentennial Celebration of the Establishment of the Psychological Laboratory of Saint Elizabeth's Hospital, April 20, 1957.

behaviors in monkeys and cats. Franz pioneered in the experimental analysis of behavior in the subhuman animal following cortical lesions, using apparatus which yielded objective records and initiating controlled experimental designs. His willingness to translate experimental methods effective in studying the behavior of the brain-injured man to the brain-injured subhuman animal remains one of the great technological and methodological achievements of this past half century.

Study of Complex Behavior

The idea that the experimental analysis of behavior is independent of behavioral complexity is important and must not be lost. No behavior is too complicated to analyze experimentally, if only the proper techniques can be discovered and developed. Complex problems evade effective experimental analysis far less frequently than experimenters evade complex problems. Unfortunately, there are many areas in which the important problems are inherently intricate. The important problems in abnormal psychology, for example, will not be solved by safe and sane research.

Actually, complexity of behavior is not set by the species or by the response under investigation. There is no limit to the complexities of experimental analysis which may be employed in studying any animal or any response system. With subhuman forms we may complicate the analysis by introducing the variables of drastically altered anatomical and physiological state, as did Franz. Indeed, even with unicellular organisms, we may investigate the biochemical variables related to the organism's behavior, and there is no forseeable limit to the possible depth of analysis.

Let us restrict ourselves, however, to the problem of the experimental analysis of the behavior of the total organism. Less than a hundred years have passed since large-scale, systematic studies of the behavior of man and of closely related animal forms were first attempted. Looking backward twenty-five, fifty, seventy-five, or a hundred years, one sees that the nature of behavorial investigations has changed, and the fundamental changes have for the most part not been sudden or cataclysmic. They have appeared as trends, and these trends now are of such temporal length that they have some predictive power with regard to the direction which the experimental analysis of behavior will take in the future.

Insofar as the behavior of the total organism is concerned, there has been a trend, at least among psychologists, to attempt to analyze ever-increasingly complex behavioral processes. Experimental psychology developed in large part from experimental physiology. One of the great figures of the era preceding the advent of experimental psychology was <u>Hermann von Helm-holtz.</u> After measuring reaction time in peripheral nerves, he studied reaction time in the intact human being, the classical reaction time situation. But von Helmholtz abandoned these studies as being outside the domain of experimental science because of what appeared to him to be the intrinsic and capricious variability of the total, intact, human *S*. Simple, choice, and complex reaction time seem to us now to be completely within the domain of experimental investigation; indeed, to many of us these problems appear to be so simple as to be relatively unchallenging. We are no longer disturbed by human variability, and we have long since developed tools which we believe enable us to handle human variability in terms of precise, analytical, experimental designs.

Again referring to White's 1907 report, let me quote:

It . . . becomes of the highest importance to investigate mental diseases upon their mental side and to study their origin and development by modifications of the methods of the psychological laboratory. While great expectations were entertained from the application of psychological methods of psychiatry, it was soon found that the accumulation of reaction time averages was of little value for the solution of psycho-pathological problems and that the methods of normal psychology must needs be modified to suit the changed conditions.

Now it may or may not be argued that we have <u>fully accomplished</u> the <u>change in methods of normal psychology</u> to such a point that all the <u>psychological problems in the psychiatric field have attained solution.</u> But, regardless of the progress made, psychological research in abnormal psychology has had a greater influence on reaction time studies than reaction time studies have had on abnormal research. The very attack on problems of complexity and importance often places specific psychological problems, apparatus, and procedures in perspective.

It is no accident that the kinds of behaviors which we classify as learning, thinking, motivation, and emotion were subjected to experimental analysis after the methods of studying more limited aspects of the behavior of the total organism had developed. Certainly the earlier experimental psychologists must have thought about these areas of human behavior, for they have long been described in common-sense language terms. The forefathers in our field must have left these areas relatively untouched, either fearful that they lacked the technical tools to investigate scientifically areas of such frightening complexity or believing that these areas were outside the pale of the *experimental* analysis of behavior.

Approximately fifty years passed from the inception of experimental psychology—the psychology of the individual—to the inception of experimental social psychology. Recourse to the pioneering textbooks in the field, such as Floyd Allport's *Social Psychology,* will make it apparent that early experimental social psychology differed in no very striking degree from the then existent experimental individual psychology. But once social psychology became an identifiable area populated by identifying people, the complexity of problems which were studied and the complexity of the groups whose behavior was subjected to experimental analysis progressively increased. There may be some who feel that the social psychologists have already gone too far in interpreting the complexities of group interactions and group behaviors which can properly be subjected to experimental analysis; but it is a very safe prediction that, even if they have gone too far in the past, they will go very much farther in the future.

It is doubtless improper for anyone to set the limits of either individual or group behavior that is subjectable to experimental analysis. It is, however, an historical fact that psychologists have been subjecting ever more complicated behavior, individual or group, to experimental analysis. It is also a striking fact that they have been quite successful in discovering new techniques to facilitate their analyses. Furthermore, they have developed a wide range of supporting techniques, including new methods of experimental design and analysis, test and interview methods, and rating techniques. Doubtless many enthusiastic investigators have gone beyond the bounds of the experimental methods, but it would take a Solomon to assess exactly where these boundaries lie.

Longitudinal Approach

A second obvious trend in the experimental analysis of behavior is the ever-increasing importance being given to developmental investigations. Probably this is not an entirely independent trend, for the introduction of a major temporal variable into any research, field-observational or experimental, results in increasing complexity in the problem studied. Obviously, we are discussing here the trend to emphasize the longitudinal as opposed to the cross-sectional approach. It is apparent that we are not dealing with a dichotomy, but a scale. If we investigate the learning of a single problem, we are studying changes operating through time, even though this is a relatively brief period of time. Any transfer-of-training study can properly be regarded as longitudinal. Yet definitional matters aside, experimental psychology per se has traditionally been more concerned with the cross-sectional than with the longitudinal approach, and there has been, I believe, a tendency for experimental psychologists to think and plan in cross-sectional terms. In part this may be tradition, and in part it may have been imposed by necessity. Longitudinal studies are expensive; they are expensive financially, and they are expensive in personal demands and personal devotions. They are not easily adaptable to doctoral dissertations. Moreover, understanding them always involves a risk that the methods will be outmoded by the time the study has been completed, for technical changes are rapid in many research areas. Regardless of the difficulties, the trend toward longitudinal orientation in the analysis of behavior will continue. All aspects of behavior—learning, thinking, emotions, motivations, and behavior deviations—are affected by developmental variables and can be fully understood only in ontogenetic perspective, and this is true at the subhuman level as well as at the human level.

It is not my intention to imply that only longitudinal studies are desirable or have validity. Many problems are not only amenable to cross-sectional methods, but must be attacked in that way. For example, if we wish to determine the effect of age per se on ability to solve an initial learning problem, we must attack it by presenting the problem to groups varying insofar as possible only in age. But if we are interested in the effects of early learning experiences on later learning facility, we must employ the longitudinal approach. It is not an accident that the increased interest in long-time developmental studies has followed decades of cross-sectional research. Aside from their expensiveness, long-time studies have another limitation: they are productive only after cross-sectional studies have provided necessary information about interrelationships among variables operating at any particular time in determining behavior. In a sense, the cross-sectional studies prepare the way for the longitudinal ones, and the trend toward longitudinal studies is in part a reflection of the coming of age of experimental psychology.

Having been raised as a pure experimentalist, in the experimental tradition, I have followed with interest the changes in my own research programs and the development of these programs. The experimental S that has consumed almost all my research time has been the rhesus monkey. When I initially approached the experimental analysis of this animal's behavior, I approached it in the classical, cross-sectional manner. My co-workers and I investigated how the macaque learned to solve a discrimination problem, a string-test problem, an oddity problem, even a single concept. If it had not been for the fact that my monkey Ss continued to live after they had solved a problem and that they were not expendable in view of the available financial support, I might still be engaged in cross-sectional studies of the monkey's behavior. In fact, one criticism about my research that I encountered repeatedly was that my monkeys were not naive: they had had laboratory experiences prior to some problem about which I was currently reporting, and therefore my results, in the eyes of my critics, must be of questionable value. These same men were, of course, using the neonatal college Sophomores and Juniors as experimental *S*s. Then I discovered that the longevity of my *S*s was an asset to my research, not a liability.

Almost as much by accident as design, I ran one group of *S*s on a long series of discrimination problems rather than on a single problem. After all, the animals were there, and no more pressing problem presented itself at the time. Out of satisfying what seemed then to be a whim, we discovered a phenomenon with broad theoretical implications: the phenomenon of interproblem learning or, to use our term, the formation of learning sets.[2]

More recently, we have planned and initiated much more extensive longitudinal studies in which we have separated infant rhesus monkeys from their mothers at birth and raised them under the controlled conditions of the laboratory. We have been successful in raising over fifty of these young animals, and we have obtained data on their learning development from birth through 3 years of age. The monkey can learn conditioned shock responses and conditioned approach responses to a feeding booth during the first week of life. The rhesus infant masters, in a few trials, the single-unit Y maze at 15 days of age, and additional days of growth effect no improvement in performance. Tested in the Wisconsin General Test Apparatus, the monkey learns to discriminate between two stimulus objects very efficiently at 60 days of age, and performance approaches maximal efficiency at 120 days. The difficulty of the delayed response has probably been overrated; effective performance on this task first appears at about 125–150 days.

The ability to solve a single problem does not mean that the animal has the ability to transfer this learning to other problems of the same kind or class. The 120-day-old monkey that solves a single discrimination problem with adult efficiency transfers little or nothing to the next discrimination problem, the next twenty-five discrimination problems, or the next hundred. Discrimination learning-set formation is still inefficient at 200 days of age, and full interproblem learning ability is not completed until late in the second or third year of life. In other words, a very considerable maturational gulf exists between single-problem learning and learning-set formation.

[2] Because this phenomenon has been frequently described, I merely refer to it in the printed form of the paper.

We know that the macaque monkey visually explores its environment from the first day of life onward, and we have some information as to the kind of stimuli which elicit these compelling responses. Both observational and experimental findings indicate that visual responsiveness to detail appears rather suddenly between the eighth and tenth days of life in individual monkeys. Associated with this development there is a burst of exploratory-manipulatory activity to detailed stimuli, and we are convinced that these externally elicited and motivated behavior patterns are dependent on maturation rather than learning. Researches presently being conducted by Robert Zimmerman show that the eight- to ten-day-old macaque suddenly becomes able to solve a black-white discrimination; and the first of these problems which it then faces, it solves rapidly. Other data obtained by Zimmerman indicate that the ability to discriminate between a triangle and a square matures a few days later; and when this transpires, the infant monkey is able to solve this form discrimination rapidly. Additional data suggest that after this first form discrimination is learned, primary stimulus generalization in the infant is similar or identical to that in the adult monkey. We believe that our data will presently end all speculation concerning the degree to which brightness discrimination, form discrimination, and color discrimination are acquired or innate.

We have found the longitudinal approach to the experimental analysis of behavior interesting and even exciting, and we are now extending this type of analysis to other areas than learning, perception, and motivation. Lorna Smith is tracing the development of the nonnutritive sucking responses. William Mason is tracing the development of social behaviors. And we are planning and conducting systematic longitudinal studies on the development of emotional responses.

Interlaboratory Research

A third trend in the experimental analysis of behavior is, I believe, the development of interlaboratory research. This is not a trend of long standing, nor is it a well-established policy developed in any formalized way discernible at the present time. But it is a trend which I believe has been developing, even if on an informal basis. Let me again illustrate from my own experience. The systematic study of subhuman primate behavior arose from the researches on the chimpanzee carried out at the Yerkes Laboratories of Primate Biology at Orange Park, Florida. When we began our researches on monkeys, we were properly and consciously influenced by the previous work of that organization. Many of our researches were designed to measure in the monkey what had already been measured in the chimpanzee. Subsequently, the Yerkes Laboratories have conducted certain complementary researches in which they have investigated in the chimpanzee certain behaviors, such as color vision and various complex kinds of learning, which we had studied in the monkey. At the present time we are initiating researches on the nature and development of patterns of emotion which are similar to, and modeled after, researches by Hebb on the chimpanzee. This pattern of interlaboratory research in particular areas of psychology has been informal rather than directed, but it represents a pattern which is, I believe, becoming evident in many areas. More recently we have seen a directed pattern of interlaboratory research which may well serve as a model for future large-scale interlaboratory researches. This is the interinstitutional research being conducted by the Veterans Administration on the tranquilizing drugs. An attempt is presently being made to initiate another large-scale interdisciplinary and multi-institutional research program on conditions affecting susceptibility to cerebral palsy. The human cases are so few at any institution that only an interinstitutional program seems likely to yield the desired information. It is true that such a program goes beyond the experimental analysis of behavior, but it will certainly incorporate behavioral researches.

One aspect of this interlaboratory "collaboration" is the increasing frequency of symposia devoted to the discussion of specific problems or problem areas. Psychologists from all parts of the country and even the world have become more and more interested in gathering together to share their information, to give leads to other investigators that might further the attack on difficult problems. This pooling of information is doubtless saving research time and effort, not to mention funds, and accelerating progress in the field of psychology.

Twenty years ago a great many scientists lived with paranoid fears that their developing ideas would be stolen by their associates; now scientists of equivalent status live more in fear that their developing ideas will be ignored than that they will be stolen, and some are even eager to have their ideas stolen if the theft will be acknowledged in a footnote. It is a happy change that the scientist has come to think of himself as a social being, and his work as part of a social process.

Communality of Experimental Method

A fourth developmental trend relating to the experimental analysis of behavior is a conceptual trend: a developing belief that the experimental method as a method for the analysis of behavior is the common property of all behavioral scientists, not the exclusive right or exclusive prestige symbol of any one particular group.

The experimental method as operationally defined by most psychologists consists in reliably measuring some response variable, the dependent variable, and determining its functional relationships to other, independently manipulated variables. Frequently, but by no means necessarily, the independent variable is a stimulus variable. It is immediately apparent that this paradigm of the psychological experiment is very broad. The dependent variable can be a verbal report or verbal judgment; it can be an eyeblink or finger flexion, a score on the two-hand coordinator or Brown spool packing test; it can be a total or partial score on the Stanford-Binet, the Rorschach, or the Szondi test. The independent variables are in all cases essentially unlimited: including scaled stimulating conditions, intervals between stimulation, conditions of past experience, alterations in physiological state, and maturational status of the Ss.

It is obvious that, although experiments are all devised by the measurement of some dependent variable and the systematic manipulation of an independent variable, not all experiments are of equal value. There are wide degrees of difference in the precision with which various behaviors can be measured, i.e., in the reliability and objectivity of the measurement of the dependent variables. Likewise, the precision with which various independent variables can be scaled and controlled is by no means identical. Experiments differ in qualitative and quantitative excellence and may be evaluated by some highly objective criteria. Above and beyond this, there are more subtle criteria for judging the quality of experiments: the criteria of values. Value criteria are social criteria: they are determined by social norms, and they change with time. Whether or not we like these criteria, they have vast significance and can doubtless be measured with significant reliability. Psychologists both independently and as a social group have subjected many experiments to such evaluating devices. They have appraised experiments, elegant and inelegant, experiments employing the introspective method, Gestalt construcɩs, the 14-unit multiple T maze, or the Szondi test; and psychologists will continue this process.

Adaptation of Method to Problems

Perhaps there is a fifth developmental trend among psychologists, or at least a considerable body of psychologists: a trend to adapt method to problems, rather than to adapt problems to method. The deification of extremely rigid experimental method once threatened to lead to the exclusion of many problems of importance from the domain of the experimental analysis of behavior. There are classical instances in the past where the premature use of limited methods has blocked rather than facilitated the development of a new research area. For many classes of problems, simple observation methods may be more productive than rigid laboratory experiments using complex apparatus, especially during the exploratory phases of programmatic research. Actually, it should be emphasized that there is no sharp dichotomy between observational and experimental methods or between clinical and experimental methods.

At the present time, for example, we are interested in tracing the development of various patterns of emotional behavior in the rhesus monkey. We began by looking for response patterns which might fit into this rather broad category and noting the kinds of situations which elicited such behavior. But this observational study, like almost any observational study, is gradually taking on the characteristics of an experiment. As we gain sophistication about the monkey's emotional responses, we become more selective in the patterns which we observe, and we define our various dependent variables with increasing precision in the expectation of getting increased reliability. We learn that independent variables might be profitably exploited and gradually arrive at crude scales for quantifying these variables. We know at this point that we are using the experimental method, but we are not sure at exactly what stage the transition occurred. We have initiated formal experiments with rigid criteria for at least one of our emotional dependent variables, and we are trying to scale some of the independent variables that are functionally related. But we are open-minded as to whether or not formal experiments will give us as complete a picture of the nature and development of emotions in monkeys as we can obtain by supplementing the experimental data with essentially "pure" observational data.

Just as I believe there is no proper hierarchical system for ordering the various kinds of psychological methods, so do I believe that there should be no such system for ordering the various kinds of psychologists. Clinical psychologists, comparative psychologists, experimental psychologists, physiological psychologists, and social psychologists, insofar as they are interested and engaged in the experimental analysis of behavior, are all one family—happy family or not. None of these groups can with propriety set itself up as a sacred scientific society and assign to the others the role of secular groups enjoying only second-class psychological citizenship.

Results of importance bearing on the experimental analysis of behavior will be discovered by the use of various methods (both within and without the formal laboratory), by the aid of complex electronic apparatus or apparatus no more complex than the human brain and eye, by the use of experimental designs that are recondite and those which are naive, by the efforts of scientists who are intellectual giants and the efforts of scientists with more modest abilities. Different kinds of psychologists using very different methods will do golden- and silver-angel research; and, although I believe there should be no hierarchies among kinds of psychologists, I am convinced that there are and should be hierarchies in the values of the products which any and all kinds of psychologists produce. It is my opinion that golden-angel research will be best achieved if every psychologist feels that he is free to work on the problems which he believes are important, in the way which he thinks is appropriate, without feelings of deference. We need not worry too greatly about the techniques used or the capabilities of the men who first secure the intellectual beachheads. They will be followed by successive waves of silver-angels who will move in the heavy equipment, the Fisher-Yates tables, the Monroe calculators, and even the IBM machines and digital computers if the assault on the intellectual island is worthy of such logistic support. The grains of gold which were already uprooted from the sandy beaches will then be arranged in rows and columns, combinations and permutations, and eventually reconstructed and reassembled into intellectual coins which will be scientific legal tender for all time and all eternity. Whether or not anyone is interested at this time in the captured intellectual island, it can at least be left at a statistically significant level of confidence. And it is a pleasing thought that meanwhile other psychologists will be searching for and engaging in the experimental analysis of other areas of behavior, using (it is to be hoped) methods of their choosing, in the ways that give them personal satisfaction.

√ 8. *Hereditary Transmission* *

PAUL H. MUSSEN
AND JOHN J. CONGER

THUS LIFE begins at conception. But what of the forces that, throughout the individual's existence, will influence his development? When do they begin? The answer, again, is at conception. For at the moment that the tiny sperm penetrates the wall of the ovum, it releases twenty-four minute particles called *chromosomes.* At approximately the same time, the nucleus, the inner core of the ovum, breaks up, releasing twenty-four chromosomes of its own.

This process is of great interest to us because it has been established through painstaking research, that these chromosomes, which are further subdivided into even smaller particles called *genes,* are the carriers of the child's heredity. All the child's physical heritage from his father and his mother is contained in these forty-eight chromosomes.

What Is Transmitted?

Long before the geneticists established the existence of chromosomes and genes, scientists were convinced that many characteristics of a child's parents were transmitted to the child at conception. People have, however, differed about what was transmitted and how. For example, one school of thought, dating back to Lamarck, a French zoologist who published a book called *Philosophie zooligique* in 1773, long maintained a doctrine known

* From Paul H. Mussen and John J. Conger, *Child Development and Personality,* pp. 28–32. Copyright 1956 by Harper and Bros., New York, and reprinted with their permission.

as the inheritance of acquired characteristics. Lamarck felt that individuals improved or weakened their own physical capacities through experience or training, and that the effects of such changes could be transmitted to their offspring. Thus, by developing a diseased lung or poor digestion, a prospective parent would be hurting his child's chances of being healthy. People began to postulate such notions as that the giraffe acquired his long neck because his ancestors had spent a great deal of time reaching into trees for food, or that the snake lost his legs as a result of his forebears' propensity for creeping through crevices.

Nor were such speculations confined only to obvious physical characteristics. Many people believed that a mother could influence her child's chances of being born with a talent for singing, if she had, in her youth, carefully cultivated her own voice. Or that if a father had previously developed an interest in mathematics, this interest was likely to be inherited by his son.

However, such early theories as these, and the inferences based upon them, were dealt a hard blow by Weismann in 1889. He presented evidence suggesting that while the rest of the body may change with increasing age or through exercise, illness, or injury, the germ cells (chromosomes and genes) which an individual harbors, and which are passed on to his children at their conception, do not ordinarily change.

In the main, subsequent research has tended to support Weismann's position. However, it has since been determined that under exceptional circumstances, genes may change or be killed, as for example, through direct radiation from X ray or from atomic blasts. Nevertheless, genes are not subject to any of the usual influences that either build up or break down our bodies or improve our minds. Thus the genes that a sick, but well-educated man of 50 possesses, are no different from those that he possessed as a healthy, but untutored youth of 17. In short, changes in the rest of the body do not affect the genetic characteristics of the germ cells which are passed on to our children. Hence there is no reason for believing that we can affect our children's biological destinies by engaging in physical education or self-improvement campaigns.

The Mechanisms of Hereditary Transmission

One of the things that must have puzzled parents in prescientific days was why two children of the same parents should be so different physically. The answer lies in the mechanics of hereditary transmission.

If each child received all of both parents' genes, we could not explain individual genetic differences between them, since all the children would then have identical heredities. The fact, however, is that each child inherits only half of each parent's genes. Moreover, different children in a family may inherit different combinations of their mother's and father's genes. Thus individual differences between them become possible.

The way in which this happens will become clear as we proceed. It will be recalled that the original fertilized ovum contains forty-eight chromosomes. As this cell divides to form two new cells, each of its forty-eight chromosomes also divides in half, by splitting lengthwise down its center (see Fig. 1). Through a process known as *polarization*, the halved chromosomes then go to opposite sides of the cell. Thus, when the cell itself divides down the center, the new cells will each contain the same forty-eight chromosomes as the original cell.

This process is repeated again and again as development proceeds. Even in the completed human being, when the myriad cells of the body have by this time taken on their special functions as tissue, bone, blood, and muscle, each cell still contains a replica of the original forty-eight chromosomes of the fertilized ovum.

Germ Cells

But if this is true, why don't the sperm and ovum, which go to make up a new individual, also contain forty-eight chromosomes each, since certainly they too are cells? It will be recalled that the new individual receives only twenty-four chromosomes from each parent.

The answer, stripped of genetic complexities, is actually quite simple. The adult organism contains, not one, but two kinds of cells—body cells which go to make up bone, nerves, muscles, and organs; and germ cells, from which the sperm and ova are derived. While the process of chromosome and cell division described above applies to the somatoplasm (the body cells), it does not apply completely to the germ cells. Throughout most of their evolutionary history, the latter develop just as the body cells do. But at the time of their final division into recognizable sperm or ova, the pattern varies. At this point, the germ cells split, but the chromosomes do not. Instead, the forty-eight chromosomes, which in reality are twenty-four pairs of similar chromosomes—one pair-member from each parent—simply divide into two groups. One member of each pair goes to one of the resulting sperm or egg cells, and one to the other (see Fig. 2). Thus the ova and sperm have only twenty-four chromosomes each and the new individual obtains a total of only forty-eight.

We can see, too, why it is that the children of the same parents do not all have to be alike. As may be seen from Figure 3, if Sperm A unites with Ovum D, the new individual will possess a different set of chromosomes than if Sperm B unites with it. (Ovum C is indicated in dotted lines since

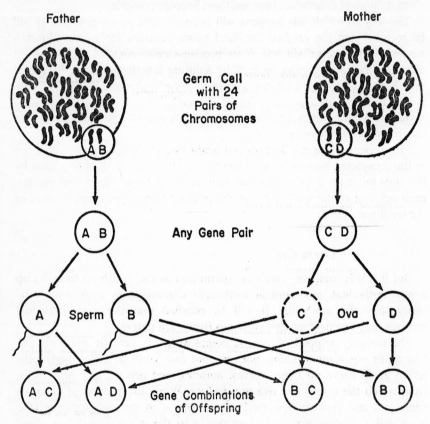

Figure 3. Schematic diagram showing possible gene combinations of offspring resulting from gene pairs of parents.

ordinarily at any one conception only one ovum from the mother is ready for fertilization. The same of course is not true of sperm. At any one mating millions of sperm are released—as many as a hundred million in one drop of seminal fluid, any one of which might potentially fertilize the receptive ovum.)

9. Biological Inheritance, Environmental Influence, and Cultural Heritage *

LESTER D. CROW

AND ALICE CROW

The Impact of Biological Inheritance

CONSIDERED genetically, both heredity and environment play important roles in the life of any individual. There must be a living organism upon which environmental conditions can exercise their influence. Contrariwise, an organism cannot live and grow in a vacuum. Human reproduction is basic to the continuance of the human species. Increased understanding of the significance of inherited potentialities exercises a potent influence upon evolving educational theory and practice. . . .

Functions of biological inheritance. Certain principles of biological inheritance are almost self-evident. As members of the human species, all individuals have many characteristics in common. Differences among personal traits tend to be quantitative rather than qualitative to the extent that individual patterns of development tend to follow what can be thought of as relatively normal progress. For example, anyone who possesses normal functioning vocal organs can learn to talk. Whether the "silver-voiced" orator is a product of superior biological heredity or of well-guided training is another matter.

Many music lovers still insist that the voice of Caruso has never been equaled. Whence came his unique vocal powers? Psychological study is attempting to find adequate answers to questions such as this. The results of such intensive study can be of inestimable value to parents and teachers in helping young people develop, to an achievable limit, whatever potentialities they may possess. As we gain greater understanding of an individual's inherited potential, we are enabled better to evaluate the potency of environmental influences.

A popular misunderstanding of the functioning of biological inheritance is evidenced by laymen who speak of a child's inheriting a characteristic from his mother or father. Studies in this field have given us the following principle: 50 per cent of a child's characteristics probably are inherited

* From Lester D. Crow and Alice Crow, *Human Development and Learning,* pp. 23, 27–33. Copyright 1956 by American Book Co., New York, and reprinted with their permission.

from the mother's line, and the other 50 per cent from the father's. It has been estimated further than one half of a child's native characteristics are inherited from his parents, one fourth from his grandparents, one eighth from his great-grandparents, and the lesser fractions in proportion down the ancestral line. These relationships between inherited traits and family potentials can explain some of the differences (apart from those caused by differing environmental conditions) that are found among siblings.

Determination of the sex of the new organism also is associated with chromosome distribution. The new life receives twenty-four chromosomes from each parent. The mother contributes twenty-four x chromosomes. If the father contributes the same number of x chromosomes, the child will be a girl. If, however, the father contributes twenty-three x chromosomes and one y chromosome, the child will be a boy. It is the one x or y chromosome received from the father that is the sex determiner. . . .

Furthermore, certain genes give evidence of being stronger than others. The stronger genes are referred to as *dominant* because traits produced by them are more likely to appear in successive generations than are traits produced by the weaker or *recessive* genes. Gregor Mendel, an Austrian Augustinian abbot, in 1866, was the first to propound the theory of dominance and recessiveness of traits, as a result of his experiments in the hybridization of peas.

Environmental and Cultural Influences upon Human Development

In the foregoing discussion of human growth and development, we attempted to show that an individual is what he is at any stage of his development as a result of the interaction that constantly is taking place between his growing self and the many factors of the environment by which he is stimulated. Biological and psychological studies of the functions of inheritance have provided a workable basis upon which to build comparable studies of the effects of differing environmental conditions and cultural influences upon native traits and maturational sequence. Some of these effects are discussed briefly.

Learning and maturation. An important characteristic of human nature appears to be the inherent ability to respond to stimulation in such ways as to bring about changes in attitudes and overt behavior. This statement implies that every individual from birth on has the power *to learn*—to adapt himself to whatever conditions seem to be of value in his life experiences. This general conclusion does not present the whole story, however. As has been mentioned earlier, what a child learns and how well he learns are dependent upon his existing stage of maturation—his readiness to learn. Moreover, there are wide differences among children, as well as among older persons, in their limits of "learnability." As native constitution differs among individuals, so does the ability to profit from learning stimulation.

A child's relative degree of success in adapting himself to his environment is closely associated with the kind of learning stimulation to which he is exposed and the ways in which he is stimulated. Here again must be taken into consideration the native constitution of the learner and his state of readiness to learn. Before attempting to guide a young person's learning experiences, parents and teachers need to understand the ways in which, and the extent to which, even the children of the same family differ in these respects. Mothers sometimes cause themselves and their children much difficulty because they do not recognize the fact that their children are not all alike.

The attitude of a woman known to the authors illustrates this lack of understanding of child nature. Her first child, a girl, was an extremely alert youngster who responded to learning stimulation so well that she sometimes was expected to react in ways beyond her maturational level. On the whole, she made a good adjustment. As often is the case with the first child, the mother kept a detailed log of the girl's developmental progress, including such matters as the child's first intelligible word, creeping, crawling, and walking experiences, toilet training, changes in eating habits, manipulatory progress, and all the other behavior changes that accompany early growth and development. The mother was very proud of her alert daughter.

Then came the second child, a boy. He was a heavier and less active baby than his sister. His developmental process also was much slower than hers. The mother did not keep a written report of his sequences of responses but day by day, almost hour by hour, she compared his behavior reactions with those of his sister when she had been passing through the same stage of development. In every instance, the boy's progress lagged behind his sister's. This disturbed the mother very much. She could not believe that a son of hers could be so "slow." She feared that he was subnormal in intelligence. The fact that he was a healthy boy who ate and slept well only increased her concern about him. Even during the elementary-school years of the two children, this mother continued to compare the boy's behavior at home and his record in his school-work with those of his sister at his age.

It was not until they both were in high school, the girl one year ahead of her brother, that the mother discovered that in some areas of study, especially in mathematics, her son was more successful than his supposedly brighter sister. Even then the mother attempted to place the blame of the girl's relative lack of success upon poor teaching, although both young persons had studied with the same teachers. Not until her two children had reached their later teens was the mother finally willing to admit that they were different, and that in many ways, the boy was superior to his sister in learning ability.

Differences in learning ability among the children of the same family become a serious matter if all the children happen to attend the same school and are taught by the same teachers, one after another. It is likely that the first of the siblings to attend the school will achieve a certain reputation for himself as a learner. Nonunderstanding teachers then will expect every other child of that family to perform similarly to the first child. If the first child had demonstrated superior learning ability, he may be held up as a model to the others, some of whom may not be able to achieve so successfully as he did. This is a frustrating experience for a youngster and is likely to inhibit the expressing of whatever other learning abilities he may have, in terms of his maturational status. If the first child were a slow learner, his reputation might result in the teacher's failing to recognize the superior abilities or more rapid maturation of the younger siblings.

The fact that children's maturational patterns do not progress uniformly should be understood by everyone who attempts to guide children's learning experiences. The child whose early maturation is rapid may appear to the teacher of the early school grades to be an extremely bright youngster, and is stimulated accordingly. The child's maturational rate may slow down, however. By the time he reaches the later grades, he may demonstrate no more than average learning ability. Because of his earlier performance, his teachers may expect more from him in the way of learning success than he can achieve. Consequently, his parents and teachers may assign other causes than the real one for his failure to meet their expectations; the child's interest in learning may be inhibited further by their treatment of him. The child who matures slowly at first but who later makes more rapid progress may not receive sufficient learning stimulation in his later childhood years because of nonunderstanding adults who do not recognize his increased learning readiness.

Environmental influences during early childhood. Many psychologists believe that the first six years of a person's life are the most important. They emphasize the effects of the physical conditions and the cultural pattern of the home on the type of attitudes and the behavior which are being developed in the child. The ways in which the young child's needs and wants are satisfied, the objects in the home by which he is stimulated, the attitudes toward him displayed by his parents and other members of the family, the language spoken in the home, habitual activities of the family, and the relationships that exist among the members of the family and between the family and neighborhood associates and family friends— all these represent some of the factors of influence by which he is surrounded. Gradually, the child learns to react in more or less expected ways to the patterns of behavior that are peculiar to the culture into which he has been born.

During this period, not only is the child being guided by his elders into specific kinds of learning, but also certain habit patterns are being developed without his being aware of them. As the result of a kind of trial-error-trial-success type of response, he learns that some of his behavior responses are approved and others are not. He develops one attitude toward his mother, another toward his father. He soon discovers that he can "get away" with certain forms of activities with one adult and not with another.

For example, a relatively cooperative one-year-old was left in the care of an unmarried uncle while the parents were away for a few hours. When they left, the child was sitting contentedly in his high chair, playing quietly with some toys. As soon as he was alone with his uncle, however, he began to throw his toys on the floor, apparently expecting his uncle to pick them up. As soon as a toy was returned to him, he threw it down again. If the uncle did not return it quickly enough, the child screamed, held his breath, or kicked until the toy was returned. No amount of pleading or scolding made any changes in the child's behavior. By the time the parents returned, both the adult and the baby were in a state of near-exhaustion. At the sight of his mother, the child started to "coo" and to settle back to the manipulation of toys, with no attempts at throwing them.

Unfortunately, we do not know what goes on in the young child's mental processes that causes him to react as he does to environmental stimuli. The best that we can do is to study the child's overt behavior in specific situations and then attempt to discover what factor in the situation is related specifically to the displayed attitude.

By the time the average child enters kindergarten or the first grade, he reflects, in his simple thinking processes, his attitudes toward people and things, and in his accustomed behavior, those environmental influences that either have helped or have hindered desirable personal and social development. At this age, some children exhibit a commendable amount of independence of action, poise, and ease in the presence of adults or their peers, an attitude of cooperation, and a considerable amount of self-control. Other five- or six-year-olds give overt evidence of continued dependence upon their mother or other adult who has cared for their needs, are shy in the presence of strangers, are demanding in their relations with their peers, and appear to have little or no self-control or ability to handle their own affairs. To some extent these differences can be explained in terms of rate of maturation; to an even greater extent they probably are rooted in the kind of home and neighborhood environment in which the children are reared.

Cultural patterns and the developing child. Every child matures in an environment that is peculiar to itself. The effect of all the elements of this environment that gradually stimulate the development of the organism into a social person can be called the individual's *social heritage*. This socializing process sometimes is referred to as *acculturation*.

Several studies have been made of the effects upon the child of the culture in which he is reared. Comparisons between relatively primitive cultures and modern, more sophisticated ones, as these affect child development, have yielded some interesting results. Social anthropologists, sociologists, and psychologists seem to agree that children all over the world are relatively similar in their growth or maturational pattern. The differences that exist in the behavior of children reared in different cultures would seem, then, to be the result of the cultures themselves rather than of the native constitution of the individuals.

In general, competition and aggressiveness among children are cultural outgrowths. Margaret Mead, as a result of her studies of life among primitive people, found, for example, that children in New Guinea were very gentle and noncompetitive, as compared to the children of modern Western cultures. In Samoa, the cultural aim was the development of uniformity of personality rather than the encouragement of many different varieties of personality, as is characteristic of our culture.

In contrast to the Samoan emphasis upon uniformity is the "flattened out" culture that, in the 1930's, was characteristic of the then relatively isolated community of Colvin Hollow, in the Appalachian Mountains, less than one hundred miles from Washington, D.C. This community consisted almost entirely of individually owned and operated farms. Each family was a social unit by itself with little if any community consciousness, or appreciation of what it means to be a citizen of the United States. The children of these families, therefore, developed a pattern of life that was unique to individual family customs and attitudes.

The cultural patterns of some peoples of Europe, Asia, and South America are neither primitive nor modern. Among them, child rearing is in a state of flux. Improved methods of communication and transportation have led to greater intermingling of different peoples, and a breakdown of many of the older cultural traditions. War periods also are responsible for the infiltration into traditional patterns of thought of what might be referred to as modern ideas. Consequently, parental attempts to foster traditional attitudes and modes of behavior come into conflict with youthful struggles to achieve democratic status in the home.

Language patterns still differ, but more people are gaining at least a minimum of skill in languages other than their own. In most cultural areas, "modern" dress is taking the place of dress styles peculiar to a particular people. American motion pictures are penetrating far-flung corners of the world; here we enjoy pictures produced outside the country, sometimes presented in a foreign language. Modern toys and games and sports are becoming universal in their appeal. Coca Cola advertisements appear everywhere. These are but a few of the ways in which a modern world culture gradually is supplanting isolated, traditional cultures.

By nature, children all over the world show similar likenesses and differences. It is possible that, as particular cultural beliefs, attitudes, and accustomed behavior disappear, there will be a comparable change in the developmental pattern of all young children. Eventually, we may reach the point where, within limits, all people will share common beliefs, attitudes, and modes of behavior.

10. Culture and Personality *

MAX L. HUTT

AND ROBERT G. GIBBY

IN OUR detailed examination of the interaction of culture and personality in early infancy, we shall begin with the proposition that there is no ubiquitous, fixed cultural pattern in which the baby is reared or even in the ways in which biological needs are met. For example, it is not always the biological mother who takes care of the baby or who feeds him. Among

* From Max L. Hutt and Robert G. Gibby, *The Child: Development and Adjustment,* pp. 51–55. Copyright 1959 by Allyn and Bacon, Inc., Boston, and reprinted with their permission.

the Alorese, an Indonesian people, the baby is frequently taken care of by the father while the mother is occupied in the fields with her chores. At other times a sibling or a grandparent may be responsible for the baby. During these times that the mother is away, sometimes as early as the second week after its birth, the baby is given premasticated food or it may remain hungry until the mother returns. At the other extreme are the Hopi Indians of our own country. These Indians are extremely indulgent in their care of the baby, who is breast-fed by its mother whenever it shows any inclination to want nourishment. In this respect, the use of the breast as a pacifier or as a comforter is also practiced by Okinawans and the Comanche. Our only point at this time is that there are great variabilities in the kinds of interactions between mother and infant which are related to culture variabilities.

Some Constancies in the Culture of Infants

Despite the marked differences that exist among cultures in respect to early patterns of child-mother interactions, there are also marked constancies. After all, the newborn child is a helpless, dependent individual who will die unless its nutritional needs are met and unless it is protected from injury and disease. Hence, with few exceptions, there has been a *minimal constancy* in the relationship between infant and mother (or the adult who takes care of him). This type of constancy makes it very difficult to know what is inborn in the infant, what is "instinctive" in the mother, and what is the learned effect of the persistent modes of interaction. An illustration of this difficulty in the case of subhuman species will make this point more explicit. Psychologists had long assumed that animals as well as humans were born with certain *instincts:* certain inborn ways of behaving to reach specified goals without opportunity of learning these behaviors. Most of the texts in psychology of a few decades ago contained the particular author's list of such animal or human instincts, and psychologists vied with each other in compiling more complete and exhaustive lists. These instincts were assumed to be present because of the apparent, unvarying behavior of the particular species. However, when in experimental studies the conditions of "minimal constancy" were varied, surprising results were obtained. For example, Schneirla found, in a review of the experimental literature of maternal behavior of lower animals, that much of the so-called instinctive maternal behavior was not instinctive at all but was the result of interactions of learning, socialization, and specific types of chemical excitation. It was learned that when a cat is prevented from licking parts of its body that are *customarily* licked during parturition or when the cat is prevented from licking at the afterbirth, its interest in licking its neonate and even its very interest in the neonate may be entirely lacking; i.e., such interests are not automatic and instinctive. Many studies have now demonstrated that, in fact, there are no true maternal instincts in animals, although some authorities do not accept this proposition entirely. In a similar way, studies have shown that what was formerly assumed to be instinctive in the infant animal was attributable to the combined effects of development, learning, and socialization. Again, merely by way of illustration, a study by Scott may be cited. In this study, it was reported that a female lamb, separated from its mother and from usual mothering experiences for the first nine days of its life, failed to respond in the "instinctive" manner of young lambs. It did not suckle and did not graze with the other lambs. (In fact, it seemed to prefer people and was rejected by other lambs!)

From the foregoing we can begin to see that the behavior of a newborn organism is considerably influenced by the early experiences to which it is subjected—by its cultural heritage. We have tried to indicate, too, that the interactions between infant and culture are highly complex, embracing such *patterns* of behavior as methods of giving nourishment, methods of giving affection and sensual stimulation, methods of control and discipline, and experiences in interactions with single individuals or with groups of individuals in constant or inconstant ways. Each of these units of interaction and many others contain many complexities within themselves. For example, methods of giving nourishment may vary in terms of what is fed, the amount of food offered, the frequency of feeding, the salient factors determining the times of feeding, the concomitant behaviors of the mother during the feeding, and the like. This complexity within the units of the pattern and within the total pattern makes it difficult indeed to isolate the precise relationship and the causal influence, if any, between an individual factor in the infant's early experience and the immediate or long-term resultants in personality. This does not mean, however, that early experience is unimportant—indeed all the evidence is to the contrary. It does mean that we shall be doomed to disappointment if we try to predict resultants in personality development from individual, isolated, specific factors in the child's cultural experience. Orlansky attempted to review the evidence on the relationship between specific aspects of infant-mother interactions, such as duration of breast feeding, and was unable to find any direct, simple correlations with subsequent personality. This might have been expected because of the reasons we have suggested above.

Patterns of Feeding

To illustrate and clarify the significance of the culture-organism inter-action, we shall now discuss two of the many patterns that are significant. Later in our treatment of the development of the infant we shall have occasion to examine some other patterns affecting the general personality and socialization of the child. Two of the most important sets of experiences for the newborn center around the intake of food and the early controls of body functions. Let us consider the nutritional intake of the baby first. As Scupin points out: "When (the infant) is hungry it sucks loudly on its fingers, but this pacifies it only for a short time. Before it is placed at the breast, its head rolls back and forth restlessly, the mouth seeks eagerly, and the eyes are open wide. When it finds the nipple, it utters satisfied grunting sounds, sucks hastily until it chokes, and sighs as if it were doing the most strenuous work." Presumably this pattern of responses by the infant is ready to function at birth. How it develops, becomes modified, and finally gets integrated into later forms of food-seeking and food intake is a matter that is very much affected by the nature of the *total pattern* of the infant's relationships with its mother. Equally important, this total pattern of relationships involves much more than the development of food intake habits; it affects the way in which the early personality characteristics of the infant develop. For, along with the intake of food, the baby "takes in" the earliest (for him) culture patterns of the mother. The nature of the attention he gets, the nature of the deprivation he suffers, the kinds of affection he is given and the amount and kind of fondling and "handling" which may be part of the food intake relationship with the mother affect his reaction patterns. As Fries, for example, has shown, when babies are taken care of by compulsive, rigid nurses they tend to develop startle (or anxious) reactions and show other signs of tension and anxiety, whereas when babies are taken care of by gentle, secure nurses they show far less of such reactions. Observations by Escalona of infants who were high-strung, showing that their mothers were also high-strung, support the same conclusion: that babies take in more than nourishment; they "take in" also many of the attributes of the mother. Exactly how this interiorization of attitudes and other behaviors occurs is not thoroughly understood as yet, but much of it is explainable by the process of *empathy*, a nonverbal means of communication through which the infant shares some of the mother's psychological experiences.

In our own American society, by and large, the feeding of the baby is now on a demand basis. Much permissiveness is practiced on the assumption that under such conditions the baby will develop more adequate emotional security and *basic trust* in its relations with the world. Such a practice, which is in opposition to the previously held practices of scheduled feedings, allows for individual differences in the nutritional and physiological needs of the youngsters and also allows for individual differences among mothers. We have apparently learned, in this country, that such a permissive relationship does not necessarily mean complete indulgence of the baby. The baby has to learn very slowly, and later the infant also has to learn, to tolerate frustrations and to compromise its needs with the needs of mother and family. If this beginning of reality-testing is not practiced, very slowly to be sure and with the individual tolerance limits of the baby or infant, the baby can learn to become the tyrannical master of the household and fail to learn methods of secure and reciprocal relationships with others.

Although the trend in this country is toward permissive or demand feeding, such a practice will not automatically solve all of the problems of good infant-mother interactions. As we have already indicated, much depends on the emotional security of the mother who can do what she feels is right for the infant because her observations of the infant, and not because some arbitrary norms from some authoritative source book, tell her what to expect and what to do. In addition, the mother is, herself, part of a culture, which greatly influences the ways that she has "available" for dealing with and relating to her child. These general culture patterns have been dichotomized as *fetusphile* and *fetusphobic* by Bernfeld. By the former term is meant a culture that attempts to reproduce the "natural" conditions of infants so that it is most comfortable, warm, and protected. By the latter term is meant a culture that traumatizes infants or shocks them so that through physical frustrations they will become hardened. These two extremes of culture patterns may be termed overindulgent and overtraumatic, respectively. Another way in which cultures may be classified with respect to the general pattern of infant-mother relationships is the following threefold division described by Honigmann: *symmetrical,* in which the infant is treated like an incomplete adult; *complementary,* in which the infant is regarded as essentially different from adults; *reciprocal,* in which the infant receives certain things from adults as due to him and owes other things to adults (such as achievement) in return. It is probable that an infant living in a particular culture will tend to form personality characteristics that are different from another infant living in another category of culture.

11. A Cross-Cultural Study of the Reinforcement of Child Behavior * [1]

WAYNE DENNIS

FEW PSYCHOLOGISTS reject the proposition that the rewarding of an act increases the frequency, vigor, and promptness with which it will recur. That the strength of a response can be increased by reward has probably been recognized from an early human period. It is likely that parents and other adults—without benefit of Thorndike, Skinner, and others—early found that reward was an effective means of social control. It goes almost without saying that they rewarded those acts of which they approved, and hence rewards had the effect of transmitting and inculcating social values.

It follows that if one knew what child behaviors were being rewarded in a society one could formulate hypotheses concerning both the values of the adults and the future behavior of the children. But in a "field situation" it is difficult to know what is being rewarded. The approval of child behavior often occurs in the home, or in some other setting in which it cannot readily be observed. We wish to report some data obtained with a method which we believe will enable a researcher to investigate in nearly any society those reinforcements which probably play a major part in the socialization of the child.

Method

The method consists in using the critical incident technique developed by Flanagan and his associates. In general, this technique involves asking the subject to describe one or more instances of behavior of a specified kind. In the present connection this means that the subject is asked to

* From Wayne Dennis, "A Cross-Cultural Study of the Reinforcement of Child Behavior," *Child Development,* 28 (December, 1957), 431–38. Reprinted by permission of the author and the Society for Research in Child Development.

[1] The research here reported was done during 1955–56 while the author was a visiting professor at the American University of Beirut, Lebanon. The writer wishes to express his gratitude to the University for making the study possible, and to the Rockefeller Brothers Fund for a grant to the University which defrayed the costs of the investigation. He wishes also to express his appreciation to those who served as research assistants in the study (Mrs. Adele Hamdan Taky Din, Miss Leila Biksmati, Mrs. Yvonne Sayyegh, and Mrs. Marie Therese Broussalian) and to the principals, teachers, and pupils who so generously cooperated.

describe instances of behavior on his part for which he has been praised. The subject is not asked to give generalizations. Instead the investigator derives generalizations from the analysis of many specific incidents.

In the present investigation all data were gathered by means of individual interviews of school children. Specifically, the procedure is as follows: The child is taken from his classroom to the interviewing room by the interviewer. After preliminary remarks to establish rapport the interviewer obtains from the subject his name and his age at his last birthday. He then says: "I am interested in knowing what things boys and girls do that cause people to praise them. Do you remember a time lately when you did something for which someone praised you? Tell me about a particular time when someone praised you."

If the response does not indicate in detail what the child did, or just who was involved or just who gave the praise, appropriate supplementary questions are asked. The interviewer records the responses as nearly verbatim as is possible. In each case, the interview is conducted in the native language of the child. In the present study the answers of children whose primary language was not English were translated by the interviewer and recorded in English.

After the first incident is recorded, the interviewer says, "Now tell me about another time when you were praised." In the study here reported only two responses were requested from each child.

Subjects

All subjects were attending schools in Beirut, Lebanon, and were between 5.0 and 10.99 years of age. The groups were as follows:

Americans. These were pupils at the American Community School in Beirut. In the main they were children of parents employed in Lebanon by American government agencies, by the American University of Beirut, or by American oil companies and other business concerns. By most standards of classification, the majority of the subjects came from middle-class well-educated parents. At the time they were tested (March–April, 1956) each child had been in Lebanon a minimum of six months. Many had resided in Lebanon two or more years. Some non-Americans attend this school; their responses were excluded from the results. The pupils of this school constituted the majority of American children of school age residing in Beirut in 1955–1956. There is no assumption that this group is typical of American children in the United States, but it is believed that many American children would give responses similar to those which we obtained. The

American subjects totalled 120 children. There was approximately equal representation of the two sexes, and of the various age levels.

Arabs. This group consisted of 240 children chosen so that they could be conveniently subdivided in various ways. The subgroups were boys and girls (120 of each), Moslems and Arab Christians (120 of each), pupils of private schools and pupils of public schools (120 of each) and three age groups, five- to six-year-olds, seven- to eight-year-olds and nine- to ten-year-olds (80 of each).

Armenians. Children of this group attended a private Armenian school which is one of the best Armenian schools in Beirut. They belong primarily to the middle class. In most cases their families emigrated to Lebanon following World War I. In this group there were 60 subjects equally divided as to age and sex.

Jews. These subjects came from a school which is attended by the majority of the children of the Jewish colony in Beirut. All social classes are represented, but it is believed that few parents fall into the unskilled labor classification. The majority of the families of these children have lived in the Near East for several centuries. Arabic is their primary tongue and they were questioned in this language. This group contained 60 subjects approximately equally distributed in regard to age and sex.

Categorization of Incidents

The incidents reported fell into certain categories. These categories, which are listed in Tables 1 and 2, are as follows:

1. *Academic.* This class includes all incidents relating to academic performance, such as being praised for doing lessons, for doing them well, for grades, for improvement, etc. Assisting teacher, however, falls in category 8, and doing unassigned creative or constructive work whether associated with the school or not is placed in category 14.

2–8. *Assistance.* These items are differentiated from each other in terms of the person to whom assistance is given. Sample items are: helped mother wash dishes, ran out and bought groceries for my aunt, etc. Item 6, assisting unfortunates, includes helping a blind man across the street, helping someone who has been injured, giving alms to the poor or to beggars, etc.

9–11. The titles of these categories shown in Table 1 are self-explanatory. "Being quiet" includes refraining from activity as well as refraining from making noise.

12. *Giving or sharing.* This heading indicates voluntarily offering a

present to others, giving food, sharing a toy, etc. It does not include alms-giving, which is included under item 6.

13. *Creative work.* Under this class is included such items as unassigned art work, making a dress, making a boat or a kite, constructing toys or models, and organizing a group activity.

Categorization of Rewarding Persons

As shown by Table 3, the persons doing the praising were classified according to their relationship to the child. These persons were mother, father, teacher, adult relatives, and other children. Some persons who were reported as praising did not fall into one of these categories; they were omitted from the tabulations. For this reason the percentages in Table 3 do not total 100 per cent.

Results

Table 1 indicates the frequency of each kind of incident in each of the four main groups. Table 2 gives the same information for the various subdivisions of the Arab group. The other groups are not large enough to

Table 1

GROUP COMPARISONS OF INCIDENTS REPORTED: PERCENTAGE OF RESPONSES IN EACH CATEGORY

	American	Arab	Armenian	Jewish
1. Academic performance	5%	28%	31%	41%
2. Assist mother	25	26	15	22
3. Assist father	6	2	0	2
4. Assist sibling	9	4	3	5
5. Assist relatives	0	2	3	0
6. Assist unfortunate	0	9	12	3
7. Assist peers	8	0	1	2
8. Assist others	7	5	3	3
9. Being quiet	1	3	5	2
10. Being polite, obedient	5	11	7	7
11. Sports and games	6	2	3	2
12. Giving or sharing	9	2	8	3
13. Creative work	13	2	8	3
14. Miscellaneous	6	5	4	7
Number of children	120	240	60	60
Number of responses	240	440	120	116

Table 2

COMPARISONS OF SUBDIVISIONS WITHIN THE ARAB GROUP: PERCENTAGE OF INCIDENTS IN EACH CATEGORY

	Religion		Sex		School		CA		
	CHRIST.	MOSLEM	M	F	PRIV.	GOV'T	5, 6	7, 8	9, 10
1. Academic performance	26	30	35	21	29	27	46	21	17
2. Assist mother	26	26	18	33	21	31	19	33	25
3. Assist father	2	2	2	2	0	4	2	1	3
4. Assist sibling	3	5	2	5	6	2	1	4	6
5. Assist relatives	2	2	2	3	1	3	1	3	3
6. Assist unfortunate	8	9	10	8	10	7	1	7	18
7. Assist peers	0	0	0	0	0	0	0	1	0
8. Assist others	7	3	5	5	5	5	2	4	9
9. Being quiet	3	2	1	4	4	2	5	1	3
10. Being polite and obedient	12	9	11	10	9	12	14	12	6
11. Sports and games	1	3	2	1	3	1	1	1	3
12. Giving or sharing	1	2	2	1	2	1	0	3	2
13. Creative work	2	1	2	1	2	1	3	2	0
14. Miscellaneous	7	4	7	5	6	4	6	7	5
Number of children	120	120	120	120	120	120	80	80	80
Number of responses	225	215	215	225	221	219	149	147	146

justify such subdivision. Table 3 compares the groups in regard to the persons who did the praising. Each set of results will be briefly discussed below.

Table 1 demonstrates that the relative frequencies of various kinds of rewarded behavior vary greatly between groups. For example, there is a large difference between the American group and the other groups in regard to the per cent of incidents which involve academic performance (item 1 of Table 1). In the American group praise for academic performance constitutes only 5 per cent of the total. In other groups it makes up from 28 to 41 per cent of the total (p of difference of 5 to 28 per cent $< .001$). This difference may be due to the fact that the American school is a "progressive" one which, between ages 5 and 10, puts very little pressure upon the pupil. By and large, the parents seem to approve of the permissive atmosphere of the school. In contrast the majority of the Lebanese schools stress academic achievement, even among five-year-olds, and the parents, too, stress school performance.

While item 1 of Table 2 shows a decline with age in the relative importance of academic achievement among the Lebanese subjects, this is probably due to the fact that other forms of praised behavior, such as assisting others, increase with age. The introduction of new behavior reduces the *proportion* of incidents concerned with praise for academic performance but does not indicate that academic work becomes less important in an absolute sense.

Among the Lebanese groups, the Jewish group is highest in respect to the emphasis placed upon academic achievement. The p of the Arab-Jewish difference is .01. The Armenian group, which is second, is not significantly different from the Arab group. Table 2 shows that within the Arab group Christians and Moslems do not differ in giving praise for school performance. But boys receive more praise for academic items than do girls.

Attention is next directed to the categories which deal with assisting or helping others (item 2–8). In all groups the child is praised for helping the mother more often than for helping other individuals. It will be noted that the values for assisting father, assisting siblings, assisting peers, and assisting "others" are appreciably greater for the American group than for any other group. Apparently American children are encouraged to enter into cooperative activities rather widely, whereas the Lebanese child's helpfulness centers chiefly upon the mother. An exception to this generalization arises in the case of assisting unfortunates, the majority of whom are street beggars who are blind or crippled or otherwise handicapped. The Near Eastern custom of giving alms to such people is engaged in by children as

well as by adults, and children are praised for their almsgiving. This kind
of charity seems to be almost absent among the American and among the
Jewish children. At any rate, they report no praise for almsgiving.

It will be noted that the American children are seldom praised for being
quiet or for being polite and obedient (item 9). The Lebanese parents and
the Lebanese teachers, on the other hand, frequently praise the child for
sitting still and making no noise. The American-Arab difference in this
respect is significant at the 1 per cent level of confidence.

Praise for performance in sports and games (item 11) has three times
the frequency among Americans as among the Arab and Jewish groups.
The *p* value of the American-Arab difference is .02.

Giving and sharing (item 12; this item does not include almsgiving)
is approximately three times as frequent in the American group as in the
Arab and Jewish groups (*p* of American-Arab difference is .001). Creative
work, such as constructing things and initiating projects, is highest among
the American children. The American frequency (13 per cent) is 6½ times
the Arab frequency (2 per cent) $p < .001$). The Armenian group is
second highest (8 per cent).

Table 3

PERSONS GIVING PRAISE: PERCENTAGE OF INCIDENTS IN EACH CATEGORY

Persons Praising	Americans	Arabs	Armenians	Jews
Mother	37	44	32	34
Father	13	17	7	11
Teacher	5	15	24	28
Adult relatives	0	9	9	8
Children	25	4	12	1
Number of children	120	240	60	60
Number of responses	240	440	120	116

Table 3 shows the relative frequency with which children are praised
by various persons. The three Near Eastern groups resemble each other in
that the major portion of the praise is administered by adults, chiefly by
parents and teachers. Near Eastern children appear not to be rewarded by
other children, the amounts of praise received from children being only
1, 4, and 12 per cent in the three groups. The difference between the
American group and each of the other groups has a *p* of .001 or less. These
facts are in accord with the earlier finding that there is only infrequent
reference in these groups to assisting peers. Among the Americans, how-

ever, approval by other children makes up 25 per cent of the total. For the Americans, teachers are responsible for only 5 per cent of the praise incidents, whereas for the Jews and the Armenians the corresponding figures are respectively 28 and 24 per cent (*p* of difference between 5 and 24 per cent < .001). The Americans appear to relate much more to their peers; the Lebanese child relates predominantly to adults.

In summary, the American children are distinguished from the other groups as follows: They receive a larger portion of their praise for assisting persons other than unfortunates (with proportionally less assistance given to the mother by the Americans than by the others). They also exceed the other groups in rewards for performance in sports and games, giving and sharing, and in creativity. The Near Eastern groups receive relatively more praise than the Americans for academic achievement, for assisting unfortunates and for being quiet, polite, and obedient.

It will be noted that while there are some differences among the three Near Eastern groups, there is a considerable degree of agreement among them. There is a generalized Near Eastern pattern of child approval which differs considerably from the American pattern. This is shown by Table 4, which contains the correlations between the rank orders of the categories for each pair of groups. It will be noted that the intercorrelations of the Lebanese groups are between .67 and .83, whereas the correlations between each of these and the American group range from −.11 to .32.

Table 4

CORRELATIONS BETWEEN THE RELATIVE FREQUENCIES OF CATEGORIES

	Arab	Armenian	Jewish
American	−.11	.06	.32
Arab		.67	.83
Armenian			.68

If adequate data on values were available, we believe it could be shown that praise is bestowed in accordance with the prevailing values of each group. For example, Near Eastern society is known to be very strongly family-centered. Accordingly we find that children are frequently rewarded for assisting relatives but seldom rewarded for assisting peers or other nonrelatives. The exception to this rule is the giving of alms. Arab children are praised for giving alms; American children are not. This difference too accords with adult values. The well-known interest in sports shown by the American adult is paralleled by rewards for participation in games in childhood. Near Eastern interest in sports is slight in comparison with the interest in America; we find Near Eastern children are seldom rewarded for achievement in sports. To give further examples from our data of the probable congruence between adult values and the rewarding of child behavior would unnecessarily repeat material previously presented. While our data do not *prove* that values and habits are inculcated by reward, they seem entirely consonant with this interpretation.

Summary

The critical incident technique was used to investigate the relative frequency with which different kinds of behavior are rewarded in three Near Eastern groups of children and in an American group. Highly significant differences were found between the American group and the Near Eastern groups. While some differences exist among the Near Eastern groups, they have a considerable degree of similarity.

It is suggested that rewarding behavior by praise, and by other means, is an important method of transmitting and inculcating social norms and values. On the basis of our experience the critical incident technique is recommended to psychologists, anthropologists and others as a useful tool in making cross-cultural comparisons. Its usefulness, of course, is not limited to the study of praise.

12. *Adolescence during the Middle Ages and Early Modern Times* *

LESTER D. CROW
AND ALICE CROW

B Y THIS TIME the concept of adolescence as a period of preparation for adult living had moved a long way in kind and age years from the pubic phase of development that was characteristic of primitive culture. As the organizational patterns of cultural groups increased in complexity, the adolescent period took on greater significance.

* From Lester D. Crow and Alice Crow, *Adolescent Development and Adjustment*, pp. 24–26. Copyright 1956 by McGraw-Hill Book Co., Inc., New York, and reprinted with their permission.

The medieval adolescent. During the Middle Ages schooling for all children and young people was the exception rather than accepted custom. In the days of "chivalry" boys of the upper class served as pages to women until about the age of 14, when they became squires and were inducted into the arts of knighthood by the men whom they now served. Adult status was achieved when, or if, a young man gave evidence of having developed those behavior characteristics that were considered to be knightly. Courage, chastity, and loyalty to God, country, and his "fair lady" supposedly were knightly qualities. The adolescent girl was prepared to be an attractive, tender, and submissive mate to her spouse. Considerable attention was devoted to the acquiring of "upper"-class youth of grace, charm, wit, and sprightly manner.

The adolescent and the beginnings of modern cultures. Through early modern times children of lower social classes enjoyed little, if any, adolescent preparation for adult responsibility, except what they received as a member of a hard-working family unit. Elizabeth Browning's poem "The Cry of the Children" presents a tragic picture of the lives of small children who worked in the mines of England. The novels of Charles Dickens and his contemporaries paint vivid word pictures of the sad experiences suffered by young people of the time, even when and where some schooling was made available for the masses. As was the situation in earlier cultures, economically and socially favored youth enjoyed superior educational advantages.

The Industrial Revolution and the Reformation, which were the outgrowths of general dissatisfaction with existing European cultural patterns, exercised a tremendous effect upon the place of the child and the adolescent in the societal group. Through the Industrial Revolution the provision of life necessities was taken out of the home, thus weakening to that extent the closeness of cooperative effort within the family unit. As a result of the Reformation, responsibility for achieving spiritual salvation was transferred from the religious leaders to the individual himself. Both of these societal upheavals were accompanied by significant changes in adult attitude toward most children and adolescents.

By the beginning of the eighteenth century some schooling had been made available for children of all social classes, including some schools for adolescents. For the most part, however, whatever educational opportunities that existed were subsidized and controlled by the Church and were established to serve religious purposes. The developmental needs of children and adolescents were not considered, however. Some two hundred years ago fundamental schooling in the vernacular started to become a state

Table 1

CHANGES IN ADOLESCENT STATUS

From	To
A short pubertal period between childhood and adulthood	An ever-increasingly longer period (four to seven or eight years) of preparation for the assumption of adult responsibility
The experiencing of rigid rites and ceremonials as tests of readiness for adult status	Relatively little emphasis upon such procedures, except for religious observances (confirmation) during early adolescence and some social recognition ("coming-out" parties) for girls at the end of the adolescent period
Early marriages and the raising of large families for the benefit of the societal group	No restriction upon age of marriage or size of family
Mating controlled by parental authority	Individual freedom of mate selection
Specialized training of upper-class boys for war or political leadership	Many-sided education as preparation to engage in one or another occupational or citizenship activity
Little, if any, education for girls beyond some training in homemaking	Increasing trend toward equalization of educational opportunities for the two sexes
Great emphasis upon superiority in physical strength and endurance	Concern about the mental as well as the physical health of young people, and decreasing emphasis upon mere physical strength and endurance
Educational advantages available to a relatively small number of young people	Educational advantages available to all
Schooling, for the most part, the responsibility of parents, religious institutions, or national organizations, usually on a fee basis, especially for adolescents and young adults	Nontuition, citizen-supported education available for all from the preschool level through adolescence and, in some communities, through the graduate-college or university level
No recognition of individual differences among children except in physical structure and constitution	A recognition and acceptance of the fact that young people are different as well as alike, physically, mentally, and emotionally
Almost complete disregard and nonunderstanding of young people's developing interests, aptitudes, and needs	Increasing interest in, and study of, the developmental pattern of the needs, wants, interests, and aptitudes of maturing children and adolescents
Emphasis upon the submission of young people to the authority and will of parents and other elders	Encouragement of individual freedom of behavior from early childhood through adolescence within the framework of the general welfare of a democratic society

function; educational opportunities for adolescents and young adults increased. Yet not until men like Rousseau, Basedow, Pestalozzi, and their followers propounded revolutionary theories concerning the education of children was recognition given to concepts that stress the unfolding capacities of the child, the natural urges, interests, curiosities, and activities of young people, and the possibility of potential differences in ability to achieve successfully.

The nineteenth century witnessed disagreements among religious and political leaders, educators, and psychologists that dealt with the growth and developmental needs of adolescents as well as children. There was difference of opinion concerning the purpose to be served by, and the extent of, education that should be made available for all young people. Considered also were the ways in which appropriate learning opportunities should be subsidized and organized. The research and experimental contributions of psychologists, biologists, and sociologists of the late nineteenth and early twentieth centuries have resulted in the gradual development, especially among the Western cultures, of a new attitude toward the maturing child and adolescent, a greater appreciation of individual differences among young people, a more intelligent understanding of the problems of adjustment that may be experienced by a young person in his struggle to achieve adult status, and a trend toward granting him increasing freedom of action and decision-making during his maturing years.

Changes in adolescent status. Summarized briefly, the gradual changes in cultural patterns from early authoritarianism to present-day widespread democratic ideology has been accompanied by changing adult attitudes toward the growing-up years, as shown in Table 1.

As we consider the changes that gradually have taken place in adolescent status and in adult attitude toward the significance in the life of the individual of his growing-up years, we must be cognizant of the fact that deviations from traditional practices can be found even among some of the earlier cultural groups. Moreover, certain traditional attitudes toward adolescence have persisted to the present. Perhaps it is possible to find in the conflict that still exists between former authoritarian attitudes of adults toward young people and modern, democratic ideals one of the most serious causes of the problems experienced by today's teen-agers.

13. Concepts of Development *

WILLARD C. OLSON

THE USE OF such concepts as *maturation, nurture, development,* and *growth* is not completely standardized. The oversimple equation

Maturation $\times$ Nurture = Development

will help the reader to understand the distinctions made in this text. We will take up each of the terms of the equation in turn. When we appraise the changes in the end product, *Development,* we are dealing with growth.

Maturation. The term *maturation* refers to the unfolding of a design which is essentially hereditary in origin. Maturation is frequently thus confined to sequences and patterns which are innate and over which no external influence has any power. Maturation includes the fact that the nervous system often anticipates a new function; that is, the environment does not create the function. The progression is assured by internal factors and the environment supports the changes but does not generate them. Thus racial inheritance is accomplished through maturation.

Changes involved in maturation are prerequisites to many achievements of the organism. For example, the ability to attain an erect posture and to walk must be preceded by many changes in gross structure, such as the ratio of leg to trunk, a shift in the center of gravity, and a differentiation of control of the separate parts of the body from the total mass movement. All of these changes require cooperation of nature and nurture but nature precedes and sets limits and, indeed, often insists on and requires the nurture when it is needed. The maturation process is so imperious that when

* From Willard C. Olson, *Child Development,* 2nd ed., pp. 17–20. Copyright 1959 by D. C. Heath and Co., Boston, and reprinted with their permission.

nurture is limited maturation may occur at the expense of life itself. Thus a child will increase in height and will die on a diet only sufficient to meet his static maintenance needs of the moment. In other words, he will maintain growth in height while losing weight and the capacity for normal activity.

Maturity is sometimes used as a word to indicate the attainment of a particular stage of development. It is again a product of both the forces of maturation and of nurture. It often has in it the idea of the completion of one phase and readiness for the next. Thus a child is described as *premature* if born before he is fully ready to cope with the outside environment. An individual may be described as mature if he is able to reproduce his kind. Maturity may also be used to describe the attainment of adult status, as in height. By extension of meaning a person is often described as mature if he fulfills the social requirements for his age and immature if he does not.

Nurture. The term *nurture* is commonly used, in the broadest sense, to embrace not only feeding but all of the complexities involved in education and socialization. The organism is in constant interaction with its environment. An available supply of food for desirable physical growth and a variety of suitable experiences for social and intellectual growth constitute two of the major concerns of society. A good environment should comprise all the essentials for optimum growth.

Earlier literature on child psychology put strong emphasis on the unfolding of hereditary patterns of behavior and instincts. Under the influence of such concepts, schools were expected to adapt programs to the particular instinct which was at its height at each age period. These concepts concerned various mixtures of what was given by heredity and what had been obtained from the culture. It now seems clear that children are born with a structure and a functioning system which produce the energy that leads to activity. A growth potential drives the child to complete a design whose ultimate destination and rate of development are strongly influenced by heredity. The troubles of the investigator of heredity begin when he attempts to ascribe details of behavior to either heredity or environment. It is seldom indeed that this can be accomplished.

Development. The complex product of the forces of maturation and of nurture, as described previously, is called *development*. In the absence of adequate nurture, development would fail and such things as increase in size, attainment of bodily skills, or the acquisition of speech would not be possible. Schools provide experiences for desirable types of development not likely to occur otherwise. Thus differences in schooling will produce individual differences in a variety of acquisitions, such as reading, arithmetic, or a foreign language.

In a culture which does not provide reading experiences there will be no development in reading and the people will be illiterate. In a culture which provides reading experiences initial success and eventual level is also related to maturational forces. The proper timing and emphasis between readiness and experience represent an aspect of teaching skill. In education the curriculum becomes the special nurture provided by schools for the development of the child.

Growth. We use the term *growth* to measure development. Growth is concerned with changes in size, complexity, and proportion, and with such qualitative changes as those which occur in muscle, bone, hair, and pigmentation. Casual observers of children are most impressed by growth in the sense of *increase,* since changes in stature and weight with time are so obvious. The term *growth,* however, also includes *internal changes in complexity,* such as the cell division that *makes* the embryo more complex without increasing its size. It also embraces change in the sense of *decrement,* such as loss in the mass of tonsil tissue or of the thymus gland, reduction in number of separate bones, or in the decrease in calories utilized by the individual per unit of weight or area as he becomes older.

As well as being used to describe physical changes in structures and physiological functions, the term *growth* is also applied to behavior and achievement. Thus the appraisal of *motor development* such as crawling, standing, walking, and running is a part of the study of growth. Similarly, the changes that occur in a child's ability to act in relation to others in the family, neighborhood, and community may be described as *social growth.* The contrast between the uninhibited outbursts of crying and of temper tantrums in early childhood and the greater self-control normally exhibited in later life is evidence of *emotional growth.* To be complete, any consideration of growth must also include *mental growth,* such as the ability to perform abstract intellectual tasks and to acquire information and skills in school subjects.

Sequence. It is possible to speak with great certainty about some of the *sequences* that occur in development. Unless drastic measures are taken to alter the sequence, a child sits before he stands, stands before he walks, walks before he runs. He talks before he is able to read and reads before he is able to spell well. His ability to read develops earlier than his ability to write.

Rate. Scientific study enables one to speak with some certainty about the rates of development. *Rate* refers to the amount of increment or increase in a structure or function in terms of units of time. Thus increase in weight proceeds at a rapid rate per year in early childhood and again in the circumpuberal period. Rates differ markedly from child to child, and there is no present knowledge which would enable any specialist to change these rates except within narrow limits. There is no magic by which the individual differences resulting from varying rates can be erased. The hopeful thing is that all can grow in all dimensions of development.

Pattern. A *pattern* of growth refers to the relationship of various measured characteristics within an individual. Thus a child of 10 who has a high mental age, a high reading age, and a somewhat lower height age, weight age, carpal age, and dental age differs in pattern from one who has high physical ages and relatively low mental and achievement ages. One might also speak of a child's pattern of growth in reading as showing a plateau period from ages 6 to 9, with a rapid increase from ages 9 to 12.

At times the word *form* is used to describe the relationship between sets of measurements such as height and weight. Terms such as *obese* and *slender* may be used to describe the relationship or form.

14. The Period of the Embryo *

PAUL H. MUSSEN
AND JOHN J. CONGER

ONCE THE growing egg has been successfully lodged in its new home, development is rapid. Its *inner* cell mass, which will become a recognizable embryo, begins to differentiate itself into three distinct layers:

1. *The ectoderm* (outer layer), from which will develop the epidermis or outer layer of the skin, the hair, the nails, parts of the teeth, skin glands, sensory cells—and the nervous system.

2. *The mesoderm* (the middle layer), from which will develop the dermis or inner skin layer, the muscles, skeleton, and the circulatory and excretory organs.

* From Paul H. Mussen and John J. Conger, *Child Development and Personality,* pp. 55–56. Copyright 1956 by Harper and Bros., New York, and reprinted with their permission.

3. *The endoderm* (inner layer), from which will develop the lining of the entire gastrointestinal tract, the Eustachian tubes, trachea, bronchia, lungs, liver, pancreas, salivary glands, thyroid glands, and thymus.

While the inner cell mass is being differentiated into a recognizable embryo, the outer layers of cells are giving rise to the fetal membranes—the *chorion* and *amnion*. These two membranes, together with a third membrane derived from the uterine wall of the mother (the *decidua*

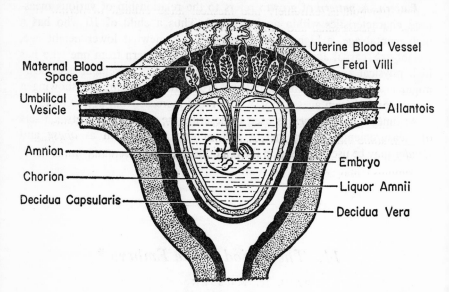

Figure 1. Diagram representing the relationship between the uterus, the membranes, and the embryo during early pregnancy. (From L. Carmichael, "Origin and Prenatal Growth of Behavior," in C. Murchison (ed.), *A Handbook of Child Psychology,* 2nd ed. Worcester: Clark University Press, 1933, p. 50. By permission of the publisher.)

capsularis), extend from the wall of the uterus and enclose the developing embryo (see Fig. 1). They form a sac which is filled with a watery fluid (*liquor amnii*) which acts as a buffer to protect the embryo from shocks experienced by the mother. It also helps to provide an even temperature for the embryo and serves to prevent adhesions between the embryo and the amniotic membrane.

Simultaneously, other fetal sacs are formed, the most important of which becomes the umbilical cord. It extends from the embryo, and is attached at its opposite end to the section of the uterine wall where the uterus and the chorion are joined. This area is called the *placenta*.

The umbilical cord might well be referred to as the lifeline of the embryo. Through it, two arteries carry blood from the embryo to the placenta, and one vein carries blood to the infant from the placenta. However, the relationship between the child's blood stream and the mother's is not a direct one. Both the child's and the mother's blood streams open into the placenta. But the two systems are always separated by cell walls within the placenta. These cell walls consist of semipermeable membranes—that is, they function as extremely fine meshes, large enough to permit the passage of gases, salts, and other substances of small molecular size, but too small to allow blood cells to get through.

We still lack a precise knowledge of all the substances which can get through a normal placenta. However, various nutrient substances from the mother's blood—chiefly sugars, fats, and some protein elements—are known to permeate it. Waste products from the infant, primarily carbon dioxide and other metabolites, can also pass through the placenta. In addition, some vitamins, drugs (including nicotine and alcohol), vaccines, and a few disease germs (notably those of diphtheria, typhoid, influenza, and syphilis) may also get through and affect the embryo's development.

15. *Approximate Timetable of Prenatal Development* *[1]

ROBERT I. WATSON

First Month

Fertilization, descent of ovum from tube to uterus. Early cell division and formation of embryonic disc from which new organism will develop. Early formation of three layers of cells—the *ectoderm*, from which sense organs and nervous systems will develop; the *mesoderm*, from which circulatory, skeletal, and muscular systems will develop; and *endoderm*, from

* From Robert I. Watson, *Psychology of the Child: Personal, Social, and Disturbed Child Development,* pp. 73–75. Copyright 1959 by John Wiley and Sons, Inc., New York, and reprinted with their permission.

[1] This is adapted largely from M. S. Gilbert, *Biography of the Unborn* (Baltimore: Williams and Wilkins, 1938). Material from other sources has been added where relevant.

which digestive and some glandular systems will develop. The ovum becomes implanted in the walls of the uterus. Special layer of cells formed in the uterus which will become the *placenta* and through which nutritive substances will be carried to the new organism and waste products carried away. Special layer of cells forms the *amnion* or water sac, which will surround the developing embryo except at umbilical cord. Heart tube forms and begins to pulsate and force blood to circulate through blood vessels in embryonic disc. Nervous system begins to arise, first in form of neural groove appearing at about 19 days. Development of intestinal tract, lungs, liver, and kidneys begins. By end of one month, the embryo is about one fourth inch long, curled into a crescent, with small nubbins on sides of body indicating incipient arms and legs. Eyes arise as two pouches thrust out from brain tube, and tissue which will produce inner ear forms.

Second Month

Embryo increases in size to about 1½ inches. Bones and muscle begin to round out contours of body. Face and neck develop and begin to give features a human appearance. Mouth becomes reduced in size, and eyes move to front of face. Forehead very prominent, reflecting precocious development of brain in comparison to rest of body. Limb buds elongate. Muscles and cartilage develop. Sex organs begin to form, though still essentially identical in both sexes.

Third Month

Beginning of fetal period. Sexual differentiation continues, with male sexual organs showing more rapid development and the female remaining more neutral. Buds for all twenty temporary teeth laid down. Vocal cords appear; digestive system shows activity. Stomach cells begin to secrete fluid; liver pours bile into intestine. Kidneys begin functioning, with urine gradually seeping into amniotic fluid. Other waste products passed through placenta into mother's blood. Bones and muscles continue development, and by end of third month spontaneous movements of arms, legs, shoulders, and fingers are possible.

Fourth Month

Lower parts of body show relatively accelerated rate, so that head size decreases from one half to one fourth of body size. Back straightens; hands and feet are well formed. Whorl patterns appear on fingers and toes; skin appears dark red, due to coursing of blood showing through thin skin, and wrinkled, due to absence of underlying fat. Finger closure is possible. Reflexes become more active as muscular maturation continues. Fetus begins to stir and to thrust out arms and legs in movements readily perceived by the mother.

Fifth Month

Skin structures begin to attain final form. Sweat and sebaceous glands are formed and function. Their secretions, plus dead cells sloughed off from the skin, form a paste called the *vernix caseosa* covering the entire body. Skin derivatives also appear—hair, nails on fingers and toes. Bony axis becomes quite straight, and much spontaneous activity occurs. Fetus is lean and wrinkled, will be about 1 foot long and weigh about 1 pound. If aborted, it may respire briefly, but will soon die as it seems unable to maintain movements necessary for continued breathing.

Sixth Month

Eyelids, which have been fused shut since third month, reopen; eyes are completely formed. Eyelashes and brows begin to develop. Taste buds appear on tongue and in mouth and are, in fact, more abundant than in the infant or adult. If born, the six-month fetus will perhaps live a few hours or longer if protected in an incubator. During brief extrauterine life, may exhibit "Moro" or startle responses.

Seventh Month

Organism capable of independent life from this time on. Cerebral hemispheres cover almost the entire brain. Seven-month fetus can emit a variety of specialized responses. Generally is about 16 inches long and weighs about 3 pounds. If born, will be able to cry, breathe, and swallow, but is very sensitive to infections and will need highly sheltered environment for survival.

Eighth and Ninth Month

During this time, finishing touches are being put on the various organs and functional capacities. Conditioning can be demonstrated, indicating the readiness of the organism for certain kinds of learning. Fat is formed rapidly over the entire body, smoothing out the wrinkled skin and rounding out body contours. Dull red color of skin fades so that at birth pigmentation of skin is usually very slight in all races. Activity is usually great, and he can change his position within the somewhat crowded uterus. Periods of activity will alternate with periods of quiescence. Fetal organs step up their activity. Fetal heart rate becomes quite rapid. Digestive organs continue to expel more waste products, leading to the formation of a fetal stool (called the *meconium*) which is expelled shortly after birth. Violent uterine contractions begin (though milder ones have been tolerated earlier), and the fetus is eventually expelled from the womb into an independent physiological existence.

16. *Developmental Changes in Needs during Infancy* *

ROBERT I. WATSON

IN CONCLUDING the discussion of needs of the neonate, we also conclude the discussion of the neonate as a base line and turn to developmental changes during infancy. We shall begin with a discussion of developmental changes in feeding, sleep, and elimination. The other neonatal needs do not show enough important developmental changes to warrant consideration.

Developmental Changes in Feeding

You will remember that neonates are reported by Gesell and Ilg as requiring about seven or eight feedings per day. By the time they are 4 weeks old typically the number of feedings has been reduced to five or six. The number of feedings is reduced further to three to five feedings in the following weeks. Beginning at 16 weeks this number of feedings, or a little less, is maintained until toward the end of the first year, by which time the

* From Robert I. Watson, *Psychology of the Child: Personal, Social, and Disturbed Child Development*, pp. 182–88. Copyright 1959 by John Wiley and Sons, Inc., New York, and reprinted with their permission.

three meals a day regime of our culture is fairly well established (along with one or two snacks).

Supplementation by solid foods has been going on from about 20 weeks of age. Cup and spoon feeding takes place during this time and by 40 weeks the infant helps himself in feeding, incidentally making a fine mess of it in the process. Even preference for certain foods is well defined at one year, for example, certain vegetables, hot as compared to cold cereals, and so on.

Scheduling and self-demand feeding. Scheduling and self-demand feeding will be discussed first in terms of some normative findings in order to place the problem in perspective; next will be a discussion of some of the evidence that led to the use of self-demand feeding; and, finally, consideration of the question of whether scheduling in very young infants is learned or not learned by them.

In general, the large group of mothers interviewed by Sears and his associates used neither a self-demand system nor a rigid schedule but something in between. Only 12 per cent of the mothers always fed the infant when he cried and permitted him to eat as much as he wanted. Only 8 per cent fed him by the clock, waking him for feedings. The remainder followed practices that were somewhere between these extremes.

It was the pioneer study of Clara M. Davis in 1928 which probably served as the original scientific impetus for changing adult attitudes in the direction of greater permissiveness toward infant feeding and self-regulation in the scheduling of infant feedings. In her study fifteen infants of about weaning age were presented with a variety of foods from which to choose as to kind and amount. In the first few days of free choice, there were great individual differences among the infants as to what and how much they ate. All of the infants gradually selected diets which, according to adult standards, were well-balanced and nutritious. Moreover, none of them developed feeding problems. In a later study, she permitted infants a free choice of different formulas at a single feeding and found that highly variable amounts and kinds were taken at different meals. Davis' studies and those that followed after helped to usher in an era of greater trust in the infant's capacity to select how much to eat, at what times, and how often. But this does not mean he cannot learn to adapt to a schedule instituted by his parents.

Infants are fully capable of learning to adapt to the feeding schedules introduced by adults. This was neatly demonstrated by Dorothy Marquis who studied the learning of a feeding schedule by infants during the first ten days of life while they were still in the hospital. Two infant groups, experimental and control, were placed on different feeding schedules. The experimental group was on a three-hour feeding schedule, except during the last day in the hospital when these infants were shifted to a four-hour schedule, while the control group was on a four-hour feeding schedule throughout its hospital stay. She measured in both groups the activity patterns (restlessness) by a mechanical device supporting the bassinets in which the infants lay. Their activity was the criterion of adaptiveness to the schedule. When the interval of feeding was changed from three to four hours in the experimental group on the tenth day, these infants showed a sharp rise in their activity during this extra hour between feedings. At the end of three hours, their heretofore habitual feeding time, body movements increased abruptly and continued throughout the fourth hour. Apparently, the infants had learned to respond to hunger cues at the end of three hours. Failure to receive their accustomed feeding markedly increased restlessness. Those control infants fed on a four-hour schedule from birth to what was now the tenth day showed only their usual gradual increase in activity as their feeding time approached. Marquis suggests that this adaptation to a schedule, as shown by the experimental group with their increased activity when the schedule was disrupted, is an instance of the earliest form of socialization. It made a difference for these infants to have to wait an extra hour for feeding, showing in a definitive fashion the learning of the newborn infant in the process of adapting to the external demands of a feeding schedule.

Breast and bottle feeding. In the Sears, Maccoby, Levin study they found 40 per cent of the infants were breast-fed, of which the majority received breast feeding for but three months. In view of the large number being fed by bottles and the relative shortness of breast feeding by those who did receive it, it is of interest, despite the somewhat digressive character, to examine the reason the mothers gave for not breast feeding. Over 40 per cent claimed they were unable to breast feed for physical reasons, such as not having enough milk or the presence of inverted nipples. Another 16 per cent reported that the doctor advised against breast feeding without specifying any physical difficulty. Thirty-five per cent did not want to breast feed, some for emotional reasons, others because they did not want to be tied down, and still others for unspecified reasons.

The two groups who gave "physical reasons" or "doctor's advice" seem quite large, too large in fact for the reasons given to represent actually the true state of affairs. There is a strong possibility that the objections they offered to breast feeding were rationalizations and that they did not want to for reasons other than the ones given. For example, "inability" may have been dislike of breast feeding.

Weaning. The sucking movements of the infant are adapted for taking liquid foods from breast or bottle. With increased maturation at about the third or fourth month, mouth movements begin to change in a direction suitable for eating solid food and biting movements begin to appear. By 7 to 9 months these movements have become stronger.

Repeated reinforcement of sucking has occurred during these early months and sucking has become a well-established habit in securing nourishment. The process of weaning means these habitual patterns must be eliminated and new activities learned.

It cannot be overemphasized that, while weaning at first glance may appear to be a simple straightforward practice, it is, in reality, a very complicated one. Even the term is used in more than one sense. Sometimes, weaning refers to a shift from breast to bottle feeding. In the sense used here, however, it means the process of giving up sucking for a new mode of food-getting through eating of solid foods and drinking (not sucking) of liquids. As Sears, Maccoby, and Levin indicate, weaning involves five tasks:

> The child must learn *not to want* to get his food by sucking. He must learn to *like to drink* the same food he formerly got by sucking. He must learn to *want solid foods*. He must learn the *manipulative skills* required for eating them—biting, chewing, and the use of fingers and utensils, as well as drinking from a cup. He must learn to do *without being held* while he is eating.[1]

Now each of these tasks may be presented to the child in an endless variety of ways. For example, solid foods can be thrust at him all at once or their presentation can be spaced almost from birth, long before the process of weaning. Frustrations arising from weaning will depend upon many things, not precisely summed up as "weaning."

In their sample of mothers, Sears *et al.* found that two thirds had started the weaning process by the time the infant was 11 months old. For the majority, the process of weaning took four months to complete. Nevertheless, at least 12 per cent took a year or more.

Developmental Changes in Sleep

As the infant grows older, his general activities increase while his sleep decreases. By the end of infancy he may be sleeping as little as eleven hours at night with one or two naps during the day. Gesell offers a detailed description of sleep behavior at various ages. At 4 weeks he reports that typically the infant gradually drops off to sleep toward the end of the

[1] Robert R. Sears, Eleanor E. Maccoby, and Harry Levin, *Patterns of Child Rearing* (Evanston, Ill.: Row, Peterson and Co., 1957). Copyright 1957 by Row, Peterson, and published with permission.

nursing period. At this age the infant has four to five sleep periods in twenty-four hours. By 16 weeks he has established something of a night sleep rhythm, falling asleep after the 6 P.M. feeding and waking between 5 and 6 A.M. He does not fall asleep immediately after each feeding and has about three naps during the day in addition to his sleep periods. At 40 weeks he tends to fall asleep after his 6 P.M. feeding and sleeps through to 5 to 7 A.M. There may be one long midmorning nap or as many as four short nap periods.

While the total number of hours of infant's sleep is decreasing, the hours are increasing in length. While hunger and pain may awaken him at any time, loud sounds and other stimuli are decreased in our culture at night and consequently, during this period he is less disturbed by environmental stimuli. This plus other socialization practices cause the interrupting of sleep to be less frequent at night. As the infant grows older, increasing stimulation from its surroundings competes with the biological demands for sleep. We arrange these in terms of cultural expectancies with emphasis on more stimulation during the day than at night. Part of the pattern is, nevertheless, that of daytime naps. He learns sleep habits in relation to the time patterns of his culture.

As Gesell indicates, the infant must learn to sleep in the same way he learns to creep, stand and walk, and grasp a spoon. He must also learn to stay awake! Although learning is undoubtedly important, maturation is also important. As he grows older he is not so subcortical (without the service of the highest nerve centers of the brain) as Gesell puts it. Millions of cortical cells, previously nonfunctional because they had not matured sufficiently, are beginning to make connections between eyes, ears, and the muscles of the eyes. Their maturation serves to keep his cortex "awake" and thus for him to be more receptive to his surroundings. Staying awake for longer periods of time (with increasing amounts of time spent in acts other than those associated with hunger and feeding) is an important part of the process of early development. These longer periods of waking afford opportunity for more intensive and varied experiences with the environment.

There are, of course, individual differences in sleep requirements among infants and in the same infant from one time to another. By and large, however, we are not too demanding in our culture and allow the child during infancy to express his individuality in this regard. He generally may be said to sleep as much as he needs to, and to wake when rested. Consequently, sleep is not a vehicle upon which extremes of social pressure are practiced.

Developmental Changes in Elimination

Gesell's normative findings will again be appealed to in connection with elimination changes. At 4 weeks the infant tends to have three or four bowel movements in a twenty-four-hour period. He may now cry when his diaper is wet and he quiets when changed. At 16 weeks there are one or two movements, most commonly after a feeding. By 28 weeks there is apt to be only one movement, usually at 9 to 10 A.M. Urination is still occurring at frequent intervals. At 40 weeks the infant may be dry after an hour's nap and sometimes an infant may respond to the pot. Changes hereafter will be described in the context of the problem of toilet training which this need engenders.

Social demands in our culture require that the child learn voluntary control of bladder and bowel so as to void at an acceptable time and place. Changes in eliminative processes under ideal conditions await the age at which neuromuscular mechanisms have sufficiently matured for them to be voluntarily controlled. As a neonate he cannot do so, even if by some miracle, he "wanted" to do so. Punishment, bribes, and scolding may go on relentlessly, but the learning remains incidental and sporadic until he is maturationally ready for voluntary control.

Both bladder and bowel control are extremely complicated processes, neurologically and psychologically. Not only are there complicated neural pathways which must mature, but also the processes and paths change from age period to age period. Moreover, they involve the entire organism, not just isolated organ systems. For example, it is not until about 15 months of age that postural immaturities have lessened sufficiently to allow the infant to sit on the toilet. Language enters into the process in that he can communicate his needs in this area at about 18 months.

The importance of maturation in bladder control is shown in a study by McGraw on twin boys. With one of them, bladder training was started at about 50 days by placing him on the toilet every hour. Until about 600 days there was little evidence of learning. After 600 days the curve of success increased sharply, and by 700 days successes were close to 100 per cent. No training whatsoever was started with the other twin until 700 days. His performance was almost immediately as good as that of the twin with the longer period of training. This rather startling difference is not an isolated phenomenon as another record of twins by McGraw shows. Evidently, training started later rather than earlier takes advantage of maturation and is more effective than trying to train earlier.

The results found by McGraw, however, should not be taken as definitive concerning the *date* to begin training or to expect its ending. This is subject to individual variation. Moreover, only one rather rigid method of training was used in her study. It is quite possible that if a more flexible schedule had been used, different data concerning timing would have been found. Her data are indicative merely of *relative* relationships in these twins and are in no way an index of what happens in sample groups.

Toilet training is a learning situation in which whatever reward may accrue to the child is not in the satisfaction of the basic need. His social eliminative needs are, if one may slip into the vernacular, learned the hard way.

17. How to Encourage Language Development *

LEIGH PECK

IN ANY FIELD of development, it is ill-advised to force a child ahead faster than his own individual rate of growth would indicate. Such pushing may be especially dangerous in language, for if we are constantly correcting a child's speech or urging him to show off by saying pieces for callers, we may create an emotional problem that will seriously interfere with speech. But while we avoid pushing a child, we want to be sure to give him the opportunities that will enable him to develop at his own best rate. In no field is this more important than in language, for a child is dependent upon other people for speech models.

In encouraging speech, the first thing is to talk to the baby in an affectionate, cheerful, companionable way as you feed him, bathe him, and do the other necessary things for him. Long before you expect him to imitate or even to understand what you are saying, talk to him about all the things you and he are doing and seeing together. He will respond first to the tones of your voice, but eventually the words will take on meaning. For the most part, one should avoid "baby talk," for obviously the child's speech will be

* From Leigh Peck, *Child Psychology: A Dynamic Approach*, pp. 182–86. Copyright 1953 by D. C. Heath and Co., Boston, and reprinted with their permission.

no better than the models he imitates. An occasional exception to the no-baby-talk rule may well be made in the case of a very young child who cannot yet speak well enough to learn the grown-up version of some expression for which he has a real need. The two-year-old can learn to say, *bathroom,* or *Go to the bathroom.* Most one-year-olds cannot make so elaborate an announcement of their needs; they and their mothers may find *tee-tee* a useful verbalization. The speech of any servants who may be in the home will, of course, have some influence on the child's speech. However, we need not feel too much concern if the maid who helps care for the child makes some grammatical errors. These are not likely to affect his speech seriously. More hazardous to good speech and to good mental health would be association with someone whose voice placement is poor, who has a strained, too high-pitched voice, very possibly caused by emotional tension. By all means, association of the child with anyone who stutters should be avoided, as that habit can be picked up by imitation and can result in a lifelong handicap.

Conversation with adults is not enough. The young child needs other little children his own age with whom he can talk and play. The need to make himself understood during cooperative play is a powerful incentive to speech. Excursions are also highly stimulating to speech, for the child wants to talk about the new things that he has seen. It is important that when we take a child on an excursion, whether next door to see a bird's nest or by plane to the Indian country, we use in our conversation with him the names of all the new things he is seeing, adjectives that express their special qualities, and verbs that tell what is being done. Otherwise, he will find himself in the unenviable position of a little girl who on her return from a plane trip was cross-questioned regarding every detail by her air-minded playmates, but was able to answer only, "I went on a plane," because her adults had failed to furnish her with verbal symbols for her new experiences. Books can also be highly stimulating to speech. Children, for example, who have had read to them books about trains, airplanes, and fire engines will find material there for hours of dramatic play.

In encouraging a young child's speech, we must remember to put first things first. Just as in food-taking we remember that enjoyment of food is the big objective and that the very minor objective of good table manners can best be attained gradually and unobtrusively, so in speech we must remember that free, spontaneous expression and communication of ideas is the important goal and that the niceties of grammar and enunciation are best picked up incidentally along the way. To nag the child about his speech, so that he feels, "Every time I open my mouth I put my foot in it," can only defeat our major objective. Often we hear the advice given, "Make the child ask for things. Don't be too ready to interpret his gestures and grunts. If he wants a drink, make him say *Drink* before you give it to him." Such advice, applied within reasonable limits and in the right spirit, may be good. The baby who is already interested in learning to talk and who at the moment is feeling comfortable and jolly (not very hungry or tired or sleepy) may, if we make a merry game of it, enjoy being encouraged several times a day to try to say the word for what he wants. But if we turn taskmasters and sternly require the busy toddler, who has so very many other things to be learning, to verbalize his needs at every turn before they can be satisfied, he is likely to associate speech with unpleasantness, and thus we defeat our own major ends.

Difficulties in Language Development

Though the great majority of children learn to talk uneventfully, the ones who have considerable trouble are numerous enough to warrant some attention to the various types of language difficulties and to the things that can be done to help children with such difficulties. It is estimated that 7 or 8 per cent of school children have speech defects that should be corrected. These defects are often classified as including: (1) defects of articulation (involving the addition, omission, or distortion of certain sounds), as in infantile speech or foreign accent; (2) difficulties of voice (such as huskiness, harshness, or shrillness); (3) difficulties of rhythm (stuttering); (4) difficulties with the symbolic aspects of language (as in aphasia, when the handicapped person has difficulty in associating meaning with the word sound or with the written symbol); (5) paralyses and crippling conditions. A briefer classification, according to cause, includes: (1) the organic (occasioned by anatomical or physiological deviations in structure); (2) the functional (deviations in speech despite normal mechanisms); (3) the psychological (particularly stuttering).

Are Twins Necessarily Retarded in Speech?

One mother says, "I read in a book that twins are generally backward in learning to talk; so I try not to worry over my boys being so slow. It's just something you have to expect with twins." She has, of course, misinterpreted the point that the author of her book was trying to make. Being a twin does not in itself condemn a child to language retardation. But it is true that twins, if they play almost exclusively with each other and lack other companionship, may come to understand each other's gestures and sounds so well that they lack incentives to learn the language of the community. Cases have been known of twins who entered the first grade speaking in a jargon unintelligible to anybody but themselves. That would not have occurred if their parents had arranged for them more experiences outside the home and especially more play with other children. Thus, the mother who was quoted at the beginning of this paragraph should be saying, "Since my children are twins, it is all the more important that they play every day with other little children. I'll put them in a good nursery school if I possibly can."

Bilingualism: Advantage or Handicap?

The bilingual child is one who early in childhood learns at the same time two languages. Often he is a child whose parents or grandparents were immigrants to this country, and the older members of his family speak some language other than English. Occasionally he is a child whose family has lived abroad during his early childhood; he learned the two languages there at the same time. Again, the bilingual child may be one whose parents have arranged for him to begin the study of a foreign language at an early age because they consider this the best way for him to acquire the correct accent. Regardless of the circumstances that have made him bilingual, we are interested in the question, "Will bilingualism be an advantage to him? Or will he become confused in trying to learn two languages, and thus be handicapped in one or both?"

It is easier to learn to pronounce a foreign language correctly if we study it in our earlier years. That is because all of us in the babbling of infancy practice making more sounds than are comprised in any one language. The little baby in an English-speaking home makes French nasal sounds and German guttural sounds and the sounds used in Chinese and Choctaw and a host of other languages. But as he learns to speak English, he ceases to practice the sounds that are not a part of the English language. When he begins to learn a foreign language, the closer he is to the babbling of his infancy, the easier it will be for him to make sounds that are not used in English. Therefore, it is easier for a preschool child or even for a pupil in elementary school to learn to pronounce a foreign language than it is for a high school boy or girl. It is still harder for a college student or for a yet older person. For the reason just explained, some school systems introduce the study of a foreign language into the elementary grades, rather than waiting until high school.

18.   If a Child Stammers *

C. S. BLUEMEL

THERE IS an old belief that children stammer because they think faster than they can talk. This is very nearly correct. Actually a child does much of his thinking in eagerness and excitement, and he has many feelings and frustrations that could never be put into words. And even if he could calm his feelings and try to think his way into speech, he would often lack the vocabulary to express himself. He would then encounter a speech block—a sort of road block in word-thinking.

Halting and repeating and backtracking are normal phases of speech in a child's developmental years, and the symptoms should cause no anxiety. This commonplace stuttering is nothing more than speech in the making. It is immature speech; it is trial-and-error speech. It is speech that is not yet organized into a pattern that the child can use and control. Yet children differ in their natural fluency. In general, girls are more fluent than boys. But apart from sex, some children are highly skilled in speech and others are peculiarly inept. It is the inept children, of course, who stutter more when they are learning to talk. But usually these handicapped children develop a satisfactory degree of fluency, and in the long run they are not far behind the more skillful pacemakers.

A child learns speech by imitation—much of it, of course, unconscious. He learns the language that he hears, be it English or Chinese or Choctaw. And he learns good speech or bungled speech according to the manner in which the words are presented to him. He cannot learn good speech from the baby talk of other children; he learns only by hearing clear speech in the adult pattern. Twins talk poorly because they listen to each other. The only child in a family talks well because he listens to the mature speech of his parents. Actually few children have the opportunity of learning good speech by absorbing good speech patterns. Most children catch their speech in much the same way as they catch measles—by being exposed to it.

The child is obliged to catch his speech because there is no natural division between words as he hears them. He is in much the same position as the beginning student who is learning a foreign language and can make nothing out of a running conversation. Yet the student understands short

* From C. S. Bluemel, "If a Child Stammers," *Mental Hygiene* (July, 1959), pp. 390–93. Reprinted by permission of the author and The National Association of Mental Health.

phrases, and the foreign words make sense when he hears someone say *bon jour,* or *guten Morgen,* or *buenos dias.*

It can be seen that the child has considerable difficulty in learning speech because the words come to him in telescoped form. Naturally his difficulty is multiplied if he has to learn two languages at once. His parents may speak German, while his playmates speak English. Or the family may emigrate just when he is beginning to learn his native language, and he is thrown into bewilderment by a new language he cannot understand.

Even when a child is learning a single language the learning process is seldom easy. In this developmental period, while the child is "making" his speech, he encounters stresses which tend to "unmake" it. His speech may seem normal enough during this period, yet it may break under the stress of excitement, fatigue, or frustration. The resistance of speech to stress is somewhat like the resistance of ice to weight. Ice that is half an inch thick on a lake looks the same as ice that is four inches thick; but while the thinner ice will barely carry the weight of a man, the heavier ice will sustain the weight of an army. One cannot, of course, compare ice with speech, but it can be said that when speech is securely organized it can tolerate the weight of considerable stress.

The thinly organized speech of a child is easily broken by such common stresses as the excitement of a party or picnic. Fluency is even more likely to break under the sustained excitement of Christmas festivities. Speech is often disturbed by the fatigue of travel, camping trips, and other tiring activities. There are many experiences which overstimulate the child and disrupt his tranquility; but while most of these stresses have only a temporary disrupting influence there are some experiences which may have a lasting detrimental effect. Such, for instance, are the experiences of shock— the shock of a fire, a flood, a fall, an automobile accident, or any misadventure which carries the semblance of disaster.

Less conspicuous influences also break a child's speech, and here we can include the sustained stresses of anxiety and frustration. The child's fluency may suffer under the stress of family discord, the daily fear of a harsh teacher, or the menace of a bullying playmate. Fluency may also be disturbed by the nervous nagging of anxious parents who constantly "correct" the child's speech and thus make him self-conscious and apprehensive. In speech, the area of stress is particularly broad, and the speech function may be disturbed and impeded by any severe or sustained stress which exceeds the child's uncertain tolerance.

The functional upsets in a child's life are not, of course, limited to speech. Stress may disturb a child's sleep, his appetite, his digestion, his bladder control and countless other functions. There are natural limits to the tolerance of stress—and this applies to the adult as well as the child. When these limits of tolerance are exceeded something is sure to give. The reaction may take the form of insomnia, night terrors, loss of appetite, vomiting, facial twitching and so on. The reaction may also take the form of stammering, the particular functional disorder that concerns us.

Though the speech disturbance of stammering appears to be simple, it is, in reality, complex. The initial disturbance, the primary stammering, is an intermittent ability to talk—or to talk with accustomed fluency. And as if this were not enough, the primary stammering soon takes on a secondary phase. When the stammerer's speech becomes blocked he tries to force the utterance of his words, and he enters upon an unnatural phase of effort and struggle, and sometimes contortion. He may even use his fists and his larger body muscles in a futile attempt to articulate. Meanwhile, his breathing is disturbed, and he holds his breath or attempts to talk after exhausting air from his lungs. In primary stammering, the thinking process is already confused, but in secondary stammering the speaker becomes more disorganized as he tries frantically to escape his dilemma by searching for synonyms and roundabout expressions. Phobia adds itself to the picture; the speaker now becomes fearful of difficult words and of ominous people and situations associated with his former speech frustrations. All of this secondary stammering is added to the primary speech disturbance, and the final predicament of the speaker may be severe and bewildering.

And now the question: How can speech impediments be avoided—the stuttering of speech in the making, and the stammering of speech in the unmaking? The stuttering of early speech, or prespeech, is normal, and ordinarily it should not cause alarm. Yet the repetition and halting may be excessive, and the broken pattern of speech may turn out to be the forerunner of stammering. For this reason impeded speech cannot always be ignored. Nervous and excitable children often make and unmake their speech in alternating phases; when the unmaking predominates, stammering is sure to follow.

At this juncture in the child's life the problem is to organize his speech—to organize it into a pattern of natural fluency. This procedure not only reduces the stuttering, but it safeguards the child against the subsequent development of stammering. The organizing process is, of course, nothing more than the learning process. To learn good speech the child must clearly distinguish the words that he hears. But commonly the words of adult speech run together—theyruntogetherlikethis. They run together like the conversation in French or German that we hear when we are traveling abroad. We can understand the child's dilemma in distinguishing speech sounds when we consider what a task it would be to read the morning paper if all the words were merged into an endless polysyllable. Yet this is the kind of polysyllable the child hears in adult conversation. To his inexperienced mind the words are all linked together in challenging confusion.

Here the child needs speech training in which the words are unlinked so that he can understand them. The parents can help the child by speaking slowly, clearly, and in short sentences. Thus by a process of ear training they present a pattern of speech from which the child learns easily and naturally. In the natural steps of learning the child first hears words with unmistakable clearness. Then he remembers the words. Then he is able to think the words. Then he can say them. Admittedly this formula is over-simplified, but it emphasizes the logic and the necessity of ear training. Of course the parents cannot engage in ear training throughout the day, but they can speak in slow and measured phrases often enough to provide the child with a stable pattern of speech which he adopts for himself.

An agreeable form of ear training consists in reading to the child from a storybook or picture book. Again the sentences are short and clear. "Once upon a time—there were three bears—a papa bear—a mama bear—and a baby bear." Here the child identifies the words, and he learns as he listens. Soon he will want to join in the "reading" as the game proceeds. Of course he follows the pattern very poorly while his speech is new; nonetheless he learns in his own way and in his own time. Meanwhile, he is not *taught* to speak. He is given a clear pattern of speech, and he does the learning by himself. When he makes mistakes he is not corrected; and when it is his turn to talk he is not interrupted.

Phonograph records can be used to promote the learning process, and they add considerably to the opportunities for ear training. Recorded songs are as useful as rhymes and stories—provided the words are clear. The mother repeats a few words as a record is played, and the child eagerly joins in the talking game. Occasionally a radio or television program can be found that will supplement the records, though the speech will have to be clear and slow if it is to have ear training value. Throughout, the sensory training is informal, and it takes the pattern of a game. Yet the games establish the function of speech in an unbreakable pattern, and they furnish the child with lasting fluency.

This process of "making" or organizing speech can also be used effectively when the child's speech is in the process of "unmaking." The speech function which has become disorganized must be repaired or reorganized. There is little need to pay attention to the stammering itself, for this is merely a symptom—like the spots in measles. In speech therapy the parents endeavor to re-establish the normal pattern of fluency. The child must hear and feel himself again talking normally, and he does this as he listens to slow and measured speech, and repeats the words or accompanies them. This repairing process should be done early in the course of the speech disorder; otherwise, the abnormal speech may itself become established as a lasting pattern.

Meanwhile, of course, the disorganizing stresses in the child's life must be identified. There may be too much activity and excitement and too little calm in the daily program. There may be too much competition for speech at the family table, and no one may be listening when the little fellow is trying to talk. Still worse, an older brother or sister may snatch speech away from him, and thus put him at a constant disadvantage. Whatever the disturbing stresses in the child's life, they should if possible be removed.

Adequate bed rest is important for the child who is overstimulated and easily disorganized. When such disturbances as facial twitching, bed-wetting or stammering suddenly appear, the child can be helped by a few days of bed rest. The rest will be more beneficial if it is fortified with a sedative—given, of course, under medical direction.

A tranquil home is important for the nervous child, for it tends to establish the inward composure that is necessary to normal speech. Yet in the child's developmental years, composure is easily lost and speech readily becomes disorganized. Fortunately, parents can safeguard the child in these situations. They can help him and guide him in the simple skills of word-thinking and thus they can assure him the fluency that he will need in daily living.

||\\/ ADOLESCENT GROWTH
AND DEVELOPMENT

19. Characteristics of Preadolescence: Ages 11 to 14 *

EDWARD C. BRITTON
AND J. MERRITT WINANS

Boys: Ages 12 and 13 (Grades 7 and 8)
Girls: Ages 11 and 12 (Grades 6 and 7)

THE GIRLS are more than a year ahead of the boys in most phases of development through this period. For both, this stage covers a quick trip from the comparative serenity of childhood to the challenges and complexities of adolescence. Powerful forces bring about sweeping physical and emotional changes. Almost one third of the girls will have begun menstruation in their twelfth year. Breasts and hips are more adult than childlike. For the boys, the penis is growing rapidly, shoulders and chest are broader and deeper, and the voice is beginning to change. Preadolescents are dependent on wise adult help if these changes are to take place without undue anxieties. Parental patience is required for the flighty and inconsistent behavior that appears from time to time.

Preadolescence is the introduction to the next developmental stage, adolescence, where children learn to come to terms with a new, challenging, and, at times, difficult way of life.

Characteristics in this chapter apply to most children in the indicated age range. But some of these children, in at least some respects, will be in either the previous or following stages. The reader is therefore advised to

* From Edward C. Britton and J. Merritt Winans, *Growing from Infancy to Adulthood,* pp. 58–67. Copyright © 1958 by Appleton-Century-Crofts, Inc., New York, and reprinted with their permission.

supplement the present chapter by reading those both preceding and following. He is again reminded that the material in this book does not enable the layman to make a dependable appraisal of any child as either retarded or gifted. This can be done only by the expert.

Physical Development

GROWTH

1. The slowdown in growth at the end of later childhood is followed in this stage by rapid acceleration.

2. Appetites may be enormous. Boys need up to 4,000 calories, girls to 3,000.

3. There is great variety in weight and height among these children due to the different ages at which they reach the growth spurt.

4. Bones and ligaments are not yet sufficiently formed to withstand heavy pressure. High pyramid formations can do permanent damage to those supporting the weight.

5. Coordination is improving though not at adult levels. The emotional problems of some may lead to coordination problems. The girls are more precise in their movements than boys.

HEALTH

6. They continue to enjoy comparative freedom from diseases. However, ears, eyes, and especially teeth, may require medical attention. Minor illnesses of short duration are fairly common. Some of these may be imagined but are very real to the child. Some may begin orthodontic treatment.

7. Some may still be fussy about foods.

8. The deterioration in posture first noted in later childhood continues through this period.

9. For most, at least nine hours of sleep are required.

ACTIVITIES

10. Endurance is usually not high, perhaps because of the rapid growth spurt. They can overtire themselves in exciting competition.

11. For many, this is a period of listlessness. The cause may be physical or emotional.

Emotional Development

GROWTH

1. The comparative serenity of later childhood is left behind and emotions begin to play a more obvious part in their lives. They frequently appear to be unable to control them and lose themselves in anger, fear, or love. There is often no relationship between the importance of the situation and the violence of the reaction.

2. They are beginning to experience rapid swings in mood, completing a cycle from extremes of elation to depression within a few hours.

3. The preadolescent's strong emotions can become an asset in developing positive social attitudes. They have strong positive feelings toward ideals that are presented to them effectively.

4. At no age will a child with unmet emotional needs change his behavior to any extent as a result of logical arguments. This is especially true of preadolescents and adolescents.

PROBLEMS: IRRITATING BUT TEMPORARY

5. Both boisterous and nervous behavior indicate the preadolescents' strangeness with new feelings. They may become less responsible and less obedient. They may be hostile to the adults most loved.

6. Frustrations may grow out of conflicts between parents and peers, an awareness of lack of social skills, or failure to mature at the same rate as others. The early-maturing girl and the late-maturing boy encounter the greatest difficulties.

7. They are much given to secrecy. They like their own room, complete with "keep out" sign.

8. Anger is very common. It may grow out of feelings of inadequacy in the face of new challenges, fatigue associated with rapid growth, feelings of rejection, or simply general feelings of uncertainty.

9. Fears, too, are common.

10. Other responses to unsuccessful experiences are overeating and overactivity.

PROBLEMS: POSSIBLY PERSISTENT

11. Overdependence on parents and constant failure to enjoy the company of others should be reviewed carefully. They may be symptoms of problems that can become increasingly serious.

12. Failure to achieve status and belonging to the peer group may lead to loneliness and self-pity.

13. At this stage those with delinquent tendencies come into conflict with the law. They have the knowledge and physical capacity necessary to commit serious offenses.

Social Development

PEERS

1. Their status with the peer group has become even more important than in later childhood. Adult approval is correspondingly less important even though they show need of it when it is withheld.

2. They feel a growing compulsion to conform to the dress, language, possessions, and general behavior of the peer group.

3. They may look down upon those who are less mature and be greatly impressed by those who are more so. Hero worship is common.

4. By the end of this stage, for the most, the "gang" with its out-of-the-way meeting place is changing into the "crowd" often found talking eagerly around the soda fountain.

5. They can be much influenced by the behavior codes of groups like the Scouts or YMCA if these groups enjoy prestige among their peers.

6. Teamwork is now readily understood and practiced. They can work together effectively on projects and enjoy games involving detailed organization such as baseball and football.

7. Most friendships continue to be formed within the immediate neighborhood or classroom. For some, common interests will lead to friendships further afield.

8. Both friendships and quarrels are becoming more intense though neither is likely to survive for a long time.

9. Boys, more than girls, choose friends from their own sex and express antagonism toward the other. Where girls have boyfriends the boys are generally from the next older age group. Preadolescent boys begin to show an interest in girls by teasing and hiding their possessions. Girls who receive such attention gain status with their peers. By the end of this period both boys and girls want mixed parties.

FAMILY

10. The preadolescent shows his concern for his family by anxiety when any member encounters poor health or any other serious problem.

However, he is working hard to achieve independence from them and his efforts in this direction are often misinterpreted by parents.

11. Some children at this stage are very much concerned if they feel that they are failing to measure up to parental expectations. Parents sometimes cause serious problems when they demand a level of performance far beyond the child's ability.

TEACHERS AND OTHER ADULTS

12. The unsuspecting adult is often confused in working with these children. The preadolescent's ideas about himself are constantly changing. One day, or even one hour, he is acting the role of an adult and the next he is a child again.

13. He may have reached the point where he looks to some adult, other than a parent, for help in understanding the complexities of life. This adult must respect his independence, make him feel that he is being treated as a peer, and be willing to listen at length as well as to talk. Such a person frequently has a strong influence on the child. This relationship becomes even more important in adolescence.

14. A crush on the teacher is common, especially the girls for the men teachers. This is a highly sentimental feeling and is much different from the relationship described in the previous point.

15. They expect a high level of skill and maturity in teachers and parents.

16. The uncertainties and insecurities of the preadolescent make it difficult for him to accept criticism.

Mental Development

ABILITY

1. While brain and other neural developments are almost complete, these children lack the experience to enable them to solve many adult problems.

2. They are still most comfortable working on immediate concrete problems though some are now ready to consider in a more mature manner concepts like *democracy*. History begins to have more meaning and they can relate it to present events.

3. They are able to apply a scientific problem-solving approach to increasingly complex problems if placed in an environment that encourages it.

4. Some will be satisfied with manipulating and learning the general

characteristics of electric bell circuits, for example. Others will go on to discover the basic laws at work and to apply them in new situations.

5. Charts, maps, and diagrams are now useful means of communication.

6. They are able to use good judgment in handling money. If properly prepared, they can budget their allowance and supplementary income without the supervision of adults.

7. The attention span continues to increase with all activities. The most striking gains are in problem-solving activities.

8. Their reading rates may be adult.

INTERESTS

9. Their interests are much influenced by their accelerating physical growth, their increasingly strong emotional reactions, and their awareness of the new roles awaiting them in society. While interest in physical science continues, especially for boys, problems of human relationships become increasingly important.

10. They have a much wider variety of interests now. Individual differences in interests become greater.

11. They respond well to opportunities for creative expression. Writing, dramatizing, and painting all allow them to explore and develop new interests and to turn to their own advantage the emotions they are feeling so strongly.

12. They like expressing their thoughts in diaries, poetry, and letters.

13. Reading and collecting equal or exceed the high rates of later childhood.

14. This is the period of much daydreaming. They pretend that they have famous parents, they have been adopted, or they are orphans. Daydreaming may become frequent enough to interfere with school work. They no longer engage in imaginative play.

15. Girls lose interest in playing with dolls. They become preoccupied with themselves and their appearance. They are more prone to wish for success in adult life than are boys.

16. Home responsibilities are expanded. They can wash the car, wash dishes, and look after younger children. They appreciate an increased voice in planning along with these new responsibilities.

Moral and Spiritual Development

1. A conscience becomes more apparent at this stage. These children exhibit strong feelings about honesty, for example. However, more of them

than formerly will steal. This may grow out of their greater need for a wide variety of articles, the greater chances of success in stealing, the greater pressure of the gang, and the general emotional instability characteristic of this stage.

2. Feelings of guilt, based on both real and imagined wrongdoings, become common.

3. Their sense of simple justice remains strong and they are quick to challenge the teacher or parent who violates it. However, with guidance, they can be led to understand the need for meeting the problems of different people in different ways.

4. Some will begin to question the religious teachings of the home. Their feelings will be intense, though changeable. By 13, boys are dropping out of church and Sunday school at a rapid rate.

5. Prayer becomes more abstract than at earlier stages.

6. Girls demonstrate superior moral knowledge. Parents spend more time with them talking about proper behavior.

7. Children of this age can assume jobs away from home and see them through.

8. By 12 many children will be able to reject an immediate enjoyment such as television for a long-term satisfaction such as earning money.

9. They are ready to accept the other person's point of view and to live in harmony with those with whom they disagree, if in an environment that values these skills. They are beginning to see the possibilities of cooperative group action.

10. They begin to exhibit more concern for others and are willing to be helpful without any tangible reward.

20. Characteristic Needs of Adolescence *

RAYMOND G. KUHLEN

THE FOLLOWING paragraphs attempt to generalize from such specific facts as just cited and to discuss briefly what appear to be the more important motives and needs characterizing the adolescent period. There are, for example, the need for social status, the seeking of vocational and material

* From Raymond G. Kuhlen, *The Psychology of Adolescent Development,* pp. 243–47. Copyright 1952 by Harper and Bros., New York, and reprinted with their permission.

goals, the desire for personal independence, the personal direction and orientation provided by codes and ideals of conduct, the need for explanation and long-time purposes, and the desires which grow from sex and other biological needs. Separate listing and separate discussion does not imply that there are separate motives.[1] A "motive" or "need" is by no means a psychological entity. Any aspect of behavior tends to be determined not by a single "motive," but by the total motivational situation. Some "motives" will reinforce each other, and some will be in conflict. And what constitutes an important motive for one individual may be relatively lacking for another. If these principles are recognized, a listing of what seem to be major adolescent needs will provide a framework within which to approach problems of adolescent adjustment, and a source of hypotheses regarding the motives of particular individuals; to this extent it will serve a worth-while purpose.

1. *The need for status and acceptance.* Perhaps no psychological need is so pervasive as the desire for social approval and social acceptance. A thousand things—living on the right street, getting in the right club, being mentioned on the society page, winning a smile of approval from parent or teacher—contribute to an individual's prestige and his personal satisfaction, to his status. The need for status and acceptance represents the common need for a secure position and a sense of belongingness in one's home and family, in one's actual or desired social set, or among one's colleagues at school or work. Such a sense of security depends upon the existence of relationships involving affection, mutual trust and confidence and respect, and freedom from threat or frustration. The emotional or social insecurity that results when status is absent or uncertain characterizes much chronic maladjustment. In fact, lack of psychological security in childhood is probably the most important cause of adolescent and adult personality maladjustment. As a later chapter suggests, the desire for status and social acceptability, though important in varying degrees throughout life, is given a special complexion at adolescence because at this age status and acceptance

---

[1] Various writers present their own formulations of the needs and motives of individuals. Symonds urges that there are two basic needs—security and adequacy. Maslow discusses needs in terms of a hierarchy of five levels of priority, lower level needs taking priority over higher level needs. Murray lists a substantial number of "needs" and "presses." And one might argue that there is but one need—tension reduction. But the latter is no more helpful than to say that personal "happiness" is the basic goal. There must be further description of the kinds of conditions that give rise to tensions and the kinds of behaviors or ends that reduce these tensions and thus become goals, of the *ways* in which happiness is found. In considering the problem of motivation in adolescence, there must be consideration of the areas in which adolescents in the American culture typically need to make adjustments.

among members of the opposite sex and among adults are much to be desired. The desire for status and acceptance is so basic that it will be reflected in many other "motives."

2. *The desire for independence.* Though people are gregarious and socially oriented, they are also highly individual and, in the American culture, "need" a certain freedom of action and decision. This is true of adults, of children (who at very early ages often go through a phase of negativism when their individuality is asserted), and of adolescents, especially in America where a great premium is placed upon individual initiative. Among adolescents the desire for self-determination and independence (to be accepted as a mature, responsible, self-directing adult) may represent one of the more important motives. To no small degree this importance derives from the fact that, like the attractive green grass, independence lies largely on the other side of the fence. Crossing this "fence" is often made especially difficult because of parents' refusal to treat the adolescent as an adult, and because of society's failure to provide a place for the young person in adult economic life. The pride with which a child attains an age which denotes a certain degree of independence—as 16, 18, or 21—illustrates the importance of this motive.

3. *Vocational and material motives.* The achievement of independence is to no small degree contingent upon the adolescent's becoming economically self-supporting. Partly for this reason, partly because new personal economic needs are arising, because schooling is drawing to a close, and because society expects it, vocational goals begin to come to the fore during the late teens. The need is apparent first in fantasy, then in vague exploratory concern, and finally in tentative decisions as to specific vocations. Vocational and material aims often develop early and in some cases seem to dominate almost every thought and action. It will be recalled that vocational achievement and material possessions represented a major portion of the content of college students' fantasy. And the importance of vocational motives is reflected in reactions to failure. To the Air Force cadet who dreamed of becoming a fighter pilot and later a commercial transport pilot, washing out of flying was a personal catastrophe. To the chap with his heart set on becoming a lawyer, inability to gain admittance to law school is a severe blow.

Vocational motives are, however, more complex than mere "job goal" may suggest. They may involve a sheer desire for mastery, as in the case of the mathematician or statistician who takes delight in solving complex problems for the thrill he gets out of having done them. They may represent primarily an avarice for material possessions, the vocation being chosen largely in terms of the promise for material rewards. Vocational goals may represent a love for a type of activity, such as the person who becomes interested in a hobby and forsakes his job for the thing he "likes to do." Or the job may be chosen because of the possibilities that it offers for social prestige and public prominence. Some of the most serious problems of adolescence and adult life grow out of the inability of young people to clarify sufficiently their vocational goals so that intelligent action can be taken toward achieving them.

4. *Adherence to codes and ideals.* Much of behavior is guided by principles of "right" and "wrong." A person who does a virtuous act gets a "lift" out of it, a feeling of self-satisfaction; the person who deviates from the dictates of his "conscience" is apt to experience feelings of guilt. As a person grows, he makes the standards and norms of his particular culture his own, and in this way a need to conform to society's demands becomes a personal need. The accepted patterns of conduct of the home and the immediate social group become so much a part of the individual's system of ideals and standards that they take on emotionalized meanings for him. Moral beliefs, codes of honesty, sex codes, group loyalty, ideals of courtesy, law observance, ideals of beauty, the perfect life, religious virtue, attitudes of admiration, hate, contempt, or pity toward various national or minority groups—these and many other personal values too numerous to mention contribute to the attitudinal complex often labeled a "value system" which plays a highly significant role in a person's motivational make-up.

In adolescence special significance attaches to the fact that habitual ways of behaving and habitual attitudes may not be appropriate to the new social group (as in high school, college, or on the job) in which the teen-ager finds himself. The young person with broadening contacts with the inconsistencies of his culture (and with a higher level of intellectual maturity which makes him more sensitive to these inconsistencies) is often faced with special problems involving readjustments of ideals and behaviors related thereto as he encounters the inconsistencies of his culture.

5. *The need for understanding and "completeness."* The fact that people are intelligent probably lies at the root of certain psychological needs that must be met if there is to be satisfaction. Man is able to think in the abstract and to reason; it is reasonable, then, that he should inquire beyond the facts immediately at hand and seek to learn things beyond. The fact that religion supplies answers to complex unknowns may account for its existence in various forms in diverse cultures. Morale is higher among troops who understand the nature of the undertaking and are not operating in ignorance of the total picture and purpose of a given maneuver. Their intellectual

need to know "why" has been met. Fears and superstitions have often developed to fill the need for "answers." The interruption of stories or tasks before their completion appears, according to some research, to create tensions that result in their persisting in memory longer than tasks not interrupted. Such examples illustrate a general need for understanding, for completeness, and for projecting of plans. Such needs are apt to characterize adolescence, in part because a level of intellectual maturity has been reached that permits broader visions, more serious questioning of things that had previously been accepted at face value and greater ease in dealing with abstract matters, and partly because abstract matters are being increasingly encountered. That some motivation exists to explore these issues and to achieve understanding is suggested by the numerous occasions on which young people discuss such questions as truth, beauty, religion, and ideals of one kind or another in "bull sessions."

6. *Sex and other biological needs.* Sexual needs represent a strong motivating force during a considerable portion of the life span. In the chapter on physical growth, special attention was directed to the advent of puberty, the physical fact of sexual maturation, and the accompanying changes in sex interest and desire. In the chapter on interests, a major trend noted was the emerging interest in sex-social activities during adolescence. In many ways the importance of sex in influencing the adolescent's behavior is evident. While emerging from biological pressures, sex expression has been so carefully directed by society that in adolescence it is most often evident in desire for dates and participation in various social activities, such as dancing, swimming, tennis, and other recreational activities in the company of members of the opposite sex. Direct sex expression outside of marriage is frowned upon in the American culture, but despite this taboo there is frequent direct satisfaction through autoerotic practices and illicit intercourse, and partial satisfaction on a semipermissible basis through petting and other intimate physical contacts. Although an earlier table has indicated that sex occupies a central position in everyday fantasy, it is probably not (as some psychologists have stressed) the dominant motive in life. But since the sex drive is not so readily satisfied in the American culture as is the tissue need for food and water, it may be expected that it will exert more pressure upon behavior generally than do other creature needs.

Other needs that grow out of the biological nature of the organism include the need for oxygen, water, food, and freedom from extreme conditions such as heat, cold, and other painful stimulations. For a large portion of the American population, these latter needs tend to be submerged beneath a veneer of cultural habits; being satisfied, they are not active as motivators. Adequate food and shelter have for many never been a serious problem; the concern more likely has been for a socially desirable type of housing in "good" neighborhoods, for food prepared in ways to which Americans have become accustomed. The urge for self-preservation in the sheer biological sense is relatively unimportant because few modern activities are matters of life or death. Though the importance of the majority of biological needs may well be minimized as far as their place in determining the behavior of many people is concerned, it is not to be forgotten that among certain groups there may be chronic want, and in some places at certain times deprivation or threat of pain or death may be so serious that the cultural veneer crumbles away in the interests of sheer life. During the war, many an individual found himself pitted against another in an out-and-out animal struggle for self-preservation. In some parts of the world, the basic problem is to keep the human animal fed, not as a social creature to be dined in socially approved ways, but as a hungry biological organism.

7. *Habits as motives.* A discussion of motives cannot be limited to a list set up a priori. Instead, there are innumerable motivational possibilities of a highly individual nature, varying to the extent that there are variations in individual habits of thinking, feeling, or doing. Biologically, the organism is so constructed as to be able to maintain a remarkably constant internal environment. Bodily temperature, for example, is so carefully regulated that even relatively slight deviations are sufficiently unusual as to be symptomatic of something wrong. Psychologically, there is a similar (though not so precise) tendency on the part of people to maintain constant external environment and a constant pattern of behavior. They tend to maintain their ways of life, to do the things they are accustomed to do, to seek out in new places of residence their *own* kind of associates. A habit or set of habits, once established, tends to carry its own motive power, to become a drive in its own right; habits which originally had adjustive value may continue because of the momentum they have acquired. Often the full significance of this principle is missed by the average person because it is not recognized that habits may be of various types and degrees of complexity, including the more complex and implicit habits of thinking and feeling, of reacting emotionally or nonemotionally.

21. Physical Growth *

AT THE TIME of the first anthropometric measurements (age 11.4 years) John weighed approximately 80 pounds and stood slightly over 4 feet 9 inches in height. Seen on the playground among his classmates he appeared approximately average in physical size and conformation. But in the following years John grew more slowly than his classmates. He lagged behind in height, in weight, in nearly every measure of physical size. With the tediously slow increments characteristic of delayed maturing (85 per cent of the boys in his group were earlier in maturity than John) he dropped to the twenty-fifth percentile in height, the fifteenth percentile in weight, below the tenth percentile in shoulder breadth. This was in the high-ninth grade, age 15, his lowest point in physical status relative to the group, and also (if the reader will recall) an exceptionally bad period in nearly every measure of social relationships as observed by his classmates and by adults.

Figure 1 presents, in silhouette form,[1] seriatim annual photographs for John. This illustration gives a clear indication of John's somewhat narrow body build, persisting into maturity; his gradual growth from 12 to 15 years; and a sudden spurt in growth from 15 to 16. Figure 2 illustrates growth in height as related to his age mates. In the preparation of this chart, the average for boys in the Adolescent Growth Study is represented by a smoothed solid line, the actual age means being shown as points on or adjacent to the line. The larger dots indicate the measurements obtained for John, at approximately six-month intervals. From 11.5 to 12.5 years of age, John is seen to be almost exactly average in height. From this point, however, he dropped progressively below the average, until at 14.5 he reached the lower margin of the shaded area which in this chart represents the middle 50 per cent of our cases ($\pm$ 1 P.E. from the mean). John was, at this time, still a "little boy" among classmates the majority of whom

* From Harold E. Jones, *Development in Adolescence,* pp. 67–74. Copyright 1943 by D. Appleton-Century Co., Inc. By permission of Appleton-Century-Crofts, Inc., New York.

[1] As a part of the program of physical studies, conducted by Dr. H. R. Stolz, body photographs, nude, were taken under standard conditions at each semiannual physical examination. For the present purpose, photographs are included only for year intervals; the effect shown in the published plate was obtained by taking a contact print of a paper positive, with overexposure to eliminate details which would reveal personal identity.

were further advanced in the cycle of pubertal development toward adulthood. By every external indication he seemed destined to become an undersized adult. But within this year a change in growth rate occurred, leading to a belated growth spurt through which he eventually caught up with the average for his group.

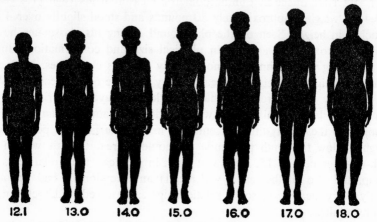

Figure 1. Silhouettes from body photographs at year intervals.

Another way in which growth data can be presented, bringing into sharper relief the variation in rates at successive ages, is to show the *increments* according to specified units of time. A convenient unit to use is a decimal part of a year. Table 1 exhibits John's growth in height and in weight with computations of (a) absolute gains per .1 of a year and

Table 1

JOHN'S GROWTH IN HEIGHT AND WEIGHT FROM AGE 12.1 TO 18.1

Age	Height			Weight		
	MM.	INCREMENT PER .1 YEAR	% GAIN PER YEAR	KG.	INCREMENT PER .1 YEAR	% GAIN PER YEAR
12.1	1489 *			38.0		
13.0	1529	4.4	3.0	38.6	.7	1.8
14.0	1580	5.1	3.3	43.9	5.3	13.7
15.0	1644	6.4	4.1	47.4	3.5	8.0
16.0	1718	7.4	4.5	53.5	6.1	12.9
17.0	1753	3.5	2.0	55.5	2.0	3.7
18.1	1765	1.1	.7	60.0	4.1	7.4

* In terms of feet and inches, John's height at 12.1 years was 4′ 10½″; at 18.1 years, 5′ 9½″. His weight at 12.1 was 84 lbs., at 18.1, 132 lbs.

(b) percentage gains per year. It can be noted that John's greatest velocity of growth in height was after the age of 15 (that is, in the year period ending at 16 he grew 74 mm., or 7.4 mm. per .1 of a year). His growth in weight was less even and regular, but with the largest absolute gain also falling in the sixteenth year.

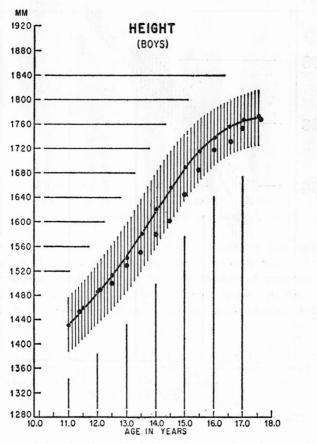

Figure 2. Growth curve for height (boys).

Skeletal Maturing

To the superficial observer (and also to John himself) his growth record during this adolescent period was exceptional almost to the point of abnormality. It had serious consequences in his ability to hold his own with his

peers—an ability already compromised, as we have seen, by other deficiencies. And yet in terms of more fundamental characteristics, John's
growth in height was entirely normal. This is illustrated in Figure 3, which

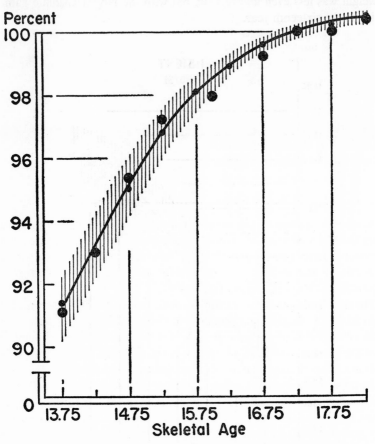

Figure 3. Relative growth in height, according to physiological age.

shows his *relative* growth, the percentage of mature height,[2] presented
according to his physiological rather than his chronological age. Physiological age, in this instance, is determined through X rays of the hand and

[2] Mature height is taken as the height reached at 17.6 years. At this time his skeletal
maturity was sufficiently complete so that further growth in height could be expected
to be negligible.

[3] The technique of X-ray assessment has been described by N. Bayley, "Skeletal
X-rays as Indicators of Maturity," *Journal of Consulting Psychology,* 4 (1940), 69–73.

knee, evaluated with reference to the Todd standards for skeletal maturing.[3] In this figure, the solid line represents the average relative height of all of the boys in the sample, classified according to their physiological (skeletal) ages. The points representing John's relative height, are close to the line of the averages, showing that in terms of basic maturation his growth in height is normal and consistent. Although apparently grossly retarded in height at 14 and 15 years of age, his skeletal maturity indices at those ages make possible the prediction that his ultimate mature height will be approximately average for his group.

In growth patterns of the type illustrated here, we note the possibility of a complete physical recovery from a period marked by deviate physical characteristics. It is not always as easy, however, to recover from the psychological consequences of a growth record which, in the adolescent period, fails to conform to group norms and group expectations.

Growth Curves Relative to the Group

Since our interest in the details of John's physical growth is primarily from the point of view of possible social implications, it will be useful to consider another type of growth curve in which each measure is expressed in terms of standard scores comparable to those previously shown for psychological traits (Chapters III and IV).

Figure 4 presents these relative growth curves for a selection of three measurements: height, stem length,[4] and bi-iliac width. In the case of each of these components of physique we note that the seriatim measurements begin near the average, recede to a lower position, and then return to the average. This is a characteristic picture of a late maturing individual.

In other measurements John showed a similar tendency to lag behind the average after age 12. Unfortunately, in some of these physical traits he failed to recover the ground lost in the early teens. Figure 10 presents relative growth curves for weight, arm circumference, and chest circumference. In these curves a more or less stable position was reached around the age of 15; this does not mean that John ceased growing in these characteristics, but merely that he failed to show an *accelerated* growth to compensate for the earlier period of deceleration. Having dropped to the lowest 15 per cent of the group, in later years he remained approximately in the same relative status.

[4] Stem length involves the measurement of the length of the trunk and head when the subject is sitting with his back against an upright measuring board, and his upper legs are at a 45° angle with the floor. Bi-iliac width is a measure of hip width; it is recorded from sliding calipers, the jaws of which are placed firmly at the iliac crests.

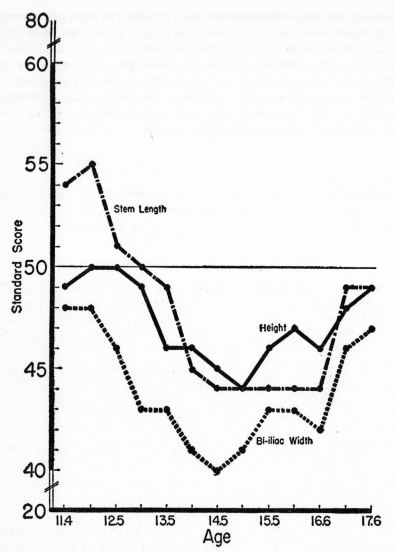

Figure 4. Standard scores for physical measurements. Stem length, height, bi-iliac width.

Thus in John's case we see an illustration of the fact that the physical growth of an individual has an individual pattern, not merely with regard to the timing of changes in the rate of growth, but also with regard to the relationship of parts. This relationship, in the case of John, is one in which his mature physique is characterized by a normal height and a fairly normal development of the abdominal trunk and legs, but a weak and fragile development of the upper part of the body comprising the arms, shoulder girdle, and chest. This can also be seen in a study of the silhouettes in Figure 1. In John's physique, and more basically, we may infer, in his endocrine organization, occur parallels to our records of his interests, attitudes, and activities, which were often characterized as differing from those of his more vigorously masculine classmates.[5]

22. *Somatic Variations* *

HAROLD W. BERNARD

The Fallacy of Types

There is a widespread tendency to attempt to classify people into distinct categories. Thus there are saints and sinners, fat and lean men, optimistic and pessimistic, mature and immature, children and adolescents, fifth graders and seventh graders. Actually, these and similar categories tend to confuse rather than to clarify. One person may have in mind a fifth grader who is quite mature while another thinks of a seventh grader who is immature—the two being quite alike in terms of interest and behavior. The man who is pessimistic about his business prospects may be quite optimistic about his children's future. In short, there is a continuousness of differences in any one respect that makes it fallacious to classify people into types.

Psychologists have attempted to classify people on the basis of body build—hoping to discover some predictable personality traits that accompany physique. One of the more notable early attempts was that of E. Kretschmer who divided physique into three categories: (1) asthenic—thin, underdeveloped body, (2) pyknic—heavy, thickset body, (3) athletic—well-developed, muscular body. The difficulty of classifying

---

[5] Various investigators have attempted to provide a systematic basis for the classification of body proportions.

* From Harold W. Bernard, *Adolescent Development in American Culture*, pp. 159–63. Copyright 1957 by World Book Co., Yonkers-on-Hudson, N. Y., and reprinted with their permission.

people into these types is indicated by the fact that Kretschmer had to add a fourth category, the dysplastic, which is a mixture—pyknic legs and asthenic trunk, for example. Kretschmer did find some relation between body build and the type of mental illness a person would have if he broke down. The asthenic was more likely to have schizophrenia and the pyknic was more likely to suffer from manic-depressive psychoses. The relationship between body build and normal personality was less susceptible to prediction.

Varieties of Physique

The fact that body types cannot be sharply differentiated does not mean that there is no relation between physique and personality. The search for relationships is continuing under the leadership of William H. Sheldon, who hopes to provide a new framework for psychology: "It has been growing increasingly plain that the situation [interpretations of human life] calls for a biologically oriented psychology, or one taking for its operational frame of reference a scientifically defensible description of the *structure* (together with the behavior) of the human organism itself." [1] His study avoids the error of discrete types by providing for continuity of measurement. Three focal types are postulated: endomorph—abdominal predominance (fat men, relatively little skin in proportion to bulk covered); mesomorph—predominance of bone and muscle (athletic type); and ectomorph —lean body, delicate bones, large skin surface in proportion to bulk. The measurements of a person's build are summarized in a three digit number, 7 indicating the maximum of that type and 1 indicating the minimum. Thus an extreme endomorph would be coded as 7–1–1, an extreme mesomorph as 1–7–1, and one who was predominantly ectomorph would be 1–1–7. Such extremes occur very rarely, combinations such as 4–3–4, 2–5–2, or 4–4–4 are more likely to be found (the sum of the digits does not have to be nine). With this flexible system Sheldon has studied at least seventy-six different combinations in terms of degree of the focal type possessed. In addition to the purely bodily differences Sheldon sometimes found it necessary to refer to such "secondary" features as hirsutism, texture of the skin, and the possession of sex characteristics typical of the opposite sex. Thus there is considerable flexibility in his approach.

[1] William H. Sheldon, *The Varieties of Temperament* (New York: Harper and Bros., 1949), p. xv. See also Sheldon *et al., The Varieties of Human Physique* (1940), and *The Varieties of Temperament* (1942), both published by Harper and Bros. Material quoted above is used by permission of Dr. Sheldon and the publishers.

Physique and Personality

The relationship between somatotype and personality is of particular interest in the psychology of adolescence.

Names have been given to the three correlated groups of traits. *Viscerotonia,* the first component, in its extreme manifestations is characterized by general relaxation, love of comfort, sociability, conviviality, gluttony for food, for people, and for affection. The viscerotonic extremes are people who "suck hard at the breast of mother earth" and love physical proximity with others. The motivational organization is dominated by the gut and by the function of anabolism. The personality seems to center around the viscera. The digestive tract is king, and its welfare appears to define the primary purpose of life.

Somatotonia, the second component, is roughly a predominance of muscular activity and of vigorous bodily assertiveness. The motivational organization seems dominated by the soma. These people have vigor and push. The executive department of their internal economy is strongly vested in their somatic muscular systems. Action and power define life's primary purpose.

Cerebrotonia, the third component, is roughly a predominance of the element of restraint, inhibition, and of the desire for concealment. Cerebrotonic people shrink away from sociality as from too strong a light. They "repress" somatic and visceral expression, are hyperattentional, and sedulously avoid attracting attention to themselves. Their behavior seems dominated by the inhibitory and attentional functions of the cerebrum, and their motivational hierarchy appears to define an antithesis to both of the other extremes.[2]

Of course, we are all acquainted with individuals whose body types would not seem to accord with the kind of personality revealed in their daily lives. There are tall, thin boys who seem to enjoy the vigorous pursuit of athletics that is purportedly more natural to the mesomorph. Some heavy-set, chunky individuals are interested in scholarly pursuits and engage in contemplative behavior. There are athletic-looking persons who enjoy eating and fellowship and who love comfort. No doubt the kind of culture in which an individual has lived, especially the tone and interest of family life, does much to shape these personality orientations. The fact of differences in personality cannot be ignored, however, and it is entirely possible that bodily structure plays a part in the *tendencies* to develop in a given direction. Certainly, those who attempt to interpret the behavior of adolescents cannot blithely endorse the behavioristic tendency to explain everything on the basis of education, environment, and experience.

[2] William H. Sheldon, *The Varieties of Temperament* (New York: Harper and Bros., 1942), pp. 10–11. Quoted by permission of Dr. Sheldon and the publishers.

"But," runs the argument, "how does one explain the fact that the athletic-appearing (mesomorph) individual does become a scholar?" Environment is the answer. Another question must be asked: "Does the development of a personality that is not in accord with a person's body type predispose him to mental breakdown?" For example, will forcing young persons into athletics, dancing, intense scholarship also force them toward emotional instability? Even if body-type is discredited as a cause, parents and teachers well might ask themselves if in their attempt to make boys and girls into musicians, serious students, competitive individuals, or social "butterflies" they do not cause an otherwise adequately adjusting person to become tense, uncertain, and unhappy. Some youngsters can be happy sitting and watching others dance, compete, and carry off scholarship awards.

There is another unanswered question: "Does not the growth of some adolescents tend to change their body build—though Sheldon believes a child can be accurately somatotyped by the age of 16?" Despite the question, the following conclusions seem to be warranted: (1) Sheldon's morphology should be viewed with an open mind because it provides for continuous variation of differences rather than discrete types. (2) Personality must be interpreted on the basis of inherent factors as well as environmental influences. (3) Young persons may be presently well adjusted and still not fit some popular stereotype. (4) Those who work with young persons should respect their socially acceptable inclinations (whether innate or acquired).

23. *Objectives of the Adolescent Period* *

LUELLA COLE

NEAR THE BEGINNING of the adolescent period the boy or girl achieves sexual maturity and, in some specific capacities, intellectual maturity as well. By the end of adolescence, physical growth is complete and intellectual growth very nearly so. Only severe deprivation can prevent a human organism from reaching adult size, shape, and function, or from growing

* From Luella Cole, *Psychology of Adolescence,* 5th ed., pp. 4–7. Copyright © 1959 by Rinehart and Co., Inc., New York, and reprinted with their permission.

into its expected mental maturity. In short, nature will provide for these two types of growth, unles some catastrophe intervenes. The real problems of adolescence are therefore emotional, social, moral, and economic.

Most adolescents solve their problems by slow degrees during the ages from 12 to 21. The adolescent with severe conflicts and violent reactions is so much more dramatic than the boy or girl who develops slowly, and without fireworks, that one is likely to overemphasize the storm and stress of the period. In the normal growth of a typical individual, childhood fades, adolescence advances, and adulthood arrives in a gradual, smooth series of small changes and with only temporary and incidental difficulties and disturbances.

The boy or girl enters adolescence with a child's adjustment to the world. No matter how perfect his emotional and social adaptation may be, it is not suitable for adult life. A child is normally dependent upon others, has little or no interest in members of the opposite sex, expects to be supported both emotionally and financially by his family, takes his judgments ready-made from those he admires, and has neither the interest nor the ability to deal with generalized principles. At the end of his adolescence he should be ready to leave his home—emotionally and actually—to maintain himself economically, to manage his own social contacts, to make up his own mind, to establish his own home, and to concern himself with the general principles behind surface phenomena.

In the change from dependent childhood to independent adulthood an individual has to approach many goals, the more important of which are to be presented shortly. These objectives have been grouped for the sake of convenience into eight areas of human interest and activity: emotional maturity, establishment of heterosexual interests, social maturity, emancipation from home, mental maturity, the beginnings of financial independence, proper uses of leisure, the development of a definite point of view about life, and the identification of one's self. These are the same objectives that hold for the years of maturity also; the adolescent can be expected to make only a beginning in leaving his childhood behind him and in preparing to enter adulthood. It is a rare person who achieves adulthood in all phases of existence. The child that one once was keeps popping up from time to time with childish, if not infantile, solutions to the myriad problems of daily life. From that child no one ever fully escapes, but the adolescent should make a beginning in the process of meeting the new requirements of adulthood. In order to emphasize the basic fact of growth, the goals—presented in the next few pages—have been stated in terms of change from a childish toward an adult level.

Table 1

GOALS OF THE ADOLESCENT PERIOD

A. *General Emotional Maturity*

From
1. Destructive expressions of emotion
2. Subjective interpretation of situations
3. Childish fears and motives
4. Habits of escaping from conflicts

toward
1. Harmless or constructive expressions
2. Objective interpretations of situations
3. Adult stimuli to emotions
4. Habits of facing and solving conflicts

B. *Establishment of Heterosexual Interests*

From
1. Exclusive interest in members of same sex
2. Experience with many possible mates
3. Acute awareness of sexual development

toward
1. Normal interest in members of opposite sex
2. Selection of one mate
3. Casual acceptance of sexual maturity

C. *General Social Maturity*

From
1. Feelings of uncertainty of acceptance by peers
2. Social awkwardness
3. Social intolerance
4. Slavish imitation of peers

toward
1. Feelings of secure acceptance by peers
2. Social poise
3. Social tolerance
4. Freedom from slavish imitation

D. *Emancipation from Home Control*

From
1. Close parental control
2. Reliance upon parents for security
3. Identification with parents as models

toward
1. Self-control
2. Reliance upon self for security
3. Attitude toward parents as friends

E. *Intellectual Maturity*

From
1. Blind acceptance of truth on the basis of authority
2. Desire for facts
3. Many temporary interests

toward
1. Demand for evidence before acceptance
2. Desire for explanations of facts
3. Few, stable interests

F. *Selection of an Occupation*

From
1. Interest in glamorous occupations
2. Interest in many occupations
3. Over- or underestimation of one's own abilities
4. Irrelevance of interests to abilities

toward
1. Interest in practicable occupations
2. Interest in one occupation
3. Reasonably accurate estimate of one's own abilities
4. Reconciliation of interest and abilities

Table 1 (cont.)

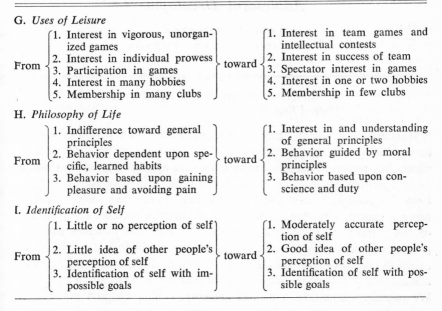

G. *Uses of Leisure*

From
1. Interest in vigorous, unorganized games
2. Interest in individual prowess
3. Participation in games
4. Interest in many hobbies
5. Membership in many clubs

toward
1. Interest in team games and intellectual contests
2. Interest in success of team
3. Spectator interest in games
4. Interest in one or two hobbies
5. Membership in few clubs

H. *Philosophy of Life*

From
1. Indifference toward general principles
2. Behavior dependent upon specific, learned habits
3. Behavior based upon gaining pleasure and avoiding pain

toward
1. Interest in and understanding of general principles
2. Behavior guided by moral principles
3. Behavior based upon conscience and duty

I. *Identification of Self*

From
1. Little or no perception of self
2. Little idea of other people's perception of self
3. Identification of self with impossible goals

toward
1. Moderately accurate perception of self
2. Good idea of other people's perception of self
3. Identification of self with possible goals

The first set of problems and goals centers around the attainment of emotional control. Children have little power to inhibit their responses, they have many fears, they are self-centered, and they run away from what is disagreeable. It is, then, one task of adolescence to emerge from childish into adult forms of emotional expression, to substitute intellectual for emotional reactions, at least in recurring situations, and to learn that one cannot escape reality.

24. The School, the Peer Group, and Adolescent Development [*] [1]

RICHARD L. SIMPSON
AND IDA HARPER SIMPSON

Introduction: Status of the Adolescent in the United States

Human biology dictates that in all societies there be a period of adolescence, during and after puberty. Societies vary, however, in the extent to
which they recognize adolescence as a separate age category and provide a
distinct pattern of behavior for it. Some distinguish adolescence sharply
from childhood and adulthood, others do not.[2] In our own society, adolescence is known as the "awkward age," while in some societies this period is
relatively tranquil and devoid of problems.[3] This fact indicates that the
problems of adolescence, where they exist, are not biological but social in
origin. A comparison of various cultures suggests that our own problems of
adolescence stem from the position of the adolescent in our social structure.
We consider adolescents a distinct category, neither children nor adults,
and we keep them in the adolescent category well into the years of biological
maturity. Yet we do not provide explicit or compelling norms to guide
adolescent behavior.

In some societies, the beginning and end of adolescence occur at definite
times, and are celebrated by collective rites of passage. Throughout Poly-

[*] From Richard L. Simpson and Ida Harper Simpson, "The School, the Peer
Group, and Adolescent Development," *The Journal of Educational Sociology* (September, 1958), pp. 37–41. Reprinted by permission of the authors and *The Journal
of Educational Sociology*.

[1] The ideas developed here grew out of discussions connected with a study conducted by Ida Harper Simpson under the direction of Professor M. E. John at the
Pennsylvania State University. Ida Harper Simpson, "Adolescent Behavior and Food
and Beverage Patterns," Report No. 1, Social Science Research Center, Pennsylvania
State University, University Park, Pennsylvania, April 1957.

[2] Ralph Linton, "Age and Sex Categories," *American Sociological Review,* 7, pp.
589–603.

[3] Until 1928, most writers agreed with Clark Hull's view that the "trauma of
adolescence" results from the physiological changes attending puberty. The "social"
explanation of adolescent behavior has gained sway since Margaret Mead, in *Coming
of Age in Samoa* (New York: William Morrow, 1928), described a society in which
adolescence took place without trauma. This approach holds that adjustment to the
biological changes of adolescence is helped or hindered by the culture's interpretation
of these changes.

nesia, for example, adolescents are sharply differentiated from children and adults. They are formally organized into age groups and, relieved of most social and economic responsibilities, are left free to pursue the tasks of courting and personal adjustment. The primary function of the adolescent groups is to entertain themselves and others.[4]

Our own society, in contrast, does not clearly specify the onset and end of adolescence, or the proper behavior during this period. This vagueness is at the root of our adolescent problem, since people adjust most easily to those situations in which their expected behavior is most clearly defined and understood.[5] The social role of the American adolescent is not clear. In school, for example, he is expected to be a diligent worker, but his peer group may prefer that he be an irresponsible pleasure seeker.

The adolescent plays numerous roles in numerous groups. Studies which have emphasized the "trauma" of adolescence have usually focussed on only one status of the adolescent: his status in the parental family in Freudian writings, and his status in his peer group in most other writings. Yet the very diversity of statuses occupied by the adolescent in modern society may account for his insecurity. He has no single "core status" or dominant role whose expectations take priority over the demands of other statuses.[6] Viewing this situation psychologically, one might say that the adolescent lacks an all-pervasive self-concept. He does not know exactly who he is or who he wants to become.

The Peer Group and Adolescent Social Needs

The social striving of the American adolescent centers around the need to develop a clear status and a gratifying self-concept which will equip him for adult life. To satisfy this need, the adolescent must do several things. He must gain social recognition on the basis of his own achievements, and in terms of the values of his age group; no longer may he depend on the assured recognition which his family gave him in childhood. He (or she) must develop a self-concept, and the behavior patterns which support this self-concept, which will differentiate his behavior clearly from that appropriate to the opposite sex.[7] Finally, he must develop certain habits or quali-

[4] Ralph Linton, *op. cit.*

[5] Leonard S. Cottrell, "The Adjustment of the Individual to His Age and Sex Roles," *American Sociological Review*, 7, pp. 617–20.

[6] The concept of core status was suggested to the writers by Professor Harvey L. Smith of the University of North Carolina.

[7] Some writers maintain that the need for sex differentiation is subsidiary to the more general need for personal achievement and the approval of the peer group. In this view, the wish of the adolescent to be desired as a date, or to be a football hero,

ties needed for successful adult living, such as initiative, responsibility, and self-reliance.

Much of the burden of adolescent socialization is placed upon the school. The adolescent spends many of his waking hours in school, or in activities connected with the school. The formal program of the school, however, is not sufficient to meet all of the adolescent's developmental needs. The demands of the curriculum make no distinction between the statuses of boys and girls, with the exception of minor portions of the curriculum such as physical education, shop work, and home economics; therefore the school program contributes little toward differentiating the sex roles of adolescents.[8] Moreover, the values of the school—diligence in study, respect for the social etiquette and moral codes of the middle-class adult world— are not necessarily those of the adolescent; and the adolescent may or may not derive great satisfaction from achievements in terms of these adult values. He needs to attain recognition on the basis of values peculiar to his own age group.

Unlike the formal program of the school, the peer group enables the adolescent to gain social recognition through his personal qualities and achievements. Its dating pattern, athletic contests, and other activities build a clear-cut sex role into the self-concept of the adolescent. The individual wins recognition for his sense of humor or his loyalty to friends. The boy asserts his maleness in athletics, or by swearing and telling sexual jokes. The girl competes for prestige through dating, and pays homage to her sex by giggling over the latest Elvis Presley record. In these ways the peer group, far more than the formal school program or even the home, defends the individual against the uncertainties of adolescence through the security of group membership. The importance of the peer group for adolescent adjustment is shown in a study of young adult schizophrenics, by N. J. Demerath. The subjects, before their schizophrenic conditions developed,

---

stems from the more general wish to achieve social eminence in the peer group. It has been noted, for example, that a high school or college girl may be more interested in what dress she wears to a party than in whom she accompanies as a date, provided that the boy be socially presentable. On this general point see Margaret Mead, *Male and Female* (New York: William Morrow, 1949), pp. 284–88. Whether the needs for personal achievement and sexual differentiation are in fact one or two needs is a question that can remain open without damage to the present analysis.

[8] See Talcott Parsons and Robert F. Bales, *Family, Socialization, and Interaction Process* (Glencoe, Illinois: The Free Press, 1955), p. 116; and Talcott Parsons, "Age and Sex in the Social Structure of the United States," *American Sociological Review,* 7, 604–16. Parsons suggests that adolescent sex roles are not significantly differentiated in the family, the community at large, or the school, and that the burden of change and differentiation of sex roles is therefore thrown almost wholly on the peer group.

had seldom participated in intimate, formal group activities. They had lacked the ability to associate with their fellow students, had felt socially rejected, and had identified with the adult norms of scholarly excellence, moral perfection, and submissiveness. Demerath concludes that the person who successfully adjusts to adult demands must first prepare himself in the informal group life of adolescence.[9]

The Role of the School in Adolescent Development

Despite the value of the peer group for adolescent development, it has its limitations. To the adolescent peer culture have been ascribed such characteristics as irresponsibility, distaste for constituted authority and established moral codes, blind conformity to group values, and a purely hedonistic approach to life.[10] If this description of the peer culture is in any degree accurate, one might question its ability to develop such habits as self-reliance, initiative, and responsibility.

The demands of the school curriculum help to meet the need of the adolescent to develop habits of self-reliance and responsibility. Schoolwork requires concentrated effort and abstention from other activities until the assignments are completed, and it represents striving for a distant goal. Where the academic program falls short is in its inability to harness the adolescent's desire for achievement and recognition among his peers. But perhaps the school is not entirely helpless in this regard. Through its extracurricular activities program, it can enable its pupils to work willingly, in natural and intimate groups, toward goals which they themselves value highly, and in ways which develop such qualities as responsibility and the facility for making vital decisions. The student council, the dance committee, even the home room clean-up committee bring adolescents together in useful or harmless projects where leadership is exercised, mutual obligations are met, and camaraderie is developed. In the extracurricular program, the benefits of the peer group and the school are combined. A balance is struck between free initiative and guidance from above, between play and work, between individual achievement and group obligation.

[9] N. J. Demerath, "Adolescent Status Demands and the Student Experiences of 20 Schizophrenics," *American Sociological Review,* 8, pp. 513–18.

[10] See, for example, Edward Y. Hartshorne, "Undergraduate Society and the College Culture," *American Sociological Review,* 8, pp. 321–31; Talcott Parsons, *op. cit.;* Robert J. Havighurst and Hilda Taba, *Adolescent Character and Personality* (New York: John Wiley and Sons, 1949), *passim;* and Arnold W. Green, "Young America Takes Over the Colleges," *Commentary,* 7, pp. 524–34. For an opposing view see Frederick Elkin and William A. Westley, "The Myth of Adolescent Culture," *American Sociological Review,* 20, pp. 680–84.

To be sure, the adolescents in their extracurricular activities will adhere to the values and mores of their peer culture. No more than at the corner drugstore or the bowling alley will they overstep the bounds of conformity to group standards. There is a difference, however, between passive conformity to the behavior patterns of the herd and active problem-solving within the framework of group values. Listening to some popular singer because one knows that one has to like this singer is passive conformity. Deciding which orchestra to employ for a dance, or how to finance the affair, is active problem-solving behavior, within the value framework of the group but requiring creative thought and initiative nonetheless. Conformity to group mores is with us all our lives, and must be with us if society is to proceed in an orderly fashion; but there are different kinds of conformity.

Like anything else, extracurricular activity programs are limited in their effectiveness. They are not a substitute for the study of books. They usually reflect the class stratification of the community with students from the more well-to-do families monopolizing the leadership and those less economically fortunate often left out or relegated to minor positions.[11] They may have little appeal to some pupils in underprivileged neighborhoods, among whom the thought of any activity connected with the school arouses feelings of dread or contempt. It seems reasonable, however, to claim some efficacy for them, as one way in which the adolescent can achieve a secure status among his fellows and develop habits of responsibility at the same time. At best, active participation in extracurricular affairs can draw together the separate roles of "student" and "member of the peer group," thus helping to clarify the uncertain status of the adolescent. It may even, in some cases, give him something resembling a "core status" as "member of the school community."

One conclusion from this analysis is that we need not, in the current clamor to tighten discipline and produce a generation of intellectuals, lose sight of the function which extracurricular activity programs may fulfill.

[11] A. B. Hollingshead, *Elmtown's Youth* (New York: John Wiley and Sons, 1949).

25. Adolescents' Views on One Aspect of Their Development *[1]

RUTH STRANG

A DOMINANT EMPHASIS in adolescent psychology is on the adolescent's concept of himself and perception of his world. Many trends focus on this emphasis. Gestalt psychology highlights the importance of the "situation-as-perceived" by the individual. All the writings on the self-concept and "self-consistency" present an individual's view of himself as a determinant of his behavior. In client-centered counseling, the individual is helped to gain an understanding of himself and his relationships. In education, too, teachers are urged to look below the surface behavior to the meaning of the behavior of the child. From this emphasis arises the need to learn more about the inner world of adolescents and to see things through their eyes.

There are many methods of getting glimpses into how adolescents are thinking and feeling. Most widely used perhaps are the check-list type of opinion survey and the adjustment inventory. The questionnaire is a little less suggestive than the check list, but still to a considerable extent channels the individual's responses. Something may be learned from informal group discussions of adolescent problems. In such discussions and in sociodramas, adolescents have expressed some important insights into their psychology. Personal documents of various kinds are another important source of understanding. In interviews, ranging from the casual to the psychoanalytic, some adolescents will reveal a great deal of their "private world." Others, without realizing it, reveal themselves in their responses to projective techniques. The slightly structured composition combines some of the values of the personality inventory and the projective method.

There are individual differences in response to these various techniques. Some adolescents are stimulated by the group to think freely; others respond best in a face-to-face interview; still others welcome the opportunity to express their thoughts and feelings in the writing of anonymous compositions. Some adolescents are far more suggestible than others and

* From Ruth Strang, "Adolescents' Views on One Aspect of Their Development," *The Journal of Educational Psychology* (November, 1955), pp. 423–32. Reprinted by permission of the author and the publisher.

[1] Paper read at the 1954 Annual Meeting of the American Psychological Association, September 6, New York City.

therefore more influenced by the items on a check list or the wording of specific questions.

In this paper, only the responses in freely written compositions will be considered. The directions for writing these compositions invite introspection on a given subject. If properly introduced they evoke frank, thoughtful, and sincere responses. Confidentialness is assured.

Questions will arise, of course, concerning the reliability and validity of the data obtained from these relatively unstructured compositions. Neither the retest nor the split-half form of reliability seems appropriate to apply to personal documents. A repetition of the request for compositions may result in showing variation within the individual rather than shortcomings of the instrument. "Very few psychologically meaningful properties ever really stay put even while the investigator is looking straight at them." [2] The split-half method obviously is not appropriate to data that are in the form of a pattern, instead of a series of discrete, comparable items.

Validity of compositions may be implied in several ways: (1) from knowledge of the rapport with the subjects in getting the data, (2) from internal evidence of frankness and lack of facetiousness, and (3) from comparison with data of a similar kind obtained from group discussions and interviews. The use of the first person ("I think," "I feel") on the basis of other evidences in the compositions seems associated with the most genuine kind of expression. The third person ("adolescents feel . . . ," "boys and girls often think . . .") seems associated with a measure of reluctance of the writer to give his own feelings freely. And the second person, when used, seems generally to be employed in a short story sense ("you should . . .") by those who appear to be merely repeating lessons that they have learned from parents, teachers, and other adults.

Over two thousand compositions of this kind, on a variety of topics, were obtained by teachers from adolescents of a wide range of ability and socioeconomic background in grades seven through twelve. Only one of the topics—"How It Feels to Be Growing Up"—obtained from 277 pupils, will be considered in this paper. Included in this sample were public high school pupils in a large city (70 in number), in a small textile town (22), in a wealthy residential suburb (19), in middle-class suburban towns (79), in a semi-rural village (14), as well as pupils in a Roman Catholic commercial high school (56) and a boys' military academy (17). The teachers presented the topic to the pupils with a minimum of structuring of the

---

[2] Dalbir Bindra and Ivan H. Scheier, "The Relation between Psychometric and Experimental Research in Psychology," *The American Psychologist,* IX (February, 1954), 70.

situation. The pupils wrote the compositions during the class period and did not sign their names.

There are obvious limitations to the data presented. Among these are (1) the very small number of compositions from rural schools, (2) the lack of supplementary information about the individual pupils, and (3) the differences in pupil-teacher relations which affect the quality of the responses. The first limitation may be quite easily removed in future studies; it is relatively simple and inexpensive to obtain these compositions from a large number of cooperating teachers. Every teacher who has co-operated has gained understanding of his pupils quite disproportionate to the amount of time spent in reading the papers before they were sent to the investigator. The second problem may be solved by giving each pupil a number previously identified with the pupil's name. Then the composition may be studied with reference to all the other items of information obtained about the individual pupil. The third difficulty may be handled by discard-

Table 1

NUMBER AND PERCENTAGE OF ADOLESCENTS EXPRESSING POINTS OF VIEW
ABOUT GROWING UP

	Grades					
Viewpoints about Growing Up	7–8–9 (185)		10–11–12 (92)		TOTAL (277)	
	No.	%	No.	%	No.	%
Concern about vocation, or about the future	85	46	31	34	116	42
Feeling of increasing independence and self-direction	68	37	40	44	108	39
Awareness of increased responsibilities	53	28	42	46	94	34
Concern with social relationships	37	20	32	35	69	25
Concern with boy-girl relationships	32	17	28	30	60	22
Feelings about religion or morality	10	5	42	45	52	19
Concern with marriage and raising a family	24	13	19	21	43	16
View of growing up as fun, or "good" experience	22	12	21	23	43	16
Feeling of frustration that independence is not recognized	23	12	12	13	35	13
Awareness of increasing acceptance in the adult world	15	8	14	15	29	10
Possible reluctance to relinquish the security of dependence	8	4	16	17	24	9
Relation of sports to growing up	18	10	6	7	24	9
Problems of sibling relationships	19	10	5	5	24	9

ing the papers in classes where the pupil-teacher relationship was apparently poor or the standard directions for writing the composition had not been given. The papers usually give clear clues as to whether the pupil is writing frankly and sincerely or facetiously.

Two kinds of information were obtained: (1) common points of view and (2) specific psychological insights expressed by individual adolescents. The "commonality" aspect is presented in Table 1, while the individuality in response is represented by the direct quotations.

The common points of view represent the thoughts and feelings uppermost in the adolescents' minds at the time of writing. To be sure, there are many other ideas that do not occur to them at the moment. Consequently, the meaning of the percentages used in this study to describe frequencies of response is not the same as in the case of check lists and questionnaires. Both present problems of interpretation. The frequency count of the compositions lacks absolute value because many individuals may hold a particular viewpoint without expressing it. On the other hand, those responding to the check list may mark a particular item with very little basis for doing so. In both instances, the nature of the sample will affect the frequency of response on separate items.

Common Responses

Common responses to the topic: "How It Feels to Be Growing Up." The tone of these compositions was generally positive and expectant. There was little evidence of the severe "strain and stress" emphasized by early writers on adolescence. Almost one sixth referred to this period as "fun" or "a nice time of life"—they had a "good" feeling about it.

Moreover, the data do not bear out the general impression of adolescent irresponsibility. They accent adolescents' desire to be independent and to take responsibility. Many of these young people thought of growing up as involving increasing independence, self-direction, and responsibility. Only a few continued to show some reluctance to relinquish the security of dependence. They are more likely to have feelings of frustration that their independence is not recognized. Some of them were aware of increasing acceptance in the adult world. The younger pupils seemed to be more optimistic and less realistic than the older group.

A surprisingly large number of junior high school pupils seemed to be concerned about vocations and the future. This high frequency of reference to vocations may be attributed to their interpretation of the topic as focused on the future instead of on the process of growing up. Another possible explanation is that the responses of some of these pupils may have been influenced by a unit on vocations recently taught in the junior high school.

The accompanying table presents, in order of frequency of mention, the categories into which the responses were classified, together with the number and per cent of responses in each. The tabulation was done by Dr. Warren Roome, who read each composition and classified each significant statement under the one heading which best described it. The headings evolved from a preliminary reading of the compositions.

The sequence of categories from junior to senior high school suggests a kind of meaningful progression in the process of growing up. As children grow older their feelings of independence and self-direction increase. They become much more concerned with religious and moral questions and with social relations, especially with boy-girl relations and marriage and family life. Their awareness of increased responsibilities grows. As they grow up physically and assume more responsibility they also become increasingly aware of their acceptance in the adult world.

Some variation was noted among the different kinds of schools in which the compositions were obtained. For example, the papers from the Catholic schools showed a high degree of uniformity. A possibly significant concept which seemed to pervade these compositions is that of sudden independence, of almost instantaneous transformation from not-adult to adult, at some specified age—either 16 or 18. Possibly also of significance is the relatively high frequency with which these pupils expressed either a reluctance to leave childhood or fear of adulthood. Their religious orientation is also marked. Nevertheless, in these and even more in the other compositions unique statements of a genuinely personal viewpoint were expressed.

Specific Responses

More valuable in understanding adolescents than the frequency of common responses are the psychological insights occasionally expressed by individual boys and girls. Those insights have the following claims to authenticity:

1. They are based on the first-hand experience of adolescents themselves, not on observation of their behavior by adults.

2. They depend less on delayed memory than many statements about adolescents made by adults.

3. They express attitudes and feelings directly, whereas most of the data about adolescents consists of inferences regarding their attitudes and feelings.

4. They may be culled from a large number of compositions written by teen-agers and representing a wide range of age, intelligence, socioeconomic status, family backgrounds, emotional adjustment, geographical location.

A few of these insights are included here as illustrations. They are grouped under five main categories, corresponding to the more detailed categories in the table: (1) reluctance to grow up or a feeling that adults do not understand, or frustration in growing up; (2) concern about physical, emotional, social, and other aspects of growing up; (3) a somewhat neutral awareness of problems and opportunities; (4) feelings of increasing independence, self-direction, and responsibility; and (5) satisfaction in growing up and awareness of their acceptance in the adult world. The quotations have been placed under what seemed to the writer the most appropriate heading, although other points of view may also be represented in a single quotation.

1. *Reluctance to grow up, a feeling that adults do not understand or frustration in growing up.* As shown in the table a relatively small percentage mentioned the feelings illustrated by the following quotations. So far as this sampling shows, these attitudes seem to be related to the individual personality more than to the age of the pupils.

"Nothing angers me more than to have someone say, 'Oh, you are still young with no problems yet.' "

"I am expected to have manners like an adult, yet have to go to bed early like a little child."

"Parents say, 'You're old enough to help out with this,' and 'You can't do that; you're much too young.' "

"More often you wonder what it will be like when there is no mother and father to guide you and it scares you."

"Growing up is a hard thing to face because childhood is so dear to our hearts."

"The feeling that comes with growing up sometimes frightens you. The thought that now you are responsible for all your actions. People can't say, "She is only a child and you can't blame her for her bad actions.' "

"My friends and I have, at one time or another, felt that our parents did not understand us, nor care to."

"Grown-ups say they remember how it was to be growing up: that they understand our problems. I disagree, as they forget the unpleasant memories; only someone who is going through the process knows what it is like to be growing up."

"When I finish growing up, which I doubt anyone really does completely,

I hope I will be able to remember how I felt so that I can understand people who are growing up then."

2. *Concern about physical, emotional, social, and other aspects of growing up.* In these quotations, which are typical of a large percentage of the compositions studied, points of view presented by psychologists concerning uneven growth and acne, boy-girl relations, swings of mood, and alternation between childish and adult interests are reinforced.

"The age of 13 is a difficult age. . . . When boys are 13 they are too old for cowboys and Indians and too young for girls. Girls are too old for dolls and too young for boys."

"Such disadvantages as legs too long, arms too long, pimples, and many other things that make a boy feel very out of place."

"Growing up has made me feel different about religion. When I try to understand and ask questions, I either get a confusing answer or my question cannot be answered."

"Growing up in the world today means an uncertain future. It means bringing our own children into a troubled world. Waiting years for boys who may never return from war results in emotional upset for many."

"One of the difficulties of teen-agers is their moods. Sometimes they get up in the morning feeling wonderful. Instead of talking, they feel like singing. Other days they feel wretched and depressed. They can hardly drag themselves around. . . . These moods come and go in a mysterious way, for just no reason at all."

3. *A somewhat neutral awareness of problems and opportunities.* Instead of concern about their problems, some of the youngsters take an understanding, accepting, and even humorous attitude toward them. This insight into the growing-up process is illustrated by the following quotations:

"Parents, it seems to me, worry too much about our welfare. But that is simply because they are under a false impression; we are grown up long before they have a chance to realize it."

"Most girls think about only one thing—boys."

"Every time a boy pays a nice compliment, I feel that I've grown up more. It makes me think that in some way I've learned to better my appearance."

"Some girls when they are quite young are regular tomboys. Then all of a sudden, something happens. They become conscious of their appearance. They start to take care of their hair . . . they start to hang up their clothes . . . they begin to notice different styles. They wear their first pair of high heels and start to apply lipstick."

"My brother is three years older than I am. . . . Wherever I go I no longer am Margaret Kerr but Sam's sister. My brother and I get along swell. Even though he calls me 'Stinkweed' I know it's just his peculiar way of showing me affection."

4. *Feeling of increasing independence, self-direction, and responsibility.* Many illustrations of this point of view might be quoted. In fact, in this sampling of adolescents it was the dominant way of perceiving the process of growing up. They expressed simultaneously their desire to be free from parental domination and restriction of childhood and their eagerness for more mature experiences.

"When a boy reaches his teens he doesn't like to be led around by his mother's apronstrings and he wants freedom and likes to feel self-dependent."

"Instead of running from mistakes as a child would, I now see the wisdom of facing and conquering error."

"I like the idea of being able to choose and make decisions for myself."

"As I grow older I can do more things without my parents having to worry about me."

"Growing up means . . . facing problems with almost no help."

"My problems are now solved by me. I no longer run to Mom to solve them unless her advice is absolutely needed."

"As you grow up you are not so much of a burden to your parents, and they do not worry about you but pass on the worries to you and you carry your worries for yourself."

"When a problem arises, big or small, you can work it out without getting yourself and everyone around you confused and nervous."

"I am beginning to understand the responsibilities of my position, and most amazing of all, to tackle them."

5. *Satisfaction in growing up and awareness of their acceptance in the adult world.* Although their desire for independence is much more frequently mentioned than their satisfaction in the process of growing up, almost one sixth referred to the rewarding aspects of adolescence and one tenth recognized their increased acceptance by adults. The following quotations refer especially to the ego satisfaction of being able to handle the problems of adolescence and being accepted on a mature level. In much of the writing on adolescence these positive feelings about growing up are overshadowed by the emphasis on anxiety, insecurity, and "problems."

"Growing up makes me feel as if I were somebody important."

"I derive a great satisfaction from the solution of my problems and even anticipate the advent of new ones with a curious mixture of anxiety and exhilaration."

"As you reach your teens you find that people will talk to you and let you give your opinions."

"I am now on eye level with adults and beginning to be accepted as a person in my own right."

The wide range of attitudes toward growing up is represented by these two responses: (1) "I think that growing up is one of the most exciting things that can ever happen to anyone," and (2) "On the whole growing up is the biggest ordeal anyone goes through. I believe I have had more trouble now than I ever had. Disappointments and let-downs are the biggest hurdle in growing up. One thing I learned to do is never build up my hopes."

The statements made by adolescents about themselves are appealing; they are directly, simply, and often vividly stated. Many of them verify the viewpoints of psychologists about adolescents. Some of them suggest positive feelings and attitudes that perhaps have not been sufficiently recognized in adolescent literature—(1) the satisfaction that comes from successful accomplishment of adolescent tasks, (2) the recognition that responsibility should accompany freedom, (3) their eagerness to assume responsibility, and (4) their insight into adults' points of view. Most of all, these compositions alert us to individual differences among adolescents and the diversity of viewpoints and feelings which they express.

26. Concepts of Motor Development *

J. M. LEE

AND D. M. LEE

THERE HAVE BEEN a large number of studies of motor development which yield some generalizations quite helpful to teachers. Many studies have been done on motor development and motor control of very young children. Other studies have been made of the ages at which various motor skills are developed. A third set has been what we might call laboratory studies of tapping, shooting at targets, etc. The fourth area from which we get our information consists of studies which have been made of the development of motor skills in industry. In spite of this great amount of research available, there are many areas in which the findings will have to be generalized in order to get specific applications to school situations.

1. Motor development proceeds from the general to the specific. Studies of infants and children have shown that there is a control first in head movements, then in the trunk, and finally in the extremities. A baby shows many random diffuse movements which later become differentiated. In learning a new motor skill, a general pattern is noted from large to finer and finer adaptations until the skill is perfected. The same pattern is followed in the use of muscles. The child first gains control over large muscles and then finally over the smaller muscles.

The use of manuscript writing in the primary grades is an example of the application of this principle. In such writing, only single strokes are

---

* From J. M. Lee and D. M. Lee, *The Child and His Development*, pp. 67–73. Copyright © 1958 by Appleton-Century-Crofts, Inc., New York, and reprinted with their permission.

needed to produce the individual letters. Cursive writing, however, requires much greater control of the smaller muscles.

The learning of new motor skills in children exhibits somewhat the same phenomenon. In attempting to learn a motor skill there is great involvement of the body and apparent struggle on the part of the youngster. These characteristic symptoms gradually disappear. The teacher should not be disturbed at the restlessness of children when they are attempting to learn a new skill. The same phenomenon is exhibited somewhat in any new learning in which the child is uncertain of the approach of the problem. One reason for this is that he does not perceive all of the details of the problem. His agitation also undoubtedly represents response to frustration as well as a bodily response.

2. *Motor skills show irregularity in development.* Over a period of time there is a gradual improvement in most motor skills. The teacher cannot expect a regular pattern of development. There will be spurts and pauses and regressions, especially in younger children.[1] It would be expected that somewhat the same pattern is apparent in older children, but perhaps it is not as obvious. Evidence is clear that muscular development and increase in strength continue throughout the school period, as does the general pattern of physical development.

3. *There appears to be a series of motor abilities, not one generalized motor ability.* Attempts to measure the various motor skills have shown that there is little relationship among the skills. This is especially true among fine motor skills. A great deal of the research in this area has come from industrial studies. These have shown by the use of various kinds of performance tests that it is difficult to predict later success. Most of the significant improvement has come from study of work methods and their improvement along with adequate motivation. Tests of physical ability such as the Rogers or the Brace measure a number of factors. Such tests help the instructor locate early the markedly superior and the markedly inferior students.

4. *Boys and girls differ in muscular control.* These differences are comparable to differences in growth. Muscular development has usually been measured by the strength of grip. The picture which is customarily found is that reproduced in Figure 1. The maximum gain taking place for girls is at age 13, while the maximum for boys is at age 16. At age 13 the differences between boys and girls begin to appear, and those differences

---

[1] For those interested in a good description of the development of infants in relation to motor abilities, see George G. Thompson, *Child Psychology* (Boston: Houghton Mifflin Co., 1952), chap. VII.

increase until maturity is reached. An explanation of this has been given by Jones.

We should not be surprised to find such differences, for strength is influenced not merely by muscular structure, but also by neural development, by skeletal factors involved in leverage and by various nutritive conditions. No doubt a partial explanation of the prolonged growth of strength in boys is in terms of the greater activity and the greater functional use of the new physical powers attained through adolescent growth.[2]

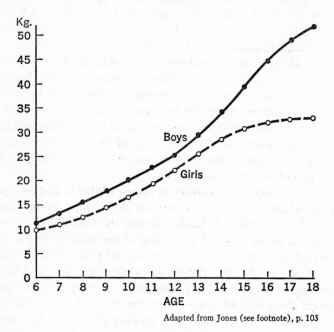

Adapted from Jones (see footnote), p. 103

Figure 1. Growth curves of strength of grip (Iowa City).

Of course it is at this time that girls become interested in many phases of life other than physical activity, while most boys continue to be interested in and concerned with activities requiring physical abilities. This difference in interest may explain some of the findings.

When finer motor and mechanical skills are measured, these six differences do not always appear. Jones and Seashore report a study of school

[2] Harold E. Jones, "The Development of Physical Abilities," *Adolescence,* 43rd Yearbook, Part I, National Society for the Study of Education (Chicago: University of Chicago Press, 1944), p. 103.

children between the ages of 11 and 15.[3] In a test which required the
selection of an appropriate finger movement in response to a series of numbers visually perceived, girls were slightly better than boys. In another test
involving an extreme degree of manual precision and steadiness, girls exceeded boys. On reaction time to sound, and in a test which required the
use of two hands simultaneously, the girls and boys were approximately the
same. In spatial eye-hand coordination and in temporal eye-hand coordination, boys showed superiority to girls.

Even where sex differences occur, they certainly are considerably smaller
than the range of variation within either sex. The authors interpret these
differences to mean that an advisor certainly is not justified in suggesting
that a given type of motor training be avoided merely because "Girls do not
take to that sort of thing." Evidence accumulated during the war in which
women participated in many complex and practical motor skills certainly
indicated that there was not the difference in motor abilities between the
sexes that there was once thought to be.

Our culture and our concept of what we want to be like have of course
placed many limitations upon the activities in which we participate. They
also influence greatly the development of certain skills. It is not expected
that girls would have the same drive to participate in athletics in high
school as would boys. Instead, in some of the girls, the important drive for
them seems to be toward dating boys who participate in athletics.

  *5. Learning and maturation are concomitant factors in motor
development.* This concomitant relationship was also discussed in Concept 9 in physical development. Some skills develop primarily as a result of
maturation while others develop primarily as a result of learning; nevertheless, the two processes are reciprocally related. In summarizing the research
on this problem, Munn says:

This relationship is especially important during early childhood when the neuromuscular system is undergoing rapid growth and when, at the same time, there
are numerous influences to encourage learning. With increasing age there is a
relative decrease in the importance of new maturational factors.[4]

The utilization of maturation and learning is of greatest importance to the
primary teacher. Most of the activities of the primary grades involve more

---

  [3] Harold E. Jones and Robert H. Seashore, "The Development of Fine Motor and
Mechanical Abilities," *ibid.,* pp. 126–30.
  [4] Reprinted with permission from Norman L. Munn, "Learning in Children,"
Leonard Carmichael (ed.), *Manual of Child Psychology* (2nd ed., New York: John
Wiley and Sons, Inc., 1954), p. 387.

than motor development; they also involve perception. An interesting study in the area of the primary grades is one by Hildreth.

Hildreth studied the ability of children from 3 years to 6 years, 5 months to write their names. The first stage is scribbling in imitation of the adults' cursive writing. Beginning with age level 4–6 to 4–11 about a fourth of the group were able to print their names so they could be recognized. Age 5–0 to 5–6 showed an increased percentage who could print their names with more regularity, better control, and alignment. The improvement continues in both regularity and speed for the next year.[5]

Samples of name-writing taken at the beginning of the first grade will give the teacher some idea of the comparative development of the children in motor control and perception. The more poorly coordinated children should be given a longer exploratory period with pencil, paper, letters, and numbers before formal writing, especially in cursive style, is begun.

In view of other data on the development of fine motor skills, improvement in the legibility in the handwriting of a child must come from an approach which analyzes the errors of the individual. Group work probably will not result in much improvement after the initial skill has been developed.

It is very doubtful that the child who enters the first grade and is still at a scribbling stage has sufficiently matured to the point where he would profit by the formal instruction in manuscript writing given to the other children. An attempt at such instruction probably would arouse frustration. His motor control should be watched very carefully, and the teaching started when it would appear he is ready.

Other motor skills which need to be developed in the primary grades are comparable to that of handwriting. The teacher needs to observe individual youngsters and start their work on the skill when it appears that they are ready. It must be realized that in motor skills, as in intelligence, there is a wide range of individual differences.

6. Learning techniques used in developing motor control make a difference. From the research on the problem there seem to be three procedures which should be followed: First, the child should be shown the correct way to perform the skill. Second, he should be given opportunities to practice it, being free to initiate his own movements, and to make incorrect as well as correct responses. Third, after he has progressed somewhat, he should be given suggestions for correcting the incorrect responses.

[5] Gertrude Hildreth, "Developmental Sequences in Name Writing," *Child Development,* 7 (December 1936), 291–303.

For the teacher this means that demonstrations of such skills can be given to the whole class at one time. The individual students can practice; but, when it comes to improvement of the skills, the teacher should diagnose each individual's difficulty and furnish him suggestions for specific improvements. This individual diagnosis is absolutely necessary with regard to such subjects as handwriting, typing, physical education, industrial arts, home economics, art, music, and other subjects utilizing motor control and development.

7. The development of motor abilities is especially important in relation to the emotional and social adjustment of boys and girls. This concept is very closely related to Concept 10 in the section on physical development. Anyone who has watched elementary-school boys and girls on the playground realizes that those who have highly developed motor skills are much more acceptable to the group than those children who have few such skills. Perhaps you were one of the last ones to be selected when groups of children "chose up" baseball teams. If you were, you can remember only too well how you felt. You can also remember how you hated to see any choosing up of teams take place because you knew just exactly what would happen. If you were the first one chosen, wasn't it because you could play ball better than most of the other children? This importance of motor skills and abilities continues for boys through the secondary school and to somewhat lesser extent in adulthood. For girls it continues through the elementary school and to a somewhat lesser extent in the secondary school.

Observing the level of development of the motor abilities of an individual child may supply an important clue in understanding his personality problems. The school may help him to improve his motor abilities, if deficient, or it may help him to give more importance to other goals. An example is Henry who had only one eye with useful vision from early childhood. Obviously he didn't make an effective baseball player in high school; but he did get his satisfactions from excelling in debate.

8. Leisure-time activities of adults involving motor skills were largely begun in childhood. Jersild made a study of the activities especially utilizing hand skills in which men in their twenties and beyond participated during their leisure time. His findings are highly significant.

In a study of men in their twenties and beyond, it was found that the things they did with their hands during their spare time was influenced to a large degree by what they had learned to do when they were children. The study revealed that men did not, as a rule, take up entirely new motor skills after they reached mature years. Moreover, most of the skills they had acquired as children and now put to use as adults were learned outside the school. Such learnings, in turn, appeared to be subject to the caprice of opportunity.[6]

This is quite an indictment for schools which declare one of their major objectives to be the worthy use of leisure time. There are many opportunities in the first six grades which could be offered to all children, each child then being allowed to follow those which he enjoyed the most. There are carving and clay-modeling, construction with hammer and nails, the building of models such as houses, trains, etc., ping-pong and tennis, the playing of various musical instruments, and many, many others. It seems that the school has a responsibility to encourage each child to find some hobby which involves work with his hands. Such activity should not, as is too often the case, be allowed only when the teacher can't find anything else to keep the child busy.

9. It would appear that motor abilities might be developed to a much greater extent by the schools. A visit to practically any public school in grades one to twelve will demonstrate that the primary emphasis is on the development of intellectual abilities. There is relatively little time or effort devoted to the development of motor abilities. The evidence indicates that children have many motor controls which are little capitalized by the school situation.

27. Motor Activities *

KARL C. GARRISON

MOVING-PICTURE CAMERAS as well as other technical devices have been used to assist investigators in studying the motor activities of infants. At birth, the infant is more than a living creature with bones, flesh, and various types of sensory equipment in a more or less immature stage. The newborn infant is an active creature. In fact, he was an active creature for several months prior to birth. Birth extends the scope of his activities and

[6] Arthur T. Jersild, *Child Development and the Curriculum* (New York: Teachers College, Columbia University, 1946), p. 135.

* From Karl C. Garrison, *Growth and Development*, 2nd ed., pp. 43–49. Copyright 1959 by Longmans, Green and Co., Inc., New York, and reprinted with their permission.

registers the beginning of vocalization in the birth cry. This is purely reflexive and results from air being drawn over the vocal cords and setting up vibrations in them.

Mass activities of infants. The first activity of infants are largely random and uncoordinated. Thus, when sensory stimuli are applied to any part of the body, motor activity will occur throughout the entire body, but in a most pronounced form in the part stimulated. Observations of the responses of infants to a pressure stimulus revealed that some make pushing movements with their feet when pressure is applied to the chin.[1] Several subjects were observed to push at the experimenter's hands with their feet. Such foot action may be interpreted as part of the defense pattern of the infant. By means of kymograph records, the number of responses in a unit of time and the intensity or strength of the responses were determined. In relation to arm and leg movement, twenty-two infants made the strongest forward leg movements with the leg opposite that of the dominant defense hand, while seven of the infants made the strongest forward movements with the same side as the dominant defense hand. Twenty-five infants had both leg and hand dominance. The average number of significant leg movements of the right side was 3.4 for an infant from birth to 99 hours, 7.7 for infants 100 to 199 hours old, and 6.8 for infants 200 hours of age and older.

Using the stabilimeter-polygraph, Irwin measured the amount of motility of seventy-three infants.[2] With the exception of one case, the ages varied from birth to 16 days. The most active infant was found to be about 290 times more active than the least active. The average number of oscillations per minute during periods when the infants were judged to be asleep and awake are presented in Table 1. It shows that during periods when infants

Table 1

COMPARISONS OF OSCILLATIONS DURING WAKING AND SLEEP PERIODS
(AFTER IRWIN)

	Infants	o/m	S.D.
Awake	71	51.5	43.3
Asleep	71	8.7	13.4
Difference		42.8	

[1] Mandel Sherman and I. C. Sherman, "Sensori-Motor Responses in Infants," *Journal of Comparative Psychology,* 5 (1925), 62–65.

[2] Orvis C. Irwin, "The Amount of Motility of Seventy-Three Newborn Infants," *Journal of Comparative Psychology,* 14 (1932), 415–28.

are judged to be asleep, the average motility amounts to 8.7 oscillations per minute; the average number of oscillations per minute during the periods when they are judged to be awake was 51.5. The ratio of activity during waking and sleep periods was therefore about six to one.

Evidence has been offered from several studies by Irwin to substantiate the observations that newborn infants are more active just before than after nursing.[3] In one study, the motility of seventy-three infants was measured by means of stabilimeter continuously from 2:30 P.M. until 5:45 P.M. The mean oscillations per minute for each of the thirteen fifteen-minute periods are given in Figure 1. This also shows how motility is distributed

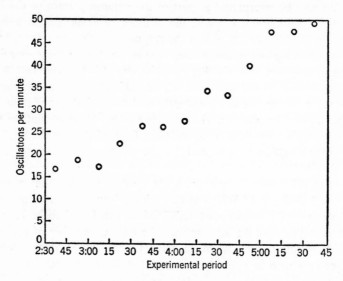

Figure 1. Average motility of seventy-three infants between two consecutive nursings. (After Irwin)

between the two consecutive feedings. The distribution between two consecutive feedings represents mean values and does not show individual characteristics. Not all of the infants showed an increase in motility at the end of the experimental period. This is indicated from a comparison of the motility of each infant for the first hour with that of the last hour. This comparison reveals that forty-nine of the seventy-three infants show an increment, while twenty-four infants or approximately one third show a

[3] Orvis C. Irwin, "The Distribution of the Amount of Motility in Young Infants between Two Nursing Periods," *Journal of Comparative Psychology,* 14 (1932), 429–45.

decrement in the amount of motility. However, the average increment of the forty-nine infants showing increased motility is 3.5 times greater than the average decrement made by the twenty-four cases showing decreased motility.

Specific activities. Specific activities have been conveniently classified into (a) reflexes and (b) general responses. Many studies have been made of the reflexes appearing during the early weeks of life. More recently, a number of investigations have dealt with responses that involve a larger portion of the body than that encompassed in a reflex. These responses may be referred to as adaptive behavior. Much adaptive behavior evolves from these early mass movements. This is quite clear in the observations of the development of locomotion, which is described at a later point in this chapter and in a subsequent chapter. It should not be concluded, however, that the infant progresses from mass to specific movements suddenly or even smoothly. The movements of the hand toward an object are at first of a circuitous nature; later, these movements become more direct, but will often reveal many characteristics of a circuitous approach in the wavering of the arms and hands. Many lateral deviations may be observed before the infant's reaching and grasping evolve into a short and a more direct approach.

As the infant develops, the functions of the arm and hand are reversed. During the early stages, it is the arm that determines the movement of the hand. At this stage, as already suggested, movements are of a mass, diffuse nature. At a later stage, the hand determines the movement of the arm. The child at this stage grasps objects. Specialized functions appear as the thumb and forefinger assume more important places in the child's repertoire of activities.

Stimulation of crying. The stimuli which arouse the crying of infants come from the immediate environment or the physical condition of the baby. Aldrich and others have made continuous observations of over one hundred infants.[4] The causes of crying and the number of crying spells for each cause are presented in Table 2. The most common cause of crying among these infants resulted from causes unknown to the observers, while hunger ranked second. However, the hunger cries were of longer duration than were those for unknown reasons. Mass activity of the infant's body accompanies crying, especially vigorous crying. No uniform cries for the different situations or conditions were noted among the newborn. The duration and intensity of the cries seemed to depend partly upon the vocal

[4] C. A. Aldrich, C. Sung, and C. Knop, "The Crying of Newly Born Babies. II. The Individual Phase," *Journal of Pediatrics*, 27 (1945), 95.

strength of the different infants and upon the nature of the stimuli which aroused them. Gesell and Ilg have suggested that they become more proficient in this ability if they are allowed to exercise it.[5] Furthermore, their proficiency appears to be promoted in the case of the hunger cries if their demands are met promptly and if the needs for food and sucking are insured.

Table 2

NUMBER OF CRYING SPELLS FOR EACH CAUSE

Babies	Days	Causes of Crying				
		A HUNGER	B VOMITING	C SOILED DIAPERS	D WET DIAPERS	E UNKNOWN REASONS
50	8	2,760.0	45.0	737.0	1,630.0	3,295.0
50	1	345.0	5.0	92.0	203.8	411.7
1	8	55.2	.9	15.7	32.5	65.9
1	1	6.9	.11	1.9	4.07	8.2

Motor development during infancy. The scope and function of the ontogenetic changes during the first year of life have been summed up by Gesell and Ames as follows:

Head

The head lifts from the floor through an arc of 90° or more.

Arms

The arms, at first sharply flexed, extend forward; later they flex inward under the chest, and come to extension from shoulder to floor at right angles to the trunk which is at first supported on the forearms and in time on the hands.

Legs

The legs extend backward, lift; later they flex forward beside the trunk, and then under the trunk, supporting its weight on the knees. In time the legs like the arms come to right angle extension, supporting the trunk on the feet.

Trunk

The trunk, at first convex, flattens, concaves, then flattens again upon elevation above the ground surface. The trunk is in horizontal or oblique alignment until the assumption of the upright posture.[6]

[5] Arnold Gesell and Frances L. Ilg, *Child Development* (New York: Harper and Bros., 1949), p. 98.

[6] Arnold Gesell and Louise B. Ames, "The Ontogenetic Organization of Prone Behavior in Human Infancy," *Journal of Genetic Psychology*, 56 (1940), 247–63.

They point out further that these changes of pattern come about gradually and concurrently. They state: "In deep perspective they may be envisaged as a single flow of postural transformations." And, although twenty-three stages have been characterized and described, these are not accurately separated as discrete stages. They state further: "During the course of a day, an hour, or indeed of a minute, he may display two or three closely related patterns or stages: (a) a pattern which he has almost outgrown but reverts to for pragmatic reasons; (b) the pattern which is most characteristic of him at his level of maturity; (c) the pattern which is so nascent that he uses or manifests it only sketchily and imperfectly." [7]

Ames conducted a study designed to compare the pattern of stair-climbing behavior with the pattern of prone progression.[8] Cinema records of their stair-climbing behavior were taken in the majority of cases at monthly intervals. Records of the prone behavior of each child were compared with the prone behavior seen contemporaneously. Typical patterns of prone behavior and climbing behavior were then compared. A definite pattern in stair-climbing behavior was observed that was almost identical with that observed in the normal creeping stage. The typical stair-climbing pattern consists, as does the creeping pattern, of almost simultaneous forward movement of a contralateral pair of limbs, followed, after a short pause, by a forward movement of the other pair of limbs. The chief difference between the two patterns is that stair climbing often starts with a single foot movement of a pair of limbs. In the typical stair-climbing pattern the infant starts with the placement of the left foot on the first stair. The left hand is then placed on the second stair, and immediately afterward, the right foot on the first stair. There is a short pause at this point, then the right hand moves to the third stair and left foot to the second. After another short pause, the left hand and right foot move up one stair. Temporal analysis of these movements shows that the left hand and right foot move almost simultaneously, as do the right hand and left foot.

The ages at which the different children observed climbed smoothly up a flight of four or more stairs are listed as follows:

One child 48 weeks
One child 52 weeks
Six children 56 weeks
One child 60 weeks
Two children 80 weeks

[7] *Ibid.*, p. 254.
[8] Louise Bates Ames, "Some Relationships between Stair Climbing and Prone Position," *Journal of Genetic Psychology,* 54 (1939), 313–25.

One child 84 weeks

The mean age for this group for first pattern climbing is 62 weeks. In contrast, the mean age for first creeping is 44 weeks. Thus, on the average, these infants crept about eighteen weeks before they were able to climb a flight of stairs.

The ability of the infant to reach for things develops through several stages. At first, he closes his fingers over any object that touches the palm of his hand. At 3 or 4 months of age, if someone offers him a toy, he moves his head, arms, and legs, and if either hand touches the toy, he grasps it. A month or so later, he is able to close in on the toy. Thus, the reaching of the arms for the toy is accompanied by fewer head and leg movements. More specialized movements are now developing out of the earlier mass movements. By the age of 9 months, he will probably be able to reach out with both hands, and with one hand leading, grasp the object that he wants. After this stage, there is a continuous development of coordination in reaching and grasping, but even at 3 and 4 years of age considerable awkwardness in reaching for things beyond his arm's length may be observed.

28. How the Infant Gains Control over His Arms and Hands *

FRIEDA K. MERRY
AND RALPH V. MERRY

As was pointed out earlier, grasping is possible even in prenatal life, and is again evident in the neonate. Early grasping, however, is quite different from the voluntary digital technique used by adults. It is, in reality, a reflex response of the hand as a whole, occurring when an object is placed in it, and, as in the case of the Darwinian grasp, often is sufficiently strong to support the weight of the body.

The exploratory activities of the hand are of inestimable value to the child in getting acquainted with the world about him. Manipulation, when

* From Frieda K. Merry and Ralph V. Merry, *The First Two Decades of Life*, 2nd ed. pp. 165–69. Copyright 1958 by Frieda Kiefer Merry and Ralph Vickers Merry and reprinted with the permission of Harper and Bros., New York.

combined with vision, touch, "mouthing," and hearing, enables him to understand size, distance, and textures, and orients him to directions.

In the development of manipulation the eyes lead and the hands follow, and until the eyes and hands are coordinated, little progress can be made in prehension. At birth the eyes are uncoordinated and the ability to focus upon objects usually does not occur before the end of the second month. It will be about another month before the child can follow a moving object with his eyes. Even in cases in which the vision is well developed at 16 weeks, one investigator at Yale University found that no infant would touch a cube placed before him, but only stared at it for about five seconds. At 20 weeks, however, one fourth of the babies touched the cube, and at 24 weeks, one half of them did so. Between the ages of 28 and 40 weeks coordination between eyes and hands is established, and by 40 weeks *all* the infants touched the cube.

The length of time spent by the baby in staring at a cube increased from 4.75 seconds at 16 weeks to 18 seconds at 28 weeks. By the end of the first year, however, the amount of time spent in looking at an object decreased to 10.75 seconds.

The manner of reaching for a cube shows definite changes with increasing maturity, and three general patterns may be recognized. Of these the earliest, or backhand type, occurs rather infrequently, while the second, or circuitous type, is the most common. The third, or straight approach, is the most mature, and is the ultimate goal in manual control.

Progress in manipulation depends not only upon the technique used in reaching but also upon the posture of the body. Reaching is dominated first by the shoulder, then by the elbow, followed by the fingers, and finally by the wrist.

The first movement used in reaching is a backhand sweep, forming an incomplete arc. This is characteristic of the child between 16 and 28 weeks of age, or at about the time he is trying to sit up.

At 28 weeks the approach to an object is very circuitous, but by 36 weeks it is only slightly so. During this time the infant may shorten the distance between himself and the object by bending forward from a sitting position and rotating one shoulder. Movements in reaching are dominated by the shoulder during the first 40 weeks after birth, but when greater participation of the elbow, wrist, and finger occurs, a straight approach is possible. This is the third and final stage in reaching, and usually is accomplished between the ages of 40 and 52 weeks. From domination by the shoulder, as in the more immature patterns of approach, the arm is now controlled and aimed by the wrist and forefinger.

These three patterns in the development of reaching are not always clearly distinguishable, and progress from one to another frequently is irregular. By the age of 1 year, however, most children have achieved a fairly mature pattern of reaching, but adult performance may not be attained until the fourth or fifth years.

In addition to reaching movements the infant goes through a number of stages in developing the ability to grasp objects. An analysis of these activities has been made by motion-picture recordings at the former Yale Clinic of Child Development. Some of the principal types of grasping are given in the accompanying illustration, Figure 1, showing ten hand positions at different age levels during the first year.

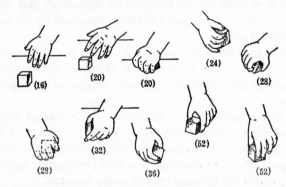

Figure 1. The development of prehension in the infant. (After H. M. Halverson, "An Experimental Study of Prehension in Infants," *Genetic Psychology Monographs,* 1931, *10:* Nos. 2, 3. By permission of the Journal Press, Provincetown, Mass.)

The first position shows that no contact is made with the cube at 16 weeks, although the child may stare at it for five seconds. The technique used by the twenty-week-old infant is illustrated in positions 2 and 3. Here he does not grip the cube, but rather corrals it with his hand and squeezes it against his body or other hand. In the literature this type of prehension is referred to as a "primitive squeeze." The "squeeze grasp," shown in position 4, which occurs at about 24 weeks, is really the first evidence of an actual but clumsy method of grasping an object. The cube is gripped between the fingers and the palm of the hand. A refinement of this grasp, known as the "hand grasp," occurs at 28 weeks, and is shown in the fifth position. Here the fingers encircle the cube somewhat more effectively than at 24 weeks, with the thumb placed parallel to them. Thumb opposition is beginning at 28 weeks, as is shown in position 6, and at 32 weeks is quite evident in the so-called "palm grasp" illustrated in position 7. The fingers and thumb cooperate to hold the cube against the palm of the hand. Position 8 shows the cube being held by the tips of the thumb and fingers at 36 weeks. A refinement of this is shown in positions 9 and 10 at 52 weeks, when a superior forefinger grasp, or pincer movement, is established. The cube is now gripped between the ends of the fingers and the thumb, and can be held without resting the hand on the table.

Similar stages are evident in the hand approaches made in an effort to secure a small round sugar pellet. Visual fixation for about two and a half seconds is characteristic at 20 weeks, and the attention is shifted to objects other than the pellet. Scratching movements occur at 24 weeks; raking movements resulting in prehension by the palms of the hands at 28 weeks; and thumb opposition and pincer movements beginning at 40 weeks.

The development in prehension during the first year is tremendous. At birth the child is unable to use his fingers as separate units, but by the end of 52 weeks he can use his fingers and thumb in pincer movements.

An excellent résumé of the development of reaching-prehensile behavior has been made by McGraw in a study of 1904 observations of seventy-three children from birth to 4 years. She summarizes her data under six so-called phases of development.

The phase that characterizes the infant during the first thirty-five days is called the "newborn or passive phase." At this stage of development the grasp is purely reflexive in nature and there is no real coordination between eyes and hands.

Around 115 days the second or "object-vision phase" occurs. This marks the beginning of fixation or regard.

The period around 210 days is called the "visual-motor phase," where eye and hand coordination of a compulsive rather than of a purposive type has been established.

Development around 360 to 375 days is characterized as the "manipulative and deliberative phase." Here the child shows sustained attention for the object and can deliberately inhibit the act.

The "visual release phase" follows. The child can appraise the situation in one brief look and then glance in another direction as he picks up the object.

The last or "the mature phase" is attained when "the child is able to appraise the location and size of the object without giving undue attention to it." He usually employs but one hand, and uses a light grip.

According to McGraw, cortical function does not enter into reaching-prehensile behavior until about the age of 8½ months, and the adult phase is not perfected before the fourth or fifth year. This latter conclusion is not in accord with those of Gesell and Halverson, who feel that the mature level is reached by 60 weeks.

The parent who understands the sequence of development in reaching and prehension will surround his child with things that are appropriate to the infant's particular level of growth. Obviously, these will include articles of food, objects, and toys suitable to grab, chew, and explore.

At 3 or 4 months the baby may place his hands on the bottle or breast while sucking, and about a month later will pat it.

From about the sixth or seventh month on, the infant may put things in his mouth, and care must be taken to prevent him from getting hold of sharp or dangerous objects. This is especially true when he is cutting teeth, and wants hard things to chew.

Usually a child at 4 or 5 months is allowed to take a sip from a cup held by someone else, but by 1 year he may be able to hold the cup briefly by himself. He may also try to manipulate a spoon, but generally turns the bowl sideways or upside down, making quite a mess of things. Adults who understand this phase of development, however, will not be too disturbed about it.

At the time that the pincer movement is developing the baby delights in poking into his cereal and in picking up crumbs from his tray. Finger feeding continues to be popular with him well into the second year.

If the year-old child is at that stage of development where he pulls himself to a standing position, he may insist upon standing up while he eats.

By the second year considerable manual progress has been made. The child does not spill so much when he eats, and usually he is rather adept in the handling of his spoon. He can manage his cup fairly well by this time, also, and his chewing has improved.

In another year he can use his fork skillfully, and can pour milk or water from a small pitcher into a glass.

Eating is a strenuous process for the young child and he tends to become fatigued and dawdles over his meals. This dawdling seems to reach a peak in most children at 3 or 4 years of age.

By the fourth year the child can eat and talk at the same time, and can now use a blunt knife. He tries to help his mother by assisting in clearing the table and putting food in the refrigerator.

The five-year-old usually gets much satisfaction from cutting his food with a knife, and his table manners are much more mature, but they still do not reach the standards some mothers expect.

The growth of arm and hand control is illustrated, also, by the development of play behavior. At 24 weeks the baby will usually grasp a rattle, and ordinarily from 28 weeks to the last quarter of the first year he reaches for objects with both hands. Thereafter, he generally uses one hand but may transfer things from one hand to the other. The ability to release objects begins around the age of 28 weeks, but dropping them *voluntarily* on the table or floor usually does not occur before the child is 44 weeks old, when he tends to keep everyone busy picking up things he drops.

At 6 months a baby may throw a ball from a sitting position, but co-operative ball play is not evident before 13 months. The child can catch and toss at 2 years, and his basic pattern of throwing is fairly well established by the time he enters school.

29. *Infant Development under Conditions of Restricted Practice and of Minimum Social Stimulation* *

W A Y N E   D E N N I S

Subjects and Experimental Conditions

In earlier communications we have described our subjects and have depicted the experimental conditions as they bore upon the special topics upon which we were reporting. It seems desirable here to present the conditions of the experiment in their entirety. We hope that the account is sufficiently complete so that no further account of experimental conditions need be given at a future time.

Our subjects were fraternal twins, but the relationship of the infants was not an important part of the study. Our original plan envisaged the use of only one subject, but the first inquiry for a subject to the Social Service Department of the University of Virginia Hospital revealed an opportunity to secure a pair of nonidentical female twins. The proffered twins were accepted because they enabled us to double the number of our subjects with considerably less than a doubling of cost and care. Thus the twin

* From Wayne Dennis, "Infant Development under Conditions of Restricted Practice and of Minimum Social Stimulation," *Genetic Psychology Monographs,* 23 (February, 1941), 149–54, 173–77. Reprinted by permission of the author and The Journal Press.

relationship of the subjects was, from the standpoint of our problem, purely accidental.

Their parents are of north-European ancestry. The father was a former taxi driver, whose whereabouts at the time of the birth of the twins was unknown. The mother had been a saleswoman in department stores. The father had no other children; the mother had two children by a former husband. We were able to obtain the twins as subjects because the mother was unable to provide for them. They came to us when they were 36 days old. The mother understood that we offered temporary care of the twins in return for the privilege of studying them. She understood the general nature of our research and was cooperative at all times.

Throughout the experiment the twins lived in our home but they were confined to the nursery. This was a second-floor room, so situated that from the infants' position only sky and treetops were visible through the windows. The room itself contained only the subjects' cribs, a bureau, a table, two chairs, and a screen near the door. No picture or decoration of any sort was permitted in the nursery. The door of the room was kept closed, and we entered the room only to care for the subjects, to observe them, and to experiment with them. The twins were never taken from the nursery except on a few test occasions and for trips to the University Hospital for anthropometric and pediatric examination. On these trips the infants' faces were covered. For three months during the summer the subjects lived in a summer cabin, seventeen miles away, in a room similar to the winter nursery. As the trip to and from the cabin was carefully supervised, and as their mode of life at the cabin was identical with that in town, this fact does not alter the principle that the environment of the subjects was limited and controlled in a very strict manner.

Although the infants were indoors at all times, we saw to it that fresh air and sunshine were plentifully supplied. Windows were opened for a period daily, the length of the period depending upon the outside temperature. The subjects, dressed only in shirt and diaper, were given sun baths before an open window. Direct sunlight came through the windows during a large part of the daylight hours. In spite of spending the first year of life indoors, the twins had a sun tan at all times.

The subjects were placed in individual cribs, of the trade name "Kiddie Koop." The cribs were placed side by side with a screen equal in height to the cribs between the two, so that the twins could see each other only when taken from their beds. During the first nine months the subjects were taken from the cribs only for feeding and bathing or when removal from the cribs was demanded for the purposes of experimentation.

With the exception of a few occasions during the latter part of the experiment the sole care of the twins was supplied by the experimenters. This means that we bathed and fed the infants, changed the diapers and bed clothing, and cleaned the room. The infants seldom saw other people, and when they did it was with our knowledge and supervision. Visitors were required to adhere to the same practices which we imposed upon ourselves.

We carefully refrained from rewarding or punishing the subjects for any action. The subjects were not scolded or spanked or treated roughly in connection with any response. We did conduct some experiments to determine the first reaction of the subjects to scolding and to a light slap on the thigh, but these stimuli came at a time when the infants were silently and quietly watching the experimenter. With a few exceptions, we never encouraged or discouraged any act of the twins. The exceptions to this rule, and to other such general rules, occurred in the last month of the investigation, when the experimental conditions were partially suspended.

Indifferent behavior toward infants is most difficult to achieve, not in respect to avoiding such overt acts as praising and fondling but in respect to the amount of attention which is given to the infant. If the infant is doing something new or interesting, the adult is likely to watch the child much more closely than usual, and this increased attentiveness on the part of the adult may act as a reward and may induce repetition of the response. In order to avoid variation in attentiveness we attempted to watch the infants at all times when we were in their presence, except when we were taking notes. In this connection it must be borne in mind that when we were in the nursery we were never engaged in anything other than meeting the needs of the subjects and observing their behavior. Routine behavior, as well as any new behavior of the subjects, was observed and recorded each time we entered the nursery. This is very different from the ordinary home situation, where the infant receives attention primarily when he engages in some unusual, or some culturally significant, response. It is our belief that we did not reveal more interest in any one act of our subjects than we did in any other act.

This leads to a consideration of our treatment of the twins' cries. In this respect our procedure was as follows: If either of the infants cried at some time other than feeding time, one of the experimenters entered the room and investigated the cause. The cause was ordinarily a soiled diaper. The diaper was changed, and we left the room. If the child cried as we left, we paid no attention to such a cry.

The feeding routine was maintained in a general way, but not with extreme rigidity. If an infant was asleep at the regular time for feeding, we allowed her to go somewhat beyond the usual period. If she fretted a great deal or cried strongly before the hour for feeding, her food was given as much as fifteen minutes early. In that sense, we may be said to have rewarded the crying of the subjects, but in so doing we could hardly have rewarded any other response. We shall see later that crying was very infrequent.

We not only avoided reward and punishment but we avoided acts which might have provided examples for imitation. With certain exceptions to be noted later our behavior in the nursery was limited to changing diapers, bathing, feeding, etc. We carefully refrained from baby talk and from babbling, as we wanted to know whether such vocalizations would occur without example. Likewise, we never performed for the twins such acts as patting their hands or playing with their toes.

Thus far we have spoken only of the conditions which remained relatively constant until the last few weeks of the experiment. We turn now to more stringent restrictions in the environment of the subjects which, in the main, were applied only for the first half year. The conditions to be described were designed to provide answers to specific questions and were abandoned when the answers were obtained.

We wished to determine whether or not the infants would smile upon hearing the voice of the adult, if speech were not associated with the care and attention which the adult supplied. For this reason, until the twins were 26 weeks of age, we never announced our entry into the nursery and never spoke to the subjects. We were not totally silent, for we occasionally commented to each other while in the nursery, but we were careful not to make comments while we were feeding or otherwise caring for the twins. Our speech when we were outside the nursery could be heard by the infants, but it had no more relation to their behavior than did traffic noises or other common sounds.

We wished also to know whether positive responses toward us would develop if we refrained from smiling at the twins and from petting, cuddling, and fondling them. In order to determine the answer to this question we avoided these expressions during the first 26 weeks. Withholding of demonstrations of affection of this sort was not an easy task to impose upon ourselves, particularly as the subjects themselves were very expressive. From the fifteenth week onward they almost invariably greeted us with a smile and a vocalization. After this fact was thoroughly established, we decided in week 27 to return their smile of greeting, and to speak to them as we approached.

The reader may ask how we could keep from rewarding various responses of the subjects when once we permitted ourselves to smile at and to fondle and play with the twins. This was accomplished by engaging in these responses only at times when no particular act of the twins could be said to be encouraged by our behavior. We romped with the children, as by shaking or rolling them only when they were indifferently employed with some response that was already well established.

During the thirty-sixth week we began placing the twins for several minutes each day upon quilted pads on the floor. This was for the purpose of giving them some experience on a relatively hard surface. At the beginning of the forty-second week we started placing the infants in high chairs for a short period each day. But even in the last month of the experiment, the larger part of the twins' day was spent in the cribs.

No toys were provided for the subjects until the forty-ninth week. At that time a rattle and a few other toys, to be described later, were introduced. Our aim in introducing the toys was to see what use would be made of them when no example, encouragement, or instruction was given by the adult.

One sort of restriction to which the infants were subjected requires special comment. In accordance with our general policy of letting the twins alone and of refraining from initiating any development, we did not put the twins into sitting or standing postures, nor provide any practice in reaching for many months. Under normal circumstances parents prop the child up before he can sit alone, hold him upright on the adult's lap before he can stand well, and dangle objects before him before he can reach with any accuracy. These responses, more than any others, require the intervention of the adult in order that early practice be made possible. Our experiment ruled out nearly all possibilities of early practice of these reactions, whereas many other responses were practiced by the twins because unlike the responses mentioned above they did not require the aid of the adult.

The three responses—sitting alone, standing with support, and reaching for a dangling object—were submitted to tests when the twins were of an age such that the responses are present in normal infants of normal environment. When these tests had been made, we no longer refrained from placing the twins in sitting and standing postures, nor did we keep all movable objects out of their reach.

We attempted to give the two subjects identical treatment. This was carried to the extent of dividing the attention of each experimenter equally between the two subjects. For convenience, the experimenters will be referred to by their initials: *W* referring to the writer and *M* referring to Mrs.

Dennis. *M* fed Rey throughout one day while *W* attended to the feeding of Del. During the next day, *M* fed Del and Rey was fed by *W,* etc. The infants were bathed one at a time, but the order of bathing was reversed from day to day. The bathing was done by *W,* the drying and dressing by *M.*

In order that the infants' positions in the room should not lead to a difference in treatment, the crib which Rey occupied during one day was occupied by Del during the next day, etc. Thus it will be seen that great pains were taken to insure that the two subjects were treated exactly alike.

A few words may be added on miscellaneous aspects of the twins' care. Before the twins came to us, the mother's milk had been found to be quite inadequate, and supplementary feeding by bottle had been resorted to. At the beginning of the experiment, bottle feeding constituted the sole means of feeding. The nursing bottle was utilized for the giving of liquid foods throughout the experiment, i.e., weaning from the bottle was not attempted, but solid and semisolid foods were given by spoon.

The diet of the subjects was chosen with the advice of Dr. L. T. Royster of the Pediatrics Department of the University of Virginia Hospital. During the early months the diet of the twins consisted of lactic acid milk, which was kindly prepared for us by the hospital staff, and of orange juice. Soup, cereal, and strained fruits and vegetables were introduced gradually after the twenty-fourth week. No elimination training of any kind was undertaken. . . .

A List of Developmental Items

A description such as that which we have just presented cannot propose to name all of the items of behavior which appeared in the course of the experiment. It seems desirable to present a complete list of new responses which made their appearance in the twins' repertoire, and to accomplish this purpose is the aim of the present chapter.

The items which follow are arranged in the chronological order in which they occurred in the experiment. That is, each item was added to the list as it occurred, regardless of the twin which first performed it, although of course the records of the subjects are separated. The two columns on the right side of the table show the age at which the response occurred. If each subject performed the response, the date of appearance is given for each subject.

This table (Table 1) is limited to items which occurred *spontaneously.* This means that the table contains responses which, so far as the circum-

Table 1

NEW ITEMS OF BEHAVIOR

No.	Behavior items	Week of first appearance	
		REY	DEL
1	Hands close on objects	7	6
2	Smile	6	6
3	Cry tears	8	6
4	Fixate *E*	6	7
5	Smile when fixating *E*	6	7
6	Frown	6	6
7	Turn from back to side	8	6
8	Tense during bath	6	
9	Arms active in bath	9	7
10	Cry at sound	18	7
11	Corners of mouth pulled down before crying	7	7
12	Vocalize vowel	7	8
13	Rub face	9	7
14	Arm startle to touch or jar	7	7
15	Tongue between lips	7	7
16	Turn head to watch *E*	8	7
17	Stop crying when *E* enters nursery	7	8
18	Stop crying when light turned on (at night)	8	7
19	Open mouth smile	11	7
20	Scolding vocalization	8	17
21	Fret	8	8
22	Coo	8	8
23	Hand to mouth	8	10
24	Vocalize when fixating *E*	9	9
25	Shake head	9	11
26	Purse lips	12	9
27	Raise eyebrows	9	9
28	Fixate objects beyond crib	11	9
29	Jerk upon hearing noise	11	9
30	Consonant-vowel syllable	9	
31	Near-laugh	10	9
32	Eyes watch *E*'s hands	10	9
33	Noise inhibits crying	10	10
34	Look for *E* when he disappears behind screen	10	10
35	Vocalize single consonant	10	36
36	Stick out tongue	10	25
37	Cry when *E* leaves crib	18	10
38	Rub eyes	10	10
39	Lift head when supine	16	10
40	Cry upon seeing bottle	11	10
41	Fixate own hand	12	11
42	Feeding inhibited by staring at *E*	11	26
43	Cry when put down without attention	15	11
44	Chewing movements	12	12

Table 1 (cont.)

No.	Behavior items	Week of first appearance	
		REY	DEL
45	Crowing vocalization	12	12
46	Attempt to turn from supine to prone	16	12
47	Turn toward sound	19	12
48	Carry object to mouth	21	12
49	Increased activity at sight of *E*	15	13
50	Watch own hands persistently	14	14
51	Kick when otherwise quiet	15	14
52	Coaxing vocalization	14	20
53	Stare at stranger	14	14
54	Stop nursing to coo or smile	17	16
55	Sob		16
56	Clasp own hands	18	16
57	Laugh	21	16
58	Gurgle	16	16
59	Raise head and shoulders when supine	18	17
60	Turn supine to prone	50	17
61	Head inclined toward approaching bottle	19	18
62	Pull at bedclothes	19	18
63	Open mouth when *E*'s finger approaches face	20	19
64	Arms extended, expressive movement	19	22
65	Pucker face at stranger		20
66	Place hands on knees	20	20
67	Smack lips when being fed		20
68	Hold legs in air	21	21
69	Grasp own ankle	22	21
70	Rising vocalization when nipple removed	22	22
71	Extend and wave arms	27	22
72	Grasp own toes	22	22
73	Laugh during solitary play	23	23
74	Place soles of feet together	23	
75	Shouting vocalization	27	24
76	Grasp own diaper	24	24
77	Cry when *E* leaves room	25	24
78	Wiggle toes	27	
79	Scratch sheet or crib	27	29
80	Open and close hands repeatedly	27	
81	Touch hands together	27	27
82	One hand clasps other hand	30	27
83	Sing-song vocalization	29	27
84	Grasp own ear	31	28
85	Grasp own hair	29	
86	Scratch own head	29	
87	Affected cough	30	29
88	Pincer prehension of bedclothes	30	29
89	Fret when bib put on	31	30
90	Arch back when supine	30	31

Table 1 (cont.)

No.	Behavior items	Week of first appearance REY	DEL
91	Grasp *E*'s face and hair	31	
92	Pat own body	31	33
93	Pincer prehension of own toes	31	
94	Open and close mouth repeatedly	31	
95	Kick during bath when otherwise quiet	33	31
96	Suck lower lip	32	31
97	Turn prone to supine	39	33
98	Roll on floor	51	33
99	Pat object	34	45
100	Throw self backward in rejecting food	34	
101	Pat own foot	34	36
102	Smack lips when not eating	35	37
103	Cross legs	35	35
104	Pat knee with contralateral foot	36	
105	Rock self on abdomen		36
106	Rest head on palm of hand when supine	37	49
107	Rub soles of feet together	37	
108	Vibrate lips by blowing	44	37
109	Toe to mouth	37	41
110	Pivot on abdomen	43	37
111	Vocalize click	37	49
112	Pat own hands		37
113	Monotonous vocalization while going to sleep		38
114	Foot push against crib	38	
115	Suck at sight of bottle		39
116	Reach for spoon when being fed	39	45
117	Snap fingers	41	
118	Bend forward and rest on elbows when supine		41
119	Go from sitting to prone position	46	43
120	Put covers on and off face	44	
121	Rubs own gums		47
122	Grasp toes while sitting	47	47
123	Bounce while sitting	48	49
124	Cry when object taken from her	49	48
125	Touch and pursue object with forefinger		49
126	Push floor with foot when prone	49	51
127	Display repertoire for stranger		49
128	Scoot backward when prone	51	
129	Splash in bath	52	54
130	Whisper	52	54
131	Rise to half-sitting, resting on elbow	52	52
132	Take nipple from mouth, plays with it		54
133	Finger lips while vocalizing		54
134	Rub self in bath	55	
135	Raise self to sitting position	56	61
136	Reach in diaper for feces	57	

Table 1 (cont.)

No.	Behavior items	Week of first appearance	
		REY	DEL
137	Cross index and middle fingers	57	
138	Pull to kneeling position	57	
139	Kneel without hand support	58	
140	Shake bedclothing		58
141	Walk on knees, holding side of crib	58	
142	Shrug shoulders		59
143	Pull to standing in crib	59	
144	Go from standing to kneeling in crib	59	
145	Put foot on tray of high chair		59
146	Rock self on elbow in half-sitting position		59
147	Scoot backward when sitting	59	
148	Rock when sitting		59
149	Get to kneeling position without pulling	60	
150	Progress by bouncing in sitting position	60	
151	Pivot while sitting	61	
152	Stand momentarily without support	61	
153	Creep	61	
154	Walk, holding to crib	61	

stances of the twins were concerned, *could* have occurred at any time. We have not placed in the list any item which required special action on our part—such as sitting when placed sitting, or supporting the body weight when held upright. Such test behavior was not included, because, since the tests were not made daily or even weekly, the period at which test behavior appeared was in large measure a function of the time at which the test was given.

The list is defective in regard to vocalizations. To have listed each distinct sound as it was produced would have extended the list beyond reasonable proportions.

In commenting upon this series of developmental items, we wish to call attention first of all to the extensive character of the list. One hundred and fifty-four distinct responses are listed. The list is by no means complete, for vocalizations were largely omitted. The record shows how marked is behavioral development under conditions of minimum social stimulation and restricted practice.

It will be seen that the order of appearance of the items was roughly the same for the two subjects. If a rank-order correlation is computed for the items which were common to the repertoires of the two subjects, it is found to be .99.

The list shows that during the early months there was little difference in the rate at which new responses were acquired by the two subjects. Del was slightly in advance of Rey. In later months, however, Rey was considerably more advanced than Del, especially with regard to locomotor items.

Finally, we may note that behavior became more individual in the later months. At the beginning, the subjects almost invariably developed the same responses. In the later months, each subject developed many items which were never practiced by the other twin.

30. *Study of Prehension in Infants* *

H. M. HALVERSON

The Experiment

METHOD, SUBJECTS, PROCEDURE

The experimental study of prehension herewith presented was undertaken in the photographic observatory of the Yale Psycho-Clinic, which, with its special arrangements and equipment for observing and photographing the infant, reduces to a minimum interference with his characteristic behavior.

The study is both a motion and frame-by-frame analysis of the cinema records of infant prehension of red cubes measuring one inch on an edge, and is both qualitative and quantitative in nature. The paper also introduces some photographic techniques for the purpose of analyzing and resolving human behavior into temporal and spatial patterns.

The subjects of investigation are twelve or more infants at each of the following ages: 16, 20, 24, 28, 32, 36, 40, and 52 weeks.

The cube situation is but one of the many test situations used in the normative examination of infants. Our subjects are selected from those who by this examination indicate that they are developing normally. In order to secure infants who are most likely to be of average development, we include only those whose fathers fall within the middle 50 per cent of the

* From H. M. Halverson, "Study of Prehension in Infants," *Genetic Psychology Monographs,* 10 (August–September, 1931), 122–23, 128–29, 270–80. Reprinted by permission of The Journal Press.

general adult population as determined by the Barr rating scale. The education of both parents is generally that of the grammar school. The infants are of Teutonic or of Celtic race, are well nourished, and the records of each reveal a normal gestation term, an approximately average birth weight, and the absence of any serious illness since the time of birth.

The procedure for the study of cube prehension is as follows. When the infant arrives at the clinic and the usual precautions with regard to his physical condition are exercised, he is brought into the photographic observatory, is relieved of all clothing, and given opportunity to adjust to his environment before the regular normative examination starts. The regular examination is about one fourth completed when the cube situations are instated, thus providing a warming-up period and complete adaptation without apparent fatigue.

The infant is seated on the platform (30 inches in height) of the experimental crib before, but not touching, a table-top which is supported elbow high on the crib's adjustable side rails. The young infant who cannot maintain a sitting equilibrium is placed in a small, specially constructed Morris chair with a supporting belt about his waist. This arrangement is elastic enough not to interfere greatly with forward or lateral movements of the trunk.

The infant faces the longer edge of the table-top, which is 30 by 20 inches, and is divided laterally into six equal lanes by lines which extend from its further edge to a horizontal line parallel with, and 6 inches from, the near edge. These lines, which aid materially in the analysis of the records, have in no way, as far as we can determine, interfered with the infant's natural behavior toward or with the cubes. The infant exhibits no self-consciousness in performing his task and enjoys the full free play of trunk and limbs, untempered by inhibitions, in his reactions to the cube before him.

There are three cube situations, each of twenty seconds' duration. In the presentation of the first cube, the examiner (E) stands on the left side of the crib, facing it, takes a cube in the palm of her left hand and carries it below the table-top to the median plane of the infant. She then takes the cube between her thumb and two first fingers and taps it against the far edge to draw the infant's regard to this point. As the infant, for the first time, fixates the cube, it is advanced along the median line at a rate which brings it to the standard median position, a point 6 inches from the near edge, in 2 seconds. E then releases the cube so that one of its surfaces fronts the infant. If, within 9 seconds, the infant gives no indication of reaching for the cube, or appears unlikely to touch it, E, at a signal from the operator

(*O*) outside the observatory, advances the cube 3 inches nearer the infant and again releases it. If, at the ninth second, the infant appears likely to touch or take the cube, the cube is not moved forward until the next signal, at 14 seconds. Of course, if the infant grasps the cube before the ninth second, *E* does nothing further with it. Thus any infant who does not acquire the cube within the first 10 seconds (it takes one second for *E* to reach the cube at nine and another to advance it to the near position) is given a second chance to prehend the cube at a point easily within his reach.

This procedure is repeated in presenting the second and the third cubes, with the exception that the second cube is presented with the infant holding the first cube in his left hand, and the third cube situation starts with a cube in either hand. The interval between successive cube instatements is about two minutes.

A motion-picture camera, encased in a near sound-proof box and aimed at the infant from an angle of 50° above the horizontal in the front median plane, records the infant's behavior. A second camera, at ear level and at right angles with the first camera, is used judiciously to furnish supplementary photographic records. . . .

Conclusions

1. There are four steps in prehension: (a) the visual location of the object, (b) the approach by the hand, (c) the grasp, and (d) the disposal of the object.

2. The amount of regard by the infants for the cube increases rapidly from 4.75 seconds at 16 weeks to 18.0 seconds at 28 weeks, and then generally decreases to 10.75 seconds at 52 weeks. The fact that the older infants grasp the cube sooner than the younger groups (less than 32 weeks of age) may account for this decrease in time. The group medians for the average duration of the individual regards for the cube, for the longest regard, and for the first regard, follow the same general rule for rise and decline of time values as does the total regard time.

3. Infants of the 16-weeks group and of the 20-weeks group usually follow the short initial regard for the cube with a second, and sometimes a third, brief regard. The other infants vary greatly in their manner of regard; some infants attend the cube throughout the duration of the situation, others regard it briefly several times, others regard it profoundly twice or three times, and some look at it but once.

4. Only slight differences distinguish the regard for the second cube

from the regard for the first cube. At 36 weeks and at 40 weeks the duration of the first regard for the second cube is greater than the duration of the first regard for the first cube. This increase in regard is due to delayed reaching for the cube, which, in turn, is due to interference caused by the presence of a cube already in the infant's possession. For the remaining groups, the first regard for the second cube is as short as that for the first cube. The brevity of the first regard is marked at 52 weeks, for these infants secure the cube quickly and look elsewhere immediately. A number of these infants grasp the cube without looking at it.

5. In the third cube situation the total regard for the cube for the five lower age groups is less than that for the first and for the second cubes, but for the 36-, 40-, and 52-weeks infants there is no difference in total regard. The presence of two cubes in the infant's hands apparently interferes with his regard for the third cube. In contrast to what we find in the first and second cube situations, there are no long regards for the third cube in any of the groups.

6. The sequence of infants' regard for objects about them varies for the three situations. The 16-weeks infants first regard the presented cube, then the table top on their hands (in fact, it is sometimes difficult to tell when it is one or the other, particularly when they scratch the table), and then the cube or the examiner. The 20-weeks group regard first the cube, then the examiner, and then the cube again, or the other cubes if they are present. The remaining age groups in the first situation first look at the presented cube, then at the examiner or the dome, and then again at the cube. In the second and third cube situations the regard goes to the presented cube, then to the other cubes or the dome, and then back to the cube.

7. The arrangement of the groups with respect to frequency of shifts of regard, beginning with the group having the greatest number of shifts, are: 36-weeks, 20-weeks, 52-weeks, 40-weeks, 16-weeks, 24-weeks, 32-weeks, and 28-weeks.

8. All infants regard the presented cube longer than they regard any other object. Interest in the other cubes waxes from 16 to 28 weeks and then weakens gradually with age. Only the 16-weeks and 20-weeks groups regard at length the hands and table. At 16 weeks infants regard the examiner extensively. There is then a gradual and rapid decrease in the amount of regard for the examiner, until at 28 weeks infants scarcely notice her. The older infants regard her infrequently. The 52-weeks infants regard the dome longer than do those of any other group, the 32-weeks group also look about them at length, while the 24-weeks group regard the dome but little.

9. After 24 weeks, the infant's first approach is likely to yield success in reaching the cube. Speed in reaching increases with age up to 32 weeks and then decreases. Bilateral approaches appear frequently at 24, 28, and 32 weeks when both hands are unburdened with other cubes.

10. Infants regard the presented cube most frequently. After this cube, the objects oftenest regarded are: at 16 weeks, the table and examiner; at 20 weeks, the examiner and the dome; at 24, 28, 32, 36, and 40 weeks, the other cubes and the dome; and at 52 weeks, the dome and the examiner.

11. Three forms of approach appear: the backhand sweep; the circuitous, which includes, besides the angular and scooping sweeps, the less circuitous reaching; and the direct (straight) approaches. Infants from 16 weeks to 28 weeks of age employ either the backhand approach, which is only the first half of the circuitous approach, or the very circuitous approach in reaching. Infants of 32 and 36 weeks use a less circuitous form of approach in reaching for the cube, and infants of 40 and 52 weeks usually employ the direct approach. Genetically, the backhand and circuitous approaches straighten out into the direct approach. Up to 24 weeks of age, the infants in reaching usually point the hand so that it will come to rest fully upon the cube. After 28 weeks, they so direct their hand that only the forefinger will pass over the mid-top of the cube.

12. The lateral view of reaching reveals three principal types of approach: (a) the slide, which is extensively employed by infants up to 32 weeks of age, (b) the loop, which likewise is employed by these younger infants whenever they do not use the slide approach, and (c) the planing approach, which is the characteristic reaching action of infants of 36 to 52 weeks of age. Combinations of these profiles also appear, such as the loop-slide, the plane-slide, and the plane-loop.

13. The unilateral approach is the common type of reaching at all ages, but bilateral approaches are about as common as the unilateral type at 24 weeks, and occur frequently at 20 weeks.

14. Up to 28 weeks of age infants raise their hands relatively high in reaching for the cube. From 28 weeks to 52 weeks the height of the approach gradually diminishes.

15. There are four adjustment stages in the approach pattern: (a) The *initial advance.* (b) In the *accelerated advance* the hand increases its speed forward and generally laterally, although the destination of the hand is as yet indeterminable. (*c*) In the next stage, *alignment,* the hand points so that its ultimate destination is no longer a matter of conjecture, for the cube is within that portion of the table-top which subtends the thumb-

forefinger angle. (*d*) The *culminating approach,* in which the hand sets itself for the grasp, follows the aligning approach.

16. From 16 weeks to 24 weeks, infants often raise the hand, thrust it forward circuitously, and lower it in a manner which suggests that the approach consists of three individual acts. At 40 weeks, no trace of these separate acts is discernible; they are incorporated into one fluent reaching movement.

17. If we except those approaches which cut in short of the cube, infants from 16 weeks to 28 weeks of age point their forearms directly above the cube at the final stage of the approach, and, while infants over 28 weeks of age sometimes direct the forearm in this manner, they usually aim it toward a point above the lateral side of the cube which is nearest the reaching hand.

18. Infants up to 28 weeks of age reach for the cube with the thumb pointing almost straight down from a pronated hand, and the older infants approach the cube with the thumb directed in medianward or semimedianward from a hand which is slightly rotated in the same direction.

19. The manner in which infants hold the thumb in reaching indicates roughly the kind of grasp which follows. If the thumb points inward, the grasp will find the thumb opposed to the fingers; if the thumb hangs down or curls under the palm, a grasp of lower order will result.

20. For the youngest infants the plane of the angle formed by the forefinger and thumb just preceding grasp is vertical. As the infant matures, the plane of this angle rotates toward a horizontal line.

21. In reaching for the cube, the hand usually remains pronated throughout its entire course, or it rotates slightly from a somewhat palm-in toward a pronated state as it sweeps in toward the cube. During the approach, the other hand usually does not rotate, regardless of its other movements.

22. Accuracy in reaching by infants improves gradually and steadily from 16 weeks to 52 weeks.

23. At 16 weeks no infants are likely to touch the cube. At 20 weeks one fourth of the infants touch the cube, and one third grasp it crudely. At 24 weeks about one half of them touch, and one half grasp the cube. At 28, 32, 36, 40, and 52 weeks we may expect all infants to grasp the cube, if they really desire it. The distinguishing differences between these older infants is in the time actually required to grasp the cube, amount of cube displacement, number of adjustments necessary for a firm grasp, and the type of grasp.

24. There are ten types of grasp which arrange themselves in a genetic

series: (a) no contact, (b) contact, (c) the primitive squeeze, (d) the squeeze grasp, (e) the hand grasp, (f) the palm grasp, (g) the superior-palm grasp, (h) the inferior-forefinger grasp, (i) the forefinger grasp, and (j) the superior-forefinger grasp.

25. The type of grasp determines the aim of the approach. The infant points his forearm directly at or above the cube to secure a palm grip, and he points his forearm at or above the near lateral face of the cube to procure a forefinger grasp.

26. Older infants grasp the cube sooner after its presentation and, after touching it, secure a firm grip more quickly than do the younger infants. The former also make fewer adjustments, and displace the cube less in grasping it, and regard it less both before and after grasp.

27. Infants from 16 to 28 weeks of age seldom grasp the cube from the *S.M.* position, while the older infants usually grasp it from this point. If we except the 16-weeks infants, who never grasp the cube, we find in general that the number of unsuccessful attempts to reach the cube varies inversely with the age of the infants. The 24-weeks group touch the cube oftenest without grasping it, and the number of grasps increases with age up to 28 weeks, after which the cube is usually grasped by all infants except when other cubes are present. No age group demonstrates clearly that one hand is preferred over the other in the prehension of the cubes.

28. Twenty-eight weeks is the critical age in infant prehension. Infants at this age have the longest single regard and the greatest total duration of regard for the cube. The hand begins to free itself from forearm control in reaching for objects. Corralling is giving way to direct reaching, and the infant, instead of directing the entire hand toward the cube, is beginning to point his hand so that only the index and medius fingers will pass over the cube. The hand is losing its pawlike behavior in favor of finger manipulation of the cube, and a vital change from palm grip to active thumb opposition is occurring in the type of grasp.

29. Infants often reach for and touch, and three of the older ones grasp, the presented cube when they already hold a cube in the approach-hand.

30. Up to 28 weeks of age the infant often invokes the aid of the second hand in grasping.

31. Infants contact oftener with the third cube than with the second cube but they do not grasp the third cube nearly as often as they grasp the second cube.

32. Active thumb opposition, which occurs only in the higher types of grasp, is a complex act which involves the coordinated action of three muscles and therefore appears relatively late in infancy.

33. The delay in the digital leadership of the forefinger is perhaps due to the late maturation of its neuromusculature.

34. The two most common forms of lifting the cube from the table are: (a) a purely elbow flexion and (b) a hand-elbow action, in which the hand, after grasping the cube, rotates on its ulnar edge before elbow flexion begins.

35. The more characteristic reactions to the cube by the infants of different ages are as follows: At 16 weeks, infants follow the examiner's hand after she presents the cube, slide their hands about on the table, and often keep one or both hands on the table during the entire situation. At 20 weeks, infants scratch the table, and attempt to get both hands about the cube after reaching with both hands simultaneously. If they succeed in touching the cube, they either push it out of reach or simply hold it. At 24 and at 28 weeks, they approach the cube in a scooping manner, sometimes using both hands, and then corral and surround the cube or push it out of reach. After grasping the cube, they hold it, take it to the mouth, inspect the cube, and release and regain it. At 32 weeks, the infants use the scooping approach to surround the cube, inspect it, take it to the mouth, release and pick the cube up again, and exchange it from one hand to the other. They often disregard the cube when there are other cubes present. At 36 weeks and at 40 weeks, the infants execute a number of bilateral approaches and shift the cube from one hand to the other. They also bring the cube to the mouth, simply hold the cube, inspect it, hold it with both hands, release and regain it, bang the table with it, exchange hands on it, execute a number of bilateral approaches, and hold it in both hands. The 52-weeks infants often put the cube down and pick it up again, bang the table, exchange hands on the cube, simply hold it with one hand or both hands and inspect it, but do not bring it to the mouth. The 16-weeks infants do not, as a rule, reach the cube.

36. From 16 to 36 weeks the range of activity of infants' hands on or above the table-top gradually increases. From 36 weeks to 52 weeks the activity decreases slightly.

37. Prehension in infants progresses in a manner which indicates the presence of developmental behavior patterns. These patterns, which in early infancy appear as very crude forms of reaching, grasping, and manipulation, develop gradually and observably into highly refined and integrated systems of sequential acts.

38. The development of reaching and grasping affords excellent examples of the progress of maturation from the coarser to the finer muscles. The early approach patterns consist largely of crude shoulder and elbow

movements in which slow and somewhat angular action predominates, while the later approach patterns employ better directed shoulder and elbow action, in addition to wrist movements and hand rotation, under the dominating influence of the forefinger and thumb. The early approach reveals a crudely functioning hand at the end of a poorly directed arm, while the later approach reveals a well-coordinated arm under the directing influence of a pretty well developed prehensile organ. In grasping we find at first a clawing type of closure in which the thumb is practically inactive and no digits predominate, succeeded by a nipping, pressing type of closure the dominating factors of which are the thumb and forefinger, i.e., a crude palming movement giving way to a refined forefingertip grasp which includes precise placement of the digits upon the cube.

39. The increase in the number of higher types of grasp and the inincrease in the amount and variety of digital manipulation of the cube in infants from 16 to 52 weeks of age are due in part to anatomical growth of the digits of the hand, in part to maturation of its neuromusculature, in part to training, and in part, perhaps, to increase in cutaneous sensibility of the fingertips.

40. This investigation demonstrates the applicability of the motion camera for the study of infant behavior.

31. The Learning of Motor Skills as Influenced by Knowledge of Mechanical Principles *

FRANCES M. COLVILLE

M ANY GENERAL PRINCIPLES of mechanics are relevant to the teaching, learning, and performance of activities included in the physical education curriculum. These principles may describe the motion of objects such as balls and racquets, movement of the body itself, or a combination of both.

* From Frances M. Colville, "The Learning of Motor Skills as Influenced by Knowledge of Mechanical Principles," *The Journal of Educational Psychology* (October, 1957), pp. 321–26. Reprinted by permission of the author and the American Psychological Association.

The question has been raised as to whether knowledge of these general principles and an understanding of their application to these activities will facilitate the learning and improve the performance of pupils in physical education classes. Also of interest are questions concerning the influence of knowledge of these principles as applied to one activity upon subsequent learning of other activities to which the same principles apply. Results of a few experiments suggest that a pupil who understands a principle related to one skill may master a related skill more readily than the pupil whose experience has been restricted to specific instruction in technique without explanation of pertinent principles.

With reference to the teaching of a motor skill in which a specific principle of mechanics is involved, then, two questions have been raised:

1. What is the effect of knowledge of a principle upon immediate learning of a skill to which the principle applies?

2. What is the effect of knowledge of a principle learned in relation to one skill upon subsequent learning of a different or more complicated skill to which the same principle is applicable?

Reported investigations bearing on the acquisition and transfer of principles are limited, and although most authorities agree that general principles are probably transferable, little strong experimental evidence is available to support such a claim. Apparently, little or no experimentation has been done in the field of physical education on the effect of knowledge of principles of mechanics in learning situations involving body movement and large muscle activities.

Judd, and Hendrickson and Schroeder reported that knowledge of the principle of refraction was beneficial in dart throwing and rifle shooting at a target under water. Cox found that knowledge of principles involved in manipulating electrical equipment facilitated the assembling and stripping of such equipment. Other experimenters have reported similar results from investigations involving mathematics, mental games, spelling, card tricks, and mechanical puzzles. In contrast to these findings are a number of investigations in which the method of including instruction in the principles involved did not appear to be more effective. In studying the effect of drill versus the learning of generalizations related to addition and subtraction, Olander found that the two methods appeared to be equally effective. Babitz and Keys found similar results with college chemistry classes, and Hendrix reported only one difference, significant at the 12 per cent level, in her experiment with teaching algebraic generalizations.

With the exception of the experiments by Judd, Hendrickson and Schroeder, and Cox, all of the reported investigations have dealt with various types of learning other than motor learning, and only Judd's experiment involved skills requiring the coordinated use of large muscles of the body as well as fine coordinations of the fingers. Judd, and Hendrickson and Schroeder, while reporting a difference in favor of instruction in principles, included this instruction in such a way that additional time was allotted to the group receiving the instruction. Thus, the experimental groups had the advantage of additional time as well as additional information. Furthermore, Judd supplied no statistical analysis of his early experiment, and the other differences reported were significant at a statistical level below that which is usually considered acceptable.

In the present investigation, an attempt was made to control these ambiguities by using an experimental design which insured that both the experimental and the control groups spent equal amounts of time in learning and performing and by considering only those differences which were significant at the 5 per cent level of confidence or above.

Method

PURPOSE OF THE STUDY

It was the purpose of this study to investigate certain questions related to the teaching of physical education activities in which specific principles of mechanics are involved. This problem was approached by: (a) selecting three principles of mechanics which are pertinent to motor skills; (b) selecting three motor skills, each of which utilizes one of the principles; (c) establishing for each skill two comparable groups of Ss, one of which was taught without reference to the principle involved, and the other of which was taught to understand and apply the principle; (d) comparing for each skill the performance of the two groups, one of which spent the entire time practicing the skill without reference to the principle involved, and the other of which spent part of the time practicing the skill and part of the time in learning the principle; (e) comparing for each skill the performance of the two groups in a similar or more complicated form of the skill to which the same general principle applies.

SELECTED PRINCIPLES AND SKILLS

The selected principles and the skills in which they are utilized were as follows:

Principle I: The angle of incidence is approximately equal to the angle of reflection. Skill: Rolling a ball against a surface, or surfaces, from which it would rebound.

Principle II: In stopping a moving object, the force opposing the momentum must be equal to the force of the momentum, and if the object is to be caught, this momentum must be dissipated by reducing the resistance of the catching surface. Skill: Catching a tennis ball in a lacrosse stick and catching a badminton bird on a tennis racquet.

Principle III: An object set in forward motion through the air by an external force is acted upon by the force of the momentum and by gravital acceleration. Skill: Archery.

PROCEDURE

Three parallel experiments were devised, each of which was designed to investigate performance of one of the three skills. The Ss for all three experiments were undergraduate women students at the University of Southern California. There were thirty-six Ss in the Ball Rolling experiment, forty in the Catching experiment, and forty-two in the Archery experiment. (The Ss in the Archery experiment included some men whose scores were treated separately from those of the women.) For each of the experiments the Ss were divided into two groups, one of which spent the entire time learning and practicing the skill, and the other of which spent part of the time learning about the principle and the rest of the time learning and practicing the skill. Each experiment consisted of two tests. During the first test the Ss of the nonprinciple group learned the skill and practiced. The Ss of the principle group learned the principle, and the skill, and practiced. The total amount of time spent by both groups was the same. During the second test both groups practiced a similar or more complicated skill. Each group spent the same amount of time and no mention was made of the principle involved.

The Ball Rolling experiment. The Ball Rolling experiment was designed to illustrate the principle describing the rebound of a ball. The apparatus consisted of a modified pinball machine plunger, a squash ball, a felt-covered table surface four feet wide and six feet long, and a target made of colored construction paper. The overall size of the target and each of its scoring divisions was determined by recording the hits made by a group of comparable Ss who were not used in the experiment. These Ss rolled the ball so that it would rebound from one side of the table as close as possible to the center of the adjacent side which was marked with a square of white paper. The rest of the side was covered with brown wrapping paper, and spots on this paper to which the balls rolled were marked in red pencil. This scoring sheet provided the basis for establishing a six-standard deviation scale, and from this scale the scoring areas of the target were derived.

The *S*s were asked during the first test to roll the ball against one side of the table in such a manner that it would rebound to the target placed against the adjacent side. For the second test they were asked to roll the ball so that it would rebound from two adjacent sides to the target set at right angles on the third side.

The Catching experiment. The Catching experiment consisted of two tests each involving the skill of catching a moving object. The first test involved catching a tennis ball in a lacrosse stick. For the second test, they caught a badminton bird on a tennis racquet. The apparatus for this experiment, in addition to balls, birds, crosse, and racquet, included a homemade device for projecting the tennis ball and the badminton bird. This device proved to have high reliability.

The Archery experiment. The Archery experiment was planned to illustrate the principle of gravital acceleration and its action on arrow flight and the relation of line of flight to line of sight. The first test involved shooting from twenty yards. The second test included ends shot from thirty yards, from forty yards, and a Junior Columbia Round.

Analysis of data. In each experiment, the reliability of the scores was established by use of the split-half technique, the odd scores being correlated with the even scores. Use of the Spearman-Brown Prophecy Formula for predicting reliability of the whole test resulted in coefficients which ranged from .81 to .94 and thus it was felt that these scores were sufficiently reliable to permit further analysis and comparison.

All of the data were analyzed by means of analysis of variance using Edwards' technique for repeated measurements of the same subjects. This technique tests differences between methods, between trials, and between the interaction of trials and methods. In each experiment the initial ability of the two groups, as evidenced by preliminary trials, was tested and found not to differ significantly.

Findings

In the Ball Rolling experiment, no significant difference in the performance levels of the two groups was found on either test. A difference between trials significant at the 1 per cent level of confidence was found on both tests.

In the Catching experiment, no significant differences were found in performance levels, and a difference between trials significant at the 5 per cent level of confidence was found only on the first test.

In the Archery experiment no significant difference in performance levels was found. A difference significant at the 1 per cent level for men and at the 5 per cent level for girls was found on the second test at all distances except forty yards.

The following general findings were noted:

1. A significant amount of learning took place under both methods of instruction.

2. This learning was not only similar in amount but also in pattern. Exceptions occurred in the second test of the Catching experiment where no significant increase in scores occurred in either group, and in the Junior Columbia Round for men in the Archery experiment, where both groups increased in scoring ability, but the group which had been taught the principle was significantly better at twenty yards.

These findings are in general agreement with those of some published investigations and are opposed to those of some others. However, most of the reported experiments have dealt with various types of learning other than motor learning. The ability to use understood principles in performing a motor skill presents a complex problem since more than one type of learning is involved. As Ragsdale has pointed out, a learner may understand a principle when applied to inanimate objects, but he may not understand and be able to apply it to his own movements. In general, it seems that the findings of this study support Ragsdale's observation, at least in the initial stages of acquiring an unfamiliar motor skill.

Conclusions

Within the limitations of the three parallel experiments which constitute the present investigation, there is no evidence:

1. That instruction concerning mechanical principles utilized in the performance of a motor skill facilitates the initial learning of the skill to any greater extent than an equivalent amount of time spent in practicing the skill.

2. That such knowledge facilitates subsequent learning as evidenced in the performance of a similar or more complicated skill to which the same principle is applicable.

However, since it appears that some part of the learning period may be devoted to instruction concerning general principles without detriment to the motor learning of the students, it would seem desirable to include such instruction in order to provide this additional opportunity for acquiring some related knowledge about principles of mechanics and the application of forces.

32. Dimensions of Ego and Infantile Identification * [1]

WANDA C. BRONSON

IT HAS BECOME apparent in recent years that, as commonly used, the concept of identification refers to at least two types of processes, each serving a different function. One of these processes, described variously as "developmental identification," [2] "emotional identification," [3] "true identification," [4] or "ego identification," [5] refers essentially to the learning and integration into the self of the patterns of a loved and respected model. The second process—labeled respectively by the same writers as "defensive identification," "behavorial identification," "imitation," and "infantile

* From Wanda C. Bronson, "Dimensions of Ego and Infantile Identification," *Journal of Personality* (December, 1959), pp. 532–44. Reprinted by permission of the author and the *Journal of Personality*.

[1] This paper is based on a portion of a doctoral dissertation offered in partial fulfillment of the requirements for the Ph.D. degree at the University of California. The author wishes to thank Dr. Jean Walker Macfarlane, Director of the Guidance Study, for her help and suggestions throughout this study. While acknowledgments are due to all Guidance Study staff members for their aid in the execution of this investigation, the author wishes to express special thanks to Edith Katten and Doris Elliott for their work in making ratings and to Dr. Norman Livson for his invaluable assistance on methodological problems.

[2] W. S. Lair, "Psychoanalytic Theory of Identification" (Unpublished doctoral dissertation, Harvard University, 1949); O. H. Mowrer, *Learning Theory and Personality Dynamics* (New York: Ronald Press, 1950).

[3] S. M. Stoke, "An Inquiry into the Concept of Identification," *Journal of Genetic Psychology,* 76 (1950), 163–89.

[4] L. M. Lazowick, "On the Nature of Identification," *Journal of Abnormal and Social Psychology,* 51 (1955), 175–83.

[5] Edith Jacobson, "Contribution to the Metapsychology of Psychotic Identification," *Journal of the American Psychoanalytic Association,* 2 (1954), 239–62.

identification"—has as its defining characteristic a behavioral similarity between the self and the model which, however, is not mediated by any underlying emotional allegiance. The difference between the two types of identification has been summarized by Jacobson as follows: "The first [ego identifications] are realistic in so far as they result in lasting changes of the ego which justify the feeling of being at least partially like the love object. The latter [infantile identifications] are magic in nature; they represent a temporary—partial or total—blending of magic self and object images, founded on fantasies or even the temporary belief of being one with, or becoming the object, regardless of reality." [6] Implicit in the psychoanalytic formulation which Jacobson represents are both the antecedent circumstances and the resultant behaviors which should characterize and differentiate the two identification processes. This study represents an attempt to make some of these characteristics explicit and to establish empirically dimensions which could distinguish infantile from ego identifications. In order to investigate the validity of the theoretically derived predictions, a circumscribed area of behavior was selected for study. Since psychoanalytic theory holds that masculine identity is developed primarily through identifications with the father figure, it is upon the problem of father-son relationship and the boy's development of masculine behaviors and attitudes that this study focuses.

Following the psychoanalytic formulation, the process of identification is defined as an outgrowth of introjection whereby the self of the individual becomes transformed by developing behaviors and attitudes with the model as the referent. Whether infantile or ego identifications are established is determined by the degree of maturity the ego has achieved. In the early stages of psychic development the images of self and object are not yet clearly distinguished: perception of reality is not yet clearly defined. At this stage the aim of identification is *to be* the security-giving object in the belief that frustrating reality can be thus excluded. Hence, under the pressure of anxiety a young child will imitate certain adult behaviors—more often than not meaningless as far as the reality of the situation is concerned—in the magical belief that they make him identical with the powerful model he is imitating.

As the ego matures, firm boundaries between realistic perceptions of self and objects become established. The aim of identification neither need nor can any longer be the *being* of the security-giving object: a mature ego presupposes not only the ability to perceive realistically the differences between child and adult but also the capacity to tolerate frustration and

[6] *Ibid.,* p. 43.

bind tension. The aim is then *to be like* the security-giving object in the *future*. The child begins to emulate significant behaviors of the important adults in his environment and blends his self and object representations on the basis of a realistic likeness.

Thus, under ideal conditions of psychic development, ego identifications should prevail. Only identifications which have remained arrested since infancy or which, though established later, have occurred under conditions tending to regress or impede the development of the ego, should maintain their infantile character. One of the main factors determining whether ego development proceeds to mature levels or becomes fixated at an early stage resides in the nature of the relationship between the child and his parents. Hence, the first assumption made in this study is that the quality of parent-child relationship—specifically, the quality of the relationship between father and son—will relate to the kind of masculine identification established by the boy: a stressful relationship leading to the prevalence of infantile identifications, a nonstressful one to the occurrence of ego identifications.

It has been asserted that the formulation "I want *to be like* this model in the *future*" underlies the process of ego identification. Such a formulation implies that the basic acceptance of what the model represents is tempered by the perception of existing differences in both the situation and the make-up of the self and the model. In terms of the present research, it implies that ego identification with the father would lead the son to an essential acceptance of himself as a male but would not result in patterns of masculine behavior identical to those of the father. Similarity in behavior should exist only to the extent of generating a feeling of solidarity but not to the point of interfering with the boy's unique development. Rather, the postulated basic acceptance of masculinity would lead to the expectation that, regardless of the specific way in which the father's masculinity is expressed, the son's behavior, while characteristically masculine, would also allow for the inclusion of occasional nonmasculine behaviors without fear of creating conflict or activating repressed fears.

The process of infantile identification, defined as essentially immature or regressive after the period of infancy, arises mainly in the attempt to cope with anxiety. The defensive character of such identifications implies that the model, while of great emotional value, represents a threat to the ego: he is imitated as a defensive measure—either intra- or interpersonal—he cannot, however, be accepted as an ego-syntonic part of the self. Hence, when a boy's main self-perceptions result from such infantile identifications with a threatening father, his attitude about himself as a male cannot fail to acquire an anxiety-provoking character so that either conflict about or outright rejection of his own masculinity should prevail. Since internal conflict tends to be expressed overtly by the adoption of rigid and extreme behavior patterns, either hypermasculinity or nonmasculine behaviors should become characteristic of such a boy. Further, the magic desire *to be* the model which defines the process of infantile identification should find expression in a lack of independence between the son's and the father's masculine behavior: the main determinants of the boy's masculine attitudes should be those expressed by his father rather than the dictates of his own needs and preferences. Since, however, the need to be the model is accompanied by an inability to accept him as an ego-syntonic part of the self, such lack of independence need not take solely the form of imitation of paternal behavior. It can equally well be expressed by an attempt at an overt rejection of what the father stands for: the present conceptualization of infantile identification requires that the father be the determinant of the son's masculine behavior, irrespective of whether it be as an object for emulation or for rejection.

To summarize the assumptions of this study: a boy develops his masculine identity primarily through identifications with the father figure. Two kinds of identifications are possible: ego identifications which arise in the course of a supportive, acceptant relationship between parent and child, and infantile identifications which prevail when such relationship is marked by conflict. The following are predicted as being characteristic of boys whose masculine identity is based on ego identifications: (a) acceptance, on covert levels, of masculine attitudes and needs; (b) masculine behavior characterized by moderation; (c) a moderate degree of similarity between their own masculine behavior and that of their fathers. Boys whose masculine identity has been established primarily through infantile identifications should be characterized by: (a) rejection, on covert levels, of masculine attitudes and needs; (b) extreme masculine or extreme nonmasculine overt behavior; (c) extreme similarity or extreme dissimilarity between their own masculine behavior and that of their fathers.

Method

SAMPLE

The present study is concerned with a sample of forty-two boys and their fathers drawn from the families participating in the Guidance Study of the Institute of Human Development. Selection of Ss for the present research was based on the sole criterion of availability of data pertinent to the hypotheses under consideration. The purpose of the Guidance Study was the comprehensive investigation of physical, mental, and personality development in a group of children from birth through the 18th year. The sample was closely representative of the population of children born in 1928–29 in Berkeley, California, an urban community containing a large state university and located within a larger metropolitan area. A more detailed description of this original sample and of the methodology of data collection for the Guidance Study is presented elsewhere.[7]

The present investigation focuses on the period of preadolescence: more specifically, it deals with materials obtained when the Guidance Study boys were 9 through 13 years of age. This particular period was selected since some of the measures pertinent to the present study were available at only these ages. Furthermore, although the theoretical formulation of the processes of infantile and ego identification assumes that they originate early in the psychic development of the child, the testing of the hypotheses generated in this investigation demands that the organization of masculine attitudes and behaviors has achieved at least the minimal stability expected at preadolescence.

DESCRIPTION OF THE VARIABLES

Father-son relationship. A measure of the nature of the relationship existing between fathers and sons was obtained from the descriptive codings of behavior made by the Guidance Study staff on the basis of half-yearly interviews with the child, the mother, and any other sources of information available at the time (teacher, father, relative). The following two scales were used in constructing a father-son relationship score:

A. Undemonstrative-Demonstrative [8]

1. Extravagantly demonstrative relationship which in part seems compensatory to strain or insecurity.
2. Shows affection easily, freely and warmly—a direct, nonexploitative response fostering security in the child.
3. Normally responsive.
4. Very seldom expresses feelings of affection, embarrassed over occasional demonstrativeness. If kissing or petting occurs, it is a matter of forced routine and doesn't appear to be a spontaneous or pleasant reaction (for example, when going away or returning home, etc.).
5. Never demonstrative, whether due to long habits of reserve or due to the straining relationship existing.

[7] Jean W. Macfarlane, *Studies in Child Guidance. I. Methodology of Data Collection and Organization,* Monograph of the Society for Research in Child Development, Vol. 3, No. 6 (1938).

[8] Since this scale is curvilinear as far as underlying health of relationship is concerned, i.e., an extremely low rating has as negative an implication for a good relationship as an extremely high one, for the purposes of this study ratings numerically weighted as 1 were arbitrarily given a weight of 4.5.

B. Straining-Easy relationship
1. Exceptionally easy relationship, happy, affectionate, security-giving. Real support and satisfaction.
2. Supporting and satisfying relationship; parent and child enjoy each other, have fun together, regard each other as individuals.
3. Normal adjustment, occasional frictions but no continued or severe strains; real satisfactions. Reactive adjustment to occasional strains but normal recovery. Mild, chronic nagging which carries no load of intense feeling behind it.
4. More or less chronic tension but not as disruptive as (5); but such a relationship exists that neither parent nor child can let down barriers, remaining on the defensive and braced against sudden eventualities. Or occasional disruptive episodes as severe as (5), but occurring intermittently, not chronically. Have practically no moments of a really easy relationship.
5. Extremely disturbing relationship, whether shown in hostility, martyred service, or in swinging ambivalence. Chronic and acute strain in the relationship, which is never easy. Parent extravagantly concerned in the minutiae of regime or any minor problems that arise. Always makes the emotional most out of what should be regarded as minor training details. Constantly on the alert to pick out the children's faults or to think they are completely faultless. Practically no compensatory satisfactions in the relationship.

On each of the two scales the ratings assigned to each child between the ages of 9 and 13 were averaged. The correlation between the two sets of averaged ratings is .57 ($p = .01$). The index of stressfulness in the relationship between the father and the son was expressed as the sum of the average ratings of undemonstrativeness and of strain in relation obtained by a given father-son pair. (High scores indicate a stressful relation, low scores, a nonstressful one.)

Sons' overt masculine behavior. This variable was measured by a method developed by Honzik (1951); it is based on the difference in toy selection between boys and girls in a play situation. Toys whose usage differentiated significantly between boys and girls over three age periods—11, 12, and 13— were used by Honzik to develop a Masculinity-Femininity scale. Although derived from the traditionally "projective" play situation, the Honzik MF scale does not utilize the projective aspects of the situation. It is equivalent to observing children in play and selecting those behaviors which differentiate the sexes empirically. The use of blocks, vehicles, and persons in uniform results in a high masculinity score; the usage of persons in ordinary dress and the use of furniture results in a high femininity score.

The overt masculinity score used in this study is the average of the Honzik MF scores obtained by the boys in the three play situations. Although the scale was derived on the basis of differences between boys and girls, it has been used here to differentiate within the group of boys.

Sons' covert masculine behavior. This measure was abstracted from TAT protocols obtained from the *S*s were 9 through 12 years old. The TAT had been given to 38 of the 42 boys in the sample. Stories told to two pictures presented at each testing (3GF of the present set and M18 of the previous one) as well as to three free-choice pictures constituted the materials used. The TAT protocols were scored on the Aron modification of the Sanford-Murray scoring scheme (1949).

Three variables were selected as reflecting different aspects of a preadolescent boy's feelings about masculinity:

1. Independent Striving: striving for freedom from dominance, for self-mastery. Active aggressive attempts at independence.
2. Controlled Aggression: responses of anger to a disagreeable (frustrating or depressing) situation.
3. Dependence Frustration: dependency needs accompanied by implied or explicit nurturance deprivation.

The first two variables were selected on the assumption that fantasy expressions of independence and aggressiveness are in keeping with the expected socio-psychological development of masculine identity and represent, for a pre-adolescent boy, a realistic preparation for the adult male role. The third variable, dependence frustration, was included in the belief that within the framework of preadolescent culture frustration of dependency needs becomes an unavoidable concomitant to a boy's development of masculine behaviors and atttiudes. Expression of such frustration is seen as indicating a realistic acceptance of the masculine role. The *S*'s score on each of the three variables is expressed as the percentage of the given type of response based on the total number of responses given to all pictures over the three-year period. High scores represent acceptance of masculine attitudes; low scores are seen as reflecting denial of masculine identity.

Fathers' overt masculine behavior. An index of the fathers' masculinity was obtained from ratings made at the time of the present investigation. Two independent raters made a subjective judgment on a five-point scale as to how masculine a given father would have been considered by others in his environment.

Results

SONS' OVERT MASCULINITY

The prediction was made that infantile identifications, which occur when the father-son relationship is stressful, would lead to the boy's adoption of extreme masculine or extreme nonmasculine behaviors while ego identifications, established in a nonstressful relationship with the father, would result in masculine behavior characterized by neither of these extremes.

The results support the hypothesis that extreme masculine behaviors are characteristic of boys with a stressful relationship to the father while middle range behaviors are characteristic of boys whose father-son relationship is nonstressful.

SONS' COVERT MASCULINITY

Concerning the patterns of covert masculinity, the prediction was made that infantile identifications with a stressful father would lead to a rejection of masculine attitudes while ego identifications with a nonstressful father would result in an essential acceptance of masculine identity. Thus, boys with a nonstressful father-son relationship should obtain higher TAT masculinity scores than boys with a stressful relationship. . . .

To obtain a more reliable composite TAT score which would consider all three variables simultaneously, the total group of thirty-eight boys was ranked on each variable and each S's sum of ranks over the three variables was obtained. On this composite score the difference between the Nonstress and the Stress groups (again evaluated by means of the U test) is significant at the .003 level of probability, lending strong support to the prediction that the degree of stressfulness in the father-son relationship relates to the son's covert acceptance or rejection of masculine patterns.

RELATIONSHIP BETWEEN FATHERS' AND SONS' OVERT MASCULINITY

It has been argued that infantile identification with a stressful father leads the son to adopt the father's behavior as the main determinant of his own overt masculinity. Hence, he will either try to duplicate the paternal pattern or act in its exact opposition. Ego identification with a nonstressful father allows the boy a choice of behaviors suited to his own unique needs. While a certain degree of similarity in behavior would be expected, it should prevail only insofar as the father's patterns are independently suitable to the son's needs.

The hypothesis requires an evaluation of the similarity of behavior existing between the father-son pairs in the two groups. The prediction is that the Stress group will show a bimodal distribution of similarity scores, one mode occurring at the extreme of similarity, the other at the extreme of dissimilarity while the scores of the Nonstress group will be distributed between the two extremes.

To test the hypothesis, the two scales of overt masculinity—Honzik MF scores for sons and masculinity ratings for the fathers—were transformed into standard scores and the absolute difference between the scores of each father-son pair was obtained. Figure 1 shows the distribution of the difference scores in the two groups. The Moses test of extreme reactions indicates that the Stress group differs from the Nonstress group in showing more extreme scores at the .0008 level of probability.[9]

In comparing the two distributions presented in Figure 1, however, it becomes apparent that while the Stress group "rejectors" (i.e., boys with large difference scores) fall at a considerable distance from the Nonstress group mode, the Stress group "imitators" (whose difference scores are small) differ from it minimally. The question must be raised, therefore, as to whether the small difference scores found in the Stress group are indicative of the "imitation" predicted for that group or of the "similarity" expected in the Nonstress group. A tentative answer can be obtained by considering whether the masculinity scores of a father-son pair who show little difference fall at the extreme or in the middle range of the masculinity distribution. Similarity at the extremes, being theoretically less likely, would have greater probability of representing true imitation than similarity in the middle range. All of the "imitators" in the Stress group (as well as the Nonstress father-son pairs with small difference scores) have standard scores on the masculinity scale falling within half a standard deviation of the group mean. Thus, while the data give clear indication of "rejectors" among Stress group boys, the presence of "imitators" cannot be considered as established.

Since the relationship between fathers' and sons' overt masculinity does differ in the Nonstress and the Stress groups but apparently assumes only one form in the latter, rather than the predicted two, a correlation can be used to describe the data. A Pearsonian r was computed between the sons' Honzik MF scores and the fathers' overt masculinity ratings separately in the two groups. The correlations are $-.74$ ($p < .01$) in the Stress group and .37 in the Nonstress group, confirming the hypothesis that in a stressful father-son relationship the son's overt masculine behavior is

[9] The Moses test of extreme reaction is a nonparametric technique specifically designed to test the hypothesis that within a given group some Ss will show extreme behavior in one direction while others will act in the opposite direction. It will be noted that a hypothesis similar to that tested here was made concerning the overt masculinity of the boys in the Stress group. The Moses test was not used in that situation because of the presence of many between-group ties which make this technique inapplicable.

strongly affected by that of the father, though the prevailing pattern found is that of rejection rather than of both rejection and imitation.

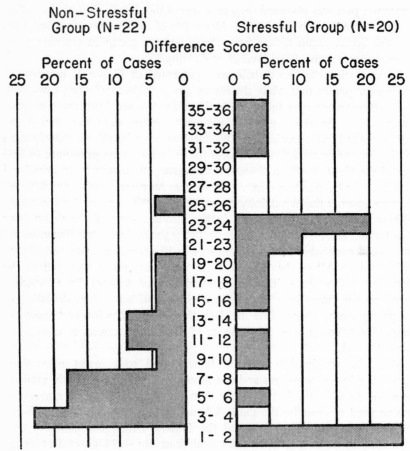

Figure 1. Distribution of overt masculinity difference scores between fathers and sons in the Stress group and in the Nonstress group. The difference scores represent the absolute difference in standard scores obtained by the sons on the Honzik MF scale and the fathers on the overt masculinity rating scale.

Discussion

The data demonstrate that the masculine behaviors of boys who have a stressful relationship with the father differ from those whose father-son relationship is nonstressful. It is of interest to note, however, that the interrelationships among these behaviors fail to differentiate between the two groups of boys. The results seem to imply, therefore, that further studies of the meaning and functions of masculinity in personality organization may find that the inclusion of some consideration of factors related to the development of masculine behaviors would prove fruitful.

The data have lent clear support to the predictions concerning both overt and covert masculine behaviors characteristic of boys who have established ego identifications with the father and of those for whom infantile identifications have presumably prevailed. In the area of the relationship between the fathers' and sons' masculine behaviors, however, the results need further clarification. While the lack of independence between fathers' and sons' masculine behaviors required by the definition of infantile identification is indeed characteristic of boys with a stressful father-son relationship, of the two theoretically possible patterns—rejection or imitation of paternal behavior—only the former has been found. Possibly wider sampling of the same boys' masculine behaviors—obtained under varied conditions of anxiety, internally or externally induced—would have allowed for the appearance of the second pattern. It is also possible that overt imitation or rejection of a stressful father varies as a function of age: had the Stress group boys' masculine behavior been compared to that of their fathers in early grade school rather than at preadolescence, it may be that a correlation similar in magnitude but in the opposite direction to that obtained in the present study would have been found. It is apparent that a more detailed investigation of this problem is required.

While the data support the hypotheses about the effect that stress in the father-son relationship has upon the son's development of masculine attitudes and behaviors, the conclusions about the differential characteristics of ego and infantile identifications must remain inferential. The conceptualization of the processes of identification has remained a theoretical construct in this investigation, mediating the formulation of hypotheses but never directly assessed. However, the empirical and theoretical consistency of the data lend strong support to the formulation offered and indicate that further research along the same theoretical lines could be productive in allowing further clarification of the concept of identification.

Summary

This investigation attempts to distinguish the effects of ego and infantile identification with the father upon the son's masculine behaviors and attitudes at preadolescence. Following psychoanalytic theory and process of ego identification is defined as a desire *to become like* the model in the *future;* that of infantile identification, as a magic need *to be* the security-giving object immediately in order not to have frustrating reality intrude.

The assumption is made that a stressful father-son relationship tends to interfere with the son's ego development and therefore results in the boy's establishing infantile identifications with the father. In a nonstressful father-son relationship it is assumed that ego identifications with the father will prevail.

On the basis of the psychoanalytic conceptualization of the two processes of identification, the following predictions were formulated as to the characteristic masculine behaviors derived from ego and infantile identifications. Ego identification with a nonstressful father should result in: (a) acceptance, on covert levels, of masculine attitudes and needs; (b) masculine overt behavior characterized by moderation; and (c) moderate similarity between the son's and father's masculine behavior. Infantile identification with a stressful father should lead to: (a) rejection of masculine attitudes and needs on covert levels, (b) extreme masculine or extreme nonmasculine overt behaviors, and (c) a high degree of similarity or of dissimilarity between the son's and father's masculine behavior.

The predictions were tested on a sample of forty-two preadolescent boys. All hypotheses were given support.

33. The Status of Adolescents in American Society: A Problem in Social Identity [*][1]

ROBERT D. HESS
AND IRENE GOLDBLATT

A DOLESCENTS OCCUPY an ambiguous position in American society. As a phase in personal and social development adolescence is a recognized period experienced by every American youth. As a status in the social struc-

[*] From Robert D. Hess and Irene Goldblatt, "The Status of Adolescents in American Society: A Problem in Social Identity," *Child Development,* 28 (December, 1957), 459–68. Reprinted by permission of the authors and the Society for Research in Child Development.

[1] Support from the Social Science Committee of the University of Chicago is gratefully acknowledged.

ture, however, it is loosely defined at both entry and exit transition points and offers a set of vague and often conflicting roles. The age behaviors expected of adolescents by adults are viewed by society with ambivalence and anxiety. With the possible exception of old age, no other phase of individual development is so clearly marked by negative connotations and lack of positive sanctions.

It is obviously one of the central objectives of socialization to bring preadult members to equal status in the adult society. However, the difficulty of achieving this transition is affected by the subordinate individual's perception of the relative position of his status group in the structure of the society and by the attitudes of adults and their willingness to permit expressions of autonomy on the part of subordinate members.

Although there has been little systematic research on the status of adolescents in American society, as viewed by adults or by adolescents themselves, it is generally assumed that the attitudes of the society toward its teen-age members are characteristically depreciatory and often hostile. Our preliminary interviews with adolescents revealed their awareness of a presumed inferior reputation among adults. Adolescents frequently expressed the belief that they are, as a group, subject to condemnation, criticism, and general devaluation by adults and that there exists among adults a stereotype of adolescents as sloppy, irresponsible, unreliable, inclined toward destructive and antisocial behavior. It was the objective of our research to explore the evaluation of adolescents by both teen-agers and parents and the relationship between opinions of parents and teen-agers within the same family.

Research Procedure

THE INSTRUMENT

To obtain evaluations of adolescent and adult reputations, a set of rating scales of twenty pairs of adjectives was constructed. These pairs were selected from comments offered by teen-agers and adults in interviews about the problems of parent–teen-ager interaction. The adjectives represent socially desirable aspects of character and personality, and define in part the standards toward which the middle-class child is directed by his elders and, to a lesser extent, the terms in which the adolescent evaluates himself. The members of each pair can be viewed as positive and negative ends of a specific behavior continuum. Each pair of adjectives was set up on a seven-point scale, 7 representing the highest, or most desirable, rating, and 1 the lowest (see Table 1).

TESTING PROCEDURE

Each subject was asked to use the scales in making ratings on (a) the "average teen-ager," (b) the "average adult," (c) "teen-agers" from the viewpoint of an adult, and (d) "adults" from the viewpoint of an adult. This resulted for each adolescent in a set of ratings on teen-agers and adults and his prediction of the manner in which teen-agers would be rated by adults.[2] Similarly, each parent was instructed to rate (a) the "average teen-ager," (b) the "average adult," (c) "teen-agers" from the viewpoint of a teen-ager, and (d) "adults" from the viewpoint of a teen-ager.

The testing procedure gave rise to the following sets of data:

A. Actual evaluation of own status group, or "self-rating"
    1. adolescents' rating of teen-agers
    2. parents' rating of adults
B. Evaluation of the other status group, or "actual reputation"
    1. adolescents' rating of adults
    2. parents' rating of teen-agers
C. Predictions of how the other status group would rate own status group, or "expected reputation"
    1. adolescents' predictions on how adults would rate teen-agers
    2. parents' predictions on how teen-agers would rate adults
D. Predictions of how members of the other status group would rate themselves, or "predicted self-rating"
    1. adolescents' predictions of how adults would rate adults
    2. parents' predictions of how teen-agers would rate teen-agers

SAMPLE

Ratings were collected in conjunction with an interview study of thirty-two families, a study concerned with exploring beliefs and attitudes about teen-agers as these affect parent-child relationships during the adolescent period. The sample was composed of thirty-two adolescents, sixteen boys and sixteen girls, and fifty-four parents, thirty mothers and twenty-four fathers. In each family, interviews and rating scales were administered to the mother and her teen-age child. The father was interviewed in slightly more than one half of the families. However, whenever possible, rating scales were obtained from fathers, even if they were not accessible for inter-

[2] The rating scales were administered twice over a three-week interval to a group of six adolescents. Ninety-two per cent of the scores shifted only one scale step or less from the first to the second administration of the scales.

viewing. All interviews were taken in the home and the rating instrument was administered in the course of the interview.

The families in the sample were upper-middle and middle-class in a metropolitan area. Twenty-three of the families were Protestant, one was Catholic, and seven were Jewish. There was one mixed marriage, Protestant and Jewish.

Average age of the boys was 15.9 years; the average of the girls, 15.5 years. The average high school grade of both boys and girls was 2.8. Two of the adolescent subjects attended private, nondenominational schools, one attended a parochial school, and the remaining twenty-nine were enrolled in a public high school.

FINDINGS
Perception of the Status Difference between the Two Groups

RATINGS OF THE TWO GROUPS ON "THE AVERAGE TEEN-AGER"

Both adolescents and parents rated teen-agers in a mildly favorable manner. Fifteen of the ratings by adolescents fell above the scale mean (4.0) and five below (Table 1). The mean rating that adolescents gave to teen-agers, on all items, was 4.38. Parents rated teen-agers above the scale mean on fourteen of the items and below on six (Table 2). Expected differences between the ratings of parents and those of adolescents did not emerge. Only three of the differences between adolescent and parent ratings were statistically significant at the .05 level of confidence (items 1, 7, 13). On one of these, the moral-immoral continuum, the parents gave teen-agers a significantly higher (more positive) rating than did the adolescents themselves.

RATINGS BY THE TWO GROUPS ON "THE AVERAGE ADULT"

Both adolescents and parents believe that adults are superior to the teen-ager on all but one (item 13) of the twenty characteristics. Not only did both groups rate the adult more favorably than they rated the teen-ager, but the adolescent subjects gave much higher mean ratings to adults than did the parents. The mean rating on all items by adolescent subjects was 5.60; that of the parents was 4.86. Adolescents rated adults higher than did the parents on each of the twenty items. Sixteen of these item differences were statistically significant. Only items 4, 8, 13, and 19 showed insignificant differences.

Table 1

MEAN ITEM RESPONSE BY ADOLESCENTS

Traits	Ratings of		Predictions of Adults' Ratings of	
	Teen-Agers	Adults	Teen-Agers	Adults
1. Neat–untidy	4.81	5.88	3.17	5.68
2. Patient–impatient	2.94	4.72	2.23	5.06
3. Cooperative–uncooperative	4.59	5.38	3.37	5.86
4. Serious–frivolous	4.50	5.56	2.70	5.41
5. Responsible–irresponsible	4.62	6.22	2.76	6.07
6. Courteous–rude	4.81	5.81	3.17	5.83
7. Mature–immature	4.62	6.06	2.87	6.00
8. Cautious–impulsive	2.69	5.44	2.10	5.28
9. Consistent–inconsistent	3.56	5.44	2.37	5.76
10. Grateful–ungrateful	4.81	5.72	3.00	5.83
11. Reliable–unreliable	5.19	5.97	3.40	5.93
12. Stable–unstable	4.35	5.47	2.90	5.93
13. Moral–immoral	5.16	5.53	3.80	5.79
14. Self-directed–easily influenced...	3.72	5.28	3.17	5.68
15. Respectful–disrespectful	4.78	5.75	3.37	5.79
16. Unspoiled–spoiled	3.97	5.03	2.67	5.72
17. Considerate–inconsiderate	4.44	5.62	3.07	5.83
18. Self-controlled–wild	4.59	5.88	2.80	6.11
19. Thoughtful–thoughtless	4.66	5.66	3.13	5.86
20. Loving–angry	4.81	5.69	3.60	5.72
Means	4.38	5.60	2.80	5.71

THE EXTENT OF PERCEIVED DIFFERENCES BETWEEN
TEEN-AGERS AND ADULTS

The difference between each group's rating of teen-agers and its rating of adults (Tables 1 and 2, col. 2 minus col. 1) can be considered an expression of the distance in status as it is differently perceived by the two groups. It has already been noted that teen-agers are rated in a mildly favorable manner by both groups, and that adults are believed to be superior to teen-agers. However, adolescents accentuate in their ratings the relative superiority of adults over teen-agers. In scale terms, the distance between adults and teen-agers is perceived by the adolescents to be almost twice as large as that seen by parents.

These differences apparently represent the different concerns of the two groups. Both groups share the opinion that teen-agers have a relatively long way to go before they reach the adult level of self-control. However, the adolescent subjects seem to feel that they are much less "responsible"

Table 2

MEAN ITEM RESPONSE BY PARENTS

Traits	Ratings of		Predictions of Teen-Agers' Ratings of	
	Teen-Agers	Adults	Teen-Agers	Adults
1. Neat–untidy	3.98	5.00	4.93	5.00
2. Patient–impatient	2.48	3.69	5.14	2.58
3. Cooperative–uncooperative	4.45	4.84	5.96	3.84
4. Serious–frivolous	4.80	5.20	5.62	5.82
5. Responsible–irresponsible	4.87	5.24	6.02	6.09
6. Courteous–rude	4.44	4.86	5.48	4.30
7. Mature–immature	3.98	5.02	5.60	5.36
8. Cautious–impulsive	2.72	4.78	4.11	5.18
9. Consistent–inconsistent	3.57	4.18	5.53	3.18
10. Grateful–ungrateful	4.59	4.82	5.60	3.66
11. Reliable–unreliable	4.98	5.10	5.91	4.93
12. Stable–unstable	4.45	4.76	5.64	4.98
13. Moral–immoral	5.98	5.46	5.87	5.51
14. Self-directed–easily influenced....	4.18	4.32	5.85	5.18
15. Respectful–disrespectful	4.50	5.22	5.56	4.70
16. Unspoiled–spoiled	3.70	4.31	5.54	4.22
17. Considerate–inconsiderate	4.22	4.78	5.66	3.77
18. Self-controlled–wild	4.62	5.34	5.32	5.16
19. Thoughtful-thoughtless	4.09	5.24	5.54	4.49
20. Loving–angry	4.83	5.14	5.32	4.57
Means	4.27	4.86	5.51	4.63

and less "self-directing" than adults, while the parents seem relatively unconcerned about these characteristics.

Expected Reputation

THE ATTEMPT TO PREDICT THE RATINGS OF THE OTHER GROUP

The adolescent's view of his status in the social system is a function of the reputation he anticipates from adults as well as his own view of his age group. It is significant, then, that the adolescents of our sample predict that teen-agers will be evaluated in a generally unfavorable manner by the adult group.

All of the ratings which the adolescent subjects anticipate will be given to teen-agers by adults fall below the scale mean (Table 1, col. 3). Adolescents expect that the lowest ratings will describe them as impulsive, impatient, inconsistent, spoiled, frivolous, irresponsible, and wild. In contrast to the unfavorable reputation adolescents believe the teen-ager has, the parents in the sample believe that their own status group has a mildly favorable reputation among teen-agers.

DISPARITY BETWEEN EXPECTED REPUTATION AND SELF-RATINGS

The difference between the adolescents' own rating of teen-agers and their predictions of the average adults' rating of teen-agers can be regarded as a measure of the extent to which teen-agers will feel underrated or depreciated. The data indicate that adolescents expect to be underrated on each of the items. On eighteen of the items (all except 8 and 14) the difference between self-ratings and expected ratings is statistically significant. (Table 1). By contrast, parents predict that teen-agers will significantly underrate adults on only six items (2, 3, 9, 10, 17, 19; Table 2, col. 2 minus col. 4).

The items on which the parents feel that adults will be underrated can be seen as relating to tension in interpersonal relationships. However, parents believe that qualities of maturity which are relatively independent of interpersonal relationships will either be accurately perceived by the teen-ager or even overrated. These ratings suggest that parents feel they will be seen as mature but unsympathetic or ill-intentioned in interpersonal affairs. They feel that they will be seen as more "uncooperative," "ungrateful," "impatient," and "thoughtless" than they really are.

Ratings Indicating Expected Perception of Status Differences

PREDICTIONS OF THE SELF-RATINGS OF THE OTHER GROUP

The disparities already mentioned are emphasized by the belief each group has about the ratings which they think members of the other group will give themselves. Two sets of predictions are involved: the adolescents' predictions of how adults will rate themselves, and the parents' predictions of the ratings teen-agers will give themselves (Table 1, col. 4; Table 2, col. 3). Both groups believe that members of the other status group will have very favorable opinions of themselves. Parents predict that teen-agers will rate themselves above the scale mean on all items. Adolescents believe that adults will rate themselves above the mean on all items. The difference between the two sets of predicted self-ratings is very small.

DISPARITY BETWEEN PREDICTED SELF-RATINGS AND OWN RATINGS

The parents' predictions of the teen-ager's favorable opinion of himself represents a belief that teen-agers will overestimate themselves on the traits in question, since the parents themselves give a generally lower rating to teen-agers. In contrast the adolescent expects that parents will see themselves in the same favorable light as he sees them. In effect, teen-agers are expressing confidence in the parents' judgment, even when the parents are evaluating themselves. By the same rationale, parents expect that teen-agers will be conceited, or, at best, unrealistic when judging themselves. This expectation is expressed by significant differences on seventeen of the twenty items (exceptions are 13, 18, and 20; Table 2, col. 1 minus col. 3). There is only one reversal: parents say that teen-agers will underrate themselves on "moral" behavior.

Comparison of the rank ordering of items revealed that parents believe teen-agers will emphasize items having to do with readiness for emancipation from parental control. Such items as "responsible," "mature," "consistent," "stable," and "self-directed" rank higher in the predicted self-estimate than in the parents' ratings of adolescents. In complementary fashion, parents expect that adolescents will rate themselves *relatively* low on "self-controlled," "cautious," "neat," and "patient." This indicates that these parents believe that teen-agers think of themselves as ready to lead their own lives—but along rather hedonistic lines.

THE EXPECTED PERCEPTION OF STATUS DIFFERENCE

A measure of predicted status differential between the two groups may be obtained by a comparison between the view the adolescent has of his reputation with adults and the view he thinks adults will have of themselves. This is the teen-ager's prediction of his relative status in the eyes of the adults.

Considered in these terms, the data show that *adolescents think adults will see themselves as vastly superior to the average teen-ager* (Table 1, cols. 3 and 4). Further, adolescents predict that adults' opinion of the status difference will be much greater than adolescents believe it is (Table 1, cols. 1 and 2 compared with cols. 3 and 4).[3]

---

[3] An indication of the characteristic adolescent attitude toward their status in adult minds is seen in the relatively small range that appeared in the predicted ratings. In rating their own group and the adult group, the range between highest and lowest mean rating is three scale steps; in the predicted ratings this range is two scale steps. The adolescents, then, are predicting that the average adult will show little discrimination in evaluating teen-agers and will underrate them even on traits on which the teen-agers feel most competent and acceptable. The parents do not make a comparable assumption in the ratings they expect from teen-agers.

Parental Attitudes and the Ratings by Own Teen-Agers

It was assumed that the ratings given by adolescents to the "average adult" and to the "average teen-ager" were not unaffected by the attitudes encountered in their own family experience. The ratings of parent-child pairs were examined, therefore, to determine the degree of association between mother-child pairs and between father-child pairs.

The resulting coefficients offer evidence that the mother's attitudes are more influential than the father's in determining the attitudes of the teen-agers. The mother's perception of status difference (Table 2, col. 2 minus col. 1) correlates significantly with the extent to which her teen-agers feel underrated (Table 1, col. 1 minus col. 3). That is, the larger the status difference that the mother perceives between adults and teen-agers, the lower the reputation that her adolescent predicts teen-agers have. This relationship is highly significant and holds for both mother-daughter and mother-son pairs (Table 3). However, the father's perception of the adult–teen-ager status difference appears to have virtually no effect upon the attitudes of his children as indicated by insignificant coefficients with both sons and daughters.[4]

Table 3

COEFFICIENTS OF ASSOCIATION (TAU) BETWEEN THE RATINGS OF PARENTS
AND OWN CHILDREN

	Children Expectation of Underevaluation (Table 1, col. 1 − col. 3)			
	Girls	*N*	*Boys*	*N*
Parents: Perception of Status Difference (Table 2, col. 4 − col. 1)				
Mother	.55*	(13)	.59*	(13)
Father	.13	(11)	.00	(10)

* $p < .01$.

Although adolescents appear to be sensitive to their mothers' evaluations, their own ratings of teen-agers are relatively independent of parental

[4] The attitudes of fathers about teen-agers are significantly related to those of the mothers in the sample (Pearson $r = .44$) but their perception of the status difference between the two groups is not (Pearson $r = .18$).

opinion. The comparison between the ratings of parents and their children on the "average teen-ager" reveals no significant association between adolescents and either father or mother (Pearson r's of .062 and .067 respectively). The teen-ager's feeling about his group's reputation among adults thus appears to be determined in part by the attitudes of his own mother toward teen-agers as a group but he resists her influence in making his evaluation of his own group.

Summary of Findings

1. Adolescents and parents agree in expressing mildly favorable opinions of teen-agers.

2. The adolescents tend to idealize adults, i.e., they have much higher opinions of adults than do the parents.

3. Adolescents see a relatively greater status difference between teen-agers and adults than do the parents.

4. Adolescents believe that the average adult has a generalized tendency to depreciate teen-agers. They feel that teen-agers have a uniformly low reputation among adults.

5. Parents anticipate that teen-agers will have a selective tendency to undervalue adults. They predict that adults will get lower ratings than they merit on items which refer to interpersonal relationships, but that they will be accurately evaluated on noninterpersonal maturity items.

6. Adolescents believe that the adults will evaluate themselves relatively accurately.

7. Parents believe that teen-agers have unrealistically high opinions of themselves.

8. Both adolescents and parents believe that the status difference between teen-agers and adults will be distorted to approximately the same extent by the other group.

9. The attitude of the adolescent about the relative status of teen-agers is significantly associated with the opinions of his mother about the adult–teen-age status difference. However, the opinion of his parents is not related statistically to his evaluation of the "average teen-ager."

10. The attitude of the father as expressed in the rating scales is not significantly associated with ratings of his own teen-age children.

Three trends in the data stand out as particularly relevant to parent-adolescent relationships and to theories of adolescent socialization: (a) the agreement between the two groups in their evaluation of teen-agers; (b) the perceptual distortions of both groups in predicting the response of the other group; and (c) the immense status difference between the groups that teen-agers believe exists in the minds of adults. The prominence of these trends emphasizes the difficulties faced by the adolescent in his effort to effect a transition from adolescence to adult roles and behavior.

From their own point of view, the adolescents credit themselves with an acceptable degree of achievement which, nevertheless, places their group in a subordinate position with respect to adults. This willingness to admit a differentiation between their own status and that of adults is in agreement with the views of adults, though it tends to exaggerate the status distance.

The assumption by parents that teen-agers have unrealistically high opinions of themselves is not corroborated by the data obtained from adolescents themselves. This parental belief may, to some extent, simply represent a response to, and acceptance at face value of, a protective bravado and air of competency which the adolescent assumes to protect himself, both from arousing parental anxieties and from his own feelings of inadequacy.

Our data suggest that one of the central problems in parent–teen-ager relations lies not so much in disparity between their respective evaluations of adolescents as in the fact that each group mistrusts or misunderstands the opinions of the other. Parents and adolescents thus interpret teen-age behavior and problems in different, and often contradictory, terms. For the adolescent, teen-age problems are expressed in terms of *ego functions*— autonomy, self-control, and judgment based upon exploratory experience with adult roles. For the parent, the problems of teen-agers are primarily concerned with control of *id impulses* for which, they believe, parental supervision and control are essential. Both views, of course, are to a degree realistic and the families of our study which displayed a minimum of parent-child conflict were those in which parents and teen-agers were willing to recognize the importance of both viewpoints.

The status difference between the groups probably serves a positive socializing function for the teen-ager. A moderate overestimation of the attributes of adults offers a lever for the parent in the socializing process and provides motivation for the adolescent towards increased autonomy and maturity. However, the extreme idealization of the adult by the adolescent, when it is joined with a belief that personal achievements he has made are not recognized by adults, may retard ego development and encourage behaviors which defeat the objectives of both parents and adolescents themselves.

34. Why Antisocial Children? *

J. RESNICK

IT IS GENERALLY accepted that most behavior problems are caused by difficulties arising in the environment. The circumstances under which a child must live contribute significantly to his adjustment. It appears that most individuals meet problems by attempting to adjust in a manner which will minimize the stress and strain and maintain for the individual a measure of self-confidence and satisfaction. Various questions present themselves in working with children whose behavior may be classified as antisocial in nature. Does the child who feels unloved differ markedly in his behavior from other children who feel that they belong? What may be the characteristics of his behavior? Does the child initially seek antisocial ways of gaining recognition?

Investigations indicate that usually the antisocial child is no more responsible for his antisocial behavior than if he had contracted a communicable disease. His inadequate social behavior is a way of releasing nervous tension arising from his unfortunate situation. Opportunities should be provided in a socially acceptable way for the child's personality needs with a chance given to perform in the areas of his interests, to contribute to the class discussion, and to be helpful to the teacher in the classroom. The relationship between the child and the teacher should be congenial with the educator realizing that the child's behavior is but the result of his environmental experiences.

Paul, a child of 10 years, was referred to the writer because his academic performance was below his ability to achieve. He also showed a strong dislike for anyone in authority and at times would strike children on slight provocation. An investigation disclosed that there were two boys in the family, Paul and a younger brother, David, aged 7 years. It appeared that David resembled his father and as a result received considerable attention and gifts. The older boy was made to feel unwanted. Oddly enough, he resembled his mother who readily admitted the father's favoritism. Paul's antisocial behavior was understandable in the light of his home situation. Considerable improvement resulted when the father became aware of the consequences of his behavior toward Paul. Improvement in this child's conduct soon became apparent with changed methods in the home.

* From J. Resnick, "Why Antisocial Children?" *The Educational Forum* (November, 1956), pp. 101–4. Reprinted by permission.

Does the child who feels unloved differ markedly in his behavior from other children who feel that they belong? What may be the characteristics of his behavior? It should be recognized that a child has a continued need for praise and attention. His self-confidence and feeling of security are affected by inadequately met personality needs. Nervous tension usually arises from this condition and manifests itself in various ways, such as restlessness, difficulty in attending to the task at hand, and being easily affected by adverse criticism. An unloved child may respond in the opposite way by readily yielding to authority and becoming quite obedient in order to gain approbation. The child who is loved and wanted does not feel the need to engage in rebellious and aggressive behavior to gain a feeling of security as does the unloved child.

Charles, a twelve-year-old child in the sixth grade, lived in a home in which his father and stepmother were quite unconcerned about his need for approval and attention. There were indications of rejection which took the form of frequent whippings as a result of the boy's conduct. The stepmother especially was quite uninhibited in this direction as shown by the child's remark to the writer, "I'm getting tired of my stepmother pounding on me. She makes prints on my back with a belt. As soon as I get old enough, I'm going to get a job and leave home." The child indicated that although he did not welcome physical pain he chose this means of being noticed which was more desirable than feeling isolated. His behavior in the classroom was of a similar nature. Where he could not obtain sufficient recognition, then antisocial behavior resulting in chastisement was chosen and, in a way, partially provided for his personality needs although the process resulted in an uncomfortable experience. To the child to feel alone and not needed is more punishing than a physical display of violence which in part recognizes his presence and for a brief moment permits him to be the figure around whom all activity revolves.

Does the child initially seek antisocial ways of gaining recognition? It may be assumed with confidence that a child's original bid for acceptance is shown in ways which are approved by his elders. By displaying love and affection, and having it returned, the young child often gains the security that he seeks. Showing what he has achieved may be used as a means of obtaining attention and praise. In the classroom, there will be found children who feel they must show superior achievement or they will turn to less acceptable ways of being noticed. Often the seed of this form of maladjustment is planted in the home. Attention and affection are bound up with academic performance. These children need to be made to feel that they are needed and wanted regardless of academic achievement. The child who feels that no one cares for him or loves him may cease to seek attention and affection. Usually when this condition prevails, it is after the child has made repeated attempts for acceptance and his efforts were rewarded by punitive measures. The child transfers his antagonistic feeling to his associates and derives satisfaction when he has aroused in others a strong dislike for himself. These children are unhappy and often uncooperative. They need many indications of love and sympathetic understanding. While their behavior is frequently of the nature that elicits punishment, they should be regarded as emotional cripples and remedial measures will usually include praise, attention, love and affection, success experiences, and a moderate amount of firmness in supervision.

Ralph, a nine-year-old boy, was a serious behavior problem in the classroom. Since the child's residence was above a funeral parlor which the parents operated, he was constantly reminded to be quiet. He was not permitted to have playmates in the home and was discouraged from visiting in the homes of other children, because as the mother stated, "The children in this neighborhood aren't very nice and my boy might pick up a lot of bad habits." Since the father was not home much of the time, it became the mother's function to remain within listening distance of the telephone, so that she rarely visited other families. The parents seemed too occupied with the business to notice Ralph's need for belongingness. The child's small successes in school were mentioned by the boy as a bid for attention. However, these attempts met with failure as they were brushed aside and went unnoticed. One time the child brought a dead cat into the funeral chapel and left it there. This action brought much censure upon the child and considerable attention. A dead rabbit, then a dead bird appeared mysteriously in the funeral chapel. Talks to Ralph were replaced by corporal punishment. The classroom also felt the result of this rejection of the boy since he was seen to push or hit children and at times speak out without respect for authority. Other children showed annoyance at his antics, but Ralph seemed to relish their discomfort.

A conference with the parents gradually revealed the child's strong need for love and affection and attention. Unaware of the damage caused by neglecting the child, the parents were eager to try corrective measures which included separating the residence from the place of business, inviting friendly children of Ralph's age group into the home, spending time each day sharing in the child's activities, regular obvious showing of affection and love, and striving to develop in the child a feeling of belongingness. The prognosis for this child's future is encouraging.

In every child's life there is a necessity for emotional security which is influenced by the people with whom he associates. Indications of inadequate adjustment are revealed by the antisocial child in his difficulty to adjust to his own age group as evidenced by frequent fights as well as name calling. These children show by their behavior that they are usually easily thwarted by obstacles in the environment and that they have a strong need for recognition. Many manifest a tendency to attract attention to themselves; however, others are reserved and withdrawn. Children who defy authority without regard to the consequences are indicating that they have not reached the point at which they feel they have been conquered by the adverse circumstances which surround them. This fighting back is a form of boldness which is usually regarded as healthier, although more disrupting, than the retiring response to a difficulty made by the reserved maladjusted child who is also a serious problem. As the child matures he adopts ways of meeting his problems which become habituated and characterize him.

The child whose behavior may be classified as being of a problem nature is commonly found in the classroom. An awareness that the pupil's conduct stems from influences over which he has had little or no control tends to give to the educator a more tolerant attitude toward the child's behavior. The teacher is inclined to view the misbehavior as a problem whose solution can be found if all of the facts are considered. Such an approach will usually reduce the possibility of nervous tension arising in the teacher as well as result in improved performance in the child. A progressive educator strives to teach the child and also improve his personality, the ultimate product being a worthy member of our American culture.

35. The New Importance at Adolescence of Social Relationships *

RAYMOND G. KUHLEN

A MARKED waxing of social interest at adolescence is apparent to any careful observer of this age group. Frequent and interminable telephone conversations, new concern about dress and appearance, demands

* From Raymond G. Kuhlen, *The Psychology of Adolescent Development,* pp. 289–91. Copyright 1952 by Harper and Bros., New York, and reprinted with their permission.

for the family car, disagreements with parents regarding frequency of "nights out"—these are the evidences so obvious in almost any household which includes adolescents. The aggregate of social pressures stemming from the adolescent's own age mates (sometimes referred to as the "peer culture") becomes increasingly influential, and often represents a major source of family conflict because of its rivalry with parental control. Several reasons may be advanced for these trends. In the first place, the adolescent has grown physically to the point where he is capable of more independent action, and consequently he spends more time outside of the home in near-adult types of social activities with his age mates. He naturally will wish to conform to the expectations of his associates.

In the second place, there is increasingly clear delineation of the cultural role which is appropriate for one sex or the other, and an increasing awareness of the opposite sex. "Status" at adolescence implies not only status with respect to being masculine or feminine, but also status in the eyes of the opposite sex. This is a new status, and heterosexual experiences are for the adolescent *new* experiences. As such they have that special flavor and significance not found in experiences which have become commonplace, and their very newness generates an enthusiasm absent in the socially more sophisticated. This *new* orientation accentuates interest in a wide variety of social activities and is one of the distinguishng features of adolescent, as contrasted with preadolescent, social life. In the third place, frustration may accentuate concern with social problems. All is not smooth sailing for the adolescent, and where sailing is rough attention is demanded. Habits (social and recreational skills) are often not adequate to the social situations in which he finds himself. Thus, early social interest may occupy the center of the stage because social "know-how" has not yet been acquired. Nor is it possible to satisfy that new organic need, sex, which has become more prominent, without running into strenuous social disapprovals. The continued social interest during the teens and early twenties may be largely a product of delayed marriage and the pressures of a biological need which can be partially satisfied through social activities. It is repeatedly evident that the social interests of adolescents are essentially *sex-social interests*.

Social consciousness is high at adolescence, in contrast to adult life, in part because school life forces adolescents into close contact with individuals from all sorts of backgrounds. In school, individuals with certain deficits rub shoulders with those who possess greater poise, better clothes, better family standing, and a more active social life—and as a result, attention is focused on such differences. And sheer presence in a school culture which abounds with cliques and more formal social groups intensifies the *need to belong* to these groups. An adolescent who sees others in social groups and hears others talking about their group activities is necessarily going to be concerned about attaining membership, and will be conscious of his lack of status if he fails of acceptance. In a nonschool environment he might be quite unaware of the existence of such groups. And once school days are over, he is no longer constantly reminded of the status he does not possess. Such reasons as "lack of proper clothing," given for dropping out of school, suggest that "quitting school" may, for some, be essentially an escape from an intolerable social situation.

It is often difficult for adults long out of school and far removed from the heterogeneous social experiences of the school situation to appreciate the extent to which particular problems in the social sphere can disturb adolescents. Adults have gained social experience, found their respective social niches, and become burdened with work or family responsibilities; often they tend to brush aside the problems of adolescents as of no consequence or to consider them only as topics for amusing comment. Usually it is extremely revealing to an adult to reread his own adolescent diary— if he wrote one and retained it—or to reread love letters which he wrote in his teens or early twenties. For those who did not keep diaries, or who burned their letters, an excerpt from an adolescent "note" is presented here to convey something of the flavor and concern generated by adolescent social experiences. Written by a boy to a girl (and picked up by the writer of this book on a city bus), the note reveals the embarrassment caused by running out of money (an adult might easily laugh off a situation like this), and hints at such teen-age problems as "going steady" and the social inconvenience of being employed on the conventional high school "date night."

I dont' know what you mean by the way I feel about things but that doesn't matter now. I brought the $.50 to school with me today to pay you back for helping me out the other night. I certainly appreciate it, and I'll bet you think I'm a rat but the way I feel now I wouldn't have the nerve to go out with you again since I borrowed that money from you. That is the reason I acted the way I did Friday nite and all this week because I have been ashamed of myself. It was silly of us to think of going steady anyway because I'm working on Friday nites and when I get out there isn't time to do anything. I hope you won't stay too mad at me because I feel the same about you that I have always felt but there isn't anything that can be done. . . . Well I guess that is all to say except that I bet I don't stand very high in your estimation but I don't deserve to, so I'm sorry for everything that's happened.

There is little question that this youngster felt badly about this incident, but doubtless ten years from its occurrence he will be relating it as an amusing incident—so soon do adults get out of tune with their own younger years.

36. *Language as a Social Skill* *

MAX L. HUTT

AND ROBERT G. GIBBY

IT IS DURING the third year of the child's life that language really emerges into its own as a social skill. We pointed out in the last chapter that by the end of the second year language has developed into the *expressive stage* and that the child has learned to use language actively for narrative purposes. In the next year there is a rapid flowering of expressive language, and language skills become significant in greatly extending the child's world. Through increased locomotion he is able to get about more actively and independently and to explore the physical world around him. Through language he can do much more. He learns to understand the world of immediate experience in many different ways, for once he has words to conceptualize these experiences he can begin to differentiate them more effectively, to compare them, and even to summarize and to integrate them. He can also extend his world beyond that of immediate experience. He uses words to remember past events and to anticipate future ones. He learns to differentiate experiences from within (*emotions*) from experiences from without (*external stimuli*) in ever more reliable fashion. He uses language to express his needs and to control the behavior of others. In these and other ways, language becomes a means of extending himself in time and space, and of enriching himself through direct participation with cultural experiences that can be shared with others. As a consequence he learns to use judgment more effectively; he can be reasoned with; he can explain himself. Although he may not always use these abilities constructively, he

* From Max L. Hutt and Robert G. Gibby, *The Child: Development and Adjustment,* pp. 155-59. Copyright 1959 by Allyn and Bacon, Inc., Boston, and reprinted with their permission.

does learn to use them in more effective relationships with people, animals, and "things."

Some inkling may be gained of the rapid increase in language skills during the third year from the following selected facts. The size of the child's evaluative vocabulary probably increases, on the average, from about 300 words to about 900 words, a gain of 300 per cent. During the same period his ability to name objects on pictures increases from about one or two to about seven words. By the end of this period he has learned to understand and use at least three different prepositions; he can readily distinguish *in* from *under* and *above* from *below*. The typical length of his sentences increases from about one word, or occasionally two words, to about four words. By 3 years of age, although he is still confused about many words that sound the same but mean different things (such as "whole" and "hole"), he has at least learned that sometimes the same sound may be used for different words and the things that they represent. He is less "concrete-minded" in his use of words toward the end of this period, so that "brother" does not only mean his own brother but may represent the brothers of other children. His sentences contain more verbs and some adjectives and adverbs. He tends to use a greater variety of words within a given space of time. These are but a few of the many research findings that have been gathered over the past three decades.

It has become increasingly clear that language development is greatly influenced, once a sufficient degree of maturation has been attained, by a variety of environmental factors. One of these is the richness and variety of experiences the child has—experiences with things and with feelings. This principle has been recognized, and the importance of rich, personal experience as a foundation for good language development stressed, by the National Council of Teachers of English. Such factors as the kind of language used by the parents and siblings and the readiness of parents to answer questions and encourage the use of better verbal expressions by the youngster play important roles. There is convincing evidence that the age of associates influences the rate and quality of language development. An important argument for placement of children in a good nursery-school environment is based on the finding that when children regularly have children of their own age to play and learn with, their intelligence in general, and their linguistic skills in particular, develop more adequately.

Perhaps more important than the concrete types and varieties of physical, linguistic, and social experiences that the child has is the type of emotional climate in which he is developing. We have noted that children placed in orphanages tend to have retarded general development. Their language development is especially retarded. Goldfarb's studies show that when children who have spent the first three years in an institution are compared with children who have spent their first three years in a foster home, the former group not only showed language development that was inferior to the latter group, but also, in terms of absolute standards, it was greatly retarded in *all aspects* of language skills that were measured. Even three to five years later, as measured on retests at that time, this retardation had not been overcome. The specific agent or agents producing this effect were presumed to be the nonstimulating, impersonal relationships of the institutional environment. Clinical studies by various psychiatrists have shown that when the child does not have a good emotional relationship with a mother, *autistic language* (noncommunicative, self-centered language) may develop as part of a total *schizoid* personality adjustment—a severely disturbed state of withdrawal. Allen has demonstrated that specific types of emotional climates may be responsible for delayed speech and other types of speech and language defects. He characterizes these types of disturbed children as: (a) the "protest child" who has learned to reject food and has emotionally tense relationships with a parent, (b) the "overprotected child," (c) the child who has had insufficient emotional support, and (d) the "throttled child" who has not been permitted to express his feelings and impulses in appropriate manner.

The general point of these and other studies and reports is that language development is closely tied in with effective personality development. This conclusion is of particular concern to us in connection with the language development of the toddler for two very special reasons. The first is that during this period of rapid speech and language development the average child customarily experiences some difficulties. Many children first begin to stutter at this time—as part of their trial-and-error learning of speech and as part of the turbulence of emotional experiences during this time. Hence, it is doubly important to be patient when the child speaks and to maintain a relaxed and accepting emotional atmosphere. Most stutterers of this period overcome this difficulty spontaneously under normal circumstances. The second reason is related to the fact that the child is going through a period of socialization (the *anal* period) in which he has to learn gradually to accept certain prohibitions and frustrations. Language development may be unnecessarily disturbed by too severe regimes of toilet-training, by too much emphasis upon regularity and cleanliness, by too great dominance in getting the child to conform rapidly, and the like. The child needs "room" for the expression of some of his "negativism" and he needs time and acceptance (understanding that this is a difficult time for him, too) in order to express both his impulses and his frustrations in language, as well as in other forms of behavior. Lewis, in discussing the increase in the child's use of questions during this period ("Why, Mommy?"), puts his finger on the crux of the matter: ". . . the growth [of the child in language] is determined by social cooperation working upon two powerful tendencies . . . to use language as play and as a means of satisfying vital needs."

One of the most fascinating aspects in the development of language of children, closely related to the general issue we have been discussing, is the gradual transition from *egocentric* to *socialized* speech. The man most responsible for focusing attention on this problem, and who has contributed a great deal by way of both theory and research, is Jean Piaget. He classified children's speech into these two main categories on the basis of the function that language plays in the life of the child. By egocentric speech he meant speech that the child uses essentially for his own purposes without any concern about whom he is speaking to and without any intent to communicate to anyone. This type of speech was further subdivided into three subcategories: (a) *monologue* (in which the child speaks without interaction with anyone), (b) *collective monologue* (in which two or more children each engage in separate but more or less simultaneous monologues), (c) and *echolalia* (in which the child repeats the sounds made by others, without any necessary comprehension or any objective to communicate to others). Socialized speech was divided into five subcategories: (a) *adapted information* (in which some exchange in thoughts is taking place between the child and another person), (b) *criticism,* (c) *commands, requests,* and *threats,* (d) *questions,* and (e) *answers.* Piaget found that children's speech is predominantly egocentric between 3 and 5 years of age. During the next two years, socialized speech develops rapidly, and by 7 years of age socialized speech becomes clearly and consistently more prominent. These findings are based on the child's spontaneous speech. It has been noted that the function of speech changes considerably depending upon the situation in which it is observed or measured.

On the whole these conclusions of Piaget's have been confirmed by other workers, although some have taken sharp issue with the kinds of interpretations of the data that Piaget made. One of those who has disagreed with Piaget's interpretations is Vigotsky, who stated that although a child's speech at 3 years of age is clearly egocentric in structure (and in this his data are in agreement with Piaget's), the function of such speech is nevertheless social in character. His essential point was that closer examination of the relations between speech functions and the social situations in which they were employed indicated that, even at 3 years of age, an important function of the child's speech was communication—or socialized speech. He did find that by 7 years of age both the structure and function of speech were clearly socialized, but he believed that previous to this there was a maturation in the structure of children's language forms so that socialized speech was clearly shown to be present in greater degree than Piaget had indicated. The major characteristics in this type of maturation to which Vigotsky called attention was that of *inner speech*. As the child grows older, inner speech increases. By this is meant speech designed to test things out for oneself, to think things through, and the like. Hence, Vigotsky believed that, in fact, socialized speech really decreases as the child matures and as he is able to use the more mature form of inner speech. To demonstrate these interpretations, he designed a series of studies in which children's speech was examined under various conditions of *reduced* social stimulation and interaction, so that speech during free play was contrasted with speech in such situations as those involving a complete stranger, those with a deaf-mute child, and the like. In such situations egocentric speech, and not socialized speech, *decreased*. It seems to the writers that Vigotsky's results are really consistent with those of Piaget, but that attention has been called to two important distinctions: that function and structure of language are two different attributes, and hence have to be defined and interpreted more carefully than Piaget defined them; and that although children's speech at the earlier level (say 3 years) is more egocentric in form than it is in later life, it clearly has important social functions in the behavior of the child.

This last point can be restated in another manner, as we have already done a few paragraphs back: the characteristics of the speech of children are greatly influenced by their social situations. Many studies have been conducted to test this conclusion and there is essential agreement that this is, indeed, the case. This fact, as we may now characterize it, also points up the importance in studies of language development of children of specifying rigorously the precise conditions under which the observations or measures of language are being made. In turn, this fact indicates the highly cautious interpretation one must make of language norms in terms of the conditions under which the norms were obtained.

There is one additional observation about the development of language in the third year to which we should like to call attention. Linguistic skill and intelligence are highly correlated with each other, providing environmental and social conditions are kept constant, the correlation coefficient usually being in the range of .85 to .95. This helps to explain why most widely used intelligence tests for children, particularly those from 2 years of age and up, are so heavily based on language items. As a matter of fact many children's language or vocabulary tests are sufficiently valid to be used as measures of intelligence, providing the conditions noted above are observed. For example, one of the fairly widely used vocabulary tests for children, which is also usable as an intelligence test, is that devised by Van Alstyne. The test consists of a series of cards on each of which there are four pictures of objects or situations. The child is asked orally to point out which of the four on each card is the appropriate answer to a question about that card, like "Show me the pen," or "Show me the boy who is running." The test takes only about fifteen minutes to administer and gives a reliable estimate of the child's evaluative vocabulary and therefore of his intelligence—providing the child's background is similar to that of the children upon whom the test was standardized and providing the conditions of testing are adequate. Another vocabulary test, and one that has had more extensive research done in devising it as well as in evaluating the significance of the findings, is the Williams and McFarland revision of a test originally published by M. E. Smith in 1926. This test, known as the *Smith-Williams Vocabulary Test,* based upon samplings of words from Thorndike's word list for children, is available in two alternate forms, and involves both a test for *recall* of word meanings and the *recognition* of word meanings. This test has turned out to be one of the very useful research instruments for estimating the size of children's vocabulary at different ages and for inquiring into the types of conditions that facilitate vocabulary development.

37. *Some Social Issues in Education* *

E. GEORGE PAYNE

THE ISSUES in educational philosophy and practice are so numerous and varied that the mere *selection* of specific ones, for emphasis, advertises one's point of view. Where there are so many possibilities from which to choose, it has seemed wise to be plain about the criteria that have guided the choosing. Two considerations have led the writer to the specific issues

* From E. George Payne, "Some Social Issues in Education," *The Educational Forum* (November, 1952), pp. 47–55. Reprinted by permission.

presented in this article. The first is the matter of timeliness. It has not been a matter of deciding which issues are the most important, but rather, a matter of identifying those issues to which one must give some precedence of attention. It is possible, no doubt, to identify issues so basic that they are always timely, but there are crises in education, as in all other fields, which change the specific pressures and needs to which one has to address himself. The principle of "putting first things first" does not always yield the same order of business every day. The second consideration has been the matter of lip service and practice. On many issues, the educational world *appears* to approach some unanimity of opinion when the "ideal" is talked about. Somewhere between the lip service to an ideal and translation of it into practice, however, there often develops an hiatus that paralyzes and confuses. Where these gaps are widest, a need for the resolution of the issue presses us most keenly.

Three social issues among the many that remain when these criteria are applied are the following: (1) the issue of "indoctrinating" for democracy; (2) the issue of individual self-reliance versus social aid and cooperation; and (3) the issue of national versus international orientation in our schools.

The basic point of view in education is concerned primarily with democratic social control as contrasted with autocratic or totalitarian control in communistic or fascist societies. If a country posits freedom as basic to its life—freedom of the press, of religion, of speech, of assembly, and the newer proposals of freedom from fear and the like—then education in its widest and most fundamental sense is the *sine qua non* of social control. The control of the individual in society and the control of society itself becomes essentially self-control, and such control depends upon the ideas, ideals, and attitudes of the individual and the society in which he functions. In contrast with the controls that are imposed by an individual or a group of individuals, in a democracy such as ours seeks to be, the controls must be built into the life and personality of children and youth so effectively that there is no need for the imposition of practices from the outside or from above, such as is essential in autocratic societies. As a matter of fact the very life of democracy depends upon the extent and effectiveness to which these controls are established in the individual through the educational process.

Obviously, these controls and essential practices are developed in the family, in the neighborhood or community, and in the schools through the formal and informal agencies operating there. The main and fundamental part of the educational process is the incorporation of the social heritage, and the cultural patterns of the community and nation and these are drilled into the life and personalities of children and youth mainly by the family and community pressures. The school, moreover, operates to supplement the family and the community in its task, but the school has a much larger task in equipping childhood and youth for effective and creative action in a developing and experimental community and nation—the essence of the democratic life. It is out of the efforts of the educational personnel to construct a program of instruction under the democratic ideal that the social issues of education arise.

The Issue of Indoctrinating for Democracy

This age old issue was recently raised again by John T. Flynn, in an article addressed to parents and citizens, in the *Reader's Digest* for October 1951 entitled: "Who Controls Your Child's Mind?" He presented the amazing view that Professors George Counts and Harold Rugg of Teachers College, Columbia University, control the minds of American youth and these professors by their writings and teachings are making communists and socialists of childhood and youth in the schools of America. The distinguished professors must feel highly honored to be accorded such a predominant influence in American education and life, and I am sure they would if the accusation were not so naive and impossible! It is not the purpose to enter into a discussion of the relative merits of Flynn versus Counts and Rugg, but rather to discuss two opposing points of view, operative in our society as an issue in education. Therefore, we will not deal with the views of these persons except as they represent two divergent political and educational points of view.

A large segment of the American public, of which Mr. Flynn is typical, regard the American concept of free enterprise in its nearly unadulterated form and as it has developed in the Colonial and early American period of our history as the ultimate in human relations in so far as our industrial and economic welfare are concerned. This segment of thinkers and writers would allow no fundamental changes in the social order, although they favor minor changes and improvements. They would accept some regulation and government control over industry and welfare; they would accept the principle of organized labor and collective bargaining, and they would on the whole accept a modified social security program, old age pensions, unemployment insurance, and such ameliorative provisions as have developed and become a part of our laws and practices in recent history, but beyond this they would not go.

This segment of the thinking and writing public, moreover, insists that education should propagandize for the *status quo,* that education should go all out for the capitalistic system as it has operated in the past with limited modifications suggested above, and that any instructors who vary from this pattern of thinking are un-American, socialistic or communistic and in general unworthy to lead the American youth, and therefore unfit to teach in our schools. Moreover, this group of the population would exclude from the schools all literature that raises any questions about the permanency or adequacy of the institutions as they have developed in the past. This group, furthermore, ignores completely the fact that the world, including America, has undergone fundamental changes in the past, that we have passed from autocratic control to an experimental democratic society, that we have passed from a feudalistic order to a capitalistic society, that we have passed through an industrial and political revolution all to the advantage of human society and welfare, and civilization. This group in a word assumes that fundamental progress henceforth must take place within the framework of the present order, and that any deviation from this concept makes the individual unfit for citizenship. Moreover, the educator who deviates becomes disloyal, unpatriotic and unworthy. This group seems to believe and hold that change, even fundamental changes in the past, is acceptable but that henceforth the whole effort of education and all the formal and informal agencies thereof must be geared to the maintenance of the *status quo.*

In contrast with the views of this reactionary or conservative group we have another segment of the population, the liberal or progressive, which takes a totally different view. It holds that we cannot determine for all time the trends or the changes that should take place in the social order, that in this changing world nothing is static, and therefore, in order to equip the youth for the responsibilities of citizenship they must understand the changes that have taken place in the past and that similar changes may take place in the future. They insist that this is a very complex world and that, to be a good citizen, one must be intelligent, one must understand the social forces in operation in the world, and one must keep an open mind in economics, in religion, and in all problems of social relations. They insist that it is not the business of the educator to propagandize for any social order, but to educate the individual for a role in our democracy. The child must learn to understand change and be prepared by his emotional attitudes to accept it when necessary. This liberal group is characterized by the reactionary group as socialistic, communistic, and atheistic because they dare to believe in change. No such characterization is pertinent.

The essential point of the liberal group in politics and education, and we would of course exclude from this group all the extremists, let us say the communists of the Soviet type and all fascists of the Hitlerite type, is that social science should become more functional and less passive, should encourage emphasis on duty rather than self-satisfaction, should excite the crusading spirit for reform and improvement rather than produce another generation of mere antiquarians. This liberal group of educators and citizens would wish to have the youth who will live in and manage the future learn to regard social change as normal and to regard it with an attitude of satisfaction if the change is in the interest of social welfare, and to allow this change to lead in any direction that will produce human satisfaction and contribute to individual and social personality.

This point of view, moreover, stems from a recognition that the world is vastly different from what it has been and that the Emersonian and Thoreauian ideal of self-sufficiency, which are still taught, just do not fully meet the requirements of the modern complex world. The day of a free man in a free society, unaffected by the actions of others departed without the help of any professors of economics or education. The liberals in education would have us notice that the original concept of *"a free man in a free society"* is not operative today as in the past and to recognize that the basic values in individualism are preservable only if there is far greater emphasis upon cooperativeness. The egoism of the individualist who assumes that what he did in one context, anyone can do in any context, is most unlovely and unrealistic. This concept of "what was good enough for me is good enough for my children and other people's children" is amazingly universal. It is operating at this very moment in my own community where the elders insist that the one-room school built fifty years ago satisfies the demands of modern education because they survived it. But what a survival!

The liberals in education, such as Rugg and Counts, do not condemn the past as a past, but condemn it as a rigid guide for the future. They insist that the words, "socialism," "race equality," "collectivism," "planned economy," and the like should not stop the thinking of the teacher and citizen, and that both must be permitted to discuss such terms in public meetings and teach their significance to our youth who will have to face them and deal with them tomorrow. It was a tremendous, though perhaps unconscious, recognition on the part of the American public of these changes when in 1936 the Congress recognized and passed the social security legislation. Here is a dramatic evidence that the Congress recognized that the day had passed, when the majority of the people, even the decent well-meaning people, could be counted upon to play a middle-class role and emerge at the age of 65 with the ability to support themselves from the yield of their savings. Is this socialistic? It is even supported by the conservatives, and even most of the reactionary would agree that it cannot be undone.

Therefore, what the liberal in education wants, and this is true also of our liberal citizenship, is realism in our teaching of children. They don't want history to be a matter of trembling over the sacredness of the past or the personal characters of great men. They want Washington, Jefferson, Lincoln, and Teddy Roosevelt to be presented with reality as they were, great men with human faults and idiosyncrasies, and they believe that youth will better serve our country if they understand them as such. They don't want economics to be a matter of geometry, misunderstood to be God-given for all times, places and circumstances. They are fully aware that as in all education, jarring someone loose from anchors is hard and dangerous, even when the anchors are proved prisons, but it must be done. Some teachers and more students are cast adrift without finding new moorings, but this is inevitable in education.

The great majority of the public-school teachers of America represent the liberal point of view as outlined here. They plead for realism, for good will, for critical thinking, for sense of duty, for crusading for improvement. They are neither more nor less socialistic, collectivistic, or unpatriotic than the times are. None of this attitude on the part of the liberals is subversive. In contradistinction to the conservative the liberals in education do not believe in indoctrination, they believe in realistically educating for the change that has come and the change that is inevitable for the future.

The Issue of Self-reliance versus Social Aid and Cooperation

This issue is clear-cut and is a conflict between those who would extend relief to the underprivileged, and they are many in virtually all communities, and those who would extend relief but would do so only with the assurance that the aid would result in the improved status of those receiving aid and ultimately the ability to survive without public support, and survive amply. This second group would insist that the acceptance of relief would exact from the recipient effort in full measure in self-support. The aid would be accompanied by, not only instruction in its use, but instruction that would aid the recipient in independent living.

The problem of the relief of the distressed who have become submerged by the complexities of the modern world and are thus on the borderline of starvation, because of their inability, unaided, to satisfy their minimum necessities of modern life; that is, the minimum requirements of food, clothing, and shelter, has become a major problem of modern society. The problem has arisen and developed to its present proportions almost wholly within the twentieth century. This is not meant to imply that poverty is a modern phenomenon, but relief, both public and private, in its present organized form is essentially of twentieth century origin and provides one of the most vital of our social and educational issues.

When I was a youth on the farm near the end of the nineteenth century, relief was purely a community matter and necessary help was accorded by neighbors who assumed responsibility for those in distress. Not even the churches of the community as organizations extended aid, for that would have appeared as charity and no one would accept charity; starve, yes! Charity, no! It was in this situation in 1895 that an epidemic of typhoid fever struck our community. Our family was socially and economically well situated, but when this epidemic hit us and all the labor personnel of our large family became ill we would have met disaster without help, for the crops were ready for harvesting and no one to work. I remember well looking out of the sickroom window and witnessing a thrilling spectacle, the neighbors, dozens of them with teams, wagons, and tools entering the fields, and when we recovered from our illnesses the crops were harvested and in the barns and we were safe for the ensuing year.

This was a typical action, but no one did this as a matter of charity. It would not have been offered or accepted as such. It was an act carried out by neighbors with the definite knowledge that each one would be secure in mind and know that in a like circumstance his needs would be met with no questions asked and no *quid pro quo* exacted. These were the days of the simple neighborhood life when there were few telephones, no radio, no automobiles and relatively few of those things that have since become necessities. In those days, moreover, there were very few if any charity organizations and there was little public relief in the cities and none in the country. Today in contrast we spend between thirteen and fourteen billion dollars annually for public and private relief, mostly public. It has become one of the major jobs of modern society to administer to the underprivileged and the cost is many times greater than that of all the cost of the entire educational program, both public and private. Moreover, this relief cost does not include the cost of the social security, old age pensions, unemployment relief and such other public functions. This enormous expenditure is for relief and welfare. We have no wish to question its extent or importance.

These are the bald facts of relief, but they involve a social and educational issue of first importance and divergent philosophies basic to the administration of the relief program and the part that education should play in it. There are two widely different points of view with reference to the treatment of the underprivileged. Roughly they are the following: First, there are those, generally the relief professionals, who hold that every person is entitled to the minimum essentials of food, shelter, and clothing, and a certain minimum of education and cultural necessities. They insist that the welfare of the body politic is best served when these minimum essentials are provided. Furthermore, they insist that these essentials should be provided in the form of money income to be spent at the discretion of the recipient with as little restriction as possible. They insist that only in this way can we maintain in the recipient of relief a feeling of independence and self-respect essential to democracy. They admit that the money provided will in many cases be unwisely spent. They know from wide experience that families will procure from the income provided nonessentials, will suffer from the want of necessities, but they believe that only in this way can the recipients of relief funds learn wisdom in the use of the income they receive. They do not object to education *per se* in the use of the relief funds but insist that the imposition of an instructional program with the relief program would restrict freedom of action essential to the citizens of a democracy.

Second, the opposing group accepts the point of view of the first as to the necessity of providing minimum essentials, but they insist that the provision of relief without education in the use of relief will lead to disaster. It will create within our body politic a group who expect a living without effort on their part. They insist that this has already happened, and that we have already, by the method of administering relief, undermined to a degree those elements of character that have made America great: that is, the rendering of a *quid pro quo,* in so far as possible, for what one receives. They believe that the policy in the administration of relief has created a group who expect something for nothing as their right and that this policy is partly responsible for the increase in crime in our society. This group believes that we must about-face in the administration of relief if we are to avoid disaster, and that education must play a vital role in the change that must take place.

What then does this mean for education and the educator? We are in an era in which we have come to assume that the whole difficulty in the world arises from the inequality of income and differences in economic status. We speak and think of economic status as the one and only condition essential to world peace and happiness. We in America, both as private relief organizations and as government, pour out lavishly of our means in the expectation that this will bring about satisfaction and solve the world's problems. We have developed welfare programs in states and communities in which we provide individuals and families, without adequate incomes, with the funds essential for complete living without any attempt to equip those receiving aid with the experience and education necessary for its effective use for insuring the welfare of the recipients and the best interest of the commonweal. Here the educator faces one of his most dramatic and vital problems.

We have no wish here to minimize the importance of adequate income to meet the needs of the families of the nation. What we wish to underscore is that income does not guarantee welfare. We can point to many nations like the new State of Israel and to individuals without number whose income is scanty and yet who rear their families and meet their obligations of citizenship effectively. Welfare in the individual depends upon the use made of his income and its use depends upon the education and intelligence he has acquired. Moreover, the welfare of the community depends upon the extent to which it has been educated to place welfare at the top of the desired objectives and to use all its resources to insure the welfare of the people. Such an achievement is the primary function of education.

The Issue of National versus International Orientation in Our Schools

The twentieth century has presented the unusual phenomenon of one world tied together by immediacy of communication and swift and effective transportation. It is no longer possible to preserve the isolation that has characterized the developing cultures in the millions of years of recorded and unrecorded historical evolution. The world has become a neighborhood in which even the ignorant, the illiterate, and the impoverished not only are aware of the rest of the world, but are familiar with the conditions of welfare and civilized living. Not even the "Iron Curtain" can contain the

CROW: Readings in Child and Adolescent Psychology-10-12-27 TR   69

happenings of the people in the remotest area and the conditions of living there. We can no longer expect the submerged and underprivileged of the earth, and they are countless, to accept meekly the imposed feudalistic controls and the accompanying poverty that have prevailed in all recorded history. The underprivileged masses of the world are in revolt.

These social changes brought about by the advance of material civilization have created an international crisis with its cold war and actual conflicts which may break into a third world war at any time. The slowness of cultural changes and the slowness of education in its action and effects have left the world confused and statesmen unprepared to deal with the problems resulting from the world changes and development. The political, educational, and social leadership is confused and uncertain.

38. On the Meaning of Intelligence * [1]

GEORGE D. STODDARD

I

It is well known that Binet developed his scale for the measurement of intelligence in response to a demand for the early discovery of children likely to fail in school. Improvement of the tests over the years was a somewhat desultory process. Theory was kept to a minimum, the tests being constructed around the simple principle that a large number of graded small tasks, each involving the higher thought processes, would approach a concept of *general mental ability*. It was clear that the items could be arranged in ascending clusters, conforming crudely to chronological age. Children readily accepted them as goals.

There has been no change in the underlying concepts of the most widely used American revisions of the Binet-Simon scales, unless the utilization of Stern's intelligence quotient could be so regarded. Certainly this quotient has done much to bring mental testing before the scientific world and the public in general. Its ease of computation and its ready application in school or clinic have indeed lulled many a worker into the feeling that now we have something mathematical and fixed, something comparable to the measures and pointer readings of our friends in the physical sciences.

In reality the IQ concept is not simple. Let us take a quick look at the numerator, or mental age, as determined, let us say, by the 1937 Stanford

* From George D. Stoddard, "On the Meaning of Intelligence," *Psychological Review,* 48 (1941), 250–60. Reprinted by permission of the author and the American Psychological Association.

[1] Presented at the meeting of the American Psychological Association, Pennsylvania State College, September 4, 1940.

Revision. Since at this point no controversial issues are involved, time can be saved by a simple enumeration of the considerations given weight in the selection of the test items:

1. Increase in percentage passing with increase in chronological age
2. A correlation of the per cent passing an item with mental ages from the 1916 revision, or with a composite total score
3. Ease of administration and scoring
4. Appeal to the child
5. Brevity
6. Lack of sex imbalance

All these variously employed and pragmatically weighted criteria were taken in conjunction with the tacit understanding that, for a sampling of American-born white children, each test and the composite should be related to pupil achievement in standard subject matter. They do not, however, throw much light on the meaning of intelligence, for we come out with the old tests familiar to Binet or to the Army workers: opposites, comprehension, analogies, vocabulary, similarities and differences, completions, absurdities, memorizing, etc. In any such omnibus, the "ability to do abstract reasoning," like Spearman's "g," is carried more like a spare tire than a paying passenger! What the primary mental abilities involved are, I do not know, but one could expect to find Thurstone's perceptual, verbal, and memory factors. Such patterns, as they are determined, will depend to some extent upon the chronological and mental age of the subjects.

Under the conditions cited above, it was possible, for a small sampling of children, to make the mean mental age equal to the mean chronological age. This would yield average IQ's of 100, for the best range of the testing (the elementary-school years), but would not guarantee a constant IQ for any child. Rather, for children somewhat removed from the mean mental ability, differences in variability up through the years have always led to marked variations in IQ. These unequal distances away from the mean for the same IQ at different age levels, together with the fact that the scales are not standardized on adults, even though applied to them, lead to obvious complications.

Certainly a mental age of 15 is no more meaningful for an average thirty-year-old than a mental age of 30 for an average fifteen-year-old. If it is helpful to say that a six-year-old is bright, knowing full well that his mental maturity is at a low level, then we can make the analogous statement about a sixty-year-old. We do not say, "the child is bright *for a six-year-old*," since that is redundant. Neither should we say that a man is bright (or dull) for 60. That, too, is redundant. Either he is bright or he is not, his age being utilized as a reference point for entering the tabulation of scores. For those still older, to be bright is to postpone senility.

Analysis of the curves of mental growth is legitimate, but it should not depend primarily on IQ's. However, successively determined IQ's, based on valid and standardized materials, could furnish a plat of a person's changing, or unchanging, intellectual status in respect to his chronological peers.

It is to be noted that in no sense does the validity of an IQ depend upon its fixity. Only if a child maintains his relative status should the IQ remain constant; to find it constant otherwise would be a mark of insensitivity and hence invalidity in the test.

II

To go into practical aspects of mental testing, however, is not my purpose. The question is, what *is* the nature of mental ability, of intelligence, as revealed by measurement? Unfortunately no answer can be given that will satisfy persons interested in child and adult development, for the subtests are not revealing. On the other hand, if you want to measure memory, reading comprehension, reasoning ability, vocabulary and general information, good procedures are available. Almost any combination of reliable measurements of these functions, accompanied by clinical observations, will give fair predictions of academic success, and of general ability to solve problems.

It has become painfully clear that without the aid of the clinic, the use of IQ's by teachers, parents, physicians or judges leads to unhappy results. The same conditions that lead to poor schoolwork may yield low IQ's; in fact, there is thus far no higher validity for mental testing than its tendency to parallel school achievement. Under cultural conditions that make schoolwork dominant from ages 6 to 18, and highly important at younger and older ages, this is to be expected. For the child, the safe, prudent, approved life involves, above all, a steady familiarity with the three R's and their up-to-date companions.

In brief, the meaning of intelligence, as it emerges from all child testing Binet in type, is *scholastic aptitude*.

To say this is not to deny the existence of a tremendous span of intelligence from idiocy to genius. There are persons so organically defective that one could not think of a free competition in which they could succeed; and others so strong as to prosper under many, but not all, social conditions. But our present tests are poorly adapted for exploring intelligence over this great range.

III

If one were, in all candor, to undertake the measurement of intelligence, it would seem helpful to define the term and then to set up the necessary operations and test procedures. Confusion has resulted from the long failure to proceed in this manner. Even errors or defects in the definition would not be as bad as what we now have, for a worker could always say, with some truth, that *if* you define intelligence in such and such a way, then here is a test of that function which meets certain criteria of reliability and validity.

For example, we could define intelligence as the ability to do good work in school. It could be estimated solely from measured achievement. As I have indicated above, this is really not a farfetched definition, testing being what it is. But, one objects, a child might get ill or neurotic or bored, thus failing. No matter; that is provided for in the definition. He ought to be better, or know better, or do better—if he is to be judged *intelligent*.

We shall never arrive at any clarity if we allow *causes* for variation to be confused with the concept under consideration. Thus *running ability* can be well measured under standard conditions. Among those with low running ability quotients would be found the lame, the fat, the ill, the decrepit, the untrained, the uninterested. But we must stick to our measurement guns—there is no point in estimating how they could have run, shorn of these disabilities. That may be the coach's job, but the tester is the timer. Similarly, it would be a theoretical and practical advance, if mental abilities could be analyzed and combined in conformance to some clear ideas of what we are trying to do.

There have been some mild attempts to do this in behalf of Spearman's principle of the eduction of relations, and the recent work of Wechsler on the Bellevue Intelligence Tests moves in this direction. The second stage of the factorial analysis of numerous mental tests illustrates the principle, difficult as it may be in actual practice. Having identified certain abilities designated primary, which may turn out to be structure-like organizations of mental processes and are at least somewhat independent clusters of abilities, Thurstone has taken the next step, namely the construction of test materials designed to measure these abilities. Whether or not it leads immediately to the improvement of scholastic predictions, at least it is promising as a potential revelation of mental organization. If you know what you are looking for, you will find it in unexpected places.

IV

Accordingly let us pay some attention to definition. During the past few years I have brought together what impress me as the principal attributes of a functional concept of intelligence. Most of the separate portions are not original, but current in psychology from Binet to Thorndike. The composite is new, at least in the sense that nobody else is likely to lay claim to it! It is based not on factors, components or special abilities, but on qualities. Each attribute springs from the whole functioning organism, but the main focus is intellectual.

Intelligence is the ability to undertake activities that are characterized by (1) difficulty, (2) complexity, (3) abstractness, (4) economy, (5) adaptiveness to a goal, (6) social value, and (7) the emergence of originals, and to maintain such activities under conditions that demand a concentration of energy and a resistance to emotional forces.[2]

As Thurstone says of a primary ability, a concept of intelligence is futile unless it reduces and simplifies. At first glance, this formulation may appear to be as big as a bus off the main highway. What do these terms mean? Let us take them up, with just a phrase for each:

1. *Difficulty* is a function of the percentage passing. Throughout any series of mental measurements, it must increase with chronological age, so long as we postulate mental growth.

2. *Complexity* refers to the breadth or area: not only how difficult the task, but how many kinds of tasks may be successfully undertaken. Attributes (1) and (2) are related in the sense that high accomplishment is pyramidal in structure.

3. *Abstractness* is a means of connecting mental ability to symbolic relationships. It eliminates, as such, physical and motor acts.

4. *Economy* is another name for speed—the accomplishment of the most mental tasks in the least time. It calls for early good choices, for faster insights.

5. *Adaptiveness to a goal.*—It is not enough to perform speedily difficult and complex tasks. There must be a goal, a purpose as against aimlessness, and plasticity as against rigidity.

6. *Social value* as an attribute is useful in keeping intelligent actions

[2] For an earlier form of this definition see Stoddard and Wellman, *Child Psychology* (New York: The Macmillan Co., 1934), p. 176.

within the normal range of human behavior. Thus insanity is not, from this standpoint, something that the human mind may endure without loss of intelligence.

7. *The emergence of originals* is included because of its special place at the upper end of any valid distribution of intelligence. It is characteristic of genius. While related to high ratings in the six preceding qualities, it is not an inevitable outcome of such ratings.

No longer are IQ's of 140 or above regarded as of "genius" level. The tendency is to place the lower limit much higher, perhaps at 170. But this will not suffice either, for the good reason that Binet testing offers little opportunity to show what new solutions or original patterns a child can produce. Binet tests, by definition, are restricted to the simple, the piecemeal, the common, the overlearned.

The next step is to place children and adults along a continuum in which a low composite score in these attributes means low intelligence, and similarly up to the appearance and development of original ideas. Until recently it has appeared quite satisfying to rest at this point, with the thought that a new intelligence scale could follow these lines. With certain improvements, learning, vocabulary, comprehension, and contractual tests could act as a vehicle carrying most of the indicated measurement load.

But now I must insert two conditions, without which it is difficult to explain why so many "intellectual" persons can be so habitually unintelligent. (These persons would do well on mental tests saturated with the demands listed above, with the probable exception of numbers (6) and (7).) The two conditions are a concentration of energy and a resistance to intrusive emotional blockings or distortions.

The first condition postulates a selecting, rejecting, recombining process moving in the direction of larger goals; sheer accumulation of information is the antithesis of intelligent activity. Intelligence, feeding upon an amorphous mass or an endless aggregation of facts, bogs down. It begins to look strangely like the "standard" school curriculum which, by overwhelming the pupil, teaches him to accept a half knowledge about a thousand things as superior to a full and clear understanding of certain basic principles in human knowledge and behavior. It enshrines half-learned, soon-forgotten details while neglecting the few dozen basic principles in the physical, biological, and social sciences that could forever inform and delight the inquiring mind. It is keen on *knowledge about,* and cool toward insight and participation.

Out of school, the failure to grasp the real significance of *intelligent* behavior leads to a wallowing in "mental stunts," to crossword puzzles, to question-and-answer superficiality. If such activities are carried to extremes, that is to say, beyond their preserves in harmless pastime, the whole effect is to make a wastebasket of the human mind. It is not in facts *per se,* nor in the first person, place or chronology that comes to mind, but in their relationship to generalized principles and to goals in human development and behavior, that order appears out of chaos.

In a world that, in and out of school, has developed contact and communication to a marvelous degree, this attribute of intelligence appears crucial. It is a guard against mental indigestion. Perhaps it can be framed as a question: How many hours has this person devoted to the systematic exploration of any mental question? That such expenditure of energy is related to motivation, is obvious. It is likely that the distinctive analyses of Kurt Lewin could throw light on its relative strengths among different individuals.

This leads directly to the second condition in the concept of intelligence. While emotional forces are excellent in their time and place, they play havoc with the decisions and actions that depend upon logic and objective relationships. If 2 and 2 are ever to be anything but 4, the change must be brought about by mathematicians, not by ignorant or neurotic persons who dislike 4.

The whole question of propaganda is a case in point. The propagandist conceals his intentions and tries to establish relationships in your mind that could not be tolerated if all were known. This is done presumably for your welfare. In other words, you are not to be trusted with full knowledge, for you might come to the wrong (that is, right) conclusions. It is a mental legerdemain employing labels, symbols, dark rooms, and favored gestures and traditions. It is not necessarily a result of international crises, although these may widen the scope and increase the deadliness. Since emotion-arousing labels are a stock-in-trade, any person, other things equal, is intelligent to the extent that he remains undeceived.

V

Thus far I have said little about the form of testing required to carry the load of such mental attributes.

Since we know that adults are more differentiated than children, expressing their intelligence in greater penetration into certain areas (such as those represented in vocations and professions), it is desirable to permit adults to make choices. In addition to a general rating, in what areas are they most at home mentally? A follow-up testing in those areas would permit greater variability among those previously judged equal and would raise the test ceiling.

So far as emotional resistance is concerned, the methods developed in recent studies of propaganda are promising. They could be adapted to a scale of intelligence. The energy concentration attribute is a hard one to measure, but approaches have been made at the preschool level. How long and how effectively will a child work at an accepted task (that is, a contract)? The test, perhaps clinical in type, must permit, at the extremes, immediate capitulation and potent long-continued application.

The new tests must give scope to originality, style, and invention. They must provide for more than a verbal medium of intellectual expression; for example, they should employ space relations, performance tasks, and scientific symbols. Theoretically the arts should be included, but this will involve practical difficulties, for it is the insights and relationships we are after and not technical skill alone. More learning-on-the-spot would appear helpful, with less emphasis on what the child already has learned and is now bringing to the test situation. Thus in a foreign language aptitude test, the ability to learn Esperanto during the testing period is an index of subsequent achievement in French and German.

The main point, however, should be emphasized. We should have *some* theory of intelligence and then construct tests consistently with it.

VI

Space does not permit me to say more than a word about nature-and-nurture in relation to intelligence. Among psychologists there is an acceptance of the idea of developmental limits along hereditary, constitutional and environmental lines. This point of view I have developed in the *Thirty-Ninth Yearbook* of the National Society for the Study of Education and it need not be repeated here. Present controversies are on matters of degree. When viewed in the light of test inadequacies, they are inconsequential. With everybody using blunderbusses, the game is difficult to bag!

To change one's IQ is to change one's mental status in a group. It does happen. Similarly subgroups may go up or down relatively to a larger group extant, or previously formed and measured. This too happens. One effect of improving the tests will be to increase this sensitivity to changes in the child's behavior, changes related to happenings in the organism. But as psychology is not and never can be physiology, so intelligence cannot be reduced to brain cells, brain waves, or genes. The higher processes involve the lower, but the sequence is irreversible.

Having pitched our definition of intelligence, now as in the early days of Binet and Spearman, high in the evolutionary and individual scale, we cannot climb down without losing meaningfulness. To say this is not to belittle but rather to encourage the investigation of all underlying conditions in the fields of genetics, anatomy, and physiology. They have their own validity and may produce insights that can be transmuted into the currency of psychological events.

Intelligence, as a system of behavioral manifestations, is culturally determined. The intact organism, grossly similar to others, may nevertheless be "feeble-minded." Such depressants as physical exhaustion, illiteracy, and other cultural impoverishments, together with the profound effects of taboos, traditions, and emotional blockings, may serve effectively to retard what we call normal mental growth.

With everything right and good in social dynamics, however, the feeble-minded will not die out. Organic defects and deficiencies exist; some, but certainly not all, are carried down in genetic lines which no guidance or favoring can bring to normality. Such persons are happy enough, provided that we do not force them through meaningless mental motions. Most of the ones I know are not only "earning their keep" (in an institution), but have developed a certain repose and charm. Like the "best people," they tend to have too few offspring to assure ultimate survival, unless their ranks are constantly restored from the large middle population.

With a clarification of concepts and the reconstruction of measurements, the old issues will take a new form. Analysis will surely become more individualized; there will be a return to what *this child* knows and does, and what he can do under optimum conditions of stimulation and guidance. Thus may we learn to bring children to their highest levels of intellectual endeavor and social richness.

39. Three Faces of Intellect *[1]

J. P. GUILFORD

MY SUBJECT is in the area of human intelligence, in connection with which the names of Terman and Stanford have become known the world over. The Stanford Revision of the Binet intelligence scale has been the standard against which all other instruments for the measurement of intelligence have been compared. The term IQ or intelligence quotient has become a household word in this country. This is illustrated by two brief stories.

A few years ago, one of my neighbors came home from a PTA meeting, remarking: "That Mrs. So-And-So, thinks she knows so much. She kept talking about the 'intelligence *quota*' of the children; 'intelligence *quota*'; imagine. Why, everybody knows that IQ stands for 'intelligence *quiz*.'"

The other story comes from a little comic strip in a Los Angeles morning newspaper, called "Junior Grade." In the first picture a little boy meets a little girl, both apparently about the first grade level. The little girl remarks, "I have a high IQ." The little boy, puzzled, said, "You have a what?" The little girl repeated, "I have a high IQ," then went on her way. The little boy, looking thoughtful, said, "And she looks like such a nice little girl, too."

It is my purpose to speak about the analysis of this thing called human intelligence into its components. I do not believe that either Binet or Terman, if they were still with us, would object to the idea of a searching and detailed study of intelligence, aimed toward a better understanding of its nature. Preceding the development of his intelligence scale, Binet had done much research on different kinds of thinking activities and apparently recognized that intelligence has a number of aspects. It is to the lasting credit of both Binet and Terman that they introduced such a great variety of tasks into their intelligence scales.

Two related events of very recent history make it imperative that we learn all we can regarding the nature of intelligence. I am referring to the advent of the artificial satellites and planets and to the crisis in education that has arisen in part as a consequence. The preservation of our way of life

* From J. P. Guilford, "Three Faces of Intellect," *The American Psychologist* (August, 1959), pp. 469–79. Reprinted by permission of the author and the American Psychological Association.
[1] The Walter V. Bingham Memorial Lecture given at Stanford University on April 13, 1959.

and our future security depend upon our most important national resources: our intellectual abilities and, more particularly, our creative abilities. It is time, then, that we learn all we can about those resources.

Our knowledge of the components of human intelligence has come about mostly within the last twenty-five years. The major sources of this information in this country have been L. L. Thurstone and his associates, the wartime research of psychologists in the United States Air Forces, and more recently the Aptitudes Project [2] at the University of Southern California, now in its tenth year of research on cognitive and thinking abilities. The results from the Aptitudes Project that have gained perhaps the most attention have pertained to creative-thinking abilities. These are mostly novel findings. But to me, the most significant outcome has been the development of a unified theory of human intellect, which organizes the known, unique or primary intellectual abilities into a single system called the "structure of intellect." It is to this system that I shall devote the major part of my remarks, with very brief mentions of some of the implications for the psychology of thinking and problem-solving, for vocational testing, and for education.

The discovery of the components of intelligence has been by means of the experimental application of the method of factor analysis. It is not necessary for you to know anything about the theory or method of factor analysis in order to follow the discussion of the components. I should like to say, however, that factor analysis has no connection with or resemblance to psychoanalysis. A positive statement would be more helpful, so I will say that each intellectual component or factor is a unique ability that is needed to do well in a certain class of tasks or tests. As a general principle we find that certain individuals do well in the tests of a certain class, but they may do poorly in the tests of another class. We conclude that a factor has certain properties from the features that the tests of a class have in common. I shall give you very soon a number of examples of tests, each representing a factor.

The Structure of Intellect

Although each factor is sufficiently distinct to be detected by factor analysis, in very recent years it has become apparent that the factors themselves can be classified because they resemble one another in certain ways.

[2] Under Contract N6onr-23810 with the Office of Naval Research (Personnel and Training Branch).

One basis of classification is according to the basic kind of process or operation performed. This kind of classification gives us five major groups of intellectual abilities: factors of cognition, memory, convergent thinking, divergent thinking, and evaluation.

Cognition means discovery or rediscovery or recognition. Memory means retention of what is cognized. Two kinds of productive-thinking operations generate new information from known information and remembered information. In divergent-thinking operations we think in different directions, sometimes searching, sometimes seeking variety. In convergent thinking the information leads to one right answer or to a recognized best or conventional answer. In evaluation we reach decisions as to goodness, correctness, suitability, or adequacy of what we know, what we remember, and what we produce in productive thinking.

A second way of classifying the intellectual factors is according to the kind of material or content involved. The factors known thus far involve three kinds of material or content: the content may be figural, symbolic, or semantic. Figural content is concrete material such as is perceived through the senses. It does not represent anything except itself. Visual material has properties such as size, form, color, location, or texture. Things we hear or feel provide other examples of figural material. Symbolic content is composed of letters, digits, and other conventional signs, usually organized in general systems, such as the alphabet or the number system. Semantic content is in the form of verbal meanings or ideas, for which no examples are necessary.

When a certain operation is applied to a certain kind of content, as many as six general kinds of products may be involved. There is enough evidence available to suggest that, regardless of the combinations of operations and content, the same six kinds of products may be found associated. The six kinds of products are: units, classes, relations, systems, transformations, and implications. So far as we have determined from factor analysis, these are the only fundamental kinds of products that we can know. As such, they may serve as basic classes into which one might fit all kinds of information psychologically.

The three kinds of classifications of the factors of intellect can be represented by means of a single solid model, shown in Figure 1. In this model, which we call the "structure of intellect," each dimension represents one of the modes of variation of the factors.[3] Along one dimension are found the various kinds of operations, along a second one are the various kinds

[3] For an earlier presentation of the concept, see J. P. Guilford, "The Structure of Intellect," *Psychological Bulletin,* 53 (1956), 267–93.

of products, and along the third are various kinds of content. Along the dimension of content a fourth category has been added, its kind of content being designated as "behavioral." This category has been added on a purely theoretical basis to represent the general area sometimes called "social intelligence." More will be said about this section of the model later.

In order to provide a better basis for understanding the model and a better basis for accepting it as a picture of human intellect, I shall do some exploring of it with you systematically, giving some examples of tests. Each

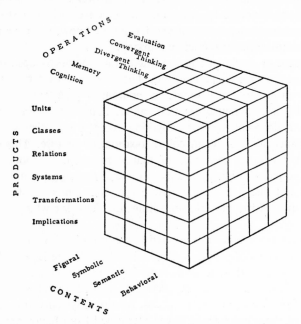

Figure 1. A cubical model representing the structure of intellect.

cell in the model calls for a certain kind of ability that can be described in terms of operation, content, and product, for each cell is at the intersection of a unique combination of kinds of operation, content, and product. A test for that ability would have the same three properties. In our exploration of the model, we shall take one vertical layer at a time, beginning with the front face. The first layer provides us with a matrix of eighteen cells (if we ignore the behavioral column for which there are as yet no known factors) each of which should contain a cognitive ability.

THE COGNITIVE ABILITIES

We know at present the unique abilities that fit logically into fifteen of the eighteen cells for cognitive abilities. Each row presents a triad of similar abilities, having a single kind of product in common. The factors of the first row are concerned with the knowing of units. A good test of the ability to cognize figural units is the Street Gestalt Completion Test. In this test, the recognition of familiar pictured objects in silhouette form is made difficult for testing purposes by blocking out parts of those objects. There is another factor that is known to involve the perception of auditory figures —in the form of melodies, rhythms, and speech sounds—and still another factor involving kinesthetic forms. The presence of three factors in one cell (they are conceivably distinct abilities, although this has not been tested) suggests that more generally, in the figural column, at least, we should expect to find more than one ability. A fourth dimension pertaining to variations in sense modality may thus apply in connection with figural content. The model could be extended in this manner if the facts call for such an extension.

The ability to cognize symbolic units is measured by tests like the following:

Put vowels in the following blanks to make real words:

P__W__R
M__RV__L
C__RT__N

Rearrange the letters to make real words:

R A C I H
T V O E S
K L C C O

The first of these two tests is called Disemvoweled Words, and the second Scrambled Words.

The ability to cognize semantic units is the well-known factor of verbal comprehension, which is best measured by means of a vocabulary test, with items such as:

GRAVITY means _____
CIRCUS means _____
VIRTUE means _____

From the comparison of these two factors it is obvious that recognizing familiar words as letter structures and knowing what words mean depend upon quite different abilities.

For testing the abilities to know classes of units, we may present the following kinds of items, one with symbolic content and one with semantic content:

Which letter group does not belong?

XECM   PVAA   QXIN   VTRO

Which object does not belong?

clam   tree   oven   rose

A figural test is constructed in a completely parallel form, presenting in each item four figures, three of which have a property in common and the fourth lacking that property.

The three abilities to see relationships are also readily measured by a common kind of test, differing only in terms of content. The well-known analogies test is applicable, two items in symbolic and semantic form being:

JIRE : KIRE : : FORA : KORE KORA LIRE GORA GIRE

poetry : prose : : dance : music walk sing talk jump

Such tests usually involve more than the ability to cognize relations, but we are not concerned with this problem at this point.

The three factors for cognizing systems do not at present appear in tests so closely resembling one another as in the case of the examples just given. There is nevertheless an underlying common core of logical similarity. Ordinary space tests, such as Thurstone's Flags, Figures, and Cards or Part V (Spatial Orientation) of the Guilford-Zimmerman Aptitude Survey (GZAS), serve in the figural column. The system involved is an order or arrangement of objects in space. A system that uses symbolic elements is illustrated by the Letter Triangle Test, a sample item of which is:

$$
\begin{array}{cccc}
 & \overline{} & & \\
d & \underline{} & & \\
b & e & \underline{} & \\
a & c & f & \underline{?}
\end{array}
$$

What letter belongs at the place of the question mark?

The ability to understand a semantic system has been known for some time as the factor called general reasoning. One of its most faithful indicators is a test composed of arithmetic-reasoning items. That the phase of understanding only is important for measuring this ability is shown by the fact that such a test works even if the examinee is not asked to give a complete solution; he need only show that he structures the problem properly.

For example, an item from the test Necessary Arithmetical Operations simply asks what operations are needed to solve the problem:

A city lot 48 feet wide and 149 feet deep costs $79,432. What is the cost per square foot?	A. add and multiply B. multiply and divide C. subtract and divide D. add and subtract E. divide and add

Placing the factor of general reasoning in this cell of the structure of intellect gives us some new conceptions of its nature. It should be a broad ability to grasp all kinds of systems that are conceived in terms of verbal concepts, not restricted to the understanding of problems of an arithmetical type.

Transformations are changes of various kinds, including modifications in arrangement, organization, or meaning. In the figural column for the transformations row, we find the factor known as visualization. Common measuring instruments for this factor are the surface-development tests, and an example of a different kind is Part VI (Spatial Visualization) of the GZAS. A test of the ability to make transformations of meaning, for the factor in the semantic column, is called Similarities. The examinee is asked to state several ways in which two objects, such as an apple and an orange, are alike. Only by shifting the meanings of both is the examinee able to give many responses to such an item.

In the set of abilities having to do with the cognition of implications, we find that the individual goes beyond the information given, but not to the extent of what might be called drawing conclusions. We may say that he extrapolates. From the given information he expects or foresees certain consequences, for example. The two factors found in this row of the cognition matrix were first called "foresight" factors. Foresight in connection with figural material can be tested by means of paper-and-pencil mazes. Foresight in connection with ideas, those pertaining to events, for example, is indicated by a test such as Pertinent Questions:

In planning to open a new hamburger stand in a certain community, what four questions should be considered in deciding upon its location?

The more questions the examinee asks in response to a list of such problems, the more he evidently foresees contingencies.

THE MEMORY ABILITIES

The area of memory abilities has been explored less than some of the other areas of operation, and only seven of the potential cells of the memory matrix have known factors in them. These cells are restricted to three rows: for units, relations, and systems. The first cell in the memory matrix is now occupied by two factors, parallel to two in the corresponding cognition matrix: visual memory and auditory memory. Memory for series of letters or numbers, as in memory span tests, conforms to the conception of memory for symbolic units. Memory for the ideas in a paragraph conforms to the conception of memory for semantic units.

The formation of associations between units, such as visual forms, syllables, and meaningful words, as in the method of paired associates, would seem to represent three abilities to remember relationships involving three kinds of content. We know of two such abilities, for the symbolic and semantic columns. The memory for known systems is represented by two abilities very recently discovered.[4] Remembering the arrangement of objects in space is the nature of an ability in the figural column, and remembering a sequence of events is the nature of a corresponding ability in the semantic column. The differentiation between these two abilities implies that a person may be able to say where he saw an object on a page, but he might not be able to say on which of several pages he saw it after leafing through several pages that included the right one. Considering the blank rows in the memory matrix, we should expect to find abilities also to remember classes, transformations, and implications, as well as units, relations, and systems.

THE DIVERGENT-THINKING ABILITIES

The unique feature of divergent production is that a *variety* of responses is produced. The product is not completely determined by the given information. This is not to say that divergent thinking does not come into play in the total process of reaching a unique conclusion, for it comes into play wherever there is trial-and-error thinking.

The well-known ability of word fluency is tested by asking the examinee to list words satisfying a specified letter requirement, such as words beginning with the letter "s" or words ending in "-tion." This ability is now regarded as a facility in divergent production of symbolic units. The parallel semantic ability has been known as ideational fluency. A typical test item calls for listing objects that are round and edible. Winston Churchill must have possessed this ability to a high degree. Clement Attlee is reported to have said about him recently that, no matter what problem came up, Churchill always seemed to have about ten ideas. The trouble was, Attlee

----

[4] R. E. Christal, "Factor Analytic Study of Visual Memory," *Psychological Monographs,* Vol. 72, No. 13 (Whole No. 466) (1958).

continued, he did not know which was the good one. The last comment implies some weakness in one or more of the evaluative abilities.

The divergent production of class ideas is believed to be the unique feature of a factor called "spontaneous flexibility." A typical test instructs the examinee to list all the uses he can think of for a common brick, and he is given eight minutes. If his responses are: build a house, build a barn, build a garage, build a school, build a church, build a chimney, build a walk, and build a barbecue, he would earn a fairly high score for ideational fluency but a very low score for spontaneous flexibility, because all these uses fall into the same class. If another person said: make a door stop, make a paper weight, throw it at a dog, make a bookcase, drown a cat, drive a nail, make a red powder, and use for baseball bases, he would also receive a high score for flexibility. He has gone frequently from one class to another.

A current study of unknown but predicted divergent-production abilities includes testing whether there are also figural and symbolic abilities to produce multiple classes. An experimental figural test presents a number of figures that can be classified in groups of three in various ways, each figure being usable in more than one class. An experimental symbolic test presents a few numbers that are also to be classified in multiple ways.

A unique ability involving relations is called "associational fluency." It calls for the production of a variety of things related in a specified way to a given thing. For example, the examinee is asked to list words meaning about the same as "good" or to list words meaning about the opposite of "hard." In these instances the response produced is to complete a relationship, and semantic content is involved. Some of our present experimental tests call for the production of varieties of relations, as such, and involve figural and symbolic content also. For example, given four small digits, in how many ways can they be related in order to produce a sum of eight?

One factor pertaining to the production of systems is known as expressional fluency. The rapid formation of phrases or sentences is the essence of certain tests of this factor. For example, given the initial letters:

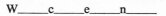

W____c____e____n____

with different sentences to be produced, the examinee might write "We can eat nuts" or "Whence came Eve Newton?" In interpreting the factor, we regard the sentence as a symbolic system. By analogy, a figural system would be some kind of organization of lines and other elements, and a semantic system would be in the form of a verbally stated problem or perhaps something as complex as a theory.

In the row of the divergent-production matrix devoted to transformations, we find some very interesting factors. The one called "adaptive flexibility" is now recognized as belonging in the figural column. A faithful test of it has been Match Problems. This is based upon the common game that uses squares, the sides of which are formed by match sticks. The examinee is told to take away a given number of matches to leave a stated number of squares with nothing left over. Nothing is said about the sizes of the squares to be left. If the examinee imposes upon himself the restriction that the squares that he leaves must be of the same size, he will fail in his

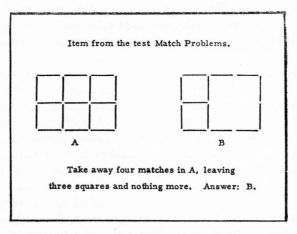

Item from the test Match Problems.

A

B

Take away four matches in A, leaving
three squares and nothing more.   Answer: B.

Figure 2. A sample item from the test Match Problems. The problem in this item is to take away four matches and leave three squares. The solution is given.

attempts to do items like that in Figure 2. Other odd kinds of solutions are introduced in other items, such as overlapping squares and squares within squares, and so on. In another variation of Match Problems the examinee is told to produce two or more solutions for each problem.

A factor that has been called "originality" is now recognized as adaptive flexibility with semantic material, where there must be a shifting of meanings. The examinee must produce the shifts or changes in meaning and so come up with novel, unusual, clever, or farfetched ideas. The Plot Titles Test presents a short story, the examinee being told to list as many appropriate titles as he can to head the story. One story is about a missionary who has been captured by cannibals in Africa. He is in the pot and about to be boiled when a princess of the tribe obtains a promise for his release if he will become her mate. He refuses and is boiled to death.

In scoring the test, we separate the responses into two categories, clever and nonclever. Examples of nonclever responses are: African Death, Defeat of a Princess, Eaten by Savages, The Princess, The African Missionary, In Darkest Africa, and Boiled by Savages. These titles are appropriate but commonplace. The number of such responses serves as a score for ideational fluency. Examples of clever responses are: "Pot's Plot, Potluck Dinner, Stewed Parson, Goil or Boil, A Mate Worse Than Death, He Left a Dish for a Pot, Chaste in Haste, and A Hot Price for Freedom. The number of clever responses given by an examinee is his score for originality, or the divergent production of semantic transformations.

Another test of originality presents a very novel task so that any acceptable response is unusual for the individual. In the Symbol Production Test the examinee is to produce a simple symbol to stand for a noun or a verb in each short sentence, in other words to invent something like pictographic symbols. Still another test of originality asks for writing the "punch lines" for cartoons, a task that almost automatically challenges the examinee to be clever. Thus, quite a variety of tests offer approaches to the measurement of originality, including one or two others that I have not mentioned.

Abilities to produce a variety of implications are assessed by tests calling for elaboration of given information. A figural test of this type provides the examinee with a line or two, to which he is to add other lines to produce an object. The more lines he adds, the greater his score. A semantic test gives the examinee the outlines of a plan to which he is to respond by stating all the details he can think of to make the plan work. A new test we are trying out in the symbolic area presents two simple equations such as $B - C = D$ and $z = A + D$. The examinee is to make as many other equations as he can from this information.

THE CONVERGENT-PRODUCTION ABILITIES

Of the eighteen convergent-production abilities expected in the three content columns, twelve are now recognized. In the first row, pertaining to units, we have an ability to name figural properties (forms or colors) and an ability to name abstractions (classes, relations, and so on). It may be that the ability in common to the speed of naming forms and the speed of naming colors is not appropriately placed in the convergent-thinking matrix. One might expect that the thing to be produced in a test of the convergent production of figural units would be in the form of figures rather than words. A better test of such an ability might somehow specify the need for one particular object, the examinee to furnish the object.

A test for the convergent production of classes (Word Grouping) presents a list of twelve words that are to be classified in four, and only four, meaningful groups, no word to appear in more than one group. A parallel test (Figure Concepts Test) presents twenty pictured real objects that are to be grouped in meaningful classes of two or more each.

Convergent production having to do with relationships is represented by three known factors, all involving the "eduction of correlates," as Spearman called it. The given information includes one unit and a stated relation, the examinee to supply the other unit. Analogies tests that call for completion rather than a choice between alternative answers emphasize this kind of ability. With symbolic content such an item might read:

pots   stop   bard   dram   rats   <u>?</u>

A semantic item that measures eduction of correlates is:

The absence of sound is _____.

Incidentally, the latter item is from a vocabulary-completion test, and its relation to the factor of ability to produce correlates indicates how, by change of form, a vocabulary test may indicate an ability other than that for which vocabulary tests are usually intended, namely, the factor of verbal comprehension.

Only one factor for convergent production of systems is known, and it is in the semantic column. It is measured by a class of tests that may be called ordering tests. The examinee may be presented with a number of events that ordinarily have a best or most logical order, the events being presented in scrambled order. The presentation may be pictorial, as in the Picture Arrangement Test, or verbal. The pictures may be taken from a cartoon strip. The verbally presented events may be in the form of the various steps needed to plant a new lawn. There are undoubtedly other kinds of systems than temporal order that could be utilized for testing abilities in this row of the convergent-production matrix.

In the way of producing transformations of a unique variety, we have three recognized factors, known as redefinition abilities. In each case, redefinition involves the changing of functions or uses of parts of one unit and giving them new functions or uses in some new unit. For testing the ability of figural redefinition, a task based upon the Gottschaldt figures is suitable. Figure 3 shows the kind of item for such a test. In recognizing the simpler figure within the structure of a more complex figure, certain lines must take on new roles.

In terms of symbolic material, the following sample items will illustrate how groups of letters in given words must be readapted to use in other

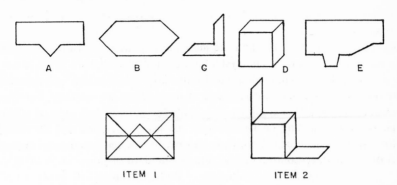

A B C D E

ITEM 1   ITEM 2

Figure 3. Sample items from a test Hidden Figures, based upon the Gottschaldt figures. Which of the simpler figures is concealed within each of the two more complex figures?

words. In the test Camouflaged Words, each sentence contains the name of a sport or game:

> I did not know that he was ailing.
> To beat the Hun, tin goes a long way.

For the factor of semantic redefinition, the Gestalt Transformation Test may be used. A sample item reads:

From which object could you most likely make a needle?

> A. a cabbage
> B. a splice
> C. a steak
> D. a paper box
> E. a fish

The convergent production of implications means the drawing of fully determined conclusions from given information. The well-known factor of numerical facility belongs in the symbolic column. For the parallel ability in the figural column, we have a test known as Form Reasoning, in which rigorously defined operations with figures are used. For the parallel ability in the semantic column, the factor sometimes called "deduction" probably qualifies. Items of the following type are sometimes used.

> Charles is younger than Robert
> Charles is older than Frank
> Who is older: Robert or Frank?

EVALUATIVE ABILITIES

The evaluative area has had the least investigation of all the operational categories. In fact, only one systematic analytical study has been devoted to this area. Only eight evaluative abilities are recognized as fitting into the evaluation matrix. But at least five rows have one or more factors each, and also three of the usual columns or content categories. In each case, evaluation involves reaching decisions as to the accuracy, goodness, suitability, or workability of information. In each row, for the particular kind of product of that row, some kind of criterion or standard of judgment is involved.

In the first row, for the evaluation of units, the important decision to be made pertains to the identity of a unit. Is this unit identical with that one? In the figural column we find the factor long known as "perceptual speed." Tests of this factor invariably call for decisions of identity, for example, Part IV (Perceptual Speed) of the GZAS or Thurstone's Identical Forms. I think it has been generally wrongly thought that the ability involved is that of cognition of visual forms. But we have seen that another factor is a more suitable candidate for this definition and for being in the very first cell of the cognitive matrix. It is parallel to this evaluative ability but does not require the judgment of identity as one of its properties.

In the symbolic column is an ability to judge identity of symbolic units, in the form of series of letters or numbers or of names of individuals.

Are members of the following pairs identical or not:

825170493_____825176493
dkeltvmpa_____dkeltvmpa
C. S. Meyerson_____C. E. Meyerson

Such items are common in tests of clerical aptitude.

There should be a parallel ability to decide whether two ideas are identical or different. Is the idea expressed in this sentence the same as the idea expressed in that one? Do these two proverbs express essentially the same idea? Such tests exist and will be used to test the hypothesis that such an ability can be demonstrated.

No evaluative abilities pertaining to classes have as yet been recognized. The abilities having to do with evaluation where relations are concerned must meet the criterion of logical consistency. Syllogistic tests involving letter symbols indicate a different ability than the same type of test involving verbal statements. In the figural column we might expect that tests incorporating geometric reasoning or proof would indicate a parallel ability to sense the soundness of conclusions regarding figural relationships.

The evaluation of systems seems to be concerned with the internal consistency of those systems, so far as we can tell from the knowledge of one such factor. The factor has been called "experiential evaluation," and its representative test presents items like that in Figure 4 asking "What is wrong with this picture?" The things wrong are often internal inconsistencies.

A semantic ability for evaluating transformations is thought to be that known for some time as "judgment." In typical judgment tests, the examinee is asked to tell which of five solutions to a practical problem is most adequate or wise. The solutions frequently involve improvisations, in other words, adaptations of familiar objects to unusual uses. In this way the items present redefinitions to be evaluated.

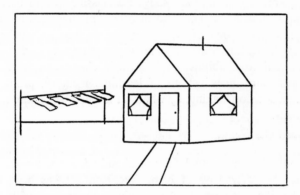

Figure 4. A sample item from the test Unusual Details. What two things are wrong with this picture?

A factor known first as "sensitivity to problems" has become recognized as an evaluative ability having to do with implications. One test of the factor, the Apparatus Test, asks for two needed improvements with respect to each of several common devices, such as the telephone or the toaster. The Social Institutions Test, a measure of the same factor, asks what things are wrong with each of several institutions, such as tipping or national elections. We may say that defects or deficiencies are implications of an evaluative kind. Another interpretation would be that seeing defects and deficiencies are evaluations of implications to the effect that the various aspects of something are all right.[5]

[5] For further details concerning the intellectual factors, illustrative tests, and the place of the factors in the structure of intellect, see J. P. Guilford, *Personality* (New York: McGraw-Hill Book Co., 1959).

Some Implications of the Structure of Intellect

FOR PSYCHOLOGICAL THEORY

Although factor analysis as generally employed is best designed to investigate ways in which individuals differ from one another, in other words, to discover traits, the results also tell us much about how individuals are alike. Consequently, information regarding the factors and their interrelationships gives us understanding of functioning individuals. The five kinds of intellectual abilities in terms of operations may be said to represent five ways of functioning. The kinds of intellectual abilities distinguished according to varieties of test content and the kinds of abilities distinguished according to varieties of products suggest a classification of basic forms of information or knowledge. The kind of organism suggested by this way of looking at intellect is that of an agency for dealing with information of various kinds in various ways. The concepts provided by the distinctions among the intellectual abilities and by their classifications may be very useful in our future investigations of learning, memory, problem-solving, invention, and decision making, by whatever method we choose to approach those problems.

FOR VOCATIONAL TESTING

With about fifty intellectual factors already known, we may say that there are at least fifty ways of being intelligent. It has been facetiously suggested that there seem to be a great many more ways of being stupid, unfortunately. The structure of intellect is a theoretical model that predicts as many as 120 distinct abilities, if every cell of the model contains a factor. Already we know that two cells contain two or more factors each, and there probably are actually other cells of this type. Since the model was first conceived, twelve factors predicted by it have found places in it. There is consequently hope of filling many of the other vacancies, and we may eventually end up with more than 120 abilities.

The major implication for the assessment of intelligence is that to know an individual's intellectual resources thoroughly we shall need a surprisingly large number of scores. It is expected that many of the factors are intercorrelated, so there is some possibility that by appropriate sampling we shall be able to cover the important abilities with a more limited number of tests. At any rate, a multiple-score approach to the assessment of intelligence is definitely indicated in connection with future vocational operations.

Considering the kinds of abilities classified as to content, we may speak roughly of four kinds of intelligence. The abilities involving the use of figural information may be regarded as "concrete" intelligence. The people who depend most upon these abilities deal with concrete things and their properties. Among these people are mechanics, operators of machines, engineers (in some aspects of their work), artists, and musicians.

In the abilities pertaining to symbolic and semantic content, we have two kinds of "abstract" intelligence. Symbolic abilities should be important in learning to recognize words, to spell, and to operate with numbers. Language and mathematics should depend very much upon them, except that in mathematics some aspects, such as geometry, have strong figural involvement. Semantic intelligence is important for understanding things in terms of verbal concepts and hence is important in all courses where the learning of facts and ideas is essential.

In the hypothesized behavorial column of the structure of intellect, which may be roughly described as "social" intelligence, we have some of the most interesting possibilities. Understanding the behavior of others and of ourselves is largely nonverbal in character. The theory suggests as many as thirty abilities in this area, some having to do with understanding, some with productive thinking about behavior, and some with the evaluation of behavior. The theory also suggests that information regarding behavior is also in the form of the six kinds of products that apply elsewhere in the structure of intellect, including units, relations, systems, and so on. The abilities in the area of social intelligence, whatever they prove to be, will possess considerable importance in connection with all those individuals who deal most with other people: teachers, law officials, social workers, therapists, politicians, statesmen, and leaders of other kinds.

FOR EDUCATION

The implications for education are numerous, and I have time just to mention a very few. The most fundamental implication is that we might well undergo transformations with respect to our conception of the learner and of the process of learning. Under the prevailing conception, the learner is a kind of stimulus-response device, much on the order of a vending machine. You put in a coin, and something comes out. The machine learns what reaction to put out when a certain coin is put in. If, instead, we think of the learner as an agent for dealing with information, where information is defined very broadly, we have something more analogous to an electronic computer. We feed a computer information; it stores that information; it uses that information for generating new information, either by way of divergent or convergent thinking; and it evaluates its own results. Advantages that a human learner has over a computer include the step of seeking and discovering new information from sources outside itself and the step of programing itself. Perhaps even these steps will be added to computers, if this has not already been done in some cases.

At any rate, this conception of the learner leads us to the idea that learning is discovery of information, not merely the formation of associations, particularly associations in the form of stimulus-response connections. I am aware of the fact that my proposal is rank heresy. But if we are to make significant progress in our understanding of human learning and particularly our understanding of the so-called higher mental processes of thinking, problem-solving, and creative thinking, some drastic modifications are due in our theory.

The idea that education is a matter of training the mind or of training the intellect has been rather unpopular, wherever the prevailing psychological doctrines have been followed. In theory, at least, the emphasis has been upon the learning of rather specific habits or skills. If we take our cue from factor theory, however, we recognize that most learning probably has both specific and general aspects or components. The general aspects may be along the lines of the factors of intellect. This is not to say that the individual's status in each factor is entirely determined by learning. We do not know to what extent each factor is determined by heredity and to what extent by learning. The best position for educators to take is that possibly every intellectual factor can be developed in individuals at least to some extent by learning.

If education has the general objective of developing the intellects of students, it can be suggested that each intellectual factor provides a particular goal at which to aim. Defined by a certain combination of content, operation, and product, each goal ability then calls for certain kinds of practice in order to achieve improvement in it. This implies choice of curriculum and the choice or invention of teaching methods that will most likely accomplish the desired results.

Considering the very great variety of abilities revealed by the factorial exploration of intellect, we are in a better position to ask whether any general intellectual skills are now being neglected in education and whether appropriate balances are being observed. It is often observed these days that we have fallen down in the way of producing resourceful, creative graduates. How true this is, in comparison with other times, I do not know. Perhaps the deficit is noticed because the demands for inventiveness are so much greater at this time. At any rate, realization that the more conspicuously creative abilities appear to be concentrated in the divergent-thinking category, and also to some extent in the transformation category, we now ask whether we have been giving these skills appropriate exercise. It is probable that we need a better balance of training in the divergent-thinking area as compared with training in convergent thinking and in critical thinking or evaluation.

The structure of intellect as I have presented it to you may or may not stand the test of time. Even if the general form persists, there are likely to be some modifications. Possibly some different kind of model will be invented. Be that as it may, the fact of a multiplicity of intellectual abilities seems well established.

There are many individuals who long for the good old days of simplicity, when we got along with one unanalyzed intelligence. Simplicity certainly has its appeal. But human nature is exceedingly complex, and we may as well face that fact. The rapidly moving events of the world in which we live have forced upon us the need for knowing human intelligence thoroughly. Humanity's peaceful pursuit of happiness depends upon our control of nature and of our own behavior; and this, in turn, depends upon understanding ourselves, including our intellectual resources.

40. *What Is an Aptitude?* *

ALEXANDER G. WESMAN

As INTEREST in any technical field becomes increasingly widespread, it is perhaps inevitable that misconceptions concerning some of the relevant concepts and terminology should appear. This seems to be especially true of aptitude testing. That the misconceptions should refer to the basic understanding of the term "aptitude" itself is of serious import; clarification of the concept and resolution of differing meanings is vital, not only to aptitude testing but to the entire field of psychological measurement.

The definition of aptitude which Dr. Bingham prepared for Warren's

* From Alexander G. Wesman, "What Is an Aptitude?" *Test Service Bulletin,* Nos. 36–40 (1948–50), pp. 2–3. Reprinted by permission of the Psychological Corporation, New York.

Dictionary of Psychology is an excellent starting point for elucidation of the concept:

> APTITUDE. *A condition or set of characteristics regarded as symptomatic of an individual's ability to acquire with training some (usually specified) knowledge, skill, or set of responses, such as the ability to speak a language, to produce music. . . .*

A complete appreciation of this definition would do away with a number of misunderstandings which are prevalent. We may note, first, that nothing inherent in this concept assumes that aptitudes are hereditary. The expression "born that way" is a dangerous fallacy which still is heard even among educated people. On the other hand, one cannot undertake to make every average person into a genius. Fortunately for our present purpose, we really do not need to determine *how much* of an aptitude is hereditary and how much reflects environmental forces. Aptitude is the result of the interaction of heredity and environment. The infant is born with certain potentialities, and begins learning immediately. What he learns makes it possible for him to learn more. It is similar to the investment of capital which bears interest, the interest then becoming additional capital which also may be reinvested to earn still more interest.

A second important feature of the definition is that it is extremely broad. As conceived herein, aptitude embraces intelligence and achievement, personality and interests as well as any other abilities and skills which predispose to learning. The use of the term aptitude as being limited only to the specialized learning capacities for music or engineering or stenography is misleading. The familiar intelligence tests have found favor because they predict the student's ability to learn to read, or write compositions, or bisect an angle, or understand social trends. In other words, they are aptitude tests which describe the student's potentiality for learning in a number of academic subjects or vocational endeavors. This has been recognized in the healthy tendency to speak of scholastic aptitude tests rather than intelligence tests. A more sophisticated understanding of the nature of intelligence and aptitude has made this trend inevitable.

Many of us who have accepted the idea that intelligence tests measure aptitude have failed to recognize that achievement tests are also aptitude tests when used most purposefully. The most important function which an achievement test can serve is to make evident what the person has learned, either so that we can predict how well he will learn additional material of a similar nature, or to indicate whether he has the skills or knowledge required for future success in a particular profession or trade. The use of an achievement test score solely for recording a person's accomplishment is relatively sterile; only when it predicts, obviously or indirectly, is such measurement maximally useful.

The importance of interests and other personality traits for learning skills or acquiring knowledge needs no exposition. How well a person will acquire proficiency depends so much on his interest in the task, on his drives and his goals, that the layman appreciates these conditioning factors as thoroughly as does the psychologist. It is only when the term aptitude is too narrowly delimited that the contributions of interest and personality are overlooked as aspects of aptitude.

The total concept can perhaps be summarized by regarding aptitude as simply a capacity to learn. When we refer to stenographic aptitude, we mean the capacity to learn those skills which make for a successful stenographer. This is a relatively specific aptitude. When we refer to academic aptitude, we mean the capacity to complete successfully a more comprehensive curriculum. This is really a broader set of aptitudes, and we frequently use so-called tests of general mental ability to facilitate our prediction. It is noteworthy that the modern trend is away from single score intelligence tests in favor of tests which yield several scores—e.g., verbal, numerical, abstract, mechanical, etc. This is a recognition that for specific courses or jobs, the best prediction can be obtained from more specific measurement than is yielded by an undifferentiated single "intelligence" score or IQ.

The measurement of aptitude, then, is the assessment of knowledge, skill, and any other characteristics which serve to predict learning success. Usually test data are the most important bases for such prediction. Sometimes background data which reveal experience, interest or personality characteristics may be equally fruitful sources of prediction. Industry's use of the weighted application blank, for example, is based on solid experience with the value of biographical data.

What, then, is an aptitude test? It is any test which is used for prediction of some type of learning. Its validity as an aptitude test depends on the extent to which it will predict successfully. We probably shall continue to categorize tests as intelligence tests, achievement tests, interest tests, special aptitude tests, etc., as though there were no overlap in their functions. However, we must not let ourselves become confused by our own practical pigeonholing. To avoid erroneous thinking about prediction, we need to keep constantly in mind the broad definition of aptitude.

41. The Intelligence Test in School Use: Some Persistent Issues *[1]

JAMES B. STROUD

THE FIRST successful intelligence test was designed with little regard to definition or theory. Binet proceeded in an empirical fashion to ascertain kinds of tests that would discriminate among criterion groups. Kuhlmann, Terman, and most of the early workers adopted the Binet procedure. On the other hand we are all familiar with various analytical approaches to the problem of intelligence test design. Thorndike's *area, altitude,* and *speed;* Spearman's *g* and *s* factors; and Thurstone's *primary mental abilities* are cases in point. Thus, Spearman wrote, "When a knowledge of *g* and *s* factors makes it possible to construct tests which measure *g* and *s* at the maximum, an accurate measure for *G* for any individual can be obtained." This, he maintained, is far better than an average derived from a miscellany of unrelated traits.

Thus, the history of the intelligence test reflects two major approaches in test design: (1) the empirical and (2) the analytical. In the former, the psychologist attempts to maximize differences among criterion groups. This is largely a utilitarian approach. In the analytical approach the psychologist investigates the nature of intelligence, with little immediate concern for the practical. Obviously it was Spearman's hope that the two approaches would ultimately amount to the same thing. As yet this hope has not been fulfilled. Test designers have generally resorted to the Binet method of maximizing differences among criterion groups. The advancement in design is reflected largely in statistical and logical refinement of Binet's general plan. Perhaps the most notable departure is the PMA battery. Here one gains the impression, from the somewhat limited research, that insofar as the tests of the PMA battery are factorially pure, most of them assess mental abilities not closely correlated with school achievement.

Binet regarded the MA as a general average. Perhaps the general average is still the most significant feature of the major tests. However, most general tests have featured batteries of subtests permitting part scores and resulting profiles. This practice tends to insure systematic sampling of intel-

* From James B. Stroud, "The Intelligence Test in School Use: Some Persistent Issues," *The Journal of Educational Psychology* (February, 1957), pp. 77–85. Reprinted by permission of the author and the publisher.
[1] Presidential Address, Division of Educational Psychology, 1956.

lectual abilities and thus to improve the "general average." Ostensibly the purpose of this feature is to provide for differential diagnosis and prediction. Although discussion of the analytical features of intelligence scores has sharpened within the last decade or so, the usefulness of the part scores in school situations still suffers from a lack of detailed research on the differential power of the constituent subtests.

Nonverbal tests came into the picture originally as a means of examining persons presenting language handicaps. Most of the new general intelligence tests within recent years have featured both verbal and nonverbal scores. Wechsler's recent and impressive Intelligence Scale for Children, affectionately referred to as the WISC, and the more recent and equally impressive Lorge-Thorndike tests are cases in point. Insofar as we know, at least insofar as I know, this trend in test design is dictated more by fashion than by empirical evidence attesting its usefulness in general school situations. I suspect one would have some difficulty marketing group intelligence tests today that did not contain nonverbal features. I also am inclined to suspect that their worth as nonverbal tests in school practice has not been demonstrated by research. What the clinical psychologist is able to make of the results of this kind may be another matter.

Most of the earlier nonverbal tests were seriously lacking in validity as intelligence tests. We have just completed a correlation analysis of the WISC on about eight hundred school children, grades three to six inclusive. In our results the nonverbal tests predicted academic achievement quite as well as the verbal tests. The attested usefulness in school situations, however, of the Wechsler nonverbal tests may well stem from the fact that they are valid tests of intelligence, rather than from their nonverbal character. Quite conceivably additional verbal tests of comparable quality might be substituted for the nonverbal ones without detriment to the battery.

Our analysis failed to yield much in the way of differential prediction of the achievement measures used, reading, arithmetic, and spelling. It is true that four or five of the eleven subtests gave better prediction than did the others of the three achievement measures. But this apparently resulted from the fact that they were better tests rather than from qualitative differences. A multiple regression analysis was performed based upon within-grades intercorrelations between the eleven WISC subtests and the three achievement measures. *Beta* weights were tested for statistical significance and least significant variables successively eliminated. It was found that four WISC subtests—Arithmetic and Vocabulary among the verbal tests, and Block Design and Object Assembly among nonverbal tests—accounted for most of the correlation between the WISC and the achievement measures. The within-grades least squares multiple correlation between all eleven WISC tests and reading, for example, was 0.74. The within-grades least squares multiple correlation between these four subtests, Vocabulary, Arithmetic, Block Design and Object Assembly, and reading was 0.73. The correlation between the unweighted raw score sums of the four subtests just referred to and Reading was 0.69. Comparable results were obtained for arithmetic achievement and for spelling achievement. It is a particularly striking fact that for all practical purposes the same four WISC subtests are the most effective predictors of each of the three achievement tests. For cross validation purposes the same kinds of analyses were carried out on a sample different from that on which the regression equations were derived, but drawn in the same way. The results obtained with the independent sample were strikingly similar to those obtained on the original sample.

Incidentally, analyses of this kind seem to be indicated for differential aptitude tests. It has been suggested that in view of the high correlations obtained between general aptitude tests and intelligence scores and also between general achievement tests and intelligence scores, the intelligence test is no longer required in school practice insofar as prediction of achievement is concerned. It is true that prior achievement predicts future achievement at least as well as does the general intelligence test. But it is equally true that the intelligence test which can be administered in a fraction of the time and at a fraction of the cost predicts future achievement almost as well. The merits of the argument must rest pretty largely upon the nature of the evidence of differential prediction. This brings us back to the intelligence score. How much have we improved upon Binet's "general average," beyond obtaining better averages? The value of pat scores on a test— verbal, nonverbal or others, depending upon the analytical properties of the test—must be assessed in terms of differential prediction, actually substantiated by research. Perhaps it is true that the general achievement test and the general intelligence test each tells us something unique about the pupil and that arguments about one replacing the other could well be forgotten. However, and for the time being, it may be well to bear in mind that the intercorrelations among achievement scores in various school subjects are relatively high. In view of this fact it will be difficult to do a great deal with differential prediction. Consider a medical aptitude and a legal aptitude test, for example. One has a medical aura, the other a legal one. But it still may be true that they could be pretty well interchanged so far as their basic purposes are concerned.

Another issue at least related to the intelligence score is the generality of the mental age. The mental age score, whether determined by Stanford-

Binet method or that derivable from Wechsler tests by multiplying the obtained IQ by CA, is, in effect, an average score. Are some MA's, say, of 10, better than others? Do MA's of a given magnitude vary qualitatively? In our work we have sought to determine whether or not MA's of a given magnitude vary qualitatively with the brightness of the pupils achieving them. A related but somewhat different question is whether or not we can make the same predictions relative to current school achievement of bright and dull pupils earning like MA's. Of course, we would predict much greater future achievement for the younger pupils. In one investigation Kolstoe formed matched pairs of bright and dull pupils achieving equal, estimated true Stanford-Binet MA's. The mean Stanford-Binet MA was 11.3. The mean CA of the dull members was 15.5, giving a mean IQ of 79. The mean CA of the bright members was 9.3, giving a mean IQ of 126. The bright and dull pupils in the sample thus formed were then compared on the basis of the eleven WISC subtests and the PMA subtests. Except for PMA subtest Number, differences between the bright and dull pupils on the seventeen subtests were small and generally not significant. The dull, older pupils were far better in performance on PMA subtest Number.

In a companion investigation, Bliesmer compared bright and dull pupils, matched in MA, on reading achievement. On reading subtests Recognition of Main Ideas, Drawing Inferences, and Total Comprehension, the bright, younger pupils excelled by significant amounts.

The school placement of the older pupils in this sample was three or more grades higher than that of the younger pupils. Owing to the hierarchical character of the arithmetic curriculum, the younger pupils had had no instruction in some of the operations which the older pupils had studied. This may account for some or all of the superiority of the older pupils in Number. One might think, a priori, that young, bright pupils would surpass (in achievement) older, dull pupils of comparable MA's. They are likely to be better motivated, they have been expected to do well in school, they are more likely to be accustomed to success. In general they have had better early home training and have had more encouragement and stimulation at home. Of course, these advantages may be offset by the fact that at the age level at which the work just mentioned was done the older pupils had spent twice as many years in school as the younger ones.

At the present time we are witnessing a growing interest in the education of gifted pupils. This is obliged to sharpen interest in the nature of the mental abilities of the gifted, especially the highly gifted. Perhaps we would be inclined to infer from the results of the work on the generality of the Mental Age that ten-year-old pupils earning MA's of 15 would behave on such tests as the WISC and the PMA much as fifteen-year-old pupils of average intelligence.

The work on the mental age concept just referred to certainly suggests that for the age ranges involved, the MA as a unit of measurement possesses a high degree of generality. This is not to defend the Stanford-Binet procedure of designing intelligence tests. I do mean to defend the MA as a highly useful unit of measurement. The Wechsler method of designing intelligence tests, while it may not produce a superior result, appears to be more efficient and more economical.

The logic of the argument that the MA as a unit of measurement suffers from known or suspected inequalities of its units is not impressive. The meaning and usefulness of height age or weight age or dental age are unaffected by the fact that these units prove to be unequal when tested by a metrical scale. A height age of 9 is scarcely more meaningful in school work because we know how much this is in metrical units. A mental age, or for that matter a reading age, of 9 is not less meaningful because we are unable to say how much intelligence or how much reading ability it is.

Moreover, the inequality of successive MA units, or our lack of knowledge regarding their equality, argues nothing with respect to the equality of IQ's obtained at successive age levels. The IQ defines a pupil's mental development in relation to the mental development of other pupils of like age in the general population. In a sense it defines the rate of mental growth. We may say that a six-year-old pupil who achieves an IQ of 125 develops at the rate of 1.25 of a mental year for each calendar year. At this age his attainment equals that of the average pupil 7½ years old. He has gained a year and a half in six years. He would be expected to gain another year by the time he is 10. We could also say he is approximately 1.5 S.D.'s above the mean for his age, or that he exceeds about 93 per cent of the pupils of his age in the general population. The fact that the MA score from which the IQ is derived at successive ages may not be equal has nothing to do with a pupil's maintaining his relative position in his age group.

Terman's concept of validity of the IQ implies an absence of systematic variations in IQ with age. Given constant means and S.D.'s over an age range, a given IQ must signify the same degree of brightness at successive age levels within this range. This assumes nothing with respect to the equality of the MA units from which the IQ's are derived. Unfortunately, test designers have not always been as careful as they should have been to publish S.D.'s for successive ages over the range of years covered. In the absence of this or comparable information we cannot tell whether or not an

IQ of a given magnitude at one age level is strictly comparable numerically to one of like magnitude at another age level.

One of the more troublesome practical problems is the comparability of IQ's obtained on different tests—one might say needlessly troublesome. It should not have been a difficult matter at all for test designers to have provided school psychologists or other school officials with the variability data necessary to the establishing of numerically equivalent scores on various tests.

In schoolwork there constantly arises the question of the significance of fluctuations in IQ from one testing to another, no matter whether the same or different tests are used on different occasions. When test designers, as Terman and Wechsler have done, provide the necessary data, the school psychologist can readily acquaint teachers with the amount of fluctuation required on a given test to become significant at given levels of confidence. There is no excuse for test authors' not doing this.

Traditionally our schools have been interested in several kinds of growth data. The variables for which we have the most satisfactory measures are mental growth, educational growth, and physical growth. It is of interest to note that these three types of growth possess considerable stability. Correlations between intelligence scores earned at 8 and at 18 years of age run around 0.85, as seen, for example, in Bayley's work. Correlations between measures of stature, obtained at 8 and at 18 years are of somewhat comparable magnitude, as are those between measures of educational achievement taken ten years apart.

We also know from an abundance of research that intelligence scores and educational achievement scores are rather closely intercorrelated, and that neither of these is closely intercorrelated with measures of physical growth. Moreover, we can improve prediction of educational achievement somewhat by combining intelligence and past achievement scores. We do not, as the work of Gates showed more than twenty-five years ago, improve prediction by combining intelligence scores with various measures of physical growth.

However, the statistical method ordinarily used, that of multiple correlation, precludes our obtaining a lower correlation than that obtained between intelligence alone and achievement. If, on the other hand, we form simple averages involving MA's and various physical growth age scores, such as height age, weight age, grip age, and so on, and correlate the averages thus obtained with achievement, we do stand to obtain a much lower correlation. Indeed, if as many as five or six physical age measures are thus combined with MA and the resulting averages correlated with achievement, the coefficient should approach in magnitude the coefficient obtained between physical growth measures and achievement.

This is not to controvert the importance of physical growth in the conduct of schools. Physical growth features in the health and well-being of children. It is probably an important factor in their social and emotional adjustment. Certainly it would appear that any serious deviations should pose personal problems to which adjustment must be made. But we do not improve, but lower, prediction of achievement by combining physical age scores with MA scores.

For about as long as I have been acquainted with the subject at hand, there has been some expressed concern about the effect of reading proficiency on group intelligence scores. To be sure this is primarily a practical problem. But I suspect it could be argued that some of us have published papers on problems that had less practical—or theoretical—significance. In a way it is a bit strange that more work has not been done on this problem, if for no other reason than that of allaying the concern of teachers and school officials.

Some work of one of our own students on an M.A. thesis suggests that a slow reader who has good reading comprehension is penalized, so to speak, on timed group tests. No evidence was obtained to suggest that the pupils scoring low on reading comprehension, whether fast or slow in rate, were penalized in any way. It seems probable that a facile reader who enjoys excellent reading comprehension would outperform on timed group intelligence tests, an equally intelligent pupil who reads slowly. Whether such an outcome would help or hinder prediction would depend upon the relationship between reading rate and educational achievement. One would suspect that the relationship is far from close. It is conceivable, as Durrell pointed out long ago, that since reading proficiency is correlated with achievement, the presence of a reading factor in group intelligence tests may actually improve their predictive power.

Obviously, we would not expect the effect of reading proficiency on group intelligence test scores to be the same for all such tests. We would anticipate that the obtained effect would, among other things, prove to be a function of the speed-power variable.

By way of closing, some brief remarks are made apropos of the social status question in intelligence testing. Without doubt, the publicity given this question by the work of Eells, Davis, and colleagues and the earlier work of Cattell should have a wholesome effect upon test construction. As a group, test authors in the past were probably guilty of some degree of carelessness with respect to this problem. It is perhaps too early to attempt to resolve the important issues raised. The need is urgent to understand the meaning of social class differences in test scores as psychological phenomena. The use of such expressions as "culture fair" and "culture bias" gives the impression that these differences are the unwitting work of test authors. I say unwitting because surely no one would have done this by design. Obviously, if these differences are chargeable to test authors, they are unimportant as psychological phenomena, save as they become something to be studiously avoided. On the other hand, we may find that the problem is really too big for the test author. It may turn out that the kinds of cultural impact associated with social class differences affect the course of *mental development* of children as well as their performance on intelligence tests.

Social class differences are real differences—substantial psychological phenomena with which schools and society must deal. It may be that we cannot build valid intelligence tests which will not at the same time discriminate among the social classes. Or, if we start the other way round by designing tests which will not discriminate among social classes, we may find that the tests are poor predictors of academic achievement.

42. Boys and Girls—Are There Significant Ability and Achievement Differences? *

WILLIS W. CLARK

T HAT THERE ARE some significant psychological differences between boys and girls, I am sure all will agree. But there are many significant differences among boys themselves and among girls themselves as well. And for most characteristics the differences between boys and girls are no greater than the differences found among boys themselves and among girls themselves. The problem is not whether significant differences exist between the sexes but whether these differences have educational implications.

* From Willis W. Clark, "Boys and Girls—Are There Significant Ability and Achievement Differences?" *Phi Delta Kappan* (November, 1959), pp. 73, 76. Reprinted by permission of *Phi Delta Kappan* and the California Test Bureau.

A recent article suggested that mental and educational achievement differences between boys and girls had the following implications:

1. If boys are admitted to school six months or so later than girls, there will be less frustration for boys, their parents, and their teachers; and there will be fewer drop-outs of boys in high school because of failing or unsatisfactory work.

2. State legislatures or boards of education should raise the legal entering age for boys (or lower it for girls). If custodial care for immature children is needed, it can be provided much less expensively than by placing such children in the schoolroom with more advanced children.

3. All mental age norms published should be revised to provide norms for each sex.

These implications require careful study and consideration in the light of other research. At the present time school entrance is primarily based upon chronological age. While it may vary from school to school and state to state, the chronological age requirements for boys and girls are the same.

The tests utilized in this study were the California Test of Mental Maturity (CTMM) and the California Achievement Tests (CAT). The CTMM measures intelligence through a sampling of mental processes in five areas: memory, spatial relationships, logical reasoning, numerical reasoning, and verbal concepts. The test also yields separate language and nonlanguage mental ages as well as a total mental age. The CAT measures achievement in the basic skills of reading, arithmetic, and language. Two test scores are reported for each basic skill area. These scores are for reading vocabulary, reading comprehension, arithmetic reasoning, arithmetic fundamentals, mechanics of English, and spelling. These two tests together provided fourteen variables which were investigated for sex differences—the five mental factor areas plus the language, nonlanguage, and total mental ages, along with the six achievement areas of the basic skills.

A further word might be said about the boys and girls selected for use in the study. The California Test Bureau had available the CAT and CTMM scores for a total of 69,354 pupils from 341 school systems in forty-eight states. These pupils constituted a stratified sample controlled both with respect to eighteen geographical areas and four community-size categories, and was representative of the total pupil enrollment in public schools. From this sample, second stage random samples of seventy-five boys and seventy-five girls were drawn at grades three, five, and eight. Some seventy-five different school systems and cities were represented in the sample for boys and girls at each grade, and the school systems represented by the boys were independent of the school systems represented by the girls. Thus, the biasing effects due to all cases being drawn from a single school or community have been eliminated, or at least occur only by chance due to the procedures used in selecting the cases.

Among twenty-four possible chances for differences between boys and girls with respect to mental ability characteristics (eight test scores at each of three grades) only three were found. All three of these were at grade three and, contrary to findings in many other studies, the boys showed superiority over the girls in each instance. These data support the conclusion that the results of the California Test of Mental Maturity are not biased in favor of either boys or girls. Accordingly, intelligence—at least to the extent that the California Test of Mental Maturity measures intelligence —is independent of sex. Any difference in performance of individuals on the tests should be interpreted accordingly as due to differences in the mental abilities of the individual as an individual and not due to the sex of the individual.

For the California Achievement Tests no significant differences were found between the performance of boys and girls at grades three, five, and eight for reading vocabulary, reading comprehension, and arithmetic reasoning. For arithmetic fundamentals, there were no differences between the performance of boys and girls at grades three and five but at grade eight the performance of the girls was slightly better. For mechanics of English, the girls did better than the boys at grades five and eight. And for spelling, the girls performed better at all three grades.

An acceptable conclusion appears to be that for reading and arithmetic there is no basic difference in the performance of boys and girls. However, in the basic skills area of language (mechanics of English and spelling) the performance of girls is superior to the performance of boys even after differences that can be attributed to chronological age and mental age are worked out of the data.

A few of the educational implications of this study are of prime importance:

1. Sex differences in the area of general intelligence do not exist. Hence there is no need to provide mental age norms for each sex. It should be stated that many previous studies have identified sex differences in certain specific groups. The hypothesis is offered that if mental ability differences by sex do exist, they arise from environmental factors. Conditions in our environment, in our mores, in our schools, and in our customs probably operate in selective ways so as to further the development of specific abilities in one sex to a greater extent than in the other sex.

2. Differences in achievement in the basic skills areas of reading and arith-

metic were not found. It follows that we must look toward the instructional materials area, toward interests, and toward other educational factors when we find differences in performance.

3. The superior achievement of girls on both the mechanics of English and spelling tests implies that significant sex differences do exist in the language area. It may be necessary to afford additional instructional time and materials exclusively to boys in the language area in order to bring their achievement to the level of girls in the same grade.

4. Finally, on an over-all basis, this study stresses the wide range in variability in both mental ability and achievement at each grade and reminds the educator of the continuing need for dealing educationally with the individual differences of students irrespective of the sex of the pupil.

43. The Relationship of Intelligence and Achievement to Birth Order, Sex of Sibling, and Age Interval * [1]

SARAH M. SCHOONOVER

THIS INVESTIGATION is a supplement to the writer's previous study of resemblances in the mental and educational ages of siblings (Schoonover, 1956). In the original study, three different methods of analysis of longitudinal growth records, i.e., means of the average differences, percentage reduction of difference by family membership, and correlation produced evidence of a substantial amount of sibling resemblance in intelligence and achievement. Resemblances in intelligence were somewhat greater than they were in achievement.

The purpose of this study is to investigate the following questions: (a) What is the relationship of the ordinal position of a child to his mental test performance? (b) What is the relationship of the sex of a child's sibling

* From Sarah M. Schoonover, "The Relationship of Intelligence and Achievement to Birth Order, Sex of Sibling, and Age Interval," *The Journal of Educational Psychology* (August, 1959), pp. 143–45. Reprinted by permission of the author and the American Psychological Association.

[1] The writer is indebted to Willard C. Olson and to Byron O. Hughes for their criticisms and suggestions in the preparation of this manuscript.

to his mental test performance? (c) What is the relationship between age interval and degree of resemblance in mental achievement of siblings?

Studies involving familial resemblances in mental ability have been numerous during the past ninety years. The contribution of the above investigations is that they employ the longitudinal approach to this problem in a manner that has not been utilized with data analyzing sibling resemblances in intelligence or achievement.

Siblings Selected for Study

The data were obtained from the records of the University Elementary School at the University of Michigan. All true sibling pairs, with chronological age overlap, and with four or more scores per sib on the Stanford-Binet test and on the Stanford Achievement test, from the fall of 1929 through the spring of 1951, were used in this study. With these qualifications, fifty-nine sibling pairs were found for intelligence; sixty-four pairs for arithmetic, education, reading, and spelling; forty-two pairs for literature and social studies; forty pairs for language; and thirty-eight pairs for science. For additional details regarding description and selection of data the reader is referred to the earlier report (Schoonover, 1956).

Methods for the Comparison of Longitudinal Sibling Records

For each family included in this study a mental growth graph and eight achievement growth graphs were constructed. This meant that 344 growth graphs and 757 individual growth curves were plotted.

The linear equation best fitting the data was found to eliminate the observed variation and to determine some constant rate of growth which may be used to characterize the observed results. The equation of a straight line, $y = ax + b$, which gives the slope and the intercept of the line used to describe the growth-age relationship, was found by the method of the least squares fit. The linear fit for each child for intelligence and for each of the eight achievement variables was plotted graphically.

For each pair of siblings the limits of the overlap of their chronological ages were found, and from these the midpoint of the age overlap was computed. From the linear best fit, the age scores of each sibling were read at these midpoints. By subtracting the score equal to the midpoint of the age overlap from each sibling's chronological age score, the average difference for the overlap period was found. In other words, each child's mental and/or achievement age score difference from the theoretical norm was obtained. The means of these differences were calculated for the older siblings and for the younger siblings.

Using the method described above, the means of the differences between mental and/or achievement age scores and midpoints of the chronological age overlap were calculated for sibs with brothers and for sibs with sisters. To ascertain the reliability of the differences between the sib-pair means, *t* tests were employed.

The chronological age difference in months and the midpoint of the age overlap were found for each sibling pair. From the linear best fit, the age scores of each sibling were read at these midpoints. The average difference for each sibling pair was found by subtracting the smaller age score from the larger age score. Correlation coefficients were computed to discover the relationship between the chronological age difference and the average score difference for the sibling pairs. A Pearson product-moment formula was used, as was a *t* test of an observed correlation.

Findings

Older and younger siblings. The results secured by the comparison of the means of the average differences from chronological age norms for older sibs and for younger sibs are given in Table 1 for intelligence and achievement.

Table 1

MEANS OF AVERAGE DIFFERENCES FROM CHRONOLOGICAL AGE NORMS FOR
OLDER AND YOUNGER SIBLINGS, EXPRESSED IN MONTHS

Mental or Achievement Age Measure	Older Sib	Younger Sib
Mental	24.8	25.7
Arithmetic	1.0	1.4
Education	9.4	8.0
Language	35.8	35.7
Literature	23.9	21.7
Reading	18.1	14.2
Science	25.1	24.2
Social studies	13.4	13.3
Spelling	−1.1	−1.4

These older and younger siblings consistently were found to have means of average differences that were very similar to each other. No differences were found to be reliable at the .05 level.

These findings are in accord with those of Hsiao (1931), Jones and Hsiao (1928), and Griffitts (1926). They are incongruent with those of Thurstone and Jenkins (1929), Willis (1924), and Koch (1954). Jones (1954) has pointed out that in normal samples, when methodological difficulties are adequately controlled, no birth order differences in intelligence occur. The findings of this study not only support this viewpoint but, in addition, reveal no birth order differences in achievement.

Siblings with brothers and siblings with sisters. The results obtained by the comparison of the means of the average differences from chronological age norms for sibs with brothers and for sibs with sisters are shown in Table 2.

Table 2

MEANS OF AVERAGE DIFFERENCES FROM CHRONOLOGICAL AGE NORMS FOR SIBLINGS WITH BROTHERS AND SIBLINGS WITH SISTERS, EXPRESSED IN MONTHS

Mental or Achievement Age Measure	Sibs with Brothers	Sibs with Sisters
Mental	26.2	23.9
Arithmetic	3.0	−0.9
Education	10.3	6.5
Language	44.3	25.8
Literature	27.6	17.1
Reading	17.9	13.4
Science	32.7	17.1
Social studies	19.5	6.7
Spelling	1.2	−4.1

Siblings with brothers consistently were found to have larger means of average differences than siblings with sisters. In other words, sibs with brothers had higher scores than sibs with sisters in all mental and achievement measures. The differences between these sib means were significant at the .01 level or lower in language, literature, science, and social studies, and at the .05 level in arithmetic. The sib mean differences in intelligence, reading, education, and spelling were not significant at the .05 level.

These results substantiate those found by Koch (1954) and are in disagreement with those secured by Tabah and Sutter (1954). As an explanation of the finding that the possession of a male sib appears to influence test performance, Koch has pointed out that possibly the more aggressive, vigorous, and competitive male alerts his sib to a greater extent than does the more passive female.

Age interval and average score difference for siblings. The results secured by the method of correlation coefficients for chronological age interval and average score difference for sibling pairs are given in Table 3. No relationship was found between age interval and average score difference for siblings, with correlations ranging from −0.09 to +0.18 for the nine mental and achievement measures.

Table 3

CORRELATIONS BETWEEN BIRTH INTERVAL AND DIFFERENCES BETWEEN SIBLINGS IN
MENTAL AND ACHIEVEMENT AGES

Mental or Achievement Age Measure	Correlation Coefficient
Mental	0.03
Arithmetic	0.18
Education	0.00
Language	0.11
Literature	0.01
Reading	−0.09
Science	−0.07
Social studies	0.03
Spelling	−0.07

It may be observed that these correlations substantiate each other and give some indication of the value of the correlations in the population, since they are all in a relatively narrow range.

These findings are harmonious with those of Conrad (1931), Finch (1933), and Richardson (1936). On the basis of the above results, it appears that variations in birth intervals are without influence on measures of intelligence and achievement.

As a suggestion for further research it may be pointed out that if a large number of comparable longitudinal sibling records could be secured, the interactions of the variables, i.e., ordinal position, sibling's sex, and spacing could be investigated.

Summary

An analysis was made of sibling performance on intelligence and achievement tests utilizing longitudinal data. (a) No significant differences were found between older and younger siblings in intelligence or achievement as measured by deviation from the norms for chronological age. Thus priority of birth in a family gave no advantage in intelligence or achievement. (b) Sibs, irrespective of sex, with brothers consistently had higher mental and achievement ages than sibs with sisters. (c) The relationship between interval between births and the average difference in intelligence and achievement for sibling pairs was insignificant.

44. The Bases of Emotional Experiences *

LESTER D. CROW
AND ALICE CROW

AN EMOTIONAL EXPERIENCE is a stirred-up state of the individual. Although there may be increasing storm and stress during adolescence, emotions are experienced both before and after this age period. Hence they are not peculiar to the adolescent stage of development. Emotional reactions during adolescence differ, however, in certain respects from earlier emotional expression.

The nature of feeling. A feeling state is an effective experience that accompanies an individual's daily experiences. The attitude of the individual at the moment has a profound influence upon the way he may react. Both an anticipatory attitude toward, and an attitude of acceptance of, the environmental conditions aid the individual at the time to experience *pleasantness* or *unpleasantness*. Of necessity, feelings are subjective and introspective. Only the individual can experience the feeling state; if the situation is accompanied by a feeling of pleasantness, there is a desire to repeat it; if unpleasantness is experienced, there is a tendency to exhibit avoidance behavior. There is a strong adolescent drive to continue activities that bring enjoyment and thus prolong pleasant experiences, and to reject, avoid, or terminate unpleasant situations or conditions. . . .

The nature of emotion. Emotions resemble feelings to the extent that the entire body participates in the reactions that accompany the experience. Both feelings and emotions are concerned with the affective experiences

* From Lester D. Crow and Alice Crow, *Adolescent Development and Adjustment,* pp. 129–30, 134–37. Copyright 1956 by McGraw-Hill Book Co., Inc., New York, and reprinted with their permission.

that involve general reactions of the individual during the time he is affected by stimuli that arouse or excite. An individual is not born with set patterns of emotional behavior. Emotional responses are the outgrowth of interactions between inherited constitution and environmental factors of influence. An emotionalized state may be accompanied by a dynamic drive to action, but the emotion cannot be regarded as the cause of the drive.

Some adults erroneously attempt to explain a young person's expressed urge "to go places and do things" as symptomatic of the strong emotions that are considered to be characteristic of adolescent development. As we know, however, the physiological and psychological changes that are taking place during the growing-up years give rise to the arousal of new wants. The extent to which these adolescent "needs" are satisfied or thwarted determines the kind and intensity of consequent emotional reactions.

The arousal of emotions. An emotion results from the fusion of complex sensory and perceptual experiences with patterns of attitudes and behavior already established. The perception of an appropriate stimulus starts the emotion, which is fully experienced as soon as the feeling tones and other affective elements have been aroused through the functionings of the autonomic nervous system. The feelings and impulses thus aroused are basic to an emotional experience. Moreover, stimulus situations that are associated with interest or desire can become emotion-arousing. For example, if an individual has developed an interest in another individual, object, or a situation, it is possible that emotional reaction will result from stimuli that emanate from the presence of the individual, object, or situation, or from thoughts about the stimulator of the emotional state.

There is a close relationship between the stimulus that arouses the emotion and the emotion itself. A particular stimulus arouses one emotion at a time; it cannot arouse two opposite emotions simultaneously. Moreover, the stimulus situation may arouse an emotion at one time and not at another, even though the conditions appear to be similar at both times. Contrariwise, similar stimuli may arouse different and even opposing emotions at different times. Difference in perception of the stimulus will change the inner reaction of the individual to it. Stroking may arouse the emotion of anger at one time; at another it may elicit the emotion of affection.

The rate of change from one emotional state to another can be rapid. A person may be aroused by anger or jealousy at one moment; if he is exposed to an appropriate stimulus, he immediately may experience a more pleasant emotional state. The intensity and duration of emotional responses depend upon the physical and mental condition of the individual as well as upon the persistency and strength of the stimulus. An emotional state is likely to continue if the stimulus that aroused the emotion is present and the individual is aware of it. If the stimulus is removed, however, or the individual's attention is distracted from it, the emotion either disappears or is reduced considerably in strength.

Physiological bases of emotion. Many physical and physiological changes accompany an emotional experience. These changes are made possible through the functioning of the endocrine glands as they are controlled by the autonomic nervous system. This nervous system has three main divisions; they are concerned with glandular action and the action of many vital organs. The *cranial* and *sacral* divisions work together and in direct opposition to the *sympathetic* branch. The cranial and sacral therefore are sometimes called the parasympathetic branch. Nerves from all branches run to the vital organs of the body, such as the heart, blood vessels, lungs, stomach, liver, intestines, spleen, salivary glands, sweat glands, kidneys, bladder, colon, and genitals.

The sympathetic branch inhibits digestion, constricts blood vessels, dilates the pupils of the eyes, causes the hair to stand erect, releases blood sugar from the liver, stimulates the secretion of sweat glands, releases adrenaline from the suprarenal glands, increases the blood pressure and pulse, and checks the flow of saliva. The action of the cranial and sacral divisions is opposite to that of the sympathetic. There is a constant struggle for normal balance between these sets of nerves. During an emotional state the sympathetic branch is in ascendance; as the emotion subsides, the parasympathetic branch assumes control until normal balance is restored.

The nerves run to the viscera and return, rather than to the muscles that are connected with the skeleton. The sympathetic nervous system is not under voluntary control; a person cannot direct his heart to beat faster, his glands to secrete more or less fluid, or his eyes to dilate. Nor can he experience an emotion unless there is an actual stimulus to arouse it. He also is unable to stop the emotion if external and internal conditions are set for its continuance. Overt expression of one's feelings can be partially concealed, but the emotion itself cannot be controlled. The keen observer can recognize certain overt signs of emotionalism, such as a bulge of the eyes, a flush on the face, a flow of tears, a choke in the voice, an attempted retreat from the situation, or a display of aggressive behavior.

An emotion, therefore, represents affective feelings tones, is characterized by inner adjustment, is conditioned by the functioning of the autonomic nervous system, is expressed overtly through behavior responses peculiar to the particular emotional state experienced, and is aroused by the interaction between an external stimulus situation and the inner mental status.

The stirred-up state of the individual, as represented by a combination of these factors, represents an emotional experience. Thus an emotion is a dynamic internal reaction that protects and satisfies the individual or causes him discomfort or annoyance. These various aspects of an emotional experience can be condensed into a summary definition of emotion as *an affective experience that results from the fusion of complex sensory and perceptual stimulation with established patterns of behavior, accompanied by inner adjustment of stirred-up states and expressed in one or another form of overt behavior.*

45. Factors Affecting Emotionality *

ELIZABETH B. HURLOCK

IN EVERY CHILD, as in every adult, the state of emotionality varies from time to time, depending on such factors as health, time of day, and environmental influences. Any attempt to control the emotionality of the child must take into consideration these factors, because emotional control can be brought about best by eliminating the factors which act as predisposing causes. The most important of the factors predisposing the child to emotionality are the following.

1. Fatigue. When the child becomes tired, owing to too little rest, too much excitement, inadequate food for his needs, or other less common causes, he is predisposed to irritability and temper tantrums. This holds true for every age during the childhood years, but is especially serious in the early years of life when the child does not recognize fatigue as such and continues to play actively instead of resting at the time when he really needs to rest. Time out to rest, accompanied by a drink of fruit juice to give extra effort and ward off fatigue, has been demonstrated to result in less negative behavior among nursery-school children than when no break in midmorning was given or when water was substituted for fruit juice (Keister, 1950). The hungrier the child, the more prone he is to angry outbursts (Dollard *et al.,* 1939).

* From Elizabeth B. Hurlock, *Child Development,* 3rd ed., pp. 253–56. Copyright 1956 by McGraw-Hill Book Co., Inc., New York, and reprinted with their permission.

2. Poor health. When the child is in poor health due to malnutrition, digestive disturbances, diseased tonsils and adenoids, defective eyes, poor teeth, or colds, he is predisposed to emotionality, just as in the case of fatigue. Any temporary condition of poor health, such as fatigue from a restless night or irregular bowel movements, tends to make children irascible and predisposes them to temper outbursts (Goodenough, 1931). Children who have a history of frequent illness are more emotionally upset and unstable than are children whose health is better (Garrison, 1952). Among healthy children, ages 7 to 11 years, there have been found to be fewer emotional disturbances and less emotionality than at other periods of childhood and than among less healthy children (Dingwall, 1949).

3. Time of day. Because the child becomes more fatigued at certain times of the day than at others, it is not surprising to find that these times are accompanied by pronounced emotional disturbances. In babies and young children, the periods preceding the scheduled eating and nap times are the ones when emotionality is apt to be at its height. If the child's schedule is interfered with and eating or nap time is delayed, the period preceding it is generally one of pronounced fussiness and irritability. This holds true for older children as well as for younger (Goodenough, 1931).

4. Intelligence. Studies of mentally deficient children of different ages have shown that there is less emotional control, on the average, among those of the lower intellectual levels than among children of the same ages who are bright (Meltzer, 1937). However, children with greater intellect have greater emotional scope. They are more able to perceive the tragic and comic, to sense and to fear omens of future calamity, to anticipate in their feelings and thoughts the future consummation of their hopes, and to acquire a wider range of interests which may be blocked or fulfilled by their experiences (Jersild, 1954a). Even among young children, those who are bright are more sensitive to things that might endanger them than are less bright children of the same age levels (Holmes, 1935; Boston, 1939; Despert, 1942; Jersild and Meigs, 1943; Jersild, 1954, 1954a).

5. Social environment. A too exciting environment, in which there is too much tension from bickering and quarreling, from too crowded a schedule, or from too many exciting experiences for which the child is not well prepared, such as radio programs, movies, entertaining, or trips, all tend to heighten the child's emotionality. More frequent temper outbursts, for example, have been found in homes where there are visitors or more than two adults (Goodenough, 1931). As Jersild (1954) has commented, "The more adults in the home, the more occasion for everyone to get in everybody else's hair." A calm, secure, happy home life, on the other hand, results in less emotionality among children (Garrison, 1952).

How the child is handled by adults, the number of restraints placed on his activities, the type of discipline used to control his behavior, and the ease with which he can get what he wants from others, all contribute to his emotionality. Furthermore, the child can develop habits of emotionality from being with others, whether adults or children, who are themselves highly emotional. Children from poor general social level, for example, have been found to be more emotionally unstable than those who come from good, middle-class homes where the home environment is generally more stable and there is less emotional tension among the members of the home environment (Springer, 1938).

The social environment of the school influences the child's emotionality just as does the social environment of the home. Nursery-school children who are urged by adults to do such things as take off their coats or wash their hands showed more mood shifts, less stability, and less happiness than did those who were given more freedom to plan their own activities (Lee, 1932). Grade placement of elementary-school children affects their emotional stability. When a child is overaged for his grade, he tends to be emotionally unstable. This is true also of bright children who are usually younger than their classmates. Such children become the target of other children's teasing, and this leads to feelings of insecurity and anger, with their accompaniments of emotional tension (Turner and Eyre, 1940).

6. Family relationships. Parental attitudes are often responsible for a child's emotionality. Emotional symptoms are most commonly found among children whose parents neglect them, who are away at work for a large part of the day, who are overanxious about their children, who constantly talk about their children's ailments or behavior, who make babies out of them by helping them too much, who "spoil" them by giving way to them too much, or who make them the center of home life. Overprotected children show more nervous symptoms, while neglected children are more often antisocial and aggressive in their emotional behavior (Cummings, 1944). "Planned-for children," many of whom have perfectionistic mothers or parents who have too great ambitions for their children, are especially subject to emotional problems (Sloman, 1948).

First-born children are, proverbially at least, "spoiled." It is therefore not surprising if the oldest child of a family is more emotional than the later-born children. The first-born has learned from experience that the use of the emotions is a quick and easy way to get what he wants, and as a result, the child develops the habit of giving way to emotional outbursts. Similarly, the youngest child of a family, if he has been "babied" by parents and older brothers and sisters, develops habits of emotional reactions as the easiest method of dominating the social situation. How great emotional stability or instability the only child will show depends largely upon parental attitudes toward him.

7. Level of aspiration. While many emotional problems arise because parental expectations are beyond the child's potentialities and the child is made to feel inadequate by parental criticism or disappointment, some emotional instability is directly traceable to the child's own level of aspiration. Children, owing to lack of experience and lack of knowledge of their own capacities, often aspire to the impossible. If they lack the abilities and the skills to achieve the goals they have set for themselves, they feel inadequate. Too many and too repeated failures result in emotional tension, an accompaniment of all feelings of inadequacy (Garrison, 1952). As Jersild (1954a) has pointed out, "Anything that lowers a child's confidence in himself, anything that threatens his self-regard or threatens to disturb the role he wishes or pretends to play or threatens to block goals which he regards as important, may increase his tendency to be anxious or afraid."

What threatens the child's level of aspiration will vary from age to age and may even vary from time to time in the child's life. While his aspirations are of his own making, they are, nevertheless, influenced by what he knows or thinks others expect of him. To illustrate how aspirations vary, Jersild (1954) has pointed out, "When he is able, or thinks he is able, to walk by himself on rough ground, he may be angry if someone tries to take his hand, whereas earlier, when this feat was beyond what he expected of himself, he was glad to take a hand or be carried, and even later, when the rough terrain is no longer a challenge, he again may be quite glad to hold a hand or to get a lift." Thus, only when an aspiration of the moment is threatened will there be any effect on the child's emotional stability.

46. Developmental Differences in the Stability of Object Preferences and Conflict Behavior *

BETTY RHEA STEWART

WHILE CHILDREN have served as subjects in a number of conflict and choice-making studies, the focus has not been on their performance, but on the testing of general conflict theory. However, the conceptual picture of the young child presented by Baldwin, Lewin, and Werner suggests that differences in psychological maturity, roughly defined as increasing differentiation in the life space, could be expected to affect the child's stability of object preference and his behavior in a conflict situation.

The young child, as they depict him, lives in a here-and-now world where perception, emotion, action, and general cognitive activities are still partially fused. As the child grows older, differentiation between and within these capacities develops. He has an extended range of emotions instead of his earlier diffuse reactions. His perceptions are less affectively tinged and are well articulated rather than global. He has a past and a future which are significant influences in his present. He is able to withhold action until he has grasped a situation cognitively without being forced to act by the pull of the immediate situation.

The study was designed to test the effects of increasing age upon stability of object preferences and upon behavior in a conflict situation of the approach-approach type. . . .

Summary and Conclusions

The experiment was designed to examine the effects of increasing age upon stability of object preferences and behavior in conflict situations of an approach-approach type, chronological age being the independent variable. Psychological maturity and valence were assumed to be intervening variables. The dependent variables were ranking times, choice times between paired comparisons of the toys, and stability of preferences over periods of a few minutes and approximately a week.

* From Betty Rhea Stewart, "Developmental Differences in the Stability of Object Preferences and Conflict Behavior," *Child Development,* 29 (March, 1958), 9, 16–17. Reprinted by permission of the author and the Society for Research in Child Development.

The two samples consisted of 30 nursery school children and 30 fourth grade school children. In the first part of the experiment subjects were shown twelve ten cent toys which they ranked by a modified ranking procedure. In the second phase the children chose between pairs of most liked and least liked toys as determined by their previous rankings. The third part consisted of a retest of ranking behavior after an eight to eleven day lapse, and a brief interview with the older children. The following conclusions were drawn from the results:

1. Young children are less consistent in their choices than older children both in an immediate choice situation and after an interval of time.

2. Young children differ more from each other in their preferences than do grade-school children.

3. Young children choose more rapidly than older children when given a whole array of toys to choose from, but less rapidly when the task is to choose one of two toys.

4. The behavior of young children in a choice situation is more indecisive than older children's behavior.

5. The choice behavior of young children is not influenced by the valence of the objects, as ranked by themselves, but older children find it more difficult to make choices between objects they dislike.

47. *Experimental Modification of Emotions* *

HAROLD W. BERNARD

THE STUDY of the experimental modification of emotional responses is of interest for two reasons. First, many of the experiments suggest some practical implications for those who work with the growing individual. Second, hope for the improvement of behavior is generated in the face of the widespread belief that personality is formed in the first half dozen years of life. In this section three kinds of experimental studies that seem to have particular pertinence for adolescence are reviewed.

* From Harold W. Bernard, *Adolescent Development in American Culture,* pp. 319–22. Copyright 1957 by World Book Co., Yonkers-on-Hudson, N. Y., and reprinted with their permission.

Frustration and Regression

Roger G. Barker and his associates conducted an experiment designed to test the hypothesis that frustration leads to the dedifferentiation of the person and hence to regression. Although the study was made on preschool children it has pertinence for the study of adolescence because it suggests a theoretical explanation of nonconstructive emotional responses. Further, it has been pointed out in many places, including various parts of this book, that adolescents encounter many frustrations—especially those imposed by culture—which complicate their problems of adjustment.

The experiment consisted of three parts. First, there was a prefrustration period, which consisted of the subject's being placed in a playroom containing a wide variety of attractive toys. He was allowed to play freely but was encouraged to explore all of the toys through demonstrations by the experimenter. A point was made of showing the subject all of the toys so that interest would be developed that would later serve as a goal. Next, there was a frustration period which consisted of the dividing of the room by means of a wire screen, behind which most of the toys were kept. The child was allowed access to a limited number of simple toys in the other part of the divided room. The experimenter answered any questions but otherwise remained aloof from the play situation. Thirty minutes later it was suggested that they leave the room—the subjects were generally quite anxious to comply. Finally, there was a postfrustration period in which the experimenter suggested to the child that they play with the interesting toys and the screen was raised. Usually the child was pleasantly surprised and returned to the toys with alacrity. He was allowed to play until he was ready to leave. This third part was not a part of the experiment; it was simply to allow the subject to satisfy his desire to play with the toys.

Two kinds of behavior appeared in the frustration period. One was termed free activities—play with the accessible toys, activities with the experimenter, looking out the window, finding other objects in the room with which to play, wandering about and giving attention to lights and noises. The other was barrier and escape behavior—physical approach to the barrier, social attempts on the experimenter, looking and talking about the toys behind the barrier and emotional expressions of whimpering and whining. Since growth consists, among other things, of a process of differentiation, regression was judged in terms of the level of differentiation expected of a child in accordance with his life age and mental age. Based on a point scale from 2 to 8, in terms of constructiveness, the children regressed from a mean of 4.99 in constructiveness to a level of 3.94 in the frustration period. This consisted of a regression of 17.3 months of mental age. Conceptually, the interruption of elaborate play and the substitution of barren, uninteresting toys caused the following: There was a decrease in the freedom of expression of the child. There was a decrease in the mood of happiness. There was an increase in restlessness and hypertension. And there was an increase in aggressive behavior—biting, kicking, and the tendency to break and destroy.

A number of thought-provoking probabilities stem from the experiment. Living continuously with a frustration may inhibit growth toward more mature emotional expression; or, if higher levels have once been obtained, the continued frustration may produce a chronic evidence of regressive behavior. It seems probable that an increasing variety of behavioral situations would foster continued differentiation of response. Frustration decreases the constructiveness of behavior. This certainly seems to appeal to those who attempt to explain delinquent behavior. Finally, and the authors point this out, the total situation must be taken into account—the physical situation, the other persons present, and the individual himself. It is also safe to say that those who are concerned about adolescents who reveal immature emotional responses would do well to see if any frustrating situation in the adolescents' lives can be located.

Autocratic-Democratic Social Atmosphere

In the study of adolescent psychology it is important to study the processes by which an individual absorbs or rejects the ideology that predominates in his social group. An experiment by Kurt Lewin and his associates throws light upon the factors that create status and security within a group. The investigation was designed to evaluate the effect of artificially created social climates on the behavior of ten- and eleven-year-old boys. By means of the Moreno test, subjects were equated for qualities of leadership and interpersonal relations. They were then divided into autocratic, democratic, and *laissez-faire* groups, each of which had distinctive character.

In the autocratic group all determination of policy was made by the leader; techniques for attaining the goal (making paper and clay masks) were dictated by the leader so that the future steps were uncertain; the leader determined the subjects who should work together. The leader criticized and praised individuals without giving reasons but was impersonal rather than hostile. In short, the leader purposely put up barriers to the free movement of the individuals in the autocratic group.

In the democratic group, policies were a matter of group determination; steps in the pursuit of the goal were discussed and explained and alternatives were suggested; members were allowed to choose the others with whom they would work; the leader attempted to be a member of the group in spirit but did not do the actual work; he gave praise and criticism on an objective basis.

In the *laissez-faire* group, complete freedom for group and personal decision was encouraged, but the leader stated that he would help when and if help were desired. The leader was friendly when he was approached but tended to remain aloof, groupings were determined by the subjects, and comments on the work were infrequent with no attempt made at interference.

After a period of six weeks of membership in these groups a number of characteristic behaviors became evident. For the *laissez-faire* group, the number of aggressive actions per meeting averaged thirty-eight, for the autocratic group there were thirty such actions, and for the democratic group, twenty. There was thirty times as much hostile domination in the autocratic group as in the democratic. In the autocratic atmosphere there was more demand for attention and more hostile subject-subject criticism, while in the democratic group there was an atmosphere of cooperation and appreciation of others. More constructive criticisms were made in the democratic atmosphere. Observers noted that boys in the autocratic group became dull, lifeless, and apathetic in actions that were not of the aggressive type. In contrast, the democratic members were more spontaneous, friendly, and fact-minded. The evaluation of the boys themselves showed a dislike for the autocratic leader but they directed their animosity to their peers. They appreciated and liked the democratic leader but felt they should have more help and direction from the *laissez-faire* leader. When the leaders left the room (which they did as a part of the experiment) constructive activities broke down almost immediately and there was a marked rise in aggressiveness in the autocratic group. But in the democratic group normal activities continued for a longer period of time. One of the interesting phenomena of the autocratic group was the creation of a "scapegoat"—a boy who was picked on by his peers. Life was made so miserable for two of the boys that they dropped out. No such occurrences were noted in the democratic group. Thus, hostility against the autocratic leader gave rise to the psychological defense mechanism of displacement. The treatment of the finished product was also noteworthy. Those in the autocratic group destroyed the product of their work, in one case using the masks for weapons of "warfare." The democratic group discussed the matter and decided to leave their masks as models for other groups. There was a much greater manifestation of a "we" feeling in the democratic group than in the other.

48. *The Role of Social Class Differences and Horizontal Mobility in the Etiology of Aggression* *

GERHARD J. FALK

IT IS THE OBJECT of this paper to demonstrate that differential aggression patterns are the consequence of social class membership. From such a demonstration it may then be inferred that the consequences of aggression such as homicide, assault, etc., are equally related to social class.

Social Controls

That there is a difference in the adaptation of the social classes to their environment was already recognized by Aristotle.[1] The philosopher advises that one class is rich, another poor, and the third "mean" and that the latter is "best." By this he meant that "he who greatly excels in strength, beauty, birth or wealth or is very poor, very weak or disgraced cannot follow rational principles." The two extreme groups, Aristotle tells us, are likely to become criminal as those who have too much good fortune are neither willing nor able to submit to authority. They are never reared to learn the habit of obedience but commit "roguery." [2] "Evil begins at home," says the philosopher. We are also told that only the middle class of citizens can be

* From Gerhard J. Falk, "The Role of Social Class Differences and Horizontal Mobility in the Etiology of Aggression," *The Journal of Educational Sociology* (September, 1959), pp. 1–10. Copyright, 1959 by the Payne Educational Sociology Foundation, Inc. Reprinted by permission of the author and *The Journal of Educational Sociology*.

[1] Benjamin Jowett, *Aristotle's Politics* (New York: The Modern Library, 1943), p. 190.

[2] *Ibid.*, p. 191.

relied upon to secure the state and to exhibit a stable and permanent influence. Aristotle also commented that children are treated in a differential manner with reference to socioeconomic class.

This phenomenon is of course still true. Thus we find that the lower classes are more severe with regard to toilet-training while American middle classes expect of their children a good deal of educational attainment.[3] The social classes also differ with respect to the feeding of infants, weaning and the use of pacifiers; bowel and bladder control and the assumption of responsibilities in the household.[4] In other words, the techniques employed in the care and rearing of children are culturally patterned and therefore tend to be similar within a social class.[5] Lower classes are reported to have a psychologically close hierarchical and rigid parent-child relationship while middle classes are more ostensibly equalitarian and flexible in this regard.[6] At the same time lower classes tend to be more permissive with respect to outside activities than the upper classes. The middle class is more concerned with fostering parentally trained independence in their children by clearly defining the extent of outside activities that may be sought. Maintenance of supervision by the withdrawal of approval makes the middle-class child aware of the importance of "proper" behavior which may be defined as conformity to class standards.

Warner [7] indicates that life in the middle-class family proceeds according to strictly established rules with reference to the outside world and that children are vigorously supervised and brought up to value the achievement patterns and moral codes of their class. Discipline exists in the lower classes also but it is often harsh and there is little supervision of children outside the home.

Differential Child Rearing and Aggression

These differences in child rearing are not confined to the home. They are carried over to the schools as well.

[3] Robert J. Havighurst and Allison Davis, "A Comparison of the Chicago and Harvard Studies of Social Class Difference in Child Rearing," *The American Sociological Review,* 20 (August, 1955), 441.

[4] Allison Davis and Robert J. Havighurst, "Social Class and Color Differences in Child Rearing," *The American Sociological Review,* 11 (November, 1946), 698.

[5] Abraham Kardiner, *The Individual and His Society* (New York: Columbia University Press, 1939), p. 147.

[6] Henry Maas, "Some Social Class Differences in the Family Systems of Pre- and Early Adolescents," *Child Development,* 22 (September, 1951), 145.

[7] Ruth Rosner Kornhauser, "The Warner Approach to Social Stratification," *Class, Status and Power* (New York: The Free Press, 1953), p. 233.

This means that there are different controls upon children from different social classes in the schools of the country.[8] Thus, as schools are now constituted, controls fall more heavily on boys than on girls and the hand of authority is much lighter upon the child of the upper and middle class than on the child of the lower class.[9] The tendency is to be harsh and rebuking to the child of the lower class, to make punishment more severe for such children and to minimize rewards for children categorized as "racial" or "ethnic" minorities. The same holds true of a child with a "bad" reputation.

The consequence of these class differentials in rearing children is of course differential personality organization as well. It is the predominant type of social relationship in a society or ethnocentric group which determines an individual's society oriented identification, his status, his demands and his expectations.[10] To these he must conform in order to preserve his social relationships.

Thus the personality of an individual becomes the organization of his drives and motives as dictated by the unconscious aspects of mental behavior. This behavior differs from class to class and is largely determined by environmental pressures.

Thus we see that personality is a function of class differentials, a view which is supported by the finding that there is a relationship between neurosis and social class.[11] This would indicate that if neuroses of all kinds are manifestations of underlying personality characteristics there is some evidence that class differentials affect adjusted as well as nonadjusted persons.[12]

Adjustment is defined as emotional conditioning to class values. Since the pressures and constraints of one class differ so much from that of another class it becomes evident that there is no objective criterion of well adjusted or "neurotic" but that these terms must be sociologically interpreted with reference to the group in which the subject operates.

Thus, lower-class children are encouraged to express aggression freely and openly. The slum culture teaches a child to fight and to admire

[8] George Psathas, "Ethnicity, Social Class and Adolescent Independence from Social Control," *The American Sociological Review,* 25 (August, 1957), 442.

[9] H. Otto Dahlke, *Values in Culture and Classroom* (New York: Harper and Bros., 1957), p. 274.

[10] Jack P. Gibbs and Walter T. Martin, "A Theory of Status Integration," *The American Sociological Review,* 23 (April, 1958), 141.

[11] Robert J. Havighurst, "Social Class and Basic Personality Structure," *Sociology and Social Research,* 36 (July, 1952), 356.

[12] Robert B. Cattell, "The Cultural Functions of Social Stratification," *The Journal of Social Psychology,* 21 (July, 1948), 25.

fighters.[13] Thus the child who shocks her middle-class teacher by telling how her uncle beat her aunt as a "Mother's Day Present" [14] gets approval from her own group for aggression while the teacher considers the same trait obnoxious. The reverse is also true. Middle classes praise children for being anxious to please, for keeping quiet and for compliance with their requests. These same traits, however, are considered the attributes of a "schemer" by the lower class. Here outspokenness is considered important and aggression is considered a token of "honesty." [15] Readiness to "tell people off" is esteemed and culture heroes are people who have long police records, particularly if they have been charged with murder.[16]

This aggressiveness is developed in children from 2 to 5 years of age so that they will be quick to fight and proud of their handiwork. Women expect their brothers, fathers, and husbands to be cocky and aggressive.

Additional light is shed on this class differential by the fact that lower-class children have less of an opportunity to rise to a higher socioeconomic position than is true for middle-class children. Therefore, the restrictions imposed by the middle-class parent on his children are purposeful because they lead to upward mobility. The lower-class child sees no such advantage and therefore resents restrictions more and is more willing to exhibit aggression or frustration.[17]

Values and Social Class

In simple folk societies most people have a rather well defined status which is sustained and reinforced by direct participation in community life.[18] Thus social forces make for a good deal of rigidity of classes and give each individual a definitive guide for behavior. In American society however, classes are less well defined than in caste societies.[19] This is particularly true in the urban community but is also true in urban oriented groups. Even while some social forces have made for more rigidity, others have tended to counteract this. As a result many persons' notions of class have

[13] W. Allison Davis and Robert J. Havighurst, *Father of the Man* (Boston: Houghton Mifflin Co., 1947), p. 14.

[14] *Ibid.*, p. 15.

[15] *Ibid.*, p. 17.

[16] *Ibid.*, p. 19.

[17] Milton L. Barron, *The Juvenile in Delinquent Society* (New York: Alfred A. Knopf, 1955), p. 134.

[18] Elwin H. Powell, "Toward a Redefinition of Anomie," *The American Sociological Review*, 23 (April, 1958), 131.

[19] Gideon Sjoberg, "Are Social Classes in America Becoming More Rigid?" *The American Sociological Review*, 16 (December, 1951), 783.

become confused and indistinct. This trend is further enhanced by the indeterminate state of the class structure as designed by such variables as occupation and economic success. Ours is an acquisitive and competitive society where individuals are admired by reason of prestige positions that are achieved. The role which the person plays first as a child in the family and then in the peer group and finally as an adult are all functions of the rights and obligations of status which is defined here as any position in any social system.[20]

These roles finally become incorporated into the structure of the self and are exhibited in self-discipline, the unconscious aspect of mental behavior.[21] Outside pressures, such as the demands of the job, the expectations of friends and relatives, and the relations to associates structure these roles even more closely and serve to keep the family together and control the individual.[22]

This then leads to the conclusion that the status of the adult white male in America depends primarily on occupation. Thus the vocation of an individual determines his general social status if determined either by himself or someone else.[23] However, status is not the same when subjectively determined or when objectively analyzed. In fact differences arise here which are a function of class membership. Therefore values are not the same from class to class.[24]

When differences between the values of people are analyzed by class it appears that differing social classes will define values subjectively in a manner which may differ from the objective measure of their class membership. This means that the criteria of occupation and economic condition, value judgments and other objective factors tend to classify individuals in a social class which is not always consistent with their self-conception of their status.

Thus class is defined both subjectively and objectively and differs on the basis of who classified an individual. Therefore the attitudes of people are determined by the class in which they believe they are. For instance, different groups in a community have a differential amount of power, but this does not mean the same thing to everyone.[25]

[20] Powell, *op. cit.,* p. 132.

[21] Havighurst, *op. cit.,* p. 358.

[22] August B. Hollingshead, "Class Differences in Family Stability," *The Annals of the American Academy of Political and Social Science,* 272 (November, 1950), 39.

[23] Powell, *op. cit.,* p. 132.

[24] Ivan D. Steiner, "Some Sociological Values Associated with Objectively and Subjectively Defined Social Class Membership," *Social Forces,* 31 (May, 1953), 328.

[25] Walter Goldschmidt, "Social Class in America—A Critical Review," *The American Anthropologist,* 52 (October, 1950), 484.

The power relationship in society is instrumental in promoting the individuality of each member of the group. Thus, the master is more of an individual than the servant, the commander more than the common soldier. Individualism grows with power and with wealth but also with responsibility. This responsibility consists both of the view which the individual has toward himself and also the opinion he has of those who make him responsible.[26]

Class Membership and the Frustration Aggression Hypothesis

In modern western societies the "proletariat" and other classes are theoretically considered equal before the law. Actually, however, and to some extent even legally, the totality of their rights and privileges is much more modest than that of other classes.[27] Thus, punishment for criminals with different social characteristics, such as social class and sex, varies according to the crime and its cultural significance for that class and sex.[28] The reason for this is that people with different life experiences are likely to make different judgments concerning the seriousness of an offense and the punishment that should be assigned for the violation of the law.

The deterrent and retributive effects of a given sentence can therefore be assumed to be different for different segments of the population. For instance, the lower-class Negro is characterized by attitudes and modes of behavior brought from the South. He has "a greater tendency to follow without anxiety an accommodative and stereotyped role with respect to whites, a more unstable and mobile employment status and a fairly casual attitude toward family and institutional controls." [29]

Law, however, was developed in an earlier and more integrated society and does not always reflect contemporary diversified values as outlined in the above quotation.[30] In addition to the differences in interpretation of social control as practiced by diverse socioeconomic and racial groups, the agents of social control also differ in their interpretation of behavior dependent of course on their class membership. Thus the background of

[26] Ferdinand Tönnies, "Stände und Klassen," *Handwörterbuch der Soziologie* (Glencoe: The Free Press, 1931), p. 58.

[27] Pitirim Sorokin, "What Is a Social Class?" *The Journal of Legal and Political Sociology*, 3 (September, 1947), 24.

[28] Arnold M. Rose and Arthur E. Prell, "Does the Punishment Fit the Crime?" *The American Journal of Sociology*, 51 (November, 1955), 248.

[29] Richard A. Schermerhorn, *These Our People* (Boston: D. C. Heath and Co., 1949), p. 148.

[30] Sorokin, *op. cit.*, p. 25.

judges is related to their judgments and the punishment they assign for various offenses differ with the sex, socioeconomic status and size of the community concerned.[31] Therefore punishments favored for criminals of different social classes and for the two sexes vary according to the crime and its cultural meaning in relation to class and sex.

Thus social controls of a legal nature are more stringent upon the less privileged groups than the more powerful groups. However, this is not the only area in which the deprivations of a low socioeconomic status operate. The nature of the work done by the "proletariat" is often highly monotonous. It is boring and little calculated to stimulate thought, to say nothing of creativeness. His share of burdensome duties including subordination and dependence on others is disproportionately large. Thus, "to be poor means to be dependent on the grace and good will of the rich." [32]

Now the problem of the place of power in the social system shades directly into that of authority relationships. Both root in the fundamentals of social interaction and become meaningful when institutionalized expectations include the legitimization of coercive sanctions.[33] This means that authority is synonymous with superiority and control over the action of others. The nature and basis of such superiority may vary widely. However, whatever its source, the superior-inferior relationship promotes a feeling of frustration on the inferior individual and generates a strong motive for conflict by imputing to the superior class responsibility for the injustices under which the inferior suffers.[34]

This does not imply that frustration for the lower classes in American society is imaginary. Instead, it is very real and self-perpetuating. Poverty means hardship. By reason of low income or dependence on relief undernourishment is common.[35] Clothing, furniture, and utensils cannot be replaced when they wear out. Life is thus a nightmare of fear and hunger, evictions and a pauper's grave. The burden of debt holds many families in poverty even if their income might otherwise be adequate. This perpetuates the deprivations of the lower-class community and creates a sense of despair. Such despair is founded on experience as a vicious circle enmeshes the poor. Their health is generally poor. Therefore their stamina is low. In addition they are culturally deficient as they lack education. Consequently employers are unwilling to hire them except for the most routine

[31] Rose, *op. cit.,* p. 43.

[32] Tönnies, *op. cit.,* p. 62.

[33] Talcott Parsons, "The Theory of Social Stratification," Bendix, *op. cit.,* p. 96.

[34] T. H. Marshall, "The Nature of Class Conflict," *Class Conflict and Social Stratification* (New York: The Institute of Sociology, 1938), p. 108.

[35] James Ford, *Social Deviation* (New York: The Macmillan Co., 1939), p. 290.

jobs. These jobs are the least stable and most subject to business cycles so that the lower-class worker is the last to be hired and the first to be fired. This in turn results in cheap rental living, overcrowded rooms and family instability.[36]

"The lower-class family pattern is unique. The husband-wife relationship is more or less an unstable one even if the marriage is sanctioned by law. Disagreements leading to quarrels and vicious fights followed by desertions by either men or women are not uncommon." [37] Thus broken homes are frequent and children begin their lives under such circumstances. This leads many lower-class persons to assume that their circumstances are hopeless, that respectable people sneer at them and that the social controls are unjust.

Admittedly, social controls always have their limitations. Abel describes how even the rulers of a concentration camp cannot insure a "foolproof" organization but must contend with the unforeseen and the weaknesses of human nature.[38] That is to say that humans cannot be molded like a robot. Thus any ruling personnel is dependent on its subject population and this dependence insures that controls can never be complete. Nevertheless there appears to be some evidence that frustrations consequent to social controls may lead to aggression.[39]

The frustrations inherent in any vertical relationship produce a number of different possible responses, one of which may be some form of aggression. Even when no specific frustrating agent is present some object may be created for the purpose of relieving aggression arising from frustrating situations.[40] This need varies with the tolerance to frustration which a thwarted individual may have. However, such frustration is often displaced upon a person or group representing a constellation of ideas that evoke hostility. Such aggressive responses as are then evoked may be spectacularly dangerous to society.

Periodically attention is focussed on a person who has committed an extremely aggressive crime.[41] Such crimes are often committed by persons

[36] Joseph A. Kahl, *The American Class Structure* (New York: Rinehart and Co., 1957), p. 211.

[37] *Ibid.*, p. 212.

[38] Theodore Abel, "The Sociology of Concentration Camps," *Social Forces,* 30 (December, 1951), 154.

[39] John Dollard, *Frustration and Aggression* (New Haven: Yale University Press, 1950), p. 134.

[40] Neal E. Miller, "The Frustration Aggression Hypothesis," *The Psychological Review,* 48 (July, 1941), 340.

[41] August B. Hollingshead, "Selected Characteristics of Classes in a Middle Western Community," *American Sociological Review,* 12 (June, 1947), 385.

feeling inferior either with regard to society in general or with regard to a specific person with whom there exists frequent face to face contact. In such cases murder may be the result of a wish to get rid of the real or imagined domination of another person, thereby removing the inferiority suffered.

Alexander [42] describes such a case, a situation which resulted in fratricide: "In the course of a quarrel Mark, who was 19 years old, shot his brother William, who was two years younger than he, and his friend Ferdinand, approximately the same age. The psychological problem that the criminal act of this boy imposes on us consists fundamentally of how this weak, somewhat introverted, not especially aggressive young man with a constant feeling of inferiority committed such a deed which no one thought him capable of.

. . . his younger brother William was physically stronger and had beaten him brutally . . . he began to give way to the feeling of being constantly the underdog. In phantasy his brother continually struck him. When he got into a controversy with anyone this picture appeared, paralyzing his power of resistance. The resulting tension caused his hatred of his brother and the shooting." This murder occurred within a family group.

Differential Mobility

An important function of our class oriented society is horizontal and vertical mobility. This presents the individual with the necessity of adapting to various social strata and different conditions in time and place throughout a lifetime.[43] Consequently a good deal of mental and emotional strain accompanies this mobility while intensive shifting from place to place also hinders considerably the promotion of rigid habits and stable morals. Thus we find that stratification creates hostility and horizontal mobility fosters the opportunity to express it. Therefore an inverse relationship exists between the degree of horizontal mobility and the strength of the social controls.

Anyone who has read *The Grapes of Wrath* by John Steinbeck finds therein an example of this relationship. This is further underscored by the high delinquency and crime rates in the slums of New York and Chicago and other large cities where high mobility is accompanied by truancy, runaway children, vagrancy and crimes of all kinds.[44]

[42] Franz Alexander, "A Double Murder Committed by a Nineteen Year Old Boy," *The Psychoanalytical Review,* 24 (June, 1937), 113.

[43] Pitirim Sorokin, *Social Mobility* (New York: Harper and Bros., 1927), p. 510.

[44] Harry Elmer Barnes and Negley K. Teeters, *New Horizons in Criminology* (New York: Prentice-Hall, 1947), p. 154.

Thus, both urban and rural mobility promotes disorganization. The country boy who comes home from the city with alien notions is a less frequent example of disorganization than the city boy who has been exposed to differential culture patterns. Nevertheless, the effect is the same and maladjustment is the result.[45]

A study of mobility in Seattle connects high labor turnover with juvenile delinquency, low school attendance, and court appearances. Thus it can justifiably be concluded that delinquency varies directly with horizontal and vertical mobility. An illustration of the degree of spatial mobility with which our society must deal is given by Sutherland.[46] Relating the circumstances of the Urschel kidnapping he says, "the Urschel kidnapping occurred in the state of Oklahoma, the victim was held captive in a remote rural section of Texas, the ransom money was paid in Missouri, a portion of the money was exchanged in Minnesota, another portion was hidden in Texas, one of the guilty parties was located in Colorado and the others in Tennessee, Minnesota, Texas and Illinois."

Conclusion

We have shown that aggressive patterns are learned as part of early childhood education and are reinforced by class membership. Consequently, violent crimes are equally related, and learned. It can thus be adequately concluded, that the preponderance of violent offenses in the lower classes is related to a *generally more violent* environment, rather than to any "criminal tendencies." Since crimes of violence are more subject to publicity, however, than crimes of a more subtle nature, it is easy to believe that crime is *per se* more frequent in lower than middle or upper classes.

This view we have thus refuted.

[45] Barnes, *op. cit.*, p. 154.
[46] Edwin H. Sutherland, *Principles of Criminology* (New York: J. B. Lippincott Co., 1947), p. 248.

CHAPTER IX

FORMATION
OF INTERESTS
AND ATTITUDES

49. *A Survey of the Attitudes, Opinions, and Objectives of High School Students in the Milwaukee Area* * [1]

WILLIAM H. BOYER

Procedure

This study began in a Psychology of Adolescence course in the spring of 1957. Both the students and the teacher were interested in obtaining more direct information about adolescents than textbooks and journals offered. The class developed lists of questions relating to attitudes, opinions, and objectives of adolescents. These questions were organized into a questionnaire and given to teen-age groups. The questionnaires provided such useful information that the study was expanded, and two members of the original class continued the project in the fall of 1957 and obtained information from high school students throughout the Milwaukee area.

The sample consists of anonymous questionnaires from 569 adolescents. All socioeconomic classes, age levels, religious groups, and sexes are represented in the sample. No precise randomizing procedure was used but care was taken to distribute the sample throughout the area. Samples were taken from public high school classes required of all students. The majority

* From William H. Boyer, "A Survey of the Attitudes, Opinions, and Objectives of High School Students in the Milwaukee Area," *The Journal of Educational Sociology* (March, 1959), pp. 344–48. Reprinted by permission of the author and *The Journal of Educational Sociology*.
[1] Special assistance on the project was provided by Betts Haven and Amy Stuart, students at Milwaukee-Downer College where the study was conducted.

of respondents (69%) were from the upper high school grades since they were the most useful in giving replies to questions about future adult plans and past adolescent experiences.

Since the sample was taken from public high school students, adolescents who dropped out of school were not proportionally included. Those who dropped out would be less likely to have favorable attitudes about education and society than those who remained in the "success ladder" of society. The study is therefore more representative of adolescents in school than of the adolescent population as a whole.

All ratios given in the findings are percentage rather than numerical comparisons. In all of the findings it is necessary to keep in mind that these are statements of opinion and may not directly correspond with active forms of behavior. The findings are not necessarily true of high school students throughout American society, but they provide an indication of patterns in one locality.

Summary of the Findings

RESPONSE TO SOCIETY

School. A majority (84%) said they were satisfied with their high school. Nearly twice as many of the dissatisfied students were boys. The most frequent reasons given for dissatisfaction were:
1. Need a broader variety of course offerings
2. Need less "regimentation"
3. Need better student counseling

Religion. About two thirds (69%) said that religion played an important part in their lives. The majority of this group was girls. There was a slight trend toward more interest in religion at the higher age levels.

The following percentages of those who list a religious preference said their religion does not play an important part in their lives:
1. Jewish   50% (based on only eight in sample)
2. Protestant   31%
3. Catholic   22%

Six per cent of the total sample said they have no religious preference.

Parents. The majority of the students (64%) said they have had wholly satisfactory relations with their parents. Of those who were dissatisfied, slightly more were boys, and there was a small increase in dissatisfaction with an increase in age.

Those who had conflicts with their parents usually complained that parents are "overstrict." Girls voiced this complaint twice as often as boys.

Yet many others wish their parents were "more strict." The main concern was for "more understanding."

Special legal restriction on adolescents. The majority were satisfied with the special legal restrictions on adolescents. The following percentages indicate those who believe present laws are unjustified relating to:

1. Employment and voting   (35%)
2. The sale of cigarettes   (25%)
3. Driving age   (20%)
4. The sale of liquor   (17%)
5. Marriage   (13%)

Guidance sources. When advice is needed the following persons were considered the most important (in rank order):

1. The mother   4. A friend
2. The father   5. A sibling
3. The minister   6. A teacher

Boys indicated no preference for either parent over the other (42% would consult either). Girls listed their mothers nearly five times as often as their fathers as the person they would be most likely to consult in making an important decision.

Response to the status quo. Most of the respondents (69%) were not satisfied with the world as it is and would like to be able to make the following changes (in rank order):

1. Reduce the threat of war
2. Improve domestic political problems
3. Reduce racial prejudice
4. Improve American education

A slightly higher percentage of girls than boys indicated dissatisfaction with the world as it is, and there was a slight increase in dissatisfaction with an increase in age. However, when "the threat of war" was excluded, the majority were satisfied with the world as it is.

Sex, Dating, and Marriage

Only a minority had any definite plans for marriage in the immediate future, and 75 per cent were not currently going steady. However, the majority (57%) of both boys and girls approved of going steady. Their main reasons were that going steady provides "security for dates," "preparation for marriage," and "learning to get along with the opposite sex." The main reason for not wanting to go steady was that "you don't meet enough people."

The majority (84%) thought sex education should be taught in the schools, but they did not believe the schools were currently doing an adequate job. They suggested that sex education should begin in the seventh or eighth grade, or no later than the ninth.

Leisure Activities

Sports were the most popular kinds of leisure activities for both the boys and girls, especially for the boys. Next in importance were social activities and then individual hobbies.

The majority (62%) read five or more books a year in addition to those required in school, and the girls read slightly more than the boys. There was a small reduction in leisure reading with an increase in age.

The following were the five most popular books:

1. *Gone with the Wind*
2. *Hot Rod*
3. *The Robe*
4. *Street Rod*
5. *The Yearling*

Future Plans

Fifty-one per cent said they expected to go to college, slightly more boys than girls. This group considered high school to be primarily a preparatory requirement for college. About 6 per cent of those intending to go to college did not expect to graduate. The majority of those planning to go to college lived in the higher socioeconomic class areas.

The following vocations were listed most often as future vocational goals:

Boys		*Girls*	
1. Engineer	17%	Secretary	25%
2. Mechanic	15%	Teacher	16%
3. Draftsman	10%	Nurse	13%
4. Air Force	4%	Housewife	8%
5. Architect	2%	Airline Stewardess	4%
6. Doctor	2%	Beautician	3%
7. Teacher	2%	Social Worker	3%

(Notice that girls designated teaching eight times as often as boys. Only 8 per cent of the girls listed "housewife" as their only vocational objective.)

A wide variety of vocational objectives were listed, often with only one or two students having a particular interest. Seven per cent had no vocational plans, and they said they were in school primarily because of "social opportunities," "interest in learning," "compulsory laws," and "parental demands" (in that order). Only 2 per cent intended to quit high school before graduation.

Nearly half (42%) of the boys expected to go into military service. Twenty-nine per cent of the boys who intended to go to college expected to go into military service before they went to college.

Eleven per cent had made plans for marriage and a majority of these were girls.

An Appraisal of the Findings

Most of these teen-age students indicated little awareness of the many critical problems of their age. Thirty-one per cent were completely satisfied with the world as it is, very probably as a result of their not really being aware of the realities of the world they live in. If "concern for the dangers of war" is excluded, the majority were willing to adjust to the world as it is. No student objected to military conscription, even though it might delay or even deter his higher education or future vocational plans.

The majority considered education to be primarily vocational preparation, an anachronistic misemphasis in a world where the development of a variety of abilities is necessary. Schools may need to give students a better understanding of the nonvocational values of education and to help counteract the class-status symbolism of much current education.

Parents may be surprised to learn how willing their teen-age sons and daughters are to follow their advice. It is not enough, of course, that parents exert a primary influence; it is the kind of influence they exert that is crucial. (The predominance of matriarchal influence may warrant consideration.)

A minority of the students made perceptive and critical replies to the questions, and their criticism was usually constructive, rarely with any indication of hostility. Future studies might profitably concentrate on these "deviants" so we may better understand how they got that way. Too often adolescents are classified as the good ones (the conformists) and the bad ones (the delinquents), yet the classification that has been omitted may include the most socially valuable group of all.

50. *Attitudes Affect Pupils' Learning* *

CYRIL R. MILL

At the 1950 White House Conference on Children and Youth, William Heard Kilpatrick made a point with a memorable illustration. In talking about "What do pupils learn?" he referred to the way that most of us were taught to go to church. When we were children we were made to go to church. Whether we wanted to or not, every Sunday, and sometimes oftener we had to dress up and go to a church. It was usually the idea of our parents that if we developed early habits of going to church these habits would stay with us for the rest of our lives.

But did we really learn to go to church? In fact, many of us learned just the opposite. We went to church while we were children because we were forced to, but as soon as we became old enough to have some control over our own behavior we stopped going to church. For many of us it was not until much later when we had rethought through the whole matter that we determined for ourselves whether or not we would be regular church goers.

As Dr. Kilpatrick said, "A child can be forced to do on the outside because we are bigger and stronger than he is, but for effective learning we must reach the child on the inside." In other words, we must have an effect on his attitudes toward what we teach if we want other techniques of instruction to take effect.

Attitudes Affect What

Kilpatrick's illustration demonstrates the important point that we do not always know what we are teaching. In fact, we may sometimes be teaching the child the opposite from what we think we are getting across to him.

A junior high boy once told his teacher, "Mrs. Jones, I think I could like you if you weren't an English teacher!" What he was really saying was that his attitude toward English was such that he could never like anyone associated with it, and she might as well stop trying to teach him the parts of speech. Many classroom teachers can tell you that they often experience a nagging sensation that they are teaching entirely the wrong thing for the pupils who happen to be facing them in the classroom. They

---

* From Cyril R. Mill, "Attitudes Affect Pupils' Learning," *Educational Leadership* (January, 1960), pp. 212–16. Reprinted by permission.

would like to throw out the curriculum, the course-work for the day, and, forgetting about external pressures, see what they could do to really reach these youngsters where they live. They have the feeling that their point of entry into the child's world is all wrong, and that as long as they continue on their present track they will get nowhere.

A child's attitude toward subject matter often sets up a process of selective attention. *What* he will learn is determined in part by his readiness to receive.

Attitudes Affect How

One answer to this problem of reaching inside the world of the learner was provided in this Journal just a year ago in an article by Carl Rogers. He pointed out the similarity between significant learning and psychotherapy. Learning is facilitated when a pupil is confronted with a situation perceived as a problem. It also helps when the teacher is able to be a real person who is not playing some sort of a role, and who can truly accept and understand the feelings of the pupil. In this situation the teacher provides resources and tools, and he includes himself among the other resources for which the pupil might discover a use. Basic to this idea of teaching is the climate in the classroom which promotes the development of natural tendencies in the pupil.

A follow-up article by Tenenbaum illustrates the intense attitudes for learning which are developed under such circumstances as those described by Rogers. Students tend to work harder than ever before, and experience changes in themselves which they would not have believed possible. This change in attitude toward learning effects a change in their learning behaviors so that their whole being becomes involved.

Attitudes are thus closely related to motivation. Fortunate is the teacher whose children are positively oriented toward him and his subject matter. He will find them working with greater vigor, learning more, more quickly.

Attitudes Affect Why

Learning is facilitated when a close, positive relationship exists between teacher and pupil. Sometimes this relationship becomes so intense that it resembles the identification phenomenon that brings a boy to emulate characteristics of his father, or a girl to imitate her mother. Pupils who identify with their teacher not only adopt his mannerisms, and speech, and feel a desire to be close to him, they also work hard to follow his directions, to be a good member of his group, and to earn and deserve his praise.

The attitude of a child toward his teacher can also hamper the learning process. If a child hates his teacher, or is irritated by his teacher's voice or some mannerism, he may really be unable to perform at his optimum level. Such instances, usually referred to as a "personality conflict," are distressing to everyone. In spite of such occurrences, teachers do not need to feel that they must woo their pupils and win them over to doing good work by being "friendly." Children react to genuineness in an adult, and pupil polls have repeatedly shown a preference for the teacher who is on the strict side—a good disciplinarian. But where a child's grades begin to fall, the alert teacher can well ask whether a deteriorating teacher-pupil relationship is the cause. If so, it is often something that can easily be remedied.

What Are Attitudes?

The importance of a child's attitudes toward learning cannot be underestimated. To understand this, one needs to go further and explore the nature of attitudes in general. What is it about an attitude that gives it strength to influence the way a person behaves?

Suppose you rate yourself on the following concepts. Give yourself a rating of 1 if you feel strongly *for* and 5 if you are strongly *against*. If you are neutral, rate yourself 3.

_____The NEA
_____A communist in the White House
_____*Lady Chatterley's Lover*
_____Small foreign cars
_____Fluoridation
_____The Catholic Church
_____Jack Paar
_____"This Is Your Life"
_____Pogo
_____A person who cracks his knuckles

It is the items which you marked "5" in which we are interested. As you read the item, did you feel a repugnance? Did you use extra effort and pressure in marking the "5" so that it is blacker than the other ratings? Did your expression change as you read the item?

These and many other reactions may have been elicited by the concepts which you oppose. They indicate an emotional response called *negative valence,* and simply reflect that you bear within yourself the tendency to react against many items which from time to time may arise in your environment. In a like manner, you possess a readiness to respond favorably toward other aspects in your environment (positive valence).

These readinesses, or tendencies, influence behavior. Because of them one works to get the things he wants, one votes for and against certain issues, one joins a cause, opposes something, attempts to influence others, and in many ways succumbs to the push and pull of attitudinal valences throughout the day.

The crucial and unique feature of attitudes and the aspect which makes them potent in the learning situation is their emotional component. People generally take a stand for or against Jack Paar or Pogo, for instance, and defend their position with heat and vehemence. A belief which lacks this emotional aspect is something else again—perhaps it may be only an opinion or judgment.

Where emotion is involved, the effect upon learning is going to be intensified. A strong positive valence for a subject will result in the quick amassing of a great deal of material in a short time. On the other hand, as above in the case of the boy and the English teacher, a strong negative valence is going to make learning difficult or impossible until the situation is restructured to bring to the fore some aspect with a positive potential. For instance, if the teacher can show the boy the similarity between the logic in grammar and the logic in an automobile engine, he may get some fun out of diagramming a sentence. Such restructuring is often more readily accomplished than effecting a change in the original attitude itself.

Whose Attitudes?

The child's attitudes are not the only ones that need scrutiny in this issue. Teachers have attitudes that are important to the learning process, as well as parents, communities, and prevailing attitudes in the nation as a whole.

In the impressionable years of childhood one might say that attitudes are catching. Anderson and Brewer found that children placed in nursery school under a dominative teacher showed significantly more dominative and aggressive behavior in the classroom and on the playground than children who were placed under more democratic and permissive (socially integrative) teachers. The following year, if the children were placed with a teacher with different characteristics, it was not long before the children's play took on these new attributes.

Parents are sometimes appalled at their children's attitudes, as reflected in dinner-table conversation, which turn out to be considerably different from their own. In fact, as the child grows older, child rearing seems to develop largely into an effort to counteract some of these family-alien attitudes picked up by the children from outside the family circle. A constant complaint of parents is, "We'd get along fine if it weren't for the influence of Betty's friends." But one cannot bring up a child in a vacuum. The early family relationships must have been built up strongly enough to withstand the later influences from outside which may occasionally be deemed undesirable.

A very difficult situation exists where a middle-class teacher (which includes most of us) is trying to teach lower-class children. The value system in lower-class homes is so different, the attitudes of children, parents, and neighborhood at such variance from those of the middle-class teacher that he often feels he is speaking in a foreign tongue.

Consider his efforts at teaching common courtesy, "please," "thank you," and "excuse me," to children who regard such niceties as affected or snobbish. The teacher regards books, and their care, with high value; the children are often unused to thinking about them at all! How many boys in manual arts classes make as their first project a bookshelf—and take it to a home where there are no books! Teachers regard fighting as a stupid way of settling differences; but many boys would not gain the respect and approval of their own father if they could not hold their own in a street fight.

Even speech patterns are reflected in this class difference. A slum boy, greeted in the morning by his teacher with "Good morning, Robert," refused to answer and threw himself into his seat. Another teacher entered and said, "Hi, Bob," to which he replied with "Hi" and a beaming smile.

Such attitudes toward school, books, teachers, and the learning situation in general are often a reflection of home and neighborhood. I am rather pessimistic about how far any teacher or school can go to effect a positive change in the situation except in the occasional case where a child and a home are atypical for the particular neighborhood culture. For instance, some families are on the move, going up the social scale. A mother or father does not accept the class mores for themselves and their children. Where such an attitude and drive for betterment exists, the teacher can do wonders to help the child get the education he and his family desire.

It is because of the existence of such children that teachers must avoid stereotyping whole groups or classes. Remaining alert for the golden nuggets which exist in almost any group and helping them to achieve a little more polish and shine, educationally speaking, are stimulating and rewarding, and keep many teachers in positions which are otherwise frustrating and dull.

Our country has a long way to go before its national attitudes toward education can compare favorably to those found in the USSR. What would we be able to achieve if it were commonly held that to obtain the highest possible training was a patriotic duty? What would happen to our teacher shortage if the teaching profession were on a par with medicine, and similarly rewarded? What changes would we see in our pupils if we implemented the concept of individual differences and gave each child the idea and assurance that he could learn all of the material of the basic course of instruction—and then provided the teachers with tools, time, and techniques to assure that the pupils would do so!

These national attitudes prevail in the Soviet Republics. They account in part for the tremendous accomplishments of their educational system in the last twenty-five years. It may be that we must leave to national organizations any program directed toward effecting a large-scale change in attitudes toward education. The immediate concern within the scope of each individual educator is to look at his own attitudes and those of his pupils so that the classroom atmosphere is such that learning can take place.

51. Teen-Age Traits, Interests, and Worries *

LESTER D. CROW

THE PUBLICITY that is being given at present to asocial behavior engaged in by some American adolescents has caused much adult concern over teen-age attitudes and interests. One area of study has to do with boy-girl relationships during the teen-age period. Probably never before in history have young people enjoyed so much freedom as they now experience in such matters as selecting friends and associates of either sex and of engaging with their peers in work and recreational activities. What are their standards of friend selection? Especially what are the personality qualities

* From Lester D. Crow, "Teen-Age Traits, Interests, and Worries," *The Educational Forum* (May, 1956), pp. 423–28. Reprinted by permission.

admired by adolescents in members of the opposite sex? What are the significant teen-age interests and worries?

Adolescents are interested in themselves and in the other teen-agers. They not only want to be liked by other members of their own sex but they also are experiencing an increasing urge to be attractive to and associate with members of the opposite sex. During this period there seem to be definite personality qualities possessed by boys that attract girls and others that repel. The same situation holds for boys' attitudes toward girls.

The personality characteristics of teen-agers are not inherited. Rather is the kind of personality displayed by adolescents the manifestation of their inner self. Herein are reflected their growth pattern and innate potentialities and the kind of training and environmental experiences to which they have been subjected during their developing years.

It is an observable phenomenon that as boys and girls approach the adolescent period they begin to develop as individuals and to display attitudes toward members of the opposite sex that gradually come to differ materially from their earlier childhood interpersonal relations. These changed social attitudes result partly from newly awakened interests and urges rooted in physical and physiological growth changes. Adolescent social attitudes are influenced also by new social pressures that affect themselves as well as their peer and older associates.

The constant interaction of these various inner and outer factors of influence tends not only to stimulate in adolescents the development of certain more or less desirable personal qualities but also to encourage in any one adolescent specific attitudes toward behavior traits by teen-agers of either sex.

Overt Expressions of Attitudes

We adults seem to believe that certain personal qualities are considered by adolescents to be highly desirable. We are prone to underestimate their power of personality evaluation. Girls supposedly stress the possession by a boy of good looks, brawn rather than brains, and a "smooth line." Boys are expected by us to fall for a "cute trick," extremes of dress and make-up, a minimum of intelligence, and a tendency on the part of the girl to be "free and easy." Perhaps we are mistaken. If so, what are the personal characteristics of boys or girls that earn for them desired popularity among their associates of the opposite sex?

In order to obtain answers to this question, an informal study was made by the writer of attitudes toward what young people consider to be desirable and undesirable personality qualities in their peer opposite-sex associates. About 4,900 young people (2,540 girls and 2,360 boys), representing a cross-section of junior high school and senior high school students in New York City and its environs were asked to write answers to the following questions:

1. What are the personality characteristics that you admire in girls (boys)?
2. What traits do you dislike in girls (boys)?
3. What do you do to increase your popularity with the girls (boys) whom you know?

The results were organized according to the age of the adolescents responding: the younger group, 12–14 year-olds; and the older adolescents,

Table 1

PERSONALITY TRAITS ADMIRED BY MEMBERS OF THE OPPOSITE SEX

Personality Traits of Girls Admired by Boys	*Personality Traits of Boys Admired by Girls*
Good personality	Good personality
Good-looking—beautiful face, dress and figure	Good-looking—not necessarily handsome
Look nice in a bathing suit	Good character
Neatness and cleanliness	Neatness
Helpful to others	Clean and appropriate dress
Consideration for others	Intelligent
Appropriate dress	Good conversationalist
Good talker	Consideration for a girl's wishes
Dependable	Respect for girls—not fresh
Good listener	Willingness to take a girl on dates
Friendliness	Boy to be older than girl
Ability to dance	Good manners
Good manners	Good-natured
Acts her age	Smart in school
Courtesy	Clean shaven and haircut
Politeness	Clean-minded
No show-off	Kind, generous, tall
Interest in hobbies of boys	Acts his age
Modest, but not shy	Has a sense of humor
Act grown-up, not like a baby	Not too shy
Clean-minded	Honest and fair
Able to take a joke	Respect for rights of girl
	Punctuality
	Not to try to be a big shot
	Able to get along with others
	Has self-control
	The way he kisses
	Good listener

the 16–18 year-olds. Most of the younger teen-agers emphasized physical characteristics and overt behavior. The more mature teen-agers stressed attitudes and behavior associated with inner motivations and character traits. There were certain qualities, however, that were considered desirable by most teen-agers. They are presented first. The characteristics of girls admired by boys, and of boys admired by girls are presented in Table 1. The items are listed in the order of frequency of expressed interest by the teen-agers responding. Personality traits of boys disliked by girls and traits of girls disliked by boys are presented in Table 2. The attempts made by each sex to impress members of the other sex are presented in Table 3.

Table 2

PERSONALITY TRAITS DISLIKED BY MEMBERS OF THE OPPOSITE SEX

Traits of Girls Disliked by Boys	*Traits of Boys Disliked by Girls*
Sloppiness of appearance	Sloppiness of appearance
Overweight or underweight	Boastfulness
Tendency to flirt or "two-time"	Act like big shots
Talk too much	Display poor manners
Extremes of dress	Stinginess
Little regard for money	Being conceited
Too much interest in self	Poorly groomed
Lack of punctuality	Laziness
Snobbishness	Foolish behavior at parties
Talk about other dates	Exhibit fresh behavior
Too much make-up	Shyness
Sulking and pouting	Smoking excessively
Being conceited	Using bad language
Bites nails	Discourtesy to elders
Smokes and drinks	Talks too much
Giggling or talebearer	Wants to be center of attention
Inability to dance	Moodiness
Immature behavior	Sponging off other boys
Mingling with a fast crowd	Asking for date at last minute

Younger girls dislike boys who want to kiss and "paw" them. Many of the younger boys like girls who have a good "figure" and with whom they can have fun, but dislike girls who are fresh and try to act older than they are. A few of the younger boys said that they don't like anything about girls or that they usually are nuisances. Girls like boys who are older than themselves. They like boys who are willing to meet a girl's parents, or who like sports and hard work. They dislike hot-tempered, rude boys who take a girl to a party and then pay no attention to her.

Table 3

ATTEMPTS MADE BY BOYS AND GIRLS TO INCREASE THEIR POPULARITY WITH
MEMBERS OF THE OPPOSITE SEX

Attempts Made by Boys to Impress Girls	*Attempts Made by Girls to Impress Boys*
Develop good taste in dress	Become careful about appearance
Participate in school activities	Try to be friendly
Avoid annoying habits in school	Develop sincerity
Be considerate of the other person	Be popular with girls also
Develop similar interests	Try not to be catty
Become lively	Not go to expensive places on a date
Be as friendly as possible	Be a good conversationalist
Eliminate all annoying habits	Go in for school activities
Always be dependable	Avoid ridicule of others
Be polite to everyone	Have respect for elders

Boys in their later teens seem to admire girls who are even-tempered, lively, less intelligent than the boy (not stupid), a good listener, modest and sincere. Many of the older boys objected to a girl's use of excessive make-up and the wearing by a girl of slacks or of sweaters that exaggerate her figure. Oddly enough, some of the boys preferred a girl's having long hair rather than wearing it too short.

Many of the older adolescents (both boys and girls) stressed as desirable the possession of qualities such as "good character," consideration for older people, mature behavior, self-respect and ambition. Some girls said that they did not want boys to spend money on them unless the boy had earned the money. Although they did not say specifically that they did not like young people having the same religious affiliation as themselves, they did seem to approve of a young person's having some religious convictions.

The results of this study are indicative of the sound thinking, high ideals, and wholesome attitudes maintained among teen-agers. Whether or not the expressed likes or dislikes actually are the motivating forces that influence their choices of girl or boy associates, they at least gave evidence of knowing what should be admired. Several sets of responses are illustrative of their general tenor. . . .

Another study of teen-age problems concerned itself with worries of adolescents. In this study, college students (120 women and 100 men) were invited to list their worries in various areas of life during their teen years, 14 through 19. Included among the life areas were school life, home life, recreational life, boy and girl relationships, friends, vocational choice, religion, health, clothes, and money. The responses of the men and the women were organized separately. In this paper consideration is given to only two of the life areas, e.g., "boy and girl relationships," and "friends." The results are presented in Table 4.

Table 4

ADOLESCENT WORRIES RELATIVE TO FRIENDS AS RECALLED BY COLLEGE JUNIORS

Male Worries	*Female Worries*
Arguments with friends	Are friends true friends
Friends may not like me	Not to let friends down
To be worthy of good friends	To be popular
How to make friends	How to be leader in a group
Friends continue good opinion of me	How to overcome inferiority feeling

In addition, 350 teen-agers (180 girls and 170 boys) between the ages of 14 and 17 were invited to respond to their worries in the area of boy-girl relationships. The obtained responses are presented in Table 5. The form of expression made by these teen-agers is somewhat different from the responses made by the college students who reported from memory. The ability level of the college students also was higher than that of the high

Table 5

ADOLESCENT WORRIES RELATIVE TO BOY-GIRL RELATIONSHIPS AS REPORTED BY TEEN-AGERS 14 THROUGH 17 YEARS OF AGE

Male Worries	*Female Worries*
How to get a date	How to meet new friends
Girls I like don't like me	Boys I like don't like me
Girls cost too much	How to be popular
How to be invited to more parties	Boys are too demanding
Friends cut in on your girl	Should I go steady?
Mother objects to my going steady	Should I go with a boy I don't like?
How to have a girl go steady	Behavior of boyfriend
Inability to dance	Boys of another religion
Does girl love me?	Nasty tongue of other girls
Girls of another religion	Girls who try to steal boyfriend
How to be popular	Parents permit more dates with boys
How to forget girl who jilted me	How to get over love for a boy
	Friends who tell personal secrets
	How to refuse a date tactfully
	How to refuse date with girl friend's beau
	Boy friend in the service

Table 6

Table 6

ADOLESCENT WORRIES RELATIVE TO BOY-GIRL RELATIONSHIPS AS RECALLED BY
COLLEGE JUNIORS

Boy-Girl Relationships	
MALE WORRIES	FEMALE WORRIES
Not being popular	Being accepted
Desire for more dates	Sexual conflicts
Inferiority	Loss of boy friend
Displease parents with date	Sexual relations to maintain
Too few girl friends	Feeling of inferiority
Persistency of female	Boy I like doesn't like me
Girl I like doesn't like me	Boy who could hold my interest
	Little mixups

school pupils. The girls indicated a greater willingness to respond than did the boys. This was noticeable both in the number of responses and in the type of expression among the members of this teen-age group.

52. *The Reduction of Prejudice through the Arousal of Self-Insight** [1]

EZRA STOTLAND,

DANIEL KATZ, AND MARTIN PATCHEN

THE THEORETICAL BASIS of the present study, elaborated in previous papers by Sarnoff and Katz (1954) and by Katz and Stotland (1959), assumes that attitudes can reflect more than one motivational source, sometimes resulting from external forces and sometimes from individual per-

* From Ezra Stotland, Daniel Katz, and Martin Patchen, "The Reduction of Prejudice through the Arousal of Self-Insight," *Journal of Personality* (December, 1959), pp. 507–30. Reprinted by permission of the authors and the *Journal of Personality*.

[1] This investigation was made possible through a research grant from the Air Force Personnel and Training Research Center. The authors wish to express their appreciation of the contribution of John J. Jochem who assisted in the collection and the analysis of the data.

sonality needs. Effective attitude change presupposes a knowledge of the conditions under which specific types of attitudes are likely to be in the service of various kinds of motivational forces. Thus attitudes can (a) serve to give cognitive clarity and control to an otherwise unstructured world, (b) function of the interest of utilitarian needs as in the case of the person who gains security or other advantages in his own group from maintaining a pattern of discrimination (Carlson, 1956), or (c) operate as the expression of ego-defense mechanisms (Adorno, Frenkel-Brunswik, Levinson, and Sanford, 1950). Experimental attempts to change attitudes should seek to clarify conceptually the motive forces at which these attempts are directed and then, at the operational level to design specific procedures and materials for reducing or rechanneling these motives. A similar analysis of the problem of attitude change can be found in Smith, Bruner, and White (1956) and in Wagman (1955).

Although the present study is concerned primarily with the modification of attitudes by methods focusing on the deep-lying motivations for holding attitudes, situational factors and group factors are also considered. In the population studied, however, they are assumed to be of lesser significance for the attitude in question—prejudice against Negroes. Hyman and Sheatsley (1954) have pointed out the advisability of not giving priority to the psychodynamics of prejudice when such attitudes are apparently the social norms of the group. In this study, however, the group investigated consisted of college students in a northern community where the ideology gave little sanction to anti-Negro sentiments. It was thus assumed that an important, but not the sole, source of prejudice against Negroes for this group would be found in deep-lying personality needs.

In previous experiments in this program in which attempts to change attitudes were geared to their assumed motivational bases, the use of self-insight procedures has had some degree of success in the modification of attitudes. Negative stereotypes toward Negroes, resistant to positive information about this group, have been modified by materials designed to give insight into the dynamics of prejudice (Katz, Sarnoff, and McClintock, 1956). This insight into the bases of attitudes is assumed to give the subject some measure of control over the function of ego-defenses, and thus reduce prejudice stemming from these defenses.

That these experimental changes came about through some breakthrough in ego-defensiveness is a plausible but not a proved conclusion. The two arguments to support it are (a) the nature of the influence procedure and (b) the effects of this procedure, which were predicted on a theoretical basis. The procedure designed to give self-insight consisted of a case study of a person which illustrated the way in which hostility toward parents may be repressed and later projected on convenient objects for scapegoating. The person showing these mechanisms was presented, moreover, in a sufficiently sympathetic manner that the experimental Ss could become involved with her problems. In brief, the materials were deliberately designed to produce self-insight into defense mechanisms.

The second reason for the inference that the materials did in fact have this effect was the confirmation of certain theoretical predictions. It was predicted that the manipulations designed to produce self-insight would have a greater effect over time than the manipulations aimed at cognitive restructuring of beliefs about the attitudinal object. Since self-insight would involve some deeper change it might take longer to become effective and it might also increase with the passage of time. On the other hand, information materials about the object of the attitude would have their maximum effect immediately and would lose their force fairly quickly. Such in fact was the experimental outcome. It was also hypothesized that the most defensive of the Ss would be the most resistant to the self-insight since these materials would be a real threat to the individual. Again, the findings supported the theoretical expectation. A third important prediction was confirmed in one experiment (Katz, McClintock, and Sarnoff, 1957), but not borne out in another (Katz, *et al.,* 1956), namely, that people who stood in the middle ranges with respect to the use of repression and projectivity would be more susceptible to change through the self-insight materials than the people who made very little use of these mechanisms. The reasoning here was that any prejudices of this group scoring low on ego-defensiveness would be due to other factors than projectivity and scapegoating. Hence understanding the nature of these mechanisms would not be expected to decrease their prejudices.

Thus, previous studies have given some support to the assumptions (a) that materials specially designed to show the dynamics of defense mechanisms as they relate to certain types of attitudes are productive of self-insight and (b) that self-insight so produced can lead to lowered prejudice. It is still of critical importance to know more about the conditions which result in the acceptance of self-insight as a process mediating attitude change. This is the problem of the present investigation—i.e., the exploration of factors which determine the arousal of self-insight as it affects prejudice toward members of an out-group.

Three conditions were assumed to be of importance in the reduction of prejudice through self-insight: (a) self-activity or self-involvement, (b) relevance of self-activity for the attitudinal object, and (c) the arousal of tendencies toward self-consistency. *Self-activity* means that the individual himself engages, to some extent, in the interpretation of the materials concerning the psychodynamics of prejudice. If the individual is to absorb fully the meaning of the information about ego-defense, as it applies to his own functioning, he should not be able to place this knowledge outside himself, to keep it at a distance from himself. Thus, if he engages in activities leading to a fuller understanding of the ego-defensive basis of his attitudes, this very activity produces ego-involvement and places the understanding within his self-system. His involvement makes him less likely to reject the information, which is no longer something imposed from the outside. Thus one prerequisite for transforming the interpretation offered the individual into insight into himself is the active involvement of the individual in the information and its consequences. The operational procedure employed in this study for inducing self-activity was a logical ordering of statements about psychodynamics in terms of cause and effect which was required of some Ss.

Relevance of the self-activity for the attitudinal object concerns the similarity in content between the attitudes referred to in the psychodynamic materials and the attitudes which the individual is expected to change. The S should find it more difficult to avoid the implications of this self-activity if this activity is directly relevant to the target attitudes.

Self-consistency is the tendency for the person to integrate his attitudes, values, and behavior into a logically congruent pattern. The arousal of this general need should lead both to the acceptance of materials, showing the causes of conflict and inconsistency, and to changes in belief and behavior. The two conditions already mentioned of self-activity and relevance should make for self-consistency, but in addition a direct appeal to the individual's realization of the importance of consistency for his self-functioning should be effective in the reduction of prejudice. Accordingly, Ss were given indoctrination about the role of understanding the emotional bases of behavior in preventing foolish, irrational, and unrealistic behavior. Rosenberg and Gardner (1958) have demonstrated the role of consistency within a single attitude by changing the affective component through post-hypnotic suggestion in keeping with Rosenberg's earlier theoretical formulation (1956).

Hypotheses

1. *An induction which combines self-activity, relevance of this activity to the attitudinal object, and the arousal of the need for self-consistency*

will be more effective in changing attitudes than an induction representing only two of these conditions.

The assumption underlying this hypothesis is that the individual is resourceful in maintaining his attitudinal structure and has many lines of defense to fall back upon (Jahoda and Cooper, 1947). Though he may acquire some understanding of the dynamics of emotional attitudes, he will not necessarily apply it to his own prejudices if he can avoid facing the problem. Thus the chances of success in changing his attitudes are increased if, after the dynamics of prejudice have been made clear by his own self-activity, he finds it difficult to escape the relevance of this knowledge for his disparaging attitudes toward out-groups and if his own tendency toward the avoidance of irrational behavior has been aroused.

No predictions are made about the relative effectiveness of each of these three conditions for producing attitude change, partly because of the difficulties of equating the degree of strength in the induction of each of these factors.

2. *The inductions designed to produce self-insight will be more effective over time than immediately after the induction—in other words, a "sleeper effect" is predicted.*

Before the studies of Hovland, Lumsdaine, and Sheffield (1949) and the more recent experiments reported in Hovland, Janis, and Kelley (1953), it was assumed that attitude change would be maximal immediately after the manipulation of forces external to the individual. But two factors may be operative to make the Yost memory curve inapplicable to attitude change. (a) Immediate resistance may be aroused to some aspect of the critical situation or attempt at induction, which may be dissipated over time, permitting the influence to manifest a delayed or sleeper effect. (b) The critical event or attempt at induction may activate internal forces which may then proceed in their own right to bring about progressive change over time. Our assumption is that the procedures and materials employed to produce self-insight are directed at the arousal of such internal processes. Hence, more change is expected over time as the individual assimilates the insights and works through the problem in his own mind.

3. *Individuals who are in the medium ranges in defensiveness will change their attitudes in response to the self-insight procedures more than individuals who are low or high in defensiveness.* While the greatest change should occur among those in the intermediate range, high ego-defenders should show even less change than low ego-defenders.

The reason for assuming the greatest susceptibility to change of the medium-range people in ego-defense is the greater appropriateness of the appeals used for this group. The low defenders, who hold negative attitudes toward an out-group, may hold them for reasons other than the defense of the ego. If lack of self-insight was unrelated to their acquisition of certain stereotypes in the first place, an increase in self-insight should not lead to a change in stereotypes now. On the other hand, it is assumed that the exposure to a set of forces at a single point in time will not be powerful enough to affect the highly defensive people in the same degree that it will affect the less defensive *S*s. Though the induction is designed to breach defenses, it is too optimistic to expect success with the most defensive *S*s.

4. *An induction or attempt to influence attitudes utilizing relevant self-activity and self-consistency will produce changes in values and attitudes related to the target attitude.*

If self-insight has been increased so that the individual shows less prejudice toward the target group, this insight should create sufficient internal restructuring to make for less prejudice in general and for corresponding changes in related value systems. Specifically, the predictions are that *S*s will show less chauvinism and less authoritarianism. In view of the expected low power of the experimental inductions, these are bold predictions. Again it is hypothesized that the people in the medium ranges of defensiveness will show the most change.

Method

The *S*s for this study were 25 white female college students from a midwestern state university and from a midwestern state college specializing in teacher training. The experiment was performed as part of the *S*s regular class work in three meetings of undergraduate courses in introductory psychology and education, although the study was administered by the authors and their assistants rather than the classroom instructors.[2] The usual precautions were taken to minimize the pressures toward conformity to what the students anticipated the *E* wanted. Private rather than public responses were encouraged, and anonymity was guaranteed to the *S*, who supplied his own code number and letter, and who was the only one who knew this identification.

The first two sessions were separated by a period of three weeks, and the third session was held three or four weeks after the second. The first session was given over to the measurement of personality variables and to the traditional "before" measures of attitudes. The experimental influences were intro-

[2] The authors are deeply indebted to Drs. Earl Carlson and Ralph Smith for making the arrangements, and to the following instructors for the use of their class time: George Browrer, Roger Callahan, Lawrence Doty, Gordon Fielder, Robert Fisher, Donald Johnson, Calvin Michaels, Frank Restle, William Smith, Wilber Williams, Israel Woronoff.

duced as the second session. *S*s were assigned at random to one of four experimental conditions. In all four conditions, they read a case study designed to give insight into the dynamics of prejudice, but were subjected to different additional influences in each of the conditions. In the third session, measures were again taken of the dependent variable, attitudes toward Negroes, and of the personality variables. In addition, a measure of attitudes was taken directly after the experimental induction in the second session.

FIRST SESSION

Each *S* was given a booklet which contained measures of personality, of stereotypes about Negroes and Jews, of attitudes toward Negro segregation and discrimination against Negroes, and of ethnocentric attitudes. The Negro stereotype measure was the same twenty-one-item Likert-type scale as used by Katz, *et al.* (1956).[3] The measure of attitudes toward Negro segregation was the same as used by these investigators—referred to as the "behaviorial scale." The measures of the Jewish stereotype and of ethnocentric attitudes were the same as used by Adorno, *et al.* (1950). The personality measures were the F-scale and selected items from the Minnesota Multiphasic Personality Inventory having to do with conformity tendencies and projectivity.[4] All booklets were identical and the *S*s were given all the time they needed.

SECOND SESSION

Each *S* received one of four different types of booklets, realizing either the major experimental condition or one of the three influence-control conditions. The types of booklets were rotated systematically in presenting them to the *S*s. The four types of booklets had similar first and last parts. The intermediate section contained the differential influence which is described below under *The Four Experimental Groups.*

In all cases, the *S*s read a six-page, double-spaced selection entitled "Emotions and Attitudes," describing various types of relationships between attitudes and emotions, such as scapegoating, projection, and compensation, with respect to the development of antiminority attitudes. This selection was the same as the first part of the "interpretation" materials used by Katz *et al.* (1957).

In addition, each booklet had the same last part, consisting of a seventeen-item scale matched to items of the Negro stereotype scale used in the first session. This matched scale was found to correlate .84 with the original scale when tested on another sample of college students. The purpose of changing the scale was to meet the problem of the monotony of answering the same scale three times and the problem of the possible development of rigid responses to the

[3] In the scoring systems used here, the *S* was given credit for agreement with a positive statement, a procedure not followed in the earlier experiment.

[4] The MMPI results are not reported here. They show the same trends as the F-scale scores but not as clearly.

items after two administrations. In addition, four of the twenty-one items used in the original scale were repeated in the second administration to provide a constant measure of attitudes. However, the measures of ethnocentricity and anti-Semitism that were administered in the first session were not given again until the third session.

THE FOUR EXPERIMENTAL GROUPS

The four different experimental treatments will be called (1) the major experimental condition, (2) the control on the self-consistency induction, (3) the control on the relevance induction, and (4) the control on self-involvement.

1. In the major experimental condition, three procedures were utilized to make effective the materials of the case study dealing with the dynamics of prejudice. (a) One procedure attempted to produce active self-involvement through making the S order statements about personality dynamics in a logical sequence. This was done by interrupting the S before she had finished the case history with a statement in the booklet that the researchers were interested in discovering what people believe to be the causes of human behavior. This statement introduced the S to a series of eight sets of five sentences each, which were descriptive of the behavior and feelings of the person in the case history. The S was then to arrange the sentences in each set of five in the order of cause and effect, as she perceived this order. All of the causal statements were to be arranged to precede all the effect statements, although they were presented in random order. After arranging each set of five statements, the S read the correct order of sentences for that set. The purpose of presenting the correct order was to make sure that all of the Ss in this and the other conditions had the same information or understanding of the psychodynamics of the person in the case history.

An example of a set of such statements as presented to the Ss follows, with numbers of the statements indicating the correct order which the Ss read on the following page: [5]

(2) Mary was ignored by her father.
(5) Mary developed an inferiority complex.
(1) Mary was rejected by her mother.
(4) Mary developed into an insecure, anxious girl.
(3) Mary was taunted by her brother.

The purpose of this procedure of arranging the sentences was to have the S become involved in the task of understanding the psychodynamics of prejudice.

[5] The Ss' orderings were not considered to be in error if the causal statements were not in the same order as the one given as correct, as long as all the casual statements preceded the effect statements. The effect statements also did not have to be in exactly the same order as the one given as correct.

(b) Another procedure was designed to make the induction *relevant* to prejudiced attitudes toward Negroes. The method here was to make four of the eight sets of statements descriptive of the dynamics of persons prejudiced against ethnic minority groups. The other four sets dealt with the person's familial relationships. Thus, the relevance of the material to the target attitudes was explicitly presented. (c) Still another procedure was designed to appeal to the motive of self-consistency. This consisted of a page and a half of material, introduced at the beginning of the booklet, which described the advantages of consistent behavior in avoiding difficulties. It introduced dramatic examples of foolhardy behavior to illustrate the effects of irrationality. The attempt here was to supplement the neutrally toned cognitive approach of discerning correct logical relationships with some realization of the failure to understand the emotional basis of behavior. There was emphasis, too, on the importance of self-understanding in achieving a rational, consistent approach to the world.

2. The control of self-consistency was achieved for one fourth of the *S*s by omitting the material stressing the advantages of consistent behavior. The second session was introduced by only a brief statement that the *S* would have a chance to learn about the emotional basis of belief and behavior. These *S*s were given only the self-activity and relevant inductions.

3. The control on the relevance induction was achieved for one fourth of the *S*s by a change in four sets of statements which the *S*s ordered logically. In the major experimental conditions four sets of statements applied the dynamics of prejudice to minority groups. In this experimental treatment, these four sets of statements were changed to apply to prejudice against townspeople around the college which the person in the case history attended. Otherwise, the experimental influences were the same as in the major experimental condition.

4. The control on self-activity was arranged for one fourth of the *S*s by omitting the ordering of statements by the subjects themselves. They were presented in the correct logical order, but in all other respects the conditions were identical with the major experimental group. The same information was given *S*s in the control condition as in the experimental, but it was given in a different way.

The design of this experiment is unusual in that there is one major experimental condition and three control conditions. Each of the three controls is identical with the experimental condition in regard to all but one feature. This feature is omitted or varied in the control. A conventional control group was provided by seventeen *S*s who attended the first session when the "before" measures were taken, were absent from the second session when the experimental inductions were attempted, and appeared again in the third session when postmeasures were taken. This is not an ideal control group because its members were not assigned by random procedure to this condition as was the case with the four groups already described. However, since the general effectiveness of insight-arousal procedures has already been demonstrated, the control group was not of great significance in the design.

THIRD SESSION

The attitude measures used in the first session were readministered, as were the F-scale and subscales of the MMPI. The three- or four-week delay between the second and third sessions provided a basis for testing for the presence of a "sleeper" effect, i.e., of changes resulting from the experiment which did not appear immediately after the experimental inductions.

ANALYSIS OF F-SCALE

In the analysis of the data, the total score on the F-scale was employed, as well as two subscales consisting of items measuring other directedness and defensiveness respectively. The division of this scale into two subscales was done on an a priori theoretical basis. The decision as to the placement of items was based upon the classification of items into categories as spelled out in *The Authoritarian Personality* (Adorno et al., 1950). Those items which were included by the authors of this work in the categories of Conventionalism, Authoritarian Submission, and Power and Toughness, were combined to form the conformity subscale. Items in the remaining categories—Authoritarian Aggression, Anti-intraception, Superstition and Stereotype, Destructiveness and Cynicism, and Projectivity and Sex—were combined to form the Ego-Defense Scale. McClintock (1958) has presented evidence which suggests that the personality syndrome of other directedness, or conformity, operates in a different fashion in attitude change from the syndrome of repression and projection. . . .

Summary

The object of this investigation was twofold: (a) to determine the conditions under which attitude change will occur through written communication designed to give self-insight, and (b) to study the relation between changes in self-insight and prejudiced attitudes among Ss differing in ego-defensiveness. The Ss were female college students and the basic experimental manipulation consisted of the reading of a case history designed to give insight into the psychodynamics of prejudice. In addition, three other inductions were used to vary the conditions which might facilitate the acceptance of the case history and its implications for the Ss' own prejudices: (a) self-activity or self-involvement in which Ss were asked to order in logical sequence statements about the psychodynamics of prejudice, (b) making the materials which were read of direct relevance to prejudice against Negroes, and (c) an appeal to the rationality and self-consistency of the individual. These inductions were arranged so that one group of Ss was exposed to all three influences (the major experimental condition) whereas each one of three other groups had one of the experimental inductions omitted. Measures of prejudice toward Negroes and related attitudes and values were taken both immediately after the experimental sessions and four weeks later.

The findings gave support to two of the predictions, no support to a third, and only partial support to a fourth, specifically:

1. The major experimental condition combining all three inductions of self-activity, self-consistency, and relevance was assumed to be the most powerful of the manipulations in that it gave *S*s little opportunity to avoid the implications of the material presented. The results showed this combination to give the most consistent changes in reducing stereotypes about Negroes of any of the experimental conditions.

2. Since the change in attitudes toward Negroes was assumed to result from self-insight, or some form of internal restructuring, it was predicted that there would be a sleeper effect. In other words, the effects of the experimental inductions would take time to manifest themselves. This in fact proved to be the case, with no significant change immediately after the inductions but significant change several weeks later.

3. Since the influences exerted in the experiment were directed at prejudice based upon defense mechanisms, the prediction was that low ego-defenders would change less than people who used these mechanisms more, i.e., those scoring in the middle ranges on measures of repression and projectivity. High ego-defenders would be less likely to change than the others because the experimental influences would be too weak to overcome their resistance. Those scoring in the low ranges on ego-defense changed as a result of the experimental inductions, contrary to the prediction, with high ego-defenders showing the expected resistance.

4. The fourth hypothesis postulated change in values and attitudes related to Negro prejudice. No such change occurred in authoritarianism, but the major experimental condition produced significant reduction in scores on the chauvinistic items of the ethnocentrism scale. These changes were correlated with low error scores on understanding the dynamics of scapegoating.

In addition to the hypotheses under consideration, the findings contain these suggestions about attitude change:

1. The material designed to produce self-insight was most effective when accompanied by an appeal to self-consistency. This induction to avoid foolish and irrational behavior, in general, gave more positive results than the self-activity or the relevance induction.

2. Though the objective of the experiment was to increase the individual's self-insight into defense mechanisms, a number of people changed

their attitudes on the basis of another type of understanding. They apparently gave serious consideration to the appropriateness of particular attitudes for the type of person they were. The process here was more one of self-recognition than of self-insight in relation to a recognition of the meaning of certain attitudes.

53. *Student Attitudes toward Child Behavior Problems* *

ROBERT M. PORTER

THE LOOK-FOR-THE-CAUSE APPROACH is accepted by mental hygienists as the method of preference in dealing with child behavior problems. That teacher attitudes toward their pupils' behavior have been moving closer to a mental hygiene point of view during the past thirty years has been chronicled by such researchers as Ellis and Miller, Mitchell, Stouffer, Schrupp and Gjerde, and Hunter. Undoubtedly much of this improvement can be attributed to Wickman's study of 1928 which had shown that teachers and clinical psychologists were some distance apart in rating the seriousness of various kinds of behavior. The former stressed overt, objective behavior while the latter emphasized more subjective manifestations of maladjustment.

Wickman's work touched off numerous subsequent investigations. Another impetus has arisen from the increasing emphasis that teacher-preparing institutions have given to child growth and development and educational psychology courses. Sparks found that teachers with training beyond the bachelor's degree more closely approached the mental hygienists' position than did those with less training. The purpose of the present study was twofold: (a) to ascertain how undergraduate students in teacher education felt that certain child behavior problems should be handled and (b) to ascertain the extent of improvement in student attitudes as they progressed through their four years of college. At what point are these students when the college gets them and how much growth toward clinicians' attitudes occurs in their subsequent undergraduate career?

* From Robert M. Porter, "Student Attitudes toward Child Behavior Problems," *Journal of Educational Research* (May, 1959), pp. 349–52. Reprinted by permission.

Procedure

In an effort to obtain some answers to these questions an investigation was undertaken at the State University Teachers College at Oneonta, New York, during the fall of 1956. Data were obtained from about sixty students in each of the four classes: Freshman, Sophomore, Junior and Senior. This study was widened to include sixty-four seniors of the local high school and sixty in-service teachers who were members of extension courses being given by the College in Albany, New York.

The data collection instrument was a test devised by Celia B. Stendler which contained twenty-five response statements describing various behavior patterns in children. Stendler had used the test to examine the problem of teacher insight into pupil behavior from a different angle than had Wickman, *et al.* She attempted to discover how teachers thought certain kinds of behavior should be dealt with. She queried 157 elementary teachers in the midwest. Persons being questioned were asked to complete the statement by describing what they considered to be the best way of treating the particular problem. They were not required to sign their names. The test was as follows:

PROBLEMS OF CHILD BEHAVIOR

Here are some statements about children which are not complete. Each statement describes a particular kind of behavior problem. For example, the first statement says, "I think the child who never finishes on time should—" You are to finish the statement by describing what you think would be the best way of treating his particular problem.

(1) I think the child who never finishes on time should

(2) I think the child who continually fights with other children should

(3) I think the child who continually steals should

(4) I think the child who bites his fingernails should

(5) I think the child who daydreams most of the time should

(6) I think the child who relies on the teacher too much should

(7) I think the child who does his work over and over until it is just right should

(8) I think the child who never works up to his capacity should

(9) I think the child who never pays attention should

(10) I think the child who is always late should

(11) I think the child who always lies should

(12) I think the child who always talks back to the teacher should

(13) I think the child who is easily discouraged should

(14) I think the child who continually shows off in class should

(15) I think the child who always feels everyone is picking on him should

(16) I think the child who loses his temper when he doesn't get his way should

(17) I think the child who uses vulgar language should

(18) I think the child who tries to cheat on exams should

(19) I think the child who is always unhappy and moody should

(20) I think the child who continually plays truant should

(21) I think the child who is a bully should

(22) I think the child who wastes school materials should

(23) I think the child who continually disobeys should

(24) I think the child who is disliked by other children should

(25) I think the child who is timid and shy should

Answers to the test were categorized by Stendler under six different categories. They were as follows:

1. Take punitive measures.

2. Talk to him. Moralize. Be shown the error of his ways.

3. Send him to a doctor.

4. Adjust the work. This included increasing or decreasing the work, or recommending any kind of project.

5. Praise or encourage him.

6. Study him to find the cause of behavior and plan a course of action accordingly.

Findings

The percentage of the total responses of each of the six groups that fell in each category is shown in Table 1. The figures obtained by Stendler are given for comparative purposes. It is readily apparent that the technique most used by the high school seniors was Category 1, Take Punitive Measures. Over a third of them elected this category. Resort to this method was decreasingly elected by the four college classes, progressing from freshmen to seniors.

About one fifth of the freshmen, but only about one ninth of the seniors, chose to take punitive measures to deal with behavior problems.

The teachers in the field reversed this trend slightly, however. This may have been due to the fact that many of them, now middle-aged, did their teacher-training work before the causal approach was stressed as much as

Table 1

PERCENTAGE OF RESPONSES FOR SIX CATEGORIES IN TWENTY-FIVE ITEMS DESCRIBING PUPIL BEHAVIOR MADE BY SIX GROUPS TESTED

Number	1 Take Punitive Measures	2 Talk to the Child	3 Send Him to a Doctor	4 Adjust the Work	5 Praise or Encourage	6 Study Him to Find Cause of Behavior	Answer No
64 High School Seniors	38.4	21.3	.35	18.5	10.7	5.9	4.4
60 College Freshmen	22.01	32.1	.34	16.8	14.1	10.6	4.3
61 College Sophomores	20.2	25.6	.46	22.7	12.5	12.3	6.2
60 College Juniors	13.5	28.1	.47	20.3	14.5	17.6	5.6
63 College Seniors	10.7	25.3	.59	25.0	14.8	19.2	4.6
60 In-Service Teachers	17.3	19.9	1.8	23.7	14.9	17.9	4.6
157 Stendler Teachers	13.9	33.4	2.7	22.5	9.1	14.6	3.8

it is today. Another explanation may well be that once away from the class-room of theory and into the classroom of reality they found that a punitive measure is the easiest "solution" to an uprising in the ranks.

For what behavior problems was Category 1 more frequently chosen than any other category? More high school seniors chose it than any other technique for fifteen of the twenty-five problems on the test. These figures dropped to five for college freshmen and six for sophomores. Behaviors for which both groups very frequently used it included being always late, talking back, showing off, bullying, and disobeying. Juniors preferred it for only two problems—the show-off and the disobedient. There were no instances in which college seniors preferred it to any other technique. In-service teachers, however, chose it very frequently to deal with the child who doesn't pay attention, is always late, talks back, loses his temper, wastes materials, or disobeys. The Stendler teachers would use it especially for tardiness, bullying, and disobedience.

These are overt behaviors disruptive of class routine and management, and the Wickman and subsequent, e.g., Stouffer, studies indicate that teachers view these as more serious behavior problems than do clinicians. (Harry Rivlin makes an interesting distinction between conduct and be-havior. "The former," he says, "is the chief concern of the teacher, while the term 'behavior problem' is more correctly applied to the area of con-cern of the psychiatrist.") Of interest would be a follow-up study to ascer-tain the views of the same college seniors tested after they have been em-ployed in the classroom for a couple of years.

The high schoolers would do considerably less "talking to" than punish-ing. Category 2, Talk to the Child, was, however, the technique most chosen by all four college classes. It was the preferred technique for all groups except the high schoolers (who chose punishment) to deal with cheating, vulgar language, temper tantrums, or wasting of materials.

Very few persons in any group tested (less than 2 per cent) chose Category 3, Send the Child to a Doctor. It is gratifying to note that students and teachers alike apparently realize that the attributing behavior problems to physical disorders very often fails to hit the mark. Stendler reported that only for fingernail biting would more teachers use this category than some other techniques. Of the groups tested in this study, the high school seniors would deal with this problem by punishment. The college classes preferred Talking to the Child or Adjusting the Work. The in-service teachers would Look for the Cause.

Category 4, Adjust the Work, would be used by a majority of the persons in each group tested in this study, and by the Stendler group, to handle the child who daydreams, relies on the teacher too much, or is timid and shy. These are not problems disrupting classroom routine; they involve personality maladjustment. For them, Category 4 was turned to by all groups. There was a slight tendency toward increased use of this technique the higher the group on the educational ladder.

Only about 11 per cent of the high school seniors turned to Category 5, Praise or Encourage, to handle the problems presented on the test. This figure rose to about 14 per cent for the college classes and the in-service teachers. Stendler had reported that about 9 per cent of her group had recourse to this method. All of the groups in the present study, and the Stendler group would use this category for the child who is easily discouraged—an obvious choice, of course. The younger groups would use it for the child who does his work over and over until it is just right. It appears significant that college Seniors, and the in-service teacher groups used in this and the Stendler study, would Talk to the Child and point out the error of his ways (Category 2). With added training and experience, it seems, comes a realization that this behavior is not as praiseworthy as it at first appears.

Mental hygienists feel that Category 6, Study the Child to Find the Cause of Behavior, is the best answer for all twenty-five problems, and in the answers given by the various groups tested, recourse to this technique increased steadily from the high schoolers (nearly 6 per cent) to the college seniors (nearly 20 per cent). (See Table 1.) One may reasonably assume, therefore, that instruction in the college investigated emphasized an understanding of causal factors of behavior and that the instruction had some effect.

For what behavior problems was Category 6, Study to Find the Cause, chosen more than was any other technique? The high school seniors preferred it for one item, the child who is disliked by other children. There were no problems for which the majority of college Freshmen would study the cause. College Sophomores, Juniors, Seniors, and the in-service teachers would have very frequent recourse to this method to handle problems involving children who fight, steal, are moody and unhappy, play truant, and/or are disliked. The teachers in the Stendler study felt that stealing, truancy, and tardiness especially would call for handling by this category.

Summary

This study endeavored to measure the growth in attitudes toward handling certain child behavior problems as students progressed through a representative teacher-preparing institution. Data were collected from a sampling of high school seniors, the four classes of a teachers college, and teachers taking in-service courses with that college.

Findings seemed to indicate that:

1. The technique most selected by high school seniors to handle the behavior problems presented was punishment. All four college classes favored talking to the child, as did the Stendler teachers. The in-service teachers of the current study favored adjusting the work.

2. There was a sharp drop in the election of the use of punishment from high school seniors to college seniors.

3. Punishment was especially chosen to deal with overt behaviors which disrupt the classroom.

4. Very seldom would any of the groups tested seek to handle a behavior problem by sending the child to a doctor.

5. There was a tendency to handle problems of a more subjective nature, involving perhaps some personality maladjustment, by adjusting the work. The older the group, the more this method was chosen.

6. The older groups recognized that it was not praiseworthy for the child to do his work over and over to seek perfection.

7. There was a decided tendency for older groups to move more and more toward the mental hygienist view that the best technique for behavior problems is to seek the cause.

8. The general consensus of the six groups tested was that the most serious behavior problems involved unhappiness and moodiness, stealing, being disliked by others, fighting, and truancy.

Further study could well be made to follow the same college seniors as they go out into their first jobs, and to attempt to see just how much carry-over there is of their college-inculcated attitudes, and just how much these attitudes are bent when they meet the reality of the outside world.

54. Life Problems and Interests of Adolescents in 1935 and 1957 *

DALE B. HARRIS

CHANGE SOCIAL and economic patterns in a society, and you change the the emphasis adolescents give to various problems and interests."

This, in effect, is the hypothesis of the present study—a hypothesis suggested by a report published in *The School Review* in September, 1936, just twenty-three years ago this month.

In 1935, Percival M. Symonds, author of the *School Review* article, submitted to high school students in New York City and in Tulsa, Oklahoma, a list of fifteen areas of human concern. The items as well as the words in which they were expressed were taken from interviews with young people. This check list, prepared almost a quarter of a century ago, is presented here:[1]

Health—eating, drinking, exercise, posture, sleep and rest, air and temperature, sunlight, clothing, bathing, care of special parts, cleanliness and prevention of disease, excretion and elimination, use of drugs

Sex adjustments—love, petting, courtship, marriage

Safety—avoiding accidents and injuries

Money—earning, spending, saving

Mental hygiene—fears, worries, inhibitions, compulsions, feelings of inferiority, fantasies

Study habits—skills used in study, methods of work, problem-solving

Recreation—sports and games, reading, arts and crafts, fellowship and social activities, hobbies

Personal and moral qualities—qualities leading to success, qualities of good citizenship

Home and family relationships—living harmoniously with members of the family

Manners and courtesy—etiquette

Personal attractiveness—personal appearance, voice, clothing

Daily schedule—planning twenty-four hours in a day

* From Dale B. Harris, "Life Problems and Interests of Adolescents in 1935 and 1957," *The School Review* (Autumn, 1959), pp. 335–43. Copyright 1959 by the University of Chicago. Reprinted by permission.

[1] Percival M. Symonds, "Life Problems and Interests of Adolescents," *The School Review*, 44 (September, 1936), 507.

Civic interests, attitudes, and responsibilities
Getting along with other people
Philosophy of life—personal values, ambitions, ideals, religion

The students were instructed to rank the fifteen items. "First . . . indicate the order in which they are *personal problems* to you," the students were directed, "and second the order of *interest* to you." Interests were described as subjects "you would like to read about and discuss or hear discussed."

Recently the same items with the same instructions were given to twelve hundred Minnesota youth, one hundred boys and one hundred girls in each grade from the seventh through the twelfth. To make it possible to compare the responses of the two groups of young people, the results of the Minnesota study were treated by the statistical method used in the earlier study. Statistical findings are presented in Tables 1 and 2. Table 1 shows mean

Table 1

MEAN RANKS GIVEN FIFTEEN ISSUES CONSIDERED AS PROBLEMS BY HIGH SCHOOL
STUDENTS IN 1935 AND IN 1957

Issue	1935			1957		
	MEAN RANK	STAND-ARD ERROR	RANK OF MEAN	MEAN RANK	STAND-ARD ERROR	RANK OF MEAN
Money	6.5	.11	1	6.4	.13	2
Health	6.61	.13	2	8.9*	.13	12.5
Personal attractiveness	7.0	.10	3	7.3	.11	4
Study habits	7.1	.11	4	5.7*	.12	1
Personal and moral qualities	7.2	.10	5	6.9	.10	3
Philosophy of life	7.5	.11	6	7.6	.12	5.5
Manners and courtesy	7.9	.10	7	8.1	.11	8
Home and family relation-ships	8.2	.12	8.5	8.0	.13	7
Getting along with other people	8.2	.11	8.5	8.3	.13	10
Recreation	8.3	.11	10	10.1*	.11	15
Mental hygiene	8.5	.12	11	7.6*	.13	5.5
Safety	8.6	.11	12	9.6*	.11	14
Civic interests, attitudes, and responsibilities	8.7	.10	13	8.2*	.11	9
Daily schedule	9.2	.12	14	8.5*	.14	11
Sex adjustments	10.0	.13	15	8.9*	.14	12.5

* Change from 1935 significant at 1 per cent level.

rank, standard error of these means, and position in the list for the fifteen issues considered as problems in 1935 and in 1957. Table 2 reports data for the fifteen issues considered as interests.

Table 2

MEAN RANKS GIVEN FIFTEEN ISSUES CONSIDERED AS INTERESTS BY HIGH SCHOOL STUDENTS IN 1935 AND IN 1957

Issue	1935			1957		
	MEAN RANK	STAND-ARD ERROR	RANK OF MEAN	MEAN RANK	STAND-ARD ERROR	RANK OF MEAN
Recreation	5.2	.11	1	6.8*	.13	3
Health	6.1	.11	2	6.7*	.12	1
Personal attractiveness	6.8	.10	3	7.0	.11	6
Manners and courtesy	6.9	.10	4	8.6*	.10	10
Philosophy of life	7.5	.12	5	6.9*	.13	5
Getting along with other people	7.6	.11	7	6.8*	.11	3
Personal and moral qualities	7.6	.11	7	7.2*	.10	8
Money	7.6	.11	7	7.4	.12	9
Home and family relation-ships	8.4	.11	9	6.8*	.12	3
Safety	8.5	.11	10	9.5*	.12	12
Study habits	9.0	.11	11	9.6*	.12	13
Mental hygiene	9.2	.11	12	8.8*	.13	11
Sex adjustments	9.3	.14	13	7.1*	.14	7
Civic interests, attitudes, and responsibilities	9.4	.11	14	9.8*	.10	14
Daily schedule	10.4	.10	15	11.2*	.11	15

* Change from 1935 significant at 1 per cent level.

Symonds reported no socioeconomic data for the young people he worked with. Therefore, a matching of samples on this variable could not be attempted. Indeed, in replicating a study made more than two decades ago, attempts to match groups on the basis of socioeconomic status may be questionable, for living standards and educational standards change over the years.

Cultural differences associated with time were one set of influences that affected the responses of the students. Cultural differences associated with geography may have also influenced the results, since the students in the earlier study lived in Oklahoma and New York, while those in the recent study lived in Minnesota.

In analyzing results, the writer relied chiefly on the statistic ρ and on Kendall's W statistic. By using correlation methods, it is possible to compare arrays of ranks of means as well as to test the significance of change in mean ranks. Fifteen items arrayed twice by one judge must have a ρ value of .535 to establish a relationship greater than chance at the 5 per cent level of significance. To interpret differences in rank orders assigned items on two occasions, comparisons of mean ranks of samples are more reliable than comparisons of ranks made by individuals. But the meaning of the magnitude of the changes thus described is still elusive. By studying various arrangements of the data, however, it is possible to add to the understanding gained from the study of any one arrangement.

For example, means of rankings assigned to items by boys and by girls from the seventh through the twelfth grade were compared grade by grade. All correlations were estimated from Kendall's W. The average rank-order coefficient of correlation between grade groups for items that boys ranked as problems was +.74; for items ranked as interests, +.78. When the same comparison was made for girls, the corresponding values were +.70 and +.72. Thus, ranks from grade to grade changed no more on the average than is suggested by correlation values in the .70's. When the data for boys and girls in each grade were combined, the values became +.65 for problems and +.63 for interests. Reliability was increased by using a larger group, but in this particular example the use of a larger group also introduced any systematic differences typical of rankings assigned by boys or by girls.

In any set of values ranked by a group of judges, there are likely to be intrinsic relationships, simply because judges from similar backgrounds are not reacting blindly or randomly to meaningful material. It is instructive, therefore, to examine some typical interarray correlations estimated from Kendall's W. If we consider the four ranks of mean values accorded to problems by boys and girls in 1935 and 1957, the coefficient of correlation for this typical interarray is +.58; for four arrays of interests, the value is also +.58. If we consider all eight arrays of problems and interests, the value becomes +.36. These values provide a pragmatic bench mark to judge the meaning of the correlation values in the following section, which have a theoretical top value of +1.00 and describe a chance relationship as .00.

According to the analysis, the young people showed greater consistency in 1935 than in 1957 in ranking issues as problems and as interests. That is, in 1957 there was little correspondence between the order of the items ranked as problems and the order of the items ranked according to interest $(\rho = -.20)$. In 1935, however, there was a noticeable correspondence between the two sets of ranks $(\rho = +.65)$.

How did these young people, separated by almost a generation, compare in the order they assigned the items as problems? As interests? The groups showed considerable similarity in ranking items as problems $(\rho = +.60)$ and slightly greater similarity in ranking items as interests $(\rho = +.73)$.

In terms of significance of differences between mean ranks accorded the same issues, there were more instances of change in value of items as interests than as problems—thirteen significant changes in interests, compared with eight in problems. However, many of the changes in mean ranks of interests represent displacements, not a rearrangement.

In each period, boys and girls ranked their problems very much alike. In 1935, the similarity in the rankings assigned by boys and by girls is expressed by a ρ value of $+.80$. In the 1957 study, the value is $+.77$. On the average, the similarity of the rankings assigned by boys and by girls was as great as the similarity of rankings assigned by boys or by girls in successive grades. When the items were ranked according to interest in 1935, the similarity of boys' and girls' judgments is expressed by a value of $+.80$. The camparable figure for 1957 is $+.58$.

Money was rated high as a problem in both periods; it had first place in 1935 and second in 1957. Physical health was much less of a problem among students in the 1957 study; they gave the item rank 12.5, while students in 1935 ranked it second. But mental hygiene rose to an appreciably higher rank on the list, from eleventh to 5.5. Recreation dropped from tenth place to the bottom of the list. Daily schedule and civic interests, attitudes, and responsibilities—while still low on the list—rose appreciably. Study habits, seen as a serious problem in 1935, had an even more prominent position in 1957: in 1935, study habits ranked fourth; in 1957, first.

In ranking the fifteen items as interests, students in 1957 gave sex adjustments a much higher place than the students in 1935 did. Home and family relationships and getting along with people were also placed higher in 1957. Interest in manners and courtesy showed a sharp drop; other declines were less dramatic. Interest in recreation and health was high in 1935 and continued so in 1957. Though daily schedule and study habits were rated as significant problems in 1957, interest in these items was low. Civic interests, attitudes, and responsibilities likewise had a low place on the list of interests, lower than the place assigned the item as a problem.

In any ranking procedure, the highest and the lowest ranks are the most differentiated psychologically and statistically. The method in this study called for the identification of positions 1, 2, and 3 and then positions 13, 14, and 15. The students were instructed: "First enter the numbers of the problems which are first, second, and third in order of being your own *greatest personal problems*. Then skip down and insert the numbers of those which are your *least personal problems*—thirteenth, fourteenth, and fifteenth in order. Then come back and fill in the rest." Similar instructions were given for ranking the items as interests.

Since the intermediate positions in each set were assigned last, they may represent, in the ranking of interests particularly, not so much intermediate significance as psychological indifference or lack of discrimination.

Since the procedure casts doubt on the validity of the intermediate positions, the conclusions based on them are likewise open to question. Symonds comments, for example, on the relatively high place the young people in 1935 gave to philosophy of life. The rank—sixth place on the list of problems—led Symonds to assert that young people crave values and goals. Students' desire for goals and values, he went on to say, presented a challenge to teachers and counselors. In the light of the procedure and the influence it may have had on results, Symonds' interpretation may require revision.

The findings of the 1957 study raise other questions on Symonds' observations. When the students in the 1935 study listed money as the number one problem, Symonds attributed their response to the depression. It is now clear that the significance of money as a problem was not merely a result of the depression years. In the 1957 study, money was the number two problem, second only to study habits.

Symonds was puzzled by the students' lack of concern with love and marriage, which he identified on his list as "sex adjustments." The low rank —thirteenth place—he ascribed to "repression." If we consider the data from the more recent study, an equally plausible explanation may lie in the hypothesis that social patterns influence adolescents' concerns.

In the 1935 study, mental health was eleventh on the list of problems. Symonds dismissed the low rank in these words: "Mental hygiene . . . is no concern of normal, healthy, growing adolescents. The crest of life is before them. Their failures and thwartings have not yet turned them back upon themselves." But mental health was a concern of the adolescents in the 1957 study. They ranked mental hygiene high as a problem. Again, social change may account for the greater significance young people now attach to this subject.

In 1935, study habits had fourth place on the list of problems but eleventh place on the list of interests. Symonds concluded that school is important but uninteresting. He pointed to the discrepancy as a "mandate to make the secondary curriculum a living reality," not a raking over of the "dried leaves of the past." Is it not also possible that young people see study habits as a problem, not because of their own conviction concerning the value of school experience, but because of pressures exerted by parents and teachers?

After these somewhat cavalier remarks on Symonds' interpretation, let us offer a few observations of our own, probably as open to challenge as his.

First, the modern high school curriculum, in contrast to the curriculum of thirty or more years ago, has tried to meet the daily life needs of young people rather than to cram their schedules with esoteric subject matter. The present study suggests that the modern curriculum has had some success in accomplishing its purpose. As students gain an adequate understanding of their problems, one might expect their curiosity about these problems to decrease differentially. Statistically, this change would appear in a lower coefficient of correlation between the rank order of problems and interests. In the present study, this coefficient of correlation seems to be lower now than formerly. That is, there seems to be a lower coefficient of correlation between the urgency with which certain experiences are felt as problems and the wish to know more about them. To cite one example, high school courses in family living are much more common now than they were in 1935. Though interest in love and marriage and family relations has risen sharply, the status of this item on the list of problems has not changed a great deal.

As for the decline in young people's interest in manners, is it possible that today's informality and casualness in teen-age social relations are responsible for the dwindling concern with "proper" behavior? Or is the change merely the result of a fortuitous shift in the ranking system occasioned by other, more psychologically significant changes?

As for the finding that physical health and recreation are less significant as sources of problems, apparently youth centers, recreational facilities, and school health programs are serving needs more adequately now than before. Today young people see mental health as a more important, a more urgent, problem than physical health.

These shifts in concerns and interests, as we have pointed out, correspond to changes in the general social scene. During the postwar years, our culture has had much to say about sex, love, and marriage problems; young people are now marrying younger; they are more interested in love and marriage. The decline in concern over manners comes at a time of general decline in formality in behavior in our society; the students' responses may reflect this decline. While young people see physical health as less of a problem, they are concerned with mental health, a subject that is now discussed far more than it was two decades ago. Finally, in recent years, study habits—listed as number one problem by today's students—have been regarded as a growing problem by a vocal minority of adults who are dissatisfied with students' school achievements.

The present study offers at least two suggestions for the high school program. Today the number of teen-age drivers is mounting. It is common knowledge that the accident rate in this age group is above average. The fact is acknowledged by insurance firms, which set higher premiums for this group, and by schools, which have inaugurated driver-training programs. Yet the high school student of 1957 was less concerned about, and less interested in, safety than the high school student of 1935.

Objectives of the high school curriculum, indeed almost all statements of educational objectives, give a prominent place to education for responsible citizenship. Yet, as a topic of concern, civic interest was ranked low by high school students in 1935 and in 1957. Both groups relegated this item to fourteenth place.

For those who are responsible for fashioning the program of the contemporary high school, these two findings alone may be well worth pondering.

55. Self: Missing Link for Understanding Behavior *

RICHARD M. BRANDT

SELF IS GRADUALLY becoming recognized as one of the most useful, integrative concepts yet developed for explaining behavior. It has far-reaching implications for teaching and therapy, for guidance and social work, for any field where human behavior is important.

Until now, however, most statements regarding the topic of self have been obscured by the technical jargon of the particular school of theory in which they were written and therefore have received less attention than they deserve from teachers, mental hygienists, and case workers. As a general exposition concerning self, this article represents an attempt to rectify this situation. It is organized around the treatment of four topics: relationship of self to behavior, characteristics of self, development of self and the teacher's role in effecting self-reorganization.

Cannot behavior be explained from a knowledge of physical functioning and cultural forces? Based on the present state of scientific knowledge, the answer is no. Despite similarities of constitution and environment (even these factors only approach similarity in real life), the stream of life experiences is unique for each individual. A brief look at the history of psychology may clarify the reason why a theory of behavior which omits the self-processes is inadequate.

During the first three decades of the twentieth century when psychology was becoming a science the stimulus-response school of thought dominated

* From Richard M. Brandt, "Self: Missing Link for Understanding Behavior," *Mental Hygiene* (January, 1957), pp. 24–33. Reprinted by permission of the author and The National Association of Mental Health.

both psychology in general and educational psychology in particular. Behavior was thought to be primarily a reflection of outside stimuli impinging on the individual and could be symbolized readily by the formula $S \rightarrow R$. Determining which S's (stimuli) most often produced particular R's (responses) was the accepted procedure for explaining behavior. Changing behavior (learning) seemed to be accomplished best by exposing people to the most suitable S's for the R's desired.

As a result, educational methodology and research put great stress on the study of various drill and demonstration techniques and on workbook and textbook formats for their effect in producing desired responses. Studies by the hundreds were made of the vocabulary in textbooks, of the numbers in arithmetic books and of the problems in science workbooks to determine their appropriateness to the educative process. Word-difficulty lists were established so that textbooks could be compared scientifically with each other. The stimuli of education received a careful screening.

This was the heyday for those who thought of education as a bag of tricks which teachers used for training children. One might well wonder if children were considered important, at least from a scientific viewpoint, mainly because they indicated the value of particular stimuli. Following exposure to the stimuli they either did or did not respond correctly. The higher the proportion of children who responded correctly, the more successful the particular teaching technique was judged to be. Little thought seemed to be devoted to the question of why some children learned acceptable responses more readily than others or why some children did not acquire them at all. Such concerns were often dismissed with statements regarding the innate differences in children's mental capacities. The educational spotlight was focused on the specifics of what was to be taught (subject matter) at each grade level and how it was to be taught (method), the desired responses and most suitable stimuli of education. Philosophers and educational policy-makers occupied themselves with determining the former, psychologists and educational experimentalists with the latter. Teachers shared in both these activities.

The fault in these activities for explaining and affecting behavior profoundly was not in what educators were doing but in what they were not doing. The formula was too simple.

Realizing the shortcomings of the formula, a few psychologists inserted a new symbol into it. $S \rightarrow O \rightarrow R$. The O stood for organism or, more correctly today, self-organization. They reasoned that the same stimulus meant different things to different people and that variation in response should be expected because of variation in the meanings of a stimulus. For instance, mention of a common word like "light" may stimulate any of the following thoughts: color, weight, wine, touch. An artist remembers the blinding light of a desert sun which he tried to capture on a recent canvas. A boxer recalls his disqualification before an important match because he was not light enough. A connoisseur of rare vintages relives for a moment his happy trip to Bordeaux. A pianist or a pickpocket reflects on the merits of a delicate touch in his chosen vocation. The story is told of the Easterner who while riding as a passenger in a car driven by a Westerner saw a tumbleweed roll into the road ahead. Unfamiliar with tumbleweeds, he thought the object was a boulder, became panicky and tried to grab the wheel. Fortunately his companion, who had seen tumbleweeds many times, realized what was happening and averted disaster by pushing his frightened companion away from the wheel. The experience these men brought to the situation colored their perceptions of it quite differently.[1]

The O of the formula has become in recent years an increasingly important part of psychological theory and investigation. More attention than ever before is being paid to such topics as interests, values, attitudes, drives, needs, levels of aspiration, and self-concepts. It is clearly recognizable that these are characteristics of organisms themselves rather than forces which surround them. The self consists of such phenomena as these.

Today personality, i.e., self, is one of the most studied subjects in psychology. Almost every current book explaining behavior either proposes or assumes a theory of personality, a description of the O in the formula. With Freud the O takes an id-ego-superego form and has conscious, unconscious and preconscious aspects to it.[2]

In contrast to this, Snygg and Combs define the O as a phenomenal field, i.e., all that a person is aware of at a particular moment, with a phenomenal self as its psychological center.[3] Lecky describes the O as a system of values which seem to the person possessing them to be consistent with each other.[4] Prescott defines the O as the organization of meanings which have been derived from past experiences. These meanings take such forms as explanatory concepts, codes of conduct, attitudes, values, and goals.[5] The significance of these theories cannot be judged from their lack of agreement. (Actually they are much more similar than superficial inspection indicates.)

---

[1] Donald Snygg and Arthur Combs, *Individual Behavior* (New York: Harper and Bros., 1949), p. 14.

[2] Sigmund Freud, *An Outline of Psychoanalysis* (New York: W. W. Norton, 1949).

[3] Snygg and Combs, *op. cit.*

[4] Prescott Lecky, *Self-Consistency* (New York: Island Press, 1945).

[5] Daniel A. Prescott, *Children and the Educative Process* (New York: McGraw-Hill Book Co.. 1957).

Their importance lies in their indication of a great interest which modern psychologists have for the O of the formula. The trend is toward making the O the largest, most significant symbol in the formula: $s \rightarrow O \rightarrow r$. Phenomenologists would even eliminate the S, claiming that behavior is determined entirely by the nature of the phenomenal field (O) at the moment of action, that outside stimuli (S) are accepted or rejected and distorted in accordance with the state of this field and therefore have no validity of their own.

Teachers likewise began to realize that the old formula was too simple. They found that children responded quite differently to the same stimuli. They observed that a particular teaching technique had a variety of effects on children and that these different effects were not always related to the "inherited capacities" of youngsters to learn. Books, for example, were eagerly devoured by some children but seemed to contain little of interest for other equally alert, intelligent children. Through trial and error teachers found that varying their techniques assured greater success than adhering to any single teaching procedure. They also discovered that classroom behavior could not be understood without knowing something about each child and how he perceived himself and the world about him. An illustration may serve to clarify this point:

The setting is a fifth grade classroom. Three boys have been "cutting up" and in the process have managed to spill a can of paint on the nearly completed mural the class has been making for the school's Christmas festival. Livid with rage, the teacher reprimands them severely in front of the entire class. Among other things she calls them stupid, disloyal, and irresponsible. She threatens to make them do the mural over after school.

Because she does not single out any one boy for chastisement, one can assume the external stimulus is the same for the three boys. Yet their responses are different because different self-concepts are involved. One boy responds with only a shrug of his shoulders. Through many similar experiences in his five years of schooling he has learned to see himself as a person who does not do what is required, who gets into trouble, who is stupid and a failure by school standards. This latest experience fits perfectly the picture he already has of himself and consequently produces little response. A second boy similarly shows no overt reaction; yet within him hot resentment flames up at being called stupid and irresponsible. Unlike the first boy his previous school experiences have been successful, happy ones. Being interested in biographies and identifying himself with George Washington, his hero at the moment, he sees himself as he perceives Washington—strong and silent in the face of adversity, one who "can take a beating and face it like a man." If in the heat of his anger he forgets this idea for a moment and blurts out some excuse for his action, he rationalizes to himself that even Washington stood against injustice and fought for what he thought was right. Only by such rationalization can he protect his image of himself as a Washington. The third boy responds still differently. A leader in physical activities on the playground, he has often played the role of bully among his classmates. He sees himself as a tough character whom "nobody pushes around and gets away with it," even a teacher. Therefore he argues with her over her remarks and claims that the paint can should not have been left near the mural. When her back is turned but when all the children can see, he sticks his tongue out at her. One stimulus but three self-concepts and three different responses—this is the relation of self to behavior.

Characteristics of Self

In thinking more explicitly about the exact nature of self, one may well begin viewing man as organization—organization of the dynamic forces which make him what he is. Clearly he is a physical organism, a complex arrangement of electrons and protons, atoms and molecules, protoplasm and cells, organs and systems, all functioning interrelatedly and as a whole. He can be visualized also as part of a larger complex of forces, the socio-physical environment which surrounds him and is affected by him. From the interaction of organism and environment, a third set of forces evolves, the psychological. To this, as it emerges within one individual, some people assign the term *personality*. Others prefer the term *self* because it connotes more of the idea of inner organization and seems less to be confused by layman's usage.

Because self (personality) has organization as a main feature some of its other qualities can be discussed by comparing it to other perhaps more obvious forms of organization. Schools may well serve the purpose.

One school differs from another because the elements of which it consists are different. By elements is meant the personnel, the physical plant, the equipment and materials, and all the other items which together make up the school. Because no two people are alike at least the personnel elements of the two schools differ; therefore the two organizations are distinct. Similarly any two self-organizations differ because of variations in the constituents: attitudes, values, goals, memories, experience, and so forth.

In school, as in self-organization, one finds a hierarchical order of significance to the various elements. Some elements are more important, more widely influential than others. For instance, a principal usually exerts a greater influence on the school than does a substitute teacher, though both contribute to its functioning. In like fashion, general feelings of adequacy and security have a more profound effect on self-organization as a whole than do such relatively specific elements as preferences for Fords over Chevrolets or for gas stoves over electric ranges. Although the elements seem to exist in a hierarchy of significance, it should not be assumed that what is at the top in one self-organization is equally placed in another self-organization. What is a high-level value for one person may be only moderately important to another and of little consequence to still another. In our culture there are few people who do not desire material wealth; yet some sacrifice personal integrity, even chance death, for it while still others put forth relatively little effort to attain it. Similarly, some principals are much more influential than others in their respective schools.

Another characteristic of all organizations, including self, is stability. If a new principal attempts to change school policies and procedures over-night, resistance and possibly bedlam result. The principal may find himself out of a job. A change in elements must overcome the inertia of organization. Many a man who looks back at what he was ten years ago finds that some changes have occurred in the interim; yet he still holds to many of his former beliefs, interests, patterns of behavior. His hair may be sparser and his figure altered but on reacquaintance with old friends he hears, "You're the same old Bill. You haven't changed a bit." And in many respects he hasn't. Preservation of the self and maintenance of personal identity seem to underly much psychological functioning and overt behavior.

Closely related to stability is the characteristic of integration or inner consistency. Without this quality there is no smoothness of functioning to the organization. The elements are in conflict with each other and the organization lacks unity. Such a state exists in schools where everyone is expending energy in battling each other and in going his own separate way. The accomplishments of traditional teaching in one classroom are annulled by those of progressive teaching in another to such an extent that the school as a whole stands for nothing. Variety may be the spice of life but too much of it causes dissolution of organization.

These statements can be applied to self also. When inconsistent values exist within the self, psychological functioning is compartmentalized and behavior often fluctuates first in one direction, then in another. Operating according to one set of values conflicts with other sets of values, and tension (anxiety) mounts. People may desire, for instance, many of the material products of our culture—television sets, vacuum cleaners, and automobiles.

To gain the money necessary to purchase these items they may decide that everyone in the family needs a job. Father works nights because the best job is available then, mother works days, and the children work after school and on weekends. But this practice breaks up family life, which they also value highly. Realization of this effect after awhile may cause them to alter their everybody-works plan and to forego some of their material wants. The real conflict in this instance is within the self and centers around establishment of a clear-cut hierarchy of importance for the elements. The self is full of such conflicts between separate desires, needs, roles and expectancies. The need to reconcile these conflicts and to attain some unity is another dynamic which underlies behavior. It represents a reason why self is never completely stable, why change is always taking place. Constantly occurring new experiences must likewise be internalized within the self-structure. These too involve conflict and change. Some theorists therefore prefer to think of self as an organized, organizing set of processes—and perhaps rightly so—rather than a system of elements. The latter is a more static concept unless the dynamic, shifting quality of the elements is emphasized.

At least one other characteristic is worth mentioning. This has to do with the reality of the elements. Just as some schools are more effective than others in promoting the development of boys and girls, some self-organizations are more rooted in reality than others. Variations exist in the effectiveness with which the self is related to the world around it. Those who saw the movie *The Secret Life of Walter Mitty* may recall how separate Mitty's dream world became with respect to the world of actuality. One may well argue that there is little difference between the psychotic person who lives in his world of fantasy and the creative genius who sees and discovers things that others before him have never seen. Perhaps the main difference is that once the insights of the genius are put before the public others can perceive the same insights and understandings. It took time but other physicists were able to test out and accept the revolutionary ideas of Einstein. The private world of self must somehow be in communication with and related to the world of selves which surrounds it. A youngster realizes to a greater or lesser degree things that others realize, i.e., that his friends think he is bossy or that he strikes out more than any other fellow on his baseball team. His self is to some extent realistic with respect to his physical-social environment.

As has been implied, there are vast individual differences between separate self-organizations involving each of the characteristics discussed. Some self-organizations are more complex than others and include many more elements. Very few, if any, of the elements themselves are identical. Some self-organizations are much more stable than others even to the point of being rigid. Some are more highly integrated and efficient in their functioning. Some are more realistic. Individual variation in observable physical features is small when compared to differences in self-organization.

Development of Self

Self emerges from the interaction of physiological and sociological factors. Perhaps a case history will best illustrate this process. At the time this history was recorded Betty Burrows was 14 years old and in the ninth grade of a junior high school. She was 5 feet 8 inches tall and weighed 137 pounds. She had menstruated at 11 and at 14 had about completed the growth cycle. Physically she had reached womanhood. Yet her parents treated her as a little girl. According to Betty's report her mother thought she still ought to be playing with dolls. Her father thought it sinful for her to attend movies or dances. In gym classes at school she was encouraged to dance with ninth grade boys who were several inches shorter than she. Boys and girls whose interests and development were equivalent to hers had long since left junior high school. Her mental capabilities were superior but her school grades were mediocre. She expressed little interest in schoolwork. She was forced to drop art, the only course in which she seemed interested. Deriving no satisfaction from a highly restrictive environment which was completely out of step with her developmental level, Betty resorted to "nonacceptable" ways of gaining attention and enhancing herself. She seemed to take delight in shocking people. One day she reportedly drank a coke after taking aspirin because she heard this would make her drunk. Either she actually became drunk or she put on a good enough act to convince people of it. She upset the school nurse another day by volunteering to bring a marijuana plant to class for the project on narcotics.

An early maturer caught in a web of home and school pressures geared only to chronological age, Betty formed pictures of herself and the world about her that were anything but conducive to sound development. The following statements, which she made to a guidance counselor near the end of the year, illustrate some of the worries and concerns that made up her developing self-organization: "I am taller than you but I don't believe I look any taller. I quit letting them measure me when I got to be 5 feet 8 so I don't know exactly how tall I am and I don't want to. . . . They think I am nuts around here but honestly sometimes I think I will go crazy cooped up with all those little kids all day. Sometimes I run every step of the way home at noon and every step of the way back because I think I will pop if I don't."

Fortunately, the school counselor understood Betty's predicament and began accepting her as the mature young woman she actually was. Adjustments were made in Betty's high school program the next year with the result that she eventually became a popular, successful student. Feelings of being out of step with the world and concern over her growth were alleviated as she received acceptance and understanding from the counselor. The self known as Betty Burrows was a product of the interaction of biological and cultural factors and in turn affected those factors.

Understanding self must of necessity grow out of awareness of the physiological and sociological processes from which it arose and to which it is always related. Self is like a river, which owes its vitality both to the physical properties of water and the geography of the surrounding countryside. No two rivers are exactly alike; yet all obey the law of gravity and flow downhill. None can support a solid brick or steel bar. In the same way man's patterns of behavior do not ordinarily include living under water or in trees because he does not inherit the anatomical equipment of fish or monkeys. As rivers vary in size with the amount of water they contain, man's physical make-up likewise varies—some people are short, others tall; some strong, others weak; some are predisposed to hemophilia, mental retardation or fits, others not so predisposed. Constitutional factors are many and varied. They contribute to the developing self-organization as they affect the experiences the person has. The analogy can be continued as one considers environmental factors. In the Colorado Rockies are seen fast flowing brooks marked by clear pools, erupting rapids, and picturesque waterfalls. In the low flatlands of the South are found sluggish silt-laden rivers; a current is scarcely visible. Just as geography differences can be seen in the individuality of rivers and streams, so culture differences are reflected in self-differences. For example, in Hopi and Zuni Indian societies youngsters are taught to be peace-loving, generous, and cooperative; in Dobuan and Mundugumor societies they are expected to be warlike, highly competitive, and individualistic.

Each culture is organized around certain standards of conduct, common beliefs and expectations for its young. The family, the school, the community, and the peer group reward and punish on the basis of how well a youngster behaves in accordance with these mores and expectations. This is in part the socialization process. It is also the process by which the child becomes a person and develops an individuality. In the American culture how much rejection does a strapping lad of 16 with broad shoulders and towering physique experience if he doesn't at least try out for the team? The self he becomes is the result of experiences he has, and they in turn are an outgrowth of both his physical make-up and the culture that surrounds him.

The Teacher's Role in Effecting Self-reorganization

In the earlier sections of this article the relation of self to behavior, specific characteristics of self, and the development of self were discussed. One important question remains. What implications for effecting change in the self-organizations of other people can be drawn from a knowledge of self-characteristics and functioning? Self has been described not as a physical entity but, like the x of algebra, as a construct standing for the unknowns of behavior. Surely, if this construct is to be useful, inferences can be made from it regarding classroom methodology and therapeutic practice.

As a partial attempt to answer this question, six hypotheses regarding self-functioning are stated below. Procedures which these hypotheses may suggest will be illustrated, although for the most part they must be left to the reader to work out in accordance with his own self-organization. They are presented here only to provoke further thinking regarding the answer to this question.

1. *The urge to learn seems to be inherent in the human organism.* One does not have to look further than the exploratory behavior of young children to find evidence for this hypothesis. The eagerness they exhibit in exploring new objects and in trying out new skills seems proof enough. But preadolescents with their endless questions about how things work and adolescents with their undercover discussions of sex and the meaning of life provide even more evidence. At whatever level of development one considers, human beings manifest a burning curiosity, a tremendous urge to find out.

Somehow school people have failed to take full advantage of this natural tendency to know. Many times junior high teachers have stated, "They don't have an idea in their heads. Ask them to plan and they just sit without a single idea." This does not have to happen nor does it always happen. In schools where it does not happen incentive devices such as gold stars have been replaced by allowing children to work on matters with which they are naturally concerned and by encouraging them to suggest and plan their activities rather than merely follow directions of the teacher. This is not to say that what the teacher thinks is unimportant. It is to say that educators must find better ways than those often used for relating things with which children are already concerned to things that teachers consider important. During the stimulus-response era educators concentrated so much on outside stimulation that they forgot to find out what motivated youngsters intrinsically and how these matters were related to what they wanted done.

2. *People strive toward feeling comfortable.* If they genuinely attempt to trace back likes and dislikes to their origins, people often recall one or more experiences which were accompanied by feelings of comfort or discomfort, satisfaction or dissatisfaction. A rather polished speaker does not like to lecture in a particular town. Several years ago a speech he made there, he felt, "really flopped." Although he has made several other speeches there since that time, he still prefers to talk elsewhere. Strong feelings of discomfort have persisted in the form of a preference to speak elsewhere.

Feelings and emotions are a part of all experience. Elements of the self therefore are emotionally loaded, as reflected in attitudes toward school and home, toward other people and self, toward reading and baseball, and so forth. Children learn more than facts and ideas; they learn to like and dislike. A youngster who is made to feel uncomfortable in reading classes time after time, possibly because he lacks the skills to read as successfully as others, may continue to resist reading even after he develops these skills. He may require numerous personally satisfying experiences to overcome this resistance. Many teachers are therefore concentrating on eliminating threat and making children feel psychologically comfortable in the classroom. Threat produces defensiveness and inhibits self-reorganization. Successful teachers are becoming increasingly alert to the way children feel about the experiences they are having.

3. *Acceptance helps a person to grow and change.* With acceptance a person learns to trust himself and to have faith in his own efforts to learn.

Rejection, on the other hand, has two possible outcomes: Either the rejector is rejected in return (often along with whatever he stands for) or inner growth is inhibited. In the latter instance, fear or some incentive device may make it seem as if change has occurred within the self when it really has not. So many facts learned in the spring have been forgotten by fall. The test of classroom discipline must be made when the teacher is out of the room. Are not teachers depending too much on external motivation to the neglect of such a powerful force as acceptance?

Real change involves frustration because it means self-reorganization.

But when personal threat is added to a learning situation the frustration often is too great and growth is stopped. Such frequently heard comments as "That's been tried before" and "You can do better than that" need to be evaluated, in light of the individual concerned, as to how much personal threat they represent. A fine line, almost a shading, exists between challenge and threat. It is suspected that external evaluation produces more of the latter than is often realized.

4. *Changes in self depend on changes in perception.* Perception changes most readily in an accepting yet stimulating atmosphere where freedom exists to explore various viewpoints and to attach personal meaning to new insights. An interesting talk often stimulates new thoughts but unless it is followed by full opportunity for discussion most of these thoughts remain half-formed and produce little permanent change in the listener. The dormitory bull-session often has a more lasting effect than the classroom lecture.

The success of the group process as a medium for affecting self results both from the stimulation one receives from hearing many sides of the same question and from the personal involvement one experiences in contributing ideas of his own. New ideas seem to "stick" best when the perceiver himself can state them in his own words (or at least think through them in his own terms). It is not uncommon to hear group members saying, "Is this what you are saying?" or "I believe we have the same idea. Would you check me on this statement of it?" Perceptual change results from such discussions, in which no one person is expected to have all of the answers and all are encouraged to contribute. The increasing use of classroom show-and-tell periods indicates that educators are aware of the value of group process. Group process does not need to be restricted to certain periods of the day, however. It can—and in many schools does—represent a new approach to the total educative process, one which markedly changes self-organization.

5. *An individual strives toward consistency and integration of the self.* This hypothesis, the heart of Lecky's theory of personality, may well be discussed by using one of his illustrations. He describes a youngster who despite considerable intellectual ability was a poor speller. Knowing that the boy saw himself as a rather independent person, Lecky managed to convince him that not being able to spell accurately made him dependent on others for help. The boy saw his own inconsistency in self-valuation and was thereby forced to modify one of his self-perceptions. Because feeling independent was more important to him than being unable to spell, he began to think of himself as someone who could spell. His spelling improved

rapidly as he strove to prove this fact to himself and thereby to maintain a picture of himself as an independent person.[6]

From an outsider's point of view every self has inconsistent elements within it. The person himself, however, is unaware of most of these inconsistencies. If outsiders can bring these inconsistencies into awareness in a nonthreatening way, self-reorganization occurs. The lower-level element within the hierarchy of self-organization is generally altered so as to preserve the higher-level element. It is possible, of course, for modifications to take place on both levels.

6. *Significant change in behavior occurs only with change in self.* Despite the handicap of large classes of thirty or forty youngsters, a truly successful teacher deals with each as an individual. By itself the practice of grouping children does not accomplish his aim. The teacher is concerned with the separate self-organizations represented in his classroom and he knows the elements in each. He provides acceptance for youngsters. He is aware of individual perceptions and of inconsistencies within each self. He has faith in children's willingness to learn. He realizes fully that effective teaching takes place only when changes occur within the self.

56. *The Motivating Effects of Exteroceptive Stimulation* *

D. O. HEBB

MY INSTRUCTIONS from the man who cracked the whip—in the role of chairman of this symposium—were to center my talk about the effects of perceptual deprivation on human motivation and the study of brainwashing made at McGill. It's obvious, no one can *really* deal with my topic in a twenty-minute paper and also go on and talk about broad implications. So I'll make no pretense at covering the field. But if I see a chance to make a broad remark, of course, I will.

[6] Lecky, *op. cit.*, pp. 103–5.

* From D. O. Hebb, "The Motivating Effects of Exteroceptive Stimulation," *The American Psychologist* (March, 1958), pp. 109–12. Reprinted by permission of the author and the American Psychological Association.

The Infant's Environment

What we are considering here is the relation of the mammal to his sensory environment. To put this in perspective I shall start with perceptual deficit in infancy, as far as it bears on motivational and emotional problems. As you know, it is now clear that such a deficit also produces intellectual defects at maturity, but this I am not directly concerned with, except as it bears incidentally on social intelligence. Also, I am going to restrict this further to the dog, an animal that shows *some* of the complexities of temperament found in the higher species—more so than the rat, certainly. The work I refer to is mainly that of Thompson, Melzack, Heron, and Mahut. These studies of temperamental variables have shown, like those on intelligence, that the normal development of behavior depends on a normal perceptual environment. The animal reared in isolation is a permanent screwball at maturity: motivationally, socially, intellectually abnormal.

These rearing experiments, of course, relate to the early observations of Spitz concerning "hospitalism" and social deprivation of the hospitalized infant, and to the later observations of Bowlby and others, also on hospitalized children. It is important to mention also such reports of single human subjects, reared in pretty extreme isolation, as those of Davis, Hill and Robinson, and Mason. But in these human cases, of course, there are a number of uncontrolled variables, making interpretation difficult indeed.

The animal experiments not only have the advantage of experimental control; they also make it possible to observe long-term effects, because the dog grows up in a reasonable period of time. It is quite practical to rear dogs in different ways and test not only at adolescence, so to speak, but also in young middle age. There is a lot of talk in the literature about how to rear the human animal so as to produce the kind of motivations ("personality") you want, at maturity; but the child psychologist sometimes forgets to what a great extent these statements depend on some theoretical formulation or other, and there aren't any theories that we can really trust that much.

There is no evidence whatsoever that shows factually, reliably, the effects of a particular kind of rearing, for the first six years of life, upon personality and so forth when the human subject has grown up. It's a long step from dog to man, of course, and we can't put much trust in this kind of inference either. The ideal subjects for experiment would be the anthropoid apes, but these take almost as long to grow up as man does, so this again is not really practical. Perhaps Harry Harlow will manage the trick in his rearing experiments with rhesus monkeys, but in the end we are going to have to depend on a better development of basic theory, combined with the data of animal experiments.

Anyway, let me summarize the dog-rearing experiments, as far as they bear on motivational questions. One point, first, is most important in the interpretation of the results. The dogs reared in isolation showed none of the physical debility and susceptibility to infection that Spitz reported. They developed exceptionally well: in fact, being nice and stupid, they made excellent show dogs; and William Ponman, who was in charge of the colony, filled a small display cabinet in the laboratory with first-prize ribbons won with our dogs, year after year, in dog shows. This physical vigor should be kept in mind in considering the motivational deviations.

The restricted dogs were markedly atypical in activity measures, exploratory behavior, and the search for variety, sharing of food in a single food-dish, social responsiveness to another dog, response to either threatening *or* friendly persons, and response to pain stimulation.

They were also low in formal problem-solving ability, of course, and this brings me to the question of their "social intelligence." Their behavior suggested repeatedly that the motivational differences, or what seemed motivational differences, were partly due to not perceiving the situation in the same way as the normal dogs and not having acquired normal ways of dealing with others. "Social intelligence" used to be in the literature, along with the abstract and mechanical varieties of intelligence, and one of the things suggested by these experiments is that it ought still to be in the literature.

How do social skills develop? It's no longer possible just to take for granted that your heredity will do it. You don't grow up to be socially perceptive, sensitive to another's attitudes, able to be friendly without over-doing it, able to conceal your own attitudes as need be, and so forth—you don't develop all the social skills that one must have to live with others simply as a matter of heredity and growth. We know, with reasonable certainty, that this aspect of intellectual function, like others, must depend on experience also. But what kind of experience, when, at what age?

This symposium of course is concerned with motivation, not cognitive processes as such; but the point is that motivation is also a function of perceptions and skills. We want to bring up children with "democratic" values; if in fact this is to be so, they must know how to put them satisfyingly into effect. It is hardly realistic for the social scientist to concentrate only on establishing desirable motivations—how long can one expect them to survive, not to extinguish, if the corresponding social skills are missing?

The Environment of Maturity

Now we come closer home, with studies directly concerned with motivation in the adult. The infant-environment work shows that the adult is a product both of his heredity and physical environment (as necessary for growth) and of his perceptual experience during the growth period. Once development is complete, does the organism then become less dependent psychologically on sensory stimulation? When a man's or a woman's character is formed, his or her motivations and personality pattern established, is character or personality an entity that exists so to speak in its own right, no matter where or in what circumstances (assuming physical health and reasonable bodily welfare)?

In the Korean war the Chinese Communists gave us a shocking answer: in the form of brainwashing. The answer is "No." Without physical pain, without drugs, the personality can be badly deformed simply by modifying the perceptual environment. It becomes evident that the adult is still a function of his sensory environment in a very general sense, as the child is.

I am not going to ask you to listen again to all the details of the experiments that have been done and are still being done in this country and Canada (though the Canadian experiments are over) to investigate the problem. The work of Heron, Bexton, Scott, and Doane began when the Defence Research Board of Canada asked us in 1952 to find out what we could about the basic phenomena, with the hope that some possibilities for protection against brainwashing might turn up. Now brainwashing, as you know, takes different forms and can involve lack of sleep, fatigue, and hunger; and it makes a lot of use of having the subject write out "confessions" (or whatever you want to call them). Only one aspect was picked out for study: isolation from the environment. The isolation was drastic, but far from complete. Visual perception was completely prevented; auditory perception was cut down, perhaps, to about a quarter of normal; tactual perceptions, to perhaps a tenth of normal (but don't ask how this quantification is done!).

The result, again in brief, was an acute disturbance of the normal personality. (The effect observed by Lilly was apparently even greater than in the McGill studies.) There were great swings of motivation, which alternated between periods of apathy and an intense desire to get back to a normal environment. Any variation of sensory input was welcomed, but with this there was a lack of energy for problem-solving; and, after leaving isolation, the subject found it difficult or impossible to get back to his normal work habits for about twenty-four hours. In addition, there were some handsome visual hallucinations, disturbances of perception of the self, impairment of intelligence test performance, changes in the EEG, and marked visual disturbances on first emerging from isolation.

With the possible exception of the effects of propaganda, the changes were reversible, disappearing in a day or so. For the problem of brainwashing we learned something of value, which should be as widely known as possible, since we do not know who will fall into Communist hands in the future and be subjected to this—appalling, indecent, choose your own adjective—this atrocious procedure; and knowing something about it may mitigate its effects.

First, the occurrence of hallucinations can itself be terrifying to the naive subject and help to break down his resistance. If he knows that hallucinations are "normal" in these circumstances and that the effects are quite reversible, he has at least a little protection.

Second, the subject should know that his critical thinking will be impaired and that he is especially vulnerable to propaganda after being in radical isolation. Knowing this may help to resist propaganda, if the subject can keep reminding himself to make an extra critical effort. Heron's group did not try to investigate means of resistance, but did demonstrate the vulnerability to ridiculous propaganda. The subject was given talks on ghosts, poltergeists, ESP, and so forth, the experimenters deliberately propagandizing and having no truck with scientific detachment or such like. He was told that scientists are biased against psychic phenomena, that there is plenty of evidence to show the existence of ghosts, and so on—the statements being made as persuasive as possible. Control subjects were paid to listen to the same stuff and were influenced by it, but the experimental subjects significantly more. Part of this was no doubt due to the subject's eagerness to *listen,* to almost anything; again, if the prisoner being brainwashed knows in advance that he will have this weakness, he may be able to some extent to guard against it.

The effects of the propaganda were the only ones that showed signs of lasting beyond the experimental period. The groups tested two weeks later were too small to establish the point definitely, in a statistical sense, but the tentative conclusion was reinforced by incidental reports from the subjects. A number of the experimental subjects, unlike the controls, went to the library to borrow books on psychical (*not* psychological) research, mind reading, and so forth; there were spontaneous reports of being afraid of ghosts, late at night, for the first time in the subject's experience; and reports of trying to use ESP in card-playing.

It is hardly necessary to say that the experiment, taken as a whole, was very unsettling to us. Our subjects were of course free to walk out on the experiment at any time they chose (as soon as they felt they could give up the $20 a day pay!), but it would be very different for a man in fear of his life, with no choice in the matter and no termination in sight. It is one thing to hear that the Chinese are brainwashing their prisoners on the other side of the world; it is another to find, in your own laboratory, that merely taking away the usual sights, sounds, and bodily contacts from a healthy university student for a few days can shake him, right down to the base: can disturb his personal identity, so that he is aware of two bodies (one hallucinatory) and can not say which is his own, or perceives his personal self as a vague and ill-defined something *separate from his body,* looking down at where it is lying on the bed; and can disturb his capacity for critical judgment, making him eager to listen to and believe any sort of preposterous nonsense.

Fundamentally, this raises the whole question of the relation of man to his sensory environment, and it bears particularly on research in personality and social processes. There are other aspects of the problem, but for those I refer you to the chapter by Thompson and myself in Lindzey's *Handbook of Social Psychology.* What I want to do now is to bring the discussion closer to everyday living.

The effects I have been talking about can occur in varying degree. Lilly has shown that making isolation more drastic produces motivational and emotional disturbance much more quickly; but he has also shown that the lonely man, in not too abnormal an environment otherwise, may suffer gross disturbances when the social deprivation is long continued. Lilly has reviewed some of the published reports of solitary sailors, Arctic groups in the long polar night, and shipwreck survivors in a small boat. These people, the ones who survive, develop one or other of the symptoms of the mentally ill—and among the many who do not survive, of course, there are those who develop outright psychosis. Mystical feelings of oneness with the universe develop; fears of being insane, or of seeming to be insane, are common. In larger groups, socially closer to normal situations, Boag has described a motivational process that parallels—but on a more extended scale—a puzzling aspect of results found in the McGill experiments. The experimental subjects were always eager to be tested, as a break in the monotony, and then paradoxically lacked the energy to work on problems even of moderate difficulty. Similarly, Boag reports that men in Arctic stations would make extensive plans for spare-time activities, exactly the sort of thing that would protect them against their lack of stimulation, only to slump later into a kind of apathy. There was:

. . . apathy, lack of interest in surroundings, motor retardation, greatly increased hours of sleep, lack of attention to personal appearance and tidiness of quarters, and disinclination to undertake extra work or odd jobs, *in spite of complaints of not having enough to do* [italics added]. An occasional man will spend a whole winter in his quarters without leaving them to visit neighbors half an hour's walk away . . .[1]

Clearly, man's motivation is a function of his exteroceptive stimulation. I don't need to labor this further, but instead draw your attention to another set of phenomena that don't get into the books. These concern the relation of our own work habits to an accustomed environment, and the ease with which motivation is broken down. How many of you, when you get back from these meetings, will be able to go on with your work on the first day, as if you had never been away? How many of you go on vacation with plans for work that do not get carried out—that is, not even to the extent that you carry out plans when you are in your normal work environment? How many of you can write only in a particular setting, after elaborate preparation, with everything just so?

It was Karl Menninger in a personal communication who drew my attention to the similarity of the deficient-environment effects and the phenomenon of not being able to get back to work after being away—I believe it is quite common, but at any rate Menninger and I suffer from it.

Being often my own best subject when it comes to the study of abnormal behavior, I have now finally to report some peculiar behavior of my own bearing on this question of the relation of motivation to the accustomed environment. I do so with the idea that others may have observed similar phenomena and may perhaps have better ideas as to how they are to be understood. The peculiarity, really, is only in certain time relations. I have repeatedly found, when I have been a visiting lecturer or away from my usual habitat in some other similar role, that my ability to write, or do other work that I jokingly call creative, runs down over a two-week period or thereabouts. It can be restored by a short period in my own laboratory setting, and then again runs down. This is presumably a function of homesickness, of what Hunt, I believe, called cryptic nostalgia—an acute

[1] T. J. Boag, "The White Man in the Arctic: A Preliminary Study of the Problems of Adjustment," *American Journal of Psychiatry,* 109 (1952), 444–49.

condition, at times, from which I as well as many other persons suffer, though it is not mentioned among adults. (Rather vulgar, one gathers.) I can understand the nostalgia, in the sense that it is part of the whole picture of man's motivation as dependent on an accustomed environment, but I have more trouble understanding why the clock, so to speak, takes so long to run down. There are some problems here for research that have the happy combination of both theoretical and practical interest. I wish someone would tackle them.

57. *Patterns of Personal Problems of Adolescent Girls* [*][1]

RICHARD E. SCHUTZ

NUMEROUS INVESTIGATORS have determined the frequency with which various problems are listed by giving samples of adolescents. However, in tabulating the problems it has been necessary to rely on a priori systems of classification. The customary procedure has been to categorize the problems by activity or functional areas; e.g., school, home, health, etc.

The purpose of the present study was to determine the pattern or structure underlying the personal problems which adolescents recognize and are willing to report on a youth problems inventory. This pattern was investigated by extracting homogeneous clusters from a sample of 156 items selected from the inventory.

Procedure

The inventory used in the study was the Billett-Starr Youth Problems Inventory, Senior Level, a check list intended to provide a means of systematically identifying the personal problems of individual adolescents.

[*] From Richard E. Schutz, "Patterns of Personal Problems of Adolescent Girls," *The Journal of Educational Psychology* (February, 1958), pp. 1–5. Reprinted by permission of the author and the American Psychological Association.

[1] Based on a dissertation submitted in partial fulfillment of the requirements for the Ph.D. at Columbia University. The investigation was carried out under the helpful direction of Robert L. Thorndike. The writer wishes to thank Roger T. Lennon and the staff of the Division of Test Research and Service, World Book Co., for making the study possible.

The 441 items which make up the Inventory include problems mentioned in the compositions and free responses of several large samples of high school students which the authors obtained in developing the instrument. The items are organized into eleven areas designated as follows:

1. Physical Health, Fitness, and Safety
2. Getting Along with Others
3. Boy-Girl Relationships
4. Home and Family Life
5. Personal Finance
6. Interests and Activities
7. School Life
8. Heredity
9. Planning for the Future
10. Mental-Emotional Health and Fitness
11. Morality and Religion

The cluster analysis was based on the responses of 500 girls in grades ten and eleven in two Pinellas County, Florida, high schools who took the Inventory as part of the national standardization program in May 1956. The schools are three-year high schools and had a segregated white enrollment at the time of the study. The Inventory was administered in regular classrooms by regular teachers. The Inventories were signed by the students.

The basic technique of analysis was that described by Loevinger, Gleser, and Dubois for deriving clusters which have maximum reliability as estimated by Kuder-Richardson Formula 20. Each cluster is obtained by starting with a triad of items having the highest covariance and adding items in succession, adding always the item for which the ratio of the sum of covariance with the items already in the cluster is a maximum. Items are added to the cluster until no more items remain which will increase this ratio. The process is repeated on the residual pool of items to form the second and subsequent clusters.

A sample of 156 items was selected to be included in the cluster analysis. The items selected have the following characteristics: (a) they are included in both the Junior and Senior levels of the Inventory; (b) they were rated as "very serious" or "moderately serious" problems by a panel of twenty guidance specialists; (c) each was marked by at least 5 per cent of the Ss in the sample. An attempt was made to make the sample of items representative of the eleven areas of the Inventory and to include as many items as possible which have counterparts in other published problems check lists.

The Inventory attempts to get at the intensity of a student's problems by allowing him to differentiate between those which bother him "some" and those which bother him "very much." For the present analysis each *S*'s "some" and "much" responses were combined into a single category.

Each *S*'s responses were multiple punched on an IBM card, and the 156 by 156 cooccurrence matrix was prepared using the counting sorter. The figures in the cooccurrence matrix were converted to percentages and the variance-covariance matrix prepared. The cluster analysis was performed, and a check was made on the factorial purity and reliability of the obtained clusters.

Results

Three clusters were extracted from the pool of 156 items. Eighty-three items are included in Cluster I, sixteen in Cluster II, and seventeen in Cluster III. An abbreviated Cluster I, consisting of thirty-seven items, was formed by eliminating thirty-five items which correlated less than .40 with the complete cluster and eleven items which nearly duplicated another item in the cluster; e.g., the two items, "I'm often restless," and "I'm restless most of the time." The items in the abbreviated Cluster I and in Clusters II and III are shown in Tables 1–3. The items are arranged in order of the magnitude of the point biserial correlation of each item with its cluster. The area and item number within the area are indicated in the first column of each table. The Kuder-Richardson Formula 20 reliabilities of the clusters and their intercorrelations are shown in Table 4.

The nature of a cluster must be determined by examining the items to discover the general attribute they seem to hold in common. The items in Cluster I cover a broad area, coming from eight areas of the Inventory. The cluster appears to reflect a general feeling of personal anxiety and insecurity.

The items in Cluster II are currently classified under seven different area headings in the Inventory. They seem to involve a feeling of nervous tension concerning relationships with other persons. This cluster is the least homogeneous of the three, and its correlation with Cluster I is nearly as high as its reliability. Both Clusters I and II reflect personal anxiety. While the items in Cluster II did not have enough in common with the items in Cluster I to be included in the more homogeneous general cluster, they shared sufficient common variance to form another with lower reliability.

Cluster III is the only cluster that does not cut across the functional area organization of the Inventory to any great extent. Fifteen of the seventeen items in the cluster come from Area IV of the Inventory headed "Home and

Family Life." The items all represent some kind of difficulty in getting along with parents.

If a cluster is factorially pure, all of its common factor variance should be accounted for by a single centroid factor. The ratio of the first factor variance to the common factor variance thus provides a basis for evaluating the factorial purity of a cluster.

Table 1

CLUSTER I

Item No.	r	Item
10–38	.59	People don't understand me.
10–10	.57	I'm afraid of making mistakes.
10–15	.55	I'm often restless.
10–43	.51	I worry about what others say.
10–37	.51	I feel I'm not wanted.
10–17	.50	I'm disgusted with myself (dislike myself very much).
10–19	.49	I need someone to give me advice.
8–3	.49	I would like to be able to do something well.
8–1	.49	I don't understand myself.
11–10	.49	Many times I don't know what is right and what is wrong.
10–39	.48	People talk about me behind my back.
10–2	.48	I feel uncertain (unsure) about everything.
10–34	.47	I spend too much time daydreaming.
10–3	.46	I need to learn to depend on myself.
10–35	.45	I feel sorry for myself.
10–46	.45	I get excited too easily.
11–6	.45	I'm sometimes troubled by immoral (bad) thoughts.
7–5	.45	I wonder if I'll pass.
10–32	.44	I don't get out and go after what I want.
9–18	.44	I wonder if I'm taking the right subjects.
7–44	.44	I'm afraid to take tests.
10–58	.44	I'd like to know how to get rid of a bad habit.
4–46	.44	I'm unhappy at home.
7–62	.43	Some teachers never encourage or help me.
6–1	.43	I seldom have anything interesting to do.
7–85	.43	I would like to know how to get along with certain teachers.
8–2	.43	I wonder what my real mental ability is.
10–13	.42	I wonder what my future will be.
10–1	.42	I'm confused by the way things change.
2–50	.42	I feel lonely most of the time.
4–40	.42	I'm afraid to tell my (father) (mother) when I've done something wrong.
10–42	.42	I'm blamed for things that aren't my fault.
2–52	.41	I find it hard to make friends.
10–30	.41	I don't know how to (pay attention) (work or study hard).
11–5	.41	I often tell lies.
10–45	.40	I'm bothered by people who find fault with me.
10–47	.40	I can't control my temper.

Table 2

CLUSTER II

Item No.	r	Item
2–11	.63	I'm nervous when I talk to people.
2–15	.60	I'm not good at talking with people.
7–38	.55	I'm nervous in front of the class.
1–19	.49	I get tired easily.
2–10	.48	(I'm afraid) (I don't like) to meet people.
2–39	.47	I want others to like me.
1–21	.44	I'm always nervous.
3–1	.44	I don't understand (boys) (girls).
2–6	.38	I'm not good-looking.
6–10	.36	I would rather be alone.
6–9	.36	I get tired from too much activity.
6–11	.36	I spend too much time on (radio) (television) (movies).
1–22	.32	I need to know more about sex (body changes at my age) (new body functions).
10–40	.31	I'm afraid I seem conceited (stuck-up).
9–25	.30	I'm not sure whether I should go to college.
2–7	.28	I (don't have) (don't know how to pick) the right clothes.

Table 3

CLUSTER III

Item No.	r	Item
4–31	.64	My (father) (mother) is always criticizing (blaming) (nagging) me.
4–43	.59	I can't discuss things with my (father) (mother).
4–33	.58	My (father) (mother) is always expecting too much of me.
4–37	.54	I'm often the cause of family quarrels (parents argue about things I do).
4–51	.52	I'm thinking of leaving home.
4–41	.52	My (father) (mother) has little or no interest in what I do.
4–39	.51	I sometimes lie to my (father) (mother) to get permission to do something.
4–60	.51	My (father) (mother) is often nervous and irritable.
4–42	.50	My (father) (mother) never asks my opinion about anything important to the family.
4–50	.49	I dislike my (father) (mother) very much.
4–25	.49	I don't agree with my (father) (mother) about my out-of-school activities.
4–48	.48	I'm sometimes ashamed of things my parents do or say.
4–38	.45	My (father) (mother) pries into my private affairs.
4–26	.44	My (brother) (sister) is always causing me trouble.
5–4	.43	I don't get an allowance.
2–19	.40	I often "stretch the truth" when I tell something.
4–49	.34	There's too much drinking in our home.

Table 4

CLUSTER INTERCORRELATIONS AND KUDER-RICHARDSON RELIABILITIES

Cluster	I(83)	I(37)	II	III
I (83)	(.94)	.98	.67	.60
I (37)	.98	(.90)	.63	.52
II	.67	.63	(.71)	.34
III	.60	.52	.34	(.81)

A complete centroid analysis was performed independently on the items in the abbreviated Cluster I and in Clusters II and III. The highest correlation coefficient in each column of the matrix was used as the communality estimate, communalities being re-estimated by this method for every residual matrix. Factoring was considered complete when both Tucker's Phi and Coombs' criterion indicated that the last significant factor had been extracted. Three factors were extracted from Cluster I, three from Cluster II, and two from Cluster III. First factors account for 80 per cent, 69 per cent, and 85 per cent, respectively, of the common factor variance of the clusters.

To investigate the extent to which the reliability of the clusters is dependent on chance factors, the Kuder-Richardson Formula 20 reliability of each cluster was computed, based on the results of a new sample of seventy-three Ss selected from the same population as the original sample. The reliability coefficients for the new sample were as follows: Cluster I, .94; abbreviated Cluster I, .91; Cluster II, .63; Cluster III, .83.

The significance of the difference between each of the coefficients for the new and the original group was computed using Fisher's z transformation. The difference for Cluster II is significant at the .001 level. There is no significant difference between the coefficients for the other clusters.

Discussion of Results

The findings of the study have implications for both the theory and measurement of adolescent problems. While the study was not designed to test the validity of the various theories of adolescent problems that have been proposed, it does provide evidence concerning the way in which problems cluster or "go together."

The cluster structure does not correspond closely to any of the theoretical frameworks which have been proposed for classifying adolescent problems.

The composition of Cluster I suggests that a single dimension of personal anxiety underlies many of the manifest problems which theorists have used several dimensions to explain.

The fact that two of the clusters cut across several areas of the Inventory indicates that the classifying of items in problems check lists into the traditional functional or activity categories is in large part an arbitrary procedure. However, even though the conventional rubrics do not all represent true functional unities, teachers and counselors may still find the categories helpful. The subdivisions often suggest programs of action related to the kinds of services that schools and other social agencies are equipped to provide. Thus, the traditional area organization often serves the purpose of suggesting foci of therapeutic action.

Although no data are yet available concerning the predictive validity of the clusters, they provide a potential means of screening adolescents in need of psychological help. They have high face validity and are reasonably pure factorially. A study of predictive validity is required to determine the extent to which they are actually related to personal adjustment.

Summary

A cluster analysis was performed on 156 selected items from the Billett-Starr Youth Problems Inventory, Senior Level, based on the responses of 500 adolescent girls. Three clusters were extracted and designated as follows: Cluster I—General personal anxiety and insecurity; Cluster II—Tension concerning relations with others; and Cluster III—Difficulties in getting along with parents. The implications of the cluster structure for the theory and measurement of adolescent problems was briefly discussed.

58. *General Characteristics of a Model of Mature Behavior* *

ALFRED L. BALDWIN

BEFORE EXAMINING the model in detail, let us take an over-all view of it (see Fig. 1). There are three main sections in the model: cognition, goal selection, and goal-directed behavior. We assume that one necessary step in behaving is to obtain a map or picture of the external world. Since behavior is adjusted to the external world, the individual must have some picture of it. We know that the unknown is frequently disconcerting, espe-

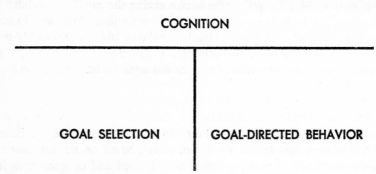

Figure 1. A schematic division of voluntary behavior.

cially to young children during the last part of the first year and throughout early childhood. We know that a certain proportion of adult behavior is specifically directed toward discovering what the external world is like. Curiosity is a common human trait. The first section of our model of behavior, therefore, is concerned with the process of knowing or cognizing what the situation is like. Cognition includes perception of the immediately perceptible aspects of the environment and also processes of making judgments or inferences about remote parts of the situation.

The second section of the model is concerned with the process of goal selection. An individual does not constantly have the same goals. In some situations the college student wants to pass an examination; in others he wants a date with his best girl; in still others he wants the football team to

* From Alfred L. Baldwin, *Behavior and Development in Childhood,* pp. 114–21. Copyright 1955 by Henry Holt and Co. (Dryden), New York, and reprinted with permission.

win its big game. In any specific situation one or several motives may be aroused. We must therefore discover what situational factors tend to arouse what kinds of motives. Not all motives are realized in overt behavior. Some are inhibited; others are ignored because they are unimportant; others are too difficult even to try to satisfy. Some motives, however, do establish a goal that the individual tries to attain.

The third section of the model is concerned with goal attainment or goal-directed behavior. Once a goal is set, there are often alternative ways of trying to achieve it. The selection of the means to a goal, the carrying out of that means, and the guidance of the ongoing behavior toward the goal are all involved in goal-directed behavior.

These three sections of the model are schematically represented in Figure 1. Later figures will fill in some of the details in each section.

INDEPENDENCE OF COGNITION FROM GOAL SELECTION AND GOAL-DIRECTED BEHAVIOR

Let us consider for a moment the reason for our having split up human behavior into these sections. One of the characteristics of maturity that has been described in an earlier chapter is objectivity in perception and cognition. The more mature an individual is, the less is his cognition of the external situation dependent upon his immediate situation, his immediate mood, his wishes, hopes, and fears. Objective cognition is determined by the properties of the external situation and not by the perceiving individual.

In our model of human behavior we shall assume that the individual constructs a picture or map of the external environment. Objectivity requires that this picture of the external world be accurate and that it be uninfluenced by the individual's motivation. To the extent that we see the world as we want to see it, or as we fear it may be, we are unable to respond to it as it really is.

Thus, in our model of mature behavior, cognition of the external world is independent of motivation. The cognition may determine the motives that are evoked and especially the motives that are acted upon, but cognition is not *determined by* the motives of the individual.

This condition is not always fulfilled in actual life. We shall see later how needs may influence perception; we all know from everyday life that our understanding of a situation may be influenced by our hopes and fears. In the model, however, we separate the process of goal selection from cognition because increasing maturity brings with it an increasing differentiation of motivation and cognition.

We assume, furthermore, that cognition and motivation are independent in another sense. Many aspects of the situation that are not relevant for goal selection or for goal-directed behavior are nevertheless cognized. The batter concentrating on hitting the ball may not be paying attention to the fact that the sky is blue, that the right-field grandstand is filled, that a bird is flying overhead, but a surprising number of these irrelevant details do apparently register. It is also true that many irrelevant details are probably not cognized; the narrowing of cognition to include only the objects of immediate relevance is especially common under strong tension. A broad unselective cognition is, however, one mark of mature behavior.

In these two senses, therefore, cognition and behavior are independent when maturity is at a maximum. For that reason they are distinguished in this model. If the distinction is made, the lack of differentiation of the two can be shown in terms of the dependence of cognition upon motivation or the narrowing of cognition by strong motivation; if the distinction is not made, it is very difficult to describe voluntary behavior in which the two are most nearly independent.

INDEPENDENCE OF GOAL SELECTION AND GOAL-DIRECTED BEHAVIOR

Just as cognition is distinguished in the model because it functions independently, so the distinction between goal selection and goal attainment depends upon the fact that they function independently. One of the important characteristics of adult human behavior is that we can use many different abilities to attain the same goal, and that we can use the same ability to attain many different goals.

To illustrate this independence of means and ends, we have only to think of some skill, such as swimming. If a person knows how to swim, he can swim for fun, he can swim to save a life, he can swim to get across a stream. The ability to swim is a skill that is acquired only once; it can function as a means to various goals or as a pleasure in itself.

It is obvious, also, that we may attain our goals in more than one way. To get to the store we may walk, drive, take a bus, or ride a bicycle. Many skills and many goals seem to be completely independent; any one of a repertoire of skills may under appropriate conditions be used in order to achieve any one of a number of goals. There is nothing in the make-up of the person himself that dictates that one goal must be reached by a certain means; it is only the external circumstances that determine the means required to reach the goal.

When this complete independence exists, then, motives and behavior are differentiated from each other, and this differentiation is one characteristic of mature behavior. Not all behavior of the adult is completely independent from goals; for the child the dependence is much greater; and in some of the instinctive behavior of animals we find almost no independence.

To note these various conditions of dependence, let us examine several behavior patterns. Crying, for example, is not differentiated from motivation in most adult behavior. We cannot cry voluntarily in the same way that we can walk voluntarily. We cannot cry every time crying would help us to achieve our goal. One of the traditional beliefs in our culture is that many women can cry as a means to an end. They can apparently let the tears stream under complete control. Whether this is true of all women is unimportant. Certainly good actors can train themselves to cry upon demand. Most of us, however, can cry only when we have certain feelings and motives.

Children may show a lack of differentiation and independence in some behavior patterns that are quite voluntary and independent for adults. Piaget reports, for example, that one child was able to clench her fist only when reaching for an object and could not clench it independently in imitation of someone else. That action had not yet become an independent act, under voluntary control and usable in the service of various motives. Children are less able to lie convincingly than are adults. To make a statement merely as a means to an end without regard for its truth requires a certain differentiation.

Some of the instinctive behavior of animals clearly demonstrates behavior patterns that are rigidly dependent upon the stimulus conditions that elicit the instinct and are unusable as a means to any other goal. The honeybee, for example, performs a very intricate dance that informs the other bees in the hive about the location of food, but as far as anyone knows, this dance is never used to communicate the location of other objects, such as an enemy. When the behavior pattern depends completely upon the conditions that elicit an instinct, it would be useless to make the distinction between motive and behavior. But there are all degrees of dependence of behavior upon motive, ranging from the rigid instinctual acts to the planned voluntary activities of the adult.

Since so much of the adult's voluntary behavior does exhibit this independence between goals and the behavior patterns that attain goals, we incorporate the distinction in the model and shall discuss separately the selection of a goal and the choice of behavior to attain it.

Thus, we see the basis for dividing the model into the sections previously described. We shall now examine the details in each of these sections, beginning with motivation rather than cognition because motivation clearly illustrates a general relationship between external stimulating factors and internal factors that is present in the other sections.

Goal Selection

In the picture of goal selection shown in Figure 2, we note first that several motives are indicated. This is necessary to represent the process by which the individual chooses among competing wishes, but for the purposes of the present section we shall consider only the process by which one motive is evoked.

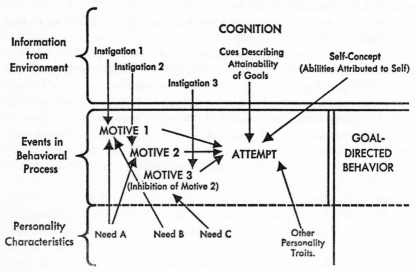

Figure 2. Goal selection.

THE DISTINCTION BETWEEN MOTIVE AND NEED

In Figure 2 a line connects each motive to cognition and another line connects each motive to some personal characteristic, or need. This same pattern of interrelation holds for every motive. The individual is made to want something partly by the external situation as he perceives it and partly because he has some personality traits which make him susceptible to the influence of the external situation. The external factor which arouses a motive is called an instigation. The internal factor which determines the individual susceptibility to instigation is called a need.

Let us look at a concrete illustration of this process. If we perceive a five-dollar bill lying on the sidewalk, our cognition of that money instigates a motive to stop and pick it up. The motive is determined, however, not solely by the external situation but also by our individual needs. If money were not valuable to us, the sight of money would not evoke the desire for it.

The psychologically active wish which is aroused in the immediate situation is called a *motive,* to distinguish it from a *need.* The selection of names for these two concepts is troublesome. The terms *motive* and *need* are not entirely satisfactory, because both words have been used by other authors in other senses. The reader should be warned that the terminology in the field of motivation is very confused and confusing; some authors use the words *need* and *motive* interchangeably.

A boy comes home from school intent upon changing his clothes so that he can play football. As he enters the kitchen door, he discovers that his mother has made a big batch of chocolate cookies. The sight and smell of the cookies motivate him to take one. His wish for a cooky is a motive. It is an active wish that affects his behavior—i.e., he takes one. Even if for some reason he does not actually take a cooky—perhaps his mother says not to touch them, because they are for her bridge club and she is not sure she has enough—nevertheless, the boy has a motive to take a cooky, and that motive affects his behavior. In this case it makes him complain, it makes him feel frustrated and perhaps makes him give up football for the afternoon so that he can wait around to see if any cookies will be left over after the bridge party.

If we consider the difference between the boy's psychological condition at the moment just before he discovered the cookies and at the moment after his mother has told him not to touch them, we can see that objectively the situations are the same; he is without a cooky. Before he sees them, however, he is not at all frustrated; he is thinking about football. After he sees them and wants them but is *then* prevented from having one, he is frustrated. The sight of the cookies was an instigation that evoked a motive; until that motive was evoked he could not be frustrated by the lack of cookies.

We can say that even before the boy saw these specific cookies, he liked cookies. This statement is just as true before as after he saw them. His liking for cookies is not, however, an active psychological want or motive. When we say he likes cookies, we mean that if he were to be given an opportunity to have cookies, he would seize the opportunity. This liking for cookies is an example of a *need.* Saying that the boy has a need is equivalent to saying that it is possible to evoke a motive by presenting him with the proper instigating situation.

The term *motive* describes the wishes that are present at any moment and are influencing the individual's behavior at that moment. The entire life of a person may be described as a series of episodes of motivated behavior. During one episode, a boy may be trying to get the right answer to a long-division problem. Then he becomes puzzled and raises his hand—now he is trying to ask the teacher a question. He notices that it is recess time, and now he wants to hurry to reach the baseball diamond so that he can have the first turn to pitch. In this way, a minute-by-minute record of his behavior can be divided into episodes (Barker and Wright, 1955). During one episode—playing baseball, for example—the motives that existed in preceding episodes are not necessarily influencing his behavior.

There is, however, in the sequence of episodes of motivated behavior, a pattern that reflects the personality of the individual. One boy may have many more episodes of playing baseball than another, and fewer episodes of reading comic books. The *need* concept is necessary to account for the fact that there is consistency and structure in the various episodes of motivated behavior that occur in the life of the individual. Thus, the appraisal of the needs of an individual is based upon the observation of consistency in recurrent episodes of motivated behavior. The appraisal of the motives of an individual is based upon the analysis of his behavior within one episode of motivated behavior.

We can all discover in ourselves some persistently recurring wishes that we recognize as being somehow characteristic of us. Some of us want prestige; we find that again and again in our daily life we behave in the way we do in the hope of gaining more respect and applause from our associates. Some of us want money—a need that manifests itself in various specific wishes for a raise in salary, for inheritance, and for other gains.

Despite the fact that we experience money-directed motives repeatedly, however, almost nobody is constantly and perpetually motivated to make money. There are at least some moments in the life of everyone when his behavior seems irrelevant to needs for money. To go to a movie, to play with the children, to read a book—these are not generally an expression of the need for money. On such occasions the motive to make money is not present psychologically; that is, it is not affecting behavior.

Some less central needs show this phenomenon even more clearly. If a man likes to play tennis, he is not continually playing or continually seeking a game; much of his time he spends working, walking home from work, or engaging in other activities that are irrelevant to playing tennis. Yet, in a sense, it can always be said that he likes to play tennis. When he is looking for a partner, or driving to the courts, or buying new tennis balls, his motivation to play tennis is active and is directing his behavior.

A motive is an active wish for something, a present psychological force toward some goal. A motive is behaviorally identifiable because it is a factor affecting behavior "here and now." This does not mean that a motive always produces movement in the direction of the goal; there may be a conflicting motive that is stronger. Even when it is not being displayed in goal-directed behavior, a motive nevertheless affects behavior. It may be the weaker side of a conflict, as we have just suggested, but in that case it is revealed in the existence of the conflict itself, which results in tension symptoms or in disturbances of the behavior that is directed toward the stronger goal. A motive is psychologically active and affects behavior.

A need, on the other hand, is a personality characteristic which can be described as a state of sensitivity or susceptibility. A motive is easily evoked if the need is strong. The person with a strong need for money can easily be motivated to get money. Thus, needs influence behavior not directly but only by predisposing the person to specific kinds of motives. Needs cannot be frustrated; only motives can be frustrated. When a motive is present but the individual is not moving in the direction of the goal, he is frustrated. Since a need is merely a state of susceptibility or sensitivity, it cannot be frustrated. Even though a person has a strong need to make money and is therefore easily and frequently motivated to make money, he is not frustrated during the time that he is motivated toward some goal other than money. If, however, he were motivated to make money and could not move toward that goal, he would be frustrated.

59. *Resolution of Frustration and Conflict* *

LESTER D. CROW
AND ALICE CROW

N O STANDARD REMEDY can be applied to assist an individual who is experiencing a frustration or a conflict. Through his developing years, the individual himself is responsible for the resolution of any frustrations or conflicts that he may experience. Parents, teachers, and community leaders, however, can assist in the building of self-realizing experiences.

* From Lester D. Crow and Alice Crow, *An Outline of General Psychology*, pp. 182–87. Copyright 1959 by Littlefield, Adams and Co., Paterson, N. J., and reprinted with permission.

An individual who is experiencing a frustration or conflict may approach the problem in one of three ways: (1) he may launch a direct attack, (2) he may attempt to effect a compromise, or (3) he may try to retreat from the annoying situation. If he uses the first approach, he attempts to do something about the difficulty. According to the second approach, he tends to utilize as many face-saving devices as possible, but he also does something to alleviate the stresses and strains present. To run away from or disregard a conflict situation in which he is involved is likely to intensify his feelings of inadequacy and frustration; his failure to resolve the difficulty may cause severe maladjustment.

The struggle to resolve frustration and conflict is a continuous process. The individual, in his attempts at adjustment during his developing years, makes use of many techniques. When his original behavior motives are blocked, he tends to react in rather definite ways. He may try to control, remove, or destroy the obstacle, or he may achieve an effective compromise. An attempt at behavior adjustment in a conflict-arousing situation is referred to as the utilization of a substitute response. The implications of such modes of adjustment are explained here briefly.

Compensatory behavior. Compensation can be interpreted as (1) the attempt of an individual to use many different forms of behavioral adjustment to failure or inadequacy or (2) the adoption of a satisfactory form of behavior to reduce tensions that result from a recognized defect or lack. For example, a small adolescent boy may engage in excessive talking or give voice to definite opinions (fact or fancy) in order to compensate for his shortness. A teen-age girl may wear startling clothes to compensate for her supposed physical unattractiveness.

Attention-getting behavior. An expression of thwarted egocentrism illustrates the attention-getting approach. Crying brings the baby's mother; the boisterous behavior of an elementary-school child commands the attention of elders who want peace and quiet; an adolescent's display of bad manners concerns all youth leaders, and adult temper tantrums command the attention of everyone. Some delinquent behavior can be traced to an immature young person's need to satisfy his urge for attention.

Utilization of introjection. Introjection is the process by which an individual acquires ideas, emotional attitudes, and ideals from others. The child gradually develops attitudes and appreciations similar to those exhibited by his parents, older brothers and sisters, and other adults. It is in this way that the beliefs and ideals accepted in the child's early cultural environment become his. Thereby, superstitions, prejudices, and moral and social values are acquired.

Utilization of identification. Identification represents the behavior displayed by an individual who regards the successful achievement of an admired person as though it were his own. An individual tends to identify himself with a person or group whom he considers to be superior to him in a field of his own interest, thereby experiencing personal satisfaction from the attainments of the others.

Identification is valuable to the extent that it helps an individual develop desirable personality characteristics. It becomes undesirable if (1) he so loses his individuality in that of his hero that he no longer is conscious of himself as a person or (2) he identifies with gangs or individuals who are organized for antisocial purposes.

Projection of blame. Projection represents the tendency of an individual (1) to place the blame on another person for errors made by himself and (2) to lack the courage to admit his own shortcomings. It is difficult for anyone to admit his errors of judgment or his inability to perform with success. It seems to be more satisfying to blame a partner in a game of bridge for errors in bidding, or a teacher for personal failure to pass an examination. To place the blame on others for personal error can become so deep-seated that the individual develops bitter resentment or becomes a chronic fault-finder.

Rationalization—self-deception. Rationalization is a form of behavior employed by an individual when he has done something that he knows is undesirable or foolish. In his attempt to protect his ego he explains his behavior in such a way that he will avoid criticism from others. Thus it becomes a form of self-deception in which the individual finds satisfying reason for his action that he knows is not the correct one. This becomes undesirable if and when he believes his own falsehoods.

Sublimation of drives. Sublimation represents substitute activity. If an individual's original interest-stimulated behavior meets with interference other, more socially desirable, ways of fulfilling his urges may be employed. For example, various substitute forms of activity are utilized to redirect the expression of the sex urge. Sublimation is concerned with the stepping up of primitive urges or emotional reactions toward socially approved goals.

Social maturity includes the ability of the individual to (1) control his strong drives toward extremes of hate, rage, love, or other emotionalized activities and (2) give them expression through behavior that follows laws, customs, and moral codes. Under certain circumstances, the normal expression of a drive may be thwarted and the individual finds satisfaction in a substitute activity, e.g., a childless woman may work toward the amelioration of ills among underprivileged children.

Daydreaming. Daydreaming occurs when the individual attempts to retreat from undesirable or frustrating situations. Through daydreams the individual is able to attain immediate imaginary satisfaction of any desired goal or purpose.

There is a constructive aspect of daydreams that is revealed in art, music, and invention. Inadequate adjustment, however, is likely to result when the individual relies too completely on the world of fantasy as a self-satisfying approach. It is especially harmful if the individual habitually retreats from reality.

Idealization. Idealization represents a tendency to place a value on something that is greater than its real worth. An individual idealizes himself, other persons, objects, or situations. Interaction between the emotions and the imagination enables him to believe that the person or object idealized is the most worth while or the most beautiful he has ever met. This explains why a person in love sees in the object of his affection many qualities that are not detected by others. Such exaggerated evaluations are frequent.

Egocentrism. Egocentrism is a form of behavior that develops as a result of the constant receiving of attention and praise, regardless of whether or not it is merited. Praise for work well done is an excellent emotional tonic. In order to instill a proper feeling of security in young children, it is necessary that they receive considerable commendation. As children mature, however, evaluations should be made and praise offered upon the basis of superior achievement rather than as a matter of course.

The child is and needs to be egocentric, but there comes a time in his developmental progress when he needs to be interested in others, in their activities, and in their interests. Frustration tolerance can be raised in these areas if the child is guided toward the experiencing of interests that are other-centered rather than self-centered.

Self-bolstering through criticism. Criticism often is utilized by an individual when he believes he does not have the ability to meet social demands as well as he would like to meet them. It is then that he delights in discovering any weakness in the adjustment armor of the more successful person.

Criticism usually takes the form of a false or an exaggerated negative approach to the behavior or activities of others. It is utilized by the individual as a "cover up" of his own deficiencies. Malicious gossip exemplifies an extreme form of criticism.

Sympathy. Sympathy is a behavior technique employed to gain the pity of others or to avoid solving a problem by convincing others that it is too difficult for him. It is one of the most difficult attitudes to control satisfactorily for the individual concerned or for others in the immediate environment.

Conversion. Conversion behavior concerns the transferring of the energy needed to satisfy a socially disapproved desire into a physical symptom. During this process conflicts often are aroused. The ideas and wishes in the unconscious sometimes come into conflict with those in the conscious. Social maladjustment then may result.

Repression. Repression concerns the deliberate thrusting aside, because of social inhibitions, of present drives that are striving for expression. An individual tends to avoid persons or places that are associated with previous unpleasant experiences.

In repression the individual deliberately *wants to forget,* although he may not be conscious of his desire to do so. This approach tends to increase tensions and to limit the individual's power of adjustment to commonly experienced situations.

Withdrawal behavior. Withdrawal behavior concerns an individual's tendency to retreat from a social situation. This tendency is rooted in temperament, personal interests, and ambitions, and situational attitudes. Three types are distinguishable: *shyness, negativism,* and *regression.*

Shyness. Shyness is a characteristic of many individuals in specific situations. The experiences of early childhood become important determining factors in shy behavior. Overprotection or too strict discipline may cause a child to become shy in the presence of strangers or persons in authority. The timid, withdrawing child may become the joy of the teacher in the classroom but his social development may be hindered by this form of withdrawal.

Too often, beneath his quiet, unassuming exterior, the child is experiencing strong feelings of frustration. A conflict exists between his desire to participate actively and the fear that he may not receive full acceptance.

Negativism. Negativism is a form of withdrawal that represents a deliberate attempt to resolve a conflict by refusing to recognize a real situation. Displayed behavior is characterized by rebellion against authority or suggestions offered by a superior. It may represent a stage in the young child's development during which he responds with a "No" even though he complies with a request. There is danger only if the negativism persists beyond early childhood years and if it is accompanied by temper tantrums.

Regression. Regression refers to the utilization of behavior tendencies that brought satisfaction during an earlier developmental period. Any shifting of the burden of decision-making may give satisfaction. Learning to acquire habitual attitudes of decision-making is valuable at each stage of individual development. The training needs to be appropriate to keep pace with the changing maturity level of the individual. Training given toward the assumption of responsibility will enable the individual to meet the demands of his environment, thereby making it unnecessary for him to revert in his behavior to an earlier stage of development, a stage in which problems were solved for him.

Neurotic behavior. Neurotic behavior is displayed by an individual in his attempt to escape frustration-producing situations or conflict in real situations by displaying symptoms of illness or of a physical disability. Neurotic symptoms frequently are symbolic. It is difficult for the individual himself or for trained persons who wish to help him to trace the causes of the displayed symptoms. Neurotic behavior is characterized by *phobias, obsessions,* and *compulsions.*

Phobias. A phobia refers to that form of behavior which evidences an individual's unusual fear of something. There is no sound reason or basis for the fear. Most individuals who experience phobias are unable to explain the cause of them or to describe clearly their own emotional behavior in relation to them.

Phobias are symbolic and are associated with unpleasant experiences. These strong, irrational states can be associated with abnormal fear of fire (*pyrophobia*), high places (*acrophobia*), dirt (*mysophobia*), closed rooms (*claustrophobia*), sight of blood (*hemophobia*), being poisoned (*toxicophobia*), and the like.

Obsessions. Obsessions refer to ideas that are unreasonable but that persist or recur. Even though they are recognized as illogical or unreasonable, they tend to persist and interfere with clear and logical thinking. For example, an individual may have an obsession to the effect that a close relative is planning his death or that the human race soon will be destroyed by insects.

Compulsion. A compulsion can be considered to be a tendency to perform, as meaningful, behavior acts that are recognized to be irrational. It is behavior that is continued because of the individual's strong desire to engage in it, without having a good reason. The urge to participate in the activity is so strong and so persistent that emotional tension is relieved only after the act has been performed.

The compulsory act may be personally satisfying and socially acceptable. For example, an individual carries a rabbit's foot to allay failure and to insure success, or he acts on the basis of superstition. The compulsory act may be personally or socially harmful, e.g., the impulse to set fires (*pyromania*) or the compelling urge to steal (*kleptomania*).

60. *Changing Perceptions in Infancy* *

MILLIE ALMY

A S THE BABY GROWS, his world becomes less and less one of diffuse sensation and increasingly one of many differentiated perceptions. This does not happen all at once, and there are probably intermittent times when he is sleepy or hungry or fatigued or anxious, when the world loses its specific qualities and he knows only vague feelings.

Can we surmise the meanings he may be acquiring at, say, 7 or 8 months as he sits in his chair and surveys the world of things around him? Perhaps he is soon to have his bath, and his mother has given him an empty powder can to play with. He grasps it in his fist, puts it in his mouth, takes it out, transfers it to the other hand, mouths it, bangs it on the chair arm, drops it, whimpers, bangs his fists instead. Mother can substitute a bath toy and the same repertoire will likely be repeated. Anything which comes within his field of vision is something to be reached for; if it is bright, all the more enticing—if red so much the better—but what is reached for is not always grasped. He is not yet a good judge of distance and does not yet see things in perspective so that a bright flower held in front of him may look about the same as the one in the pattern of his mother's apron. Whatever comes into his hand is twisted and turned, held now this way, now that, and eventually tasted and banged. How else can any object be exploited if he is to learn its size and weight, its form, its texture, its temperature, or its sound? Some objects have already acquired an emotional investment for him. Thus he may respond with much cooing and babbling to the sight of the bath toys with which his mother lets him splash, but with

* From Millie Almy, *Child Development,* pp. 132–37. Copyright 1955 by Henry Holt and Co. (Dryden), New York, and reprinted with permission.

grimaces and protests to the approach of a washcloth which has been known to get soap in his eyes.

By the time he has lived another four or five months and reached his first birthday, the world of objects will have taken on many new meanings. If we look in on him before his bath, we're less likely to find him sitting in a chair than to find him crawling underneath it. There's a tiny but intriguing bit of fuzz there that he must capture. This bit of behavior suggests a major change in the nature of his perception. He is capable of considerably finer discrimination. He now sees objects in perspective, and everything has taken on greater complexity. He is more aware of details. The powder box is not merely round, hard, and good to bang, but it has intriguing holes into which he tries to poke his index finger. He seems, too, to have a dawning sense of relatedness. If he drops the powder box (and he likely will), he is no longer so vague and unconcerned, but may go after it—probably on all fours. If you sit down beside him and roll the can to him, he may even roll it back to you. If the box has a cover which comes off, he may twist and turn the two parts together as though he senses their belongingness.

One sees, too, some sense of "before" and "after" in repetition which is no longer completely aimless. Memory is growing apace. One day, Mommie accidentally drops the beloved red bath toy behind the laundry hamper. Baby is fussy, wonderfully elated when it is found. Next day, Mommie says, "Where's duckie?" and he crawls to look for it behind the hamper.

Space, time, and reality meanings are shifting. But just as the world of things takes on new meaning, so is the world of people invested with increasing significance.

When the baby was 5 months or so, faces became more than mere configurations, and he began to notice strangers. Whereas previously, as a serene happy baby, he had more or less accepted all comers, he now became sensitive to differences, and according to Spock [1] might "take alarm at anything unfamiliar such as a visitor's hat or even his *father's* face." Upsetting to family equilibrium as such behavior may be (of course not all babies will manifest their growing abilities in precisely this fashion), it marks the beginning of a new sensitivity to people which is essential for the child's social learning. It seems likely that out of it develops the baby's readiness to imitate. . . .

This capacity, we think, has a strong emotional component. The baby's satisfaction in the use of his body is enhanced by his pleasure in the relationship with the adult. Until he has had the repeated experience of having his

[1] Benjamin Spock, *Common-Sense Book of Baby and Child Care* (New York: Duell, Sloan and Pearce, 1946), p. 149.

own body needs met, he cannot to any marked extent develop the capacity for modifying his behavior to fit the patterns set by someone else.

Changing Social Relationships

In any event, by the time he is a year old, the fortunate infant, with whom we are immediately concerned, is likely to have developed a considerable degree of sociability, at least with the members of his family and people he is accustomed to seeing every day. With strangers he may warm up slowly. This fact in itself suggests that in a sense a core of resiliency is beginning to develop within his personality. He can, in his own baby way, fend off the adult whose demeanor indicates that he regards infants as puppets to be manipulated rather than human personalities.

Relationships to adults. There is, unfortunately, not much evidence about the effects on the infant of relationships with adults other than his mother. There is ample testimony that tremendous risks to physical, mental, and emotional development arise whenever any infant is deprived of his mother. But we still do not know very much about what happens when care of the baby is shared by several adults, nor about the extent to which other adults may influence the baby's development when the mother is the one who takes most of the care of the infant. For example, the role of the father, at least during the infancy period, has generally been thought to affect the baby only indirectly. . . .

Relationships to children. Similarly, we need more information about the infant's reactions to the child members of his family. Particularly in lower-class groups, one often sees girls of 9 and 10 caring for small baby brothers and sisters. Do they represent to the infant an extension of the parental protection? One would expect that the older youngster would be able to give warm, protective care only to the extent that she herself had had the same. But there is also the possibility of a small infant offering certain satisfactions to a child who had herself suffered some deprivation. It is a fact that in our culture brothers and sisters can and usually do experience much jealousy, rivalry, and competition. But our studies of the matter have perhaps tended to look too much at the hostile aspects of the relationships, thus losing sight of the positive potentials in it. In most families the experience of the infant is likely to be mixed. He may be subjected to certain personal indignities, as was the case of a one-year-old who was liberally salted and peppered by his two-year-old brother. But he is also played with in ways which may very well add to his pleasure and enjoyment and perhaps also facilitate development. For example, a six-year-old boy was the first member of the family to excite a "dancing" response from his five-months-old sister. The baby's laughter and the way in which she caught his rhythm in the motion of her hands appeared to excite considerable joy not only in him, but also in the watching parents. In another instance, a three-year-old frequently quieted her one-year-old sister.

The question of how the infant feels about a smaller infant in the family is equally complex. It is sometimes assumed that because he "is not old enough to understand," he may not experience any jealousy (if that word correctly describes the experience of a one-year-old). What seems more likely is that what "new baby" means to him will depend pretty much on family circumstances. If *his* infancy has been pretty serene, if he has had his share of satisfactions and has developed an ability to socialize a little, *and* if his mother has sufficient resources (emotional and domestic), his equilibrium may not even be disturbed. Sometimes, however, the mother finds it impossible to give the detailed attention the small baby needs and the equally important but different attention the year-old needs, and then the older baby may feel deprived and unhappy.

The infant growing up with a twin has experiences quite different from the singleton. To what extent these affect his perceptions in the first year of life is not too well known. There have been numerous studies of twins, but relatively few focused on personality development in its very beginning. This again seems to be an instance which depends on the mother's ability to cope with multiple demands and give each infant full satisfaction. In addition, each baby constantly sees himself in the other (particularly in the case of identicals) and appears to tend to imitate him. The need for social response is in a sense taken care of in a closed circle. Under these circumstances, one would expect that differentiation might take place relatively more slowly and some sense of *me-ness* be more difficult to achieve.

The fact that a considerable degree of socialization, but not necessarily a sense of personal identity, can develop within the twin relationship raises some interesting questions about the ways in which infants in general tend to relate to one another. Genuine socialization—a give and take and mutual appreciation—is generally believed not to develop until sometime in toddlerhood or beyond and then to be dependent on prior good relationships with adults. However, Freud and Dann observed intense group relationships within a group of six orphans who had experienced severe deprivation since they were less than a year old, but who had evidently found solace in each other. Although their behavior was in no sense "normal" or typical for their age, they were able to acquire a new language and gave other evidence that they had survived their experience comparatively well.

The study lends support to the idea that under certain circumstances the infant's relationships with his peers may be a source of considerable satisfaction and support to him.

61. The Development of Thinking and Reasoning *

LESTER D. CROW
AND ALICE CROW

WHETHER VERY young children engage in the kind of mental activity that is termed *thinking* is a moot question. The child is born with a nervous system that, if it has experienced normal growth during the prenatal period, is ready to function. Nevertheless, most of a neonate's early responses are more or less reflex in nature.

The development of thinking. With the gradual maturation of the sensory mechanisms, the young child begins to associate his various sensations, with resulting perceptions, or meaningful sensations. At first, the baby's percepts are simple and often incorrect or inadequate. Repeated experience with the limited environment of his home helps him gain more adequate and satisfying recognitions of the relationships that may exist among these environmental stimuli.

There is disagreement among psychologists concerning the amount or kind of mental manipulation of perceptual materials that takes place during the very early years of the growing child. There is evidence that, before he can talk, the child seems to express in his actions the results of what resembles conceptual thinking in the older person. He responds to one person differently than he does to another. He appears to recognize and to respond to things in the home with which he has daily experience. Some children learn early that, by refraining from the kind of behavior for which they have been punished, they can avoid being chastised for misdeeds.

By the time he is 6 months old, the child displays some awareness of

* From Lester D. Crow and Alice Crow, *Human Development and Learning,* pp. 67–70. Copyright 1956 by American Book Co., New York, and reprinted with their permission.

himself and appears to be able to recognize some of his body parts. He gradually develops a more or less adequate understanding of space relationships. These begin by the baby's reaching his arms above his head and saying "up," or by squirming off an adult's lap as he iterates, "down," or "baby down." Orientation in time is difficult, even after the child has begun his school life. As his language patterns develop, the young child gives evidence through his questioning and storytelling that he is developing concepts and that he is relating these concepts to one another through mental association, or thinking.

The development of reasoning. Whatever reasoning the child attempts is limited by his experiences. Even the young child gives some slight evidence of understanding the relationship that exists between cause and effect. He seems to be able to vary his behavior in accordance with expected adult reactions. Because of his meager experiences, the direction that his reasoning takes is very different from that of the adult. Often, to the bewilderment or distress of the child, his reasoning is judged by adults according to their own standards.

Differences between child and adult reasoning may be the basis of much friction, even between adolescents and their parents. Frequently the adolescent's difficulty is that he has developed ideas of right and wrong behavior that differ widely from those the parents evolved as a result of their years of experience. The child, however, may want to do what he believes his mother wants him to do.

For example, a mother took her four-year-old child just outside the home and, pointing to the other side of the street, admonished him not to cross the street unless an older person were with him. Thereafter, he was careful to stay on his side of the street. The mother was satisfied that he had understood her admonition and would be obedient. Imagine her amazement and chagrin when a neighbor told her that the child had been seen crossing a busy highway at the end of the street, with no one there to escort him. When the boy was asked by his mother how he could be so naughty, he answered, "I wasn't naughty. You told me not to cross here at the house. You didn't say anything about the corner." The child was sincere in his explanation and was much hurt because his mother thought he had disobeyed her.

The number of similar examples of differences between adult and child reasoning is legion. Unless parents and teachers are certain that a child understands adult patterns of reasoning, they must take care lest they arouse emotional tensions in the child by accusing him wrongly of doing things he should not have done or of leaving things undone.

Important factors of learning to think. A child's conceptual thinking, reasoning, and problem-solving, like his language development (to which mental development is closely related), have as their bases the general pattern of his physical maturation and the kind and amount of his experience. Families of high socioeconomic status usually can provide for their children a wealth of experiences that lie beyond the reach of the underprivileged. Parental differences in objectivity and accuracy of judgment and reasoning also exert a powerful influence upon the direction taken by and the relative success of a child's mental activities.

The parent who answers his child's questions concerning the reasons for one or another condition or situation with a casual, "Oh, I don't know—just because," is encouraging lazy mental habits in his child. The parent may be busy or wearied by his child's barrage of questions, but it takes only a few minutes to think of a simple answer which will be satisfying for the moment, at least. A parent who consciously tries to satisfy his child's curiosity through short but accurate answers not only is helping the youngster to carry on desirable mental activity, but also is developing in the child an attitude of faith in and admiration for his parent's store of knowledge.

This situation holds for teachers as well as for parents. Teachers should not discourage children from asking questions that they fear may upset the class routines, which some teachers hold so dear. The average and bright (and sometimes the slower) elementary-school child is so intrigued by his enlarging world that he wants to know all about it—the what, the why, and the how.

An especially bright and thoughtful child may ask a question the answer to which the teacher may not know at the moment. The teacher should admit his ignorance frankly. He should follow this by telling the child where he can obtain the information and/or look it up himself and later discuss the matter with the pupil, or with the entire class, if that is appropriate. The teacher can use this procedure occasionally without losing the respect of the children. In fact, they may like him the better for it, since it shows that he too can forget. The teacher who aspires to be a leader of children, however, cannot make a general practice of admitting ignorance concerning matters not directly related to the content of class study, or of brushing children's questions aside. The pupils soon will come to consider him ineffective as a teacher and, perhaps, lose interest in learning what he attempts to teach them.

62. *Individual Differences in Memory* *

JAMES B. STROUD

AND LOWELL SCHOER

ONE OF THE persistent problems in the field of memory has been that of individual differences in retentiveness. Historically, differences in retentive ability have been linked with differences in learning ability. For example, McGeoch and Irion (1952) wrote: "By and large, individual differences in learning are reflected in individual differences in retention."

When subjects have been given equal amounts of practice and amount learned has been used to define differences in acquisition, learning scores have been found to be positively related to retention scores. This is probably what McGeoch and Irion had in mind. Another facet of the problem concerns the relationship between learning and retentive abilities when all *S*s attain a common performance criterion and differences in the rate at which this is done are used to define differences in learning ability. The evidence pertaining to this aspect of the general problem is less conclusive. It is with this aspect that the present paper is concerned.

The main body of evidence in support of the proposition that retentive ability is positively related to learning ability has been derived from analysis of learning and relearning scores. There is little doubt that there exists a positive and substantial correlation between trials to learn and trials to relearn upon the part of an array of *S*s. This type of analysis, however, seems to be a questionable procedure. Relearning scores reflect learning ability to some extent, perhaps to a considerable extent. We would expect that *S*s who learn rapidly would relearn rapidly because, if for no other reason, they are rapid learners. Similarly, those who learn slowly would be expected to relearn slowly, because they are slow learners. At best, relearning scores reflect both learning ability and retentive ability.

On the other hand, the relationship between recall and rate of learning is far from close, when all *S*s achieve a common trials-to-learn criterion, as Underwood's (1954) data, for example, and those herein reported show. In the customary verbal learning experiment, it is possible for the slow learner to achieve a level of mastery equal to that of the rapid learner if he takes enough time. In many types of learning situations, especially those

* From James B. Stroud and Lowell Schoer, "Individual Differences in Memory," *The Journal of Educational Psychology* (December, 1959), pp. 285–92. Reprinted by permission of the authors and the American Psychological Association.

regarded as most significant educationally, it is, of course, not possible for all learners to attain equal mastery. Some will achieve levels of insight, or levels of skill, not attainable to others. Under these circumstances, we would expect to obtain wide differences among good and poor learners in performance on retention tests.

In the problem at hand, we were interested in individual differences in retention among *S*s, all of whom have attained a common criterion. Demonstrating that recall scores are unrelated to rate of learning, when all *S*s achieve the same level of learning, is not, of course, equivalent to demonstrating that significant differences in recall do not exist. A basic question facing us today is whether or not individuals differ reliably among themselves in retention of materials which have been mastered equally well by all. If it could be shown that *S*s do differ reliably in recall ability and that these differences are not associated with differences in learning ability, then recall, and possibly retention, would be established as an independent variable—especially so if the differences possess some degree of generality.

Procedure

With these thoughts in mind the senior author planned and carried out the experiments reported in the following pages.[1] Originally it was planned to have each of a number of *S*s learn, recall, and relearn four or five different kinds of material. Later, since it seemed desirable to have the *S*s learn pairs of comparable lists so that some kind of assessment of the reliability of the scores could be made, this plan was given up. The materials adopted consisted of two lists of paired adjectives, twelve pairs per list, and two lists of picture-name pairs, ten pairs per list. All lists were presented by the paired-associate anticipatory method.

Adjective pairs of low associative, synonymity, and familiarity value were selected from the Haagen (1943) list. These were arranged in two comparable lists as mentioned. In the preparation of the picture-name pairs, a suitable number of photographs of senior, male students in the College of Engineering were selected from a pool of pictures just taken for the University Student Annual. Paired with each such picture chosen was a fictitious first and last name. The adjective pairs and the picture-name pairs were then reproduced on motion-picture film in such a way that the first member of a pair could be exposed on a screen for two seconds to be followed immediately by a two-second simultaneous exposure of both mem-

[1] The author wishes to acknowledge the assistance of the following persons in conducting the experiment: L. J. Carter, A. J. Edwards, Clifford Howe, and S. Muehl.

bers of a pair. In the case of the adjective pairs, the second member, the response member, appeared just to the right of the first or stimulus member. In the case of the picture-name pairs the name, the response item, appeared directly under the picture, the stimulus item. An interval of .5 second intervened between exposures of adjacent pairs within a list. An interval of five seconds occurred between trials.

The items in each list were presented in two different serial orders, the two orders alternating in a given series of trials. After the first trial, the *S*s' task was to anticipate (orally) the response member within the two-second interval in which the stimulus member alone was exposed. This was repeated for each pair within the list, trial after trial, until the learning criterion (a trial without error) was reached.

The items comprising each list, in two different serial orders, were filmed separately, making each of the four reels consisting of some fifty feet of film. Each such length of film was made into a loop and mounted in a winder. The films thus ran continuously during any one learning session for as many trials as required to reach the criterion. Once the running of the film was started for a given *S* the experimenter had no duties beyond recording the responses and stopping the projector at the end of the learning session. The four lists were presented to the *S*s in a counterbalanced order.[2]

Table 1

PRACTICE EFFECTS UPON LEARNING AND RECALL

Day	Mean Trials to Learn [a]				Mean Recall			
	PA_1	PA_2	PN_1	PN_2	PA_1	PA_2	PN_1	PN_2
1	13.28	12.31	14.79	17.17	8.93	9.27	6.29	6.66
2	10.69	11.15	12.51	13.05	8.38	8.15	5.78	5.14
3	10.38	9.39	12.18	13.81	8.14	9.46	6.83	6.12
4	10.56	9.40	11.19	12.38	7.56	7.33	5.31	4.65

[a] Does not include first presentation trial.

The *S*s were given five practice trials, on a six-pair list of adjectives, just prior to the learning of the first paired adjective list. They were given five practice trials on a four-pair list of picture-names just prior to learning the first picture-name list.

[2] The method of presenting the materials just described was adopted because of its convenience in handling the picture material. It proved to be quite as satisfactory as a memory drum in handling the verbal materials. The method permits a great deal of flexibility.

The Ss ($N = 149$) were Sophomore students enrolled in the Introduction to Psychology course, State University of Iowa. They reported one at a time for five consecutive days, starting on a Monday. On Mondays the Ss learned the experimental list appropriate to each for that day. On Tuesdays the Ss first recalled and relearned Monday's lists and proceeded to learn Tuesday's list. This procedure continued until Friday, on which day the Ss only recalled and relearned Thursday's lists. . . .

Summary

This paper has recounted some of the salient features of an investigation of individual differences in memory. One hundred forty-nine Ss, in individual sessions, learned and recalled and relearned four lists each, two of paired adjectives and two of paired picture-names. Significant correlations, ranging from .23 to .41, were obtained among the various recall scores. On the two paired adjectives lists, r's between trials to learn and words recalled (after twenty-four hours) were not significant. Significant r's of −.23 and −.25 were obtained between these variables on the two picture-names lists. Ss were divided into fifths upon the basis of trials to learn on each of the four lists. No significant differences were obtained among the recall scores of the various fifths on any of the lists. At best, the results of the various analyses suggest no more than a slight relationship between rate of learning and recall.

The data have been analyzed with respect to differences in habit strength among Ss of varying rates of learning, all of whom attained a common trials-to-learn criterion. It was found that the mean number of reinforcements bore a fairly constant ratio to the number of item presentations (or number of trials) for the different levels of learning ability. The mean number of reinforcements accomplished by the slowest fifth of Ss was 3.6 times as great as that by the fastest fifth. Further analysis of specific items showed that the slowest fifth required five reinforcements to establish a probability of making a correct response on the succeeding trial equal to that established by the fastest fifth after one reinforcement. The important question of whether or not Ss who have learned to a common habit strength criterion differ significantly among themselves in retention is unanswered. The data are in accord with the proposition that significant differences in retention do exist among Ss who have achieved a common trials-to-learn criterion.

Practice effects reduced the trials required to learn, but did not result in increased recall scores.

63. Cognition in Infancy *

ALFRED L. BALDWIN

Cognition in Infancy

THE PERCEPTION OF THE NEONATE

People have frequently speculated about what the world looks like to the newborn child. Some have pictured perceptual apparatus as a camera that accurately records the incoming stimuli. The child may lack understanding of the picture, his actions may be immature and poorly coordinated, but the reception is clear. Others have pictured the baby's view as a "big blooming buzzing Confusion" (James, 1890). Still others have pictured the child's world as a sort of vague totality in which sights and sounds and touches are indistinguishable; objects are not separated from each other; everything is fuzzy and unclear.

The evidence for any view about the qualities of the child's subjective experience is almost impossible to obtain. It is more realistic to ask how the child's perception affects his behavior rather than how the world looks to him. We can study his discriminations and the behavioral adjustments that depend on cognition.

SENSITIVITY OF THE NEONATE TO STIMULI

There is no doubt that the newborn child can see, but it is not at all clear what he can see. His ability to distinguish colors is doubtful. It is even more doubtful whether he can distinguish forms. For one thing, there are frequently hemorrhages of the retina that cloud vision, and the eyeball is so shaped that clear vision is unlikely. It also seems that the accommodation mechanism to permit clear vision of objects at various distances is not functional at birth. He can respond, however, to different intensities of light. There is considerable evidence to show that the neonate is quieted by moderate light as compared with darkness. It suggests that the presence of a visual stimulus focuses his responsiveness and leads to a decreased responsiveness in other respects.

Although there is still some doubt about the sensitivity of the neonate to sound, the existence of hearing has been reasonably well demonstrated. Possibly there is some relative insensitivity during the first few days. It is

* From Alfred L. Baldwin, *Behavior and Development in Childhood,* pp. 335–40. Copyright 1955 by Henry Holt and Co. (Dryden), New York, and reprinted with permission.

doubtful whether he can discriminate among pitches of sound. He does, however, respond differently to different intensities of sound. Just as with vision, the baby responds to the beginning of the sound stimulus, but, as the sound continues, his activity level gradually declines. This has been described as "listening."

Smell and taste, especially smell, are difficult to investigate. It is doubtful whether neonates respond to any odors as such. Some substances irritate the mucous membrane of the nose and produce facial grimaces, but probably the smell receptors are not involved. It has been shown, however, that the sucking behavior of the neonate can be modified by introducing salt into his milk. It is doubtful if he can detect other tastes, such as sweet, sour, and bitter. At any rate infants are less able to discriminate among tastes than are adults.

Infants respond to the temperature of the milk and show in other ways that they are sensitive to temperature. They definitely respond to touch, movement of the body, and posture. Since none of these external factors accounts for all activity and since all action is assumed to be evoked by some stimulus, it is generally assumed that neonates are responsive to internal stimuli.

The infant's sensitivity does not tell us anything about the organization of his perception. If an adult looks at a black circle on a white field, the black area is localized in the white, the contour is sharp, and the shape of the black figure is distinguishable. The adult can distinguish between a circle and a triangle. Are these same statements true for young infants?

The best evidence we have is indirect, coming from the reports of adults who have been blind since birth and obtain their vision in adulthood (Senden, 1932). These adults have developed quite adequate understandings of the properties of objects from the other senses; furthermore, their visual apparatus has developed as much as it can without external stimulation. It may even have atrophied or become abnormal through lack of stimulation. The congenitally blind may have lost sensitivities that they once possessed. Nevertheless, we can make a reasonable guess that infant perception is no better than the visual perception of these people.

They report that some aspects of visual organization are present when they first recover sight. They can distinguish between one area of the visual field and another. If a black figure on a white ground is presented, they can tell which is which. On the other hand, they have tremendous difficulty in distinguishing one shape from another. Although it is immediately obvious to the normal adult that a triangle has corners, these people have to search and search to discover whether or not a figure has a corner. It takes them several months of visual experience to begin to make these obvious discriminations. Another curious difficulty they experience is in transposing learning. If they learn to name correctly a square made of white cardboard, they may be unable to recognize it when it is colored yellow, despite the fact that they have little trouble distinguishing colors and learning to recognize them.

So we see that it is not surprising that infants take so long to develop some of the simple ideas of space that we take for granted. They do not at first even have the clear information that would make it possible to identify the properties of objects. The development of form perception has been studied in some detail. It seems that by perhaps 6 months of age, the child can distinguish forms. He cannot verbally name them, of course, but his discrimination can be tested by rewarding one type of choice to see if he can learn to solve the problem. In this experiment (Ling, 1941) two forms are presented to the child. The incorrect one is fastened down, whereas the correct one is removable and if sucked gives a sweet taste because it has a small amount of saccharin on it. The child not only distinguishes these forms but continues to distinguish them if the forms are turned around or made larger and smaller. This is one type of transposition that persons with recently obtained vision have difficulty in performing.

THE DEVELOPMENT OF COGNITION OF SPACE

Before we can truly say that a cognitive representation of the external world exists, the child must demonstrate certain behavioral signs of cognition. First, the object must be cognized as a permanent object that exists outside the child and that continues to exist even when the child does not perceive it. Secondly, the child must distinguish between properties of the object and its spatial relations. Properties such as size, weight, color, etc., are unchanged when the object is moved around, whereas its spatial position is changed by movements. The independence of these two kinds of properties is required for the object to have permanence. Thirdly, the child must have some knowledge of movements in space. It is very important for him to know that locomotions in space and also turning movements of an object around an axis are reversible, and that any movement can be reversed. Also, he must recognize that, to find an object, he does not need to take the same path it did to reach its present location. If the location is known, any path to that point will locate the object.

Fourthly, the various senses—vision, touch, etc.—must be integrated so that they give the person information about a single external world. Fifthly, the child must have recognized that objects and movements occur outside of himself, and he must distinguish between the movements in the external world, which he observes, and his own movements, which are adapted to the world. It is obvious, as soon as we think of it, that it must not be easy for the child to distinguish between the actions that have external effects, such as hitting, moving, etc., and the actions that have no effect, such as looking or listening. Lastly, and this may be the same as the fourth, the child must have some cognition of himself in this space that he cognizes. He must be one of the objects in his cognitive map.

Piaget has described the stages in the infant's development of cognition of the external world and has described the parallel developments of cognition and goal-directed behavior.

Stages 1 and 2. During the first two stages of infancy, which correspond to the period before the child is able to reach for a visually perceived object, none of these criteria for a cognitive map is met. The permanence of perceived objects is best investigated by studying the child's reaction to the disappearance of an object. During this period the child does not search for an object that is gone, nor does he anticipate where it might have gone. At best, he continues to feel or look at the place where it disappeared —*i.e.,* he continues doing what he was doing at the time it disappeared. During this period, there is some integration of the senses. The child learns to look at an object that is making a noise; he can tie together tactual sensations from the hand, kinesthetic sensations from limbs, and tactual sensations from the mouth. He can put what he touches into his mouth and suck it.

This is not yet space or object perception, but it is the beginning of them. When the same object is involved in two different schemata, or behavior patterns, so that it is touched by the hands and also sucked, the child gets two sources of information about it. Gradually this recognition that something fits into all the various schemata leads to its being unified into an object, but this does not happen for some time.

The fact that the infant cannot distinguish between causing an event and merely observing it (this is implied by his being unable to recognize its being external to his own actions) means that the child feels, in a way, omnipotent. Psychoanalysts (Fenichel, 1945) have pointed to this early feeling of omnipotence in children. It is not omnipotence in the sense that an adult might feel that he was so powerful he could make anything happen. The adult would see himself as outside the event and causing it. The child does not distinguish the external objects from his own actions that involve them. Thus, his omnipotence is perhaps better described as failure to distinguish between what he can cause and what he cannot.

Stage 3. Moving on now to stage three, corresponding to the period between the acquisition of visual motor prehension and the ability to engage in goal-directed means-end behavior, we find that the various senses are much better integrated than before. This is one of the characteristics signified by visually guided reaching for an object. This same behavior also puts the child in the position to observe the relationship between two objects rather than merely the relation of an object to his own actions.

Secondary circular reactions imply the same thing. The child produces a causal sequence in the external world and is able to reproduce it. This attracts his attention to the external events and makes him more sensitive to them. Secondary circular reactions are also part of stage three of infancy.

The child in stage three still does not search for an object that has disappeared, but he does show some behavior patterns which indicate that he is beginning to conceive of an external object. Piaget describes Jacqueline's behavior when she holds an object that is slowly pulled away from her. If this process causes the hand to follow the movement of the object, then when she finally loses contact with it, she may continue groping along the trajectory she has already begun. If, however, the object is jerked away rapidly or made to disappear by screening it, there is no search for it. Similarly, the eyes may follow a falling object in the first part of its fall. If this movement is begun, then when the child loses sight of it, he continues the downward movement of the eyes and eventually may rediscover the fallen object. This depends, however, according to Piaget, upon the eye movement's or the hand movement's having been initiated by the moving object. The searching is merely an extension of the activity that was going on at the time the object disappeared.

The child also shows an advance in another respect. If the object is not hidden completely by a screen, but is left so that a tiny portion protrudes, the child can at this stage recognize it and retrieve the partially hidden object. When it disappears completely, however, it is not recovered. It is not that the child's search fails; he does not even miss the object, as the following striking observation shows (Piaget, 1954):

At the age of 6 months and 19 days, Laurent was whimpering and fussing because it was just before a meal. When Piaget showed him his bottle, Laurent immediately began to cry lustily. Now Piaget repeatedly hid the bottle, either under a table or behind his hand. As soon as the bottle was out of sight, Laurent stopped crying; as soon as it reappeared he began to cry once more. Each time there was calm as long as the bottle could not be seen. After he had been teased this way several times, Laurent became very angry. His anger was in a sense a response to the frustration even though his motive to have the bottle disappeared when the bottle was invisible. If he had in any way cognized the bottle under the table, his behavior would have been quite different, as illustrated by the effect of making only part of the bottle disappear. When Piaget partly covered the bottle, Laurent's cries remained strong; if anything, they increased in strength.

Further observations show clearly the peculiar situation that exists in the child's cognition at this time. Laurent is unable to turn the bottle around if the nipple is invisible. As long as the nipple can be seen, he is quite capable of rotating it to get the nipple to his mouth, but if he sees only the bottom of the bottle, he does not turn it around but tries to suck from the bottom. Similarly, he recognizes the bottle no matter which part of it protrudes from under the cloth; it does not need to be the nipple in order to set off the crying. Thus, Laurent recognizes that the bottle is to suck and he wants it. If the nipple is visible at all, he recognizes that it is there and he must suck; but, if the nipple cannot be seen, he then sucks the bottom as though he does not recognize that the bottle has a nipple or that a nipple is necessary for effective sucking.

Stage 4; search for absent objects. As well as failing to attribute permanence to objects, the infant in stage three does not recognize the paths an object may follow. He acts as though the only movement an object could make is in the direction of the child's movement at the time it disappeared. In stage four we observe true searching behavior when an object disappears. This corresponds to the period when the child puts two behavior patterns together in a means-end relationship. At this time the child's search for a vanished object is, in a sense, halfway to a full understanding of disappearing objects.

64. Problem-Solving *

LESTER D. CROW
AND ALICE CROW

A PROBLEM ARISES when an individual is confronted with a situation in which he must respond, but realizes that his habitual patterns of response are not adequate for satisfactory adjustment to the "problem situation." We have pointed out that many minor problems can be solved more or less satisfactorily by the application of trial-error-trial-success techniques. Much waste of time and effort may be involved in such haphazard approaches to the meeting of problem difficulties, however. Hence, through their learning experiences, children need to develop a more orderly thinking procedure toward the solution of problems that are suited progressively to their maturing and developing stages of thinking ability.

Problem-solving and reasoning. In order for problems to be solved adequately, a person's concepts and memory must reflect correct perceptions of materials with which the problem deals; fruitful relationships then must be achieved through the tracing and retracing of thoughts until a satisfactory solution of the problems is reached. Such mental manipulations are characteristic of reasoning. Hence reasoning can be regarded as a form of thinking that is concerned with the orderly manipulation of memory images and concepts or ideas, until workable relationships are discovered. The science of valid and accurate thinking or reasoning is known as logic. According to the nature of the problem one of two approaches can be employed—the *inductive* or the *deductive*.

Inductive approach. Induction is the process of inferring or aiming at the general from observation of the particular. A law of causational connection can be inferred or derived from observing and analyzing some particular instances which appear to the reasoner to have either one or more characteristics in common.

Many scientific laws or principles are inferences based upon many accurate observations of certain phenomena that, upon analysis, give evidence of a common factor that then is assumed to be a general characteristic of the group observed. For example, Thorndike first promulgated the Laws of Exercise and Effect in learning as a result of his maze experiments

---

* From Lester D. Crow and Alice Crow, *Human Development and Learning,* pp. 310–14. Copyright 1956 by American Book Co., New York, and reprinted with their permission.

with hungry rats. Pavlov's explanation of learning as conditioning was based upon his observation and analysis of the carrying over of a habitual response from the stimulation situation that included it to a new stimulus. Through his observation of the behavior of many adolescents, G. Stanley Hall concluded that adolescence is a period of storm and stress.

The validity of a general conclusion reached by utilization of the inductive approach depends upon the number of instances observed and the actual similarity among them. Lay people and even men and women trained in their field may draw conclusions from too few cases of a large group that then are accepted as generalizations for the entire group. Consequently, young learners are encouraged to draw conclusions from several isolated studies. Teachers should be careful that their pupils do not make "snap judgments" without adequate observation and analysis. Perhaps one of the learning areas in which inductive thinking or reasoning is likely to produce inadequate or partially adequate conclusions is that of the social studies.

Deductive approach. Deduction means reasoning from the general to the particular. If a conclusion or principle is assumed to be valid, the problem becomes one of discovering whether the general principle applies to particular phenomena or instances. This approach to problem-solving is referred to as the logical form of reasoning. Formal logic takes the form of syllogistic reasoning. A syllogism consists of three propositions. The first two are called the premises (accepted facts or generalizations) and the third is the conclusion, in which the common term in the premise disappears, after furnishing the logical connection between the premises.

Problem-solving through logical reasoning implies the evolving of an adequate solution of the problem. Much of our thinking follows the syllogistic pattern, but subtle elements in the premises may not be recognized, thus leading to erroneous conclusions. Insight into the significance of each idea is needed. Unless children are helped to discover the actual implications of a stated idea, thinking and reasoning continue to be fuzzy even on the college level.

Although the syllogistic approach to problem-solving is helpful in that the syllogism deals with relationships in thinking, syllogisms are constructed upon relatively artificial materials. Logic, as it usually is taught, does not necessarily induce the student to apply syllogistic reasoning to his own life situations. Logical reasoning places emphasis upon *techniques* of thinking, rather than upon the *materials* of thinking. The application of syllogistic techniques has value, however, in helping an individual gain insight into thought relationships. A few examples of syllogisms may help to clarify this point.

Major premise—All men are mortal.—(correct general concept)
Minor premise—He is a man.—(correct specific idea)
Conclusion—Therefore, he is mortal.—(correct conclusion)

This syllogism represents accurate reasoning. Let us change the wording of the syllogism:

All mortals are men.—(incorrect generalization)
She is a mortal.—(correct specific idea)
Therefore, she is a man.—(incorrect conclusion)

In the second syllogism, the generalization is factually incorrect; therefore, the conclusion cannot be correct. Here is another syllogism:

Some flowers are red.—(correct partial generalization)
Violets are flowers.—(correct specific idea)
Therefore, all violets are red.—(incorrect conclusion)

The error in this syllogism is caused by the fact that the first premise tells us about the colors of *some* flowers, not all. Hence there may be flowers that have other colors. One cannot conclude from the ideas included in the premises that violets are red; they may be any color.

Phases in problem-solving. In Chapter 10, we referred to John Dewey's belief that children learn by thinking their way through problem situations. In his book, *How We Think,* Dewey presented five phases or steps that are involved in the solution of a problem. These can be described as:

1. Awareness and comprehension of the problem. (Realization of the problem.)
2. Localization, evaluation, and organization of information. (Search for clarity.)
3. Discovery of relationships and formulation of hypothesis. (The proposal of hypothesis.)
4. Evaluation of hypothesis. (Rational application.)
5. Application. (Experimental verification.) [1]

In scientific experimentation these five phases usually are clearly indicated. The scientist becomes aware of a problem that requires careful reflective thinking. He then interprets the problem in order to make certain that he understands the implications that are inherent in the problem situation. If he possessed ready-made responses to all of these elements, the situation would be no problem to him. Since the situation involves unrecog-

[1] Adapted from J. Dewey, *How We Think* (Boston: D. C. Heath & Co., 1910), pp. 106–15.

nized implications, however, he attempts, through research and perhaps experimentation, to gather all of the information for understanding that he believes he needs. He then organizes and reorganizes relationships among all of the concepts until he comes up with what seems to him to be a workable answer or hypothesis, or tentative solution. He mentally checks the hypothesis against the elements of the problem situation. He may modify and remodify his original hypothesis by reflecting upon the extent to which his tentative solution meets the requirements of the problem.

When the reasoner is satisfied with the rational validity of the hypothesis, he attempts to verify his conclusions by applying the hypothesis in the solution of problems that are similar to the one on which he has been working. If the hypothesis "works" in many situations, all of which contain the problematic element or elements, the hypothesis becomes a scientific law or a principle. The law then is applied generally until it fails to solve difficulties that are found to be common to problematic situations in which the principle is supposed to function adequately.

At this point a new problem is posed: What problematic elements are there in these situations that require solution? The five phases of problem-solving then are repeated until a better solution of the difficulty is achieved.

Factors of adequacy in problem solutions. If problem-solving is to result in correct and usable solutions, problem-solvers must possess an adequate background understanding of the elements of the problem. They must be able to discover sources of necessary information and to relate that information to the requirements of the problem until a workable hypothesis emerges, which then is thought through to check its validity. The verifying of the hypothesis through its application in appropriate problem situations may be the responsibility of the original problem-solver or of other persons who are experiencing problems in similar situations.

The verification of an hypothesis is as important as the development of the hypothesis itself. Too often a principle or law is evolved and accepted without sufficient verification through application in many situations. Consequently, the principle, law, or conclusion is found to be inadequate for general application.

We have lived through the establishment of many educational policies and philosophies that appear to function successfully in certain limited educational situations but fail to bring about expected results when they are applied in larger or different learning situations. For example, every educator is vitally interested in the problem of learner stimulation toward successful learner achievement. Consequently, many attempts have been made to solve this problem. Learning situations and learning activities can be controlled somewhat adequately in relatively small school systems. Hence many principles, techniques, and approaches to learning have been evolved and applied in small school communities or in selected schools of a larger community. When these apparently workable solutions to an educational problem have been applied to learning situations that represent mass education, they usually fail to function, or they need to be greatly modified before they are usable. In the field of standardized measurement, the same difficulty may be experienced. A test is devised to measure a certain area of learning. Unless its usability is verified by application to a large cross section of the learning level for which the test has been constructed, its value will remain local rather than general.

Reasoning that is applied to the attempted solution of a problem may be ineffective because the reasoner does not have sufficient power of insight or richness of background experience to recognize the elements of or the extent of the problem. Learners on all levels, from the elementary school through the college graduate level, may find it difficult to comprehend the problems which they are attempting to solve. Children experience this difficulty when they are motivated by their teachers to engage in the solving of problems that are associated with learning content. They might find a way to solve the problem if they understood its meaning and significance.

It is good learning procedure to challenge children with questions or problems that require the establishment of new or different conceptual organizations. The teacher must be certain, however, that a posed problem is suited to the understanding level of the children who are expected to solve it. Especially does the teacher need to be careful concerning the thought problems he assigns for home solution. The learner soon becomes discouraged if he does not understand the statement of a problem. Either he returns to school the next day with uncompleted homework, or, before the school session begins, he attempts to copy the work of another pupil, without any understanding of what he is copying.

65. The Multidimensional Contexts of Learning *

NATHANIEL CANTOR

THE RECENT STUDY by Dr. Philip E. Jacob for the Edward W. Hazen Foundation will prove disconcerting to many college teachers.[1] The study showed no significant changes in student values resulting from the character of the curriculum or from the basic courses in social science which students take as part of their general education. The quality of teaching had relatively little effect upon the value-outcomes of general education.

Some students have a set of mind so rigid, an outlook on human relations so stereotyped, and a reliance on authority so compulsive that they are intellectually and emotionally incapable of understanding new ideas, and seeing much less accepting, educational implications which run counter to their preconceptions. This particularly limits their responsiveness in the social sciences and the humanities whenever controversial issues arise. Such students quail in the presence of conflict and uncertainty. They crave "right answers." They distrust speculative thought, their own or their fellow students'. They recoil from "creative discussion."

One does not need elaborate statistical studies to risk the conclusion that most professionals, along with the graduates of schools of business administration, the teachers' colleges, and the colleges of arts and sciences, do not continue to learn in significant, vital ways, to "grow," or even to engage in much serious reading which is related to their professional work.

I confess after thirty-five years, during which time I have tried to discover what effective teaching and learning are, that I remain puzzled and challenged. The advertising copy, the statement of objectives and purposes found in the Bulletins of the Schools, are, of course, not to be taken too seriously. Faculty members of the colleges and professional schools of this country are aware of the lack of clarity and even disagreement regarding goals. If the objectives of higher education are not clearly stated, agreed upon, and striven for, it is difficult to ascertain what "effective" teaching means.

For the purposes of developing the thesis of this paper I assume that a

* From Nathaniel Cantor, "The Multidimensional Contexts of Learning," *The Educational Forum* (March, 1958), pp. 299–305. Reprinted by permission.

[1] *Changing Values in College:* An Exploratory Study of the Impact of General Education in Social Sciences on the Values of American Students.

college education should help a person to become aware of the nature of the world in which he lives, of the people with whom he associates, and of his responsibilities and obligations to others. A college education should help one to appreciate his own traditions, to heighten his appreciation of the different forms of beauty, and to learn how to make satisfactory sense out of his living.

I recognize my own biases in these value judgments but I fail to see how I can remain acceptably sane and avoid ethical commitments.

The spiritual roots of American teachers extended more or less deeply into the soil of American democracy. We have to live by some values. Historically, we are democratically oriented. That is the given. Our democratic postulates are not derived from science but from our society, more directly from our parents and teachers. They are not derived from science, but their implications and consequences can be rationally examined by science. In the light of our limited, but best, knowledge, what consequences are likely to follow from moral direction A, B, or C, and how can they be realized? The desirability of the consequences is judged in accord with our given democratic beliefs. There is no more need to ground our given values on ultimate moral "principles" than scientific judgments of facts need to be based upon first truths or the final logical proof for induction.

Our teachers alone cannot rebuild society, but they can prepare future leaders by helping them to assimilate ideas and to develop attitudes which can make some difference in meeting the concrete critical issues they now face and will face. The temptation of the fleshpots may be modified by the visions of Plato —and their own.[2]

Learning which might modify the accepted norm of "success" in American society would be, in my opinion, effective learning. It would present opportunities for many young people to become more sensitized to the meaning and implications of the data to which they are exposed and to make somewhat different choices in their life experiences. The question is can this be accomplished in the colleges? I do not know whether it is possible for any large number of students. I am certain, however, that failure to do this is due in part to the traditional "knowledge approach" on the part of a majority of teachers to the teaching-learning process.[3] The "ideas" one is exposed to in the colleges do not seem to make any vital difference in the life of the students.

[2] N. Cantor, "The Teacher in a General Education Program," *Journal of General Education* (April, 1952).

[3] I am concerned here with the colleges of arts and sciences. The graduate and professional schools present other problems.

What actually takes place in the teaching-learning situation? How many teachers are aware of the tangled web of interpersonal relations which entrap both teacher and learner? How many of us sense the vital interests of our students? Are *they* concerned with the abstractions we fool around with? Who does most of the kidding, the "profs" or the students? How much honest, meaningful communication takes place between teacher and learners? How deeply and truly concerned are we, the teachers, with what is happening to our students because of our performance? Do we fret about our lack of skill in the classroom, or is that no problem? Just what is each one of us doing in the classroom besides dealing with our specialized field of interest?

These are only a few questions regarding the realities of the learning situation. More formally I should like to discuss four different levels (there are many more) which operate in a teaching-learning group experience, namely, the social, ethical, professional, and scientific.

Social Norms

When two or more people meet there can be no communication between them unless they share certain values. Social relations as opposed to chance physical contact imply that individuals possess expectations regarding one another's behavior. A perceptive teacher will become aware of the expectations of the group he leads, and of what he expects as he leads them. I speak now of his awareness, not of his judging the desirability of the expectations. It is normal, for example, for a teacher to be aware of his status and position. He is inclined to be a bit of a *prima donna*. He is expected to possess superior knowledge and wants to display it. It is also generally understood that the teacher controls the class. He is in charge. He leads, students follow.

The student "learns" how to meet the regulations and requirements of the course and the professor. Over the years, both in primary and secondary schools, the pupils have learned what to expect and how to meet the demands of the classroom and instructor. They quickly learn, through the help of the experienced fellow students, the techniques to be used for the several instructors, which teachers demand deference.

The experienced teacher is aware of these folkways. He realizes how much of the classroom experience is an ongoing contest of wills between the traditional authority of the teacher and the resistance of the student. He understands that it requires many weeks to modify student expectations and his own traditional teacher attitudes. New classroom norms can be established but only after periods of confusion. Students do not easily surrender their lifelong distrust of the inquisitorial instructor. They sense the mumbo-jumbo of required assignments, passing grades, and the lifelessness of texts and teachers. The skilled teacher, in time, can lessen their fears and defensiveness. Through his own genuine, spontaneous involvement in helping them learn he challenges and excites the creative effort of students. New expectations on the part of teacher and learner become the pattern. The teacher expects to help, that is his function. The student's responsibility is to learn.

Ethical Assumptions

Our culture teaches us to conform to a series of religious and ethical beliefs. These are the absolutes of our society. Our ideals of Justice, Truth and Goodness are so taken for granted in our literature, official utterances, secular schooling, and, of course, religious instruction that it requires considerable cultural sophistication to recognize the arbitrary character of these usually unexamined premises. These sacred and taken-for-granted beliefs and ideals must be recognized by the teacher, how they have come about, how they function, how they help or hinder the objectives of learner development.

There is a growing acceptance of a goal in modern life, which, some of us think, threatens the development of individuals. I refer to the idea of teaching students "to adjust." The "life adjustment courses" in many of the secondary schools of the country rest squarely on the idea of conformity. In fact a new social ethic in contradiction to the Protestant ethic is developing in this country. This is the central thesis of a recent study, *The Organization Man,* by William H. Whyte. Candidates for executive positions are expected to conform to the group, to adjust to group norms. It is not merely the conformity which is dangerous, it is the fact that leaders in industry and many teachers believe that it is *morally imperative* that the individual should learn or be taught to conform for his own good. Getting along with everybody and being "well-rounded" are, it is taught, much-needed goals of modern life.

A teacher who becomes aware of this basic ethic of conformity which is rapidly creeping up on us in many segments of our life (industrial relations, moral, socioeconomic, political, and educational beliefs) will be shocked to discover the degree to which he, too, has been manipulated toward or has unwittingly succumbed to conformity. He cannot, therefore, be expected to help the learner develop creatively, or to be understanding, when the student tries out his differences with the instructor, or the packaged classroom programs. The instructor needs to accept his own differences before he can easily permit the expression of student differences.

No premium is being offered for the encouragement of ill-mannered, hostile, cantankerous, neurotic misfits. Conformity to some group standards, loyalty to organization, respect for tradition, cooperation, these are all valuable and necessary qualities of organized social activity. The problems relate to the degree of conformity, to what standards, what organization, respect for what traditions, cooperation with whom under what conditions, *and at what cost to the integrity of the individual?* In brief, we are concerned with the shifting balance between the social and individual aspects of the learner. The development of maturity requires that the learner accept a deal of the responsibility for the judgments *he* makes and the risks *he* undergoes.

A skillful teacher is aware of this dilemma, the need for the preservation of traditional values and the need for maturing individuals to determine the nature of a changing order, and the roles he chooses to play.

The Science of Human Relations

If skilled teaching has a sense of direction, a purpose, and a structure, one should be able *to describe* it. This does not mean the description will adequately cover all of the dimensions. It does mean that one should be able to state the assumptions upon which one is carrying out the process, the results which follow, whether one can predict general uniformities, and whether certain principles of helping others can be communicated and further tested. There is little precise knowledge about how people learn, how groups operate, and how one teaches. People do differ in teaching skills and in learning potential. Except in the rare case skills are developed, and learning is facilitated. There have been some great "natural" teachers and some insatiable learners. The majority of teachers, however, must acquire ability, and the majority of learners must be helped to develop. It is a serious mistake to believe that anyone is qualified to teach others (in the area of development of potential) without the available understanding of what is involved in learning.

The various methods and contents of educational programs are based upon certain assumptions, expressed or implied, regarding how people learn. No one method or content or combination is objectionable in itself. What is troublesome and misleading is dogmatic insistence on clichés and rules and verbal principles. Many teachers, unsure of themselves, and of what they are doing, that is, possessing little skill, seek security through the *Word*.

It is important that inquiry and research into how people learn and develop be supported. Without this knowledge the exercise of skill becomes personal idiosyncrasy. The teacher who seems to be consistently helpful will be exercising great skill, that is, he will possess the best available knowledge, and will understand how inadequate it is. Furthermore, the skilled teacher understands that even if our knowledge of human relations and learnings were more reliable and valid the logic of ideas rarely parallels the lust for living. The teacher discovers what is "wrong" with the learner. The teacher knows what "should" be done. It's a wise teacher who keeps that knowledge to himself until such time as the student wants to or is helped to become ready to avail himself of the teacher's wisdom.

Professional Level

This dimension is little understood by teachers. In every learning experience the helper must become sensitized to his own feelings toward the learners. What use does he make of himself for the benefit of the learner? What needs of his own are being fulfilled or frustrated? What are his biases which color his interpretations and distort his perceptions? The teacher is hard put to discover what the feelings of the members are toward him, toward each other and in relation to the data. What do they really want in their classes? Are they communicating or engaging in the usual *fol-de-rol* of pleasant intellectual amenities where no one is in danger of getting or being really hurt?

Most of us, leaders and students, fear to examine these pretty pictures of ourselves which we carry around and the pretty language with which we so clearly and simply describe our opinions, judgments, and excellent reasons for acting as we do. The individual who examines himself and others is embarking on a dangerous journey. It is hard to predict where this examination will lead one.

Skills in teaching require the development of a professional self.

By professional level I mean the teacher's understanding of how to use himself in the learning situation for the sake of the learner. The teacher's function is to assist in the development of others. Ideally the teacher's personal needs for satisfaction, approval, or control are irrelevant in the teaching-learning situation. The teacher is not being paid to use the classroom as a clinic for the expression of personal tensions. The teacher is engaged to help the learner.

No teacher, however professional in outlook, can avoid personal involvement at times. Each of us feels the need to win, to control, to dominate, to be right, that is, to make the other over in our image. If our "help" is rejected we become hostile or resentful. Or, if sometimes we succeed in dominating, we experience guilt.

The more sensitive the awareness the more disciplined will a teacher become in dealing with personal involvement. Indeed the re-creation of the professional core of a teacher rests upon the discovery that one is using the student for one's personal needs. The teacher gains satisfaction not in becoming popular with students but in redirecting and disciplining personal feeling. This continuous intrapersonal struggle can lead to more skilled, professional use of one's self.

This is, in the final analysis, the soundest test for a teacher's performance. A teacher's competence is not formed through what the learner learns but through the skill with which the teacher encourages the student to want to learn. Everyone learns only when *he* wants to learn. No one can be motivated by another. The teacher helps by creating the most favorable circumstances in which learning can occur, if the student wants to learn. For one reason or another beyond the control of the teacher he may not want to learn. The teacher's task is to encourage, to help, to put himself at the disposal of the learner. In brief the teacher's job is to perform skillfully as a teacher. The learner's responsibility is to learn. The chances are favorable that if one performs skillfully as a teacher the learner is more likely to want to learn. Nevertheless, skillful teaching need not necessarily lead to genuine learning. Poor teaching, sometimes, cannot block learning, and excellent teaching often fails to challenge those who do not want to learn.

Verbal Magic

Most college students do not comfortably understand the physical and mathematical foundations of the universe. They do not understand the meaning of scientific methods. Their social science understanding is undigested claptrap. The college of arts and sciences graduates, and professionally trained adults outside of their area of competence, are frightfully ignorant.

I do not mean to recriminate or to scold or to appear righteous. I am presenting my considered opinion of what the colleges of arts and sciences accomplish. The study of Dr. Jacob supports what many of us suspected. Part of the failure of education, it seems to me, is the confusion between knowledge and understanding. Understanding is not to be confused with specious verbal magic, hollow concepts. All of us have attended innumerable faculty meetings characterized by the dull amenities where no one risks anything or learns anything significant. What is true of faculty meetings is true of classroom meetings. The same conspiracy of silence continues. Teachers pretend to know more than they do; they talk a great deal repeating the talk of the texts. The students repeat the talk of the talk of the text talkers. Mark Twain opens his autobiography:

. . . His (a person's) acts and his words are merely the visible, thin crust of his world, with its scattered snow summits and its vacant wastes of water—and they are so trifling a part of his bulk, a mere skin enveloping it. The mass of him is hidden—and its volcanic fires that toss and boil, and never rest, night or day. These are his life, and they are not written, and cannot be written.

Understanding, genuine learning, is made up of much more than knowledge. Compassion, tragic futility, illusory hope, humility, confusion, worry, hope, love, creativity, wisdom—all of these operate in the classroom. These multidimensional factors are the matrix of vital learning. Ideas are the spark. They should enter not as vacuums but as hot filaments illuminating the dark recesses of our being. Teachers need to understand what learning involves.

66. *Animistic Thinking among College and High School Students in the Near East* *

WAYNE DENNIS

Introduction

In an earlier publication the writer reported that approximately one third of the students in several American colleges and universities attribute life to one or more inanimate objects. This finding has been corroborated by several other investigators.

* From Wayne Dennis, "Animistic Thinking among College and High School Students in the Near East," *The Journal of Educational Psychology* (April, 1957), pp. 193–98. Reprinted by permission of the author and publisher.

In comparison to many countries, the level of education in general, and the level of scientific knowledge in particular, are high in America. If animistic thinking is present in one third of American college students, it seems likely that it is even more prevalent in countries in which the educational levels are lower, and in which natural science concepts and information are less widely disseminated than in the United States. The present paper reports data relative to this deduction, derived from college and high school students in the Near East.

Procedure

Each subject was given a mimeographed sheet containing the following instructions:

"In connection with each of the objects listed below, indicate whether it is living or not living. Give a reason for each answer. Please answer the questions in the way that you think they would be answered by a biologist. For each object, the question is, is the object living in the same way that animals and plants are living?"

Below the instructions appeared the names of seven objects. For the subjects who were college students the objects were: a lighted match, the sun, the wind, the sea, lightning, a pearl, and atoms. On the blanks given to high school students, "a river" was used instead of "the sea" and "petroleum" instead of "atoms." In the case of college students, the questions were presented and answered in English, which was their language of instruction. Since the teaching of the high school subjects was in Arabic, in their case the questions were presented and answered in that language.

Subjects

The college students were enrolled in a women's college and a university in Beirut, Lebanon. Although these institutions are located in Lebanon, their students come from many Near Eastern countries. In the university, only male students were used as subjects. The majority were students in the college of arts and sciences. High school data were obtained from three public high schools in Iraq. Two of these schools were located in Mosul and one in Baghdad. The latter school and one of the Mosul schools were day schools; the other was a night school attended primarily by adults who had discontinued their earlier education before the completion of high school.

In the colleges the animism questionnaire was given in the introductory psychology course. Since the majority of students at these institutions take this course, the sampling is believed to be representative of students at these institutions. In the high schools, the questionnaires were administered to first-, second-, and third-year students in required courses, and consequently, the results are believed to be representative of these levels in these schools.

Results

The number of subjects tested in each school and the per cent giving one or more animistic answers are indicated in Table 1.

The most arresting fact about Table 1 is the generally high frequencies of animistic thinking found in all groups. The lowest figure (53 per cent) was obtained for men in the university. All other percentages lie between 74 per cent and 95 per cent.

Table 1

NUMBER AND PER CENT OF STUDENTS GIVING ANIMISTIC ANSWERS

	College Women	College Men	Baghdad Students	Mosul Day Students	Mosul Night Students	Total
Number of students	130	75	115	286	141	747
Per cent giving one or more animistic answers	77	53	95	81	74	79

The difference between the college men and college women is probably due to differences in the institutions from which they come in regard to student selection and required science courses. Sex comparisons in the high schools, in which admission policies and science courses for the two sexes are identical, indicate no sex differences. Comparisons of Christian and Moslem students, not included in Table 1, indicate these two groups do not differ in frequency of animistic answers.

Table 2 indicates the frequency with which each object was said to be living by the members of each group. It will be noted that the lowest percentage obtained was for lightning. Among the university men only 16 per cent stated that it was living. The university men yield a response frequency of 21 per cent for both the burning match and the wind. The highest per cents obtained were 75 per cent and 78 per cent. In both cases these refer to the pearl, and the scores were made by the Iraqi high school groups. It will be noted that in four of the five groups one third or more of the total responses were animistic.

Table 2

PER CENT OF RESPONSES TO EACH QUESTION WHICH WERE ANIMISTIC

	College Women	College Men	Baghdad Students	Mosul Day Students	Mosul Night Students
Match	47	21	50	27	42
Sun	38	26	66	36	35
Wind	34	21	56	24	35
Sea	41	24			
Lightning	30	16	32	23	25
Pearl	26	24	78	75	42
Atoms	55	31			
River			54	28	42
Petroleum			49	23	40
Per cent of total answers animistic	39	23	55	34	37

In the case of two groups, the college women and the Baghdad students, the reasons given for positive answers have been examined and classified. The results are shown in Table 3. It will be noted that in the two groups, respectively, 39 per cent and 38 per cent of the answers are what Piaget would call stage two or stage three answers: the object is living because it moves, either by itself or from some other cause. These Piaget classifies as nonadult answers. While these answers occur frequently in our group, the simplest sort of answer obtained from children, namely that an object is living

Table 3

REASONS GIVEN FOR ANIMISTIC ANSWERS

	College Women	Baghdad Students
	PER CENT	PER CENT
Moves, changes, does something	39	38
Supports or produces life	21	7
Has a beginning and an end	14	4
Grows	16	23
Uses oxygen, produces energy	6	16
Miscellaneous	4	12

because it is useful, was rarely encountered among college and high school students. Informal studies of Lebanese elementary-school pupils which will not be reported in detail show that stage one answers (answers in term of use) predominate at the earlier age levels in Lebanon, as they do elsewhere.

The statement that an object is living because it grows should perhaps not be listed as an instance of wrong reasoning. The reasoning is not incorrect; only the facts are wrong. Among the Iraqi subjects this answer was often given in respect to the pearl.

The statements that an object, such as the burning match, is living because it is using oxygen illustrate the fact that science education does not always operate to reduce animistic answers. Apparently the students had learned that living things use oxygen, and they reasoned that whatever uses oxygen, must be living.

College and high school students give two types of answers which are seldom given by children. The answers occur among American college students as well as in the present sample. One is that the sun, or the sea, or some other object is living because it produces, or is necessary for, life. This answer seems to result from the premise that like produces like, and therefore, that whatever is responsible for, or necessary for life, must itself be living. The second notion is that since life has a beginning and an end, all things which have a beginning and an end, as do a flame and a flash of lightning, are therefore living. These answers have not been reported by Piaget in his four stages of animism, presumably because he questioned only children. They represent categories or "stages" in excess of his four.

Discussion

It is obvious from the present study, as well as from earlier ones, that Piaget's assumption that animism is limited to children is incorrect. It seems probable that a degree of animistic thinking can be found in some adults in any society. The actual percentage of animistic replies will differ from question to question and from group to group.

While the cultural area in which the present study was conducted was a center of one of the earliest civilizations, extensive modern educational programs have been introduced only recently. Science education, as compared to linguistic, literary, and historical instruction, is undoubtedly still weak. These two facts probably account in the main for the high incidence of animistic replies to our questions.

We do not believe that the prevalence of animistic thinking in our subjects is due to positive cultural influences. Christianity and Islam, to which our subjects belong, both reject the view that objects of nature and forces of nature are themselves alive. Both of these religions would reject such ideas as tending toward idolatry.

We have indicated earlier our belief that animism arises autogenously in individuals who lack an adequate background in modern biological concepts and knowledge. The persistence of animism into the adult years, in the Near East, is to be accounted for in terms of educational handicaps rather than in terms of a positive animistic tradition.

Summary

Seven hundred and forty-seven Near Eastern college and high school students were questioned in regard to whether each of several objects is living or not living. Seventy-nine per cent gave one or more animistic answers. In the various groups the frequencies of animistic answers were much higher than those obtained among American students of comparable educational placement. The differences are presumed to reflect the differences in diffusion of scientific concepts and information in these populations.

Acknowledgment

The writer is indebted to Miss Suad Wakim, Mrs. Ada Khaza'al, and Mr. Abdul-Kadir Hubayti for obtaining the student responses on which the present paper is based, and to Mrs. Yvonne Sayegh for analysis of the data. The study was conducted in 1955–56 when the author was a visiting professor at the American University of Beirut, Lebanon. Expenses of the study were defrayed by a grant to the American University by the Rockefeller Brothers Fund.

67. Sex Differences and Judgment Processes *[1]

MICHAEL A. WALLACH
AND NATHAN KOGAN

SEVERAL RECENT STUDIES report significant differences between males and females in various kinds of judgment situations. A comparative examination of these studies, however, does not yield any simple pattern of results; and indeed, the findings, at first glance, seem to be mutually contradictory. On the one hand, some investigators have found males to be more extreme and daring in their judgments, females more restrained and conservative. On the other hand, there are studies in which the very opposite pattern is alleged to distinguish the sexes.

Consider first those papers that report greater conservatism in judgment on the part of women. Pettigrew (1958), in standardizing his category-width scale, reports a significant tendency for category estimates to be broader for males than females. "Broad" as opposed to "narrow" categorizing in the present case means that an *S*'s estimates are closer to the given extremes of a number of diverse categories, such as whale length and number of tornadoes in the United States. Using sixth grade children, Wallach and Caron (1959) found boys more willing than girls to call ambiguous figures similar to a key figure in a situation where the likelihood of error was greater when those figures were judged similar than when judged not similar. In addition, Wallach and Caron administered a children's form of the category-width scale and found sex differences consistent with those obtained by Pettigrew.

Let us turn next to those studies where women were found to be less conservative than men in their judgmental responses. Shapiro and Tagiuri (1959) compared the inferences men and women make about a person's

* From Michael A. Wallach and Nathan Kogan, "Sex Differences and Judgment Processes," *Journal of Personality* (December, 1959), pp. 555–64. Reprinted by permission of the authors and the *Journal of Personality*.

[1] This research was supported by grant M-2269 from the National Institute of Mental Health, United States Public Health Service, and was conducted under the auspices of The Age Center of New England, Inc. Grateful thanks are due Albert E. Beaton and Harvey Willson for machine processing of the data. For making classes available, we are indebted to Bernhardt Lieberman, A. Bertrand Warren, and Harold S. Zamansky of Northeastern University, and to Stephen R. Deane and Donald S. Dunbar of Simmons College. We also wish to thank Albert J. Caron and Henri Tajfel for their critical comments on the manuscript. The junior author is now at Educational Testing Service.

traits from a given single trait. For example, an S who received the statement, "People who are intelligent," was asked to specify whether such people "very often are," "tend to be," "may or may not be," "tend not to be," or "seldom are" aggressive, active, etc. The results indicated that women were more inclined than men to make extreme positive or negative inferences. In a paper on sex differences in social desirability ratings of personality traits, Cowen (1958) reports results consistent with those of Shapiro and Tagiuri; women made more extreme positive or negative judgments.

How can these findings be reconciled with the results cited previously in which females were found to be more conservative in their judgments? An obvious factor is the particular content area in which the judgment lies. The Pettigrew and Wallach-Caron studies are based on quantitative and geometric judgments, respectively, while the Shapiro-Tagiuri and Cowen investigations concern personality trait judgments. There is considerable evidence (Tyler, 1956) indicating women's inferiority to men in dealing with quantitative and spatial relations problems. On the other hand, Allport (1937), among others, has stressed women's superiority in judging other people. In sum, men's superior quantitative skills and women's superior "intuitive" abilities may account for a greater willingness on the part of both sexes to go out on a limb and risk the consequences of error in their respective spheres of competence.

While this interpretation is a reasonable one, it does not take sufficient account of the complexity of the judgment situation. A judgment or decision has two analytically distinguishable components. These are the level of certainty with which a decision is made and the decision itself. The latter, in turn, may be more or less extreme or risky in its nature. While level of certainty and extremity of decision will be positively correlated, it is entirely possible to examine variations in one of these dimensions with the other held constant.

Consider again the empirical studies cited earlier. With the category-width scale and the figure judgment procedure, decisions, by and large, are made under conditions of uncertainty. We have no way of knowing, however, whether sex differences in these tasks are attributable to certainty or extremity differences. In other words, males and females may be equally uncertain in their judgments, with males more willing to venture extreme judgments under these conditions; or males may be less conservative in their judgments for the very reason that they are more certain. Comparable problems of interpretation arise with respect to the trait-judgment procedures described above.

It is evident, then, that a thorough assessment of conservatism in judgment requires us to consider not only the particular decisions made, but also how certain or uncertain the individual's decisions seem to him. While both certainty and extremity of judgment may be a reflection of some more basic process such as risk-taking, it is no less essential that we specify more exactly the factors that may underlie sex differences in judgment. Accordingly, the present research will explore the extremity of judgments for men and women when made at varying levels of certainty. The study will also contrast various realms of content, and inquire as to possible sex differences across areas of subject matter in willingness to choose a risky alternative.

Method

SUBJECTS

A total of 357 undergraduates enrolled in introductory psychology courses served as *S*s. The males ($N = 225$) were drawn from Northeastern University; the females ($N = 132$) attended Simmons College. Both schools are located in the metropolitan Boston area and have a fairly comparable student body from the standpoint of socioeconomic status and intelligence.

PROBABILITY AND CERTAINTY TEST

This test consisted of fifty items; thirty-two originally used by Brim (1955) and eighteen new items identical in form to the Brim items and varying over a wide range of content. The test was enlarged in order to increase the reliability of an *S*'s mean probability estimate for items at each certainty level. Instructions to *S*s were as follows:

"This questionnaire will help us find out people's opinions about various things. The following sentences describe various events. We want your opinion as to how likely each event is. You indicate your opinion by estimating the number of chances out of 100 that the event will occur. Thus, if you felt an event was very likely, you'd write a number close to 100; if you felt an event was very unlikely, you'd write a number close to 0; and if you felt an event was about equally likely and unlikely, you'd write a number close to 50.

"We also want you to indicate how sure you are of your opinion. So, after you've filled in how likely you think an event is, we want you to indicate how sure you are of this opinion by circling one of the phrases below the sentence.

"All the sentences will be of the following forms:

" 'The chances that such-and-such event will occur are about _____ in 100.

| very | quite | moderately | slightly | not sure |
| sure | sure | sure | sure | at all' " |

As probability estimates for the various items move away from the extremes of 0 or 100 chances out of 100, the likelihood of error declines and, hence, judgments become more conservative. By subtracting S's estimates from 0 or 100 depending upon whether the estimate is below or above 50, scores on the probability estimation variable can range from 0 to 50.

To provide a single over-all estimate of conservatism tendencies, Brim's scoring system was used as the first method of analysis. This involved assigning numbers from 1 to 5 for the certainty categories, 1 being scored for a check of "very sure," 5 being scored for checking "not sure at all." When each item's extremity estimate (between 0 and 50) is multiplied by its certainty level (between 1 and 5) and the product summed across items, then the smaller the total score, the greater the risk-taking and/or certainty of decision; and the larger the total score, the greater the conservatism and/or uncertainty.

Since this single score confounds the two variables of probability estimate and level of certainty, the data were also treated in a more detailed way. This involved (a) finding the frequency distribution of S's certainty checks across the five levels of certainty and (b) finding S's mean extremity estimate for those items which he placed at each level of certainty. We hence could compare men and women in terms of certainty levels and mean extremity of estimate for items marked at each level of certainty.

DILEMMAS OF CHOICE QUESTIONNAIRE

In the second instrument, twelve situations were described, each containing a central person faced with a choice between two courses of action. One of these courses posed a greater risk, but also was more rewarding if successful. The reader had to advise the person in the story by deciding what probability of success would be sufficient to warrant choosing the risky alternative. Brief descriptions of the twelve situations are presented below.

1. Mr. A, an electrical engineer, has the choice of sticking with his present job at a modest, though adequate, salary or of moving on to another job offering more money but no long-term security.

2. Mr. B, who has developed a severe heart ailment, has the choice of changing many of his strongest life habits or undergoing a delicate medical operation which might succeed or might prove fatal.

3. Mr. C, a man of moderate means, has the choice of investing a sum of recently inherited money in secure "blue-chip" stocks and bonds or in more risky securities offering the possibility of large gains.

4. Mr. D, captain of his college football team and in the final seconds of a game with his college's traditional rival, has the choice of a play that would be almost certain to produce a tie score, or a more risky play that would bring victory if successful, defeat if not. . . .

Summary and Conclusions

In a study of 357 college students on extremity and conservatism of judgment at varying levels of decision certainty, women were found to be more conservative than men when unsure of their decisions and more extreme than men when very sure of their decisions. The author concluded that feminine conservatism is learned through fear of punishment in subjectively ambiguous situations. On the other hand, when a situation is perceived as highly certain, a counterphobic release of boldness seems to occur. Regarding the content of decisions, women were more conservative than men regarding risks of income loss, death, and football defeat, while women were bolder than men concerning risks in the areas of marriage and art. This finding suggests that women may take greater risks than men regarding fields in which such boldness particularly furthers a woman's fulfillment and expression. In sum, one can make no simple generalization about sex differences in judgment and risk-taking, but rather must analyze the level of certainty of the decisions in question, and the subject matter they concern.

CHAPTER XII

PERSONALITY
DEVELOPMENT
AND THE SELF

68. How the Home Affects Personality Development *

FRIEDA K. MERRY
AND RALPH V. MERRY

SINCE THE FAMILY GROUP has greater influence upon personality develop-ment than has any other cultural agency, we shall outline some of the ways in which it affects the individual, especially during childhood. The extent to which an adult is accepted socially depends greatly upon the kind of atmosphere that prevailed in his home during his growing years.

Home Ratings

In the past there was much theorizing about the social responsibility of the home, but more recently active research has been carried on. Scales have been devised for rating homes, and trained observers have been placed in them to make direct assessments of interpersonal relationships.

These procedures have been used especially in Ohio in order to ascertain how the behavior and fundamental attitudes of parents are related to the developing personalities of their children. A longitudinal study was con-ducted on 150 children, the oldest of whom was 15 at the time the report was compiled. A trained observer visited each home for a two-hour period twice a year, during which she talked with the mothers and noted the children's behavior in relation to their parents. Two reports were made:

* From Frieda K. Merry and Ralph V. Merry, *The First Two Decades of Life,* 2nd ed., pp. 462–69. Copyright 1958 by Frieda Kiefer Merry and Ralph Vickers Merry and reprinted with the permission of Harper and Bros., New York.

one a description of what took place, and the other in the form of a rating scale.

From the data that have been collected, it has been shown that although each home has its own individuality, many have enough characteristics in common so that they can be designated by certain patterns. These patterns depend largely upon the emotional attitudes of parents toward their children and also upon the parent's general philosophy of child care. *All* families, obviously, could not be classified according to one or another of these various patterns. In fact, 25 per cent did not fit in with any of them. Many of the homes, however, could be characterized as showing different degrees of rejection, indulgence, and democratic behavior. Graphic and interesting descriptions are given of homes representing different classifications. Of the various types of acceptant behavior exhibited by parents, that which most nearly approached the ideal was thought to be a democratic home where each child is respected as an individual, and the parents show that they are fond of him. It has been found that such a home situation makes children more creative, imaginative, and constructive. Generally speaking, adolescents from democratic homes identify with their parents to a greater extent than do those from authoritarian homes. In a survey of 5500 high school seniors from the State of Washington it was found that 53.9 per cent of those in democratic homes wanted to be exactly like their parents, whereas this was true of only 23.4 per cent of those from authoritarian homes. Only 15.3 per cent of the seniors from democratic homes wanted to be completely different from their parents, while this was true of 38.6 per cent of those from authoritarian homes. As might be expected, the home is largely a reflection of the parents' personalities, particularly the mother's. Personality ratings of the parents, therefore, might be as revealing as elaborate home rating scales.

What Is a Good Home?

In a good home the child's sense of security is promoted by an atmosphere of affection and mutual respect. He is made to feel that he is a valuable and desired member of the family group, and when matters of importance are discussed, his ideas, no matter how naive, are given consideration. In one family, for example, a council was held concerning choice of pets by two children aged 4 and 6. When asked what pets they would like to have, six-year-old Janet replied, "I'd like a pony and a hen." Teddy, the four-year-old, thought that he would like to have a whale and a Scottie dog. Considerable discussion then ensued between the children as to where they could keep the whale, and Teddy thought they could keep it in the back yard if they had a place with water in it. When they appealed to their father, he told them that a whale could not live in fresh water, even if they could get it there. This seemed to convince Teddy that a whale as a pet was out of the question, and he suggested instead a choice of a lamb or a Scottie dog. The important point in all this is that the parents did not ridicule any of the children's ideas, but accepted and discussed them seriously. Eventually, the children, Teddy and Janet, without feeling disappointed or humiliated, came around spontaneously to the decision that it was not practical to have a whale for a pet.

A similar plan, in one large household where each member has a voice in the family decisions, was called a family corporation. These "talk it over" sessions are held each Sunday afternoon and minutes of each meeting are kept. Routine chores, rewards, punishments, and family projects, such as the type of new car to buy or where to spend vacations come up for discussion. Members vote on fines, penalties, and punishments. Each member of the family is entitled to one vote for every year of his age. Thus, the current voting status is: John, 38; Martha, 37; Frank, 17; Albert, 15; Tom, 13; Mary Louise, 7; Margaret, 4; Michael, 2; and Stephen, 1.

In a good home, also, the child's confidences are respected; he is introduced to strange adults as well as to strange children; and his friends are welcomed and made to feel at ease. He is accepted on his own merits and is expected to contribute something to the welfare of the group. This may take the form of helping with the dishes, running errands, or doing certain other household chores. He is taught to respect the rights of others, even when he disagrees with them. The child should be proud of his family and its accomplishments, but he can be so only when it is accepted in the neighborhood. This does not necessarily mean that the family must be wealthy, but its circumstances and conduct must conform to the social and economic class to which it belongs.

Parental Rejection

Unfortunately, the ideal conditions that we have just described do not always exist. Sometimes there is little *real* affection in the home, and the child may feel unwanted or rejected. At birth, a mother may assume a rejective attitude toward her child, especially if it is illegitimate, and may refuse to nurse it, name it, or even look at it. The effects of such early maternal rejection upon a child's personality development are said to be significant and far-reaching. Apparently, infants deprived of normal psychological interchange either with their mothers or mother substitutes are seriously retarded physically, mentally, and socially, and have a high mortality rate. The widespread practice in maternity hospitals of separating mothers from their infants (whether legitimate or illegitimate) has been condemned by some writers because of the importance attached to early mother-child relationships. It is advocated, instead, that the baby be kept in the same room with the mother, and when this is done, it is claimed that the infant's breathing, feeding, and elimination are improved. In the George Washington University Hospital, for example, plastic bassinets for the newborn are hooked on the side of the mothers' beds. Double rooms with picture windows are provided, also, so that mothers, by sitting up in bed, may view their infants in the nursery. Other writers believe, however, that there has been a tendency to overemphasize the seriousness of the consequences resulting from this temporary situation. It has also been claimed that there is no scientific basis for the assumption that maternal rejection interferes with an infant's normal development. The father may reject a child if the mother dies at its birth, or if he has reason to doubt its paternity. Sometimes there is rejection by one or both parents because of economic conditions or marital maladjustments, or because the child's care may interfere with social activities.

Parents are not always fully aware of the rejective attitudes that they have toward their children. Giving a girl a boy's name or using a girl's name for a boy is often an instance of disguised rejection. For example, naming a girl Perseus or calling a boy Shirley may be a reflection of parental disappointment in the sex of the child.

Highly imaginative children sometimes develop feelings of rejection when there is no realistic basis for them.

Whether or not extremely early rejection is as serious as some people believe is still to be determined by further research. There is no doubt but that a consistently rejective attitude by parents and others during the developing years has a marked effect upon a child's personality. He may become aggressive and rebellious, and may resort to stealing, lying, and truancy in order to get attention as a substitute for the affection denied him. On the other hand, he may become withdrawn and asocial, refusing to enter into normal activities and to cooperate either with other children or with adults.

As we have mentioned already, the attitudes and standards, particularly those of the mother, who plays the dominant role in family life, have a lasting influence, too, upon the child's developing personality.

Patterns of Family Life

In Vienna an interesting investigation was made of the parent-child relationships in seventeen families, including thirty children. Twelve observers were sent into these family groups to study both the children and the parents. The latter knew that their children were being observed but were unaware of the fact that they, too, were being studied. Each observer took part in the regular family life, eating and playing with the children and helping with the housework. The validity of the findings was based upon the "extent of agreement between the records of different observers."

Each of the families studied emphasized somewhat different sets of values. One was child-centered; in another household interests predominated. A third family stressed "order, mutual assistance, and sociability," whereas education was the center of interest in a fourth group. A fifth family showed affection and sociability; in a sixth, these were absent. Despite these differences in standards, *all* families placed great emphasis upon good school marks and acceptable manners. A summary of the observations showed that home instructions concerning practical behavior were given only about one tenth as frequently as those concerning schoolwork and one twentieth as frequently as those concerning manners. This overemphasizing of school marks and manners is typical, also, of middle-class American families. It constitutes a major source of friction between parents and children and undoubtedly has permanent effects upon the child's attitudes and behavior.

Another writer has pointed out that a child's personality will vary with the mother's attitude toward certain kinds of behavior. With the development of walking and prehension there is an increased desire for manipulation and exploration. This spontaneous activity in the child may be inhibited by some mothers because they fear that he may break something, make a mess, or hurt himself. This is true especially when children are brought up in small apartments, in overcrowded tenements, or where space is limited. In such cases the child may react by being destructive or by doing forbidden things. Some parents are delighted when their children begin to talk, but later may be annoyed by their chatter or boisterousness. Conversely, there are mothers who apparently do not mind noise or dirt but who are greatly upset if the child sucks his thumb or wets his clothes.

In general, children from the lower social classes are less inhibited than are those from the middle classes. Lower-class families are more permissive in their attitudes toward sex (except masturbation), religion, manners, education and school progress, fighting, swearing, and stealing. As a consequence, the child meets fewer frustrating situations, develops a greater sense of freedom and independence, and probably is less tense than the middle-class child.

In a study of 400 twelve-year-old California children divided equally between high and low status levels, distinct differences in social behavior values as well as sex differences were found. In the upper status groups both boys and girls gained prestige by conforming to adult standards. In the lower status groups, however, greater prestige was accorded to those who did not conform to middle- or upper-class standards. In the lower-class group the boy with a reputation for fighting was the one who was popular with the girls. On the other hand, it was the "little gentleman" who had the most prestige with the "little lady" in the upper-class groups. Girls from both upper and lower classes, however, conformed to adult pressures more readily than did boys.

This greater conformity of girls to adult values was evident, also, in an intensive study of thirty early adolescent children of upper-lower and lower-middle social classes in a Midwestern city. What is expected of early adolescent children is determined largely by the mother's standards, which ultimately are derived from her social class background.

Sibling Rivalry

Rivalry among brothers and sisters is found in most families. In our chapter on emotional development we called attention to the fact that the arrival of a new baby may be a cause of jealousy among siblings if the situation is not handled wisely. If the older child feels that he is being displaced in his parents' affections, he may resort to bizarre or regressive behavior in order to gain attention. On the other hand, if the first child is allowed to "boss" the younger ones, or if he gets an undue proportion of new clothes and privileges, he may feel superior and attempt to dominate the entire family. This attitude may persist throughout life and may color all his social relationships. Such behavior has an undesirable effect upon brothers and sisters. They seek to compensate for their sense of inferiority by "ganging up" on the older child, and constant bickering and fighting result. Parents may avoid this sort of thing if they will refrain from giving older children too much authority and responsibility. Family budgets should be planned so that each child will experience the joy of having some new clothes occasionally and no one will always be compelled to wear "hand-me-downs." By not making invidious comparisons about physical appearance, intelligence, school success, etc., and by encouraging children to extend their friendships beyond the family circle, parents can avert many occasions for unpleasantness, and more tolerant attitudes can be developed.

Foreign Homes

Conflicts that arise as the result of being reared in a foreign home are probably less frequent than those brought about by sibling rivalry. When they do occur, however, they may leave an indelible impression upon the personalities of those concerned. The child may be brought up according to "Old World" standards, which are different from those prevailing in American culture, and after he goes to school he may become painfully aware of these differences. Often he feels ashamed of the dress, foreign customs, and broken English prevailing in his home and will not invite children to visit him because he fears their ridicule. He smarts under such names as "Wop," "Dago," or "Hunky," and may become antagonistic and belligerent in order to overcome his feeling of inferiority. He may even resort to joining a delinquent gang to bolster up his ego.

Bilingual freshmen, from a foreign background, attending the American International College were compared with a nonbilingual group on the basis of scores from five types of personality tests. As a whole, the bilinguals held more extreme views on social issues, did not accept members of their own group, felt socially inferior, and experienced more intense family conflicts. It was concluded from this study that, although some of the maladjustments in the bilingual group stemmed from outside social pressures, the major problems arose over the clash between two cultures existing in the same home.

Sectional Differences

Moving from one section of our country to another, which requires adjustment to various regional social codes, is another important factor in personality development. In the South, for example, certain ethical standards and social virtues valued by "quality folks" are stressed, and these may differ markedly from the the values emphasized in the West. In the South, "manners, respect for authority, unselfishness, honor, hospitality, morality, and family background" are supremely important, whereas in the West, beauty, wealth, and education are upheld as standards, and the individual is judged on his own merits without relation to his family tree. Southern families, therefore, who move to the western part of the country may experience difficulty in mingling with and being accepted by those native to

the region. Such problems in cultural assimilation may be particularly difficult for adolescent boys and girls, to whom social acceptance is so vital a
matter.

69. The Self-Image: A Theory of the Dynamics of Behavior * [1]

CAMILLA M. ANDERSON

IT IS increasingly accepted that the final word has not been said in psychiatry in regard either to the dynamics of behavior or to the technique
of achieving therapeutic results in any given case. In an effort to contribute
somewhat to the thinking in psychiatric fields, I wish to present a concept
of the dynamics of behavior that seems to me to be the simplest, the most
comprehensive, as well as the most practical that has been evolved to date.
It is one that experience has shown to be useful to the medical practitioner.

While no attempt has been made either to include or to exclude the ideas
or theories characteristic of any psychiatric frame of reference, the formulation, as might be expected, contains words and ideas that are present in
various schools of thought, outstanding among which are those of Sullivan,
Adler, Freud, and Schilder. It is reasonable to expect that any theory
worthy of being taken seriously will have concepts that are valid and that
will, therefore, be an integral part of any progressively more accurate or
more precise theory.

No attempt will be made to clarify the source or background of the concepts or to give credit to any one who has held the same ideas previously.
However, it is freely acknowledged that there is really nothing new under
the sun. The primary aim here is to present a useful tool for understanding
and for treating individuals—and perhaps cultural groups—rather than to
make acknowledgments or to pay tribute to any authority. As far as I have

* From Camilla M. Anderson, "The Self-Image: A Theory of the Dynamics of
Behavior," *Mental Hygiene* (April, 1952), pp. 227–44. Reprinted by permission of
the author and The National Association of Mental Health.

[1] Sponsored by the Veterans Administration and published with the approval of the
chief medical director. The statements and conclusions published by the author are
the results of her own study and do not necessarily reflect the opinion or policy of
the Veterans Administration.

been able to determine, the concepts as set forth here have not previously been *organized* in this particular manner by psychiatry.

Every one has an image or a concept of himself as a unique person or self, different from every other self. This concept pertains to one's self both as a physical person and as a psychological person—i.e., each one has a physical self-image and a psychological self-image.

Neither of these images is complete and neither is more than roughly accurate. The development of highly reflecting surfaces, of scientific tools for investigation, and of language have made possible increasingly accurate physical self-images, though even these aids do not eliminate obfuscations arising from the attitudes and feelings of significant people. For example, it is not uncommon to find adults who regard themselves as ugly or unattractive or excessively fat or thin or weak because their parents imbued them with these beliefs in regard to themselves while they were young, and no amount of contrary evidence can disabuse them.

The development of techniques for the clarification of psychological self-images is still far from complete, but Freud would seem to stand in approximately the same relationship to the psyche as Vesalius does to the soma.

The self-concept or image is composed of many parts, and each part is conceived of as having both structure and function or as having both anatomy and physiology. Every organ or member that is conceived of as doing a specific job is included in the individual's physical self-image. Organs are also given different values, depending on the conceived functional value of each one. The heart, for example, is ordinarily more highly valued than is the hand.

It is likewise true that every character trait that carries with it the implication of a result to be obtained through its use is a part of the psychological self-image. Every portion of the psychological self-image thus also has both anatomy and physiology, structure and function. As in a physical area, so in the psychological, there is a hierarchy of traits, some having great value in the individual's conceptual thinking and others having less.

Whereas we have been thinking and talking for years in terms of the division of the self-structure into id, ego, superego, and ego ideal, these concepts are, in my opinion, far too broad and general, if not actually erroneous, for application to any specific individual, with any hope of understanding or treating him. We need to think with more precision than these terms imply.

The structure-function concept is, however, as essential in dealing with the psyche as with the soma, since this is the only concept that can lead to logical thinking and prediction. Just as the thinking in somatic medicine has become increasingly precise and refined, so the thinking in psychological medicine needs to move toward more precise definition and understanding of the *detailed* structure of the psyche, together with the function of *each* structure.

The characteristics of the psychic structures are as general and also as specific or individual as are those of the somatic structure. Everything that pertains or relates to "I," "me," "my" conceptual thinking is included here. These structures have to do exclusively with interpersonal relations and effects and are morally oriented—i.e., they are accounted as good or bad. This moral orientation is due to the moral pressures under which the traits were structuralized, wherein "good" or "right" is what significant people demand and 'bad" or "wrong" is what they reject. We might clarify further by saying that whatever made the significant people feel more comfortable is accounted right and whatever made them feel more uncomfortable is accounted wrong.

For every "bad" portion of the self-concept, there are other "good" portions which are emphasized and enhanced: "I may not be pretty, but at least I am honest." To the extent that a baby finds himself inadequate to cope with life or is inacceptable to the people on whom he depends—e.g., is not pretty—he will feel the threat of danger or he must structuralize such traits —e.g., honesty—within himself as will restore the balance toward safety and survival. We thus have character traits actually becoming defense mechanisms in the interest of physical survival.

We are dealing in each individual, therefore, not with the basic self, which is all too often overlooked entirely, but with the conceptual value of the self as determined by the attitudes of significant people toward the child (the parental price tag), and with his efforts to counteract this appraisal, the composite of which is the character structure or psyche with which we deal in psychiatry.

Because this whole process takes place before language and higher thought processes are well established, we have the roots of character structure in the unconscious or the unlabeled. Were children born with language facility and the conceptual thinking that goes along with labeling, the domain of the unconscious would be far smaller than it is. It thus becomes clear why psychotherapy must render the unconscious conscious.

Just as structure and function are a conceptual unit in the soma—e.g., eyes-vision, ears-hearing—so will any structuralized trait in the psyche *and* the response it has characteristically engendered become a conceptual unit or assumption in the psychological image—e.g., obedience-acceptance.

For every trait structuralized, there is an assumed function to be obtained through the use of it, and this function is interpersonal—that is, the function is supplied by another person. The fact of the assumed function of a trait is usually overlooked, but is of vast importance in understanding any person's behavior. Every character trait put into action is designed to bring about some *specific* response (functional result) from some person outside the self. This response may be in fact or in phantasy, as when one feels that one has some person's approval even though that person may be dead.

The function of any trait is not arbitrarily assumed, but is established only after experience has led to the conclusion that it is useful. A certain trait or behavior will have been found to bring a certain result from significant people. Let us say that "I am obedient" has been structuralized because this has brought maximum security and freedom from the threat of annihilation. Henceforth, the structural trait of obedience will have a certain functional value associated with it, depending on early experience, which might be something like this: (1) "People will accept me," (2) "People will not punish me," or (3) "People will give me a certain coveted reward." The specificity of the assumed function is coexistent with the individual's psychic structure.

Those traits which have not had a recognized interpersonal function are not included in the self-image, just as those physical structures which have not had a recognized function are not included in the individual's physical self-image. It is function that determines not only structuralization, but the inclusion or exclusion of the trait in the psychological self-image.

Common traits in the psychic structure are such as, "I am honest," "I am dependable," "I am helpless," "I am acquiescent," "I figure things out for myself," "I keep out of the way," "I make no demands." The structures or traits are unique to the individual because they arise out of his own particular relationships.

The anticipated functional result of any trait may be found in the specific *feelings of entitlement* which are present in each individual. No two people have duplicate traits and entitlements. One may feel entitled to acceptance because he is meek, while another will feel so because he is aggressive. Common examples of these entitlements are entitlement to cooperation, to assistance, to freedom from criticism, to being left alone, to special consideration, or to endless varieties of special privilege or protection.

The feeling of entitlement is seldom recognized by the individual or causes any difficulty unless or until it fails to be gratified. This fact makes many of us believe that we are not neurotic! The bases of the entitlements are often very subtle. Everybody behaves with symbolic patterns, and everybody is supposed to understand the symbolism, is what we, in effect, say throughout our lives.

Whereas the over-all function of the components of the psychological self-image was the maintenance of life through obtaining "love" or the gratified dependency of an otherwise helpless individual, and, therefore, freedom from fear of annihilation (perhaps "anxiety" would be a better term here, because the fear was nonlabeled and, therefore, unconscious), the individual parts come to have specific functions as varied as do those of the physical self. A comparable situation exists in the physical area in which all parts of one's physical self in combination are oriented toward contributing to the maintenance of life, yet the individual component parts have functions that in themselves are over and beyond this goal.

The reason the psychological traits were structuralized was to secure the life of the child during the period of absolute or relative helplessness, when he was dependent on the people of his environment to prevent his annihilation through neglect or rejection. The psychic structure may, therefore, be thought of as a particular combination of behavioral elaborations developed for the purpose of maintaining life—i.e., for their survival value. Without these traits, the child would have been at the mercy of the hostile elements in his specific interpersonal environment, and, therefore, unable to withstand the physical dangers of his situation by reason of his inadequacy. The reason humans have an elaborate character structure is the exceedingly long early period of helplessness as compared with that of all other animals.

The psychological self-image is thus formed early in life as a result of the succession of experiences of the child with significant people in his environment. It is built out of interpersonal experiences *for survival*. It is no wonder that people cling so desperately to the character traits (defense mechanisms) that they have structuralized.

No consideration of the development of character can afford to disregard the basic protoplasm out of which the child is made. There are those who are weak and those who are strong, those who are anatomically and physiologically sound and those who are not, those whose physicochemical make-up is such as to make them "reactors" or "nonreactors." The intellectual equipment is also vastly important, and both the physical and the intellectual factors are important not only in and of themselves, but in relation to the endowments and attitudes of the significant people. The character structure will be determined by the resultant of the interplay between the child, with his physical and intellectual capacities, and the total personalities, physical and psychological, of those people who are significant to the child.

By significant people is meant those persons who are important or who have significance to the child by reason of his sensing their ability to allay insecurity or to intensify it—to increase or to decrease his sense of helplessness, to promote or to diminish his sense of well-being.

The sex of the significant person or persons is important chiefly in so far as identification is affected. If the significant person's values are not in harmony with the cultural norm, there may be confusion later because of the discrepancy between the structuralized traits and the cultural demands. It is not the "strength" or "weakness" of the particular significant person that is so important, or even his sex, but the security-insecurity resultant that evolves. Whereas mother-son, father-daughter attachments may develop into the proverbial Oedipus complex, this is not a normal or an inevitable result, but is engendered out of the neurotic libidinal needs of the parent. This is in accordance with the earlier statement that the child develops those traits which satisfy the needs of his significant people.

Factors that will be reflected in the traits structuralized are the capacity or incapacity of the child to meet specifications, either innately or through the use of effort; the basic acceptance or rejection by the significant people; the self-images of the significant people; whether the significant people are capable of giving love or only of promising it. Neurotic (nonself-accepting) parents bring insatiable pressures to bear on their children, since they are dependent on their children to make up their own deficiencies. Structuralization of traits may take place out of such feelings as love or gratified dependency, out of fear, out of hope, out of a sense of futility, out of simple fear of being overlooked, or out of rebellion.

The most rigid (nonadaptable) structures are built out of the greatest insecurities. Those who have to become something in order to merit acceptance will have to build elaborate structures, and these tend to be more precarious. There is much potential energy stored within these traits; the greater the cost to build and to maintain, the more energy is stored and the greater the danger of breaking. The energy set free if they are disrupted in either structure or function may be compared with the energy set free with the disruption of the atom.

When love or acceptance at any price is sensed to be futile, the child can fall back upon his nuisance value to be sure of not being neglected, and he may incorporate such nuisance traits into his structure. It is commonly regarded as more threatening to be overlooked than to be punished.

If the demands and assumptions of the significant people are in harmony with those of the cultural norm, and within the capacity of the individual to achieve with relative ease, and if the rewards given by these significant people are satisfactory, the individual may be expected to have a relatively stable and contented life experience. We ordinarily speak of such people as normal, but the fact is that they are normal or without symptomatology only because they are suited or adjusted to their specific cultural assumptions. Change any of these, and the "normal" label will no longer apply.

Whatever traits are structuralized, it will be found not only that they are logical—given the particular circumstances—but that to have failed to structuralize these particular traits would have been to court disaster. To the extent that the significant people give satisfactory rewards (sense of security), the child will tend to structuralize acquiescence (identification). If the rewards are not satisfactory or the demands tax his limited capacity, he will tend to structuralize rebellion, or acquiescence with resentment.

In the development of the self-image, the first year of life is the most important, each succeeding year becoming of lesser importance, until the image is essentially completed before adolescence. This is not due to the fact that the earliest period of life is the most plastic or the most impressionable, but rather to the fact that the helplessness and dependency of the child is maximum in the earliest period and, therefore, his necessity is so much greater. The greater the sense of helplessness, the more surely will structuralization take place in order to insure survival. Structuralization may take place in later years, but primarily out of a sense of helplessness. To the extent that a person feels inadequate, he can be taught.

Whereas people outside the family, such as contemporaries or teachers, may become the significant ones, their influence and their impact tend to be less because of the more advanced and, therefore, less helpless age at which they usually enter the picture. The process of structuralization is then less buried in the unconscious and is more amenable to scrutiny by the higher intellectual faculties and easier of modification. The less language and labeling enter the picture, the more difficult of access it is for appraisal or evaluation.

The assumptions and standards of the significant people tend to be accepted without critical judgment (Mother knows best!). If there is any discrepancy between these values and those of the culture in which they live, it will be the standards of the significant people the child will structuralize, provided he derives a sense of security from these significant people. Behavior that is contrary to these patterns will be accounted as morally reprehensible rather than practically unsuitable.

The basis of or the reason for the particular traits in the self-image is almost invariably not registered clearly, since language has been minimally developed. In addition, the significant people who inculcate the patterns have usually received their own standards in the same way in which they are passing them on to their children—i.e., with moral judgment—and to that extent are incapable of transmitting them with anything but feeling. The details both of the structure and of the function of the component parts of the image are the individual's fixed convictions and are removed from the realm of the questionable or the debatable. They are the specific and unique beliefs in regard to one's self and other people that every person lives by. This is equivalent to each person's having his own private religion.

Once the psychological self-image has been formed, behavior loses its free or experimental nature (in search of security) and becomes compulsive, because it has become in effect structuralized. Once having structuralized any specific trait (assumption), each individual proceeds through life behaving according to his structure and expecting the succession of people in his subsequent environment to treat him in the same manner as the original significant people treated or regarded him. This automatic maneuvering of people into reactions and responses toward him that are familiar is the essence of the transference phenomenon of Freud or the parataxic phenomenon of Sullivan. Considering the variety of experiences and situations to which each individual is exposed, it is really remarkable that there are as few changes in the course of the years as there are. A large portion of therapy has to do with discovering and clarifying these maneuverings, since they arise out of assumptions that are not valid.

To alter one's patterns of behavior is to court the anxiety which common idiom has described in the phrase, "As uncomfortable as a fish out of water." One might expect that a person who has structuralized the assumption that he is incompetent would be eager to change. This is not according to fact, for *it is the familiar rather than the hypothetically desirable that is the comfortable role.* Likewise, *everybody behaves symbolically at all times,* and each one succeeds in making whatever he does into a virtue or something that is morally correct, and this effectively precludes change. We see that freedom of choice is largely a myth.

The fact of structuralization and the fact of the need to maintain the structure (one's moral standards) intact, produces the consistency of behavior with which we are familiar in all people. *The pattern of life of every individual is a living out of his self-image;* it is his road map for living. People can be counted on to behave according to their own patterns. This consistency is not voluntary or deliberate, but compulsive, and generally is outside of awareness.

People compulsively (unawaredly) maneuver themselves into situations, behavior, and feelings that are habitual and natural, and thus avoid the anxiety that would otherwise be their lot. It is failure to do this that causes misery. It is well known by therapists that whatever anxiety an individual may be experiencing, it is less than he would experience if he behaved in any other manner. The only way to alter behavior—that is, the symbolic value of it—is to alter the assumptions that lie back of it, since assumptions determine behavior.

The pattern of behavior may be a simple living out of the basic image provided by the attitudes of the significant people (the price tag), and be associated with smug feelings of being actually better than the surface appearances (the need to be "discovered"), or it may be the persistent attempt to deny the validity of this basic image by some form of overcompensation through the defense mechanism of the self-image, but the *need* to deny it is sufficient evidence of the acceptance of its validity. Otherwise the individual would not be concerned with it. Every defense mechanism (sensed virtue) implies an assumed inadequacy or self-devaluation (non-self-acceptance). *Associated with every neurotic trait is a felt need that is insatiable,* for the individual never ceases to try to gratify this need, and the discovery of these insatiable needs is the discovery of the defense mechanisms.

The structure of the self-image (neurotic defense mechanisms) determines the day-by-day and the moment-by-moment behavior. Decisions, choices, activities, and reactions are all determined in such a fashion as will best retain the image intact (satisfy the needs), rather than as reality calls for. This need to maintain the image (the defense structure or moral standards) intact is the true neurosis. We might say that the compulsive need to keep one's skirts clean is the true neurosis.

If "I am compliant" has been structuralized, every detail of every interpersonal relation will be lived in such a way as to enable the individual to continue to regard himself in these terms, and the slightest variation from this pattern will provoke anxiety. If "I am competent" has been structuralized, the individual's life patterns will be such as to harmonize with this image, for he will "need" to keep his defenses intact.

Without significant people, or without their pressures and assumptions and attitudes to cause the self-image to be formed and have content (a hypothetical situation), the growing child and, later, the adult would have nothing to measure up to, to rebel against, or to stop him. He would have no compass and no landmarks to help him chart his course, and life would become chaotic. In the course of therapy, one of the real difficulties of patients is the sense of helplessness they feel in moving into a pattern of life that will be their own or that they choose for themselves, and that does not have as its basis the old compulsive defense mechanisms.

As long as a person can maintain his self-image intact and functioning according to anticipation, he will be free from anxiety. But whenever a person feels that there is a threat to the integrity of the whole or to any portion of his self-structure (physical or psychological), or whenever a part of his structure does not function in the anticipated manner, he will experience psychic pain, which is anxiety. Anxiety, thus, is the feeling produced whenever there is a *sensed* threat to survival, physical or psychological. When the sensed threat is recognized and labeled, we call it fear; when it is not labeled, we call it anxiety.

There is still another source of anxiety, one in which the structure is not broken nor is the function disturbed, but rather there is a sense of being overwhelmed or of being incapable of dealing with the danger with the resources at one's command. The primary feeling here is one of helplessness. This sense of helplessness is at first attached only to the physical resources, but as the psychological self becomes increasingly structuralized, it may be applied to the psyche exclusively.

In the physical area, we are familiar with anxiety produced through threat to the integrity of the structure, as witness the feelings generated by war, accident, mutilations, or diseases such as cancer. Also, anxiety is the usual result when any organ or part of the physical structure does not function in the accustomed or anticipated manner, as in heart irregularities, paralyses, pains, impotence, or other physical symptoms. The physician who deals with organic medical problems deals with these anxieties every day and in the majority of his patients.

This concept of anxiety produced by threat to the integrity of the structure and disturbance in the anticipated function of any part of the structure is as valid for the psychological image as it is for the somatic. It is a concept of the origin of anxiety so simple and so reasonable that it is intelligible to anybody. It is likewise valid as one analyzes individual people, both those with a psychiatric label and those without. The important thing to bear in mind is the uniqueness of individual character structure, and the symbolic nature of each detail of behavior. Two people may be doing what appears to be exactly the same thing, yet the symbolic value of what they are doing may be entirely different in the two people. We cannot take it for granted that anything any one does means any particular thing until we know the individual's own particular symbolic language.

Anxiety is minimal in obsessive-compulsive patients because they have been able up to this point to maintain both their structure and the anticipated function intact. They tend to be oriented toward a fixed, incorporated set of values and are, therefore, less dependent on the external world for gratification. The hysteroid character structures are oriented toward no such fixed values, but more toward immediate, external gratification of their dependency, and are thus more subject to disturbances and to transient anxieties. The development of these particular types of character structure, with the evolution of symptomatology with decompensation of their usual defense mechanisms, will provide material for a subsequent paper.

Analytic psychotherapy itself will inevitably produce anxiety in all patients because the process of treatment must necessarily produce a sense of helplessness, destroy assumptions, and thus produce disruption of both structure and anticipated function in any individual who seriously undertakes treatment.

As frequently happens, structure has been built at vast cost to the individual. He may have done that which almost exceeded his capacity, either because the functional result was satisfactory or because it seemed as if it would be satisfactory if only he exerted himself a little more. Any discrepancy between the energy required to build and maintain the structure, and the product or functional result that it delivers, will be interpreted as psychic pain.

A child who has obtained deep satisfaction out of acting like a burden-bearing adult—being "mother's big girl"—may eventually find such rewards increasingly unsatisfactory, but being structuralized as a person who undertakes much, she will find herself in a dilemma: if she continues according to her structure, she gets anxiety from disturbed function, and if she ceases living out her pattern and takes it easy or is obviously self-seeking, she gets anxiety from broken structure.

This inability to move in either direction—toward living out one's image or departing from it—is the essence of conflict. With conflict we have a sense of helplessness, and helplessness is the mother of anxiety.

It is as important to every individual that he maintain his psychological self-image intact as it is that he maintain his physical self-image intact. Every one is familiar with the concept that maintaining one's honor is more important than maintaining one's life or physical integrity. The problem as to which self should be sacrificed—the physical or the psychological—is ever present among G.I.'s. It is worthy of note that no one but the person himself can destroy the psychological self-structure, so in psychological medicine we deal not with psychological homicide, but with psychological suicide. No person's standards can be destroyed without his sanction.

In the beginning of life we have character structure developing in order to insure physical survival. Then, as the character traits become "set," these defense mechanisms in and of themselves take over dominance, so that maintenance of the psyche becomes the dissociated goal. The anxiety experienced when the psyche is endangered in any way is felt as comparable to the anxiety produced by threat of physical disintegration or nonsurvival, like the terror of a child on being lost or left alone.

Whenever the *structure* of the psychological self-image is broken or threatened, the anxiety felt is known as guilt. Since the structure is composed of the many traits demanded by the significant people, there is attached a value to each one which is that of "good" or "right." The nature of the trait is of little consequence, but only the acceptability of the trait to the significant people. It may be inadequacy, dependency, sexual infantilism, or some hostility that is structuralized (and these traits are, indeed, often structuralized), but it took place out of necessity (having these traits made the significant person feel more comfortable), and the trait is highly regarded morally. To break one's structure, therefore, implies breaking one's moral code, and the result will be a feeling of guilt.

To the extent that changes can be made in behavior with little or no difficulty or guilt, we are dealing either with superficial changes and no change in the symbolic value, or with traits that are not a part of the defense structure and are merely habits, with no moral implications attached to them. These have often been the traits that did not come under the moral judgment of the significant people during the growth process. It was not necessary to structuralize them in order to insure survival.

Whenever the anticipated *function* of the psychological self-image is disturbed, the anxiety feeling aroused thereby is felt as frustrated entitlement or outraged virtue. Since the use of any character trait implies some conceived virtue in action, it is clear that if it does not bring about the anticipated response from the other person or get the "correct" functional results, the disturbed feeling that is generated in the individual will be that he is the innocent victim of a malignant assault. Since no two people necessarily have the same assumptions, it is easy to see why there is so much outraged virtue in any interpersonal relation. Perhaps more occurs in marriage than in any other relation.

If one has structuralized "I do right by others" and the assumed function is "Others will do right by me," and if the actual functional result in a given circumstance is that the other person fails to give the anticipated response, and, instead, takes one for a sucker, the anxiety produced is felt as outraged virtue. To some extent such disturbed functioning is equated with a psychologic homicidal attack.

This whole area is commonly very difficult both to spot and to grasp because the very culture in which we live has structuralized the assumption that virtues merit rewards. Our culture is, in effect, in a childhood state wherein cause-and-effect relationships are scarcely grasped, but life is lived on the basis of moral judgments wherein "being a good boy" results in an extra piece of pie. The whole fabric of our culture is morally, rather than practically, oriented. Many people behave with the utmost practicality, but they have confused morality with practicality and so proceed on their way with unrealistic and unnecessary feelings of virtue. This whole cultural coloring with moral assumptions explains why few people can successfully practice psychotherapy, for to the extent that the moral judgment cannot be relinquished, one cannot be objective.

Whenever one becomes aware that such feelings as guilt or resentment or outraged virtue or helplessness are present, one may be led directly to important information about the self-image, and, therefore, to the defense mechanisms and the true neurosis that one harbors. The assumptions thereby uncovered are actually portions of the self-image. The entitlements will disclose both the structure and the implicit function of the image. These strong feelings are evidences of minute decompensations. The discovery of the "needs" will show how the individual attempts to maintain himself so as to be in no danger of decompensation.

Whenever anxiety has been aroused, it may be experienced as pure anxiety, varying in degree from mild discomfort to stark terror. But generally one of, or a combination of, three reactions occurs: (1) there may be reaction against or attack upon the anxiety-provoking situation or agent, with some degree of rage or resentment (hyperkinetic activity); (2) there may be withdrawal from the anxiety-provoking situation or paralysis of attack responses (hypokinetic activity); (3) there may be a conversion of the forces for attack into some type of physical symptom. In fact, physical symptomatology may represent merely a partial rather than a total response. Muscles and glands may be expressing the over-all psychic response with hyperkinetic or hypokinetic activity. . . .

To conclude, the concept of the dynamics of behavior presented here, as it works practically, has several advantages over current theories: The concepts and the terminology are simple. It unites the psyche and the soma in a common language and conceptual thinking, so that it is teachable and meaningful to medical students, to physicians, to beginners in psychotherapy, as well as to thoughtful people in unrelated fields. It makes survival basic, rather than sex, and in this respect adheres to established concepts. It is applicable to all people—those regarded as normal as well as those who are labeled with a psychiatric diagnosis. Its applicability is not local or restricted to any one particular culture, but is general and timeless. It clarifies the common meeting ground of Psychiatry and Religion. It is practical as a map or chart in the conduct of psychotherapy, and seems to be a definite factor in cutting down the time required for successful therapeutic results.

I suspect also that the theory is applicable on a wider scale than the individual, and may apply to groups within a culture and to international relations, an area in which current theories of behavior have been sorely lacking.

70. The Adolescent Personality *

LESTER D. CROW
AND ALICE CROW

THE TERM *adolescent personality* probably is a misnomer in that it seems to imply that all teen-agers display similar personality traits, or that any one adolescent's personality pattern remains relatively consistent during his growing-up years. Nothing could be further from the truth. To the adult who regards himself as the victim of inconsistent adolescent vagaries, sensitivities, rebellions, and intolerances, the more correct term would be *adolescent personalities,* with emphasis upon the chameleonlike changes in behavior and attitude that may seem to occur almost momentarily.

Although an adolescent's reactions often are unpredictable, this apparent inconsistency is evidence of the dynamic behavior motivators that are rooted in the physical, mental, and emotional phases of the growing-up process. Interpreted in terms of the meaning and purpose of adolescence, we can describe adolescent personality as a syndrome that represents the symptomatic aggregate, not of a physical disease but rather of a mental and emotional struggle for the achievement of adult maturity.

Adolescent personality development. Personality development during adolescence can be expected to continue in the form that it has been fol-

* From Lester D. Crow and Alice Crow, *Adolescent Development and Adjustment,* pp. 169–74. Copyright 1956 by McGraw-Hill Book Co., Inc., New York, and reprinted with their permission.

lowing during the childhood years, but will be conditioned by more and more of the social influences that help the individual attain status in his peer group. Although individual differences appear at birth, they are not always recognized as such. The process of personality development begins with what the individual possesses in the way of heritage and continues to develop, even though the process is much more irregular and complex than is the development of specific skills and habits.

Self-awareness, self-realization, and self-assertion develop gradually. From a relatively vague recognition of an urge to fulfill certain physical needs, the child gradually comes to achieve understanding of the objects and persons in his environment that are associated with his developing feelings of comfort and discomfort. He enlarges his needs to include satisfying relationships with many environmental factors and to discover that he is a recipient of adult-dispensed attention. Thus he develops an awareness of self, and becomes self-assertive within the confines of his relatively narrow social environment.

Throughout adolescence the developing individual becomes increasingly cognizant of the impact upon himself and his expanding needs and urges of the customs and mores of his culture, its rules and regulations, and the accepted patterns of behavior that are peculiar to the group of which he is a member. He is confronted with the necessity of evaluating his behavior in terms of the social standards and ideals of his group. His personality is undergoing vital changes during this period. The success of his activities depends upon his ability so to adjust himself and his urges and interests to group demands that he can become an active, accepted member of the group.

Fundamentally, the personality traits displayed during childhood do not change suddenly with the onset of puberty. The alert, cheerful, and cooperative ten-year-old can be expected to give evidence of similar behavior characteristics when he is 15 years old. The adolescent who, as a child had learned to get what he wanted by "throwing a temper tantrum," probably will continue to employ tantrum behavior when or if his strong desires are thwarted. An individual's general pattern of personality organization is relatively consistent throughout the growing years. Yet personality differences appear to become more marked with the changing awareness of self that accompanies pubescent physical changes, combined with a growing recognition of the significance of cultural values.

Some general characteristics of adolescent personality. Although certain needs, wants, urges, and interests are common to the majority of adolescents, it should be emphasized that the overt expression of these behavior motivators differ from one young person to another. These differences are the resultants of societal or cultural influences upon developing personality patterns. Adolescents tend to be exceedingly active in their attempts to satisfy their wants and needs according to the standards of their group. In the words of Landis, "The adolescent-youth group wants what all people in our culture want: (1) recognition and status, (2) respect and social favor, (3) response and happy social interaction, (4) security and group acceptance, (5) experience and expression, (6) achievement and success, (7) happiness and freedom." [1]

As has been noted earlier, the expression of deeply rooted personality traits varies with environmental atmosphere. From childhood onward an individual's personality is shaped by culture-dominated influences. Probably at no other period in his life is he so susceptible to societal pressures as during the teen years. Again quoting from Landis, "In our own culture some of the major compulsives which explain the direction personality formation and individual wants take are (1) the competition-success pattern; (2) the desire for bigness, strength, growth, greatness; (3) individual freedom and personal expression; (4) the notion of progress, reform, improvement, and change; (5) epicureanism, the desire for pleasure, sensual enjoyment." [2]

Anyone who is closely associated with adolescents can recognize the extent to which all or most of these compulsions function to influence personality traits of youth. The expression of a culturally directed want varies with individual personality patterning and differing value emphases. We shall comment briefly concerning the effect upon adolescent personality development of each of the listed compulsions.

The competition-success pattern. Most adolescents display a spirit of competitiveness but the area of competition is not the same for all. Some high school and college teachers display an attitude of believing that their students' major want should be competition for success in scholastic attainment. Although some young people meet their teachers' expectations in this regard, many adolescents are more concerned about striving for superior status in their peer group, especially with members of the opposite sex.

The desire for bigness, strength, growth, and greatness. Competition is implicit, for example, in an adolescent boy's desire to excel in school sports. Thereby he can demonstrate his superior strength and power. The

[1] By permission from P. H. Landis, *Adolescence and Youth* (2nd ed.; New York: McGraw-Hill Book Co., Inc., copyright 1952), p. 79.
[2] *Ibid.*

physically small, undeveloped lad who is denied the opportunity to compete in athletic activities with bigger, stronger boys, directs his efforts toward the achievement of greatness in other areas. He consciously may imitate the dress, manners, and other supposed personality characteristics of a small but admired friend or acquaintance, or of a small man who has achieved current or historic fame.

Individual freedom and personal expression. One of the strongest of an adolescent's behavior drives is the urge for freedom of decision, action, and self-expression. The manner in which he displays this felt need depends partly upon his previous experiences and present adult example. An adolescent who as a child had developed attitudes of cooperation and of submission to adult authority may be so conditioned by his own temperament and his earlier training and experiences that he finds it difficult to give overt expression of his need for independence. Outwardly he may appear to be the same submissive, cooperative individual that he had been during his earlier years; inwardly, however, he gives vent to feelings of deep resentment and frustration, thereby undermining his mental health and discouraging the development of a constructive, outgoing personality.

The effect upon an independence-seeking adolescent of contacts with differing cultural standards is well illustrated by the experiences of the teen-age children of foreign-born parents. During their childhood these young people usually develop personality patterns of the family's close-knit subcultural neighborhood group. As secondary-school students, however, they are exposed to the more permissive, self-determining influences of American democratic standards of behavior.

The struggles that the young person experiences as he attempts either to achieve a compromise between differing cultural mores, or to disavow the old for the new, may induce the development of aggressive and defiant attitudes, especially toward his parents and their ideals. Further, he may fight for a place in his chosen cultural group without a realistic understanding of the group's standards. Hence he may engage in what he considers to be acceptable behavior but discovers that he is earning the strong disapproval of his new associates, rather than the acceptance which he had sought. Consequently, he becomes an insecure, confused young person who may be driven to satisfy through asocial acts his natural urge for freedom and self-expression.

Equally serious is the situation of a teen-age boy or girl who in the family circle has been and continues to be granted extreme freedom of behavior. If he has been encouraged by his parents and other relatives to develop a self-regarding personality to the extent that he is concerned almost entirely with the satisfaction of his own wants and urges, he is likely to suffer many deflating experiences when he attempts to dominate or defy the wishes of his own-age associates.

The notion of progress, reform, improvement, and change. At one and the same time an adolescent may be a self-centered realist and a selfless idealist. A growing boy or girl may become very much concerned about human welfare. His sympathies go to geographically near or more distant groups that are regarded by him to be oppressed, to suffer economic lack, to deviate from acceptable behavior standards, or to give evidence of any form of underprivileged status. The idealistic boy or girl is motivated to change "this sorry scheme of things."

The direction of his emotionally stimulated urge to serve humanity depends upon the strength of environmental influences. Hence an adolescent variously wants to become a social worker, a physician, a missionary, a great statesman, a chaplain in a penitentiary, a philanthropist, a labor leader, or an adolescent-understanding teacher. Yet an adolescent who is filled with ardor to save or help the world may disregard almost completely the many opportunities for service that he could find in his immediate environment.

For example, the adolescent grumbles when he is asked to perform a family chore; he teases siblings or neighborhood children and torments cats or dogs; he selects the most comfortable chair in a room; he pushes his way into a crowded streetcar or dives for a seat in which he sprawls himself so that other passengers fall over his feet, to his vocalized annoyance; he plays tricks on his teacher and then resents deserved reproof. These are a few of the many evidences of adolescent thoughtlessness that unfortunately are condoned by some adults who, at the same time, may express amusement or ridicule of adolescent idealism. There are young people, however, who combine their idealistic dreams of service with realistic appreciation of the many ways in which they can and do help the members of their home, school, and community groups. These adolescents gradually are developing personality traits that impel them as adults to become our humanitarians or our social and civic leaders.

The desire for pleasure and sensual enjoyment. An individual of any age needs "time out for play," and opportunities to satisfy his desire to gain emotional satisfaction from the contemplation of natural and man-created beauty or to desire pleasure from participation in relaxing activities. The adolescent is sensitive to the elements in his environment that stir him emotionally. He wants to satisfy his craving for that which he believes will release him temporarily from the pressures of work or study responsibilities, or that will free him from environmental restraints or personal adolescent worries.

The environmental influences by which the adolescent's interests and activities are motivated, and his own developing tastes and appreciations, condition him to derive pleasure from one or another form of emotionally satisfying activity. He may spend many hours in an art gallery; he may carry around with him and, at convenient times, lose himself in the writings of his favorite poet; he enjoys singing, dancing, and listening to music that stirs him emotionally. Usually an adolescent's preferred form of leisure-time activity reflects his general temperament. However, his degree of physical energy, his intellectual level, his emotion-stimulating needs, and the kinds of pleasurable activities in which he engages are representative of the interests of his cultural group.

One cannot fail to recognize the potent, sometimes subtle, influence upon adolescent personality of the interaction that constantly is taking place between individual desires and cultural factors. During the growing-up years the relative significance of inner motivation and of outer stimulation varies from person to person. It is impossible to predict with certainty that one type of cultural influence pattern provides the most favorable environment for personality development. Moreover, youthful potentialities and drive may differ so greatly among individuals who are reared in the same cultural environment that evolving personalities vary considerably.

Effect of adolescent goal-seeking. Changing adolescent interests and attitudes can be regarded as both the causes and results of personality changes that occur during the teen-age years. Basically, these personality changes are effected as innate needs, wants, and urges find expression in developing interests and attitudes. The kind and strength of an adolescent's interest is dependent upon the nature of the goal toward which he is striving. The degree of successful goal achievement that the young person experiences exercises a powerful influence upon his attitudes and consequently upon the evolving pattern of his personality. The seven adolescent wants, as listed by Landis,[3] represent the major areas of goal-striving that, in varying degrees of potency, influence the thoughts and acts of all or most young people.

Vocational ambition is a specific adolescent goal that is included in Landis' list only by implication. Most children tend to think and talk about what they are going to do when they grow up. Childhood vocational ambitions usually are fleeting, temporary interests, however, and are motivated by changing personal wants or by admired adult example.

[3] *Ibid.*

The child's vocational ambitions usually are unrealistic in that they reflect a desire to possess something in which he is interested at the moment, or to be like someone who seems to him to be very important. At various times a boy may decide to become a candy store owner, a fireman, a policeman, a rich businessman, a veterinarian, or a famous public figure. He may want to follow his father's vocational activities. A seven-year-old youngster, for example, insisted that he is going to drive a bus when he is a man; his father deals in the buying and selling of buses. When the child was asked if he were going to sell his father's buses, he was vehement in his assertion that he would keep all of them because he wants to have more buses than anyone else in the world.

Little girls dream about their future. A young "mother" of many dolls is going to have a lot of babies; especially is this the ambition of an only child or one who has only one brother or sister. Variously, girls also may want to be a teacher, a nurse, a motion-picture star, a singer, an airplane hostess; girls tend to be interested in vocations that represent service or glamour.

A childhood vocational interest may become so much a part of a youngster's developing personality that it persists and reaches adult fulfillment. Usually children's attitudes toward adult vocational choice are ephemeral and change with experience. Adolescent interests in this area of goal-striving are likely to be more meaningful; they reflect to a greater degree the direction being taken by certain aspects of the developing personality. Yet changing ambitions are characteristic of the adolescent years as well as during childhood.

71. *Boys Who Run Away from Home* *

WILLIAM W. WATTENBERG

TRUANCY from school is known to vary in its significance as a symptom. On the one hand we have the "circus" truancies and "swimming hole" truancies, which appear to represent an effort by relatively "normal" boys to add a bit of variety to the drab routine of day-to-day existence. On the

* From William W. Wattenberg, "Boys Who Run Away from Home," *The Journal of Educational Psychology* (October, 1956), pp. 335–42. Reprinted by permission of the author and the publisher.

other hand, we have the escape from school of the youngster whose pressing emotional problems will later find outlet in serious delinquency.

Truancy from home includes during the regular school year truancy from school as well. On the surface at least it would appear to be even more significant. To the extent that it represents escape from unsatisfactory living it would appear to mean that the youngster's life is irksome in all areas, not merely in the classroom. It also represents a very drastic break with what should be the young person's chief sources of security—his family. The runaway cuts himself off from a sure supply of food and shelter. In exchange for what?

It is no wonder, then, that to answer so puzzling a question we find much speculation and some research. The theories range from those looking at inward drives to those stressing multiple causation of environmental forces.

One interesting explanation, reminiscent of G. Stanley Hall, was put forward by Staub on the basis of a psychoanalysis. He felt that running away harks back to the childhood of mankind when humanity was in a migratory stage.

Taking a rather different tack, Jahr saw in running away an attempt by young folks to express themselves in an environment over which they had little control. When present surroundings appear burdensome, distant places might seem to offer an opportunity to exercise curiosity, imagination, and love for romance or adventure.

Most of the serious fact-gathering took place in relation to the appearance of large groups of wandering youth during the great depression of the 1930's. Lovejoy attributed the runaways of that era to the breakdown of relief services and to local failures to provide vital schooling or adequate recreation. Nylander felt that the trouble was due to failure in school, family disorganization, and the breakdown of religious institutions and moral codes. Adding to these lists, Sullenger declared that children leave home because of emotional crises, school problems, too complex a social life, and failure to achieve satisfying social relationships.

On the basis of a study of 3,350 runaway boys who registered with the Los Angeles Office of the Federal Transient Service in 1934 and 1935, Outland tended to exonerate the schools. He declared that basic economic and social conditions were much more important than educational factors for boys going on the road. Almost half the group had been out of school more than two years before leaving home.

In many ways the most careful studies were the series reported by Armstrong on 660 boys arraigned in the Children's Court of New York City.

Since her group had run away between 1926 and 1930, the influence of economic forces was not as strong as in Outland's. She found that escape from current pressures was the basic motive in most cases. As compared with boys involved in theft or charged with incorrigibility, the runaways were younger and had higher IQ's. The runaways came largely from homes of low economic level, where the mother was working. More than half came from disrupted families. The group seemed to be high in its proportion of only children. There was also a marked tendency for oldest children to be runaways. Seventy per cent of the group said they left because of trouble at home; 37 per cent mentioned trouble at school. Armstrong regarded running away as a psychoneurotic reaction in which irresponsible or unfit parenthood was the basic cause and the precipitating events might arise from either school or family factors.

Procedure

The present study is based on records of 575 cases of runaway boys dealt with by the Crime Prevention Bureau of the Detroit Police Department.[1] Whenever a boy was reported missing, a trained police officer visited his home to gather information, which included his parents' ideas as to why he had run away. When the boy was found or after he had returned home, he was interviewed as to his reasons for leaving home. As a final measure, the boy was again interviewed in a family conference setting. This not only served to produce better family planning for the future, but the interplay of explanations added to the officer's understanding of the forces leading to the truancy. All the data thus gathered were recorded on a thirty-item checklist.

It should be pointed out that the population studied was quite different from those used in the studies previously reported. In contrast to the Outland population, this Detroit group was investigated during a period of relative prosperity and high productivity. In contrast to Armstrong's cases, few of the Detroit group were delinquent in the official sense. These were not court cases but rather a group reported as "missing." In the vast majority of instances, no official charge was made. The parents were happy to have their sons back, the boys were relieved to be home again, and no official action was taken against anyone.

[1] Acknowledgment is due a large number of individuals who aided in this study. The procedures were inaugurated by Inspector Sanford Shoults, the inquiry form was developed by Inspector Ralph Baker, the statistical work was performed by Lieutenant Francis Davey and the data were gathered by the patrolmen assigned to the Bureau.

Findings

The peak chronological age of the runaway boys was 15. Of the 575, the fifteen-year-olds accounted for 169. The age distribution of the entire group is set forth in Table 1. It would appear that truanting from home is an adolescent rather than a preadolescent phenomenon.

Table 1

AGE OF RUNAWAY BOYS

Age	Number
10	24
11	29
12	49
13	82
14	109
15	169
16	110
17	3

The matter of broken homes was checked by two different techniques. One was to inquire regarding with whom the boy was living; the other to record the marital status of the parents. Of the 575 boys, 330 were recorded as living with both parents. In eighty-three cases, there was a step-parent in the home; nineteen boys had run away from institutions, boarding homes, or foster parents. In the remaining cases, the boys came from households where there was only one parent present, or where there were relatives. The detailed story is given in Table 2.

The reports as to the marital status of parents presented a substantially similar picture, although there were discrepancies due to the ways in which the questions were interpreted. The main point is that slightly more than 300 of the homes were recorded as intact; approximately 250 had been broken in one way or another. The details are presented in Table 3.

An effort was made to check Armstrong's findings relative to sibling relationships. Only children accounted for forty-four of the cases. Census figures indicated that approximately 10 per cent of Detroit children had no siblings. On this score Armstrong's findings were contradicted by the Detroit group. Of those with siblings, 175 were the oldest; 132, the youngest; and 224 occupied middle positions. The slight preponderance of first-born as compared to last-born would bear out that portion of her conclusions. Sex of siblings was not a significant factor: 386 boys came from homes

Table 2

WITH WHOM BOY WAS LIVING WHEN HE RAN AWAY

Living with:	Number
Both parents	330
Mother	83
Father	24
Father and stepmother	42
Mother and stepfather	41
Grandparents	12
Uncle and aunt	6
Brother	4
Sister	2
Cousin	3
Rooming-house owner	1
Foster parents	4
Boarding home couple	11
Institutions	3

where there were one or more brothers; 380, where there were one or more sisters. Where parents had remarried, there was a slight tendency for running away to be linked to the presence of stepsisters: forty-three boys came from such homes, as compared with thirty-six from homes where there were stepbrothers.

Table 3

MARITAL STATUS OF PARENTS

Status	Number
Real parents living together	310
Common-law relationship	2
Mother remarried	71
Father remarried	64
Parents separated	70
Father dead	30
Mother dead	14
Not stated	14

The matter of deciding the reason for the running away was not easy. In most cases, as the evidence unfolded it became apparent that there was an interaction of several factors. However, an effort was made to determine the chief or precipitating cause for the incident itself. On this basis, it was the judgment of the investigating officer that search for adventure was immediately responsible for 124 of the truancies. Rebellion against parents figured as the main cause for 115 boys. Escape from school conditions led to eighty-seven incidents; and fear of punishment for some misdeed appeared in seventy-six cases. The truancy was part of an attempt to evade the police in thirty-two cases. The remaining boys gave a wide range of reasons.

School conditions did not appear as either a major or a contributing factor in 250 cases. Where school was involved at all, the trouble was likely to be attributed to poor marks; these were mentioned by 181 of the boys. Twenty-five boys complained that they were unable to keep up with the class; twenty-eight felt teachers were persecuting them; and eight left home to escape an examination. Seven boys felt they were objects of ridicule by classmates; seven were swamped by being in too large classes.

As to home conditions, these were found not to blame in 257 cases. Where they were mentioned, there was a wide range, as indicated in Table 4. Linked to most such conditions was rebellion against severe treatment or, by contrast, distaste for laxity.

As previously mentioned, the search for adventure figured as a main reason in 124 cases. It was mentioned one way or another in 267 interviews. In 120 cases, travel was described as being alluring in its own right; in 100 cases the adventurous element was too vague to pin down more definitely. For sixteen boys, an exciting job was the goal. Fourteen ran away to go camping; eleven, to go fishing; three, to go hunting; and three, to join the armed services.

In a number of cases, the abrupt departure from home was motivated by the need to escape the aftermaths of some other delinquency. In twenty-three cases, this was an auto theft; in eighteen cases, a larceny; in seventeen cases, a burglary; in the remaining twenty-six instances, a miscellaneous collection of misdeeds.

Not too easy to classify were the other reasons brought out in the interview and conferences. A few of these merit mention. For seventy-two of the boys, the running away was an effort to spite someone; indeed, a number were found hiding where they could witness and revel in the anxiety created by their absence. In sixty-four cases, part of the picture was desire by the boy to keep the good opinion of a companion who had his own reasons for taking to the road. For forty-eight boys, the destination was the home of some relative whom they felt would treat them better than their parents. Employment was the goal of forty-three. Another thirty-seven were influenced by a bad gang. For twenty-seven boys, the running away was intended to provide proof of self-sufficiency.

At the time of the initial contact, when the boy was missing, the officers rated the attitudes of the parents. With few exceptions, these were cooperative. Of the entire group, only nineteen parents could be described as indifferent; four were secretive; one, arrogant; and one, antagonistic.

Table 4

HOME CONDITIONS MENTIONED AS CAUSES FOR RUNNING AWAY

Condition	Number
Broken home	42
Parents too lax	42
Parents too strict	27
Nagging by members of family	27
Home too crowded	26
Blocking of boy's plans and desires	16
Ridicule by members of family	15
Neglect by parents	12
Home too dirty	12
Siblings pick on boy	12
Parents too bossy	10
Parents pick on boy	9
Stepmother picks on boy	9
Stepfather picks on boy	8
Parents too old-fashioned	8
Mistreatment due to drunkenness	9
Parents baby boy too much	6
Too many chores	5
Parents refused spending money	5
Friends not permitted in home	5
Boy not allowed to drive car	4
Jealousy of other family members	5
Immorality in home	2
Boy not allowed to have pet	1

After the boy was recovered, rather few parents changed their tunes. The police officers described 237 as forgiving; 116, understanding; seventy-three, as seeking assistance in doing better with their sons; and forty-eight, as intent on showing affection. On the less favorable side, forty-three turned punitive; eighteen became openly rejecting; eighteen were over-protective; and three refused assistance.

The boys showed an equal range of reactions upon their return: 278 were repentant; 163, indifferent; forty-five, sullen; twenty-seven, defiant; twelve, fearful; and twelve, boastful. The remaining thirty-eight were harder to describe in a single adjective.

Discussion

It must be stressed that the 575 boys under study probably represent a fair sample of all boys who run away from home. They became known to the police not because of complaints, but because their parents were worried and wanted them back. Few were delinquent in the official or legal sense of that term. For most, no complaint was filed. Rather, the incident led to a rallying of family forces which seemed to portend a happy outcome. In such cases the experience of the Youth Bureau has been that less than 20 per cent ever came again to the attention of police authorities.

A very striking fact is the large proportion of the group for whom the main motivation would seem to be a search for adventure, an effort to exercise independence. For this portion of the sample, the truancy seems to have had a positive significance. It appears as an index of striving, perhaps ineptly, for a more adult status.

More concern must be given to those instances where poor home or school conditions had reached the point where the youngster found the situation intolerable, and his personality organization was such that he fled from it. Here, one can well wonder how much other damage accompanied the development of the forces leading to the running away, and to what extent the boys' personality structure would lead to even graver incidents.

The prognosis for these boys seems linked to the reaction of their parents. Granted that the effects of home changes will have limited influence on an adolescent close to adulthood, yet one gets the impression that most of the fathers and mothers conducted themselves in a way to give hope that in most instances they would be as helpful to their sons as possible.

It would be interesting to have as full a report on the way school people reacted to these same boys upon their return to school. Did they also take a forgiving attitude? Did they see the truancy as a sign they had a job to do? At this point the police records are silent.

Summary

An investigation was made of 575 boys reported missing from their homes. There seemed to have been an interplay of several home and school factors leading up to the truancies. Outstanding was the frequency with which search for adventure was a key factor. In most instances the aftermath found parents trying to better their relationships with their sons.

72. Toward a Concept of Personality Integration * [1]

JULIUS SEEMAN

THIS PAPER concerns the subject of personality integration. It is chiefly an essay in conceptualization rather than a report on research. The purpose here is to see whether some useful structure can be imposed upon the process of personality integration, so that we can understand the phenomenon more fully and study it more meaningfully.

But first, a word about the area itself. We may ask why it is that, in spite of high interest in this area of psychology, so little research has thus far been fostered. The reason is simple. Many people have said that we should concentrate on psychopathology less and on normality more. Our theories of psychopathology may not be very good, but at least they are there. How about a theory of normality? This is a fine, upright thought and quite irrelevant to the central issue. For we are confronted, not with a problem of morality, but with a fact of history. What, after all, creates a scientific theory? Several things, but first we must observe something that makes us ask questions. We must have a laboratory, either conceived by nature or contrived by man, in which to study events. The laboratory of the clinician historically has been the hospital or clinic. There he has observed personality in conflict. That is what he observed, and that is what his theories were about. This is the natural course of scientific development.

But we have not had an equally visible laboratory where we can study persons of high adjustment and optimal integration. This is not a basis for organizing groups in our society. People do not gather in groups just because they are well adjusted. And so inevitably we have had little observation, little research, and little theory about the highly effective person.

The issue seems clear. If we wish to study personality integration, we must seek out its natural habitat or create the laboratories in which the process may be studied. I do not mean to suggest that the problem is only one of providing physical space. In point of fact we may assume that processes of personality integration exist somewhere today in most groups

* From Julius Seeman, "Toward a Concept of Personality Integration," *The American Psychologist* (October, 1959), pp. 633–37. Reprinted by permission of the author and the American Psychological Association.
[1] Presidential Address delivered at the Annual Convention of the Tennessee Psychological Association, November, 1958.

of our society. Our laboratory will need to be not only a physical one, but a conceptual one. We shall have to sort out in our own minds what it is we wish to study. When we have done that, the groups will be there.

What do we wish to study? How can we conceptualize personality integration in a way which will permit us to understand it better? Let me say first how I shall not conceptualize the problem. The term "mental health" is in some ways a useful one. It contains a big idea in two words. It has also been a basis on which many of our colleagues have organized their careers. But the term does not help very much at a conceptual level. For one thing, it places the focus on an often irrelevant dimension of illness and health when that is not what we are talking about at all. For another, it is so far removed from behavioral reference points that it has limited utility for psychological description. And so this paper will employ terms more immediately derived from the language of psychology.

As I think about the phenomenon of effective behavior, I find it useful to use an organizing concept which, for want of a better name, I shall call organismic integration. This term may not find wide acceptance. It will be much too muddy for many behaviorists and not dynamic enough for many clinicians. But the term does two things which I consider useful. First, the term *organismic* suggests that we are talking about an inclusive phenomenon. Second, the term *integration* is intended to suggest some form of interaction which takes place among subsystems of the organism—more specifically, an interaction which is adaptive or self-enhancing.

We are now at a crucial point in understanding this conceptual model. I am saying that personality integration is a many-vectored thing, that it is defined by events which go on within a variety of specific behavioral planes within the organism. Our next step then is to arrive at some logical method of identifying and grouping these specific behavioral systems so that we can study them in some organized way. Here I find it convenient to group these systems on a continuum ranging from microcosmic to macrocosmic, or from molecular to molar, or even from the inside of the organism out. Whichever of the terms we use, we shall come out at about the same place.

Starting at the molecular level, we may some day find it useful to begin our description of the person from the world of physics and study the relation of atomic structure to personality integration. But we are not quite ready for that yet. At present we shall have to begin our molecular-level study with the biochemistry of personality integration. From there we move to the somewhat grosser plane of physiological observation and then on to perception, affective behavior, and cognitive processes. Moving further now into the large units of observation, we shall wish to utilize the sociopsychological level of description and, finally, the sociocultural plane of description. These perspectives of observation, taken together, round out our conceptual model.

We may next illustrate the ways in which these descriptive categories enhance the understanding of personality integration. You will understand that these illustrations will be most fragmentary in comparison with the total task of analysis that will some day have to be done.

A recent study done by a former student at Peabody illustrates a possible area of exploration in physiological behavior. Starkman (1958), in reviewing the literature of the EEG, was impressed with the possibility that alpha waves might be construed as an index of stability. Increased activity or interruption of the resting state usually leads to decreased alpha. Starkman hypothesized that, within a normal group, those individuals with the greatest incidence of alpha would show the greatest physiological stability, the least reactivity in a stress situation. He used the galvanic skin response as his index of physiological reactivity. In the experimental stress condition the experimenter produced a noise by dropping a wood block on the floor. The subjects then reacted according to their natures. Starkman found the predicted relationship: that is, the persons who showed a high incidence of alpha on the EEG (in his terms, stability) also showed less reactivity on the GSR during the stimulation period. The relationship was a relatively strong one, with a well-defined though nonlinear covariation slope.

This is an intriguing result. It lends support to a concept of stability which goes beyond pathology: no pathology. Further, it has not only physiological properties but other properties besides. For the physiologically lawful behavior took place in what was after all an interpersonal situation. This kind of study illustrates very well the interaction among behavior processes which will help us define the integrative process in humans.

The area of perception has undergone considerable development within the past ten years. The new research has underlined strongly the relation between perception and personality. There is no need to labor this point here. But I should like to describe briefly just one study, the techniques and results of which add meaning to the model I am trying to develop here.

Chodorkoff (1954) studied the relationship, within a normal group, between personal adjustment and perceptual defense. His method of assessing adjustment level was quite ingenious. He defined adjustment as the congruence between a person's self-description and a description made by a clinician on the basis of psychological test evidence. He argued that high agreement between self-description and clinical description implied high self-understanding. Chodorkoff's measure of perceptual defense was tachis-

toscopic recognition time for neutral and threatening words. He hypothesized a direct relationship between perception time and personal adjustment level—that is, the higher the adjustment, the shorter the perception
time for threatening words.

Chodorkoff found the predicted relationship between adjustment level
and perceptual behavior. But beyond this, he found that the individuals in
the upper adjustment group recognized the threatening words more quickly
than they recognized the neutral words. This phenomenon did not take
place in the lower adjustment group. One might thus conjecture that the
higher adjustment person could come to terms more adequately with
environmental threat—that is, he was able to differentiate and symbolize the threat more adequately than the persons rated lower in adjustment.

If we now consider together Chodorkoff's study and the study by Starkman, we are in a position to examine a more general concept and its relation to the integrative process. Here the idea of an internal communication
network is useful. In such terms the integrated person may be described as
having an effective network of internal communication. You will note that
the concept of an internal communication network simply underlines and
extends the dominant theme of this paper, namely, the theme of interaction
between the organism's subsystems.

One function of this communication network is to provide information
on which to act. The amount of information provided is related to the
effectiveness of response. In Chodorkoff's study we saw that the high
adjustment person facilitated receipt of information, whereas by comparison
the lower adjustment person inhibited receipt of information.

Another function of the internal communication network seems to be
that of *synthesizing* experiences, of providing useful and workable response
blends drawn from smaller units of stimulation. In an earlier paper on
psychotherapy (Seeman, 1956) I spoke of this synthesizing process as an
"integrative act." In psychotherapy we find two complementary processes
at work: an experiential-affective process and a perceptual-cognitive process. The core of therapy lies in the appropriate blending of the two—that is,
in the process of experiencing with meaning. The "aha experience" in
psychotherapy arises from the appropriate blending of affective and
cognitive data. The client has been able to symbolize accurately a hitherto
formless and unknown phenomenon. To be more concrete about it: a client
under certain conditions experienced rising internal tension in the presence
of his friends. The physiological tension was formless and nameless to him;
but when during therapy he was finally able to say of this experience, "I

felt abandoned by my friends," he created a synthesis of affective and cognitive processes which gave form and meaning to his experience.

This blending of affective and cognitive processes which I have called the integrative act of psychotherapy may be quite recognizable to you in a somewhat different setting. The Rorschach sign *FC* refers not just to any blend but to an appropriate blend of form and color (that is to say, a blend of cognition and affect) and is considered a perceptual response indicative of emotional maturity. Thus the concept of synthesis or appropriate blending within the organism has been described in various contexts and may be seen as a general integrative phenomenon.

A concept concerning emotional maturity put forth by Henry (1956) seems to pull together the two elements of internal communication to which I have referred—that is, the amount of information available and the adequacy of the synthesizing process. Henry has referred to a concept of affective complexity which he ascribes to the emotionally mature person. This may be defined in the terms I have been using here as the person who can make available to himself a maximum amount of information and who can also synthesize the information effectively. These processes would lead to behavior which, on the one hand, has high variability and complexity and, on the other, has clear boundaries and adequate control.

The sociopsychological perspective of description is the next domain to consider. The work reported by Crutchfield (1955) is unusually pertinent to this topic. His study is one of the relatively few in the literature which chose superior performance as an independent variable. His sample consisted of men in a profession where leadership was a primary qualification. These men were arranged in groups of five and asked to make a number of judgments on matters ranging from simple perceptual discrimination to complex opinions. The items were contrived so that, in a number of cases when a given response was actually correct, each man, nevertheless, seemed to be alone in his judgment in contrast to the other four men. He was faced with a conflict between his own clear perception and the apparently contradictory consensus of all the other men. Should he now rely on the evidence of his own senses, or should he defer to the judgment of the group?

I believe that our model of integrative behavior yields a prediction in such cases. If we postulate a tendency toward congruence of organismic subsystems as an integrative phenomenon, we would predict that the integrated person would respond in congruence with his own perceptual system. This is precisely what happened. When Crutchfield separated the conformers on the one hand from those who followed independently their own perceptions, here is what he found: "As contrasted with the high conformist, the independent man shows more intellectual effectiveness, ego strength, leadership ability, and maturity of social relations. . . ." Crutchfield's study is of interest, not only because of its findings, but because it has a competent design which might well serve as a paradigm for future inquiries in integrative behavior.

The next study takes an entirely different aspect of the social psychology of personality integration and deals with preliminary results of some work which I have been doing at Peabody. The study concerns the differential description of high and low adjustment as given by teachers. For this purpose a teacher rating scale adapted from Radke-Yarrow's work (1946) was used.

With regard to the low adjustment children we see some interesting things. First of all, there was a three-to-one ratio of boys to girls. These proportions are consistent with the disproportionate number of boys referred to clinics and identified as reading problems in school. They are nevertheless puzzling commentaries either on our concepts of adjustment or the genetic history of the male sex.

What about the high adjustment children? Does the sex ratio reverse itself here? And how are they characterized by their teachers? For the first part, the sex ratio does not reverse, although it certainly shifts. In the high adjustment group there was no difference in sex ratio. Boys were as likely to be selected as girls. Another fact which emerges is that the teachers were not confusing adjustment with conformity or "good" behavior. The teachers picked just as many children who tended to be assertive as those who tended to be reserved. The single characteristic most often chosen to describe the high adjustment child concerned response to his immediate environment. Whereas the low adjustment child was characterized as either highly distractible by his environment or impervious to it, the high adjustment child was characterized by the awareness of and lively interest in his environment but without the diffusion of the highly impulsive child. Other characteristics which stood out for the high adjustment child were stability of mood, self-assurance, efficient organization without finicky attention to detail, and acceptance of and by other children.

This study of teacher judgment is clearly limited to the perspective of external behavioral description. Yet the pattern of high adjustment which emerges here is strikingly reminiscent of the patterns discerned in the physiological and perceptual studies. The teachers saw stability, high environmental contact, and ease of communication. These were the very kinds of phenomena recorded by the EEG, the GSR, and the tachistoscope.

Let us move now to the final category of description, the sociocultural aspects of personality integration. This is the most difficult domain to deal with, and an uncomfortable one. In some ways it threatens the whole structure described up to this point. Considerable emphasis was placed on intraindividual factors in integration. Yet the behavior of individuals in different cultures is so different, the behavioral norms so disparate from one culture to another, that one might well despair of any effort to find general laws of human nature and be tempted by a theory made up of pure cultural relativism. Such a theory would look for explanations of personality integration, not within the individual, but in the individual's relation to the milieu of which he is a part. Such a theory would give up the quest for universal explanations of personality and focus on patterns of person-to-group interaction which might be different for each culture.

You can discern, however, that this is not what I intend to do. Partly this is because I think that nature rarely polarizes events into either-or patterns. The very existence of the Gaussian or normal model assures us that nature often distributes events in forms finer than a simple yes-no. And so I am usually willing to place a small bet that the answer to almost anything lies somewhere between the extremes. I would not press my luck on this point too far. When the minister asks the groom if he wishes to take the woman beside him as his wife, some kind of categorical answer is indicated. But there are not very many true dichotomies in nature. And so I do not think that we shall need to choose between a culturally determined definition of personality and an individually determined one.

We shall, however, have to select with care the categories we use to define integration. In this connection I find it useful to distinguish phenotypic and genotypic classes of description. Perhaps some of the manifest normative differences which we see so readily as we compare cultures are phenotypic differences, the derived aspects of motives and drives which genotypically are far less variable from culture to culture. Consider, for example, the well-known illustration of the highly passive primitive culture on the one hand and the aggressive culture on the other. On the face of it, there is little to bind these cultures into a common definition of adjustment. Yet there may be underlying regularities if we observe the appropriate behaviors. For instance, is there an identification process which governs role acquisition, whatever the role? Are there differences among individuals in the effectiveness of role acquisition? What is the individual's conception of his role and of himself? And again, how full and effective is the person's internal communication network as between physiological, cognitive, and affective behavior? Perhaps much of the dilemma of studying personality across cultures will be resolved when we determine which are the right questions to ask.

This then completes the model for the study of personality integration which I wish to suggest. The model covers events from a single heartbeat to the behavior of peoples. As a model it is not a very modest one. Whether it has any truth value, we cannot yet say. But if it leads us in any way closer to discerning the true order of nature, it shall have amply served its purpose.

This paper presented a conceptual structure for the study of personality integration and suggested several variables which seem related to the integrative process. The conceptual structure leads to a multivariate analysis of behaviors which may be related to integration. The variables tentatively identified as relevant to personality integration include stability, high environmental contact, high internal communication, and affective complexity.

73. Discipline: Its Psychological and Educational Aspects *

HIRSCH LAZAAR SILVERMAN

THE DIRECTOR of the National Education Association's research division sums up the matter of discipline in these words: "Any assumption that most of today's children and youth are going to the dogs is a serious mistake." This conclusion by Dr. Lambert is based on the responses to a questionnaire mailed by the NEA to a stratified sampling of classroom teachers, in which teacher opinion on the topic of discipline was asked. But much that is psychological, scientific, objective, and technical in the area of discipline certainly needs expression, analysis, integration, and ultimately implementation.

We know that in dealing with the administration of pupil personnel boards of education have the authority, either expressed or implied, to make and enforce any rule or regulation governing the conduct of pupils which is not unreasonable. It should be pointed out also that the authority of the school board extends to the pupil while off the school grounds if the act in question is such as to affect directly the discipline and good order of the school. It is well established that a board of education may discipline a pupil to the point of suspension or expulsion for disobedience of reasonable rules and regulations.

But parents, adults everywhere, and even teachers and school administrators are now deeply concerned over the kind of generation of children our schools are producing. Pronouncements in the press, in magazines, in

* From Hirsch Lazaar Silverman, "Discipline: Its Psychological and Educational Aspects," *Mental Hygiene* (April, 1958), pp. 274–83. Reprinted by permission of the author and The National Association of Mental Health.

books, and by parents themselves are often strongly critical of the schools and their effect on modern young people. The great confusion existing in the minds of parents and critics alike is owing in part to the change in the very nature of discipline itself. Because the so-called rod is ceasing to be the symbol of authority, and punishment is no longer the basis or impetus of schoolboy effort, many people assume that discipline is disappearing.

A school of psychologists believes that perhaps America needs more than anything else at this time a generation of parents who accept as fact that their most important business in the world is the raising of children with proper and appropriate discipline. Our life today is far more complex, more demanding, and more mobile than ever before, and parents often unwittingly rush their children into the obligations and doings that are inappropriate for them, simply to satisfy the whim and wish of the parents themselves. This too causes lack of discipline and lack of control in the pupils later in life.

Let us examine the area, problems, factors, and ramifications of the field of discipline.

What is discipline? Educationally and psychologically, Smith's definition is rather appropriate here, since its application is direct in most of our democratic classrooms: "School discipline is merely social control within the school group; it includes all the forces that mold attitudes and inspire conduct of pupils. Its essence is that subtle thing called school spirit. Thus in every phase of schoolwork, the problem of discipline or social control must enter as part of the educative program, not incidentally."

In part, earlier concepts of discipline aimed to teach conformity and obedience. A pupil who questioned the word of a teacher was regarded as an upstart who deserved immediate and harsh punishment. The teacher's word was law, and failure to conform was punished by use of the hickory stick.

Both the method and the aim of discipline in today's school are different from those of former years. Today the aim is to secure good order and socially oriented self-direction. Order which stems from purposeful activity will not always be "pin-drop" silence, but it will persist without adult control. When given an opportunity, children continually surprise adults with their ability to be intelligently self-directive.

Let us examine the matter objectively and in psychological terms. One important aspect of discipline in the schools today is that punishment is largely directed toward the symptoms of misbehavior instead of being useful as a means of getting at the causes. The present view in psychological thinking leans in the direction of mental hygiene, i.e., that causes must be determined before an attack on symptoms can be very successful. Authoritarian discipline often gets the desired result of conformity, but in far too many cases the tension takes some other form of expression. A teacher may get silence in the classroom upon demand, but the suppressed tension of the students finds vent in varied ways, e.g., in writing on the hallway walls or in defacing the desks.

Psychologists feel that before an individual pupil's behavior is condemned harshly the causative factors in the social climate and the standards of the group should be analyzed. Behavior patterns are acquired during the total learning situation and consequently an individual's conduct cannot be judged apart from his social environment. Discipline, instruction, and environmental factors are interactive; in this, educators are in agreement with psychologists. If the child is to acquire rational behavior, he must have, as in other types of learning, the satisfaction of right responses and the related annoyance of incorrect responses. The type of activities from which a child derives his satisfactions certainly is an important consideration in guiding his behavior. The child who finds his greatest satisfaction from self-centered activities displays a lack of social maturity.

Misbehavior requires treatment and control no less than physical illness. However, treatment that breaks down self-confidence in a child and makes him overly fearful of rebuke can seriously retard his educational and emotional growth. Disciplining by parents or teachers that creates constant fears and anxiety will inhibit children by stifling their natural tendencies to explore and to experiment. Certainly punishment at times is warranted, but if punishment is inflicted it should have a corrective value as well as provide the child with a sense of having learned something that will guide him in the future. Punishment should not be inflicted for its own sake, nor merely as a quick emotional flare-up in response to a particular act of bad conduct.

Also, acquiring proper patterns of behavior involves self-activity on the part of the learner. For children to be able to grow in self-discipline, they must have ample opportunity to secure this growth. Where children are working cooperatively under the guidance of a teacher to achieve goals they have planned to work toward, there is no thought of conduct except to determine the best method of achieving the group's objectives. Discipline here is inseparable from teaching. Wholesome growth in discipline takes place as children gradually assume more and more responsibility.

The teacher may well be concerned with the sum total of temperament, outlook, and habitual choice which involves the personality of the child. Children should be given the tools of analysis and should be given the opportunity to pass judgment on conduct just as they are given a basis for passing judgment on the merit of a piece of literature. Growth in proper behavior must be based upon the insights and understandings of how individuals may become better judges of good and evil.

If it is to be effective, discipline must be predicated on certain basic rules of conduct. If our future society is to be strong and sound mentally, emotionally, physically, and educationally, parents and teachers would do well to acquire fundamental knowledge and sound habits in the training of children. Regular hours of rest and sleep, coupled with wholesome food, are requirements not only of the home but of the school in its indoctrination of children. Parents must be consistent in their handling of children, loving them yet being firm, and must give of their time to explain the responsibilities of daily living. Discipline is also based on proper home environment, a home in which religion is made the cornerstone, not merely given lip service. This must, of course, include parents who truly love each other and live together in mutual respect. Discipline of children also requires a father who feels his responsibility for participating in the training of the child, in all possible ways.

In diagnosing children's behavior the teacher must come to recognize the part that emotional factors play in determining human conduct. Many of the important decisions made by our pupils, particularly by the more immature among them, are largely on an emotional basis. Fundamentally, the function of education is to lead the child toward greater mental maturity and thereby assist him in making more of his decisions on a rational basis. Yet one who takes a realistic view of human behavior cannot fail to recognize the critical impact of the emotions upon conduct.

The child needs practice in learning to behave appropriately in various situations. It is no more reasonable to assume that errors in behavior may be eliminated by verbal instruction alone than it is to expect that errors in grammar may be eradicated so easily. Only as the child is presented with numerous opportunities for correct action, together with an understanding of its real meaning, does he learn to behave in a better manner. He then must practice continuously so that acceptable behavior becomes more or less automatic and habitual, even involuntary.

Another important psychological principle is this: Only when the individual understands the implications of his acts do they become significant and aid in his character development. When the teacher acts merely as a censor for outward mannerisms, she thwarts the child's growth in accepting moral responsibility for his actions. The teacher should play the role of stimulator to right behavior, rather than critic. Certainly learning to behave properly is among the most complex of all learnings. It is achieved only by constant effort. Children need guidance, not dictation, in establishing habits of good conduct.

Many factors and conditions influence child behavior. In order to understand and direct a child's behavior in an intelligent manner, the teacher should recognize that individual behavior is in part the result of many forces in the community. Some of these forces are economic; others derive from the standards of conduct of other children and adults. Particularly significant in the thinking of the child and his overt behavior are the standards of values held by the children of the group with whom he associates. Where a community sets wealth as a standard of personal value, a child's acceptance by various social levels or units may be mainly (and unfortunately) on an economic basis. Even if he has a sound personality, possesses qualities of leadership, and is able to gain admittance into the so-called exclusive circles, he may still be confused in his thinking and even be handicapped in his activities. The point we are making is, nevertheless, that the teacher has the responsibility of assisting pupils in the developing of a sound set of values.

Studies of children enrolled in schools reveal that too many are handicapped by serious defects or illnesses. Many more have minor defects. It is to be remembered that problems of behavior may often be traced directly to the child's physical handicaps. Even feelings of physical inadequacy result in social maladjustment and acts of misbehavior. This is particularly true if the handicap is serious enough to prevent the child from taking part in gym work or sports.

Many factors account for restlessness in children. Malnutrition, poor vision, and defective hearing contribute to poor achievement and the child then is irritated with the school situation. The teacher should not be too quick to punish, and should be able to recognize signs of malnutrition and of possible mental and physical fatigue.

Just as the teacher should understand child behavior, she should recognize the basic needs of her pupils. Every child needs to have feelings of security, a sense of belonging and a growing realization of adequacy or success. If he does not satisfy these needs in some part at least, his need for satisfaction may manifest itself in negative behavior, at school and in the home. Emotional blocks may even develop in a school situation in which the child is subjected to strongly rigid requirements of conduct.

Essentially, the so-called "problem child" may often be the product of heredity rather than environment. New findings in human genetics may in time nullify the prevailing tendency to blame all defects in personality on a child's early environment and conditioning. According to some teachers and other adults who work with delinquent and seriously undisciplined children, too heavy a burden of blame and responsibility is often placed on the parents of children who were supposedly "just born that way." There is mounting evidence that heredity produces degrees of susceptibility or resistance to innumerable traits and characteristics which often are regarded as purely environmental. These children who are delinquent may have been born with tendencies which incline them much more than other children to abnormal behavior or functioning. In fact, psychological thinking would prevail upon teachers, parents, and adults to avoid calling everything "environmental" or "psychosomatic" or "conditioned." Needless to say, then, the greatest and most immediate hope of the field of education should be in reducing human defectiveness in whatever area and also in improving environmental factors.

The seriousness of behavior difficulties is often determined by the mental maturity of the individual. A child of low intelligence is often susceptible to the suggestions of other persons and might find himself in a behavior situation without discriminating as to the seriousness of the difficulty or its implications. But many problems requiring discipline often arise among children of high intelligence, too. If the school situation fails to present a challenge for the bright child to exercise his mental abilities, boredom and restlessness may cause him to misbehave.

Parents can learn a lot about dealing with their children's behavior by becoming familiar with disciplinary lessons that every teacher is expected to know. The object of discipline is to help an individual to do what is expected of him; and if a child is to do what is expected of him, he must first be helped to understand real goals and limitations. Children need the security that comes from feeling there is a guide, a protective authority that will watch over them. Basic to good discipline also is the function of helping the child develop a feeling of personal worth. The good teacher and the good parent should provide the kind of discipline all children need; that includes, among other things, giving the child a limited area in which to experiment and make mistakes, helping him understand his mistakes, and showing how the problems of living call for certain kinds of behavior.

Let us not overlook this fact, namely, that a child's behavior is greatly influenced by his home environment. The standards of conduct of his parents are usually reflected in the child's acceptance or rejection of their behavior patterns. Discord in the family resulting from parental differences over the severity or the methods of punishment often results in confused and inconsistent child behavior. Bickering and arguments in the home are conducive to emotional disturbances in the child. The presence in the home of a more talented or a more gifted brother or sister, or a favorite child, may cause deep resentments on the part of the child less fortunate or less favored. The child of an immigrant or foreign-born family which may have been subjected even inadvertently to acts of discrimination in the community may be unable to make a satisfactory adjustment to school life. The rather important point here is that, even if it may be necessary at times to correct a pupil's actions immediately, the teacher has the responsibility to search for and, if possible, to find the causal factors of misbehavior.

Estes states: "After punishment is administered the effect on the organism is to produce an inhibition of behavior." Although a teacher may prevent a pupil from sucking his thumb by shaming him, the teacher may not notice that the pupil's insecurity may now show itself in his withdrawal from the groups in which the teacher works. Repressions may serve the needs of teachers at times, but does not help the child to become more self-directing.

Study of the psychology of the school group reveals many factors contributing to antisocial or unsocial conduct of individual pupils. In an analysis of the structure of the school group, Sheviakov and Redl suggest six factors which may cause undesirable individual conduct. The following is an adaptation of their viewpoint:

Dissatisfaction in the work process. The subject matter may be too easy to challenge the abilities of the students, thereby causing them to seek other outlets; or the subject matter may be too difficult and produce student indifference or irritation. Also, assignments may be poorly planned.

Emotional unrest in interpersonal relations. Tensions growing out of strong friendships or animosities among pupils may supersede work interests. Competing cliques may become emotional disturbances. Clashes of personality between pupils and teachers often result in serious maladjustment.

Disturbances in group climate. By the term "group climate" Sheviakov and Redl mean the basic feeling tone which underlies the life of a group, the sum total of everybody's emotions toward each other, toward work and toward the organization.

They give the following examples of different types of group climate:

Punitive climate: One in which pupils are accepted or rejected on the basis of the teacher's behavior code.

Emotional blackmail climate: In this situation the children develop a strong emotional dependence upon the teacher and there is strong rivalry between the children who conform and those who are not close to the teacher.

Hostile competition climate: Everybody is whipped into competition with everybody else. The result is extreme uncooperativeness among members of the group.

Group pride climate: In its extreme form, feelings of group vanity and conceit may result. The individual who does not meet all the requirements of group loyalty may be made an outcast subject to group persecution.

Mistakes in organization and group leadership. During the period of adolescence there is need for the gradual emancipation of the child from adult domination. Some of the features of the school organization which disregard this need of youth are too much autocratic pressure, too much organization, and group organization out of focus with the age, maturity, background, and special needs of the group.

Emotional strain and sudden change. A member of a group may become unduly excited about examinations, athletic contests, or community events. Sudden changes in behavior requirements, techniques and leadership frequently result in emotional upsets of both individuals and group.

The composition of the group. Frictions and discipline problems may develop unless children are grouped on the basis of criteria relevant to group life.

Parents and teachers sometimes place too much faith in the rational process in trying to get across to children the importance of certain rules of behavior. There are times when the adults should simply say to children that a rule must be insisted upon only because the adult knows better what is good for the child. The democratic way is, of course, vital in working with children, but we must not make the mistake of thinking that children will follow rules and regulations just because they have been carefully explained and discussed. Discipline cannot be totally permissive; yet ruling children haphazardly through fear and punishment can be damaging. Within a framework of adult-set limitations and controls, the child must still have freedom to make mistakes and to experiment, for only in this way can he develop the inner controls necessary for self-discipline.

To be sure, the amount of freedom suitable for a child depends upon the child's age and maturity. The ideal situation in terms of discipline is one in which areas of freedom are inconsistently widened over the years. Also, an atmosphere of love and acceptance is the first essential for helping children grow in self-discipline. Along with conditions stimulating to free action, there is a need for careful organization of the child's life at school; as children grow and mature, they should take increasing responsibility for helping to establish their own limitation and rules. In many situations in a child's life, however, the teacher, the parent, the adult generally, must assume final responsibility; and in such situations, vagueness or confusion make for poor discipline.

We feel that all pupils should not be disciplined in the same manner. The shy pupil may well be treated kindly while the deliberately mischievous child may require more vigorous methods of control. There is certainly need at times for placing restraints upon the activities of individuals and groups of children but the manner in which the restraints are imposed is especially significant. There are a few basic considerations which teachers may find helpful in preventing individual violations of good behavior. Bernard lists several of these, again keeping in mind that mental hygiene is the basis of good discipline.

Teachers must understand the nature of children. It should be remembered that growth takes place on uneven fronts; because pupils may have gained independence in one area does not necessarily mean that they can reasonably be expected to be independent in all activities. The degree of pupil control usually varies with the situation. It is natural for children to desire freedom of movement; to restrict this freedom unnecessarily or injudiciously is to ignore one of their innate drives. The teacher should recognize the individuality of each child. Every child is unique and the teacher should understand this just as she understands that every pupil's learning interest varies. All pupils cannot be forced into any one particular kind of mold, intellectually, academically, emotionally.

Strict domination should be avoided. While there must be order underlying productive work, the lock-step procedures all too often used in classrooms do not bring about continuously productive activity. Work done under compulsion develops a distaste in the pupil.

Discipline should be appropriate and consistent. Appropriate discipline takes into account the individual, the time, the total situation and the degree to which the behavior differs from the individual's typical responses. As to consistency, one should not overlook a given response at one time and deal with it decisively and abruptly at another time.

Shaming, sarcasm, and ridicule should be avoided. Any procedures which belittle another person may tend either to undermine his own sense of worth or to stimulate resentments that are destructive to a cheerful classroom atmosphere. When sarcasm and ridicule are used, it is not likely that the child will get the security needed from the feeling of companionship with his teacher, his school, and his fellow students. Any words or actions which undermine his feeling of personal worth must be strongly condemned from the standpoint of good discipline.

Pupils should be kept busy with interesting tasks. If the child is interested in his work there will be less need for imposed discipline. Busy and interested pupils have no time for acts that could keep them from reaching their objective.

A good adult example should be set. Much behavior is learned by direct imitation and much by unconscious imitation or suggestion. Pupils try to imitate their admired teachers. Especially in high school, boys and girls consciously aim to pattern their behavior after teachers whom they have selected as heroes. Because of this, a teacher's attitude toward aspects of discipline (lying, cheating, work habits, etc.) has direct influence on the conduct of his students. Not only the words he speaks but the attitudes he reveals may be taken as models by the pupils.

Friendliness, fair-mindedness, and respect for others—or suspicion, jealousy, and bigotry—are learned from one's intimates. This does not mean that a teacher has to be perfect. If a teacher cannot always be a sound example of self-discipline, he or she can at least make a consistent effort to grow better toward self-control.

Seek the cause of misbehavior. At times a student does something just because he can get away with it, but usually misbehavior is generated by some tension or deprivation felt by the child.

Have confidence in self and pupils. Autocratic procedures by the teacher are likely to grow out of personal feelings of insecurity. The teacher may demand strict conformity because of the fear that things will get out of hand; he must be confident that the pupils are capable of assuming responsibility. Children enjoy living up to expectations. If they know mature conduct is expected, they will strive for it; but if they know the teacher suspects them of incompetence, it will not likely hurt their feelings to show the teacher that he or she is right.

Use reasoning. Understanding is necessary to self-discipline. The teacher has the responsibility of explaining to erring students the reasons for rules and regulations in general and the reason for a specific requirement in a specific case. This reasoning should take place when the teacher is emotionally calm. If reasoning is attempted at a time of emotional stress, there is too great a likelihood that what is said will degenerate into wrangling, even nagging. Teachers should not expect youngsters, even of high school age, to understand their own motivation; it is therefore not very practical to try to reason with them by asking, "What makes you do this?"

Too often, the pupil honestly does not know the answer to such a question. It is better psychology to try to have the pupil place himself in the situation of another. Try to get him to see how he would feel on the receiving end of the very behavior in which he has been indulging.

Authority must be positive. In many schools pupils participate in the making of disciplinary policy and share in carrying out the policy. However, the teacher is accountable for classroom conduct. Specialization carries with it authority that can be and should be used constructively.

Provide for substitute behavior. Instead of forbidding the child to interrupt what another is presenting in class, the teacher may ask him to wait his own turn and then make some thought-out contribution. Instead of telling him only that he must study, the teacher should make an attempt to discover why he is not interested in the project and help him find some aspect of it that will challenge him. Providing substitute activities is not being educationally or psychologically "soft." Rather it is recognition of the fact that behavior is caused; that the ultimate aim of discipline is self-direction; that growth is an individual process; and that a mature individual must get along without constant supervision.

Discipline should be democratic. Democratic discipline has a triple advantage. It is in accord with the objectives and principles of our society, and thus provides preparation for more effective adulthood. It tends to capitalize on individual assets, and thus provides a means of stimulating growth toward independence and self-direction. And it lessens the chances of generating habits and tensions that are harmful to mental health.

Wholesome discipline can be developed when the teacher's direction is not only positive but also cooperative, fair, consistent, and attentive to individual differences. Such discipline depends on teachers who have a thorough knowledge of growth principles in general and an appreciation of the specific causes of behavior in terms of the school and out-of-school backgrounds of individuals.

Too often discipline is thought of in the school only. Essentially, discipline must have its impetus and origin in the home. Only those children with parents or guardians who are themselves well disciplined may be expected to be soundly disciplined as individuals. No greater mistake can ever be made by parents than to attempt to discipline children by temper and by screaming at them, or by pushing children around in a bullying fashion. Parents actually set the example through their own personal conduct of the standards they profess to want for their children; there are too many parents who preach one thing and do another, however. Discipline of children requires parents who are honestly interested in their children's activities; who try to find out what the natural interests and activities of their children are; who encourage their children to discuss problems with them; and who try to help their children to find opportunities for development of those aptitudes and interests that the children too, at the time, feel to be important in their lives. Basically and fundamentally, disciplined parents will have disciplined children if they encourage their children to accept responsibility and allow them to share consistently and intelligently in family planning within the family group.

Those of us concerned with the entire field of discipline and its psychological implications should realize that there are at least a number of aims of education that we should strive for in the foreseeable future. Not only psychologists but teachers working directly with pupils of all ages may well give much thought and planning to teaching children to be critical observers and listeners. Children should learn to live and work together harmoniously. They should be taught functioning skills in such academic subjects as reading, writing, and arithmetic, to help decrease the possibility of delinquent action and behavior in later years. They should be taught how to seek facts and to find answers. They should understand human geography; they should develop a thorough understanding of the peoples and cultures of the world, however different and varied they may be from their own. Children should be taught to adjust to change without fear. They should learn to express themselves clearly in order to communicate with others. They should learn to respect leadership and learn to regard authority not with defiance but with sufficient respect for the experience, the training and the knowledge that proper leadership requires. They should be encouraged to meet their fullest potential; they should not just learn to read, for example, but learn to read as well as they are capable of reading. Finally, they should be taught by parents, teachers and other adults to develop a sense of responsibility to each other in their roles as citizens of the community.

74. Moral and Spiritual Values *

HENRY NEUMANN

W HEN PEOPLE add the word "spiritual" to the values they want schools to develop, they have good reason. They wish children to begin acquiring morals early, yes. But only "morals"? Somehow the word has its unlovely overtones. It suggests Mark Twain's "Be good and you will be lonesome." Even where it does not imply being a kill-joy, it may mean thinking or acting out of fear of a policeman or of disapproving neighbors; or performing mechanically, without heart, compassion, understanding, or concern for true justice.

Though "spiritual" too can have its undesirable flavors, it speaks nevertheless of attitudes much more affirmative, much warmer in the sense of coming out of deep and fine aspirations. At the very least it betokens a more reflective way of regarding conduct than "moral" does, a genuine feeling for basic decencies, a sincere response to the call of high ideals, firmly cherished, and earnestly and often pondered. Though to some persons, "spiritual" may suggest "effeminate" or "too good for this world," today's frequent use of the term by men neither womanish nor otherworldly reminds us how important indeed is this educational emphasis.

Serious as delinquency in the young can be, much more is needed than saving them from wrongdoing. Nothing so drives out the poorer ambitions as a genuine feeling for the better ones. And far more common than crime is ethical mediocrity, which leaves people, as Mary Webb said, "not bad but empty of good." How can schools help to cultivate a finer grain to their pupils' lives, growth in sensible, responsible, considerate self-direction in a world where living with other people will always call for this major need? Certainly no one approach to instruction, training or inspiration within the school can be expected to do this, nor even the life of the school as a whole, without help from the home and other influences for spiritual growth. But some gleanings from the experience of the schools which this writer knows best may be of use to other teachers.

Stories which capture the imagination of young people are an excellent medium for helping them to clarify their values. Through discussions based on tales that appeal to their natural sympathies, hero worship, and concern

* From Henry Neumann, "Moral and Spiritual Values," *The Journal of Educational Sociology* (April, 1957), pp. 367–69. Reprinted by permission of the author and *The Journal of Educational Sociology*.

for justice they are encouraged to form habits of moral reflection, to look at conduct over long range, to understand as clearly as they can what issues are involved in the choices which free people are expected to make with their eyes open. This medium can be employed by teachers of almost any subject in almost any school, with material adapted to different age levels.

One example of the sort of stories which we have found helpful is that of Colonel Roebling, the engineer responsible for building the Brooklyn Bridge some eighty years ago, who discovered that one of the contractors had supplied cables which came short of the required number of wires for each strand. He thereupon ordered a whole year's work to be ripped out and any questionable cable replaced by a dependable one. Various instances were mentioned of how and why we trust people. For example, children trust their own parents. We also trust doctors, druggists, the engineer on the train, the airplane pilot. Father deposits money in his bank and pays for insurance with confidence that the people handling his money are trustworthy. The discussion also brought out the fact that cheating poisons the atmosphere of mutual confidence needed for healthy living. Thus the children saw that we owe our happiness, our security, often our very lives, to the fact that there are people in the world who are utterly dependable.

Chances for increasing such ethical understanding lie at hand in teaching most, if not all, of the subjects already in the curriculum. For example, an English class which had enjoyed an essay by Charles Lamb was told by the teacher about the tender, patient care with which Lamb treated his sister Mary, who was mentally ill. The pupils were then asked to discuss why it is that sometimes people are better friends with outsiders than they are with their own brothers or sisters. This involved a discussion of why friendships are formed, why they break, what may be reasonably expected of a friend. History, too, can be highly fruitful for ethical guidance and exploration when it is used to distinguish what in our heritage needs most to be cherished and to be carried forward to still finer application.

Through various kinds of dramatic activities, which call on every possible resource for beauty in sound, speech, mass and color that the children can contribute, ethical concepts may be demonstrated in several different ways. Sharing and planning together develops responsibility in students, increases their appreciation of one another's talents, and reaffirms their faith in one another's honesty and fairness. The subject matter presented may also inspire a lesson in spiritual values. For example, in one of our Thanksgiving festivals, several classes presented episodes in the history of man's cultivation of food. The closing scene showed food going to hungry neighbors here and abroad. In the classrooms the teachers talked over with their pupils the basic ethical principle that the best way to show thanks, and especially to our forebears, is to put their gifts to excellent use. A festival celebrating the history of light ended with scenes showing high moments in the spiritual history of the human race.

In schools situations often arise which test the maturity and ethical values of students and faculty alike. The way they measure up depends to a large extent on the way in which their understanding is enlisted as well as how the project fulfills their own sense of moral values. One of our schools once undertook a project to raise money for sending much-needed food to foreign countries. Every class discussed the part in the whole program for which it would make itself responsible. When teachers had to leave their pupils, class behavior did not suffer. The children understood clearly how the success of the project required each to restrain himself or others from taking advantage of the teacher's absence. Through this experience they learned the importance of accepting individual responsibility for one's special part in the big enterprise. Such sharing, to the fullest possible extent for each age in the collective life of the school—not merely in its "government," offers much to growth in the best of democratic relationships.

As in all teaching, much depends on the individual instructor, on his power to grasp opportunities, his understanding and appreciation for young minds, his personal contribution to the important role of mentor. The following description by one of our students of his ethics teacher might equally apply to thousands of other conscientious, imaginative teachers in schools all over the country: "When he came to our classes, he did not try to force anything into our heads; but he came and went like a quiet breeze, gently leaving a thought with us. It was not a set of rigid precepts, it was a way of life, a mural of experience, projected ahead, out of the wide past and into the expanding future. Each time he left, I had a feeling of a certain peace and a quiet self-confidence as well as a humility and a feeling of enthusiasm. I always looked forward to his talking about the Greeks, or the Romans, or the Jews, and other people, about what life and history were, and what they could become for us if we retained our curiosity, our creative drive, our inner exuberance."

75. The Nature of Religious Controls *

MORTIMER OSTOW

THE NEED to influence and indeed control human behavior has been an important issue probably since man began to live in groups. I shall make no effort in this paper to consider the moral problems created by the prospect of influencing human behavior. Suffice to say that such influence already exists in coercive political persuasion and in commercial promotion. Hopefully overt exposition and circulation of knowledge about the subject will enable those on the side of the angels to devise adequate defensive methods. Certainly there is little to be said for permitting all the information on the subject to remain entirely in the hands of the malevolent.

Religion is certainly one of our most important institutions for influencing human behavior. Since religions, of one form or other, occur so regularly in almost all known human societies, one may examine the proposition that religion performs an important biologic function for the group, which creates survival value for the religion. The pagan, and especially the animistic, religions attempt to control nature for human advantage and protection by means of magic. We cannot concede that these magical performances have survival value for the group. On the other hand, religious experience may afford relief from psychic distress to individuals, for example, by offering social sanction to unrealistic attitudes and beliefs or by providing æsthetic gratifications above and beyond those encountered in daily life. The spiritual monotheism of biblical Judaism added a new dimension to religion: the idea that ethical behavior can be a central religious requirement. With this revolution in religious orientation, man began to entrust his safety to the stability of his society rather than to cultic magic or devices for diminishing the area of his contact with the real world. Though the use of religion to stabilize society became one of the most important functions in biblical Judaism and its derivatives, this function appears to some degree in many if not most other religions—and perhaps the universality of religion may be ascribed both to whatever group survival value the social regulatory action of religion may confer and to the need for an opportunity to express psychic tendencies more overtly than a purely realistic *Weltanschauung* will permit. At any rate, if we are to work out a

* From Mortimer Ostow, "The Nature of Religious Controls," *The American Psychologist* (October, 1958), pp. 571–74. Reprinted by permission of the author and the American Psychological Association.

theory of the control of human behavior, it is proper to examine religion to see how it has handled this problem hitherto and to check our theory against its findings. This is a task of some magnitude. Here, I shall attempt merely to demonstrate an approach, to show how one may seek in religious principle and practice exemplification of a theory of the control of human behavior based upon general biologic principles and psychoanalytic meta-psychology.

One of the most universally potent forces for the control of behavior in lower social animals is imitation. Imitation is also part of the archaic equipment of the human psyche. It is the *modus operandi* of identification, the process whereby the individual makes his image of himself congruent with his image of another person. Children identify with their parents, lovers with each other, and members of a group with their leader and with each other. In each case, the identification is given effect by imitation. It is possible to influence the behavior of large numbers of people by taking advantage of their unconscious desire to identify with each other and with a leader by imitation.

A second means for influencing human behavior also rests upon the tendency to identify one with the other. It is similar to imitation but consists not of a need to repeat the words or gestures of others but to assume the emotional attitudes of others. The contagiousness of emotion in humans by facial expression, by gesture, and by posture are well known. A sober face tends to make us sober, a joyous one tends to make us joyous, and so on. In other words, we respond to the facial expression of a person who is moved, as though we were confronted by the original moving stimulus—we identify by accepting the affect communicated to us.

A third method of influencing behavior is simply to take advantage of the constantly pressing need for instinctual gratification. The instincts of man press insistently for nourishment, for sexual gratification, for shelter, for freedom from pain and threat, for sleep, and for all the derivatives of these instinctual needs, such as the need for wealth, prestige, possessions, attractive clothing, social position, and so on. When by virtue of superior strength, strategic position, or more fortunate endowment one individual acquires the power to determine whether the needs of others will be gratified or frustrated, he becomes able to induce these others to comply with his demands.

Exploiting the biologic tendency to obey is a fourth method of influencing behavior. The need to be obedient seems to depend upon the need of the young to accept the protection and instruction of the parents and later to avoid triggering the aggressive tendencies of the parents by appeasing them. Lorenz derives from the deference of the young to the parent both the obedience of the adult animal to the pack leader and the loyalty of the domestic animal to his master. The phenomenon of hypnosis is based upon the tendency to obey. Probably much of the stability of society is to be attributed to this tendency to accept and obey authority.

It follows from the foregoing paragraph that, in deference to the parents, the young may curb some of their own wishes. But there is a special mechanism which provides for the suppression of aggressive instincts under certain circumstances. In flocking animals it is clear that intraspecific aggressiveness would soon deplete the flock if it were not controlled. It seems that, when in intraspecific combat one animal acquires sufficient advantage over its antagonist to be able to destroy it, the loser performs a gesture which is stereotyped for the species and which is interpreted by the victor as a surrender. Usually the gesture involves giving up one's defenses and making oneself completely vulnerable. When confronted with such utter vulnerability, the victor becomes unable to pursue his advantage and abandons the fight. A similar controlling mechanism is probably involved in the complete immunity of the young of each species to attack by older animals. In both instances the exhibition of vulnerability disarms the potential killer. It seems to me not an extravagant speculation to suppose that the human affects of mercy, compassion, and pity are homologous to the biologic mechanism for inhibiting intragroup aggressiveness; and so are the codes of chivalry, ethics, and morality which are involved in the superego.

We have now considered five devices by means of which behavior can be influenced: imitation, communication of affect, intervention in the pursuit of instinctual gratification, obedience, and disarming by vulnerability. It requires only a few moments' thought to discern the operation of each of these mechanisms within organized religion.

The lives of saints and religious heroes are described in religious literature for the express purpose of inviting imitation. The clergy in each religious group is expected to set an example of good behavior. In Buddhism, the cultivation of tranquility is encouraged by the display of images of Buddha which portray meditative tranquility; it is hoped that the worshipper will identify with his God by imitating his attitude.

Affects, in religion, are communicated in two ways. First, affect is communicated from individual to individual by facial expression, posture, voice, and manner. For example, the goodwill of the Christmas season is so contagious that even non-Christians who are exposed to it find themselves participating. Religious congregations, worshipping together, share feelings of dedication, solemnity, remorse, invigoration, inspiration, shame, guilt, or obedience, as the case may be. Revival meetings depend for part of their effectiveness on the contagiousness of emotion. Second, affective attitudes are communicated to the congregation by perceptible configurations which are associated with religious ideas and values. Some of these configurations are displayed in religious rituals and sacred objects. Others appear in religious art forms including painting, sculpture, or literature, music, poetry, and prose. These artistically exhibited percepts create affects of awe, reverence, respect, inspiration, enthusiasm, or aversion, horror, or despair. By exploiting the contagiousness of human feelings and the power of percepts, religion evokes desired emotions.

Religion intervenes in the pursuit of instinctual gratification by promising rewards for good behavior and threatening frustration and injury in return for bad behavior. Promises of reward sometimes apply to the here and now, and sometimes to an afterlife. Some religions reassure against danger, disease, and death. While modern religion generally combats the superstition of animism and paganism, it is often tempted to suggest that the impact of natural forces can be altered by one's behavior. The reason for this is that man is more ready to respond to threats and promises dealing with immediate pleasure and pain than to such remote desiderata as social stability.

The invoking of obedience is a primary concern of religion. God and his surrogates are seen as parental figures who require and deserve obedience. Humans are seen as refractory children. Moreover, religious scriptures and authorities suggest the rules which actual parents should teach and then supplement parental instruction. They play a part in determining the ego-ideal by indicating which instinctual needs one should gratify—by instruction, by example, and by parable, myth, and legend.

Religion also exploits the susceptibility to signs of vulnerability. Weakness, innocence, humility, suffering are displayed constantly; the humanness of potential victims of aggression is emphasized; immunity for the widow, the orphan, and the suffering are prescribed; affects of pity, compassion, mercy, and sympathy are encouraged; codes of chivalry and fair play are sponsored.

There is still another mechanism for influencing behavior which requires separate discussion. We know that adult humans occasionally revert under stress to forms of regressive behavior and attitudes which were employed more appropriately in childhood. By the application of certain pressures, regression can be induced, with encouragement of passive rather than active tendencies. In a state of regression with passivity, an individual is readily induced to forego his own desires and accept control by authority out of a need to secure affection by appeasement and ingratiation. Such techniques have been sadistically elaborated and developed in modern brain-washing and doubtless in campaigns of coercive persuasion in the historical past.

While regression implies the abandoning of the intellectual maturity and the pride of responsible adulthood, and while it is a disabling consequence of neurosis, it is by no means a wholly deplorable phenomenon. It plays a significant role in normal adult life. Psychic regression is a necessary condition for sleep. Participating in sexual orgasm requires the abandonment of psychic restraint, and the experience of severe pain enforces a discarding of all other psychic considerations. A certain degree of regression accompanies the gratification of physical needs such as eating and excreting so that a formal etiquette is required to prevent too great a regression for social living. Kris emphasized that an ego regression—that is, an abandonment of reality and logic as criteria for thinking—is a necessary component of artistic and even scientific creation. The very appreciation of art and humor requires some slight regression.

It is my impression that this controlled regression, which is such an important element in daily life and in human creativity, is encouraged by religion to facilitate the regulation of behavior. Fasting and cessation of sexual pleasure are often prescribed for the entire populace. Confession, sermons, prayer, and self-degradation are employed to induce feelings of shame and guilt. And religious ritual recurrently intercepts the self-seeking pursuits of one's own goals and requires a brief surrender of autonomy. The result of this partial regression induced by religion is that the individual becomes more compliant to religious authority and hence to religion's effort to control human behavior to the end of social stability. Distortion or repudiation of reality can make behavior inappropriate and seriously impair response to real problems. However, certain kinds of distortion or denial of reality are salutary. To be aware every day of the fact that each of us must die some day, perhaps today, perhaps of a painful, protracted illness, seems to serve no useful function and may in fact be so depressing that interest and enthusiasm are obliterated. This blunting of the edge of the pain of reality can therefore, when wisely done, be a reward to the religious man for his observance and can strengthen his loyalty to religion.

I should like to conclude this discussion with three final observations. First, if my thesis is true—that is, if we can find in the institution of religion techniques for influencing human behavior—then it seems likely that a careful study of the history of religion will yield to the student of psychic function a treasure of recorded experiments on the regulation of behavior.

Second, as members of society, we may draw some comfort from the fact that human instinctual goals and tendencies can not be completely obstructed nor permanently distorted. At most, they can only be deferred or deflected for a limited period of time. Protracted restriction and supervision does not stifle the yearning for freedom, it strengthens it; while years of political freedom often lead to a neglect of liberty as a value. The effects of coercive, political persuasion, brainwashing, are never permanent. Trilling in his recent Freud lecture, "The Crisis of the Culture of Our Time," makes the point that no matter how great the cultural pressure for conformity, compliance, and homogeneity, the ultimate goals of man's instinctual apparatus are constitutionally determined and human strivings can never be completely and permanently arrested. If religion, then, has failed to obtain complete control over human behavior, if its effect is merely one of influence and modulation, it is not because of poor technique, but because of the ultimate independence of the human spirit and the essential autonomy of the instinctual apparatus.

Finally, I should like to ask a question which is irrelevant to science but urgent to humanity: assuming that we are able to learn and to use effective techniques of behavior regulation, are we sure that we can use them more wisely than religion has?

76. A Code of Moral and Spiritual Values *

PAUL S. ANDERSON

IN 1951 the National Education Association published the report of its Educational Policies Commission on "Spiritual and Moral Values in the Public Schools." As a teacher I found this statement stimulating but complex and indefinite as to specific ideas which might be emphasized in classroom work. The problem of changing the report to a code becomes important when one wishes to examine instructional materials to note which values are stressed.

* From Paul S. Anderson, "A Code of Moral and Spiritual Values," *The Educational Forum* (May, 1956), pp. 401–6. Reprinted by permission.

In some cases a statement in the original report is definite, such as "Each person should feel responsible for the consequences of his conduct." Others require simplification or interpretation.

Since the usefulness of such a code depends upon the way it might be interpreted by teachers, nine graduate students who had teaching experience evaluated the selections of several fifth grade textbooks in terms of the values listed in the code. They were asked to indicate the specific concepts that the teacher or child might discuss as a result of reading the material in the textbooks.

While individuals making these judgments differed as to the total number of values that might be present in a selection, there was a high degree of consensus concerning those listed. For example, one person might list only statements in the code that concerned devotion to truth while others would list those and also some stated in the code under Moral Responsibility.

The code as completed is divided into the ten major areas of the Commission's report.

I. *The basic value of human personality.*
   1. Every human being should have opportunity to achieve by his own efforts a feeling of security in dealing with problems of daily life.
   2. The individual can acquire a capacity for moral judgment and a sense of moral responsibility.
   3. Every child should have the opportunity to grow to his full physical, intellectual, and moral stature.
   4. Individual needs and aspirations differ.
   5. The child should feel that he can do things of value, that he belongs and is wanted.
   6. The strong and able have no superior moral status but have more definite moral responsibilities.
   7. Each individual should have a profound sense of self-respect and personal integrity.
   8. Every tendency toward despotism should be resisted.

II. *Moral responsibility.*
   1. Each person should feel responsible for the consequences of his own conduct.
   2. Moral responsibility and self-discipline are marks of maturity.
   3. An individual must learn to make decisions and accept the consequences.
   4. The defeats of life should strengthen character and make one more able.
   5. While the individual should seek help from organized codes and other individuals, one should not become completely dependent upon them.

6. During childhood there should be a balance between protective authority and delegation of responsibility.
7. Self-reliance should be tempered by social conscience.
8. Self-discipline should enable one to deal firmly with oneself and gently with others.
9. A person should have self-confidence and respect for himself as well as others.

III. *Institutions are the servants of men.*

1. Domestic, cultural, and political institutions are not in themselves suitable objects of veneration, except as they contribute to the moral values of life.
2. A family should be linked by affection rather than authority.
3. Institutions justify their existence as they contribute to the well-being of individuals.
4. Governments are established to promote individual rights.
5. Institutions should be subject to adjustments according to the needs and values of the individuals.
6. Education should encourage continuing appraisal of the suitability of existing institutions.
7. Young people should develop a strong sense of responsibility for community well-being and a willingness to devote themselves unselfishly to it.
8. One protects the institutions one values.

IV. *Common consent.*

1. Mutual consent is better than violence.
2. Voluntary cooperation is essential in all forms of life.
3. No partisan interest is authorized to overreach the popular will.
4. Force, tempered by humanity, regulated by law, and safeguarded by justice, must restrain those who reject the methods of peace.
5. The principle that group decisions should be made and enforced by common consent applies to all relationships of life.
6. The educational program should give opportunities for friendly cooperation.
7. Within limits set by degree of maturity, the reasons for established controls should be made clear to those who are subject to them.
8. Controls should be applied only when needed for the well-being of the group.
9. The administration of controls should be tempered by due regard for the imperfections of human nature and the rights of minorities.
10. Citizens should vote.
11. Citizens should vote without fear.
12. Citizens should be informed about issues of controversy before they vote.
13. Through education we can keep our form of government.

V. *Devotion to truth.*
   1. A person should have freedom to express his convictions.
   2. When a man can be punished for speaking his mind, he is tempted to say what is safe and not necessarily what his convictions direct.
   3. The right and opportunity to learn or seek the truth should not be denied.
   4. We should seek to know the truth.
   5. The arbitrary use of power to establish truth should not be permitted. (Real truth has basic power.)
   6. Loyalty to methods of rational discussion should be established.
   7. Truthfulness to facts in human relationship is essential.
   8. Criticism should be based on truth.
   9. Freedom to speak does not mean freedom to speak falsely.
   10. Everyone makes mistakes in observation, memory, etc., but to deliberately change the truth to prevent others from securing knowledge is wrong.
   11. A person should admit his errors.

VI. *Respect for excellence.*
   1. Excellence in mind, character, and creative ability should be fostered.
   2. Our welfare depends to a considerable degree on the extent to which we lift into positions of power and trust our most gifted representatives.
   3. Men should be governed as equals but we recognize that men differ in qualities.
   4. Wealth or ancestry do not guarantee superiority.
   5. It is as bad to prevent the full development of a superior individual's ability as it is to deny others an opportunity for growth.
   6. The school should stimulate and recognize the achievement of excellence in every sphere of life.
   7. Routine tasks or products can possess excellence.
   8. Students with superior ability should be recognized and receive appropriate educational guidance.

VII. *Moral equality.*
   1. All persons should be judged by the same moral standards.
   2. No man has the right to injure, persecute, or exploit others.
   3. One should treat others as one would wish to be treated.
   4. Americans seek justice and fair play.
   5. Americans are hostile to arrogance.
   6. In school there should be no discrimination based on family, race, nationality, religion, or wealth.
   7. Differences should be a means of enriching the common life.
   8. Americans resent special privileges or servility.
   9. Every man is entitled to equal rights before the law.

      10. We seek a world society of free people living under a regime of peace and fair play.

VIII. *Brotherhood.*

      1. Brotherhood should take precedence over selfish interests.

      2. Each adult citizen should strive to provide through his own efforts for the comfort and well-being of himself and those who are dependent upon him; however, those who are prevented from doing this through no fault of their own are a responsibility for all.

      3. One should not only share with the needy but attack the causes of want and suffering.

      4. A feeling of brotherhood is the result of understanding others' needs and problems and working together in a common cause.

      5. Humanitarian efforts should preserve the self-respect of those helped.

      6. Individuals should cooperate to protect the unfortunate.

      7. The school should strengthen the cooperative impulses but also insist that individuals assume responsibility.

      8. The school should encourage participation in humane and constructive community activity.

IX. *The pursuit of happiness.*

      1. Each person should have the greatest opportunity for the pursuit of happiness, provided that such activities do not interfere with similar opportunities for others.

      2. Lasting happiness is derived from deep personal resources and from the affection and respect of others.

      3. The cultivation of happiness may demand deferment of present pleasure for future satisfactions.

      4. Happiness cannot be bought.

      5. Happiness is more than temporary pleasure.

      6. Experience that satisfies spiritual needs and noble achievement brings happiness. This is especially true in creative expression, literature, music, and creation of beauty.

      7. Happiness depends on being accepted socially and needed.

      8. Financial success should be the result of one's own ability and effort.

X. *Spiritual enrichment.*

      1. Each person should be offered the emotional spiritual experiences which transcend the materialistic aspects of life.

      2. Spiritual values arise from many sources:

          Creative artistic expressions
          Noble buildings
          Religious ritual
          Memories of heroic lives
          Contemplation of Nature

Simple ceremonies of human relationship
Poetry and music
Faith

3. Public schools should not teach creeds, but should stress spiritual elements in all experience.
4. The schools should provide an environment of beauty and refinement.
5. Creative abilities should be sought out and fostered.

The value of such a code may be only for those who made it in that it created a need to evaluate the basic report in terms that had a meaning in classroom behavior. However, a wider use may be illustrated by its application to a specific selection in a fifth grade reader. The following is the summary of a story titled, "Josie's Home Run."

Josie's Home Run

Josie likes to do everything her twin brother does—especially play ball. But her brother does not like having her along all the time. Her Mother says that Josie should not play with the boys but with a few friends in the neighborhood. Finally Lowell School had only to beat Whittier to become champions. Since she cannot play, Josie coaches her brother. On the day of the game, he is sick as is another star of the team. Josie has her hair cut short and plays as her brother—eventually winning the game. All this time the crowd thinks she is Joe. When her father recognizes her, he asks, "Do you think your brother would be willing to take credit for something you did?" But she is cheered and forgiven and at the next game cheers so loudly that Joe's team wins.

The story contains a stated value:
"Do you think your brother would be willing to take credit for something you did?"
This would be classified under the general value of *Devotion to Truth*. The specific concept involved is "Truthfulness to facts in human relationship is essential."

The basic theme involves Josie's desire for equal recognition with her brother. This would be classified under the general value *Respect for Excellence*. The specific concept involved is "Equality of opportunity must be in terms of different abilities."

Josie's devotion to her school and team would be listed under the general value *Institutions Are the Servants of Men*. The specific concept illustrated is "One protects the institutions one values."

Josie's disobedience to her mother involves *Moral Responsibility* and specifically "Moral responsibility and self-discipline are marks of maturity."

The action of the parents might illustrate the specific concept that "A family should be linked by affection rather than authority" under the general value *Institutions Are the Servants of Men.*

There is a question in the minds of many teachers concerning the advisability of such "moralizing." Certainly evidence exists that verbalizing such concepts does not necessarily influence behavior. Many educators refuse to consider such instruction concerning values at all on the ground that they represent subjective judgments which cannot be verified. Indeed, Arthur Murphy has observed that some educators "would rather be caught with an incendiary bomb than a moral preference."

While agreeing that there is much to be learned concerning the development of attitudes and the value concepts of an individual, the awareness of such values as presented in the code by both teachers and students can be justified by educational experience. M. E. Sadler, after an intensive study of moral training in England, among other conclusions, states, "Study and analysis of values is important. History and literature can help organize the goals and aspirations of youth."

The use of the story for such purposes can be illustrated by the parables of the Bible, the fables of Æsop, and the Chinese classics. The story is probably the human race's oldest curriculum. Dr. Stanley Hall has said, "Let me choose the stories for a nation and I care not who makes its laws."

If the testimony of children themselves is worth anything, the story is one important force in the life of the pupil. J. W. Searson investigated the judgments of 22,000 elementary-school pupils and 6,000 high school pupils as to the influence on their own ideals exerted by the literature they had studied. The majority believe that they had been definitely helped, that their ideals were perceptibly higher because of the stories they had read.

Tuttle points out that it is one thing to praise integrity; it is quite another thing to control forces which integrate a child's interests. One of the most effective forces that does this is the story. Through the play of imagination the child can see how one habit aids another, how one act implies another, how one trait includes others, how an idea implies many traits. The reading of many stories, each of which makes vivid the relationship of two or more patterns of conduct, eventually constructs a network of relationships that unifies meaning and organizes values into a great hierarchy of loyalties.

Conduct moves surely in the direction of its dominant imagery. An ideal is a conscious image made personal and a likeable personality in fiction is a symbol of an idea. The story has power to improve conduct not by merely attaching approval to wholesome conduct, but by doing it without implying that the hearer has been guilty of less worthy behavior.

The usefulness of such a code as presented here will depend upon the teacher as she uses it to redefine behavior of those with whom she works. There are implications in each statement which must be discovered by the student as he builds his own code of values.

77. *Psychosexual Development* *

L. JOSEPH STONE
AND JOSEPH CHURCH

E ARLY in the preschool years, the child's awareness of his own sex membership plays little part in his identity. The child can say readily enough whether he is a boy or a girl, but the designation probably lacks any profound significance or stable anchorage for him. As we have already mentioned, most young children in their play feel free to take on male or female roles as the occasion demands, without reference to their own biological make-up and without the embarrassment a school-age child would feel. At age 4, even those children who know about genital differences between boys and girls regard them as secondary to styles of coiffure or dress in determining sex and sex differences. One four-year-old, visiting a family new to the neighborhood, observed their small baby creeping about the sunny lawn in the nude. Reporting on the new family to her mother, she was asked whether the baby was a boy or a girl and replied, "I don't know. It's so hard to tell at that age, especially with their clothes off." The curiosity of three- or four-year-olds about sexual matters, and their ventures into sex play, are likely to be brief. Toward five, children take genital differences more seriously and begin to be aware of personality differences related to sex. In groups of five-year-olds, one can see boys pursuing masculine interests in predominantly masculine company, and girls banding together in feminine activities. Here we have a foreshadowing of the pronounced cleavage of the sexes that takes place during the school years. We should also add that awareness of sexuality and sex roles comes earlier, as Rabban

* From L. Joseph Stone and Joseph Church, *Childhood and Adolescence; A Psychology of the Growing Person*, pp. 164–70. Copyright © 1957 by Random House, Inc., New York, and reprinted with permission.

has pointed out, to lower-class (and to most primitive) children than to middle-class children. Not only does the lower-class child tend to lead a less sheltered life, but masculine and feminine roles are more clearly defined for him than in our middle-class society of many overlapping activities for men and women.

Although the social implications of being a boy or a girl seem to outweigh the sexual ones up to the time of puberty, five-year-olds are likely to be quite persistent in their questions and experiments, and seem to be on the threshold of clear-cut sexual experience. Indeed, Kinsey cites evidence to show that some children—it is all but impossible to know how many—are able to attain sexual climax as early as age 3. Our discussion of self-awareness thus brings us to a consideration of the psychosexual crisis of the preschool years.

The Freudian View of Sexual Development

Freud's formulations of the role of sexuality in development are accepted in differing degrees by professional people in the fields of psychiatry, social work, and psychology. There can, however, be no doubt that Freud's ideas have been enormously influential, so that even those workers who reject the general framework of Freudian theory still find many of his concepts useful, and those who reject his concepts are obliged to find new ways of accounting for the facts he brought to light. Because Freud's thinking was so influential, and because his ideas have become a part of our general culture, we feel that it is necessary to present, at least in brief outline, something of the original Freudian doctrine. We have already sketched in Freud's notions about the oral and anal stages of development. Here we shall deal with what was for him the most crucial period of all, the *phallic stage,* culminating in the *Oedipus complex.*

The term "Oedipus complex" comes from the Greek myth of King Oedipus, who unwittingly, but in fulfillment of an old prophecy, killed his father and married his mother. Analogously, the small boy is seen as falling in love with his mother and turning against his father as a rival for her affections. Naturally, these strivings are opposed by the realities of the situation, by the child's sense of danger in competing with an all-powerful father, and by contradictory impulses of affection for the father and resentment (as when she disciplines him) against the mother. The normal outcome of this (in Freud's view) universal *conflict* of opposing forces is to align and identify oneself with the father, submerging (i.e., *repressing*) the unacceptable wishes. It will be noted that here and in what is to follow, we speak largely in terms of the boy. In general, it is safe to say that the girl follows a roughly equivalent sequence, with the opposite parent substituted in the relationships of attachment and hostility. However, Freud was never quite satisfied with his description of the female Oedipus complex (sometimes referred to as the "Electra complex"), and at various times developed its details in different ways.

This view, based originally on work with adult neurotics, has found some confirmation in—or at least is not inconsistent with—the behavior of both normal and disturbed children. In regard to turning against the parents, although adults were long loath to accept the fact, children are *ambivalent* about their parents; that is, they blend or alternate hostility with affection. It likewise seems to be true, as Freud proposed, that children feel guilty about their anger and conceal or deny it. In regard to the Oedipus complex itself, we should make explicit that for Freud the attachment to the mother includes specifically sexual feelings, coinciding with the shift of focus of *erogenous zones* (parts of the body susceptible to sexual stimulation) from oral and anal to genital during the latter half of the preschool years. Freud calls this stage *phallic*, however, to distinguish it from the true *genital* stage of adult sexuality. Even though Freud acknowledged a real difference between infantile and adult sexuality, his ideas were highly repugnant to his contemporaries. Nevertheless, subsequent observations of children have shown the ubiquity of masturbation and other indicators of sexual interest and activity. It is, as we know, commonplace for little boys to announce that they will one day marry their mothers, or little girls their fathers. One little girl, at age 5, went through the house systematically turning pictures of her mother to the wall. Such behavior may well reflect Oedipal strivings of the kind Freud postulated.

The repression of dangerous wishes that ends the Oedipal phase was thought by Freud to be a product of threats of castration by the father. (Freud did not use "castration" in the literal sense of removal of the gonads, but in the sense of any implied or actual injury to the genitalia, especially to the penis itself.) Unlike some other societies, ours has placed powerful taboos on masturbation, and there is no doubt that many irrational threats have been made by adults to check its practice, even, according to widespread testimony, to "If you don't stop, I'll cut it off!" Perhaps such threats were more common in Freud's day: they seem to be present in the reports of all his patients. Freud concluded that even if the father did not make such threats openly, they were sensed by the child and associated with sexuality, with yearnings toward the mother, and with guilt for hostility against the father, and hence became one of the major forces in the repression of these unacceptable feelings. In the Freudian view, therefore, the fears of young children that we discussed earlier are seen as *castration anxiety,* open or disguised representations of fear of mutilation at the hands of the potentially angry and vengeful father (often symbolized in dreams or fantasies or dramatic play as a large animal). The underlying threat is always seen as the threat of bodily attack, specifically against the genitals. Thus, alarm like Stuart's over the intactness of his body, "even to the littlest tonsil," would be seen by the Freudian psychologist as veiled castration fear.

According to Freud, the infant is born with primitive desires and rages. Freud called this primitive aspect of the personality the *id,* and conceived of it as wholly wishful, demanding, and wholly uninfluenced by the demands of reality. In another Freudian phrase, the id functions solely in terms of the *pleasure-principle.* In the course of growing up, the id components of the personality are always present in their unmodified state (we may become aware of them in some of our dreams and daydreams), but their expression is limited by two other "sectors" of the personality, labeled *ego* and *super-ego.* The ego is the reality-oriented part of the person: the person as perceiver, rememberer, reasoner, doer, and mediator of id-impulses in terms of what is realistic and feasible. In Freud's terminology, the ego is governed by the *reality-principle.* As the child becomes more aware of his parents as people whose love is crucial to him, his concerns with their admonitions and rules of behavior become something more than a recognition of reality in terms of what he can get away with. In the process of resolving the Oedipal conflict, the child buries his early overattachment to his mother (if he is a boy) and substitutes for the hostility toward his father a strong identification with him. This is said to involve an actual incorporation of certain aspects of the father's image, including the authority-wielding ones. The internalized paternal authority becomes the superego (roughly speaking, the conscience), which influences the kind of behavior the child now allows *himself.* It is as though a bit of the parent were inside him saying—but saying in the child's own voice—"Thou shalt" or "Thou shalt not": these are now *his* standards of good and bad. He is now capable of experiencing *guilt,* the product of self-condemnation, as opposed to the shame produced by parental rebuke or ridicule.

Freud's view that all children normally experience passion, hostility, shame, anxiety, and conflict is surely closer to the mark than the "sweetness and light" viewpoint that he did so much to undermine. At the same time, Freud was an extremely moral man and emphasized the importance of guilt. Conscience, the voice of guilt, is the necessary basis of much of the self-regulation required for sound social relationships. According to Freud, this is the time when one can throw in one's lot with other people or else become alienated from them and, as an inevitable consequence, from oneself. A healthy and complete superego incorporates parental love and dependability as well as threat. The failure to establish close ties of affection may lead to the development of a "psychopathic" personality, a person for whom the feelings of others are important only as something to be manipulated, and for whom right and wrong are measured in terms of personal gain. On the other hand, excessive threat by parents, producing excessive guilt in the child, causes different disturbances, including constriction of spontaneity and initiative. Erikson, whose rephrasing of basic Freudian concepts we have drawn on in describing the critical issues of infancy and toddlerhood, makes the key issue of the preschool years development in the direction either of initiative or of guilt. (While we share his view that there is a danger that initiative or spontaneity may be crippled at this period of growth, this single issue, as we stated at the beginning of the chapter, does not seem to take in enough of the developmental phenomena, or even the developmental problems, of the preschool years.)

Freud's views on parental roles may have been influenced by the Middle European family structure of his time, with its emphasis on the father as a powerful, authority-laden figure. Many writers, including psychoanalysts, have pointed out that this picture does not precisely fit the contemporary middle-class American father. We have come a long way since Clarence Day's time, when, according to the image we now hold, Father was a remote, Olympian figure who dispensed counsel, commands, rewards, and punishments (most often the last: "Just wait until your father gets home!"). During the day, he disappeared to a vaguely hallowed place known as The Office. Nowadays, he may still be remote, but he surely cannot be Olympian. There is a distressing trend in some families for father to become a dissociated supernumerary whose life does not really intersect with those of his wife and children. There is yet another trend in which father is, in his off-duty hours, submerged in family activity, playing a much more intimate role in household management, changing diapers and giving bottles, running the appliances that make mother's lot easier, and doing the weekly shopping. He would not think of handing down decrees from on high, as in the Clarence Day era, but shares the decision-making process with his wife and, as they get old enough, the children. The Office has lost its sanctity—indeed, mother has probably done a term of service in an office, too.

Not everyone, however, is totally enthusiastic about this second trend in being a husband. The husband himself may feel somewhat cut off from the masculine world he knew as a soldier or young bachelor. Along with this goes the changed significance of his work, which was at one time a separate compartment of male existence with gratifications quite different from those of having a family; the lessened value of work contributes to the husband's decreased sense of personal worth. Whatever he may be on the job, back home in the suburbs he may be in danger of becoming an assistant mother and of losing his specifically masculine identity. At first glance, studies of unemployed men in Austria during the 1930's might not seem too relevant to today's prosperous young American husbands, but findings by Lazarsfeld and his associates about the loss of prestige these unemployed men suffered in the eyes of their families may be comparable to a loss of prestige because work has low esteem. There is evidence in the content of radio programs and comic strips that father, in descending from his pedestal, has lost his dignity and become a figure of fun, a lovable, well-intentioned incompetent who is more to be tolerated than condemned. Some psychologists feel that the process has already gone too far and that in some versions the modern father does not give his children a sufficiently clear picture of masculinity, that he is not sufficiently differentiated from the mother to provide a model of the manly virtues for his sons to identify with and his daughters to relate to. Needless to say, our description of the contemporary middle-class father is a composite caricature, and the trends we have spoken of are not universal. Besides which, we should not overlook the very real gains for fathers and children in the increase of companionship between them. We are not advocating a return to the stern, Freudian father, but an understanding, participating kind of fatherhood which is nonetheless paternal and masculine, and not a second-rate, part-time motherhood. In any event, fathers are worth having, a view recently reinforced by Stolz's study of children separated from fathers in military service. By comparison with children not so separated, Stolz's children showed a greater number of feeding and similar problems, reduced independence, poorer relations with their age-mates, increased anxiety, and other such indications of maladjustment.

78. The Nature and Origins of Psychological Sexual Identity *

THOMAS COLLEY

Persons do not exist; there are only male persons and female persons—biologically, sociologically, and psychologically. This is a fact which, in everyday life, is as evident and important to the Australian aborigine as it is to the professional psychologist. The psychologist, however, often ignores this while acting in his professional capacity—especially when designing experiments or developing theoretical systems. Nevertheless, there is no human identity uncomplicated by sexual identity. Personality evolves as either masculine or feminine, or as some combination of the two.

Despite the obvious importance of the area of sexual identity for understanding personality, there has been very limited progress in theory of sexual identity since the formulations of Sigmund Freud.

The purpose of this paper is to advance a theoretical explanation of the nature and origins of *psychological* sexual identity, which will use a more contemporary language than other theory in this area and will achieve better integration with modern methods and knowledge. It relates to modern trends of psychological thinking in its emphasis upon interactional interpersonal relations, the self, and what is presently being called "person perception."

THEORY IN SEXUAL IDENTITY

It does not seem necessary to review here the various theories of "psychosexual development" and sexual identity; [1] however, a few comments will be appropriate.

Modern psychology is in debt to Sigmund Freud for his forceful assertion that there was, despite what one might like to believe, something of a sexual nature in the parent-child relationship. Also, he saw implications in this relationship which were of importance in explaining the evolution in the child, and later in the adult, of personality characteristics and disorders.

This driving, formative force that he saw in operation was not restricted

* From Thomas Colley, "The Nature and Origins of Psychological Sexual Identity," *Psychological Review*, 66 (1959), 165–77. Reprinted by permission of the author and the American Psychological Association.

[1] For a review of different theoretical views of sexual identity and development, see Blum (1953) and Mullahy (1948).

to the ignorant, weak, or "wicked" persons, but seemed present in the history of the development of every person. Freud then faced the task of explaining the causes of this sexual, and in his day reprehensible, relationship. If there was something sexual going on between parent and child, the child had to be responsible for it. Likewise, if every child had these "base" desires, the forces behind their origin had to be beyond the control of either parent or child. The most suitable explanation available to Freud at that time was that what he saw in operation was an inborn or basically instinctual phenomenon. By proposing the theory of inborn infantile sexuality and the Oedipus situation, he opened the door to further investigation into the way in which sexual urges modify and are modified by individual personalities and societies.

Today, many clinical practitioners take as their theoretical orientation the Freudian theories of "infantile sexuality," "Oedipus complex," and "stages of psychosexual development," either in their original form or in some reformulation (Freud, 1938). This may seem surprising in view of advances made in personality theory since Freud, particularly those made by the "social-psychological" theorists. Freud's thinking, although it forms the basis for so much of modern clinical practice, is only one source to which clinicians may turn for theoretical support.

The work of the cultural anthropologists, notably Margaret Mead (1935, 1949), has exerted a great modifying effect. Further modification has been brought about by the "neo-Freudians," especially Erich Fromm (1941) and Karen Horney (1937). The net effect of these contributions was a shift in emphasis from the inner determinants important in the genesis of personality to the sociocultural or outer determinants.

More recently, in the writings of Carl Rogers (1951), George A. Kelly (1955), and Harry S. Sullivan (1953), the emphasis has begun to swing back toward a position somewhere between these viewpoints, drawing on both, yet adding new meaning. This is the emphasis upon interactional interpersonal relations and the "self" as useful explanatory concepts.

Despite their many merits, these post-Freudian contributions have not found their way with ease into the clinical setting. They have not provided a means of talking and thinking about those aspects of personality which are so important in problems of mental health, sexual interaction, and sexual identity. This has left us with the Freudian concepts as often the most practical clinical tools. They have been modified, but age is beginning to show on many of them. It is hoped that the present approach will take the first steps toward providing some newer, more useful concepts in the area of sexual interaction and sexual identity.

IMPORTANCE OF SEXUAL IDENTITY AND ITS DISCRIMINATION

Most subhuman mammals seem capable from birth or seem quickly to learn ways of discriminating one sex from another within their species. The cues to which they respond are varied, but probably most often involve olfactory and visual perceptual patterns. It is probable that the man animal in its earlier evolutionary stages also relied heavily on such, rather fixed, cues for information as to the gross sexual characteristics of another.

For modern man, however, much more information than odor or appearance is required for comprehensive discrimination of human maleness or femaleness. Human sexual identity is vastly more complex than that of subhuman animals—it does not emerge exclusively from biological origins, and thus it cannot be discriminated on the basis of biological information alone. It is necessary, for example, to know of another not only that he is male, but also what sort of maleness he possesses.

Close interpersonal relations generally involve the interaction of only two persons. For this intimate type of interaction to be meaningful, each person must "identify" the other in certain areas, so that each may respond appropriately to the stimulus the other presents. Probably the most important area for which meaning is sought is that of sexual identity. Unless fairly accurate sexual discrimination is accomplished, interpersonal interaction is likely to be fraught with difficulty and anxiety. An individual's social adjustment, as well as perpetuation of the species, depends upon accurate discrimination of the sexual identity of others.

Sexual Identity

TOTAL SEXUAL IDENTITY

Although terms such as "identification" and sexual "role" have often been defined, the definition of "sexual identity" has been neglected.

As used here, *sexual identity* refers to *the pattern of positions on the biological, sociological, and psychological continua of the maleness-femaleness dimension which characterizes an individual in relation to others of his sociocultural milieu.* This is *total* sexual identity, and is, therefore, rather unwieldy as a concept. We will need to analyze it into several major components.

Description of an individual's sexual identity requires statements covering at least three important factors: a statement of biological sexual identity, a statement of sociological sexual identity, and a statement of psychological sexual identity.

By biological sexual identity (this shall be called *sexual biomode*) is meant the characteristics of heredity and organic structure and function which distinguish the biologically male from the biologically female. Such organic features as the primary and secondary sex characteristics and the endocrine functions are probably most important here.

Sociological sexual identity (or *sexual sociomode*) applies to such things as gross behavior, dress, interests, attitudes, social standards of beauty and strength, and some personality characteristics, which when taken together constitute what a particular society contributes to the concepts of maleness and femaleness.

Psychological sexual identity (or *sexual psychomode*) is meant to include characteristic ways of perceiving one's sexual interactions with others who are identified as being of the same or of opposite sexual identity.

The separation of total sexual identity into the three "modes" is done for clarity in discussion and economy in theoretical organization and does not imply clear-cut types or independent operation of these variables. The modalities of male and female characteristics are, without doubt, complexly interrelated in any person's sexual identity.

The use here of the suffix "mode" intends a meaning similar to its statistical use as "most typical" or "most frequently occurring." The terms *biomode, sociomode,* and *psychomode* may be used to refer to what is typical for an individual, for the population, or for both. For example, if it is stated that a biomodally and sociomodally male person has inappropriate identity in sexual psychomode, this means that his typical psychological identity is different from that typically occurring among males, but that physically and in social ways he is appropriately male. A person's identity may be inappropriate in one, two, or in all three modes.

It is felt that these three new terms will aid in avoiding the confusion which, in the past, has plagued the use of such blanketing terms as "identification," "psychosexual role," "masculine (or feminine) identity," and others even less precise in meaning.

PSYCHOLOGICAL SEXUAL IDENTITY

Description of an individual's sexual psychomode requires statements covering at least two important factors: a statement indicating the individual's characteristic ways of perceiving his interactions with persons of the same sex; and a statement indicating the individual's characteristic ways of perceiving his interactions with persons of the opposite sex.

Here it is meant that there are relatively enduring patterns of sexually differentiated expectations, largely out of awareness, which a person carries into his interpersonal interactions, and that we must specify the nature of these expectations *for each sex respectively*. If, for example, we know that a male characteristically sees his interactions with other males as being quite sexual in nature—that is, if he sees himself as appropriate for the sexual attentions of other males and sees other males as appropriate for his sexual attentions—this does not necessarily mean that, conversely, he will see females as inappropriate for sexual interaction. We need to know *sexual identity in relation to whom*.

In the present formulations, the emphasis will be on that part of the personality which the writer has called *psychomodal sexual identity*. The theoretical proposals will apply mainly to individual interactions and more or less exclude the contributing factors on the biological or broader sociological levels.[2] Further limitations will be that this formulation will deal with "normal" rather than pathological or deviant trends in psychomodal sexual growth, and that idiosyncratic aspects of sexual identity will be excluded from our present concern.

Theory of Sexual Identity

The following postulates are advanced as the preliminary statements of a theory of the origins of psychological sexual identity. Admittedly, they are speculative, but it is hoped that they will prove useful in describing and possibly in understanding sexual identity.

Postulate 1. The sex drive in humans derives originally from biophysical phenomena which the individual is equipped to experience.

By this is meant simply that sex need originally occurs in tissues related to sexual functions and spurs the individual to action. This "spurring" has as its goal the reduction of tension and satisfaction of the need. The resulting behavior may or may not accomplish this goal.

Postulate 2. In humans, reduction of tension and resultant satisfaction of the sexual need may normally be accomplished in a variety of ways.

Here it is assumed that there are, to all practical purposes, neither specific sexual actions (motor response patterns) nor specific sexual objects (perceptual response patterns) that in any organically predetermined way become part of the response repertory of the developing human. Remote biological cues, though they undoubtedly exist in humans, seem to be of

---

[2] Margaret Mead, in *Male and Female* (1949), gives careful attention to the effects of sociocultural influences upon sexual identity. Family group influences are evaluated by Talcott Parsons and Robert Bales in *Family: Socialization and Interaction Process* (1955).

little consequence in the discrimination of persons appropriate for sexual interaction, and in the acquisition of ways of achieving sexual satisfaction.

Postulate 3. Patterns of perceptual and motor response which are appropriate for satisfaction of the sexual need, and which are appropriate for psychomodal sexual identity, come to exist in the individual through the process of learning.

This theory of the processes involved in the determination of the psychological aspects of sexual identity assumes the occurrence of relatively enduring modification of the individual as a result of experience, and that this modification determines both the manner in which sexual satisfaction is achieved and the nature of psychomodal sexual identity.

At this point we shall have to abandon the topic of sexual satisfaction. The variety of sexually satisfying behavior which has been demonstrated to exist among apparently normal persons suggests that such sexual behavior and sexual identity are not closely interdependent. A discussion of sexual satisfaction is apart from our present aims and its inclusion would clutter our view of sexual identity.

Postulate 4. Psychomodal sexual identity is acquired as a result of interpersonal interaction.

The ability to respond to oneself as an object appropriate for sexually differentiated response from others and the ability to respond to others differentially as to sex are acquired as a direct result of having experienced the response made to one, by at least one other individual.

Postulate 5. The earliest and the most important elements which are part of the unique self are those which derive out of the modalities of maleness and femaleness.

Aside from the facts that it is living, human, and helpless, the next most important observation that parents can make about an infant that will give them a basis for meaningful response to it, is that it is either male or female. Maleness-femaleness is the nearest thing to a dichotomy that man can discern in animate nature—and dichotomies are so satisfying.

When a child is born, parents are quick to reify its sex by adding meaning to the clues nature has provided. Colors, clothing, toys, and name are kept appropriate to the child's sex. The one universal set of *differential* expectations which parents bring to the parent-child interaction is that which is based upon the sexual dichotomy. For a child, this differential coloring of parental response provides the first major data for approximating his position as a unique personality. It is evident to him that there is something that is uniquely his that is consistently influencing the responses others make to him.

It would seem that if we could describe the character of the parents' interpretation of the sexual dichotomy to the child we would be far better able to predict that child's future sexual identity. Perhaps we would also do a better job of predicting the nature of many of his interpersonal interactions, both sexual and otherwise. We would hope to know what is the meaning of maleness to him, and what is the meaning of femaleness, for it is into this framework that new human experiences are related such that the individual comes to have characteristic ways of seeing and of responding to others. Humans never simply interact; they interact with males and with females.

Sexual Interaction

Before going further, some definitions will be helpful. As used here, sexual interaction refers to those interactions in which maleness-femaleness is of central importance in shaping the interaction. In daily interpersonal relations, frequently the initial phase is largely a sexual interaction, and thereafter such interactions may reappear in momentary or prolonged fashion.

The term *sexual interaction* is a broad one. It subsumes many intricate behaviors, including those in which physical sexual need is satisfied. In the following discussion, however, the emphasis will be on "social" sexual interactions which, although potentially capable of it, do not ordinarily lead to physical sexual satisfaction. Opportunities for sexual interaction can occur most readily around emotional or physical experiences, and thus they may be found coincident with such child tending activities as feeding, bathing, elimination, punishment, and play.

Although it can be said that all interpersonal experiences of a newborn infant are in a vague sense sexual interactions, there may be no male-female differentiation to them. At first he is not aware of the differentiation in the responses others make to him, nor does he respond in any sexually selective manner. At that time there is merely an unselective *sexual-emotional approach* response on his part. With time, however, the character of these interactions may become differentiated into two general classes: *prosexual* perceptual response patterns and *antisexual* perceptual response patterns.

By *prosexual* perceptual response is meant the characteristic perception of certain interpersonal situations as appropriate for sexual *approach* behavior.

By *antisexual* perceptual response is meant the characteristic perception of certain interpersonal situations as appropriate for sexual *avoidance* behavior. The term *antisexual* implies more than a mere lack of sexual approach quality in a person's relations with others—it mplies the presence of perceptual operations which function to counteract or avoid sexual approach responses which survive from the earlier undifferentiated sexual-emotional approach phase. Much but not all antisexual response will take the *form* of what is presently called hostility. In many instances, however, restrained interaction and "pseudohostile" responses denote the presence of antisexuality.

In addition to these two classes, it is expedient to mention a third: the *confused* perceptual response pattern. This will be used to refer to a person whose sexual interactions with others are characterized by ambiguity.

The Nature of Appropriate Sexual Identity

The view of sexual interaction just presented provides a sexual approach pattern, a sexual avoidance pattern, and a sexual approach-avoidance conflict pattern. Prosexual perceptual response is appropriate with biomodally opposite sex individuals, whereas antisexuality is appropriate with biomodally same sex individuals. This is the sexual paradigm of nature.

Postulate 6. It is a basic necessary (but not sufficient) condition for appropriate psychomodal sexual identity that a person must bring to his interactions with the biomodally opposite sex the expectation that there should be something prosexual in the nature of these interactions.

Postulate 7. Conversely from Postulate 6 and also necessary (but not sufficient) for appropriate psychomodal sexual identity: a person must bring to his interactions with the biomodally same sex the expectation that there should be something antisexual in the nature of these interactions.

The expectations mentioned in these postulates exist universally in human society as the general rule. Although they are necessary, taken individually, neither is sufficient for appropriate sexual identity. Also, in some cultures it is the males that must be aggressive, while in others it is the females—but these are aspects of the sexual sociomode. Sociomodal characteristics may vary greatly from time to time and place to place; however, our assumed universal expectations should prevail. As a corollary to Postulates 6 and 7 we may say that, *to the degree that there is lack or disturbance of the expectations stated under Postulates 6 and 7, there will be inappropriate psychomodal sexual identity.* Such difficulty could be due to either failure to acquire appropriate expectations or to the acquisition of expectations which are at a variance with what is appropriate.

In order for a male, for example, to possess adequate psychomodal sexual identity, he must perceive biomodally female persons as *potentially* conducive to the satisfaction of certain needs which are predominantly sexual in nature. He should also view females as persons who expect *of him* the very kind of expectations which he brings to interactions with them. Adequate psychomodal sexual identity implies the seeing of oneself as having prosexual valence for opposite sex persons and no such valence for same sex persons, and it implies the seeing of opposite sex persons as having prosexual valence for oneself, and same sex persons as not having such a valence.

The Origin of Psychomodal Sexual Identity

BASE IN PERSONALITY THEORY

How does an individual acquire the expectations of appropriate psychomodal sexual identity? In order to answer this question, we must first establish a base in personality theory which will integrate with what we know about social behavior. The ability to respond to oneself as male or as female should come about by the same basic processes by which one comes to have identity in the more general sense of becoming a personality, coming to have a "self."

The theoretical assumption which we shall accept, and which is basic to much of what follows, is that a human comes to have a self—to experience personal identity—only through interpersonal intercommunication, and by learning to call out in himself the same meanings which he calls out in others, through the use of symbols, gestures, and other means of communication, both conscious and unconscious. We incorporate into our own newly forming personality pattern the meanings inherent in the communications of those around us, coming to see ourselves as others see us. Thus the "self" is largely a social product, dependent upon the process of communication for its development. Much that is called personality can be viewed as a result of the meanings and expectations others bring to their interactions with us. Much of personality, then, is a result of "perceptual conforming." [3]

Postulate 8. Psychomodal sexual identity comes about as a result of a process by which the child comes to perceive and respond to itself as it is first perceived and responded to by the significant figures in its early life.[4]

---

[3] The theoretical views presented here are somewhat similar to those of H. S. Sullivan (1953), C. H. Cooley (1922), A. N. Whitehead (1929), and particularly G. H. Mead (1934).

[4] Here and eleswhere in this paper, the term "significant figures" is intended to include persons who are sufficiently close to the child for long enough time to be considered parental equivalents; and other, usually older, persons who, although they do not take the place of parents, are nevertheless present for sustained interaction.

This is the postulate that is basic to our theory, and it will bear elaboration. Calling on the previous postulates, it is possible to assert more clearly that it is not the child who brings to the parent-child interactions the complex of values and expectations related to sexuality. Neither is the child able to identify the sex of parent figures, much less to respond to them differentially as to sex. Another way of stating this postulate would be to say that the parent "projects" psychomodal sexual identity into the child—the male parent projecting maleness into male children and femaleness into female children, and the female parent projecting femaleness into female children and maleness into male children. In addition, the parent will contribute something of his own by projecting distortions, personalized interpretations, and other unique perceptions which have become part of his conception of what is appropriate for male with male, male with female, or female with female interaction. These parental perceptual response patterns occur largely outside of awareness.

From the first time a mother looks at her male baby she knows that he is male and her responses will, in many subtle ways, communicate to him that this is how she sees him. The tone of her voice, the way in which she handles him, the special prolonged interest in his developing genitalia, and countless other responses communicate to the male child that his mother is interested in him in a special sort of way. Later he will learn that she is interested in him as she is interested in others who are like him in one very important manner—they are biomodally male.

A mother brings to her male child all the complex of sexual responses which she has learned. The child in turn responds to the mother in a very free, emotionally uninhibited manner. The child may bring some "instinctual" sexual response to the parent-child relationship, but the parent brings a prosexual interest which has been repeatedly frustrated and heightened by social values, taboos, and other socially contributed sex values which have not yet affected the child.

As a male child matures, he is responded to by others, some of whom are similar to mother and some of whom are different and respond to him differently. From the ones similar to mother, he gets recurring patterns of response that are, in many important ways, like that of the mother. From a different sort of figure in his hazy little world, he begins to get response patterns which are very unlike those of the mother. From these, the males, he gets responses which, in some vague way, tell him that he is one who will be in competition with them—that they view him as inappropriate for the kind of emotional treatment that the mother provides. Thus it is that the male child learns the expectations which the two major classes of adult figures have for him. He learns to expect of mother, and thereafter of other females: a flirtatiousness, a seductivity, a teasing sort of approach and withdrawal that says in unspoken language that prosexual interaction is appropriate here. He learns to expect of father, and thereafter of other males: a rivalry, a measure of hostility, a curtailment of mutual emotional interaction that lets him know that something almost the opposite of pro-sexual interaction is appropriate here.

The generalizations which have been made in the above discussion are very useful ones for a child to make and are necessary for our purposes in explanation. It might appear that when the parental role requires discipline, control, and maintenance of the incest taboo, it tends to contradict these generalizations. In keeping with the present approach, even physical dis-cipline is normally accomplished differentially in relation to sexual identity, and it may even provide an especially fine opportunity for differential parental response—either during or following a disciplinary interaction.

The incest taboo may be maintained by the setting of limits beyond which prosexual interactions may not go. By gentle rebuffing, a normal mother may tell her son that intense prosexual interaction is not appropriate *now* and *with her,* without irrevocably damaging his prosexual expectations con-cerning females.

For a female child, there is little difference in the way sexual meaning is conveyed. In the case of a daughter, it is the father who responds seduc-tively. The mother lets her daughter know that prosexual interaction is inappropriate between females and that she views the daughter as a miniature rival for the attentions of males.

The fact that the female child is at first intimately associated with the mother in a need-satisfying relationship does not seem to pose a serious problem for her psychomodal sexual identity. From the very first, the mother has been aware that this is a little female and that prosexual interest in her is inappropriate. Also, this little female is physically similar to the mother, and therefore not likely to call forth the special interest in the sexual apparatus and sexual function that the mother has for a male child. Despite the fact that the mother is satisfying certain of the daughter's needs, she is able to make it clear that there is little that is prosexual in this relation-ship. It is just that discrimination of the sexually seductive ones may come later for the female than for the male child, depending upon how early a father begins to engage in close interaction with a daughter.

Perhaps it will serve the purpose of clarity and emphasis to point out two implications which arise in relation to Postulates 6, 7, and 8.

I. A certain *optimum* of seductive behavior on the part of the opposite sex parent in interaction with the child is necessary for appropriate psycho-modal sexual identity to occur.

II. A certain *optimum* of hostile and rivalrous behavior on the part of the parent of the same sex in interaction with the child is necessary for appropriate psychomodal sexual identity to occur.

Variation in Psychomodal Sexual Identity

Psychomodal sexual identity can vary from what is biomodally appropriate as a result of several conditions: insufficient contact with a parent or parents whose psychomodal sexual identity is appropriate; physically the child fails to call out differential parental response; and contact with a parent or parents whose psychomodal identity is in some manner inappropriate.

The *first* condition could come about if a parent is absent either physically or psychologically from the family scene.

It is important to note here that our theoretical plan allows for the total absence—physical or psychological—of one parent without disturbing the child's psychomodal identity, provided there is one appropriately identified parent with whom the child experiences close interaction. One parent may supply sufficient differential response to the child for appropriate identity to occur. Even in a father's absence, an appropriately identified mother will respond to a boy "as if" he were a male and will expect him to treat her as a male would treat a female. When she and her son are together in the presence of other males she will expect of him some competition, hostility, and lack of sexuality in his relations with the other males regardless of their ages. Her interpretative approval or disapproval of his play with other male children at home, or of incidents he recounts from peer relations when not at home, also serve to let him know what she expects of male with male interactions. *Thus, a child may learn appropriate identity in sexual psychomode in the absence of a parent like himself.*

Most other theory in sexual identity differs from this approach in that it conceives that a child comes to "be" sexually as a result of *identification with* the parent of the same sex, and if this relation is disturbed or lacking, then psychological sexual identity is weakened or blocked. The term "identification" used in that manner requires the presence of a model after whom the child can pattern his behavior. Behavior in imitation of a model is important: however, its main contribution to sexual identity seems to be in the acquisition of appropriate identity in sexual sociomode.

The *second* condition, that of lack of sexual stimulus value on the part of the child, can result from such biomodal factors as lack of physical vigor, gross deviation in physiognomy, or incapacitation of the child due to mental or physical factors. It is possible for only one or for both parents to be affected by conditions such as these.

Although lack of sexual stimulus value on the part of the child can cause difficulties in sexual identity, the presence of too intense sexual stimuli emanating from the child, or projected into the child, can be just as detrimental to sexual adjustment. This situation might result in "over-identity" as a sexual being.

The *third* condition which can result in inappropriate psychomodal sexual identity—contact with a parent whose identity is inappropriate—can best be understood by examining the possible combinations of parental response and by describing the resulting types of psychomodal sexual identity. We shall assume that, in the following descriptions, there are no unusual biomodal or sociomodal circumstances which could influence sexual identity.

EXAMPLES OF PSYCHOMODAL SEXUAL IDENTITY

By using the three general classes of sexual perceptual response, we may hypothesize nine characteristic patterns of parental response, and thus nine types of psychomodal sexual identity in relation to male and female figures. Table 1 illustrates the possible types of male identity. The letters P, A, and C designate *prosexual, antisexual,* and *confused* perceptual response, either *from* the parent or *to* another figure. A Type I male, for example, is provided by his father with antisexual (A) expectations which he carries into interaction with other male figures. His mother provides him with prosexual (P) expectations concerning interactions with females.

Table 1

EXAMPLES OF MALE IDENTITY IN SEXUAL PSYCHOMODE

Figure with Whom Interacting	Type of Identity								
	I	II	III	IV	V	VI	VII	VIII	IX
Male	A	A	C	A	P	C	C	P	P
Female	P	C	P	A	P	C	A	C	A

The variety of male identities that can occur range from the most appropriate—that in which sexual biomode and psychomode are parallel (Type I)—to the least appropriate—that in which psychomodal sexual identity is inverted in relation to biomode (Type IX). In the latter case we may hypothesize the true psychomodal invert, and, because approach-avoidance confusion is absent, this type may characterize the rare psychologically "adjusted" homosexual.

Between these two types we may hypothesize others in which there is bilateral prosexuality, bilateral antisexuality, bilateral confusion, or some combination involving confusion. A male of Type II, for example, would have appropriate identity in relation to males, but would experience confusion in relation to females. He may be at ease in interaction with males but quite anxious in interaction with females. The *kind* of maleness he possesses is different from that found in Type III, but the *degree* of inappropriateness is similar.

Types of resultant feminine identity may be described similarly; however, the relations involved would be reversed.

The examples illustrated suggest that a number of predictions are possible, provided we are able to describe the psychomodal sexual identity of the parents. Postdiction of parental identity may be possible if we can determine the character of a person's perceptual responses to male and female figures.

Contact with others who are psychomodally unlike the parents may decrease the accuracy of predictions somewhat. However, it seems reasonable to assume that the early years of close interaction with parent figures largely determine the expectations of sexual psychomode and that these expectations dictate the selection of persons for close interaction. Peers who are very divergent in psychomodal expectations probably exclude each other from close interactions because such interaction would be chaotic or threatening.

It should be clear that the types of identity we have illustrated do not describe degrees of "homosexuality"—they refer to inner psychological sexual identity only. Overt homosexual sex experience does not imply inappropriate psychomodal sexual identity any more than overt heterosexual sex experience implies appropriate identity.

In the theoretical description presented in this paper, one can see a rather different approach to understanding sexual inversion than that proposed by psychoanalytic theory, and it is believed a more predictive one. Fenichel (1945) says of homosexuality, "The homosexual man identifies himself with his frustrating mother in one particular respect: like her he loves men" (p. 331). In keeping with the present approach, it is proposed that the mother of such an inverted male might not love men and might communicate to her son that prosexual interaction with females is inappropriate.

More recently, Erikson (1950) has indicated an orientation which again reflects a prominent difference. Erikson states that the "utopia" of developmental stages, "in a woman, is that ability to partake in and identify with the male's procreative role, which makes woman an understanding companion and a firm guide of sons" (pp. 88–89). The present theory suggests that the understanding companionship and firm guidance of sons should be a paternal contribution and that a mother such as Erikson proposes could easily supply the son with inappropriate expectations regarding women.[5]

Biomode and Sociomode

Any of the "types" of psychomodal sexual identity mentioned can occur in relation to any combination of biomodal and sociomodal identity. For example, a woman may be employed in a profession where "mannish" behavior and dress are desirable, if not necessary. Despite this inappropriate sociomodal sexual identity, she may still be quite feminine psychologically, in sexual psychomode, and physically, in sexual biomode. In like manner, many biomodally deviant males may possess appropriate sociomodal and psychomodal sexual identity.

We may speculate that the three sexual *modes* occasionally interact so as to modify one another. A male who deviates greatly from appropriate biomode and sociomode, whatever the causes, may with time come to develop inappropriate psychomodal identity. Also, a male who is deviant in psychomode and sociomode may with time develop deviations in sexual biomode, such as alteration in endocrine function and the accompanying changes in secondary sex characteristics.

Applications

It is beyond the scope of the present paper to make extensive suggestions as to how the theory may be applied; however, several applications and implications deserve mention.

The present approach may provide for earlier and more accurate diagnosis of disturbance in psychomodal sexual identity. Conventional projective tests might be used in such diagnosis, or special instruments may be devised to measure a child's characteristic perception of males and of females.

[5] Marked differences between the present approach and that of psychoanalytic theory will be discussed fully in a subsequent publication, and the theory will be extended and applied to problems of hostility and guilt.

Once the nature and degree of inappropriateness are determined, it may be possible to provide corrective experience so as to bring about reorganization of perceptual response to self and to others. An implication here is that, in therapy of problems of sexual identity, the *kind* of psychomodal identity possessed by the therapist may be a more important factor than what is talked about or how much "insight" is gained.

Along lines of psychopathology, one might examine the possible relation of certain disorders to certain kinds of psychomodal sexual identity.

Summary

In this paper an attempt has been made to construct a theoretical formulation which will be helpful in understanding and describing the nature and origins of sexual identity. The approach taken is an interactional and interpersonal one.

In the beginning it was indicated that sexual identity can best be understood if it is analyzed into three major components: the *sexual biomode,* the *sexual sociomode,* and the *sexual psychomode.*

It was asserted that to be a person, to have a self, implies the presence of maleness or femaleness—perhaps even depends upon it.

A person's inner or psychomodal sexual identity is held to come about as a result of a person's learning to call out in himself the same response that he calls out in the significant other persons in his early life. Because of the sexual dichotomy, he calls out either *prosexual* or *antisexual* responses in each parental figure.

Emphasis was placed upon the part that *both* parental figures play in responding differentially to the child in terms of sexual identity. The child then carries this differential of expectation into his interactions with others in later life.

It was indicated that different kinds as well as different degrees of psychomodal sexual identity are possible, and that we must describe the nature of a person's sexual identity in relation to males and in relation to females separately.

79. *Treated Sex Offenders and What They Did* * [1]

LOUISE VIETS FRISBIE

THIS PAPER is an interim report based on data being assembled over a five-year period on factors in recidivism among psychiatrically treated sex offenders. To date there has been an excess of conjecture rather than documented fact from both a medical and legal standpoint on the issue of sexual psychopathy. The Atascadero State Hospital, opened in June 1954, offers a unique research opportunity because it was designated as the one California facility for the observation and treatment of sex offenders in accordance with statutory requirements.

It is usually assumed by the general public that the molester of female children is an old man more or less in his dotage, that an incestuous relationship between father and daughter seldom occurs, and that such a relationship between father and stepdaughter also is rare. The molester of male children is assumed to be the middle-aged tramp or hobo who entices little boys into culverts or vacant buildings. These assumptions are exploded by examination of the records through October 31, 1957, of 1,114 convicted sex offenders who were discharged from Atascadero State Hospital after psychiatric treatment with a statement to the committing court that the patient had improved and was no longer considered a menace to society.[2]

Under the California law on sexual psychopathy [3] the superintendent of the Atascadero State Hospital has the privilege of selecting for treatment only those convicted sex offenders who are deemed treatable and who qualify under the law as having a pattern of abnormal sexual desire and are a menace to the health and safety of the public. The child molester is the prototype of this definition and thus should properly make up the largest group of Atascadero State Hospital patients.

The first discharges from this hospital during 1954 and early 1955 comprise those patients who were originally admitted for observation and treat-

* From Louise Viets Frisbie, "Treated Sex Offenders and What They Did," *Mental Hygiene* (April, 1959), pp. 263–67. Reprinted by permission of the author and The National Association of Mental Health.

[1] This paper expands pertinently on the general information supplied by Paul Kivisto in his article, "Treatment of Sex Offenders in California," *Mental Hygiene,* 42 (1, 1958), 78–80.

[2] Section 5517-b, California Welfare and Institutions Code.

[3] *California Welfare and Institutions Code and Laws Relating to Social Welfare* (Sacramento, 1955), Div. 6, chap. 4, sec. 5500, p. 283.

ment at Mendocino and Metropolitan State Hospitals. The philosophy and interpretation of the law by the superintendents and staffs of those hospitals was somewhat different from that at Atascadero State Hospital in respect to an offense of rape or assault with intent to commit rape on adult females. The superintendent and staff at Atascadero State Hospital usually regard these sexual offenders more properly as criminals within the meaning of the law, for in such cases the offense ordinarily represents absence of control over normal temptation and normal sexual desire. Furthermore, we consider the precise definition of the legal term *sexual psychopath* as inapplicable in instances of homosexuality between two adult males where there is in effect a willing partner, not a victim. This is private abnormality, not publicly menaceful behavior. It is therefore obvious that among the patients committed to Atascadero State Hospital for observation and treatment a minimum number will represent those convicted of rape of the adult female or of adult homosexuality, and presumably only when such convictions are symptomatic of a pattern of other uncontrollable neurotic sexual misbehavior. The effect of this selection process will be more clearly disclosed as the volume of discharges increases.

The degree of menacefulness is debatable in those sex offenses where there is no physical contact. Society, however, is annoyed by the habitual exhibitionist who mocks propriety and convention, the Peeping Tom who invades privacy, and the maker of lewd telephone calls who forces his vulgarity upon a victim usually selected at random. Obviously these persons have abnormal and uncontrolled desires. Incarceration in jail or prison serves no useful purpose since the deterrence factor is not applicable to the man who has neurotic compulsive behavior. Treatment in a psychiatric setting serves society more advantageously.

For purposes of clarity, in Table 1 the categorizing of patients by type of sex offense is in arbitrary groupings according to physical contact or no physical contact. Of 1,114 cases, 76 per cent are child molesters.

In Table 2 the age of the patient is computed in relation to the date of his admission to Atascadero State Hospital. This is reasonably accurate in assessing the patient's age at the time of his conviction because the pre-trial jail period rarely exceeds ninety days and is usually shorter. Hospitalization follows rapidly after the superior court hearing on the issue of presumed sexual psychopathy. Among those cases transferred to this hospital from Metropolitan and Mendocino State Hospitals, however, the patient would actually have been younger when the crime was committed because the admission date to Atascadero State Hospital is less closely related to the conviction date.

Table 1

FREQUENCY OF TYPE OF SEX OFFENSE

Characteristic of Offense	Number of Cases	Per Cent of Cases
PHYSICAL CONTACT	905	81
Molesting child	846	76.0
Molesting adult female	49	4.0
Molesting adult male	10	1.0
NO PHYSICAL CONTACT	209	19
Indecent exposure	136	12.0
Vagrancy *	27	2.4
Peeping Tom	18	2.0
Transvestism and/or stealing women's lingerie	13	1.1
Lewd telephone calls	10	1.0
Arson	4	0.4
Possession of narcotics	1	0.1

* Includes masturbating in car; loitering in park or near swimming pool or school grounds; masquerading as a woman.

Table 2

AGE DISTRIBUTION OF SEX OFFENDERS

Years of Age	Number of Cases	Per Cent of Cases
15–19	25	2.2
20–29	314	28.2
30–39	323	29.0
40–49	179	16.1
50–59	130	11.7
60–69	93	8.3
70–79	46	4.1
80–89	4	0.4

It is apparent that these sex offenders are predominantly young men whose median age is 36.7 years with 59.4 per cent of the total number falling into the age grouping below 40 years. This closely parallels findings on British sex offenders where 64.6 per cent in a study group of 1,985 men were under 40 years of age.[4]

Special attention will be directed to the characteristics of the child

[4] Radzinowicz, L., *Sexual Offences—A Report of the Cambridge Department of Criminal Science* (New York: The Macmillan Co., 1957), p. 113.

molester since these men represent 76 per cent of our study group. The actual conviction may represent an offense varying from one extreme of holding a child on the lap and/or kissing him or her, through digital manipulation of the genitalia, to forcible rape. Whatever the act, there is assumed to be some degree of sex gratification experienced directly or indirectly by the child molester. The ratio of cases of molestation of girls is approximately two and a half times as frequent as molestation of boys, but it must be remembered that in many cases of both sexes there is more than one victim.

Table 3

FREQUENCY OF CHILD MOLESTATION BY SEX OF VICTIM

Sex of Victim	Number of Cases
Girls	579
Boys	229
Girls and boys	38

That the child molester is not necessarily a senile old man becomes clearly demonstrated in Table 4. Fifty-three per cent of the child molesters are under 40 years of age. This is compatible with the median age of 36.7 years for all sex offenders in the study group.

Table 4

AGE DISTRIBUTION OF SEX OFFENDERS COMPARING ALL OFFENSES
WITH CHILD MOLESTING

Years of Age	All Cases	Child Molesting Cases
15–19	25	13
20–29	314	191
30–39	323	247
40–49	179	147
50–59	130	116
60–69	93	85
70–79	46	43
80–89	4	4

To what extent is consanguinity a factor among child molesters and female victims? No attempt is made here to differentiate between fondling and actual incest with penetration because of the lack of uniformity by the courts in the application of the term *incest*.[5] For study purposes, then, all daughter and stepdaughter victims are categorized broadly as child molestation cases and represent 26 per cent of the total child molestation cases involving females. In one third of the 98 cases involving a daughter, the father (patient) was between 30 and 35 years of age.

Table 5

FREQUENCY OF CONSANGUINITY AMONG FEMALE VICTIMS

Relationship of Victim	Number of Cases
Daughter	98
Stepdaughter	56
Daughter and male child	8

The median age of the child molester's female victim is 8.8 years and of the male victim is 12.3 years. The total number of victims in Table 6 is based on statistics through August 31, 1957, and hence does not coincide exactly with figures cited previously.

Table 6

AGE AND SEX OF VICTIMS OF CHILD MOLESTERS

Age of Victims	Sex of Victims	
	GIRLS	BOYS
0– 2	7	0
3– 5	76	12
6– 8	228	44
9–11	192	67
12–14	71	108
15–17	18	39
18–20	2	1

Summary

The findings in this inquiry [6] show:

1. Eighty-one per cent of the offenses involved physical contact.
2. Seventy-six per cent of the offenses represented child molesting.

---

[5] *Deering's Penal Code of the State of California* (Revised 1949), Sec. 285, p. 85.

[6] For an earlier report, see Louise V. Frisbie, "The Treated Sex Offender," *Federal Probation*. 22 (March, 1958), 18–24.

3. The median age of the sex offenders was 36.7 years.

4. Approximately two and a half times as many girls as boys were victims of the child molester.

5. Among the cases of female victims of child molesters 26 per cent were daughters or stepdaughters.

6. The median age of the female victim of the child molester was 8.8 years.

7. The median age of the male victim of the child molester was 12.3 years.

80. *Mate Selection and Marriage* *

LESTER D. CROW
AND ALICE CROW

THE SELECTION of a marriage partner has had an interesting history. Respective cultures have imposed specific regulations concerning who shall marry. Political, religious, economic, and family restrictions of one kind or another have controlled and still control mate selection among differing societal groups.

Marriage concepts. Polyandry (one woman with several husbands) and polygamy (one husband having several wives) still are conventional forms of marriage among some of the more primitive peoples. The so-called civilized world, however, is committed to the concept of monogamy, or one mate for each person. Moreover, in those cultures in which only the monogamous form of marriage has legal status most marriage rituals imply, through the words "till death do us part," that the one marriage shall be a permanent relationship until the death of one of the mates.

Traditionally, the female mate was expected to be chaste before her marriage. The discovery by her husband, during the couple's first sexual intercourse, that his wife's hymen had been broken was legal cause for an

* From Lester D. Crow and Alice Crow, *Understanding Our Behavior; A Psychology of Personal and Social Adjustment.* Reprinted by permission of Alfred A. Knopf, Inc. Copyright 1956 by Lester D. Crow and Alice Crow.

annulment of the marriage. Real or imagined evidence of a wife's infidelity to her husband also constituted grounds for the husband's dissolving the marital relationship.

With a few exceptions societal groups always have and still continue to display a generally accepting attitude toward male sexual activities. This attitude probably is rooted in a traditional belief that for the male sexual intercourse is a necessary activity for the maintenance of good health, strength, and virility. The female, as we noted earlier, was expected to be the passive recipient of the male's sexual aggression; she subjected herself to, rather than desired, the sex act. We now know, of course, that the sex desire is as strong in the female as in the male.

There still are parents who attempt to guard jealously the chastity of their unmarried daughters, but they prefer sons-in-law who have had considerable experience in sexual activity or "have sowed their wild oats." The implication of this expressed parental attitude was the fact that an "experienced" man probably would be less likely to engage in extramarital sex relations. The possibility of the man's having contracted a venereal disease before his marriage was not considered a significant factor of suitability for marriage. Many states, however, have enacted legislation requiring that both the man and the woman submit to a premarriage physical examination to detect symptoms of venereal disease.

Traditional bases for mate selection. In many of the older cultures marriages were arranged by parents on the bases of parent-determined suitability of the match. Socioeconomic status and degree of prestige of the families concerned often were considered to be the determining factors of suitability; the girl's parents supplied the dowry, the man's contribution was his superior social status. In many instances the man had the privilege of selecting a girl to whom, at the time, he was sexually attracted or who would be likely to bear him children and establish a comfortable home environment. Whether the girl was emotionally stirred by her suitor was not important. It was taken for granted that the marriage relationship would stimulate in the woman the development of wifely attitudes of loyalty to and respect and liking for her husband.

In spite of traditionally established controls over mate selection, many young people managed to marry persons of their own selection. History has given us stories of great lovers, either married or unmarried. Romantic love, as a generally accepted basis of mate selection, however, is a relatively recent concept. At present a mate may be selected for reasons other than strong emotional attachment; yet it is customary for friends and relatives of the couple to express the conviction, at least superficially, that the contemplated marriage be based on "true love." Many problems of marital adjustment stem from this sentimental attitude toward the marriage relationship in conjunction with the social acceptance of freedom in mate selection as a democratic ideal.

Modern bases of mate selection. Each state enacts legislation concerning the age at which a young person may marry without parental consent. When a young man or woman has reached the legal status of an adult, as prescribed in his or her state, the person is at liberty to marry and to be unrestricted in the choice of mate. In fact, except in cases of extreme sex perversion or of venereal disease infection, much latitude is permitted an individual in connection with his sexual activities and relationships.

Thoughtless mate selection and "quick" marriages are the resultants of various sex-stimulated phases and conditions of modern life. Some of the inducers of mate selection that are likely to give rise to marital problems of adjustment can be summarized briefly as:

1. Increased freedom of opportunity for the two sexes to participate in social activities of their own choosing without older adult chaperonage.

2. Increased participation by adolescents and young adults in cocktail parties and similar social activities.

3. Twosome night automobile drives and stops on deserted roads.

4. The tacitly accepted, though openly disapproved, participation by "respectable" girls in premarital experimental heterosexual activities.

5. The knowledge that the broken hymen does not necessarily represent loss of virginity.

6. The impact upon sexually developing young people of glamorous and detailed newspaper, radio, and television reports of the love life of national celebrities, of unrealistic love stories in some of the popular magazines, of highly sexual novels and motion pictures, of sexually arousing music, representative art, and dancing, and similar exciting media of entertainment.

7. The decrease of religious influence in some homes.

8. The apparently easy procural of a divorce and the high divorce rate.

9. The knowledge about an availability of contraceptives.

10. The seeming ease of setting up a home by means of instalment-plan buying.

11. The exposure to examples of lack of sexual control among older adults, married or unmarried.

12. The confused state of world conditions and the possible outbreak of war, especially the fact that young men who have no family responsibility are required to do their stint in military service.

Not all young people are motivated by these influences toward hasty, nonconsidered mate selection and marriage. Other stabilizing factors can offset the effects of unwholesome or abnormal sex-stimulating situations, conditions, or experiences. It cannot be denied, however, that changes are taking place in man-woman relationships, bases of mate selection, pre-marital attitudes, and marriage status.

The equalization between the sexes of educational, occupational, and political opportunities and freedom of behavior has led to the development in members of each sex of a better understanding of and respect for members of the opposite sex. The "veil of mystery" in which one sex was enshrouded for the other has given way to the possibilities of objective evaluation of one another. During the early days of the feminist movement some older, conventionally minded men and women expressed the fear that equalization of the rights of men and women would cause women to lose their femininity and men to become less masculine. Inherent physical and temperamental differences between the sexes are such, however, that, with few exceptions, each sex apparently is continuing to maintain his or her particular sex role.

Problems of mate selection. From the societal and religious point of view the fundamental purpose of marriage is to establish a home and raise a family. In earlier times the selection of a mate and consequent marriage followed this pattern. An important factor of the woman's choice of mate was the man's ability to provide a good living for his family; the man sought a woman who would bear him many children, and be an efficient wife and mother. When the home constituted the center for the provision of life necessities, a large family was an asset. Especially was this the case on a farm. Religious teachings encouraged this attitude toward the function of marriage; among some societal groups a large family was also regarded to be parental insurance against a destitute old age.

During the past half century or more the marriage function changed. Life necessities were made available through mass production outside the home; as a result of their increased educational and career opportunities, women no longer accept marriage as their only ultimate destiny. They have come to exercise greater freedom of choice concerning mate selection and marriage. Successful career achievement and economic independence, especially among more able women, have altered the bases of mate selection, marriage relations, and size of family. For the economically secure woman, the choice of a mate who will be a good provider is not imperative. Moreover, a woman who can or wishes to continue to be gainfully employed after marriage usually is interested in having a small and planned family. This attitude is strengthened by the fact that many couples believe that they owe their children whatever luxuries and success-achieving educational and vocational opportunities are available. Hence, in urban areas especially, there are many childless couples or families that consist of two gainfully employed parents and one or two children.

In rural areas the establishment of a home that contains a large family, financially provided for by the father and cared for by the mother, continues to be a purpose of mate selection and marriage; at present there is also an observable trend in this direction among city dwellers. Various personal desires, interests, or conditions determine an individual's decision to marry and the choice of mate.

Among the factors that are basic to mate selection in our modern American culture can be included one or more of the following: sexual attraction, romantic love, companionship, emotional security, desire for home and a family, escape from an unsatisfactory home situation, parental influence, loneliness, adventure, social position and prestige, financial security, gratitude, urge to reform (especially among women), notoriety, example set by members of one's intimate social group, premarital pregnancy, self-assertion in face of parental opposition, military or occupational pressure, and a felt need to regain self-esteem that may have been lost or severely damaged by being "jilted" by the first selected mate.

Unless the mate has been selected in terms of mutual attraction and respect, and similarity of interests and ideals, the chances are slim for the achievement of marital adjustment. If other factors are favorable, it is generally believed that a marriage is likely to succeed if the woman is younger than the man (optimal age for the woman is between 20 and 25 years, actual median age is 21.6 years at marriage); for the man it is between 22 and 27 years (actual median age is 24.3); if both have the same religious affiliation; if they have equal intelligence and educational status, or if the man's is slightly higher than the woman's; if the couple became acquainted in educational or occupational surroundings rather than in a social situation only; if the marriage represents freedom in mate selection; if the parents of either mate accept the other mate, and if the socioeconomic level of both mates is similar.

Important as these factors may seem, many marriages have been successful regardless of the lack of one or more of the favorable factors listed. The possible marital problems that might arise from differences in age, socioeconomic or educational status, religious affiliation, parental attitudes, or any other differences can be recognized before marriage by both the man and the woman, discussed frankly by them, and agreement reached concerning their solution. Marriage counselors have discovered that the primary cause of marital discord and mate incompatibility appears to be rooted in the personal inadequacies of either or both mates.

The emotionally uncontrolled, self-centered, and self-indulgent child and adolescent becomes the uncooperative, adversely critical husband or wife who displays an inconsiderate and rejecting attitude toward the mate. As we have said earlier, sexual incompatibility or an abnormal attitude toward marital sex relations is conducive to sexual unfaithfulness to the spouse. Too great difference in ideals, interests, or behavior habits may give rise to feelings of boredom, lack of respect, or disgust. It is during the period of courtship that the couple can evaluate each other's personal characteristics and decide whether they can be tolerated. If not, a broken engagement is better than an unhappy marriage or a marriage that ends in separation or divorce.

Problems of courtship. The nature and intensity of the adjustment problems that may arise during the period of courtship are closely related to personality characteristics of each of the two persons concerned and the bases upon which mate selection is founded. The term *courting* can be interpreted to include an older adolescent's or an adult's relationships with members of the opposite sex which may eventuate in mate selection and marriage. In a narrow connotation of the term, courtship refers to behavior during the period of time between final mate selection and marriage, commonly referred to as *the engagement period.*

In either case, the length of time that elapses between first acquaintance with the future mate and marriage and the extent of knowledge about each other that is achieved during that period of time are important factors of marital adjustment. Some research studies in this area of human relationship yield results that would seem to indicate that the optimum period is at least one year in length. According to statistical data, a whirlwind courtship followed by marriage after a brief period of acquaintance is provocative of marital incompatibility. Regardless of the cause, an engagement period that is prolonged beyond the point of emotional involvement also constitutes inadequate preparation for successful marriage relationships. These conclusions apply generally; yet, in some instances, too short or too long a courtship period in no way interfered with the success of the marriage.

Intensity of sexual attraction is closely related to the effectiveness of courtship as preparation for marriage. Petting is coming to be considered a normal accompaniment of courtship. Holding hands, embracing, and occasional kissing are accepted activities of young people who think that they are "in love." Such physical contacts can arouse strong sexual urges unless both individuals possess considerable self-control. To control further erotically stimulated physical activities short of the point of coitus is a tension-arousing and frustrating experience. The exercise of sexual control is particularly difficult for the engaged couple.

The engaged man and woman desire physical contact with each other. They become emotionally and physically stirred through their petting activities. Then arises the question concerning the possible harm of coitus, especially if the marriage date has been set for the immediate future. There is difference of opinion concerning premarital sexual intercourse. Its advocates assert that the young couple thereby can discover the extent to which they are sexually compatible. On the debit side, however, must be taken into account the possible results of coitus: arousal of guilt feelings, fear of pregnancy, repulsion, or lack of interest in the experience on the part of one of them. Strong feelings of frustration may result if the situational factors make coitus impossible or unsatisfying; the frustrated partner may decide that he or she is sexually impotent or unfitted for marital sexual relations.

There are other problems that are associated with engagement: what one should tell the other concerning his past; whether an engaged person should limit his or her social activities to those which can be shared with the other; the extent to which the engaged couple should plan ahead concerning income and budgeting, the continuation after marriage of the present occupational activity of the woman, the bearing and rearing of children, the kind of home which they shall establish, and the elaborateness of their wedding. The final decisions vary with conditions and individual interests of the couple. To attempt a satisfactory settlement of these issues becomes a test of the ability of each to cooperate and to compromise. It provides each with an opportunity to evaluate the other's degree of emotional control and intelligent approach to problem-solving, and alerts each to what may be the marital attitude and behavior of the other.

The exercise of personal restraint in all phases of premarital adjustment is important. In no area is it more important, however, than it is in sex-stimulated behavior during courtship and marriage. Hence we shall conclude this discussion of adjustment problems associated with sex by suggesting that sexual restraint is not suppression, inhibition, or denial of one of the strongest human urges. In every culture and during every period of history, can be found a few men and women who have completely sublimated their sex desires and behavior. For many others youthful control of these desires have earned for them later satisfying outlets through marriage and the raising of a family.

81. The Unmarried Mother of School Age as Seen by a Psychiatrist *

FLORENCE CLOTHIER

THE PROBLEM of illegitimate pregnancy captures the imagination. It always has and I suspect that it always will—human drives and cultural inhibitions being what they are. Ancient ballads (and some not so ancient), novels and plays of every generation, and kitchen, parlor, and locker-room gossip all attest man's interest in this very common biological phenomenon.

The universal popular interest evoked by the girl or woman who has become pregnant outside of marriage has an excited, furtive quality that marks it as charged with strongly ambivalent affect. We humans do find vicarious gratification for our own forbidden impulses in the phantasies aroused by the individual who has not only transgressed the social code but "been caught" and thus merited punishment. Illicit sexual relations, pregnancy, and childbirth touch off in all of us repressed and guilty wishes, frustrations, and anxieties. It is these feelings which condition society's attitude towards the unmarried mother and her child.

In cultural groups where rigid patterns of morality prevail, repressed impulses for sexual gratification run in a strong current. Individuals, to protect the social structure against their own submerged desires for forbidden sexual gratification, direct aggression and punishment against the unmarried mother and her child who have mobilized those wishes. The "fallen woman" and the "bastard" are viewed by society not as individuals but as projections of strong desires and even stronger defenses against those desires. Because women even more readily than men are threatened by identification with the unmarried mother, they are usually the more vociferous in their condemnation and more cruel in their punishment. Though churchmen, educators, social workers, and parents may consciously deplore it, mankind likes its wrong-doers whose acts give them indirect satisfactions while at the same time providing an opportunity for righteous indignation and even at times relief of tension through aggressive expression. The unmarried mother, herself a part of the cultural background, readily allies a part of herself with the punishing public and often welcomes ways

* From Florence Clothier, "The Unmarried Mother of School Age as Seen by a Psychiatrist," *Mental Hygiene* (October, 1955), pp. 631–46. Reprinted by permission of the author and The National Association of Mental Health.

of expiating her guilt, which lies deeper than her offense against the cultural mores.

Churchmen, educators, social workers, physicians, and the do-gooders are also human beings with forbidden impulses and strong culturally determined defenses against those impulses. Our professional literature, institutes, and activities in behalf of unmarried mothers and their children bespeak our nicely sublimated preoccupation with the same dynamic struggle that concerns the rest of mankind. Our professional orientation allows us not only unusual (but still indirect) gratifications of primitive impulses, but also provides us with the direct tension-relieving activity of doing something for society and for society's scapegoats—the unmarried mother and her child. It is well to remember that though consciously we find satisfaction in doing something for the unmarried mother, she unconsciously is doing something for us!

The old attitude still prevalent outside of professional circles that the unmarried mother is a bad and fallen woman is our society's most direct defense of its culture which is built around family life. The pseudo-psychologically oriented attitude that "to understand all is to condone all," indicates an identification with the unmarried mother's forbidden indulgence, or neurotic acting out of phantasies, rather than an identification with society's need to preserve for itself and the mother and her children the pattern of family life. It has been said that psychiatrists, particularly psychoanalysts, were to blame for social workers having turned away from an interest in serving society to an interest in serving individuals who are disturbed and whose activities disturb society. Social workers in becoming case workers are by definition focusing their attention on the needs of the individual client. But the unmarried mother and society can be well served only if the case worker can identify both with her needs and with society's needs.

Psychological understanding of the individual client must be used to help the client so that her impulsive or neurotic behavior will not further jeopardize her own future or that of the child. Her needs must be so fully met that she will not again be impelled to violate the social order. Too often psychological understanding is exploited by psychiatrists and case workers for their own glorification. Instead of using our energies and knowledge to protect immature or neurotic girls from a form of symptomatic behavior with particularly far-reaching social implications, we talk and write papers and present cases. We have made some progress in protecting the unmarried mother and her baby from having to bear the full brunt of man's projected defense against his own guilty impulses. But our own emotional

involvement still limits our best efforts particularly in the direction of prevention. Psychological sophistication can serve as a smoke screen covering
envy of the girl who has captured a man—even a phantom man—and who
has achieved motherhood. This envy is not to be tolerated consciously and
is reacted to with furious but satisfying activity in behalf of the unmarried
mother, her child, or prospective adoptive parents.

Even now with all our vaunted psychological understanding and indi-
vidualization of every case, we fall into the trap of classifying all immature,
neurotic, and psychologically healthy girls, who happen to have become
pregnant outside of marriage, in the category of unmarried mothers. Such
classification has social meaning but no more diagnostic value than to
classify all patients who throw up as vomiters. Unmarried motherhood is
a symptom of culture-psychological disharmony. It is only one of countless
possible manifestations of an individual's immaturity or of her conflict with
her environment or within herself. Only an encyclopedic study of both
sociology and psychology could hope to cover adequately the possible
dynamic or etiological factors involved in producing the symptom—unmarried motherhood.

Our own personal and professional experience confirmed by a survey of
the literature teaches us that the unmarried mother does not exist as a
stereotype. She is many women. She may be feebleminded or highly intelligent. She may be at the end or at the beginning of her child-bearing period.
She may come from a background of apparent security and wealth or she
may have had no home she could call her own. She may be struggling to
solve a neurotic conflict or she may be a pawn moving under the dictates of
psychotic phantasy or delusion. She may, like the psychopath, be acting
out primitive impulses without regard to society or future implications for
herself and her baby, or she may be psychologically mature and healthy
caught in a reality cultural dilemma. If we wish to generalize, all we can
say is that the unmarried mother is the girl or woman who because of her
own constellation of environmental and psychological factors has violated
the social mores of our culture and has accidentally or with deep intention
become pregnant. In the eyes of society having become pregnant, regardless of why she became pregnant, places the woman in the culturally
dangerous but psychologically useful category of unmarried mother. Once
pregnancy has called our attention to an unmarried girl or woman, it is time
to try to understand the dynamic factors which in her particular case produced this particular symptom. Only when we have an understanding of the
personality make-up of the individual unmarried mother and of the cultural
factors in her background can we hope to help her to plan wisely for her

own future and for the future of her baby. Regardless of our own emotional involvement with the problem in general or with the individual client in particular, we must hold to the goal of serving society by wisely serving its children and its offenders. Wise therapy requires consideration of all determinants.

Of all groups of unmarried mothers, the teen-ager represents the most challenging problem. She is still a child herself whose problems cannot be separated from her parents and whose treatment must include consideration of the family on whom she is still dependent. Her personality is not yet fully crystallized and society still has a chance to win her into satisfying acceptance of its mores. The schoolgirl unmarried mother is an adolescent and psychological factors peculiar to adolescence always play a role in her having become pregnant—just as these same factors frequently play a role in the older but still immature unmarried mother. Before discussing a possible particular symptom of disturbed adolescence—illegitimate pregnancy —it is well to review briefly that turbulent period between childhood and adulthood which is part of everyone's experience in the process of growing up.

Adolescence is a critical period because of two strong confluent currents —one biological and the other psychological. The system is bathed with sex hormones producing rapid reproductive maturity and impelling sexual demands in an individual who in our culture is still far from emotionally or socially mature. The more highly developed and complex the cultural pattern, the wider is the gap between lusty biological maturity and social maturity. It is this gap which is so often filled with discordant sexualized activity. But this gap can be utilized to prepare youth for life in our increasingly complicated world, if energies biologically released can be diverted into the sublimated channels of education.

As the girl begins to undergo profound biological changes affecting her feelings as well as her physique, she becomes frightened and insecure, and she clutches at the dependency which in her infantile development stood her in such good stead. She wants and tries to remain a child secure in her dependence on mother and father. But she is no longer a child. Her relationship to mother and father has been complicated by the Oedipal development. She has formed new identifications outside of the family and she is pulled along in the tide of her peers' increasing struggle for independence. The drive for emancipation from family becomes as impelling as the sexual drive, and often the two drives serve each other's ends. Neither the biological nor the psychological drive can achieve realistic, mature, and satisfying expression without overcoming the conflict barriers implicit in the girl's earlier childhood relationships. Certainly it is doubtful that an individual can attain satisfying independence if she has not savored fully the gratifications of infantile dependence. Where dependent needs have not been met, the drive for independence is tentative or is so colored by anger and frustration that it can lead only to distorted or aggressive activity against an unloving and therefore unloved world.

Adolescence is a period of strain in which the girl must integrate her conflicting sexual and emotional drives with the conflicting demands of her widening social horizons. If childhood emotional development was beset with difficulties so that the little girl felt herself rejected and unloved, we can expect a disturbed adolescence. The old anxiety "mother does not love me" reappears as the adolescent complaint "nobody likes me." Feelings of loneliness, anxiety, hostility, and frustration can intensify sexual urges already strong. The girl who suffered in childhood from guilt because of sexual curiosity or play will inevitably suffer from more guilt and more anxiety when sexual interests become so strong that they can no longer be repressed. Ungratified dependent needs, affection, and acceptance are sought outside the home. The adolescent who has not experienced the giving and taking relationship of love with her parents, or who has had only casual interest on the part of substitute parents mistakes the attention or the casual interest of boys for love. If she has not had relationships, she cannot evaluate relationships.

The adolescent, in her drive for emancipation, needs to form new attachments outside the home and inevitably meets new authorities (often she takes her peers as authorities) and new standards of behavior. She strains to live up to the new patterns of behavior and to integrate them with the patterns and standards which until recently she had accepted as the only way of life. The greater the discrepancy between the standards of her home and the standards which she meets in the broader community, the greater the likelihood of her feeling unloved or that something is wrong and peculiar about her. "I'm not like other people." "Nobody feels like I do." "Nobody understands me." Driven by inner fears of inadequacy or by feelings of guilt, the adolescent tries frantically to make herself somehow acceptable and to build up her self-esteem through winning attention or approval not from her family but from her new attachments. The conflict element is particularly sharp where the adolescent has strong loyalties to her past and where she has the capacity for loving and admiring those who introduce the new ideas. This conflict of standards is the typical and normal psychological conflict of adolescence. The girl is challenged against a background of biologically sexualized emotionalism to reconcile authorities and to come into some satisfactory working relationship with her own conscience.

It is small wonder that the adolescent feels overwhelmed not just by the nature of her conflicts and feelings, but by their very intensity. Her capacity to feel, which she interprets as a capacity to love, has been heightened. When emotions and problems begin to get out of control the individual is overtaken by anxiety which the adolescent girl experiences as uneasiness, apprehension, and moodiness and which her parents experience as petulant and irrational behavior. Her changeable, inconsiderate, and stormy behavior are her distorted defenses against anxiety as she tries to integrate new standards with old, to liberate herself from old dependencies and to form new attachments, and to so manage her sexual feelings that she can find satisfactions without being overwhelmed by guilt.

Perhaps the best defense against feelings of self-doubt and inadequacy is an air of self-assurance. Adolescents can be positively frightening in their "know-it-all—you're-an-old-fogey" manner. But that defense is brittle and behind it the adolescent longs for help—hence the popularity of the "Tips for Teens" type of newspaper column, magazine, and books. Today's anxious parents, unsure of their own standards and frightened of their seemingly competent teen-age daughters, shy away from inevitable rebuffs and fail to help their daughters to learn how to "get along" with boys, what to talk about, and how far to go. There has been a cultural change in the direction of permissiveness which has not necessarily made adolescence easier.

In general, adolescence is easier where the girl within her own family circle has experienced a normal Oedipal development with a strong identification with her mother and a strong attachment to her father. The formation of new, meaningful attachments can occur only where there have been past fully experienced relationships. The personality is adequate to cope with the stress and strain of adolescence if there is incorporated into the structure of personality the not-too-rigid authority of an adequate, loving parent. Where love has not existed and identifications have not been formed, or where love objects have themselves been inadequate, we cannot expect to find an adolescent with strong enough inner authority and assurance to meet the strains of growing up without symptom formation which is likely to jeopardize her relation to society. In cases where the girl's childhood has been spent in an institution or where she has been shifted from foster home to foster home, there has been no opportunity for the building up of enduring attachments. Secure and adequate identifications have not been formed and the adolescent with a weak and confused superego is

easily influenced by any and every new association which she may mistake
for an authority or for a love object. It is this adolescent, who has never
known love and who has no incorporated standards, who is constantly and
without good judgment seeking attention, approval, and acceptance.

The most disturbed adolescents are those who have been deprived of
their parents' love, particularly the mother's love because of death, separation, or rejection. A satisfying tie between mother and daughter helps to
control sexual urges and to direct those urges toward marriage and a
family. An underlying wish to conform to her mother's and society's con-
ventions provides a stable basis on which to meet the strains of adolescence.
But a satisfying tie must not be confused with an overdependent relationship to the mother which will inevitably block emancipation efforts. The
mother, whose guilt forces her to compensate for her rejection of her
daughter by overprotection of her, sets the stage for adolescent anxieties
and tensions. The daughter is likely to feel rejected, but because of all her
mother does for her and because of her identification with her guilty
mother, she always carries an extra burden of guilt which may become too
much for her when forbidden sex impulses overwhelm her.

An intrapsychic conflict which every girl must solve in the course of
growing up is the so-called masculinity-femininity conflict. The road to
feminine maturity is not straightforward. There are many girls who do not
easily accept the satisfactions implicit in femininity and who strive for
masculine goals in a distorted effort to live out an underlying wish to be a
boy. Other girls attempt to revenge themselves on their mothers or on mankind for having cast them into what they feel to be an inferior and
humiliating role. The active tomboy girl in particular resents menstruation
and the physical changes of puberty. Deep conflicts stem from the bisexual
nature of man and woman. These conflicts should be solved in the course
of the Oedipal development when the little girl finally accepts an identification with her mother in spite of her jealousy and hostility. Then, too, she
takes her father and subsequently another masculine prototype as a love
object. This psychological achievement can only be fully accomplished
where the girl can accept passive rather than active libidinal aims. Feminine
narcissism and feminine masochism when properly integrated into the personality become sources of normal satisfaction, but like any other trait
they can get out of balance so that society or the individual is damaged by
them.

Psychic conflict is normally cushioned and made bearable by escapes
into phantasy. Adolescence is a period when phantasies play a particularly
important role. Life then is tolerable only because the girl or boy can for

periods escape from both intra- and extrapsychic conflicts into a world where wishes stemming from the id, the ego, and the superego can prevail. Conscious phantasies, like neurotic symptoms, partake both of impulse gratification and guilt-relieving punishment for that gratification. Active and passive, aggressive and masochistic aims can be satisfied in phantasy, but denied reality expression because of the individual's respect for the social consequences of his behavior. Typical daydreams of the adolescent girl are phantasies of being raped, of acting as a prostitute, or of having a baby like the Virgin Mary without sex relations. In the rape phantasy, masochistic aims are deeply gratified. In the prostitute phantasy, the girl succeeds in playing the aggressive masculine role and perhaps further in symbolically castrating the man by taking his money or giving him a disease. In the parthenogenetic (virgin birth) phantasy, the girl denies the need of sex or of a man and focuses her hopes on having a baby and being a mother.

The development of a sense of reality or a strong ego is one of the most important accomplishments of childhood. The girl who can accept the world as it is and not as she wishes it to be, and who has the flexibility to adapt herself to our cultural standards, while at the same time finding satisfactions, has achieved some degree of maturity and stability. It is this respect for reality implications and for our cultural standards that normally prevents an adolescent girl from acting out the phantasies which accidentally or purposefully might lead to her becoming pregnant. This same reality sense should protect her from impulsive gratification of her sexual needs heightened by the hormonal changes of puberty. A good reality sense and a strong ego should not be so overwhelmed by neurotic conflict that the girl acts out in a way that can only bring disaster on herself.

Unmarried motherhood in our culture almost always represents a distorted or unrealistic way out of inner difficulties. It is thus comparable to a neurotic symptom on the one hand or to impulsive delinquent behavior on the other. The adolescent girl who has sexual relations with men or boys is lacking in a capacity to protect herself. Her reality sense is not sufficient to cope with her biological drives or with her conflicts centering around her struggle for emancipation. Wishes, conflicts, or phantasies are acted out and by accident or design the girl may become pregnant.

Obviously the ego may be weak and the reality sense inadequate for a great variety of reasons. From what has been said about adolescence it does not seem surprising that unmarried motherhood should occur as a not uncommon symptom. United States Children's Bureau statistics indicate that approximately 46 per cent of illegitimate births are to mothers between

15 and 19 years of age. Adolescence is a period of crucial stress and it requires a strong ego to weather the biological and psychological storm with equanimity. Our adolescent unmarried mothers are usually bewildered, struggling girls who have never achieved an inner harmony. Constitutional factors and even more significant factors in the girl's own family life determine whether her reality sense will be strong enough to protect her from her impulses, and whether her ego will be free enough from neurotic conflict so that she will not hazard her future in a distorted effort to solve her conflicts.

Dr. Margaret Gerard has described the commonest type of unmarried mother as the "impulse-ridden character." This is the childish, irresponsible, pleasure-seeking girl who with little thought as to future implications yields to temptation or to her wishes. To this girl reality consequences to herself, her baby, and her family are insignificant in comparison to her need to find the satisfactions which she feels she has missed. Because of her own emotionally neglected childhood, she has not established personality strengthening relationships and identifications. Her personality structure is flimsy and she is not capable of protecting herself or of making adequate plans for herself or her baby. In the childhood histories of these impulse-ridden girls, we find gross evidence of family disorganization. They come from broken homes or bitterly unhappy homes, or from institutions, or from a series of foster-home placements. If there have been consistent objects for identification, it is likely that these have been with socially maladjusted individuals. As Dr. Viola Bernard has stated, we find a high incidence of mothers of socially disturbed adolescent girls, including those who become illegitimately pregnant, who provide as models for identification only confusion, inconsistency, and frightening unpredictability. The daughters of these mothers have been crippled by the lack of an essential need for healthy personality development. It is interesting how often a girl who was herself illegitimate produces at an early age an illegitimate baby, whether or not she has actually lived with her own mother. It is as if the mother's destiny forced itself on the daughter by actual identification, or by the daughter's groping for an illusory happiness.

The impulse-ridden girl may have been bred in such a hostile environment that she has no conception that love can exist between people or that in responsibility there can be satisfactions. Her relations to people are clamorous efforts to squeeze from them some satisfaction for her still impelling need for gratifications of a dependent sort. She wants, at any cost, attention and approval and material evidences of acceptance. But because she cannot give herself into a relationship with another human, she cannot love. Her relations with both men and women are colored by the same mistrust and lack of warmth that poisoned her childhood. Yearning for something which her circumstances have made it impossible for her to achieve, this personality-crippled and vulnerable adolescent remains naively hopeful that through her sexual powers she will find a man who will compensate her for her deprivations and who will give her self-assurance. She submits gratefully to any man who is friendly and gives her a good time, or even to anyone who excites her—and because of her unhappiness and weak ego and superego development she is easily excited! The impulse-ridden character is emotionally immature and her primary motivation is to find someone to give her what she mistakes for love. During the love-making and the sexual act, even though intercourse in itself is not satisfying and perhaps unpleasant, the adolescent has the short-lived and frustrating phantasy that she is needed, wanted, and loved. Her judgment and reality sense are so poor that she cherishes the hope that each new man may bring her that for which she is searching.

The impulse-ridden character is likely to be promiscuous and if she becomes pregnant it is by accident. Because she is herself essentially unresponsive, her relationship to the father of her baby has no reality base. It is the derivative of a dream and the man has for her an ephemeral phantom character. He is what Ruth Brenner speaks of as a "ghost lover." Such a girl, who has not been loved as a child and who cannot relate to other girls or to boys and who is driven by strong though selfish sexual drives, has no true maternal feelings for her baby. If she is interested in it at all, it is only in the hope that through it she can gain satisfactions for herself. The capacity for full maternal love is granted only to the mature and satisfied woman who because she has received much can give generously and joyously. Physiological motherhood in our culture, even in the healthiest of girls, can occur years before maternal feelings assume the same strength as sexual feelings. The adolescent impulse-ridden character is incapable of the overwhelming and satisfying and sustained tenderness of maternity.

Married or unmarried, these immature girls make poor mothers. They transmit to their children through the emotional climate they provide for them the same primary emotional disturbances which crippled their own development. The indication would seem to be to make it easy for them to give up their babies in the hope that better provision can be made for the baby than was made for its child-mother. Society's traditional punishing attitude that keeping the baby will force responsibility on the mother and make her "settle down" is doomed to bring only tragedy to the baby and the young mother whose fundamental needs are still unmet.

It is interesting how often these girls, who are oriented only toward achieving their childhood goals, block out of consciousness the man, their pregnancy, and eventually the baby. For months they deny to themselves and to the world that they are pregnant. Dr. Viola Bernard describes one teen-age girl who even when in labor insisted that she was merely having an attack of appendicitis. When these emotionally immature girls finally do admit that they've "been caught," they do what they can to derive satisfaction from the situation for themselves. Being cared for by a case worker can be utilized to satisfy dependent needs. If the girl's personality is not too rigid in its distortion, the case worker has a challenging opportunity to contribute of her own strength and integrity to the girl's superego, so that she will no longer be ridden by impulses and dissatisfactions. The case worker's role with such a girl is to establish herself firmly as a needed object of identification. It is her aim first to meet dependent needs and to strengthen the girl's reality sense, and then to help her towards a satisfying independence. Many of these impulse-ridden characters are inaccessible to help because of their total inability to relate and because of a complete absence of inner conflict in regard to their way of life.

The adolescent unmarried mother who goes to a maternity home can often find tremendous satisfactions in this group situation where she is cared for and where for once she is like everyone else. Boarding schools and group placements have definite positive values for many types of disturbed adolescents, and under wise leadership the months spent in the maternity home can have emotional and educational value, particularly if both group treatment and case work services are available. It is tragic that so many of our maternity homes regard themselves and are used as shelters for unmarried mothers with no effort at segregation of the women and girls on the basis of their psychological and cultural needs. The continued existence of such homes is good evidence of society's unwillingness to recognize that unmarried motherhood is a symptom of cultural-psychological disharmony rather than a diagnostic category.

The reality sense may be undeveloped because love relationships and adequate identifications have not occurred and the superego is unformed, or it may be distorted because of unresolved intrapsychic conflict. In the latter case, a guilt-ridden, punishing superego holding the whip-hand may direct the development of a neurotic symptom which may take the form of illicit sexual relations and/or unmarried motherhood. It has been my experience that in clinic work many more adolescent unmarried mothers fall into the impulse-ridden character group than into the psychoneurotic group. In private practice I have seen a larger proportion of the adolescent psychoneurotics. Of the older unmarried mothers, even in clinic practice, one sees not only impulse-ridden characters but also a number of psychoneurotics. Among these older girls and women there is a noticeably larger group where the primary unconscious goal is to have a baby, rather than the baby's being an accidental complication.

When unmarried motherhood in the adolescent is on a psychoneurotic basis, one can be sure that, as in every neurotic symptom, these are elements of deep instinctual gratification and of punishment for that gratification. The underlying conflict may center around ambivalent feelings towards the mother so that the girl defies and punishes her mother while at the same time punishing herself. Or the conflicts may result from a variety of attitudes towards the father. Leontine Young has discussed the influence both of weak passive fathers and of too dominating fathers. On the one hand the girl is compelled to turn to men in order to dominate them as her mother dominated her father. On the other hand she chooses men who will hurt and humiliate her. Perhaps her guilty wish to revenge herself on her father has led her to submit masochistically to his prototype. In some cases, the father figure has been absent or lacking and the girl's phantasies about him and his relationship to her mother and to her have remained uncorrected by reality. Other girls caught in their Oedipus relationship have failed to make a transfer from father to other boys or men. Guilt feelings are strong because of the incest taboo and in this situation rivalry and identification with the mother and the longing to have a baby by the father makes the having of a baby under punishing circumstances a primary motive. Distorted feelings of guilt connected with the adolescent's drive to become emancipated from demanding rigid parents can play a significant role.

The psychoneurotic individual suffers from an impaired reality sense because intrapsychic conflicts are so impelling that psychic energy which should be available for perceiving and dealing with reality and for making plans on the basis of long-time values is absorbed by the inner conflicts. In promiscuous sexual relationships, or in an out-of-wedlock baby, the anxiety-ridden girl tries to find an answer to her unconscious conflicts and needs. It is this girl who may act out her rape, or prostitute, or parthenogenetic phantasies. Where neurotic mechanisms are so powerful as to produce symptoms destructive to the self and to others, psychotherapy or psychiatrically oriented case work, extending many months or years beyond the lying-in period, is advisable. Among older unmarried mothers in this category there may be a real question as to whether they should keep their babies. I have never seen a school-age, neurotic, unmarried mother who I have thought would gain by keeping her baby, or who would be able to provide well for her baby.

The adolescent girl, unprotected by a firm reality sense, is predisposed to sexual relationships and illegitimate pregnancy by her biological sexual drives and by the conflicts stemming from her struggle to integrate new standards with old. Where infantile needs have remained unsatisfied, or where infantile conflicts are still unresolved, adolescence is disturbed and an illegitimate pregnancy may be a particularly virulent symptom of that disturbance. A predisposition to a disturbed adolescence fortunately does not mean that illicit sexual relationships or unmarried motherhood will occur. Pregnancy out of wedlock is always overdetermined and both sexual and nonsexual motivations play important roles. The adolescent girl, driven by sexual feelings, may attempt to meet long-standing nonsexual needs through promiscuous relationship with boys or men, or through motherhood.

The emergence of this tragic symptom may be precipitated by any one of a variety of causes which has served to mobilize old frustrations, anxieties, and conflicts. Current reality situations may exist which strike at the adolescent girl's feeling of security and self-esteem. The adolescent's uncertainty and self-doubt renders her vulnerable to even trivial trauma. She is touchy and easily hurt by loss of love or by criticism so that her tenuous equilibrium is readily upset. Forbidden sex relations will still not occur unless conditions in the external environment are favorable for the symptom—though unfavorable for the girl and especially for her potential child. The influence of the social milieu cannot be disregarded. Where sexual relations are not uncommon among high-school-age boys or girls, the girl can more readily allow herself "to be laid." When there is available a sexual partner who urges necking and intercourse, and who may even provide a car or a hotel room, the girl, who is predisposed to impulsive or neurotic acting out and who believes that the man may assuage her needs, succumbs to his attentions.

As an attempted solution for frustrated love and security needs, or as a way out of neurotic conflict, unmarried motherhood is doomed to hopeless failure. To the girl's original frustration and confusion are added stupendous responsibilities which she inevitably will have to evade. Her old feelings of rejection, "Nobody likes me," are given a firmer reality base. She has lost her "ghost lover" and society has branded her a bad woman. The symptom "unmarried motherhood" has numerous highly individual psychodynamic determinants. Particularly in the case of the adolescent girl it has also important psychodynamic consequences affecting not only the future adjustment of the baby but also of the mother—herself a child.

82. How Can the Home Help a Child Make a Good School Adjustment? *

HAZEL F. GABBARD

FIRST BIRTHDAY to first grade! Important years. A time of robust growth, development, and security. Parents are the teachers in this wonderful period of childhood when miracles happen overnight, or so it seems, watching a child grow up.

It is really "at a parent's knee" that children begin to get ready for school. Parents may have no conscious thought of school as they gradually drop off doing for the child so that he may do more for himself. Nevertheless, they are encouraging the child to learn by what they do or do not do for him.

How does the child learn to be self-reliant? By his very nature he starts out feeling that dressing himself, brushing his teeth, and putting things away are exciting and grown-up things to do. Small children can learn to be a real help around the house. Putting away the silver, setting the table, helping mother wash the vegetables are all delightful occupations for the young child and give him a great sense of independence and responsibility. And the child who takes an active part in family life is more likely to cope with situations outside the family than is one who has never helped.

With praise and encouragement from his parents he delights in a chance to embark on even more difficult things, such as going on errands, clearing the table, and tidying his room. He wants to have a part in important jobs and please his mother and father. He has a sense of satisfaction when he has

* From Hazel F. Gabbard, *Preparing Your Child for School*, Pamphlet No. 108, U. S. Department of Health, Education, and Welfare, U. S. Office of Education (Washington, D. C., 1957).

been able to do things which are needed by the family. Through the completion of simple tasks in the home the child grows in independence and acquires skills which carry over into school life.

Sometimes adults are in so much of a hurry they fail to let children have a chance to share and carry responsibilities. This was what was happening in one home where four-year-old Alice, an active, alert child, was eager to help her mother with the cleaning, baking, and housework. "Let me help, Mother," was her constant plea. But the mother found Alice in the way and preferred to do her work by herself.

"Go and play with your toys, Alice, and stop hindering me," she would say. "No, I don't want you fussing around while I am baking. I'll give you one of the cookies when they are done."

Thus, the desire to be helpful and to satisfy normal curiosity is often nipped in the bud when children are deprived of entering into the household chores.

Children learn how to take care of their things largely through the example set by their family. Given a place for their toys and some help in putting them away, they will learn to be orderly, and to carry their part in the family group. They need time, of course, to do this, and they need adults who recognize when fatigue may interfere with their cooperation.

Parents can help a child grow in independence through allowing time and opportunity for him to carry responsibility for such simple things as:

> Dressing and undressing himself
> Hanging up his wraps
> Caring for his toileting needs
> Putting his toys and personal possessions away
> Helping in simple family chores
> Going on errands
> Answering the telephone
> Meeting visitors in the home
> Entering into the table conversation

Very early it is possible to allow children to have choices and to make decisions within their range of experience and development. A little three-year-old girl was delighted when her mother said she might choose the dress she would wear each day. The mother started first by limiting the choice between two dresses and gradually led up to having her go to her closet to pick from several. There are many matters on which young children may also be taken into the plans, such as letting them decide whom they will invite to their parties, the kind of present they will buy for Daddy, or the way they would like their room arranged. Simple problems put before the child will help him learn to make more difficult choices and decisions, and his willingness to take the responsibility for his own acts will grow with each experience.

The years before school is the time to lay the foundation for good health. In this period much can be done to pave the way against future illness, build a sturdy straight body, and develop a happy frame of mind to meet each day's tasks. During these formative years children establish their routine health habits, such as eating the right kind of foods, getting sufficient sleep, having regular habits of elimination, and getting exercise and fresh air through play out-of-doors. If children are dressed for different kinds of weather when they play out-of-doors, they learn to adjust to changes in temperature and to build resistance to illness before entering school.

Early establishment of a routine in living helps a child to devote full attention to new experiences as he faces them. Fortunate is the child whose parents assist him in carrying out a schedule where routine habits fall into their proper relationship with the rest of his daily program.

So important is active play to the child's growth needs in the years before 6 that it cannot be overemphasized. A wise parent fits up the back-yard, if he has one, or finds a play area for his child in a neighborhood play-group to provide the space he requires for using his body. Swings, ladders, sandboxes, planks, and boxes are the tools of play, wonderful aids for muscle building, too. Inevitably this equipment will attract other children to the yard, and the result will be to provide lessons in sharing, exchanging ideas, leading, and following, all of which are necessary experiences for a child in learning to get along well with others.

Certain precautions need to be taken to protect the child's health. An annual health check-up with the doctor should be arranged to make sure that any physical defects are discovered early and corrected. Most pediatricians advise that children be vaccinated and immunized for certain childhood diseases in their preschool years. A visit to the dentist is also a matter not to be overlooked. Since all of these health matters require time and preparation of the child for them, they should not be left until school begins. Planning for them at intervals will eliminate strain on the child and enlist his cooperation.

Living in a family circle, a child absorbs many things incidentally He will notice, for example, that adults cover their mouths when coughing, use handkerchiefs, and keep things out of their mouths. These are important health lessons to be practiced before the child enters a group. Usually parents need only to set a good example for children to imitate in order for these patterns of social practice to be acquired.

Children living in cities learn much about safety in their day-to-day living. Very early they are intrigued by the traffic lights and the police as they travel with their parents on shopping tours or other trips. This is an excellent time to answer questions concerning the safety regulations of the city. Much incidental learning needs to take place and a background of information should be acquired before the child begins to travel alone to school or do small errands for his parents. A four-year-old son was guided by his father who allowed him to give the signal when he should go and stop as they crossed the downtown streets. By the time he was 5 he had learned to be cautious and steady in those decisions affecting his safety. He knew why he should walk on the sidewalk, cross streets at corners, watch the lights, and obey traffic controls.

Getting along with others is more or less expected as children begin to live as a member of a group. Perhaps the surest way to success in school is to help children learn to make friends. Early experiences with different people who do not force themselves on a child but let him make the overtures, will start him on the way to enjoying others. The stage is set for children when parents show an interest in other people and are friendly in their contacts with them.

A certain amount of experimentation, however, must go into the life of every child before he finds his place in a group. Through play with other children his own age he learns the rules of give and take and of making friends. In the beginning years children need to experience fair play, learn to recognize the property of others, share, ask for turns, and get over the first hurdles of learning cooperation. When children are left to their own devices to work out difficulties in their early years, often the stronger and more aggressive child will try to dominate. For this reason children need supervision in their play until the rules of fair play have been learned.

Parents may notice that children with interesting play ideas naturally attract followers. As children are taken on excursions to the airport, the railroad station, the zoo, a dairy, a farm, or other places of interest, they come back to relive these experiences in their play. Not only is their play stimulated, but such trips increase the child's vocabulary and add to his information and understanding of the world in which he lives. He begins to reach out to encompass a new horizon as he gradually masters the immediate surroundings. Stretching his sights into the unknown by trips challenges and provides important experiences for him before he starts to school.

After a child has been on a trip he can be observed reliving the experience at home in various ways. His impressions of what he saw may come out in his block building or as he paints or draws. Time may elapse before he talks much about the trip, but when he does, parents will be interested to listen to what he saw and learned from the experience. Sometimes he will have questions which have come up after he has thought about the trip. If so, another visit may need to be taken to help him check on what he saw or some help be given to enable him to get answers to his questions. Finding the answers is so much more fun than being told by adults.

Books provide another avenue for reliving the experiences a child has had. They also help him to satisfy his longing and hunger for new words, new ideas, or more about the familiar. It is possible to develop in children a feeling of delight and love for books which will greatly influence their success in school. Much depends on the parents' approach even from the first picture books. Fortunate is a child whose parents see that he has some well-chosen books of his own, who take time to read to him, to tell him stories, and listen while he retells experiences or stories of his own. These are ways to help the child acquire skill and ease in self-expression. An appreciation of books fostered in the early years will also become a treasure to cherish throughout his entire life.

The child's response to sounds and movements finds a natural outlet in rhythms and songs during the years before school. Music brings so much pleasure that it should never be omitted in the life of any child. Singing, listening to music, and playing on simple musical instruments develop a feeling for music which may provide a background for musical study or personal enjoyment in the later years. Parents need not be musical themselves to give children these experiences. The stage can be set if he has among his play materials, possibly, a drum, xylophone, glass tumblers, and other rhythm instruments.

Taking into account the many phases of child growth perhaps none is more basic to school success than emotional well-being. As judged by teachers, readiness in this aspect of development rests heavily upon the child's assurance that he is loved by his parents. A child needs, more than anything else, a happy home where mutual love and respect abound and where he feels he has a place in his parents' affection. This means parents who love and enjoy each other as well as loving and enjoying him.

Parents give a child security in his home through the many things which happen to him. For example, he needs to know that his parents love him whether or not he is a good child. There may be days when he is uncooperative, when he throws his toys, gets into mischief, and destroys valuable things. As a parent meets this behavior he will not condemn the child, but focus on the act when handling these situations.

There are many ways of showing that children are loved besides displaying affection. One way is to see that the things they do well are rewarded through praise and approval by the parent. A child will strive to repeat the good things which bring him satisfaction. Recognizing when a child has done a job well, not by an adult's yardstick, but by what the child is able to do, is the fairest way in measuring his achievement. The relationships which are established between a child and his parents do more to build his sense of values than anything else.

In watching the adjustment of hundreds of school children, the observation has been made that a child who knows there is no place like home is a child who finds school a good place, too. He can leave his parents and go into the new experience confidently; he can put his full attention on the tasks ahead. The child who is uncertain of the love of his parents, who is unhappy at home, is torn within and can give only a part of his attention to his schoolwork.

83. *Reactions of Parents to Problems of Mental Retardation in Children* * [1]

EDMUND W. GORDON
AND MONTAGUE ULLMAN

THE FOLLOWING DISCUSSION of parental reactions to problems of retardation is based on a review of data obtained over a five-year period at the Morris J. Solomon Clinic for Retarded Children and a recent exploratory study of the responses of parents to young Mongoloid children.

The parents of retarded children, like those of normal children, may be classified into three groups with respect to their total life adjustment. There are those whose resources and balance enable them to cope with even the most excessive stresses in an effective and constructive manner. Family units in which this situation obtains are, unfortunately, in the minority. By

* From Edmund W. Gordon and Montague Ullman, "Reactions of Parents to Problems of Mental Retardation in Children," *American Journal of Mental Deficiency,* Vol. 61, No. 1 (July, 1956), 158–63. Reprinted by permission.

[1] Presented before the American Association of Mental Deficiency. Annual Meeting, Detroit, April, 1955.

far the greater number of parents seen have succeeded in making an adequate general adjustment but are nevertheless harassed and confused by the problems their children present. There is a final group in which one or both parents show neurotic or psychotic dispositions. Under these circumstances additional burdens tax the limit of their resources and often challenge their capacity to make any adjustment at all.

It has been our experience that parents in the first two groups are greatly helped by short-term contact in which general management problems are discussed and specific information is given. The first group benefits by such additional support and rapidly integrates it into their own effort and program. Parents in the second group stand in greater need and utilize the contact in order to establish a consistent and workable program. While it is true that parents in the third group are often benefited by well-structured situations and specific information the severity of the problem often necessitates more intensive help at a personal level.

Many of the concerns of these parents derive from a lack of basic information concerning the condition of the child. It is of interest to note the apparent relief with which some parents accept a diagnosis of cerebral damage as less distressing and shame provoking than a diagnosis of constitutional lack of endowment. Not infrequently they have been the recipient of contradictory and inadequate proposals in the past. The search for adequate facilities for treatment and education has been difficult and at times futile. In addition, these parents are often saddled with feelings of shame and guilt, as well as attitudes of defensiveness, self-recrimination and self-pity. Mismanagement arises from ignorance, overprotectiveness and in some instances denial of the extent and reality of the problem. Parents may withdraw socially and isolate both themselves and their children. Others, moved by shame, guilt, and misinformation, seek institutionalization as a solution. Many parents falter around the problem of handling sibling relationships between the retarded child and a normal child. In almost every instance economic pressures and inadequate financial resources add to the burden and limit the parents in their search for the special care and attention so many of these children require.

Some of these problems will now be considered as they emerged in an exploratory study of the responses of parents to young Mongoloid children.

A series of eight group sessions was held weekly with the parents of Mongoloid children under the age of 5 years. Six parents maintained a fairly regular attendance, whereas four others appeared at the group meetings from time to time. The study was designed, first, to elucidate the impact upon the family setting of the birth and presence of a biologically defective human organism, and, secondly, to help the parents define more accurately the nature and extent of their role and responsibility and to develop a clearer awareness of the self-defeating influence of neurotic attitudes elicited or heightened in the situation.

In a group limited to parents of young Mongoloid children, the problems of acceptance and rejection of the child, as well as those of integration into the existing family unit, were in the foreground. The general problems which emerged fell into the following broad categories: First, the complaints the parents had relative to the professional help and guidance which they had sought and received; secondly, ignorance concerning the nature of the disturbance and the consequent limited ability to plan effectively for the child; thirdly, the clarification of the realistic social, family, and personal problems, and fourth, the emergence of neurotic difficulties complicating the picture.

1. *Complaints the parents have relative to professional help and guidance.* Three of the parents expressed resentment concerning the way in which notification had occurred and the subsequent lack of reliable guidance from their medical adviser. They were particularly resentful of the way their physicians had glibly advised institutionalization without adequately preparing the parents and without regard to their ability or desire to keep the child. In one instance, the father was informed of the child's condition and the responsibility of telling his wife was left up to him. He could not bring himself to do it until a period of three months had elapsed. All of the parents felt that they should have been informed as soon as the diagnosis had been made, and it was felt that the role of the physician was to help the parents themselves to make the decision about placement after they had been sufficiently oriented to the nature of the problem, the possible prognosis, and all of this considered in relation to their current life situation. Most of the parents resented what they regarded as arbitrary and premature pressuring to have the child institutionalized. The attitudes varied from wavering indecisiveness on the one hand to the affirmative rejection of any idea of institutionalization on the other. This was expressed by Mr. A: "This is our child. We don't want to give him away. We want to find out how to help him." At the time the group started at least two of the parents were still undecided about the question of placement, but all were agreed that the parents have to be given sufficient time and help to come by this decision in their own way and at a time when they themselves felt ready. In at least one instance, the pressure on the part of medical advisers and family to have a child institutionalized resulted in a contrary impulse on the part of the parents in a situation where, all things considered, it became

apparent that institutionalization would have been the wiser course and the one really desired by the parents.

2. *Ignorance concerning the nature of the disturbance and the consequent limited ability to plan effectively.* Despite a history of exposure to medical advice, all of the parents expressed great uncertainty concerning what to expect with regard to the development of the child. There was almost total unfamiliarity with the developmental pattern of Mongolism, the nature of the defect, and the type and extent of variations that one might expect. The awareness and concern with the intellectual limitations in terms of the formal IQ scores stood out in marked contrast to the lack of understanding of the concept of social adjustment and the manifold factors which enter into this. Instead, there was a mechanical overestimation of the handicap in terms of the formal IQ and insufficient appreciation of the more flexible and complex factors that determine the level of social adjustment. Other questions concerned the actual nature of the physical defect itself, the cause, and the life expectancy of these patients. These were dealt with at a general educational level. The indirect factors influencing the physical prognosis were discussed and illustrated for the parents. The concept of lowered resistance following or dependent upon the limited muscular activity, poor muscular tone, difficulties in maintaining adequate self-protective activity because of the limited intelligence, all were brought to the parents' attention. The extremes in behavior or outcome were discussed and exemplified and the possibilities of realistic work adjustment in later life were discussed.

The emphasis in relation to these problems was along the following lines: The parents were urged to place their stress on the potential of the child rather than on its limitations, and the need to understand the responsibilities that can be carried by each child at its particular stage of development, and the need to orient themselves to a program of active stimulation in order to fulfill these potentialities. As one mother expressed it, "The more you can treat the child as normal, the less trouble you have." By this she meant that although his handicaps must be taken into consideration, they are not highlighted and do not elicit catering or a special attitude on the part of the parents.

3. *Clarification of the realistic social, family, and personal problems.* Here initially the discussions centered about the problems of social stigma, community adjustment, and family and sibling relations. Stress was placed on the cultivation of honest and matter-of-fact attitudes. The question of stigmatization was discussed in relation to the general problem of the prevalence of superstitious and irrational attitudes toward mental disturbances

of all kinds, and the fact that these attitudes cut through all strata and levels in the population. Again the emphasis was placed on the degree of progress made generally in combating these attitudes, in the greater recognition which psychiatry has achieved, and in the more humane and tolerant atti-, tudes toward all forms of mental disease and handicap. Nevertheless, the continued existence of these attitudes called forth the need of every concerned person for a program of actively overcoming one's own reticence and the urgent need on the part of each parent to take advantage of every opportunity to further the socialization of their particular child. With regard to the many questions which arose concerning the problems within the family itself, the effort was made to concretize the concept of action in relation always to considering the needs of the family as a unit. The vulnerable areas here are related to the resentment of other siblings at the amount of attention given to the Mongoloid child, and further, the handling of the attitudes and questions of the other children concerning the Mongoloid child. As for the question of how to inform the other siblings, opinions varied from letting the child find out by himself to carefully gauging explanations based on the introduction of the concepts of differences of development, disease, and mental handicap, etc. The general principles which were elaborated in connection with all of these points were as follows: (1) All questions should be answered at the child's own level of development. (2) The parents should take the initiative in introducing the problem to the sibling through the use of analogy as well as direct information. (3) Further unfolding of information should be gauged by the child's responses and questions, and (4) the example should be set by parental activity rather than by verbalization with regard to the approach, handling, and general attitudes toward the Mongoloid. A special session was devoted to the educational problems faced by these parents and was conducted by the special tutor at the clinic. The problem of nursery facilities was explored and the parents were informed of the importance of showing the child to the school officials rather than risking rejection at a distance. They were also informed of the importance of placement at the functioning level of the child and further educated as to the particular nature of the learning difficulties experienced by these children, for example, the difficulty with abstraction and the difficulty encountered by these children in making the shift from thinking at a concrete level to thinking at a symbolic level. This generally becomes manifest at the time vocabulary and writing come into the picture in the third grade.

4. *The neurotic problems.* Interfering parental attitudes were discussed in their impact on the child and as they were reflected in other siblings. The

question of parental guilt was discussed in relation to a realistic appraisal of the actual responsibility of the parents, of the nature of the organic and hereditary factors believed to be responsible for the condition, and of the basis for feelings of guilt in anxiety and in the insecurity arising in response to the challenge posed by the condition. The challenge may strike at any one of the number of vulnerable areas, both realistic and neurotic. The most commonly expressed neurotic attitudes have to do with overprotection and the inability to make realistic demands on the child. One member of the group, who showed considerable emotional instability, seemed perpetually lost in a morass of self-pity and hopelessness and all her comments in relation to her child revealed clearly her very chaotic and self-centered approach. Another parent revealed her concern about the unusually quiet attitude of an older sibling, who rarely if ever seemed to talk about the problem of her younger sister. This was clearly related to the mother's own stoical and self-contained attitude toward the sick child. At the other extreme, Mr. A seemed genuinely concerned only with what he could do for the child and with what he could learn that might possibly benefit the child. A helpful point was the ability to relate many of the problems to those faced by parents of normal children, and that far fewer were unique to the Mongoloids than the parents had assumed.

5. *Response to the group*. It was felt that although the group was conducted on an exploratory and limited basis, it proved eminently worth while and met with a very favorable response from most of the participants. Mr. C felt that he had benefited most in terms of a clearer concept of what to expect and hence a greater ability to plan for the child. The group proved of help to Mrs. B in overcoming her reluctance to leave the child with neighbors and also in becoming less compulsive and less solicitous in relation to him. Mr. A felt that he benefited most in his grasp of the nature of the intellectual limitations and his greater appreciation of the time factor in the development of the child. Mrs. R, whose own disturbance prevented her from absorbing any real information, used the group as a sounding board for her own need to be pitied and sympathized with. In brief summary, the attitudes of the parents varied from one extreme, as represented by Mr. A, to the other, as represented by Mrs. R. Mr. A exhibited intelligent, healthy, constructive, and selfless attitudes in relation to the problem. Mrs. R, whose level of functioning prior to the birth of the Mongoloid child was probably at a borderline level, was precipitated into a state of abject helplessness and confusion out of which the child became the focal point of her overwhelming feelings of inadequacy. In several of the others, the problem of relating to the child was certainly not fully resolved. In the case of Mr. C, the group

discussions seemed to have helped him to arrive at the decision to work with the child in contrast to a previous indecisive feeling about placement. Mrs. G, who was the oldest member of the group and a grandmother with two grown children, was very emphatic about her rejection of the idea of placement, but on closer examination of her attitudes, it was apparent that beneath the surface acceptance she was deeply rejecting and had sought refuge in a kind of subtle martyrdom in relation to the responsibility of caring for the child. She got little from the group because of her own defensive attitudes of placing herself beyond reproach and in a kind of all-knowing position.

Conclusion

This group experience emphasized the possibility of and necessity for helping parents to discern the realistic problems and to differentiate them from the superimposed problems resulting from their own distortions and defensive attitudes. The group experience provides an effective means of mobilizing the struggle of the parents against the prevalent myths and stigmatizing influences which they meet up with. It further fortifies them in their efforts to socialize the child in an assertive and fearless manner and defines for them their responsibility in relation to the child and the other members of the family. It is felt that the experience was a profitable one, even though it was limited to pointing up directions rather than presenting specific solutions.

The problems which emerge in this brief review underscore the need for expanded services through which preventative, informational, diagnostic, treatment, educational, and custodial requirements may be met. Many of the sources of parental mismanagement and confusion can be eliminated when the scope and dimension of the problem is more generally recognized and greater participation occurs at the level of public health agencies. In not a few instances the parents themselves have taken the initiative in challenging the prevailing social attitudes and inadequacies. They have risen above their individual hardships and handicaps to work together to mobilize resources for the care and treatment of retarded children and to awaken public opinion to the unmet needs of such children. These parents form an invaluable ally to the professionals working in the field in molding a community-wide approach to the problem.

84. Parent-Child Conflicts *

JOHN E. HORROCKS

Overindulgence

Extremes of parental reaction tend to have unfortunate results on adolescent behavior and development. Indulgence up to a point makes an adolescent's adjustment considerably easier, and gives him a real sense of security, creating a permissive atmosphere in which the teen-ager may move toward personal independence and gradual emancipation. When, however, indulgence becomes overindulgence, or when overprotectiveness appears, the consequences tend to be unfortunate. Hattwick writes, "Children whose homes reflect overattentiveness are liable to display infantile, withdrawing types of reaction." The same investigator notes that "children who are babied or pushed by their parents have more social difficulties than children from well-adjusted homes—such children also have greater difficulty in work habits, and consequently in matters of purely academic progress." Hattwick points out the inevitable vicious circle engendered by such a situation. "The parents are overattentive, the child gets along poorly at school, the parent, conscious of this poor school achievement, becomes even more attentive, and so on."

The adolescent whose home history has been one of overprotection and overindulgence experiences greater difficulty than usual in adjusting to the outside world. The overattentiveness of his parents has led him into the habit of expecting help and attention from others. In a real sense such an individual has never relinquished the egocentrism of his early childhood, when he conceived of the world and everything in it as created especially for his benefit and exploitation. All his life he has been used to getting attention, and he expects that such attention is his by right. Outside the home he will endeavor to make himself the pampered center of every situation he enters. Naturally, he does not always receive the attention he wants, and his reaction, aggressive at first, may if aggression fails to work, change to withdrawal. Such individuals look to others for aid at each stage of their development. In school the teacher is expected to assume the role of an indulgent parent and to act, in effect, as a parent surrogate. Out of school and employed, this kind of adolescent often makes a nuisance of himself

* From John E. Horrocks, *The Psychology of Adolescence: Behavior and Development*, pp. 50–57. Copyright 1951, by John E. Horrocks and published by Houghton Mifflin Company, Boston. Reprinted by permission.

endeavoring to establish the same kind of a relationship with his boss. Frequently he will try to assign a quasi-parental role to older boys or girls, and finally, in marriage, the husband or wife of this kind of person is expected to behave much like a parent.

The overindulged adolescent typically finds great difficulty in separating himself from his parents. Many newly married girls do not want their husbands to get jobs outside the town in which their parents live. They may insist upon living in the same block or even in the same house with their parents so that they can continue to depend upon them, seek advice, and in general perpetuate the comfortable child-parent relationship. Householders unfortunate enough to be on the same telephone party line with such a mother-daughter combination can testify to the long hours spent on the phone discussing the minutiae of each other's day. The daughter receives advice on exactly how she ought to handle the day's work, her husband, and many other matters. On those rare occasions when adolescents attempt to break away from such relationships, the parent usually resists and the adolescent has guilt feelings.

The reasons for an overprotective attitude on the part of one or both of the parents are various. Essentially, as Bossard points out, the emotional needs of the parents themselves are "one of the most powerful determinants of the attitude toward children." Investigators have advanced numerous reasons for overindulgent or overprotective parental attitudes. Baldwin for example, includes, among other things, a wish to play the good fairy, a need to be kind-hearted, an attempt to conceal rejection, or to gain social approval as a "good" mother. Symonds lists an unhappy childhood for the parent accompanied by a determination to protect the child from similar unhappiness and frustrations arising out of marriage. The protection may take any one of numerous forms. Often an adolescent will find himself the victim of a conflict between his parents; in such a conflict one parent may attempt, usually unconsciously, to enlist the support and affection of the child by standing as his advocate against the other parent. In more extreme cases he may even encourage the child to resist authority in order to annoy his spouse. The normal result of this activity is problem behavior on the part of the adolescent.

An unhealthy familial relationship may also arise between a child and a parent when the parent selfishly uses the child as an emotional substitute for disappointment in the actualities of marriage. The same sort of thing may occur in a home which has been broken by death or divorce; the remaining parent may turn to the child for companionship and emotional security. Such an attachment may become pathological in its intensity, particularly if the child is so closely identified with his deceased parent that he becomes in effect a surrogate for him. The child is now overprotected, and his efforts to break away are usually resisted so vigorously that he either succumbs or his revolt is accompanied by intense guilt feelings. Often the adolescent in such a situation is less and less able to associate satisfactorily with other people, more particularly members of the opposite sex, and finds himself isolated and unable to cope satisfactorily with the realities of adult life.

One of the most selfish and pernicious reasons for maternal overprotection prolonged out of all reason is the mother's fear of losing her role as "protector." This is particularly true of older women whose homes have become the center of their universe and the only source of real satisfaction in life. Many people, after marriage, devote themselves exclusively to their homes and their children. As year succeeds year the mother may give up all outside activities until there is nothing left for her but the home. Then, some time in her forties, she finds that her children are growing up and are about to leave the home and fend for themselves. Since their departure would leave her nothing to do and would in effect remove her only real interest and motive for living, the mother might tend to tighten the apron strings, enlist sympathy, inspire guilt feelings, and in general resist the emancipative process. Her resistance will be even greater if her marital relations have been unsatisfactory and her devotion to her children has taken the place of devotion to her husband. Such a reaction on her part is understandable, but it will have an unfortunate effect upon the adjustment of the adolescent who must submit to it. Some adolescents will under such circumstances make real efforts to break away, and many succeed, but it is usually at the expense of real guilt feelings on their part, particularly if they recount "all the things that mother has done for them." That such a situation is far from unusual is evidenced by some statistics cited by Glick: "The average woman is 21.6 years old (median age) at her first marriage—has her first child within about a year, and her third (last) within about 5.6 years after marriage. Her children marry when she is between 45 and 50 years old—the couple may expect to live one fourth of its married life together after the children marry."

The ordinal position of the child also may become a factor in parental overindulgence. The *first*-born or the *last*-born are most likely to be treated with the greatest indulgence. The first-born child in a family, especially, is often in the unfortunate position of being overaccepted by his parents. They adopt a most unrealistically lenient attitude toward him, granting his every wish and permitting him to adopt the role of a tyrant in the family scene.

Frequently overindulgence may result from a child's chronic illness or weakness. However, Levy feels that illness as such is not particularly productive of maternal overprotection unless some type of emotional pity or perhaps guilt feelings on the part of the mother are present. Overmagnification may stem from any number of causes ranging from overconscientiousness and perhaps compulsiveness to the behavior of well-meaning parents who have looked forward to "sharing the growing-up process" with their child and who insist upon participating in nearly every activity with him. In the latter case, some parents are obviously more successful than others, but even the parent most acceptable in the eyes of his adolescent offspring can carry such participation to the point where it is not only embarrassing to the adolescent but definitely unwelcome.

In an interesting study by Kasanin of forty-five cases of schizophrenia a considerable percentage of history of overprotection was found. He notes that "The biological inferiority of the schizophrenic child is easily detected by the parents and serves as one of the principal causes of overprotection— overprotection establishes a vicious circle in the life of the schizophrenic child because, on the one hand, the child needs the extra care for his development, but on the other hand, receiving of this extra care hinders his final development, his emancipation from his parents, and his psychosexual development."

Levy lists four basic indexes of overprotection which the student of adolescence may accept as symptomatic of an overprotected adolescent: excessive contact of mother with the adolescent, prolongation of services rendered customarily to children, prevention of development of independent behavior, and lack of excess of maternal control.

Parental Domination

Parental domination is probably the leading block to the normal course by which the adolescent emancipates himself from parental control and eventually or reasonably early, acquires the ability to take his place as a mature individual in the economic and social world. Symonds defines dominating parents as those who "exercise a great deal of control over the child by being very strict and authoritative with him, who punish the child or threaten punishment, who are hard on the child and hold him to standards which are not suited to his age and development, who criticize the child, who unnecessarily frighten the child, who plan extensively for him, or, in some cases, who care for the child's needs to an unusual degree and give him unnecessary toys or advantages or special privileges."

The reasons for a dominating attitude on the part of a given parent are numerous, but very frequently the end result of domination is the same, whatever its cause. Typically, the adolescent will tend to resent domination, and his struggle against it will often become a struggle for ascendancy between himself and his parent. There are, of course, many factors impinging upon this struggle, among them the adolescent's isolation from outside influences, the degree and kind of dominance practiced, the degree of independence the adolescent has been accustomed to in the past, the consistency of the dominance, and whether or not the dominance attitude comes from one or from both parents. Possibly the most important consideration of all is whether the adolescent feels that the dominance is reasonable and whether he accepts or rejects the motives of his parents. Both Bernard and Levy indicate that when parental dominative treatment is harsh, unusual, or irregular, severe reactions on the part of the child are likely to follow. This becomes particularly true when the parent's attitude is overly protective or overtly rejectant. Reinhardt and Fowler cite unjust punishment as a contributing factor in juvenile delinquency. In their study they note that twice as many delinquents as nondelinquents regard the father who whips his children as the "meanest man." Meyers writes that "if the dominated child is at the same time wanted or accepted, and if the domination is steady, deliberate, and probably not harsh, the result is continued attachment to parents, along with a lack of normal social development outside the family." He makes the further point that "authoritarian parenthood will not necessarily stir an adolescent to rebellious activity against the sources of his control—certain kinds of domination may actually result in a continued acceptance of authority on the child's part—his social behavior is quite benign (courteous, obedient, submissive, polite, docile. Dominated children have few friends; they are not independent; they lack confidence). When the aggressive pattern is found, it is most likely to occur . . . when the discipline is strict, inconsistent, and harsh." Horney notes that "children, as well as adults, can accept a great many deprivations if they feel the deprivations to be just, fair, necessary, or purposeful." She goes on to say that punishment can be accepted or at least borne by an adolescent if he "feels the punishment to be fair and not done with the intention of hurting or humiliating—the question of whether frustration as such incites to hostility is difficult to judge—what matters is the spirit in which frustrations are imposed rather than the frustrations themselves." A number of writers have fallen into the logical fallacy of assuming that domination will inevitably be followed by aggression and rebellion, but the facts of the case and the available data do not appear to bear out their contention.

Inconsistency on the part of the parent, both in his attitudes and his discipline, do appear, however, to have definite repercussions. Meyers found that "if two adults agreed on a command, the child complied; when they disagreed the child tended toward disobedience, or other overt manifestations of aggressive reaction." The reasons for such inconsistencies are varied, ranging from the guilt feelings of a rejected parent, which lead to occasional modifications of his behavior, through emotional instability and sporadic and temporary attempts on the part of the parent to "do something" about his son or daughter. This last usually occurs when the adolescent for some reason or other gets into difficulty, becomes especially annoying, or causes the parent some kind of public embarrassment.

Rejection

In terms of aggression or withdrawal response, the most serious type of parental attitude which may lead to dominating behavior is rejection. Newell defines the behavior of the actively rejecting parent as characterized by "severe punishment, neglect, nagging, indifference, irritation, mother threatening to send the child away, handling the child inconsistently, suspiciousness, resisting spending money on the child, and comparing the child unfavorably with a sibling."

There are many different reasons advanced for parental rejection, most of them firmly fixed in a highly emotional base. One basic reason is the fact that many children come to their homes as unwanted additions. There may have been too many previous children, in which case the parental reaction tends to be one of discrimination against the child in favor of his older brothers or sisters. The unwanted child may be the target of unusually severe discipline. He may also have to accept the discarded clothing and toys of his older brothers and sisters without ever being permitted to have anything new of his own.

The child who finds himself in such a situation is usually quite aware of the attitude toward him, and he attempts to use every means at his disposal to gain the affection and security which he lacks. When this does not work he may become resentful, bitter, and discontented, not only within his home, but outside it as well. His overt response to this feeling may take the form either of withdrawal or of aggression, but in both cases he will probably have difficulty in adjusting to the demands that society will eventually make upon him both as an adolescent and as an adult. In his attempt to gain parental acceptance, he may continue to act like a child long after he has passed beyond that stage. Unfortunately he may generalize from his parents to his teachers, his employers, and other adults and view them as parent substitutes, continuing to behave with them in the same childish manner in order to gain their acceptance. Such a person is extremely difficult to get along with and unless his motives are recognized and understood he will receive scant sympathy from his teachers or other youth workers.

Possible rejection may result when the adolescent becomes a cause of conflict between husband and wife. One of the parents may resent the child because he feels that he was high-pressured into having the child originally. The child may possess unwanted attributes or be of the opposite sex from the one desired. If the parents are particularly selfish and immature, the child will represent too great an economic sacrifice. He may be forced to live with relatives who feel he is a burden; living with grandparents during wartime is an example. Finally, the behavior of the adolescent may bring him into conflict with his parents.

Davis lists several universal situations which cause conflicts between parents and their children. Among these are a basic age or birth cycle differential between parent and child and the decelerating rate of socialization with advancing age. Younger people tend to be vigorous, noisy and to like continual companionship and activity. An older person, for many reasons tends to decrease the amount and scope of his physical and social activity as he grows older. He is usually in less need of groups of people and prefers from time to time a period of "peace and quiet." In seeking such a period he will frequently be at cross-purposes with his children who want to "have the gang in and get something doing." There is also the matter of changing mores. Things that are widely accepted in the modern world would once have been strictly taboo. Smoking is one example. The girl who smoked in the 1890's was branded as an immoral, "loose" woman and the parent who permitted it would find himself disgraced. In this connection it is interesting to note that since the growth of individual freedom and the relaxing of taboos in heterosexual relations, the modern adolescent has in that area at least less severe reasons for conflict with his or her parents. It is certainly easier for the modern girl to approach her mother on matters such as sex or smoking than it was for her mother to approach hers. Since, however, we are talking in terms of the mean, a word of caution is appropriate. It is wise to remember that there are many families whose values and points of reference are still those of several generations ago. From such families little can be expected in terms of sympathy with, or acceptance of, modern values, mores, and relinquishment of the taboos and preconceptions of another day.

Davis also points out that situations causing parent-child conflict may be considerably more severe in some societies than in others, depending largely upon the societal organization. The variables operating in any given society that enhance parent-child conflict are the rate of social change, the complexity of the social structure, the degree of cultural integration, the velocity of movement (vertical mobility) within the social structure, and the relation of this mobility to the values of the culture.

Consequences of parent-child conflicts and rejection include many more elements than harsh treatment or lack of attention to the child. These may range all the way from out-and-out physical abandonment through placing the child in an institution such as a reform school, a boarding school, a convent, or a military school, to various acts of deliberate omission such as failure to provide adequate clothing and allowance or educational opportunity. However, despite the obvious nature of these extreme acts, authorities are nearly unanimous in affirming that withholding emotional acceptance has far more serious repercussions than withholding physical things.

85. Parent Education Groups in a Child Guidance Clinic *

HAIM G. GINOTT

IT HAS BEEN pointed out time and again that progress in all fields of human endeavor does not depend so much on the overrefinement of existing procedures and implements as on the development of new techniques and tools. The best arrow does not fly so far as a bullet nor the swiftest conventional plane so fast as a jet.

This observation pertains also to the field of guidance and psychotherapy. Clinics all over the nation are flooded with an ever mounting stream of applications. To meet the vast demand for service, clinics have increased either the staff or the case load, but have done relatively little to introduce new tools of treatment or new methods of attack. Only a few clinics have introduced, as an integral feature of service, group methods such as group

* From Haim G. Ginott, "Parent Education Groups in a Child Guidance Clinic," *Mental Hygiene* (January, 1957), pp. 82–86. Reprinted by permission of the author and The National Association of Mental Health.

play therapy and activity group therapy for children or group counseling and group psychotherapy for adults.

Clinicians who are successful in individual therapy seem reluctant to venture into group treatment. Perhaps it is a reflection of the general climate of our society, which does not encourage departure from the familiar, or perhaps there is a deep fear of giving up the security of solutions that have worked well in the past for procedures that are threatening in their newness. Whatever the reasons, if our science and service are to advance we must not allow accepted solutions of the past to hinder the search for more realistic solutions for the future.

The aim of this article is to describe the efforts of one clinic to face new demands with new methods.

Three years ago there were about two hundred names on the waiting list of our clinic. Parents who called for service were told, in a very sympathetic voice, that we understood they had a problem but the best we could do for them was to put their names on the waiting list. When one mother was told that her enuretic son could not be seen for at least a year, she retorted, "By next year I hope my son will have stopped wetting without your help." We shared the mother's hope and assured her that the frustration was mutual.

Indeed it was discouraging for the staff to feel that all that could be done in response to urgent needs was to register them. It became obvious that if the clinic was to avoid the feeling of impotence it had to devise some kind of approach that would enable parents to be *seen* in treatment the year they *called* for treatment. The idea was then born that something other than individual appointments could be offered to the waiting and eager public, on the assumption that any treatment conducted by qualified personnel is better than no treatment.

After much fumbling and many mistakes we have evolved two new devices—group screening and the parent education group—and introduced them as integral parts of the clinic's manifold service. Group screening was reported in a previous article.[1] This paper will describe the aims, scope, and limits of the parent education group and the basic elements that differentiate it from group therapy and group counseling.

It is almost superfluous to state that the parent education group differs from group psychotherapy. Group therapy is aimed at bringing permanent changes in the intrapsychic balance of nosologically selected patients grouped for the therapeutic effect they have on each other. To paraphrase

[1] Haim G. Ginott, "Group Screening of Parents in a Child Guidance Setting," *International Journal of Group Psychotherapy*, 6 (1956), 405-9.

Slavson: Group therapy through transference, catharsis, insight, reality testing, and sublimation brings about a new balance in the psyche of the patients, with an enhanced ego, modified superego, redistributed libido, and corrected self-image.

The parent education group's more modest goal is to improve the everyday functioning of parents in relation to their children by helping them to a better understanding of the dynamics of parent-child relations and of the basic facts of child growth and needs. This aim is achieved by sensitizing parents to the needs of children, increasing their awareness of the role of feelings in human life, and promoting understanding of the latent meanings of children's activities, play, and verbal expressions.

Focus and Method

The parent education group differs from group counseling both in focus and method. In the parent education group there is a definite problem-centered plan of discussion that is focused entirely on child-parent relations. In group counseling there is no planned discussion and the subject matter is concerned with the daily adjustment problems of the adult client.

The immediate aim of the parent education group in a clinic setting is to render service to parents without serious personality disturbance, instead of—or in preparatiton for—more intensive treatment. We refer to the parent education group those mothers who basically like their children but have difficulty in getting along with them because of ignorance, faulty expectations, or confused cultural and social standards.

The parent education group comprises twenty to twenty-five mothers who meet weekly for ninety-minute sessions over a period of ten weeks. It is desirable to have separate groups for mothers of preschool children, school children and adolescents. Homogeneous age groups bring out common problems. This increases the intragroup identification, augments catharsis and facilitates empathetic communication.

At the first meeting the mothers are asked to state their complaints about their children as fully as they can. One by one they relate their problems. Their stories are usually tinged either with self-blame or projection of fault on the school, the neighborhood or the hereditary background of the husband. It is surprising that even at the first session the mothers talk quite freely. Their identification with each other is almost immediate. When one mother talks the others nod their heads sympathetically as if to say, "We know what you are talking about." A frequent remark is, "That's exactly the situation in my home. For a minute I thought you were talking about my child." It is apparent that they feel greatly supported by the tales of woe of the others. As one mother puts it, "Being in the same boat is half a consolation."

When all have had an opportunity to relate their complaints, they are asked to mention all the methods and "tricks" they employ to insure discipline in their children. They are also asked to formulate a reason why their persistent disciplinary measures have failed.

The parents list the whole array of standard measures used either with or against children in our society to insure discipline and obedience. The list includes spanking, deprivation, bribery, scolding, threatening, withholding of allowances, and withdrawal of love with scores of variations and embellishments, some original and some ancient.

The reasons they give for the failure of these disciplinary methods are numerous and contradictory. They attribute it to their being either too strict or too lenient with the children, to "babying" them too much or too little, or to the presence or absence of playmates in the neighborhood, etc. When they hear the same reasons given by other mothers, however, they become aware of the spuriousness of their explanations. The one who thinks she was too lenient with her child hears about the problem of the mother who was a strict disciplinarian. The one who claims she has not used but "should have used" corporal punishment learns of the problems of the parent who spanked the child too much. The one who is afraid she reared her child in "too great freedom" hears the complaints about the overprotected and oversupervised child. And the one who blames all disciplinary problems on the crowded conditions of the city hears of the hardships of the rural and suburban mothers.

When the contradictory reasons are brought out, anxiety mounts in the group. Mothers turn with pointed and often hostile questions to the staff, demanding immediate solutions to long-standing problems.

No attempt is made to answer any of the questions at this point. The parents are informed that the first sessions will be devoted to *understanding* rather than to solving problems. They are told, half seriously, that any "what-do-you-do-when?" questions will not be answered.

The Leader

It cannot be overstated that the person leading the parent education group must possess all the skills and sensitivities demanded in all therapists. The leader must be aware at all times of the latent implications of parents' communications and should be expert in what not to say as well as in what to say. This is necessary in order to avoid arousing disruptive tensions and deep anxieties.

During the first sessions the leader takes a minimal part in the discussions. He asks two or three central questions and stimulates the parents to participate freely. His first chance to "lecture" comes in answering the general question: "Why do the various disciplinary measures fail to bring lasting results?" The idea is presented that "one acts mean because he feels mean." Feelings are the cause, actions the result. Discipline that deals with actions and ignores attitudes only deepens the mean feelings and increases the chances for mean acting-out, thus creating a perpetual vicious circle.

Dealing with Feelings

This seems to be a new idea to the mothers. They have never considered the children's feelings as an essential part of the disciplinary problems. The question they raise next, quite naturally, is, "How are mean feelings changed?" The leader turns the question back to the group. Again one becomes aware how inadequately our homes, schools, church, and culture have prepared people for dealing with feelings. One realizes how afraid parents are of children's expression of true feelings, how quick they are to deny, disown, and suppress them. The total failure to comprehend the nature of feelings is best illustrated in the short sentence of a young mother who said quite sincerely, "I try to spank out hate and spank in love."

We draw on parents' own experiences to gain insight in how feelings change. Through leading questions and examples parents come to recognize that feelings accepted with understanding and loving care tend to lose their sharp edges. Many sessions are devoted to the clarification of this idea. Each mother searches within herself to answer for herself whether she really believes that a person has a right to negative feelings. For the first time in their lives parents think through these basic problems in nonmoralistic terms and in concepts that perhaps run contrary to all that has been taught to them at home, school, and church.

Parents begin to recognize that children as well as adults have both positive and negative feelings. There is love and hate, jealousy and friendliness, fear and security, and they are all legitimate feelings. There comes a realization that expression and acceptance of feelings is more healthful and more helpful than their rejection and denial. When the mothers fully understand that emotions are better channeled than dammed, the group begins searching for methods which will enable children to express troubled feelings in nondestructive ways. The parents themselves point out many ways through which children can express and liquidate angry feelings.

Through self-derived insight mothers come to grasp the value of non-critical, empathetic mirroring of feelings. Therapeutic understanding and reflection of feelings cannot be taught but it can be "caught" by individuals who experience them. The parents learn to perceive more keenly what children communicate, not only in words but in activity and play. The parents begin to see their children as *reacting* individuals and they become sensitized to the impact of their own attitudes and actions on their children's conscience and conduct.

Parents are introduced to many specific techniques that help "in times of peace reduce times of stress." These procedures are described in detail in Dorothy Baruch's *New Ways in Discipline*,[2] which was found to be an excellent guide for the discussions.

At the end of the parent education group an evaluation session is scheduled with each parent and it is decided whether further help is needed.

The most significant effects of the group experience, as reported by participants, were the diminished tensions and greater harmony between them and their immediate families. The change in the participants, as evaluated by the staff, can be described as their greater recognition of children as reacting individuals and a more positive view of their role as parents.

Our experience with the parent education group has been confined to mothers, primarily because the group met during working hours. Many mothers have complained about the difficulties they encountered in communicating their increased insight to their husbands. They have requested parent education groups for fathers—an idea worth consideration.

As a result of the parent education group experience some mothers have come to recognize the need for more intensive treatment for deeper problems. For these mothers the parent education groups served as a rehearsal in introspection and catharsis and prepared them for individual or group psychotherapy.

Parent education groups were started in our clinic as an emergency tool and substitute service. They have emerged as a method of choice on par with other major services. Parents who were at the end of the rope in their relations with their children found in the group new vistas of help and hope. After experimenting with such groups for the last three years we can state with a degree of certainty that they justify a place on the clinical roster. The main advantages of the parent education groups as we see them are:

[2] Dorothy Walter Baruch, *New Ways in Discipline* (New York: McGraw-Hill Book Co., 1949).

Parents become aware of the existence in themselves and in their children of an inner world of feelings and of its significance in making or breaking happiness.

For the first time in their lives parents take time to think through and wonder about the right of people (including themselves and their children) to have negative as well as positive attitudes, and they become aware of a new freedom—the freedom to feel.

Parents learn new methods of relating to children. They become sensitized to children's expressions of attitudes and learn to accept and reflect rather than reject or deny troubled feelings.

Parents acquire, if not digest, a large body of factual information concerning the nature of child behavior.

Parents become aware of, even if they do not fully assimilate, the meaning and value of noncritical acceptance and genuine respect.

Parents learn to be more objective and less ego-involved in their everyday relations with their children and gain an ability to handle daily problems with more confidence and less guilt.

Parents learn many new methods of dealing more adequately with the specific problems of their children.

Finally, parent education groups enable even a minimally staffed agency to provide extensive service to the community. Under competent therapists the parent education group can become a potent tool in helping a selected group of parents modify old attitudes and beliefs, develop new values and sensitivities, and bring about a greater enjoyment of family work and life.

86. *Parents and Teen-agers: Differing Perspectives* [*] [1]

ROBERT D. HESS

LEARNING to answer the questions, "Who am I? What do I do? What do I want to be?" is basically the task of adolescence—a conflict in which the young person must come to terms with himself and his capabilities, commit himself to a career and an occupation and to an individual way of

[*] From Robert D. Hess, "Parents and Teen-agers: Differing Perspectives," *Child Study* (Winter, 1959–60), pp. 21–23. Reprinted by permission of the author and the Child Study Association of America.

[1] The research project reported here was conducted at the University of Chicago with the support of its Social Science Committee.

looking at himself and relating to others. At heart, it is the highly personal job of growing up, and teen-agers must deal with it by themselves—no one, not even their parents or the closest friends—can be of much help.

At the same time, the values and attitudes he absorbs, the expectations of his parents and friends, teachers and community all help to shape the final image a youngster creates. Moreover, to be successful, he must win his society's approval. Achieving identity, then, is really a mutual process—an individual's commitment to a personal pattern of inner and outer life—and the community's acceptance of him as a unique but recognized and respected member.

Whether it's a matter of late hours or homework, "going steady," or the "crowd," politics or a job, the adolescent's attempts to assert his individuality notoriously lack grace; perhaps inevitably (and sometimes quite accurately) he may seem to his parents rebellious or rejecting. In part, however, the traditional parent-child conflict of this period stems from the apparently contradictory responsibility of parents to provide both "growing room" and guidance: on the one hand, to protect the adolescent, limiting his behavior for his own (and the family's) best interests, and, on the other, to help him move toward independence and the right to make his own decisions and even mistakes.

As the teen-ager begins to assume authority over his own life that his parents had previously held, the contradictions are apt to become more troublesome. The boundaries become even less certain, the question, "Just how much freedom is manageable?" more perplexing for parents and teen-agers alike. And behind these uncertainties lies an important fact: the difference in the way parents and teen-agers look at life and at adolescent behavior. *The two generations are absorbed with different problems and thus tend to misunderstand and misinterpret each other.*

In a project supported by the University of Chicago's Social Science Committee,[2] my colleagues and I recently had a chance to take a close look at these differences in outlook and approach. In personal interviews and a series of written questions, we tested some thirty-two adolescents and their parents on their attitudes towards "teen-agers in general" and "adults in general." Asking the youngsters (whose ages averaged a little over 15½ years) first to describe themselves and their parents, we then asked them to mark the questionnaires as they thought most parents would fill them out. For parents, we repeated the procedure, asking them to estimate

---

[2] Robert D. Hess and Irene Goldblatt, "The Status of Adolescents in American Society: a Problem in Social Identity," *Child Development,* Vol. 28, No. 4 (December, 1957).

the response of most teen-agers. In this way, we not only discovered the general attitudes these youngsters and their parents held about adolescents and adults but—what was more revealing—*the attitudes each thought the other held about himself and his friends.*

For Parents: a High Rating

To a surprising degree, the two groups agreed in their general descriptions of teen-agers. Both described the youngsters in moderately favorable terms; both gave them credit for a fair degree of responsibility and judgment; yet both also made it clear that teen-age behavior fell considerably short of adult standards. In fact, a quick glance at these findings would suggest that American parents and teen-agers had achieved a remarkable harmony.

Yet when we compared these descriptions with the *predictions of how the other group felt* about adolescence, a less peaceable picture emerged. The vast majority of parents had predicted that most of the youngsters would describe themselves in highly positive terms, *overestimating* their capabilities and maturity: yet their teen-agers seemed certain that parents would *underestimate* adolescents and disparage them. In one way or another, the youngsters seemed to be saying, "Adults don't trust us—they think we're much less mature than we really are." At the same time, the parents were saying, "Teen-agers think they're much *more* mature than they really are."

The findings showed, however, that on some questions (seriousness, reliability, morality, for example) parents actually had given more credit to the teen-agers than the youngsters gave themselves—and, on the whole, were within a few points of the teen-agers' own self-evaluation. More strikingly, perhaps, on *every* item tested, the teen-agers rated parents far higher than the parents rated themselves.

What Does Teen-age Behavior Mean?

How then did such an apparent failure in communication and understanding come about? If parents and teen-agers really agreed on a favorable —but moderate and realistic—appraisal of adolescents, why did they so completely misinterpret and mistrust each other's motives?

An important answer may lie in the very different meaning that teen-age behavior has for the two generations. In one telling instance in our interviews, for example, we discovered that both the youngsters and their parents felt that double-dating was definitely preferable to single-dating in the teen years. But when we asked *why,* the difference in the replies was startling.

For the parents, double-dating was a safeguard: youngsters on double-dates were less likely to "neck" or "pet" or "get into trouble." But the teen-agers, we learned, had more immediate problems in mind. As one youngster put it, "With four people together on a date, there's nearly always someone who can find something to say!"

Differing Perspectives

It would be misreading the evidence here to conclude that these parents were all too ready to "think the worst" of their youngsters. The gap between the two answers seems to be part of the nature of the differences between generations, the differing perspectives of the experienced and the novice.

Taking for granted the social ease acquired over three or four decades, a parent is apt to forget the very real tensions and embarrassments of the early dating years. At the same time, his experience makes him acutely aware of the long-range consequences, the hazards and problems facing adolescents. In addition, he faces the complex problem of reconciling the conflicting demands of his own needs as a parent, his child's need to grow and mature, and the demands and standards of society.

The teen-ager, on the other hand, is typically absorbed with the immediate problems of moving toward adult responsibility and maturity. He still lacks the experience to easily judge the long-range consequences of impulsive behavior. The need to prove to himself and others that he is adequate and competent, "grown-up," "popular," or "cool" is too pressing, too compelling to admit any long-range view. Paradoxically, too, his awareness of a real and considerable gap between his own level of maturity and that of adults often brings him into conflict with adults—for he is likely to disguise his feelings of immaturity with bravado.

Almost inevitably, then, the two generations bring a widely differing perspective to teen-age problems. As the adolescent attempts to redefine himself, to move toward autonomy and establish an adult identity, his tendency to overestimate adult competence may prove a useful spur. But his feeling that adults devalue his achievements and deprecate his efforts can only hold him back. So long as teen-agers mistakenly believe that adults seriously underrate them, it will have a significant impact upon their behavior and complicate the task of learning and internalizing adult roles.

87. Separation of the Parents and the Emotional Life of the Child * [1]

GEORGE E. GARDNER

IN THIS PAPER I shall confine myself to the effects on the emotional development of the child of the prolonged and essentially permanent absence of one parent from the home, and comment only to a limited degree upon those even more unfortunate situations where both natural parents are absent, presumably permanently so. I shall consider only those situations, too, where the absent parent, though away from home, is still living and may or may not be accessible to the child at stated intervals. Furthermore, because of the fact that in 75 to 90 per cent of any series of broken homes coming to our attention it is the father of the child who is absent, my remarks will be primarily directed to the effect of his absence on the child's development. To be sure, a certain percentage of mothers do desert their children, or their children are taken from them by direction, and when this happens the basic problems set for the child vary in kind and in intensity; to these I shall lend some emphasis. Yet the prototype of the broken home is that where the father is absent and the mother has the sole care of the children. In the fourth place, I shall not attempt, except tangentially, to outline the different effects of the absent parent on boys and on girls as such. Rather I would select for our consideration some universal effects upon children regardless of sex and some fundamental problems in emotional development that are affected by the absence of the parent.

Specifically, I shall speak of the effects of parental separation upon: (1) The child's developing "concept of self"—the ingredients that go to establish his own inner sense of separateness, integrity, worth-whileness, and security as an individual. (2) The child's "concept of human beings" that comprise his outer world—human objects to which he must make a definite feeling orientation and to which he is expected to respond, as a child and later as an adult, in an acceptable and an efficient way. (To the technically minded perhaps it is correct to say that I am directing my attention to the possible effects of parent absence on the ego development of the child.)

* From George E. Gardner, "Separation of the Parents and the Emotional Life of the Child," *Mental Hygiene* (January, 1956), pp. 53–64. Reprinted by permission of the author and The National Association of Mental Health.

[1] Presented at the Massachusetts Conference of Social Work.

We shall begin our discussion by a glance for a moment at what the parent is to the child; i.e., what are some of the most important attributes of the parent as far as the child is concerned and as he or she is seen through children's eyes and feelings at various stages of development. In the light of these many parental roles (and they are many and complex), we ourselves shall be better able to appreciate the effect of deviations from these roles which are brought about when a parent leaves. To the child at any age—and particularly in earliest childhood—the parent (both parents) is the source of life itself in the form of food and clothes—the one single factor of basic significance in establishing within him a sense of security and in indicating probable continuing survival. He predicates his physical integrity, including later his sense of anatomical integrity, upon the presence of parents who will care for his bodily needs and will protect him from aggressive and mutilative attacks by others.

To this basic feeling of security of body and its associated concept in the child's mind that parents through their presence alone will maintain it are added other elements in the child's over-all estimate of his parents. They are the givers of gifts that may be used as objects for gratification and the givers of love in and by itself or as symbolized by these gifts. They are in great measure the omniscient givers of information that explains his world and omnipotently protects him in it. In their seeming omniscience and omnipotence also they control his life, direct his behavior, and emphasize ideals of conduct in individual and group living.

These are the elements of the fundamental concept of the parent as it exists in the mind of the young child. Obviously many modifications of this biological or strictly "dependency-need" concept of the parents must take place as the child advances toward the establishment of a necessary concept of himself as an independently (relatively independently, of course) behaving individual or "self," at which point he is expected to refer his behavior to inculcated or incorporated mental images of these parents which, for good or ill, are to be the most powerful models that he will have within him.

It should be emphasized, too, that these parental concepts will in large part determine what the child's notions of human beings as a whole in his world of the present and the future will be like. The human objects to which he will direct, or from which he will withhold, his love in the expectation of gratifying and satisfying experiences will be determined in large part by his infant and childhood concept of the parent figures. These are models of the human love objects in his environment.

On the other hand, it is not difficult to conjecture that the child's basic concept of self is also determined by the variations in behavior on the part of his parents as they relate to the security feelings mentioned above. His worth-whileness and his intrinsic value of himself as an individual is first, and hence most crucially, demonstrated to him by the expression of his parents' own love, care, attention, protection, gifts, companionship, etc., through their presence (in the earliest years almost omnipresence) in his vicinity. One's concept of one's worth of self is inevitably a product of another's expressed need or want.

If these hypotheses and assumptions of the importance to the child of these parental relationships in the formation of both his concept of self and his concept of human beings are correct, it is possible to examine and outline the effect upon the child of any and all deviations of parents from the most efficient model for which we could hope.

We have selected for consideration one trauma, the deleterious effect of a prolonged or permanent parent absence upon these concepts. These varying effects in varying situations are brought to our attention through numberless clinical observations.

Let us start, first of all, with the child whose parent left the home before the child was 2 or 3 years of age. He has, let us say, never seen the father or cannot remember ever seeing him. It is natural for such children, at 4 or 5 and thereafter, to note the difference in their own homes; and their questions as to "Where is my father?" or, more pointedly, "Who is my father?" are either answered evasively or are virtually ignored by the remaining parent. Naturally the mother is in a very difficult position because she is caught in a conflict which she knows she has, in part, and which, regardless of what she answers, she is going to transmit with full force on the child. If she tells the child that the father left because he did not love them, the child himself feels—just as does she—for the first time a sense of worthlessness. He feels that he must have been (and still is) of little worth or his father would never have left. There is, too, a questioning of the absolute worth of his mother, for she too was left. If the mother states that she left the father because they "could not get along together"—thereby trying to minimize the shortcomings of the father in the eyes of the child— the child may very well feel that perhaps his father was all right, perhaps even better than mother really, that mother is keeping his father from him, and that the latter really would like to be home if mother would only let him. In this situation the child's concept of the mother is that she is in some part a depriving mother—depriving him of the love and companionship of a father, not because he, the child, is at fault, but because the mother and father didn't like *each other*.

Assume for a moment that the mother tries to soften the blow by taking it out of the realm of personalities or of likes or dislikes and placing it instead in the area of economics. She states, for example, that father left "because he could not support us," really meaning of course in many situations that "he *would* not support us." Immediately the child's concept of his father, of fathers in general, and of men in general is that they are unable to care for mothers or children and that under such circumstances men in general may leave their children or—even worse—ladies may leave or abandon the fathers of their children. To go beyond this rumination of the child: in the clinical setting it is not unusual for a further equation to be arrived at, namely, if mothers can so easily abandon husbands, they perhaps may at some time, if provoked enough, just as easily abandon the small prototype of husband, the male child, i.e., himself. And this certainly does not add to the child's sense of security, nor does it add to his estimate of his own worth in a world populated by human love objects.

Another explanatory device is based on the assumption that all such feelings may be prevented if the child is led to believe, through either expressed or unexpressed hints, that the absent parent is dead. This is a solution used more often than one would suppose. By such a technique the remaining parent escapes an expression of her feelings only temporarily, and the child does not escape for long either. Almost inevitably the child learns or has to be told that the absent parent is not really dead; and the acute, drastic, and painful modifications that he must make at that time are equally traumatic, if not more traumatic than the changes in concepts and feelings that must occur in the light of the other explanations commented on above. They involve, too, a marked change in his estimation of the trustworthiness of all human beings. If a parent can lie about a thing so important to him, the parent certainly cannot be trusted in all other explanations which he has received or in the future expects to receive on demand.

There is a specific anxiety that is aroused in the child as he grows older —and particularly in adolescence—following a spurious explanation that the absent parent is dead. As the child begins to doubt this explanation or as he is later given indirect or direct inklings as to the truth, he is tortured by the possibility that he is an illegitimate child: that his father left before he was born because his father and mother were never married or that he was illegitimately conceived and the marriage took place merely "to give him a name." This is a very logical deduction on his part when the remaining parent attempts to correct the original falsehood by explaining that the father disappeared before the child was born or shortly thereafter.

Finally, there is the possible deduction too—in separations taking place in the child's infancy and earliest years—that his father and mother got along reasonably well and lived together until he was born. In this situation it is very easy for the child to assume that if he hadn't been born the parents would be together—that he was the *cause* of the separation. They wanted each other but did not want *him*. One can estimate the child's own sense of worth as an individual human being in the midst of such logical ruminations. And such ruminations are the only logical ones the child can make in the light of the information that he is allowed to receive in many broken homes.

As I stated above, the mother's position following a separation in the early life of the child is a difficult one when she is asked to explain to the child the absence of the father. My thesis is that there is no explanation that will not have an adverse effect on the developing self-concept and human-being concept of the child. These effects may be and should be minimized, but they probably cannot be entirely eliminated.

Let us turn now to the effects on the child of a separation of the parents at a later stage in his development, placing the separation at a time after the child has received the benefits of an unbroken home and has had the opportunity of forming positive relationships with and concepts of both a father and a mother. I need not tell you that there is usually a long period of strife and discord in the family to which the child is subjected before the separation actually becomes a fact. He has formed to a certain degree a working relationship with both parents; both have satisfied his needs to some extent as love objects, and with respect to each he has formed a definite concept of his own self-worth and also a notion of the worth to him of father and mother—and of the value and worth of adult male and adult female human beings.

The positive aspects of both of these self and not-self concepts come under severe attack during the distressful times preceding parental separation. If the child is inclined to believe or take sides with his mother perforce in her continued and severe devaluations of his father, he may acquiesce, but he does so with poignant feelings of guilt because of the necessary modification of the concept of himself as one who must show expected love of and devotion to his father. The same arousal of guilt is caused as he listens to his father's complaint of his mother and to the citing of her deficiencies as a mother. The "good child" picture of himself that he has constructed for himself as the best source of security obtainable in this world demands that—if he is to remain a "good child"—he must retain his love for both parents. Circumstances just won't allow him to do this.

Even worse for the child is the feeling that his basic and fundamental security may be in large part swept away if either parent leaves him. Both parents are necessary to take care of his needs, the satisfaction of which he has ascribed as being particularly and peculiarly the role of one and not the other parent. Despite repeated attempts at reassurance on the part of the parent who is to remain with him, he is rarely convinced that that parent alone has the power to supply all his needs—and, of course, this intuitive feeling of the child is essentially a correct one and is so proved in time.

When we turn at this time to the other aspect of our discussion, namely, the effect of these devaluative maneuvers and strife between parents on the child's concept of human beings as a whole, we again note some necessary modifications in his estimations of human worth. These are serious and can be far-reaching. For the child the behavior and worth of parents are the models for his evaluation of the behavior and worth of all men and women. Particularly do they constitute the only closely and intimately available model of the expected love of one human being for another and of one man for one woman. The expected and hoped-for stability of love relationships of all persons—including those directed by and directed toward *him* —must be drastically modified at this period. Love relationships with human beings no longer appear sufficiently stable—they may be hazardous and lead to eventual hatred and abandonment. At least the child will henceforth be forced to consider them extremely conditional and capricious, and his reluctance to enter himself into such relationships and his attitudes toward them when he does may be patternized at the time of his parents' separation and lead to considerable future distress.

In short, if one has the opportunity to study a child intensively just before, during, and after parental separation, one is struck by the similarity of the child's reaction to the well-known "grief reaction." He tries desperately to withdraw the emotional investment he heretofore had in the now absent parent and struggles to place it elsewhere in other persons, objects, or interests in his environment. He cannot allow such positive feelings to persist or he feels guilty in respect to his negative feelings or hate for the *remaining* parent. His normal ambivalence toward the parent who has left him is heightened and his guilt becomes greater. To acquire any kind of security and peace he must get rid of both his positive and his negative feelings regarding the latter—and this process, like the mourning process, is a long and painful one.

Following the essentially permanent separation of the parents, other problems arise which in the main are more or less directly related to the possibly changed attitudes toward him on the part of his parents and to the difficulties involved in his attempts to maintain a desirable relationship with both of them—with the present parent in his everyday life and with the absent parent whom it may be possible (or expected of him) to see at stated intervals.

Assume for a moment that the child stays with his mother. Any number of changes may take place in her attitude toward him, and they are easily detectable.

1. For example, he may become to the mother—and he may sense that he has become—a burden. He may be regarded as an economic burden making it necessary for the mother to work both outside and inside the home. Or the fact of his existence and his presence may become to the mother a definite block to her desire for social relationships with adults of both sexes, or to her desire to marry again, or to the carrying out of a previously desired career that had been thwarted by her marriage in the first place.

2. The presence of the child may be a continuing example to the mother of her own deficiencies—notably her failure in her attempt to maintain a home, to satisfy a husband, to be a completely adequate wife and mother. Doubts concerning her abilities along these lines may have existed before her marriage, and its breakup may have confirmed them. The child in turn is a continual reminder and reactivator of these long-existing doubts and fears.

3. Directly associated with these changed attitudes toward the child on the part of the mother is the tendency for her to identify the child with the absent husband, and particularly to identify the child with all the bad and undesirable aspects of the father's make-up. This may happen whether the child is a boy or a girl, though obviously it occurs more often when the child is a boy. Here again the causes may reflect the mother's deep, unconscious, and unrecognized feelings about all males and only secondarily her feelings concerning a particular one—the child's father.

In short, the child may have become an economic burden, a social burden, and an emotional burden to the mother and he begins to realize it. In this situation the child necessarily fears that he is in danger of being abandoned, deserted a second time, this time by the mother. His feelings and his responses when he is seen clinically are those of the terribly insecure and fear-ridden child who in his behavior is attempting all the maneuvers that he can to attain or to maintain what to him seems to be a security position. He may try docility, passivity, and quiet withdrawal to make himself into the "good child" that the mother must love. More often he will fight back with hyperaggressiveness, hostility, and insubordination. He may attempt a regressive move to the behavorial levels of infancy when, he remembers, he was really loved and wanted, or resort to frequent feigned illnesses to regain an attentive response of love and care. Whichever one of these security tactics he may try—and any given child will usually attempt all of them in turn—he usually is unsuccessful in meeting these newly expressed hostile attitudes on the part of the mother.

On the other hand, it sometimes happens that the mother's changed attitude is one of increased positiveness and devotion to the child—and overwhelmingly so. The mother, in her attempts to demonstrate that she is an adequate mother in the face of a separation from the father (with all that this involves concerning her estimate of her own worth) may become extremely oversolicitous and overprotective of the child. His every wish has to be satisfied and his every need gratified in order that her child may appear before the world as a happy and contented youngster. He is figuratively smothered with love and gifts so that the mother may prove to herself and to him that she has not failed and will not fail in her role as a mother. In the absence of the father the child becomes the single, all-inclusive libidinal investment that the mother makes, to the exclusion of an investment of any part of herself in other people or other interests. I need not emphasize the harmful effects that such an excessively overprotective attitude on the part of the mother has on the child because, in the first place, of the impossibility of complete reciprocity of feeling toward the mother on his part. Such reciprocity is not possible in the case of the child in the intact home, nor is it possible when one parent is permanently absent.

You are aware too, I am sure, of the harmful effects of such maternal behavior in relation to the orderly development of the child—to the necessity for eventual separateness and individuality and to the initiation and beneficial completion of those maturity thrusts that depend on the widest possible association of the child with other human beings, both children and adults. And, finally, there is always to be considered the deviated and unrealistic conception of self-worth and self-value that is inculcated within the child when he is the sole object of the mother's love and overprotectiveness.

In short, when this becomes the relationship of the mother and child, the mother's needs rather than those of the child become the real motivating factors in maternal behavior.

There are additional problems set for the child whose parents are separated which, though I shall mention them but briefly, are extremely important in that they may involve the child in acute conflicted feelings resulting in guilt and a consequent modification of his internal notion of his own worth.

The child of the broken home feels "different" from other children. He is continually asked by his colleagues to explain the absence of the parent, to answer the question as to where the parent is, to give judgments to them as to which parent he feels is or was at fault, and to declare which of them he likes the more. In addition to his not knowing the answers to all these factual questions, he is not able without considerable guilt to express his true feelings in the matter. Children in general are particularly curious about broken homes and the causes of them, their curiosity arising, of course, from the possibility—however remote it may actually be in reality—that such a fate may befall their own homes. The child of separated parents is a source of information for them about facts and feelings that they hope may lead to their own reassurance and security, and they can be unwittingly cruel in their approach. At any rate, the child is made to feel "different."

Then there are the conflicted feelings that arise at the time of necessary visits to the absent parent: the child feels guilty if he leaves his remaining parent and he feels particularly guilty if he feels he had a better time there than he ever has at home. On the other hand, if he does not wish to visit the absent parent, he also feels he is a sinful child. Unfortunately he is subjected many times by both parents—by the one at home and by the one he visits—to expressed or unexpressed hostility toward, and devaluation of, the other parent. He becomes an instrument for each parent to prove that he is the better parent, that he loves the child more, that the other parent's care of him is inadequate and the cause of all his unhappiness and deficiencies in conduct or attainments. The child attempts, if he can, a double, mutually exclusive attitude of love and devotion to both parents, in order to prove to himself that he has two good parents who love him; but he rarely succeeds in this and his attempts are usually transitory and are inevitably guilt-laden.

Such visits to absent parents—their time and duration—are sometimes set by law and occasionally they are badly set. One suggestion that I might make in this respect is that visits, if demanded at all, should not be restricted to occasional single days or week-ends or to one or two holidays a year. Such short visits merely result in compulsion on the part of the parent to shower the child with innumerable gifts, and with attendance at a score of entertainments of various sorts to try to indicate to the child that this is the kind of idyllic life he would lead if he lived there all the time—a much happier existence than he now has in his permanent residence. The child returns home with little or no real appreciation of the real worth of this parent and with no feeling that the parent really loves him for his own sake.

Visits should be long enough for the child to appreciate both, and particularly for him to maintain a feeling of really belonging somewhat to the other parent and to feel that there can be a meaningful continuity of this relationship.

88. Parental Attitudes toward Boy-Girl Relations *

ALICE CROW

A MOTHER of two teen-agers recently was heard to say that she mistakenly had thought that babyhood days were the most difficult ones for parents. Baby troubles were mild as compared to the difficulties that she now is experiencing with her growing son and daughter. Adolescence appears to her to be an almost impossible period for parents.

This woman's children are two fine young people whose earlier years, filled with childish activity and fun, were relatively serene and peaceful. Although they are active at school and at home, and successful in their high school studies, they are having difficulty in adjusting in their relations with members of the opposite sex. Their parents are sharing in these youthful struggles for desirable social status.

The sixteen-year-old girl is attractive but tall for her age. Her over average height combined with an attitude of shyness and reticence has resulted in her failure to achieve as many dates as she would like to have. High school boys seem to be too immature or not tall enough to suit her. She is in that period of adolescence during which a girl's interest centers in older men. At the same time, she realizes that the objects of her sentimental attachment would not bother with a high school junior. The girl's mother feels that she is going frantic trying to interest her dreamy, dissatisfied daughter in social activities appropriate to her age and maturity status.

The second child is a fifteen-year-old boy. He, too, is tall for his age and is successful in athletics. His problem is quite different from that of his sister. It seems to his mother that every girl in his high school wants to date him and be known as "his girl." Hence, as this mother attempts to draw her

* From Alice Crow, "Parental Attitudes toward Boy-Girl Relations," *The Journal of Educational Sociology* (November, 1955), pp. 126–33. Reprinted by permission of the author and *The Journal of Educational Sociology*.

daughter into social activities, she is kept busy protecting her son from designing females.

Patience and Understanding Required

The problem of this mother is not an uncommon one. We adults sometimes lose patience with adolescents. We expect them to be both dependent children and independent adults. Too often we forget our own adolescent growing pains, especially in relation to members of the opposite sex. Teachers sometimes act as though a young person's complete interest and attention should be given to school studies. Parents are torn between pride in their developing children and annoyance caused by the fact that the parent no longer seems to hold first place in adolescent affection.

Adolescent interest in members of the opposite sex and the urge to gain their attention are as old as the human race. Parental concern about boy-girl relations is not new. The primitive father's delight when a chosen suitor dragged the daughter by her hair to the marriage cave finds an echo in the modern father's sigh of relief when he has settled the bills for his daughter's wedding. Fathers as well as mothers hope that the marriage of their children releases them from further responsibility for the welfare of the young people. Sometimes such parental attitudes are correct. If they are wrong the cause may be found in attitudes developed during adolescence toward the opposite sex.

One characteristic of our present culture is the freedom that is enjoyed by boys and girls in their social life. Although most parents believe that this freedom is generally wholesome, they sometimes wish that we might return to the former custom of arranged marriages. Left to themselves, young people may become the victims of their own emotional urges. As they struggle toward fulfillment of their innate desires and interests they may engage in activities that are harmful to themselves and disapproved by society. If they experience too great parental supervision of their social activities, they may develop attitudes of resentment which result in nonconforming behavior that result in disastrous aftermaths.

Freedom but *not license* in boy-girl relations should be encouraged by parents of adolescents. It is sometimes difficult for parents always to draw the fine line between acceptable freedom of boy-girl behavior and participation in unwholesome social activities. Parental problems in this area of human relationships are many. They include such matters as the age at which a boy or a girl should begin to date and with whom, the kind of date that is appropriate at the respective stages of adolescent development, the time for returning home from a date, and all the details of dress, grooming, use of the family car, amount of money to be spent, and other accompaniments of the dating process.

Boy-girl attraction develops gradually. Teen-age interest in the opposite sex does not appear suddenly with the onset of puberty; yet, it does increase in intensity during the adolescent years. Too often parents act as though they believed that childhood and adolescence are two separate and related phases of development rather than that development is a continuous process. Attitudes and behavior begun during childhood usually continue with modifications through the adolescent years.

Wise parents are forward-looking. They begin early in the child's life to encourage those attitudes toward himself or herself and toward associates of both sexes that will help the young person to maintain emotional stability as he or she gradually comes to be stimulated by those sexual urges that constitute an important phase of adolescent development.

Parental Attitudes toward the Child's Social Relations

As soon as the young child begins to give indication of social awareness, he or she should experience opportunities in work and play with members of both sexes. Hence coeducation is desirable from the nursery school through all the years of a young person's school life. During childhood, boys and girls tend to participate in activities common to both sexes insofar as physical and mental abilities make such sharing of experience possible and desirable.

The sex factor is not likely to affect children's attitudes toward one another unless adults encourage the youngsters to differentiate between their boy and girl companions. By their supposedly jesting remarks, adults may develop attitudes of self-consciousness in the growing child. For example, no adult comments are made if two small girls walk home from school together, but if a little boy accompanies one of his little girl schoolmates to her home, some adults immediately seem unable to refrain from teasing the youngsters about their "girl" or "boy" friend. The situation becomes more serious if the boy happens to carry some of the girl's books or if, perchance, the boy fails one day to walk home with the girl. In the latter case, foolish adults are likely to make remarks such as "What's the matter? Has Henry stood you up?" or "Doesn't Mary like you any more? Has she a new boy friend?"

Comments such as those referred to in the foregoing and others of their ilk cannot fail to influence developing children. They learn to recognize the fact that adults expect them to act differently toward members of the opposite sex from the way they behave with those of their own sex. Sometimes, an attitude of shyness, reticence or embarrassment in the presence of the other sex is a resultant of such behavior. A seven-year-old girl was very fond of a young man who was a close friend of her parents. Their relationship was pleasant and wholesome. On one occasion, however, when her parents were encouraging him to marry, he said, laughingly, "Oh, I'm waiting for Jane (their little daughter) to grow up. Then we're going to get married."

Although marriage meant no more to Jane than that parents are married, she became very much embarrassed and retorted with "I'm never going to marry." This led to further adult jesting. The little girl continued to be fond of her parents' friend, but she felt that she had lost that free companionship with him that she formerly had enjoyed. Unfortunately this child, like many others, was too inexperienced to appreciate adult humor.

Children should be allowed to associate on an equal basis with companions of both sexes, yet as soon as they are old enough to recognize certain differences between the sexes, their questions should be answered simply and accurately by their parents. It is not the purpose of this paper to treat in detail this area. Various good books and pamphlets on the subject are available for parents' use. It is sufficient to say here that a child's beginning questions such as "Where do babies come from?" or "Why does my brother (or sister) look different from me?" as well as his later more thoughtful questions concerning matters dealing with sex should be answered simply and accurately. Parents are responsible for helping their child to become well-informed about his own physical structure and sexual functions and to develop wholesome and constructive attitudes toward boy-girl relations, marriage, and parenthood.

As we know, attitudes are caught as well as taught. This fact applies especially to the kind of social attitudes developed by impressionable young people. Children are sensitive to the relationship that exists between their parents, parental attitudes toward adult friends of both sexes, as well as parental attitudes toward children's relations with their peer groups.

Fortunate is the child whose home life reflects parental understanding, family cooperation, and wholesome social attitudes. The home may be simple, but if it is clean and neat and the child is encouraged to bring to it his young friends of both sexes, he is experiencing the beginnings of those social attitudes that will be of great value to him during his adolescent period of increased interest in boy-girl relationships.

A teacher of a sixth grade class in elementary school was shocked by the sophisticated attitude displayed by her pupils toward members of the opposite sex. She had not realized that these youngsters who are encouraged to be alert to current events do not limit their learning interests to civic and economic matters. They thrill to newspaper and radio reports of the love life of persons prominent in the news. They listen to adult comments concerning man-woman relations, divorce, and other matters having sexual import. Unless home attitudes and parental training are wholesome these immature young people are more than likely to engage in daydreaming, with themselves as the heroes of a love story, or even to experiment fumblingly with their schoolmates in one or another form of sexual behavior. Even though their behavior is socially satisfactory, they may believe that they must assume an attitude of worldliness and sophistication.

Parental Attitudes toward Adolescent Relationships

A child does not suddenly become an adolescent. Physical growth and physiological changes develop gradually. Some children give evidence of these growth changes during later childhood. Their attitudes toward themselves and their peer associates give evidence of subtle differences that are not completely understood by themselves. Girls become shy in the presence of their former boy pals. They may "moon" over the picture of popular motion-picture actors or television performers. Little cliques of preadolescent girls may display silly, giggling attitudes in the presence of boys or may seem to evince an attitude of superiority to boys of their own age.

The preadolescent boy suddenly seems to lose interest in girls of his own age. With his boy pals, he tends to engage in games and other activities from which girls are excluded. Both boy and girl behavior represents a kind of "battle of the sexes" which is rooted in a developing but not fully recognized awareness of one another that results from the glandular changes that are taking place within them. As the child approaches puberty, he realizes that his attitude toward the other sex is different from what it was during childhood. His newer social approaches are uncertain unless his parents have prepared him intelligently for his new social status.

The young adolescent can be helped to make satisfactory adjustment during this critical period if his parents recognize the factors of influence that are affecting the young person and do their share in guiding his behavior and attitudes. The more sensible their own attitudes were toward boy-girl relations during their child's earlier years, the easier it will be for them to win the confidence of their adolescent son or daughter and to influence adolescent attitudes and behavior.

Although children, adolescents, and adults are more alike physically and psychologically than they are different, there are many variations or differences among individuals and within the individual himself. All adolescents seem to want to assert a rightly developing attitude of independence and release from earlier accepted adult control. They are neither children nor adults. The more they recognize their anomalous position, the more likely they are to indulge in one or more of the vagaries that are characteristic of the adolescent period of development. The teen-ager may seem to flaunt adult authority in spite of or perhaps because of a realization of his insecurity.

The boy may become unduly aggressive; he may act as though his parents' chief function is to serve him and to cater to his wishes; he may tend to wear sloppy or overconspicuous clothes; he may assume a superior attitude toward younger children as well as toward adults; at the same time, in various ways, he may attempt to impress his peer groups—both boys and girls. An adolescent boy may become moody and unduly sensitive to the attitudes displayed toward him by others in his group, or he may develop a boisterous, self-assured attitude that serves as a cover-up of his inner feelings of insecurity.

For a teen-age boy to "lose face" among his peers is a major tragedy. Adults are not always aware of the things that may be tragic incidents. For example, a baby girl was born into a family of an eighteen-year-old boy. The lad loved his baby sister and was very proud of her. In fact, her cute ways became the subject of many talks between him and his pals. His mother made the mistake, however, of expecting this boy to take the baby for a daily airing in her carriage. Much as he liked her, this was too much for the sensitive adolescent. What would his pals think of his being a nursemaid? He was too well-trained to disobey his mother's request, but, as he laughing said later, he could have throttled the child. The fact that his friends admired the baby he was wheeling along the streets did not lessen his embarrassment. Perhaps this incident indirectly caused him later to major in pediatrics and place emphasis in his professional career upon child care and parental attitudes toward children.

The behavior of growing girls is as unpredictable as that of their brothers, if not more so. They too struggle for self-realization, usually in more subtle ways than boys. Since the girl tends to mature earlier than do boys, she is likely sooner to become sensitive to changing relations between the sexes. Her tentative attempts to attract boys' attention may take various forms such as: coyness; affected mannerisms and speech; daydreaming, apparent indifference to boys or rudeness in their presence; extremes of dress, make-up, and hair-do, or even encouragement of and participation in more or less serious petting activities.

Whether a growing boy or an adolescent girl causes parents greater concern is a moot question. Since the girl usually is expected to be more amenable to parental direction than is the boy, the teen-age girl may find her problem of growing up to be different from that of the boy but no easier. Her forms of adolescent rebellion are likely to be centered in the home. Home customs and conditions sometimes gain teen-age girl disapproval. She may be "ashamed" of her parents' mannerisms, speech patterns, and dress modes. Furniture arrangement or the presence in the home of old-fashioned furnishings may "make it impossible" for her to bring her friends into the home. The presence of younger children in the home, especially when they engage in to-be-expected teasing of their young lady sister can be a cause of youthful frustration unless parents are able to cope with the situation.

A teen-age girl seems to tend more than a boy toward the development of intense but short-lived fads and fancies. Joan, the fifteen-year-old daughter of socially and economically middle-class parents was fortunate enough to have her own room. She decided that her room was entirely too conventional. Her mother wisely agreed to redecorate the room if the girl herself did the work and kept the cost low. Joan gleefully accepted the challenge. Months were spent by her in planning, painting, and rearranging. The result? The room was a startling study in severe black and white: black walls and floor, white furniture, inexpensive white drapes and bedspread. No hint of any other color was permitted. Never before had Joan been so careful about keeping her clothing in closets and dresser drawers. Nothing must interfere with her color scheme. For another month the room was the object of great admiration among her girl companions, some of whom received permission to follow her example.

During this period, Joan's mother commented upon the fact that Joan's interest in the ultramodern would wane. The woman was right. Before a year had passed, the girl began to be annoyed by her earlier "childish" ideas and the room was again redecorated. This time it oozed dainty, lacy femininity.

Many examples could be cited similar to the foregoing. Manners, dress, hair-do, and objects of adoration keep changing as the adolescent attempts in one way after another to assert himself as a person with all the rights and privileges that is owed him by adults. Parents need to understand their teen-age children, but, at the same time, with kindly firmness, control adolescent vagaries. No rigid rules can be constructed whereby all parents can be expected to guide all adolescent behavior. The mental and emotional characteristics of both parents and children need to be considered. There are, however, certain general principles that, if modified to meet individual situations, can be of value to parents who are sincerely interested in boy-girl relations.

1. The parents' own attitudes toward sexual matters and man-woman relations should be wholesome and worthy of imitation.

2. The adolescent should understand physical structure and physiological function as related to mating and parenthood.

3. Parents should do whatever they can to help adolescents meet desirable members of the opposite sex.

4. The adolescent should be encouraged to participate in group activities including members of both sexes. They also should have the privilege of entertaining mixed groups in the home, but under parental supervision.

5. The adolescent gradually should experience independence from parental control in such matters as selection of clothes, furnishings of own room, spending of money allowance, assuming responsibilities in and outside the home, and the like. The extent to which the adolescent is allowed freedom in these matters is dependent upon the economic status of the family. The adolescent should know about family finances and how much money is available for his use.

6. Adolescent vagaries of dress, grooming, food tastes, mannerisms, and the like should be understood by parents. Unless the young person carries his eccentricities to a point of social disapproval, parents should be patient, realizing that adolescent "fads" wear themselves out and disappear.

7. The young adolescent should be encouraged to limit his social activities to group situations or double dating.

8. The older adolescent should be permitted to engage in two-some dating, but should be encouraged to want parents to meet the boy or girl who is being dated, especially if the two are dating consistently.

9. The hour of return from a party or a date should be a matter of general agreement between parents and adolescents. Such factors as age of the adolescent, geographical distance, kind of party, and needed time of arising the next day should be given consideration. Most adolescents are amenable to suggestions if parental approach seems to them to be intelligent and based upon sound reasoning. They resent what they term "adult intolerance toward and lack of understanding of adolescent needs and interests."

10. Finally, adolescents can be led but not driven. Attitudes developed during childhood become crystallized during adolescence. Sooner or later,

every normal boy or girl develops an intense interest in boy-girl friendships or more intimate relationships. Fine ideals formulated and wholesome attitudes developed in the home from childhood onward act as safety valves that help prevent the young from becoming involved in "messy" situations. Such developed attitude habits aid him or her in maintaining self-control and personal dignity and in experiencing wholesome, satisfying relationships with members of the opposite sex.

89. *Parent-Youth Code* *

THE Parent-Youth Code is a guide which was prepared by the Youth Fitness Committee of the Montgomery County Council of Parent-Teacher Associations and approved by the full Council as well as the Inter-High Student Council in May 1959.

The Code Itself:

1. BASICS

Parents should know where their sons and daughters are while they are away from home. They should know WHAT they are doing, WITH WHOM they are spending their time and WHEN they will return. Any unexpected CHANGE of plans or DELAY should be discussed with the home by telephone.

The home should be the center of young people's social activity. They should be encouraged to bring friends into the home.

2. DATING

Generally speaking, there should be no dating on a night which precedes a school day.

On nonschool nights (Friday and Saturday), a definite time for return and details of transportation should be agreed upon between parents and students. It is better to start early enough so that one can return at the

---

* From *Helpful Hints,* pp. 22–24. Community Delinquency Action Committee, 12813 Georgia Ave., Silver Spring, Md. Reprinted by permission.

time agreed upon. The following times are the latest hours at which students should return to the home:

	Grades		
	10	11	12
Regular dates	Midnight	12:15 A.M.	12:30 A.M.
Special occasions	1:00 A.M.	1:30 A.M.	1:30 A.M.

Of course, the boy must accept the responsibility of seeing to it that the girl is returned home early enough so that he, too, can be home on time.

A short stop after a dance or party for food is not improper, if the students return to their homes within the hours agreed upon.

Dancing should be only at properly chaperoned places (school dances, affairs at the County Recreation Centers, private homes, church-sponsored dances).

IF A YOUNG PERSON IS DELAYED FOR ANY REASON, HE SHOULD TELEPHONE HOME.

3. HOME ENTERTAINING

Parents or a responsible adult should be at home at all times while a party is going on. They should be introduced to each guest, either upon arrival or early in the evening. They should be in the room occasionally.

A party should be planned. The type of dress should be designated. The time of beginning and ending should be fixed in advance. It is the responsibility of a courteous guest to leave on time.

Open house. For the purpose of definition, an open house party is open to all students of the same age group, irrespective of school affiliation. It has been found in the densely populated areas of Montgomery County (perhaps due to the proximity of many large high schools, including District of Columbia high schools) that "open house parties" are vehemently objected to since they frequently result in property damage, cause annoyance to the neighbors and the host and sometimes culminate in police action. They are therefore not recommended.

Party crashers. A closed party is limited to a specific group. Party crashers should not be admitted.

(We realize that these situations are not applicable to those portions of Montgomery County which are not near a great number of high schools.)

It is in poor taste to leave one party in search of another if one is not having a particularly good time at the first party.

LIGHTS OUT has no place at a well-arranged party.

Smoking. The consent of the host should be obtained before smoking.

Drinking. Under the Maryland State Law, no minor may be served any alcoholic beverage. The host has a responsibility to see that no alcohol is consumed by minors. Any guests who are under the influence of alcohol should not be admitted.

4. PUBLIC DISPLAY OF AFFECTION

A show of affection in public (beyond holding of hands) is in poor taste.

5. USE OF THE CAR

Permission to use an automobile should be based on the maturity and responsibility of the student, not simply on the ability of the driver to obtain a driver's license (minimum driving age in Montgomery County is 16 years). If the use of a car is permitted, parents should know at all times the destination and purpose and the time of return.

A car should be used only to provide transportation, and not for "joy riding" or "parking."

6. REVIEW OF PARENT-YOUTH CODE

This Code should be reviewed at least once a year by the Senior High School Student Councils.

CHAPTER XV ADJUSTMENT TOWARD
MENTAL HEALTH

90. Adjustment for What? *

GAIL M. INLOW

ONE OF THE SIGNIFICANT LANDMARKS of the present century has been the preoccupation of people almost everywhere with the process of adjustment. Today such terms as mental health, the integrated personality, self-adjustment, and maturity are commonplace. Many organized groups have made their imprint on the quest for maturity. Psychiatry, mental hygiene, psychology, guidance, educational psychology, social service, and child development are just a few of the movements or disciplines which have made significant contributions to the field of maturity.

Laymen as well as professionals share the preoccupation. Newspapers daily fan the spark of interest in the area of adjustment by carrying articles written by "authorities" on such topics as: "Are You a Whole Person?" "How to Improve Your Personality," "How Well-Adjusted Are You?" Books, both scholarly and popular, have literally flooded the market during recent years in an avowed attempt to help the readers escape the pitfalls of maladjustment and find their way to the top rung of maturity. Nor have teachers and ministers failed to keep the quest for adjustment and maturity alive in the minds of their respective audiences.

More important than the external fanfare about maturity is the basic problem which has to be faced today by every student of maturity, namely, that of determining the criteria of maturity. Yet this problem is too often ignored by the professional or lay individual who talks to you and me over the radio, through the medium of television, in the daily newspaper or in

* From Gail M. Inlow, "Adjustment for What?" *The Journal of Educational Sociology* (February, 1957), pp. 262–67. Reprinted by permission of the author and *The Journal of Educational Sociology*.

a book. Writers and speakers glibly refer to adjustment but rarely define what they mean by the term. To whom and to what should one be adjusted? When is the individual adjusted or mature and what are the standards that determine adjustment and maturity?

Personally, I envision maturity as a relative term and conceive of different levels of adjustment on the road toward maturity. The most primitive level of positive adjustment is the ability of an individual to maintain contact with the more elementary and primitive phases of perceptual reality. A schizophrenic individual may see a tree as a shadowy threat to his security or may not see it at all, whereas a better adjusted individual will react to its commonly accepted physical or psychological properties. Perceptually, he will recognize it perhaps as a provider of shade and comfort; or as a fruit-producing shrub; or as a possessor of roots, trunk, bark, branches, and leaves. The sheer act of recognizing a tree as a phenomenon of nature possessed of certain recognized properties is in and of itself an indication of elementary adjustment. But this is just the first step. Most people go through life recognizing the limited physical and psychological properties of objects and people, but they are not necessarily adjusted individuals as a result. However, they are obviously better adjusted than the catatonic who is almost completely withdrawn from reality.

A second level of adjustment may be identified as that which an individual makes to his immediate social environment. John Jones is born into a race-hating neighborhood. As he grows into adulthood, he adopts the prejudices of his associates and lives a narrow existence in a provincial setting. He eats, sleeps, earns a living, marries, seems to enjoy life, but rarely questions the values to which he and his neighbors subscribe. Probably a psychiatrist, if he were permitted to examine John Jones, would give him a clean bill of mental health. In effect, John is adjusted to a local environment. He is in contact with the less subtle forms of reality, responds to the normal physical and social drives, and is a reasonably well organized individual. But he is not mature because he is oblivious to values other than provincial ones. He adopts from his environment without question and makes no effort to evaluate the attitudes which he has and the opinions which he possesses. Or if he does think about his attitudes and opinions, he relates them only to a local milieu.

A third level of adjustment may be considered as that which is achieved by an individual who not only is in contact with basic sensory and perceptual reality and his immediate environment but one who validates his value system against the standards of a larger community—the city, the state, the country, the world. The individual at this so-called third level of adjustment who is confronted with controversial attitudes as those related, for instance, to such concepts or clichés as "white supremacy," "Asia for the Asiatics," "dirty foreigners," and "blood will tell," immediately evaluates them first of all against fact and, just as important, against the values of a larger community. He might reason that if Whites with the upper hand persecute Negroes, Negroes with the upper hand might well persecute Whites. Sooner or later the world resultant would be chaos. Therefore, as a result of his maturity, he would have to rise above race prejudice because such prejudice could not meet the standards of the inherent value system of a greater world culture. He would have to reject the import of the slogan "Asia for the Asiatics" lest he be forced to accept such other slogans as "England for the English," "Chicago for the Chicagoans," or "Suburbia for the Suburbanites." This type of compartmentalization of part or all of the greater world society could not stand the glare of a sound value system and would consequently have to be rejected.

The question of what should go into a value system of a greater world community is a problem of no mean proportions. I personally would settle for the Judeo-Christian ethic but would respect the value system of a different religious philosophy which would reject any major actions that would have an adverse effect on other countries and peoples. Each idea, principle, or attitude which the mature person tentatively accepts must be extended for validation further and further away from a provincial into a world setting of all the people of the world. Only with this extension will maturity be reached.

The mature person, far from being merely devoid of deviate personality phenomena such as projection or transferrence, is a positive "doer" in terms of his philosophy. Not only does he belong to the human race but he also shares the problems of the human race and helps to solve them. His role might be that of a local, state or national public official; a social worker; a physician; a voter in an election; John Q. Citizen participating in a worthwhile community project; a teacher, or a good neighbor. For practical reasons, he will probably have to confine his service efforts to a local setting, but in terms of validating his actions, he must not lose sight of the world around him. In effect, he accepts a local service role because it is available, but he plays the role with one eye on the immediate situation at hand and the other eye on people everywhere. As a public official, he rejects bribes because bribery is not part of a sound value system for all the people. As a physician, within the limits of his capacities and resources, he helps those who need help regardless of time and fee because this approach to life can be validated against a greater system of public values. On the contrary, if as

John Q. Citizen he condones corruption in politics, refuses consistently to buck the majority when principle is at stake, subscribes to in-groupism, and is satisfied with mediocrity, he sells short the human race and himself and delays the cause of maturity as a result.

The mature person not only must be a positive doer, he must be a positive doer to the extent of making the most out of his God-given capacities. Man has been blessed with physical, mental, and social attributes. Although heredity places absolute limitations on the extent to which he can develop his God-given powers, he is dedicated to develop them to a reasonable optimum. The human drives may be suppressed by the ascetic who because of religious belief considers the body a necessary evil; or the drives may be overstimulated by the hedonist who also lacks a sound system of values. Both the ascetic and the hedonist limit their usefulness to themselves and to others because they refuse to develop their physical capacities to the utmost in terms of a people-oriented philosophy. The mature person, on the other hand, develops his body, emotions, mind, and social capacities to a high level of efficiency because maturity performs better when qualitative standards have been met. The immature individual is the one who can do well in school but does poorly; who can influence others positively but withdraws from them; who overindulges in food, drink, or sexual behavior at the risk of limiting his usefulness to self and others. In effect, he does not develop his capacities according to the demands of a greater system of values. He may be adjusted in a limited sense, but he is rudderless in a broader sense.

Not only must the mature person have a sound value system, be a positive doer, and press toward optimum development, but he must be consistent in what he does, what he thinks, and how he acts. Every person plays many roles in the course of life and plays them in varying social situations. The church member who thinks in terms of absolutes on Sunday and settles for relativity on Monday is not consistent. The individual who is a gracious host in his home but a tyrant in his office also fails the test of consistency. On the contrary, when I as an individual can be consistent with my philosophy wherever I am or whatever I am doing or thinking, I am to that extent more mature. Thus I must be essentially the same person on the athletic field, in the presence of a social scion, while visiting with a poverty-stricken neighbor, in the church, in the home, in school, or wherever else I may be. My behavior may vary in small part because of differing cultural expectancies, but as a person I shall not vary fundamentally. I cannot be effusive and saccharine in the home of a wealthy neighbor and gruff with a fellow worker; pious when talking with a member of the clergy and profane with other associates. To be mature, my behavior in whatever the situation must measure up to standards of consistency.

Although maturity may be required to meet the test of certain identifiable standards, practically it must be considered as relative and not absolute. In one sense it is relative in that individuals of different backgrounds and levels of ability and interest are mature in different degrees. They start at a higher or lower stage of development and progress at different rates because of varying hereditarian and environmental factors. Thus John Jones with a deficient constitutional structure and a poor home environment may seem very immature according to an absolute standard; yet his progress toward maturity may be relatively greater than that of Dick Smith who has been blessed with a well-balanced central and autonomic nervous system, born into a home with many cultural advantages, but who has made little progress toward the goals of maturity.

Maturity must also be considered relative in terms of its relationships to a local culture. The major conflict which regularly confronts a mature person is that which arises between local customs and attitudes on one hand and the philosophy of maturity on the other which extends to all the people of the world. A few illustrations are in order. In the United States, maturity continuously is in conflict with the authoritarianism of parents, teachers, and public officials; with religions which deny the individual the right to question dogma; with human values that are lost to materialism; and with the preoccupation of individuals with themselves, their local cultures, and status quoism.

To what extent does the mature person have to condone cultural attitudes and actions which are inherently wrong, as judged by a people-centered philosophy, before he draws the line and says: "This I believe. This I will fight for"? Obviously, no one answer will suffice for all mature people in all situations. The determining factor is what action in the long run will best foster the cause of maturity. Jesus decided that a frontal approach by means of shock treatment was the effective way for Him to electrify people into reanalyzing their way of life. Moses, Socrates, Plato, Roger Bacon, Galileo, Darwin, and others with firm conviction based on fact and broad vision made a similar decision. Of the many leaders in the history of the world who have changed it for the better, a significant number have been crusaders. But these dedicated spirits spent many years preparing for their crusades. They were gifted, well-informed people; their plans of action were carefully thought through; and their timing was opportune. For the individual less gifted by nature, it is suggested that he conform to social mores which do not conflict with his important principles. At the same time, he should be encouraged to let his nonconformist views be known at the right time and in the right places—but he should not shout them from the housetop. If one goal of the mature person is to win others to the cause of maturity, he must select legitimate and practical ways of getting the job done. They will vary of necessity from time to time and from situation to situation. Of greatest importance is that they bear the stamp of maturity.

The road to maturity must be envisioned by thoughtful aspirants as difficult to travel. Yet each person must be encouraged to travel it in his own unique way and with confidence that he will reach limited if not larger goals. He must first of all join the human race if he is to have a marked influence on a segment of it. As he presses further along the road to maturity, he will realize that the problems of the cultural hinterlands are as important as those of Main Street; that hunger in Thailand is as important as hunger in Tobacco Road; that the intolerance of a nazi, a communist, or a Mau Mau is not any worse than the intolerance of poorly informed people in America who support the causes of race prejudice, ultranationalism, and other types of bigotry and ignorance.

If an individual is to serve humanity well, he must first of all serve himself well. Self-love of a wholesome kind must be based on the higher qualities of personality. A chronic neurotic has difficulty loving himself because he is blinded to values by his neuroses. He cannot love his neighbor because he projects his negativism to his neighbor. If he is to serve the cause of maturity, he must press toward better adjustment. But this goal of adjustment cannot be achieved with optimum success apart from a value system. Even if the higher processes of the cerebral cortex control your behavior and mine, we cannot be whole personalities without a sound philosophy. Even if the autonomic nervous system deviates seldom from the ideal of homeostasis, the resultant is socially sterile unless grounded in a value system.

Thus it is my firm conviction that writers of books and articles on mental health, adjustment, and maturity must begin to restructure their thinking away from the purely physical and psychological mechanics of process and begin to delve more deeply into the question: Adjustment or mental health for what? Probably psychiatrists, psychologists, mental hygienists, and educators have dominated for too long the field of adjustment and need more often to look for help to leaders in the other disciplines. The psychiatrist and the philosopher, the psychologist and a member of the clergy, or all of these along with the educator, sociologist, and anthropologist need to think together about maturity. It is a complex process, the road to it is tortuous, and all available resources must be tapped if our culture is to become mature. Maturity is a difficult taskmaster, but its rewards are the higher spiritual qualities of personality and decency in human relationships. These goals are worth striving for, whatever the cost, but let the various disciplines begin to relate mental health or adjustment to spiritual and philosophical as well as to physical and the more primitive psychological outcomes. Through a coordinated effort, we shall then be able to say that more mature approach has been taken to the concept of maturity.

91. Helping Young People to Deal with Their Problems *

WILLARD JACOBSON

1

Our young people are faced with many problems. These problems are the difficulties and dilemmas which they recognize and about which they express a personal concern. Young people do not leave these problems behind when they come to school. They carry these concerns with them as they come and participate in our classrooms, and these problems will affect everything that they do and learn there. In many cases we now recognize that we actually experience and learn in terms of what we recognize to be valuable in relation to the problems with which we must deal. If two youngsters are involved in a consideration of what would constitute an adequate diet, the youngster who has not had the opportunity to eat good, warm food will necessarily have a different experience than the youngster who will always have a tasty, nutritious meal. These two youngsters will have different learning experiences as they participate in this activity. In other cases a failure to solve a particular problem may prevent a young person from living and working effectively in other places and with other concerns. A concern in one classroom may be carried over into another class and affect

* From Willard Jacobson, "Helping Young People to Deal with Their Problems," *The Educational Forum* (January, 1953), pp. 219–25. Reprinted by permission.

work there. Or, a serious problem in the home may be transposed into the school and stifle any possible creative work. In this case a youngster may have to devote all his nervous energy and attention to one particular problem. The way that he deals with this problem may have a social effect. It can affect all of us. The youth who seeks group status and prestige through smoking "reefers" threatens everyone in the community. Everyone, and especially the teacher, has a stake in the methods that this young person chooses to deal with his particular problem.

We may identify several general types of problems. For example, a young child may point his finger at some object and ask, "What's that?" To be able to relate some object or experience to other experiences may be very important. On the other hand, adolescent boys have been known to express a great concern over the lack of a beard at a time when it is necessary for social prestige and position in the adolescent gang. We also have records of individuals who have been perplexed over problems that may not seem as closely related to their own needs and concerns. For example, some adults at one time were greatly perplexed by the problem of how to separate two kinds of the chemical element neon that were identical except for a slight difference in mass. This was a very serious and meaningful problem, and many men devoted a great deal of their time and energy to an attempt to solve it. This, as well as all of the other examples, could be considered a problem. The one common aspect that can be identified is that the individuals who were involved recognized a difficulty and made an attempt to deal with it and improve the situation.

The problems that young people have are those matters about which they are concerned. An individual cannot be told what his problems are. Instead, they are the difficulties that he recognizes. In the same sense, students in our classrooms cannot be assigned problems. The teacher who asks a student, "What is the percentage composition of sulphur trioxide?" is not stating a problem for the student; in some cases such questions become a kind of puzzle. However, if the question is accompanied by any kind of threat to the student, he may be faced with a difficulty. However, in such cases, the student may have to find some means to divert or cushion the threat. He may want to find some method of handling the question in order to be able to bring home the kind of report card which will ensure the use of the family car on Saturday night. Or, he may try to place the teacher in a ridiculous position in order to gain the good will and admiration of other members of his group. In either case the actual problem that is recognized by the individual student is certainly much different from the question that was raised by the teacher.

II

To work effectively with young people the teacher must become aware of the problems they recognize. This means that the teacher should try to understand their difficulties and help them to cope with these problems. In this case the teacher's questions and actions will be directed and phrased to help the young people as they investigate and meet their problems. This means that the teacher should have developed certain abilities and competencies in order to understand young people and help them work with their problems. Some of these abilities can be described.

1. A teacher should be able to work with young people to help them recognize difficulties and obstructions and to determine the relative importance of the various problems. We are involved in many problems. Therefore, we must choose the direction in which we wish to expend our energies. One group of youngsters was studying typhoid fever. A deliberate attempt was made to find the relationships between the availability of good drinking water, the difficulty of waste disposal and the incidence of typhoid fever. Throughout the discussion, questions concerning polio were raised. "Is polio caused by germs in the water we drink?" "Is it safe to go swimming while a polio epidemic is on?" "My sister is in the hospital with polio. What kind of treatment will she receive?" In many places typhoid fever is no longer a serious menace. Polio unfortunately is. In this case very little effort had been made to investigate and locate the problems that were of concern to these young people. As a result, the youngsters were dealing with matters that they judged were of lesser importance to them, and a problem of deep concern—polio—received inadequate attention.

2. A teacher should be able to help young people to recognize and consider some of the general aspects of our method for solving problems. Because we do know something about solving problems, students should not be forced to learn everything in the harsh school of trial-and-error. Instead, they should be given the opportunity to consider and accept or reject some of the tested methods involved in problem-solving. We know, for example, that it is generally inefficient to collect facts at random. Instead, it is better to search for facts and evidence while using some unifying tool or hypothesis. It was Darwin who said, "How odd it is that anyone should not see that all observation must be for or against some view, if it is to be of any service." When our automobile doesn't start, we don't immediately begin examining the entire car. Instead, we may say, "It might be the spark." We can then proceed to test whether or not there is any spark.

In this case the hypothesis becomes a tool whereby we locate our difficulty. In other problems we can use hypotheses or suggested answers in a similar fashion. They can be tools with which we can direct our investigation.

3. In helping young people deal with their problems a teacher should be able to assist them in locating necessary information. A teacher should have a picture of some of the possible sources of information that exist within the community. If an attempt is made to ascertain what kinds of trees can be grown in the local climate, it may prove to be fruitful to talk to the man who has been collecting local weather data over a period of years. He may be able to give a very good picture of the extremes in temperature and rainfall which have been experienced in the locality. Bulletins of the state department of agriculture, on the other hand, may prove to be a fruitful source of data on the climatic conditions necessary for the cultivation of various plants. The teacher should be prepared to help students to locate such sources of information. It is especially important that he have as broad a picture as possible of the sources and resource people that are available in the local community.

4. The teacher should be able to help young people criticize and evaluate evidence and information. The process of criticizing and evaluating may be understood as an attempt to predict which information will be reliable and valuable in determining which course of action has the greatest possibility of success. In almost all cases it is profitable to develop an attitude of a "demand for evidence."

5. The best approach to many problems, especially in a school situation, is through group work. If a teacher is to help young people deal with their problems he should be able to help young people to work together. He should assist young people to become aware of what is involved in group work and to help them to understand some of their difficulties. When there are conflicts within the group, some attempt must be made to clarify the conflicting positions so that the group can evaluate them in terms of the group goal. Members of the group can be helped to understand each other. For instance, the shy person who hesitates to make a contribution can often through the assistance of other members of the group be helped to participate in group discussions and projects.

6. Perhaps, the most important competence that a teacher needs is the ability to help young people to learn from their experiences in dealing with their own problems. As a result of their experiences they should learn and hence be able to deal with future problems in a more efficient and effective manner. This is a very complex process, and yet, it is fundamental. It involves gaining an awareness of the process in which we are involved in

dealing with a problem. This awareness is in terms of seeing a relationship between our experiences in dealing with a particular problem, past experiences with other problems and possible difficulties with future problems. One high school group proved to themselves that the cheapest and most effective way of providing for pedestrian safety at a street corner near the school was to erect an automobile traffic signal. They proceeded to inform the city council of their findings, of the overwhelming evidence supporting it and of their surprise that such an august body as the city council had not long age arrived at the same conclusion. They were, of course, very chagrined when their report was ignored. If they had been aware of what is involved in making a report to another group, they might have altered the nature of their study and certainly the form and tenor of their report. However, an analysis of such a situation could lead to fruitful results. They might generalize and say that, if the results of a study must be accepted by another group, the chances for acceptance are improved if that group is involved in planning and making the study. If such a generalization could be abstracted from this experience, their chances of fruitful action in the future would have been improved. It is of course at least equally important that successful experiences be examined. If their report had been accepted by the city council, they might question: Why were they successful? What aspects of their procedures were crucial for success? Learning is centered around these generalizations by which we direct our future behavior. The teacher should be able to help the student in this process of generalization.

These points are not only a list of some of the abilities that a teacher should have if he is to help young people to deal with their problems, but it is also a limited description of the role of the teacher in this problem-solving process. Many teachers have not had the opportunity to develop some of these abilities. For others, the role of the teacher in problem-solving may be strange and even frightening. These abilities can, however, be developed, and the teacher's role can prove to be interesting and very fruitful. How can these abilities be developed? From what kinds of experiences can teachers gain the security and knowledge necessary to help young people to deal with their difficulties?

III

To determine how some of these abilities may be developed and what may be the nature of some of these experiences in which teachers may gain security and knowledge, we can refer to some of the criteria generally used to select and plan for learning experiences. For example, the experiences must be such that the teacher will be able to draw upon them when he is working with young people and their problems. It is generally recognized that our ability to generalize from one situation into another is directly related to the degree of similarity between those situations. When a person can see some connection between a problem that confronts him and some experience that he has previously had, the educational experiences become valuable to him. The greater the similarity between the educational experience and the problems that will face the teacher, the greater the possibility that some connection or relationship will be recognized. The teacher's educational experiences should be as closely related as possible to the problems that he will meet in helping young people to deal with their problems.

As has been mentioned, we must also have a certain kind of security if we are to help young people as they deal with their problems. We are not dealing with questions to which the answers are already known, nor is there a definite, step-by-step procedure to follow. Instead, we are working in situations in which the youngsters must find some kind of answer to guide them in their future actions. The answers are closely related to the student's life; the answers will determine how he will act, and in this sense, they will determine the nature of his future. Therefore, it is essential that he should find the best possible answers. The teacher should have experienced the insecurity of dealing with problems to which the answers are not already known. He should also have experienced the security that comes from dealing with questions that are meaningful and significant in the eyes of the students.

The ability to help young people to deal with their problems is not segmented or made up of distinct parts. We may segment for the purpose of more detailed description. However, we cannot, for example, learn how to evaluate information in the abstract. We learn how to evaluate information as the need arises in order to work in a specific situation with a recognized problem. Teachers should have had experiences in which they can learn not only how to evaluate information, work with groups, identify important problems, but they should also see the interrelationships between these abilities and the part they play in helping young people to deal with their problems.

On the basis of these criteria it may be suggested that the teacher's ability to help young people deal with their problems can best be developed by having the experience of working in an organized fashion with a problem which he recognizes and which has meaning for him. In dealing with this problem a continued attempt should be made to recognize the process that is involved in problem-solving and to relate it to other problems that may be predicted in the future. In a sense security is developed by experience and success. If a teacher has had the experience of dealing with important problems and in recognizing some of the elements involved in coping with problems, he may be less hesitant to help young people deal with theirs. Also, it is in working with such a problem that we are able to see and understand the relationships between the various abilities that are involved in working with problems. We can, for instance, see the necessity for evaluating information when a decision as to what we should do in terms of our problems depends upon the value we place upon the information available to us. The need for predicting what kind of information and the development of hypotheses or suggested answers is related to the problem as a whole. We can learn these various things as well as the relationships between them in the process of dealing with our problems.

Young people also learn how to deal with their problems as they have actual experiences in coping with the problems which they recognize. There are many problems which must be dealt with in some way by all individuals. We all must have the basic necessities for human living: food, clothing, shelter, and relationships with other human beings. Other problems are more unique. These problems are related to the goals and aspirations that are peculiar to us as individuals. Young people will have to deal with both of these types of problems. The teacher should work with young people as they deal with these problems, and also help people to learn from these experiences so that problems of the future will be dealt with in terms of our experiences with our problems of the past.

This suggested process of learning through dealing with significant problems has several implications for the work of both the teacher and learner. One implication may be called the futility of artificiality. That which is to be learned cannot be dictated by the teacher. We can for instance make a passing grade contingent upon the memorization and regurgitation of the atomic weights of all isotopes of all elements heavier than hydrogen. Passing the course may be necessary for entrance to college. As a result, a student may alter his behavior and devote time to the memorization of atomic weights. It should be remembered, however, that in this case the information about the atomic weights is only valuable because he wants to go to college. Needless to say, he may also learn other things. He may learn to dislike artificial means for increasing the value of certain information. Or, he may learn to accept without question various impositions of value which determine what he must do. In a sense, he learns not to be critical, or, we may say, how not to be scientific. The teacher can help young people to become aware of what may be important to be learned. The decision as to what will be learned is made by the learner. In this it is implied that the learner should be involved in the process of determining the nature of the educational activity.

This approach does not mean that every morning the teacher should ask, "Children, what are your problems today?" Instead, it means that the teacher and students should work together and investigate to determine what problems are of importance to them. When a student says "Let's study typhoid fever," it does not necessarily mean that the class will direct its attention to typhoid fever. It does mean that the class will consider this along with suggestions from other students, teachers, and parents. It means that an investigation will be carried out to determine the different interests in the group, the relative importance of various suggestions, and also the resources that are available for handling various problems. What is done in the classroom should not be the result of sudden, unexamined impulse, but should be the result of investigation and study.

These problems are important. The solutions that are found and the methods that are used may have a profound impact on the future of each individual that participates. The importance of these problems accents the necessity for finding the best possible answers. To do this all available resources must be utilized. It is not enough to rely upon whatever information the teacher may have on hand that relates to the problem. Information should be sought wherever it can be found. The information from one source should be checked with information from other sources. This search for information leads the teacher and young people outside of the classroom into the laboratory, library, and the community. Resources from the community, library, and laboratory are also brought into the classroom. This can lead to intensive investigation. All of these activities become important as the teacher helps young people to deal with matters which they say are meaningful and insist are important.

92. How to Deal with Your Tensions *

GEORGE S. STEVENSON
AND HARRY MILT

Tensions Are Natural and Useful

Anxiety and tension are essential functions of living, just as hunger and thirst are. Without the experience of anxiety we would not be prepared to avoid or overcome situations harmful to ourselves and our families. Without the ability to tense ourselves we would fall short in emergencies, often to the peril of our lives.

Tension serves, too, as a stimulating source of excitement. It is to gain this kind of pleasure that we play or watch competitive games, pursue adventurous outdoor recreation, and follow drama on stage, screen, or television.

Primarily, tensions and anxiety are our self-protective reactions when we are confronted by threats to our safety, well-being, happiness, and self-esteem—threats like illness, accidents, violence, financial trouble, trouble on the job, trouble in family relations.

We tend erroneously to think of such dangers, and the tensions they arouse, as something new. While it is true that we live today under pressure of intense competition, economic uncertainty, and the possibility of total war, we must remember that our ancestors faced other perils of equal magnitude—famine, pestilence, attack by savages, as well as full-scale war.

There is this difference, however. Life today is much more complex. Many conflicting demands are made on us. The old counsels handed down from father to son in the farming and handicraft days no longer apply to conditions of intricately organized work and constant change. Our world changes so rapidly that the answer to "what to do" in the face of a threat to security of life or peace of mind can no longer be found in a traditional code of "do's" and "don't's," or even in those of our own earlier experience. The answer must often be thought out on the spot, even in the instant. What is right one day may be wrong the next. What is an acceptable response

* From *How to Deal with Your Tensions,* 1957. Reprinted by permission. This booklet is part of a joint education project of The Advertising Council and The National Association for Mental Health written by Dr. George S. Stevenson in collaboration with Harry Milt, Information Director of The National Association for Mental Health.

in the home may be unacceptable in school or business. What may be correct in one social group of which we are a part may bring ridicule and resentment in another. We are in the predicament of a traveler suddenly transported to a strange world, with little understanding of how it works, no notion of how to behave, and no one to brief us.

Everybody is confronted by threats; hence, everybody experiences tensions. Yet there are times when we become tense and anxious where no adequate threat exists. This may happen when we have been through a siege of trouble or exhausting work, are worn out and on edge and cannot reason things out or control our feelings as we do when we are rested and in good condition.

Other times this may happen when we are caught up in a conflict which we cannot work out: for example, a conflict between an outraged sense of justice and an urge to bow to the injustice because it is safer to do so, or a conflict between the impulse to do something unethical and the prompting of our conscience, which forbids it.

Very often, too, anxiety and tension may be provoked as a result of some experience in a person's background which has made him particularly sensitive to a threat which may have little effect on others. For example, a man who suffered extreme poverty as a child may react with panic when there is even a casual mention of a possible layoff from the job. Another instance is that of an adult who becomes greatly upset over a minor illness because when he was a child his parents reacted to any illness as though it were a major tragedy.

The average human being has the capacity to live through emotionally upsetting situations—even crises—and to bounce back when they are over. It is important to recognize, therefore, that an occasional bout of anxiety and tension is quite normal, and, while it may be unpleasant or even painful, it need not be a cause for additional concern.

There are, however, some people for whom life is a series of little and big crises. In such instances we may expect more than an occasional passing emotional upset. We may expect to see signs of prolonged and intense anxiety and tension. The time to become watchful, therefore, is the time when emotional upsets come frequently, shake us severely, and fail to wear off after a while.

Expect a Few—Act If Too Many

How do you recognize when this is happening? Here, in the form of questions, are some of the effects that show. If any considerable number of the reactions listed below are getting to be the rule with you, that does not mean disaster. But it does indicate the need to deal with the situation constructively.

Do minor problems and disappointments throw you into a dither?

Do you find it difficult to get along with people, and are people having trouble getting along with you?

Do the small pleasures of life fail to satisfy you?

Are you unable to stop thinking of your anxieties?

Do you fear people or situations that never used to trouble you?

Are you suspicious of people, mistrustful of your friends?

Do you have the feeling of being trapped?

Do you feel inadequate, suffer the tortures of self-doubt?

If your answer is "Yes" to most of these questions, there are several things you might do. There are, to begin with, certain simple, practical, constructive things you can do for yourself.

These measures are for the most part positive forms of action. And action, of course, is nature's instinctive response to a threat of any kind. Primitive reactions like flight or combat can rarely serve us in a modern world. Undirected reactions, such as pacing the floor, are only indirectly helpful as releases of nervous energy helping a worrier regain balance to decide on more important things to do. Much more effective is action which helps to solve a problem.

Here are a few simple, ready-to-hand actions which may help you. But remember as you read them that success will not come, even in these, from a halfhearted effort. Nor will it come overnight. It will take determination, persistence, and time. Yet the results will certainly be worth your best effort, whether yours is an occasional mild upset, which most of us experience, or one that is more lasting and severe.

Eleven Things You Can Do

1. Talk it out. When something worries you, talk it out. Don't bottle it up. Confide your worry to some levelheaded person you can trust: your husband or wife, father or mother, a good friend, your clergyman, your family doctor, a teacher, school counselor, or dean. Talking things out helps to relieve your strain, helps you to see your worry in a clearer light, and often helps you to see what you can do about it.

2. Escape for a while. Sometimes, when things go wrong, it helps to escape from the painful problem *for a while:* to lose yourself in a movie or a book or a game, or a brief trip for a change of scene. Making yourself "stand there and suffer" is a form of self-punishment, not a way to solve a problem. It is perfectly realistic and healthy to escape punishment long enough to recover breath and balance. But be prepared to come back and deal with your difficulty when you are more composed, and when you and others involved are in better condition emotionally and intellectually to deal with it.

3. Work off your anger. If you feel yourself using anger as a general way of behavior, remember that while anger may give you a temporary sense of righteousness, or even of power, it will generally leave you feeling foolish and sorry in the end. If you feel like lashing out at someone who has provoked you, try holding off that impulse for a while. Let it wait until tomorrow. Meanwhile, do something constructive with the pent-up energy. Pitch into some physical activity like gardening, cleaning out the garage, carpentry, or some other do-it-yourself project. Or work it out in tennis or a long walk. Working the anger out of your system and cooling it off for a day or two will leave you much better prepared to handle your problem intelligently and gainfully.

4. Give in occasionally. If you find yourself getting into frequent quarrels with people, and feeling obstinate and defiant, remember that that's the way frustrated children behave. Stand your ground on what you know is right, but do so calmly and make allowance for the fact that you *could* turn out to be wrong. And even if you're dead right, it's easier on your system to give in once in a while. If you yield, you'll usually find that others will, too. And if you can work this out, the result will be relief from tension, the achievement of a practical solution, together with a great feeling of satisfaction and maturity.

5. Do something for others. If you feel yourself worrying about *yourself* all the time, try *doing* something for *somebody else*. You'll find this will take the steam out of your own worries and—even better—give you a fine feeling of having done well.

6. Take one thing at a time. For people under tension, an ordinary work load can sometimes seem unbearable. The load looks so great that it becomes painful to tackle any part of it, even the things that most need to be done. When that happens, remember that it's a temporary condition and that you can work your way out of it. The surest way to do this is to take a few of the most urgent tasks and pitch into them, one at a time, setting aside all the rest for the time being. Once you dispose of these you'll see that the remainder is not such a "horrible mess" after all. You'll be in the swing of things, and the rest of the tasks will go much more easily. If you feel you can't set anything aside to tackle things this sensible way, reflect: are you sure you aren't overestimating the importance of the things you do—that is, your own importance?

7. Shun the "superman" urge. Some people expect too much from themselves, and get into a constant state of worry and anxiety because they think they are not achieving as much as they should. They try for perfection in everything. Admirable as this ideal is, it is an open invitation to failure. No one can be perfect in everything. Decide which things you do well, and then put your major effort into these. They are apt to be the things you like to do, and hence those that give you most satisfaction. Then, perhaps, come the things you can't do so well. Give them the best of your effort and ability, but don't take yourself to task if you can't achieve the impossible. Give yourself a pat on the back for the things you do well, but don't set yourself records to break in everything you do.

8. Go easy with your criticism. Some people expect too much of others, and then feel frustrated, let down, disappointed, even "trapped" when another person does not measure up. The "other person" may be a wife, a husband, or a child whom we are trying to fit into a preconceived pattern—perhaps even trying to make over to suit ourselves. Remember, each person has his own virtues, his own shortcomings, his own values, his own right to develop as an individual. People who feel let down by the shortcomings (real or imagined) of their relatives, are really let down about themselves. Instead of being critical about the other person's behavior, search out the good points and help him to develop them. This will give both of you satisfaction, and help you to gain a better perspective on yourself as well.

9. Give the other fellow a break. When people are under emotional tension they often feel that they have to "get there first," to edge out the other person, no matter if the goal is as trivial as getting ahead on the highway. If enough of us feel that way—and many of us do—then everything becomes a race in which somebody is bound to get injured—physically, as on the highway, or emotionally and mentally, in the endeavor to live a full life. It need not be this way. Competition is contagious, but so is cooperation. When you give the other fellow a break, you very often make things easier for yourself; if he no longer feels you are a threat to him, he stops being a threat to you.

10. Make yourself "available." Many of us have the feeling that we are being "left out," slighted, neglected, rejected. Often, we just imagine that other people feel this way about us, when in reality they are eager for us to make the first move. It may be we, not the others, who are depreciating ourselves. Instead of shrinking away and withdrawing, it is much healthier, as well as more practical, to continue to "make yourself available," to make some of the overtures instead of always waiting to be asked. Of course, the opposite of withdrawal is equally futile: to push yourself forward on every occasion. This is often misinterpreted and may lead to real rejection. There is a middle ground between withdrawal and pushing. Try it.

11. Schedule your recreation. Many people drive themselves so hard that they allow themselves too little time for recreation, an essential for good physical and mental health. They find it hard to make themselves take time out. For such people a set routine and schedule will help, a program of definite hours when they will engage in some recreation. And in general it is desirable for almost everyone to have a hobby that absorbs him in off hours, one into which he can throw himself completely and with pleasure, forgetting all about his work.

The Philosophy of Mental Health

Underlying these concrete suggestions there is a basic philosophy fundamental to good emotional health. That is the philosophy of faith: faith in ourselves; faith in others; faith in the ability of each person to improve and grow; faith in the desire and the capacity of human beings to work out their problems cooperatively; faith in the essential decency of mankind. As the Bible puts it, we are "members of one another."

This is our way of life. It is the philosophy of sound mental health. When it is joined to faith in the great spiritual and moral values, it will carry us through stressful situations that might otherwise shatter us.

If You Need Help—Get an Expert

Often emotional difficulties *arise out of* problems, such as financial difficulties, trouble on the job, problems of children and parents, marital trouble.

But just as often a person's long-standing habits and attitudes may *produce* conflict in the home, on the job, or in school.

These interacting forces outside him and within him tend to have a cumulative effect, each making the other worse—perhaps rapidly so. In that case, any one of us needs more help than he can give himself by following simple suggestions such as the eleven made in the preceding pages. He might wish to seek the help of a counseling or guidance service which specializes in helping people work out their practical problems. Such services may be found in family welfare agencies, schools, churches, industrial plants and offices, settlement houses, public health departments. They help people clear up practical problems, and thus they help relieve emotional strains. It is always well to seek such practical help first. Too often, people whose problems could be solved this way seek the assistance of already overburdened psychiatric treatment services.

However, if emotional disturbances become too distressing to the person or those around him, we should recognize and deal with them as mental illnesses requiring professional treatment, just as we do with a cold when it becomes very severe.

If you are concerned about yourself or a member of your family or a friend who shows signs of severe prolonged emotional disturbance, the thing to do is to seek professional help. Go to your family doctor. He may advise visiting a psychiatrist, a medical doctor specializing in the treatment of mental diseases. Or he may recommend treatment at a psychiatric clinic, a mental hospital, or the psychiatric department of a general hospital. To find out about the counseling, guidance and treatment services in your community, get in touch with the mental health association in your state or locality.

Index

ability: of boys and girls, 247–50
  teachers', 573–78
achievement: of boys and girls, 247–50
  relation to various factors, 250–55
  study of sibling, 19–25
acrophobia, 358
adjustment: and attitudes, 567
  of child to school, 516–21
  of children, 438
  for maturity, 565–85
  and motor abilities, 131
  parent-child, 516–64
adolescence: changes in status during, 62–63
  characteristics of, 87–93
  as a critical period, 505–9
  emotions during, 256–57
  growth and development during, 87–125
  in Middle Ages and modern times, 60–63
  objectives of, 108–11
  and social relationships, 192–95
adolescent(s): and adults, 179–88
  in American society, 178–88
  attitudes and opinions, 278–82
  dynamics of behavior of, 320–58
  and emotional development, 89–90
  interests of, 92, 312–19
  learning of, 359–98
  and life problems, 312–19
  mental development of, 91–92
  moral and spiritual development, 92–93
  needs of, 93–98
  objectives of, 108–9, 278–82
  and parent perspectives, 541–44
  parent and relationships of, 558–62

  and parental conflict, 534–35
  personality of, 419–25
  social development of, 90–91
  social needs and peer group, 113–15
  status in United States, 112–13
  study approaches to, 1–36
  traits, interests and worries of, 288–94
  as unmarried mother, 502–15
  views on growing up, 117–25
  worries of, 293–94
adolescent development, and school and peer group, 112–16
aggression, 269–71, 273–76, 533
animism, 388–93
anxiety, 579–80
aptitude: and intelligence, 210–55
  and intelligence tests, 238
  meaning of, 237–39
aspiration, level of, 262
asthenic, 105
athletic, 105
attention-getting, 354
attitudes: and adjustment, 567–69
  changes in, 295–99
  toward child behavior, 305–11
  formation of, 278–319
  of high school students, 278–82
  and learning, 283–88
  meaning of, 285–86
  overt expression of, 289–94

behavior: adolescent, 320–58
  characteristics of mature, 346–53
  child, 441–52
  of child and adolescent, 305–7
  children's antisocial, 189–92

behavior (*continued*)
    conflict, 263–64
    dynamics of, 320–58, 406–19
    experimental analysis of, 26–36
    influences on, 456–61
    integrative, 437–38
    kinds of compensatory, 354–58
    motor, 149–52
    problems of child, 306–7
    psychosexual, 468–515
    teen-age, 543–44
Bellevue Intelligence Tests, 213
bilingualism, 81
biological factors of development, 37–40,
    41–42
biological inheritance, impact of, 41–42
biomode, 477, 486, 488
birth order, and intelligence and achieve-
    ment, 250–55
boy-girl relationships, 289–94, 554–62

California Achievement Tests, 248–49
California Test of Mental Maturity, 248–
    49
case study, 13–19
cerebrotonic, 107
character, formation of, 441–68
Character Education Inquiry, 10–11
child(ren): antisocial, 189–92
    behavior problems of, 306–7
    choices of, 263–64
    discipline and, 441–52
    dynamics of behavior of, 320–58
    emotional life of, 545–54
    growth and development of, 64–86
    and infants, 361–63
    and language, 195–200
    learning of, 359–98
    parent adjustment, 516–64
    and parent conflicts, 528–35
    problems of retarded, 521–27
    school adjustment of, 516–21
    and sex, 478–80, 483–86
    and sex offenses, 490–95
    social relationships of, 556–58
    student attitude toward behavior of,
        305–11
    study approaches to, 1–36

childhood, emotions during, 256–77
    See also child.
Children's Apperception Test, 10
chromosomes, 39–40, 46
chronological age (CA), 243
claustrophobia, 358
Code of Moral and Spiritual Values, 461–
    68
cognition, 221, 223–25, 346–50, 370–75
college students: animistic thinking of,
    388–93
    judgment processes of, 394–98
compensatory behavior, 354–58
competition, 583
concept: of personality integration, 425–
    32
    of self, 409–19
conflict, 263–64, 353–58, 534–35
conversion, 357
cooperation, 205–8
courtship, 500–501
criticism, 356, 583
cross-cultural study, of child behavior,
    52–60
cross-sectional studies, 2–3
crying, stimulation of, 135–36, 349
cube(s): infants' control of, 139–41
    manipulation of, 153–61
culture: constancies of, for infants, 48–49
    effect of, on adolescents, 314
    factors and development of, 42–47
    and morality, 502–3
    patterns of, 46–47
    and personality, 47–51

Darwinian group, 138
dating, 280–81
daydreaming, 356
deductive reasoning, 377–78
defense mechanisms, 296–98
democracy, indoctrinating for, 202–5
development: during adolescence, 87–125
    adolescent, and peer group, 113–15
    adolescent, and school, 115–16
    biological and cultural factors of, 37–
        63
    and child growth, 64–86
    concepts of, 64–67

in infancy, 72–78
in language, 78–81, 195–200
meaning of, 65–66
motor, during infancy, 136–38
of personality, 399–440, 419–25
prenatal, 69–72
progress in motor, 126–66
psychosexual, 468–73
diaries, of adolescents, 6, 194–95
discipline, 441–52
dynamics of behavior, 320–58, 406–19
dysplastic, 106

ectoderm, 67
ectomorph, 106–8
education, social issues in, 200–209
ego, 167–78, 471
egocentrism, 356
elimination, developmental changes in, 77–78
embryo, period of, 67–69
emotion(s): adjustment of, 131
  arousal of, 257–58
  of child, 545–54
  during childhood and adolescence, 256–77
  and discipline, 447–48
  experimental modification of, 264–68
  nature of, 256–57
  physiological bases of, 258–59
emotional experiences, bases of, 256–59
emotionality, factors affecting, 259–62
empathy, 50, 540
endoderm, 68
endomorph, 106–8
environment: during early childhood, 44–46
  influence on development, 42–46
escape, 581–82
ethical assumptions, 384–85
experimental method, 7–8, 26–36
exteroceptive stimulation, 332–39

father-son relationships, 171–78
fatigue, 259
feeding: developmental changes in, 72–75
  motor activities during, 134–35

patterns of, 50–51
feeling(s): dealing with, 539–41
  nature of, 256
frustration, 83–84, 265–66, 273–76, 353–58, 580–81

Gates Reading Test, 19
genes, 40, 46
germ cells, 39–40
girls, problems of adolescent, 339–45
goal(s): of adolescence, 108–11
  of high school students, 278–82
  list of adolescent, 110–11
  seeking of, by adolescents, 424–25
  selection of, 346–50
goal-directed behavior, 346–50
growth: during adolescence, 87–125
  curve of, 101
  and development of child, 64–86
  and the group, 103–5
  meaning of, 66–67

habits, 98
hands: developing control of infant's, 138–43
  use of, by infants, 153–61
health: emotionality and poor, 260
  mental, 565–85
hemophobia, 358
heredity: and aptitude, 238
  transmission of, 37–40
high school students: animistic thinking of, 388–93
  problems and interests of, 312–19
  See also adolescent.
home: boys running away from, 425–32
  foreign, 405
  and personality, 399–406
  and school adjustment, 516–21
horizontal study approaches, 2–3
human relations, assumptions of, 385–86

idealization, 355
ideals, 80, 96
individual differences, 366–69
indoctrination for democracy, 202–5
inductive reasoning, 376–77

infancy: changes during, 72–78
  perceptions in, 359–63
infant(s): and control of arms and
    hands, 138–43
  culture and, 48–49
  environment of, 333–34
  motor activities of, 133–38
  motor development of, 143–53
  prehension in, 153–61
infantile identification, 167–78
integration, of personality, 433–40
intellect: structure of, 220–22, 234–37
  three faces of, 219–37
intelligence: and aptitude, 210–55
  components of, 219–37
  and emotionality, 250–55, 260
  and linguistic development, 199–200
  meaning of, 210–18
  study of sibling, 19–25
intelligence quotient (IQ), 210–12, 215–
    17, 239, 243, 244, 245
intelligence tests in school use, 240–47
interests: of adolescents, 92, 288–94
  formation of, 278–319
  of high school students, 312–19
interviews, 52–60
introjection, 354

judgment, sex differences in, 394–98

language: development in, 78–81
  as a social skill, 195–200
learning: and attitudes, 283–88
  child and adolescent, 359–98
  and human organism, 329–30
  and maturation, 42–44
  in motor development, 129–31
  of motor skills, 161–66
  multidimensional contexts of, 381–88
Lebanon: study of animism in, 388–93
  study of children in, 52–60
leisure activities, 281
longitudinal studies, 3–4, 19–25, 29–32,
    251–55
  See also vertical studies.

masculinity, 170–78
maturation: and learning, 42–44

in motor development, 129–30
  nurture, 64–65
  skeletal, 101–3
maturity, 565–71
  emotional, 437
measurement, method of, 7–8
memory: abilities, 225–26
  differences, 366–69
mental ability, tests of, 7
mental age (MA), 240, 243, 244, 245,
    246
mental development of adolescents, 91–92
mental health, adjustment toward, 565–
    85
mesoderm, 67
mesomorph, 106–8
*Minnesota Multiphasic Personality In-
    ventory* (MMPI), 300, 303
mongoloids, 522–27
moral and spiritual development of ado-
    lescents, 92–93
motivation, and exteroceptive stimula-
    tion, 332–39
motives, 94, 95–96, 98, 350–53
motor activities, 132–38
motor development: concepts, 126–32
  in infants, 143–53
  progress in development, 5, 126–66
motor skills, learning of, 161–66
muscular control, 127–29
mysophobia, 358

needs: adolescent social, and peer group,
    113–15
  of adolescents, 93–98
  and motive, 350–53
negativism, 357
neonate, 370–72
neurotic behavior, 358, 525–26
normative study, 2
nurture, meaning of, 65

objectives. *See* goals.
observation, directed, 4–5
obsessions, 358
opinions, of high school students, 278–82
organism, 321–24
ovum, 39–40

parent(s): and adolescents, 186–88
  and antisocial children, 190–91
  and attitudes, 286–87
  attitudes toward boy-girl relations, 554–62
  child adjustment, 516–64
  and child conflicts, 528–35
  and child's emotionality, 261–62
  and child's thinking, 365
  and discipline, 441–52
  domination by, 531–33
  education groups for, 535–41
  high school students' attitudes toward, 279–80
  language of, 96
  and mate selection, 496
  overindulgence by, 528–33
  rejection by, 401–4, 533–35
  and retarded child, 521–27
  separation of, 545–54
  and teen-agers' perspectives, 541–44
Parent-Youth Code, 562–64
peer group, and adolescent development, 113–15
perception: in infancy, 359–63
  of neonate, 370–72
personality: adolescent, 419–25
  effect of home on, 399–406
  development of, 399–440
  integration of, 433–40
  traits of adolescent, 289–94
  value of, 462
phobias, 358
physical growth, 89–90, 99–105
physique: and personality, 107–8
  varieties of, 106–7
pictorial techniques, 9–10
placenta, 68–69
plans, for future, 281–82
practice in motor development, 143–53
preadolescence, 87–93
prehension, in infants, 153–61
prejudice, reduction of, 294–305
prenatal development: in embryo, 67–69
  timetable of, 69–72
principles in learning motor skills, 161–66
problems of young people, 571–78

problem-solving, 376–80
projection, 355
projective techniques, 8–11
propaganda, 336–37
psychomode, 477, 482–88, 489
psychosexual: behavior, 468–515
  development, 468–73
  identity, 474–89
pyknic, 105
pyrophobia, 358

questionnaires, systematic, 5

rationalization, 355
reasoning: development of, 364–65
  and problem-solving, 376–78, 380
recreation, 579, 584
regression, 265–66, 357–58
rejection, 533–35
religion: controls of, 456–61
  high school students' attitudes toward, 279
repression, 357
research, interlaboratory, 32–33
retrospective reports, 5–6
rewards, effect of, on children, 52–60
Rorschach technique, 9

scapegoating, 267, 296, 300
school: and adolescent development, 115–16
  intelligence tests in, 240–47
  orientation in, 208–9
security and young people, 576–78
self: characteristics of, 324–27
  development of, 327–32
  and personality development, 399–440
self-activity, 302–4, 397–99
self-concept, 117–25, 409–19
self-consistency, 297, 299, 302–4
self-image, 406–19
  See also self-concept.
self-insight, 256–57, 294–305
self-reliance, 205–8
sex(es), 42, 97–98, 250–57, 280–81, 394–98
sex offenders, 490–95

sexual development, Freudian view, 469–73

sexual identity, 474–80

sexual interaction, 480–81

shyness, 357

sibling(s): differences among, 22–25
   intelligence and achievement of, 250–55
   language of, 197
   resemblance of, 19–25
   rivalry among, 404–5

situational tests, 10–11

sleep, developmental changes in, 75–76

social adjustment, 131, 566

social aid, 205–8

social atmosphere, 266–68

social class differences, 268–77

social development, of adolescents, 90–91

social identity, a problem of, 178–88

social issues, in education, 200–209

social norms, 383–84

social relationships: changing, 361–63
   development of, 167–204
   and emotionality, 260–61
   importance of adolescent, 192–95
   parental attitudes toward child's, 556–58

society, attitude toward, 279

sociometric techniques, 11–13

sociomode, 477, 488

somatic variations, 105–8

somatoplasm, 39

somatotonia, 107

somatotype, 107–8

son-father relationships, 171–78

S→ O→ R, 321–24

speech: socialized, 198–99
   and stammering, 82–86
   of twins, 80–81

sperm, 39–40

spiritual values, 453–55, 456–61, 461–68

stammering, 82–86

Stanford Achievement Test, 19–20

Stanford-Binet Revised Scale, 20, 210–11

status: during adolescence, 193
   adolescent and adult, 179–88

stress: versus nonstress, 173–78

tolerance of, and speech, 83–84, 86

study approaches: child and adolescent, 1–36
   commonly used, 1–4
   current methods of, 4–8

stuttering, 82, 84, 197

sublimation, 355

superego, 471

syllogism, 377–78

sympathy, 356–57

teachers, 91, 284–88, 305–11, 323–24, 365, 383–87, 438, 441–52, 455, 573–75

teen-agers. *See* adolescents.

tension, 579–85

Thematic Apperception Test, 9–10, 173, 176

thinking, 226–31
   animistic, 388–93
   development of, 363–65

toxicophobia, 358

traits, of teen-agers, 288–94
   See also personality.

trauma, 113

twins: motor development of, 143–53
   speech of, 80–81

umbilical cord, 68–69

United States, adolescent status in, 112–13

unmarried mother, 502–15

vertical study approach, 3–4

viscerotonia, 107

weaning, 75

Wechsler Intelligence Scale for Children (WISC), 241–44

withdrawal, 357, 533

worries of teen-agers, 288–94

Yale Clinic of Child Development, 140

young people: and mate selection, 496–500
   and their problems, 571–78
   and values, 453–55
   See also child *and* adolescent.